S0-AIR-791

Macmillan/McGraw-Hill READING

Mc
Graw
Hill
Macmillan
McGraw-Hill
New York
Farmington

Contributors

The Princeton Review, Time Magazine, Accelerated Reader

The Princeton Review is not affiliated with Princeton University or ETS.

Students with print disabilities may be eligible to obtain an accessible, audio version of the pupil edition of this textbook. Please call Recording for the Blind & Dyslexic at 1-800-221-4792 for complete information.

Macmillan/McGraw-Hill

A Division of The ***McGraw-Hill*** *Companies*

Published by Macmillan/McGraw-Hill, a division of The McGraw-Hill Companies, Inc., Two Penn Plaza, NY, NY 10121

Printed in the United States of America

/2, Bk.2, U.3

2 3 4 5 6 7 8 9 073/043 05 04 03 02

Authors

James Flood
Jan E. Hasbrouck
James V. Hoffman
Diane Lapp
Donna Lubcker
Angela Shelf Medearis
Scott Paris
Steven Stahl
Josefina Villamil Tinajero
Karen D. Wood

New York Farmington

Managing the

Classroom

TEACHING TIP

MANAGEMENT

Provide children in each group with their own list of centers they will go to. Children can check off each center after finishing their work. Early finishers can read a book from the Reading Center.

Sample Management Plan

Group 1	Group 2	Group 3	Group 4
With Teacher	Reading or Writing Workstation	Working with Words Station	Cross-Curricular or Computer Station
Reading or Writing Workstation	**With Teacher**	Cross-Curricular or Computer Station	Working with Words Station
Working with Words Station	Cross-Curricular or Computer Station	**With Teacher**	Reading or Writing Workstation
Cross-Curricular or Computer Station	Working with Words Station	Reading or Writing Workstation	**With Teacher**

Creating WORKSTATIONS

Establishing independent workstations and other independent activities is a key to helping you manage the classroom as you meet with small groups.

Reading

Set up a classroom library including the Leveled Books and other independent reading titles that have been previously read during small-group instruction. See the Theme Bibliography on pages T88–T89 for suggestions. Include titles based on discussions of students' fiction and nonfiction preferences.

- Self-Selected Reading
- Paired Reading
- Student Anthology selection from the Listening Library

Computer

Students can access the Internet to complete the Research and Inquiry activities suggested throughout the unit. Look for Internet connections in the following Research and Inquiry projects:

- Find Out More project at the end of each selection
- Cooperative Theme Project: Class Vacation Guide
- Cross-Curricular Activities
- Bringing Groups Together project

Writing

Focus the unit's writing projects on story writing. Weekly writing assignments related to the core selection are found at the end of each selection. The unit writing process project, Writing a Story, can also be the focus of the Writing Station. Equip the Writing Station with the following materials:

- Samples of published stories
- Story Writing samples, available in the **Teacher's Writing Resource Handbook,** pages 26–27

Working with Words

promise success explore

Selection Vocabulary
Have students write stories using as many selection vocabulary words as possible. Tell them to replace the vocabulary words with small pictures of the words. They should include a line under the picture so a partner can write in the correct word.

High-Frequency Words
Have students create a "scrambled words" puzzle for a partner to solve using these high-frequency words: *while, always, into, each, once, off.* Also have them create an answer key with the words written correctly.

TEACHING TIP

MANAGEMENT

If the classroom space is limited, incorporate workstation suggestions into a class assignment chart.

Shelve materials for each project in the classroom and distribute them as you assign an activity.

Have students work in groups, in pairs, or independently at their desks.

Cross-Curricular STATIONS

Set up a Cross-Curricular Station to help extend selection concepts and ideas. Cross-Curricular activities can be found throughout the unit.

Science

- Dog Breeds, 270
- Recycling Matters, 296
- An Inventor's Life, 330
- Learn about Food Chains, 344

Social Studies

- Safety Awareness, 262
- America Working, 288
- Who Helps? 320
- Oceans of the World, 348

Math

- Add the "Thank You's," 266
- Tiger Tips, 294
- Finding the Space, 322
- The Biggest and the Smallest, 346

Art

- Be the Illustrator, 300
- Illustrate a Feeling, 314
- Sponge Painting, 354

Additional Independent Activities

The following independent activities offer students practice exercises to help reinforce the concepts and skills taught within the unit.

PUPIL EDITION: READER RESPONSE

Story Questions to monitor student comprehension of the selection. The questions are leveled, progressing from literal to critical thinking.

Story Activities related to the selection. Four activities are always provided: one writing activity, two cross-curricular activities, and a research and inquiry activity in the Find Out More project that encourages students to use the Internet for research.

LEVELED PRACTICE

Each week, Reteach, Practice, and Extend pages are offered to address the individual needs of students as they learn and review skills.

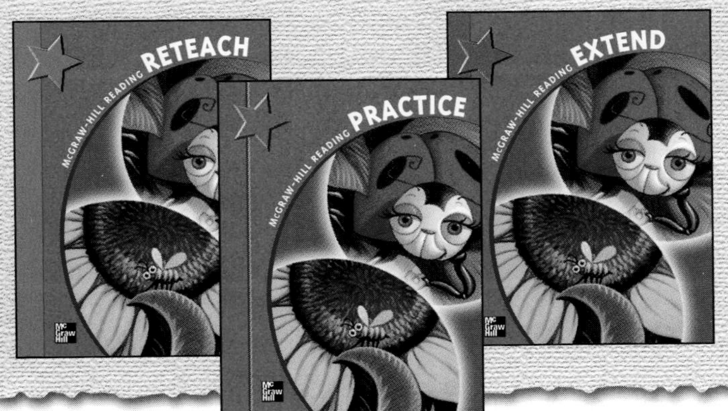

McGraw-Hill Reading

Theme Chart

GRADE LEVEL	Experience	Connections
	Experiences can tell us about ourselves and our world.	Making connections develops new understandings.
Kindergarten	**My World** We learn a lot from all the things we see and do at home and in school.	**All Kinds of Friends** When we work and play together, we learn more about ourselves.
Subtheme 1	At Home	Working Together
Subtheme 2	School Days	Playing Together
1	**Day by Day** Each day brings new experiences.	**Together Is Better** We like to share ideas and experiences with others.
2	**What's New?** With each day, we learn something new.	**Just Between Us** Family and friends help us see the world in new ways.
3	**Great Adventures** Life is made up of big and small experiences.	**Nature Links** Nature can give us new ideas.
4	**Reflections** Stories let us share the experiences of others.	**Something in Common** Sharing ideas can lead to meaningful cooperation.
5	**Time of My Life** We sometimes find memorable experiences in unexpected places.	**Building Bridges** Knowing what we have in common helps us appreciate our differences.
6	**Pathways** Reflecting on life's experiences can lead to new understandings.	**A Common Thread** A look beneath the surface may uncover hidden connections.

MULTI-AGE Classroom

Using the same global themes at each grade level facilitates the use of materials in multi-age classrooms.

Themes: Kindergarten – Grade 6

Expression	Inquiry	Problem Solving	Making Decisions
There are many styles and forms for expressing ourselves.	By exploring and asking questions, we make discoveries.	Analyzing information can help us solve problems.	Using what we know helps us evaluate situations.
Time to Shine We can use our ideas and our imagination to do many wonderful things.	**I Wonder** We can make discoveries about the wonders of nature in our own backyard.	**Let's Work It Out** Working as part of a team can help me find a way to solve problems.	**Choices** We can make many good choices and decisions every day.
Great Ideas	**In My Backyard**	**Try and Try Again**	**Good Choices**
Let's Pretend	**Wonders of Nature**	**Teamwork**	**Let's Decide**
Stories to Tell Each one of us has a different story to tell.	**Let's Find Out!** Looking for answers is an adventure.	**Think About It!** It takes time to solve problems.	**Many Paths** Each decision opens the door to a new path.
Express Yourself We share our ideas in many ways.	**Look Around** There are surprises all around us.	**Figure It Out** We can solve problems by working together.	**Starting Now** Unexpected events can lead to new decisions.
Be Creative! We can all express ourselves in creative, wonderful ways.	**Tell Me More** Looking and listening closely will help us find out the facts.	**Think It Through** Solutions come in many shapes and sizes.	**Turning Points** We make new judgments based on our experiences.
Our Voices We can each use our talents to communicate ideas.	**Just Curious** We can find answers in surprising places.	**Make a Plan** Often we have to think carefully about a problem in order to solve it.	**Sorting It Out** We make decisions that can lead to new ideas and discoveries.
Imagine That The way we express our thoughts and feelings can take different forms.	**Investigate!** We never know where the search for answers might lead us.	**Bright Ideas** Some problems require unusual approaches.	**Crossroads** Decisions cause changes that can enrich our lives.
With Flying Colors Creative people help us see the world from different perspectives.	**Seek and Discover** To make new discoveries, we must observe and explore.	**Brainstorms** We can meet any challenge with determination and ingenuity.	**All Things Considered** Encountering new places and people can help us make decisions.

UNIT 3

Contents

Starting Now

Unexpected events can lead to new decisions.

SKILLS			
Phonics	**Comprehension**	**Vocabulary**	**Study Skill**
• **Review** Digraphs *ph, tch, ch*	• **Introduce** Form Generalizations	• **Introduce** Multiple-Meaning Words	• Library/Media Center: Do a Subject Search at the Library

FICTION

SKILLS			
Phonics	**Comprehension**	**Vocabulary**	**Study Skill**
• **Review** Long *e*, Long *i; tch, ch*	• **Introduce** Main Idea	• **Review** Multiple-Meaning Words	• Library/Media Center: Read a Library Floor Plan

BIOGRAPHICAL FICTION

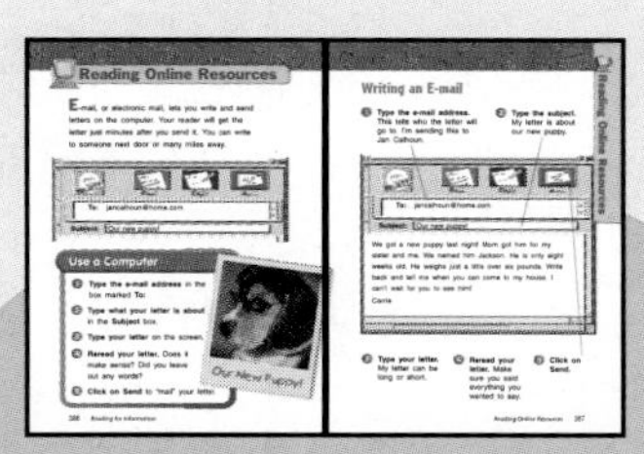

INFORMATIONAL TEXT

UNIT 3

Unit Planner

	WEEK 1 Officer Buckle and Gloria	WEEK 2 Tomás and the Library Lady
 **Leveled Books**	**Easy:** *The Seeing Eye* **Independent:** *A City Horse* **Challenge:** *My Name is Nura*	**Easy:** *A Voice for Her People* **Independent:** *Adventure in Arabia* **Challenge:** *Dance the Flamenco*
Tested Skills	**Phonics** Review Digraphs *ph, tch, ch,* 250G–250H, 281E–281F, 281G–281H **Comprehension** Introduce Form Generalizations, 281I–281J **Vocabulary** Introduce Multiple-Meaning Words, 281K–281L **Study Skills** Library/Media Center, 280	**Phonics** Review Long *e, i,* 282G–282H Review Long *e, i,* 309E–309F Review Long *e, i*; Digraphs, *tch, ch,* 309G–309H **Comprehension** Introduce Main Idea, 309I–309J **Vocabulary** Review Multiple-Meaning Words, 309K–309L **Study Skills** Library/Media Center, 308
Minilessons	**Phonics and Decoding:** Review /ər/ and /əl/, 257 **Make Inferences,** 263 **Context Clues,** 269 **Summarize,** 271	**Make Inferences,** 289 **Phonics and Decoding:** Long Vowel: /ū/, 293 **Context Clues,** 295 **Summarize,** 303
Language Arts	**Writing:** Writing a Story, 281M **Grammar:** Adjectives, 281O **Spelling:** Words with Double Consonants, 281Q	**Writing:** Writing a Story, 309M **Grammar:** Using *a* and *an*, 309O **Spelling:** Words with Digraphs *sh, ch,* 309Q
Activities		
Curriculum Connections	**Read Aloud:** "The Lion and the Mouse," 250E **Phonics Rhyme:** "Scratch My Itch," 250/251 **Social Studies:** Safety Awareness, 262 **Math:** Add the "Thank-You's," 266 **Science:** Dog Breeds, 270	**Read Aloud:** "The Library," 282E **Phonics Rhyme:** "Magic Ticket," 282/283 **Social Studies:** America Working, 288 **Math:** Tiger Tips, 294 **Science:** Recycling Matters, 296 **Art:** Be the Illustrator, 300
CULTURAL PERSPECTIVES	Working Animals, 258	Stories, 290

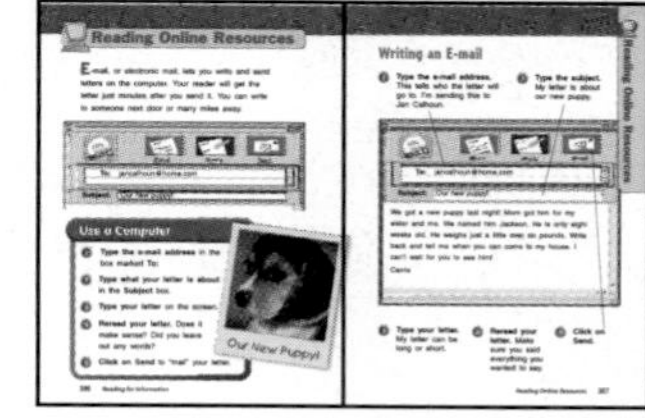

WEEK 3 Princess Pooh	WEEK 4 Swimmy	WEEK 5 The World's Plants Are in Danger	WEEK 6 Review, Writing, Reading Information, Assessment
Easy: *Everybody's Happy* **Independent:** *Karen and the Red Shoes* **Challenge:** *The Wright Brothers Learn to Fly*	**Easy:** *Billy Fish* **Independent:** *Dolphins* **Challenge:** *Giant Foam Sea Creatures*	*Self-Selected Reading of Leveled Books*	*Self-Selected Reading*
Phonics Review Long *a, o,* 310G–310H Review Long *a, o,* 339E–339F Review Long *a, o, e, i;* Digraphs, *tch, ch,* 339G–339H **Comprehension** Review Form Generalizations, 339I–339J **Vocabulary** Introduce Figurative Language, 339K–339L **Study Skills** Library/Media Center, 338	**Phonics** Review Soft *c* and Soft *g,* 340G–340H Review Soft *c* and Soft *g,* 361E–361F Review Soft *c, g;* Long *a, o, e, i,* 361G–361H **Comprehension** Review Main Idea, 361I–361J **Vocabulary** Review Figurative Language, 361K–361L **Study Skills** Library/Media Center, 360	**Phonics** Review Soft *c, g;* Long *a, o, e, i;* Digraphs *ph, tch,* 362G–362H **Comprehension** Review Main Idea, 371E–371F Review Form Generalizations, 371G–371H **Vocabulary** Review Figurative Language, 371I–371J Review Multiple-Meaning Words, 371K–371L **Study Skills** Library/Media Center, 370	**Assess Skills** Digraphs *ph, tch, ch* Long *e, i* Long *a ,o* Soft *c* and Soft *g* Form Generalizations Main Idea Multiple-Meaning Words Figurative Language **Assess Grammar and Spelling** Review Adjectives and Adverbs, 373I Review Spelling Patterns, 373J **Unit Progress Assessment** **Standardized Test Preparation** **Reading Online Resources** 373A
Phonics and Decoding: Long *e,* 317 **Context Clues,** 321 **Summarize,** 323 **Make Inferences,** 333	**Main Idea and Details,** 345 **Phonics and Decoding:** /ē/ spelled *y,* 347 **Make Inferences,** 349 **Context Clues,** 353 **Suffixes,** 355		
Writing: Writing a Story, 339M **Grammar:** Adjectives That Compare, 339O **Spelling:** Words with Digraphs *th, sh,* 339Q	**Writing:** Writing a Story, 361M **Grammar:** Adverbs, 361O **Spelling:** Words with Digraphs *th, wh,* 361Q	**Writing:** Writing a Story, 371M **Grammar:** Synonyms and Antonyms, 371O **Spelling:** Words from Science, 371Q	**Unit Writing Process:** Writing a Story, 373C
Read Aloud: "ME I AM!" 310E **Phonics Rhyme:** "Little Sister," 310/311 **Art:** Illustrate a Feeling, 314 **Social Studies:** Who Helps?, 320 **Math:** Finding the Space, 322 **Science:** An Inventor's Life, 330	**Read Aloud:** "The Discontented Fish," 340E **Phonics Rhyme:** "Party Time," 340/341 **Science:** Learn About Food Chains, 344 **Math:** The Biggest and the Smallest, 346 **Social Studies:** Oceans of the World, 348 **Art:** Sponge Painting, 354	**Read Aloud:** "All Living Things," 362E **Phonics Rhyme:** "The Plan," 362/363	GROUP **Cooperative Theme Project Research and Inquiry:** Class Vacation Guide, 249
Going Far, 328	Origami Fish, 350		

UNIT 3

Unit Resources

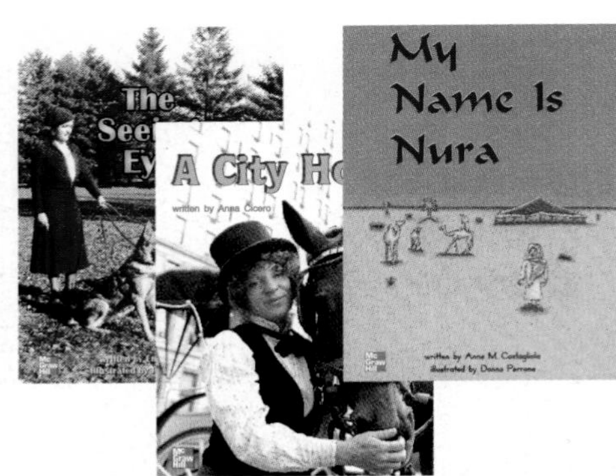

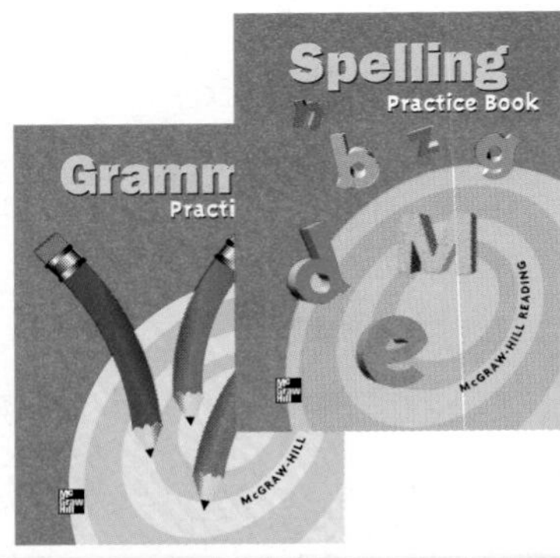

LITERATURE

LEVELED BOOKS

Easy:

- ***The Seeing Eye***
- ***A Voice for Her People***
- ***Everybody's Happy***
- ***Billy Fish***

Independent:

- ***A City Horse***
- ***Adventure in Arabia***
- ***Karen and the Red Shoes***
- ***Dolphins***

Challenge:

- ***My Name Is Nura***
- ***Dance the Flamenco***
- ***The Wright Brothers Learn to Fly***
- ***Giant Foam Sea Creatures***

THEME BIG BOOK

Share *Aunt Flossie's Hats (and Crab Cakes)* to set the unit theme and make content-area connections.

LISTENING LIBRARY

Children can listen to an audio recording of the student selections and poetry.

Macmillan/McGraw-Hill

Easy Leveled Books
Skills Intervention Guide
Phonics Intervention Guide

SKILLS

LEVELED PRACTICE

Practice: Student practice phonics, comprehension, vocabulary and study skills; plus instructional vocabulary and story comprehension. Take-Home Story included for each lesson.

Reteach: Reteaching opportunities for students who need more help with each assessed skill.

Extend: Extension activities for vocabulary, comprehension, story and study skills.

TEACHING CHARTS

Instructional charts for modeling vocabulary and tested skills. Also available as **transparencies.**

WORD BUILDING MANIPULATIVE CARDS

a b c Letter and word cards to utilize phonics and build instructional vocabulary.

LANGUAGE SUPPORT BOOK

ESL Parallel lessons and practice for students needing language support.

PHONICS/PHONEMIC AWARENESS PRACTICE BOOK

Additional practice focusing on key phonetic elements.

FLUENCY ASSESSMENT

Evaluation and practice for reading fluency.

LANGUAGE ARTS

GRAMMAR PRACTICE BOOK

Provides practice for grammar and mechanics lessons.

SPELLING PRACTICE BOOK

Provides practice with the word list and spelling patterns. Includes home involvement activities.

DAILY LANGUAGE ACTIVITIES

Provide brief, practice and reinforcement of grammar, mechanics, and usage skills. Available as **blackline masters** and **transparencies.**

WRITING PROCESS TRANSPARENCIES

Model stages of the writing process.

HANDWRITING HANDBOOKS

For instruction and practice.

McGraw-Hill School

TECHNOLOGY

CD-ROM Provides phonics support.

interNET CONNECTION Extend lesson activities through research and inquiry ideas. Visit ***www.mhschool.com/reading.***

Vocabulary PuzzleMaker Provides practice with instructional vocabulary.

Handwriting CD-ROM Provides practice activities.

Mind Jogger Videos Review grammar and writing skills.

Resources for

Meeting Individual Needs

UNIT 3	EASY	ON-LEVEL	CHALLENGE	LANGUAGE SUPPORT
 *Officer Buckle and Gloria*	**Leveled Book:** *The Seeing Eye* Reteach, 211–218 **Alternate Teaching Strategies,** T64–T76 **Writing:** Make a Poster, 281N Phonics CD-ROM Intervention	**Leveled Book:** *A City Horse* Practice, 211–218 **Alternate Teaching Strategies,** T64–T76 **Writing:** Diary Entry, 281N Phonics CD-ROM	**Leveled Book:** *My Name Is Nura* Extend, 211–218 **Writing:** Write a Scene, 281N Phonics CD-ROM	**Teaching Strategies,** 252A, 252C, 253, 254, 256, 265, 273, 274, 281N Language Support, 226–234 **Alternate Teaching Strategies,** T64–T76 **Writing:** Write a Gloria Story, 281N Phonics CD-ROM
 *Tomás and the Library Lady*	**Leveled Book:** *A Voice for Her People* Reteach, 219–226 **Alternate Teaching Strategies,** T64–T76 **Writing:** Summary, 309N Phonics CD-ROM Intervention	**Leveled Book:** *Adventure in Arabia* Practice, 219–226 **Alternate Teaching Strategies,** T64–T76 **Writing:** Letter, 309N Phonics CD-ROM	**Leveled Book:** *Dance the Flamenco* Extend, 219–226 **Writing:** Newspaper Article, 309N Phonics CD-ROM	**Teaching Strategies,** 284A, 284C, 285, 287, 291, 297, 299, 302, 309N Language Support, 235–243 **Alternate Teaching Strategies,** T64–T76 **Writing:** Write an Adventure Story, 309N Phonics CD-ROM
 *Princess Pooh*	**Leveled Book:** *Everybody's Happy* Reteach, 227–234 **Alternate Teaching Strategies,** T64–T76 **Writing:** Picture This, 339N Phonics CD-ROM Intervention	**Leveled Book:** *Karen and the Red Shoes* Practice, 227–234 **Alternate Teaching Strategies,** T64–T76 **Writing:** A Day in the Life, 339N Phonics CD-ROM	**Leveled Book:1** *The Wright Brothers Learn to Fly* Extend, 227–234 **Writing:** Penelope's Wish, 339N Phonics CD-ROM	**Teaching Strategies,** 312A, 312C, 313, 317, 319, 325, 339N Language Support, 244–252 **Alternate Teaching Strategies,** T64–T76 **Writing:** Write a Story, 339N Phonics CD-ROM
 *Swimmy*	**Leveled Book:** *Billy Fish* Reteach, 235–242 **Alternate Teaching Strategies,** T64–T76 **Writing:** Let's Pretend, 361N Phonics CD-ROM Intervention	**Leveled Book:** *Dolphins* Practice, 235–242 **Alternate Teaching Strategies,** T64–T76 **Writing:** Plan a Day, 361N Phonics CD-ROM	**Leveled Book:** *Giant Foam Sea Creatures* Extend, 235–242 **Writing:** Conversation, 361N Phonics CD-ROM	**Teaching Strategies,** 342A, 342C, 343, 351, 353, 361N Language Support, 253–261 **Alternate Teaching Strategies,** T64–T76 **Writing:** Write a Story, 361N Phonics CD-ROM
 *The World's Plants Are in Danger*	**Review** Reteach, 243–250 **Alternate Teaching Strategies,** T64–T76 **Writing:** Make a Poster, 371N Phonics CD-ROM Intervention	**Review** Practice, 243–250 **Alternate Teaching Strategies,** T64–T76 **Writing:** Make a Comic Strip, 371N Phonics CD-ROM	**Review** Extend, 243–250 **Writing:** Write an Editorial, 371N Phonics CD-ROM	**Teaching Strategies,** 364A, 364C, 365, 371N Language Support, 262–270 **Alternate Teaching Strategies,** T64–T76 **Writing:** Write a Story, 371N Phonics CD-ROM

UNIT 3

Unit Assessment

INFORMAL

Informal Assessment

- Phonics, 250G, 277, 281F, 281H; 282G, 305, 309F, 309H; 310G, 335, 339F, 339H; 340G, 357, 361F, 361H; 362G, 367, 371F, 371H
- Comprehension, 276, 277, 281J; 304, 305, 309J; 334, 335, 339J; 356, 357, 361J; 366, 367, 371J
- Vocabulary, 281L, 309L, 339L, 361L, 371L

Performance Assessment

- Scoring Rubrics, 281N, 309N, 339N, 361N, 371N
- Research and Inquiry, 249, 373
- Listening, Speaking, Viewing Activities, 250E, 250, 252C, 252–277, 281D, 281M–N; 282E, 282, 284C, 284–305, 309D, 309M–N; 310E, 310, 312C, 312–335, 339D, 339M–N; 340E, 340, 342C, 342–357, 361D, 361M–N; 362E, 362, 364C, 364–367, 371D, 371M–N
- Portfolio, 281N, 309N, 339N, 361N, 371N
- Writing, 281M–N, 309M–N, 339M–N, 361M–N, 371M–N, 373C-H
- Fluency, 276, 304, 334, 356, 366

Leveled Practice

Practice, Reteach, Extend

- **Phonics**
  - Digraphs *ph, tch, ch,* 211, 215, 216, 224, 232, 243
  - Long *e, i,* 219, 223, 224, 232, 240, 243
  - Long *a, o,* 227, 231, 232, 240, 243
  - Soft *c* and Soft *g,* 235, 239, 240, 243
- **Comprehension**
  - Form Generalizations, 217, 233, 248
  - Main Idea, 225, 241, 247
- **Vocabulary Strategies**
  - Multiple-Meaning Words, 218, 226, 250
  - Figurative Language, 234, 242, 249
- **Study Skills**
  - Library/Media Center, 214, 222, 230, 238, 246

FORMAL

Selection Assessment

- **Skills and Vocabulary Words**
  - *Officer Buckle and Gloria,* 101–104
  - *Tomás and the Library Lady,* 105–108
  - *Princess Pooh,* 109–112
  - *Swimmy,* 113–116
  - *The World's Plants Are in Danger,* 117–118

Unit 3 Tests

- **Phonics**
  - Digraphs *ph, tch, ch*
  - Long *e, i*
  - Long *a, o*
  - Soft *c* and Soft *g*
- **Comprehension**
  - Form Generalizations
  - Main Idea
- **Vocabulary Strategies**
  - Multiple-Meaning Words
  - Figurative Language

Grammar and Spelling Assessment

- **Grammar**
  - Adjectives and Adverbs, 191–192
- **Spelling**
  - Unit 3 Assessment, 191–192

Fluency Assessment

- Fluency Passages, 50–53

Diagnostic/Placement Evaluation

- Informal Reading Inventories
- Running Record
- Phonemic Awareness Assessment
- Placement Tests

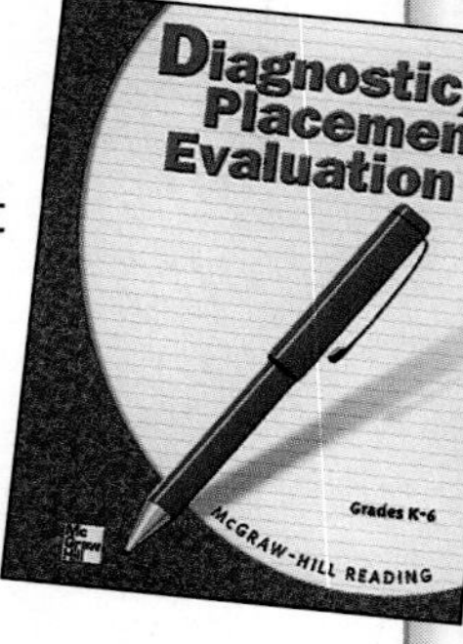

Test Preparation

- See also Test Power, 281, 309, 339, 361, 371
- Additional standardized test preparation materials available

Reading Test Generator

- Assessment Software

Assessment Checklist

Student .... **Grade** ....

Teacher ....

	Officer Buckle and Gloria	Tomás and the Library Lady	Princess Pooh	Swimmy	The World's Plants Are in Danger	Assessment Summary
LISTENING/SPEAKING						
Participates in oral language experiences						
Listens and speaks to gain knowledge of culture						
Speaks appropriately to audiences for different purposes						
Communicates clearly						
READING						
Uses phonological awareness strategies, including • blending, segmenting, deleting, substituting sounds						
Uses a variety of word identification strategies: • Phonics and decoding: digraphs *ph, tch, ch*						
• Phonics and decoding: long *e, i*						
• Phonics and decoding: long *a, o*						
• Phonics and decoding: soft *c* and soft *g*						
• Multiple-Meaning Words						
• Figurative Language						
Reads with fluency and understanding						
Reads widely for different purposes in varied sources						
Develops an extensive vocabulary						
Uses a variety of strategies to comprehend selections: • Form Generalizations						
• Main Idea						
Responds to various texts						
Analyzes the characteristics of various types of texts						
Conducts research using various sources: • Library/Media Center						
Reads to increase knowledge						
WRITING						
Writes for a variety of audiences and purposes						
Composes original texts using the conventions of written language such as capitalization and penmanship						
Spells proficiently						
Composes texts applying knowledge of grammar and usage						
Uses writing processes						
Evaluates own writing and writing of others						

+ Observed   – Not Observed

Introduce the Theme

Starting Now

Unexpected events can lead to new decisions.

DISCUSS THE THEME Write the theme statement on the board. Read it aloud to the children. Explain that unexpected events can lead us to make new choices and decisions. Ask:

- What do you do when you need to make a decision? Invite volunteers to share personal experiences about how they make choices.
- Have you ever read a book, seen a movie, or heard a song about making decisions? What was the decision in question? Are some decisions more difficult to make than others?

SHARE A STORY Use the Big Book *Aunt Flossie's Hats (And Crabcakes Later)* to help establish the unit theme. Have children discuss how the children's discovery that crab cakes are better after Aunt Flossie's stories relates to Starting Now.

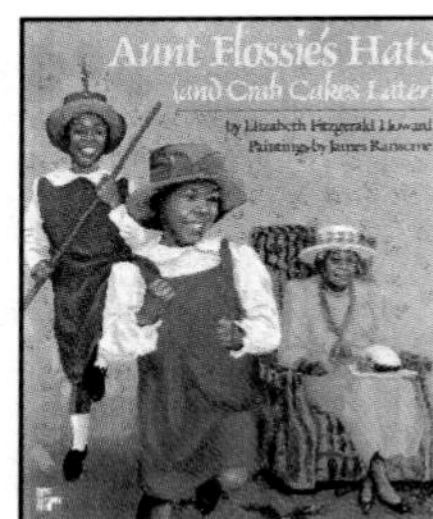

PREVIEW UNIT SELECTIONS Have children preview the unit by reading the selection titles and looking at the illustrations. Ask:

- How might these stories relate to the theme, Starting Now?
- How are these stories alike and how are they different?
- What do you think will be the important decision or choice in each selection and why?

As children preview the selections, encourage them to compare the characters, settings, and events that develop the unit theme.

THEME CONNECTIONS

Each of the five selections relates to the unit theme, Starting Now, as well as to the global theme of Making Decisions.

Officer Buckle and Gloria A police officer makes an important decision about his dog.

Tomás and the Library Lady Tomás discovers the library and makes a decision that affects his life.

Princess Pooh A girl makes an unexpected decision about her sister.

Swimmy A little fish decides how he will keep himself and other little fish safe.

The World's Plants Are in Danger We all need to decide how to save plants starting now.

Research and Inquiry

Theme Project: Class Vacation Guide Have children work in teams to brainstorm places where they would like to vacation. They will then select one vacation spot and make a class vacation guide. Their challenge is to convince their classmates that the chosen destination is the perfect vacation spot.

Make a Resource Chart Once the team has picked a place, have them list what they already know about it. Then have them create a three column chart. In the first column, have them list questions they need to answer in order to prepare their guide. In the second column, instruct them to list possible resources. When their research is complete, they will write their answers in the third column.

Create a Presentation When their research is complete, have children discuss possible formats for describing a vacation at the place they have chosen. Suggest that they find pictures that best illustrate their chosen spot or create an audiovisual presentation.

QUESTIONS	POSSIBLE RESOURCES	ANSWERS
• How do you get to this place? • What is the best time of year to visit? • What do people do there?	• Travel brochures, encyclopedias, Internet • Travel brochures, encyclopedias, Internet • Travel brochures, Internet, magazines	

See **Wrap Up the Theme**, page 372.

Research Strategies

Children may wish to research and verify information pertaining to their vacation spot. Share these tips:

- Check the library or bookstore for books about your vacation locale.
- Skim through magazines that are devoted to travel and look for relevant information. These may be found in your local library or bookstore.
- Consult the local tourism office. You may request information from the office if you do not live near it.
- Visit local travel agencies and collect brochures about your vacation spot.
- Identify and visit web sites on the Internet that may be helpful.

*inter***NET** **CONNECTION** Children can find more information about travel by visiting ***www.mhschool.com/reading.***

Poetry

Read the Poem

READ ALOUD Read "Which?" by James S. Tippett aloud to children.

- How does this poem relate to the unit theme, Starting Now?
- What is the choice or decision to be made in this poem? Is it a difficult decision for the author?
- What do you notice about the poem's structure? How does the way it is written communicate choosing between two things?

Listening Library Children can listen to an audio recording of the poem.

READERS THEATER Divide the class into two groups. Have one group read only the lines that begin with or contain the words, *I like.* Have the other group read the remaining lines aloud.

Learn About Poetry

REPETITION Review that repetition occurs when a word or phrase is repeated for emphasis.

- Have children identify which word or words are repeated for emphasis in the poem, "Which?" *(I like)*
- Discuss how emphasizing these words by repeating them contributes to the overall meaning of the poem.

PATTERNED STRUCTURES Review that patterned structures are formed by the repetition of a variety of elements, in a poem.

- Help children identify the patterns formed by these repeated elements, such as sounds, words, and punctuation.
- Write the poem, "Which?" on the chalkboard. Invite volunteers to circle each pattern with a different colored chalk.
- Discuss how the patterned structures convey to the reader that a difficult choice is being presented.

MEET THE POET

ABOUT JAMES S. TIPPETT James S. Tippett was born September 7, 1885 in Memphis, Missouri, and died in 1958. Tippett grew up in a homespun environment and enjoyed the simple pleasures in life, such as gardening, dogs, and reading. He had a long and successful career as a teacher and school administrator. Tippett wrote many books for children. *Crickety-Cricket! The Best-Loved Poems of James S. Tippett* was published in 1970.

READ TOGETHER

STARTING NOW

UNIT 3

Which?

When I am in the country
I like the trees and grass.
I like the cows and horses,
I count them as I pass.

When I am in the city
I like the city streets.
I like the trucks and taxis
Passing by in fleets.

"The city or the country?"
I sometimes say to Mother,
"I cannot say which one I like
Better than the other."

by James S. Tippett

249

WRITE A POEM

Patterned Poem Encourage children to think of things they like equally, such as certain foods or games. Children can write a poem about what it would be like to choose between two things they like equally. They can use the same format as "Which?" or you may choose another patterned poem for them to follow. Consider modeling the process by writing your own poem about this subject for the class first.

Poetry Reading Host a "Poetry Reading" for your grade level. Invite family members to come share in the fun. Encourage children to share their poems at the event.

Poetry

RHYME PATTERN Review that rhyme pattern is formed by the repetition of certain sounds in certain places of a poem. Remind children that Rhyme Pattern creates a distinct rhythm.

- Have children identify the rhyme patterns in the poem, "Which?"
- Reread the poem aloud with children and guide them to notice the distinct rhythm that the rhyme patterns create.

Oral Response

SMALL-GROUP DISCUSSION Have GROUP children share personal responses to the poem and discuss these questions:

- What does the writer like about the country?
- What does the writer like about the city?
- Why is the title of the poem "Which?"
- What do you like about the country? What do you like about the city?
- Do you prefer the country or the city? Why?
- Is this a difficult choice for you to make?

Lesson Overview

Reaching All Learners

Concept

- Animals at Work

Phonics

- Digraphs *tch, ph, ch*

Vocabulary

- accidents
- audience
- cheered
- slips
- station
- wipe

Anthology

Officer Buckle and Gloria

Selection Summary **Officer Buckle's safety lectures start to take on a life of their own when he is joined by the talented dog, Gloria.**

Scratch My Itch

Help! Help! Please help!
I need an extra hand or two.
I have an itch that I can't reach,
I don't know what to do.
And so, I have phoned you,
To kindly help me catch
That middle-of-my-back itch
That I cannot seem to scratch.
What's that? You say
You also need help feeling fine?
Well, I'll be glad to scratch your back
If you will then scratch mine.

Rhyme applies to phonics

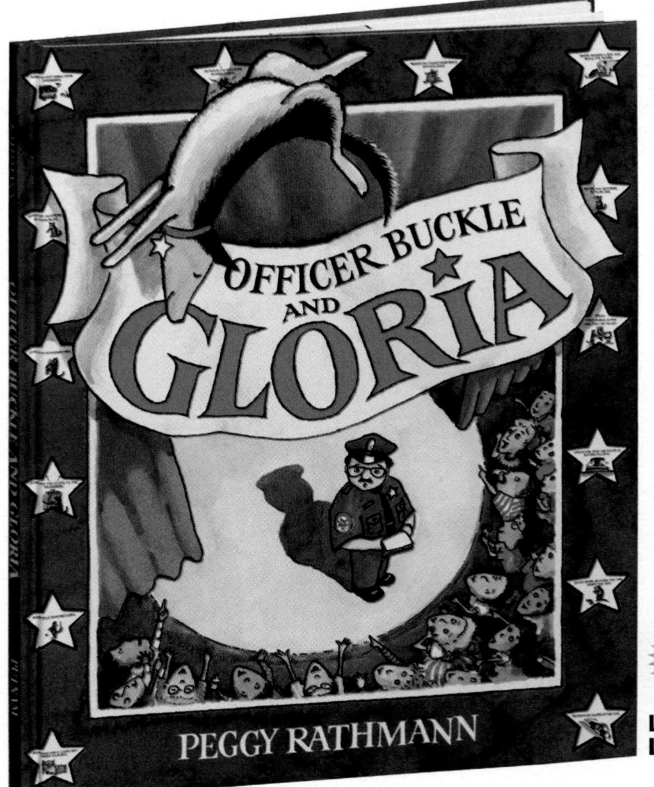

Listening Library

INSTRUCTIONAL pages 252–281

About the Author/Illustrator Peggy Rathman was born and raised in Minnesota, where one of her first art projects was creating middle-school campaign posters for her brother, who was running for student-council president. She later studied art and children's book writing. "The teacher convinced me," Rathman says, "that even a beginning writer can create an original character if the character is driven by the writer's most secret weirdness. Eureka!" Rathman has won a 1996 Caldecott Medal for *Officer Buckle and Gloria*.

Same Concept, Skills and Vocabulary!

Leveled Books

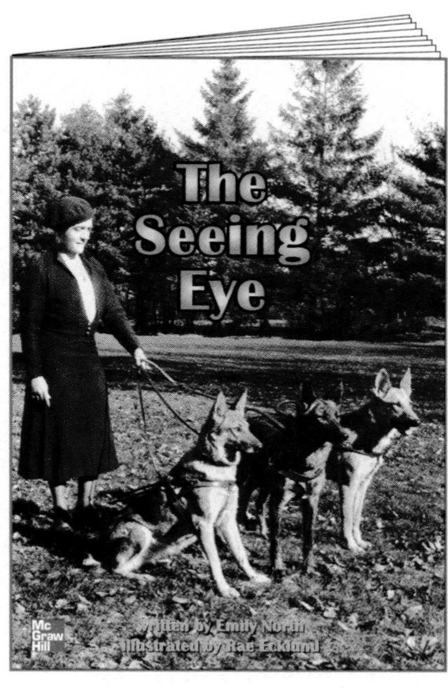

EASY
Lesson on pages 281A and 281D
DECODABLE

INDEPENDENT
Lesson on pages 281B and 281D

Take-Home version available

CHALLENGE
Lesson on pages 281C and 281D

Leveled Practice

EASY

Reteach, 211–218 Blackline masters with reteaching opportunities for each assessed skill

INDEPENDENT/ON-LEVEL

Practice, 211–218 Workbook with Take-Home stories and practice opportunities for each assessed skill and story comprehension

CHALLENGE

Extend, 211–218 Blackline masters that offer challenge activities for each assessed skill

Quizzes Prepared by  Accelerated Reader

WORKSTATION Activities

Social Studies	Safety Awareness, *262*
Science	Dog Breeds, *270*
Math	Add the "Thank You's" *266*
Language Arts	Read Aloud, *250E*
Writing	Write a Gloria Story, *278*
Cultural Perspectives	Working Animals, *258*
Research and Inquiry	Find Out More, *279*
Internet Activities	www.mhschool.com/reading

Suggested Lesson Planner

READING AND LANGUAGE ARTS	DAY 1 Focus on Reading and Skills	DAY 2 Read the Literature
Phonics Daily Routines	**Daily Phonics Routine: Fluency,** 250H Phonics CD-ROM	**Daily Phonics Routine: Segmenting,** 252A Phonics CD-ROM
Phonological Awareness Phonics *ph, tch, ch* Comprehension Vocabulary Study Skills Listening, Speaking, Viewing, Representing	**Read Aloud: Fable,** 250E "The Lion and the Mouse" ✓ **Develop Phonological Awareness,** 250F *ph, tch, ch* ✓ **Review Digraphs *ph, tch, ch*,** 250G–250H **Teaching Chart 176** **Reteach, Practice, Extend,** 211 **Phonics/Phonemic Awareness Practice Book,** 135–138 Read **Apply *ph, tch, ch*,** 250/251 "Scratch My Itch" Intervention Program	**Build Background,** 252A Develop Oral Language **Vocabulary,** 252B–252C ***accident*** ***cheered*** ***station*** ***audience*** ***slips*** ***wipe*** **Word Building Manipulative Cards** **Teaching Chart 177** **Reteach, Practice, Extend,** 212 Read **Read the Selection,** 252–277 Comprehension ✓ ***ph, tch, ch*** **Genre:** Fantasy, 253 **Cultural Perspectives,** 258 Intervention Program
Curriculum Connections	Link **Language Arts,** 250E	Link **Science,** 252A
Writing	**Writing Prompt:** Did you ever listen to a boring speech? Why was it boring? What did you do?	**Writing Prompt:** You are going to tell someone who gave a boring speech how to make it interesting. Write your advice. **Journal Writing,** 277 Quick-Write
Grammar	**Introduce the Concept: Adjectives,** 281O Daily Language Activity: Write an appropriate adjective. **Grammar Practice Book,** 161	**Teach the Concept: Adjectives,** 281O Daily Language Activity: Write an appropriate adjective. **Grammar Practice Book,** 162
Spelling *Double Consonants*	**Pretest: Words with Double Consonants,** 281Q **Spelling Practice Book,** 161, 162	**Explore the Pattern: Words with Double Consonants,** 281Q **Spelling Practice Book,** 163

 **Intervention Program Available**

Meeting Individual Needs

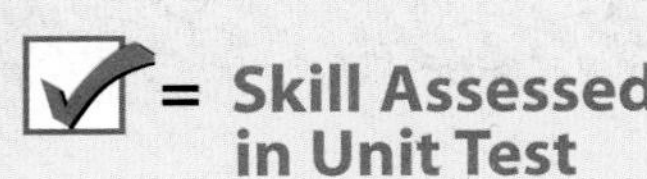
= Skill Assessed in Unit Test

Intervention Program Available

DAY 3 Read the Literature

Daily Phonics Routine: Discriminating, 279

Phonics CD-ROM

Rereading for Fluency, 276

Story Questions and Activities, 278–279
Reteach, Practice, Extend, 213

Study Skill, 280
☑ Library/Media Center
Teaching Chart 178
Reteach, Practice, Extend, 214

Test Power, 281

Read the Leveled Books, 281A–281D
Guided Reading
☑ *ph, tch, ch*
☑ Instructional Vocabulary

Intervention Program

Activity Social Studies, 262

Writing Prompt: You have been asked to talk to children about safety. Choose a topic, such as how to cross the street or how to ride a bike safely. Write what you would say.

Writing a Story, 281M
Prewrite, Draft

Review and Practice: Adjectives, 281P
Daily Language Activity: Write an appropriate adjective.

Grammar Practice Book, 163

Practice and Extend: Words with Double Consonants, 281R

Spelling Practice Book, 164

DAY 4 Build Skills

Daily Phonics Routine: Words in Context, 281F

Phonics CD-ROM

Read the Leveled Books and the Self-Selected Books

☑ Review Digraphs *ph, tch, ch,* 281E–281F
Teaching Chart 179
Reteach, Practice, Extend, 215
Language Support, 231
Phonics/Phonemic Awareness Practice Book, 135–138

☑ Review Digraphs *ph, tch, ch,* 281G–281H
Teaching Chart 180
Reteach, Practice, Extend, 216
Language Support, 232
Phonics/Phonemic Awareness Practice Book, 135–138

Minilessons, 257, 263, 269, 271

Intervention Program

Math, 266

Writing Prompt: Write three things everyone should do to ride a bike safely. Choose one of the things and tell why it is important.

Writing a Story, 281M
Revise

Meeting Individual Needs for Writing, 281N

Review and Practice: Adjectives, 281P
Daily Language Activity: Write an appropriate adjective.

Grammar Practice Book, 164

Proofread and Write: Words with Double Consonants, 281R

Spelling Practice Book, 165

DAY 5 Build Skills

Daily Phonics Routine: Writing, 281H

Phonics CD-ROM

Read Self-Selected Books

☑ Introduce Form Generalizations, 281I–281J
Teaching Chart 181
Reteach, Practice, Extend, 217
Language Support, 233

☑ Introduce Multiple-Meaning Words, 281K–281L
Teaching Chart 182
Reteach, Practice, Extend, 218
Language Support, 234

Listening, Speaking, Viewing, Representing, 281N

Minilessons, 257, 263, 269, 271

Intervention Program

Activity Science, 270

Writing Prompt: Think about a time someone talked to you about safety. Describe the person. Tell what he or she said.

Writing a Story, 281M
Edit/Proofread, Publish

Assess and Reteach: Adjectives, 281P
Daily Language Activity: Write an appropriate adjective.

Grammar Practice Book, 165, 166

Assess and Reteach: Words with Double Consonants, 281R

Spelling Practice Book, 166

Language Arts

Read Aloud

The Lion and the Mouse

a fable by Aesop adapted by Eve Rice

One day, a mighty Lion was fast asleep in the woods. Thinking he was just a rock, a little Mouse ran up his back. The Lion woke at once and took the poor Mouse by the tail.

"How dare you wake me up?" he roared. "I am going to eat you!"

"Oh, please," the Mouse said. "Let me go, and someday I will repay you."

"Don't be silly!" Lion roared. "How will you repay me? You are just a little Mouse—too small to be much use to me."

Then he laughed. "All right. Go on."

He put the Mouse down and she ran off into the woods.

When many days had passed, the Mouse ran by that place again. And hearing an awful roar, she soon found Lion, caught in a trap made of rope.

Quickly Mouse ran to the trap. She took the rope in her teeth and chewed and chewed until she chewed right through the rope and set the Lion free.

Continued on page T2

Oral Comprehension

LISTENING AND SPEAKING Read aloud this fable of a small but helpful mouse. When you have finished, ask, "Would the ending have been different if the lion had not gotten trapped in the net? Why or why not?"

GENRE STUDY: FABLE Discuss the literary devices and techniques used in *The Lion and the Mouse.*

- Remind children that animals in fables often have human characteristics. As a class, make a list of adjectives to describe the lion and the mouse.
- Ask children to describe the setting of the story. Ask, *Could the story take place someplace else? Is the setting critical to the fable?*
- Remind children that fables often teach a lesson. Ask children what lesson *The Lion and the Mouse* teaches.

Activity Have children think about how the mouse and the lion might continue their friendship. Encourage children to imagine what could happen next, and to draw a picture about the mouse and the lion's new adventure. Encourage children to introduce a new animal friend into their pictures. Remind them that animals in fables often symbolize human traits. ▶ **Visual**

Develop Phonological Awareness

Blend Sounds

Phonemic Awareness

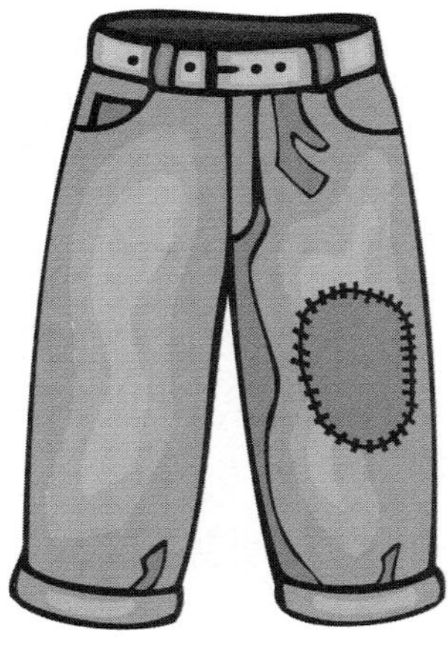

Teach Invite children to play a sound game. Say a sentence. For one of the words in the sentence, say only the sounds of the word. Ask children to put the sounds together to guess the word. For example, say: *His pants have a /p/-/a/-/ch/ on the knee. What's on the knee of his pants?* (patch). Repeat, saying a sentence with the word *phone*.

Practice Continue the game by using the following words in sentences: *catch, photo, fun, back, pitch, graph, peach, chime, wood,* and *bath*.

Segment Sounds

Phonemic Awareness

MATERIALS
- classroom objects

Teach Tell children they are going to count the sounds in words that name objects found in the classroom. Demonstrate by pointing at a wristwatch and saying /w/-/o/-/ch/. Simultaneously, hold up one hand and count the sounds on your fingers. Say: *The word watch has three sounds /w/-/o/-/ch/.*

Practice Walk around the classroom, pointing to or holding up the following objects: *chalk, photo, desk, coat, switch, pen,* and *graph*. Have children say the words, and then count the sounds using their fingers.

Delete Sounds

Phonemic Awareness

MATERIALS
- magazine or storybook pictures

Teach Hold up a picture of a truck. Say: *truck.../t/-/r/-/u/-/k/. Now I'll say some sounds in the word.../t/-/u/-/k/. What sound did I leave off?* (/r/) *If I leave off the /r/ sound in truck, the new word is tuck.*

Practice Continue the activity with the words below, leaving off the sound in parentheses. Challenge children to name the missing sound and say the new word.

frog (r)	blotch (l)	skip (k)
plant (l)	stick (t)	crab (r)
snap (n)	bleach (l)	

Observe children as they blend, segment, and delete sounds. If children have difficulty, see Alternate Teaching Strategies on p. T64.

Children will:

- identify letter combinations *ph, tch,* and *ch.*
- blend and read letter combinations *ph, tch,* and *ch.*

MATERIALS

- **Teaching Chart 176**
- **Word Building Manipulative Cards**

Skills Finder

Digraphs *ph, tch*

Introduce	B2: 92G-H
Review	B2: 115E-F, 116G-H, 281E-F, 281G-H
Test	B2: Unit 2

SPELLING/PHONICS CONNECTIONS

See The 5-Day Spelling Plan, pages 281Q–281R.

TEACHING TIP

MANAGEMENT When possible, invite volunteers to take on the role of teacher, running their hands under words on the board as the class blends the sounds together.

Review Digraphs *ph, tch, ch*

PREPARE

Review *ph, tch,* and *ch* Remind children that when some letters appear together they represent a single sound. Write *ph, tch,* and *ch* on the chalkboard. Elicit from children that the letters *ph* make the /f/ sound; the letters *tch* and *ch* make the /ch/ sound.

TEACH

BLENDING Model and Guide Practice with *ph, ch,* and *tch* Words

- Display **Teaching Chart 176**. Point to *ch*. Tell children that these letters stand for the /ch/ sound.
- Write the letters *ch* in the blank space in the first example.
- Blend the sounds together to read the word *speech*. Have children repeat after you.
- In the next row, write *ch* in the space to form the word *chill*. Repeat the process you used for *speech*.
- Have volunteers suggest letters to help you complete the first column of the chart, making a word that contains the /ch/ sound. Ask volunteers to read the completed word.

ch	tch	ph
speech	watched	telephone
chill	itch	graph
chair	stretch	elephant
reach	pitcher	phonics

Teaching Chart 176

Use the Words in Context Have volunteers use the words in sentences to reinforce their meanings. *Example: Snowy weather can cause you to feel a chill.*

Repeat the Procedure Follow the same procedure to complete the remaining columns on the **Teaching Chart**.

PRACTICE

SEGMENTING Build *ch, ph,* and *tch* Words with Letter Cards

Divide the class into small groups. Read aloud the words *reach, chair, photo, graph, catch, patch*. Have groups use **Word Building Manipulative Cards** to build each word. Ask children to then copy each word on an index card and circle the letter combinations that make the /f/ or /ch/ sounds. ▶ **Visual/Linguistic**

c h i m e

ASSESS/CLOSE

Build and Read *ch, ph,* and *tch* Words

To assess children's ability to build and blend words with letter combinations, observe them as they work on the Practice activity. Then have children use two *ph, ch,* or *tch* words in a sentence.

ADDITIONAL PHONICS RESOURCES

Phonics/ Phonemic Awareness Practice Book, pages 135–138

McGraw-Hill School TECHNOLOGY

CD-ROM activities for practice with Blending and Segmenting

Meeting Individual Needs for Phonics

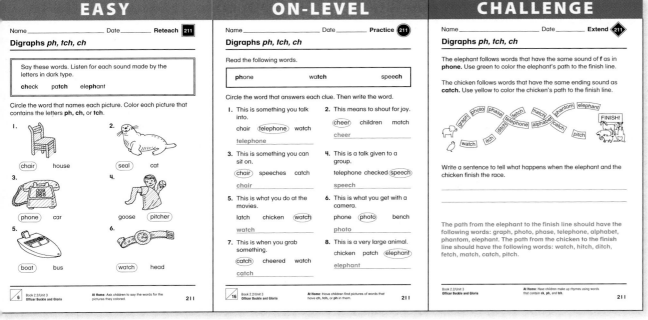

EASY

Name __________ Date ______ **Reteach 211**

Digraphs *ph, tch, ch*

Say these words. Listen for each sound made by the letters in dark type.

check pa**tch** ele**ph**ant

Circle the word that names each picture. Color each picture that contains the letters **ph, ch,** or **tch**.

1. (chair) house
2. (seal) cat
3. (phone) car
4. goose (pitcher)
5. (boat) bus
6. (watch) head

6 Book 2.2/Unit 3 **Officer Buckle and Gloria** — **At Home:** Ask children to say the words for the pictures they colored. 211

Reteach, 211

ON-LEVEL

Name __________ Date ______ **Practice 211**

Digraphs *ph, tch, ch*

Read the following words.

phone wa**tch** spee**ch**

Circle the word that answers each clue. Then write the word.

1. This is something you talk into.
   chair (telephone) watch
   telephone
2. This means to shout for joy.
   (cheer) children match
   cheer
3. This is something you can sit on.
   (chair) speeches catch
   chair
4. This is a talk given to a group.
   telephone checked (speech)
   speech
5. This is what you do at the movies.
   latch chicken (watch)
   watch
6. This is what you get with a camera.
   phone (photo) bench
   photo
7. This is when you grab something.
   (catch) cheered watch
   catch
8. This is a very large animal.
   chicken patch (elephant)
   elephant

16 Book 2.2/Unit 3 **Officer Buckle and Gloria** — **At Home:** Have children find pictures of words that have **ch, tch,** or **ph** in them. 211

Practice, 211

CHALLENGE

Name __________ Date ______ **Extend 211**

Digraphs *ph, tch, ch*

The elephant follows words that have the same sound of **f** as in **phone.** Use green to color the elephant's path to the finish line.

The chicken follows words that have the same ending sound as **catch.** Use yellow to color the chicken's path to the finish line.

graph photo phase fetch match phantom elephant telephone alphabet catch ditch itch watch pitch FINISH!

Write a sentence to tell what happens when the elephant and the chicken finish the race.

The path from the elephant to the finish line should have the following words: graph, photo, phase, telephone, alphabet, phantom, elephant. The path from the chicken to the finish line should have the following words: watch, hitch, ditch, fetch, match, catch, pitch.

Book 2.2/Unit 3 **Officer Buckle and Gloria** — **At Home:** Have children make up rhymes using words that contain **ch, ph,** and **tch**. 211

Extend, 211

Daily Routines

DAY 1 Fluency Write the following words on the chalkboard: *reach, telephone, watch, chair*. Point to each word, asking children to blend the sounds silently. Ask a volunteer to read aloud each word.

DAY 2 Segmenting Write on the chalkboard the following list: *tea_, pa_, _one, _ange, _eck*. Call volunteers to the board to add the letters combination *ch, ph,* or *tch* to complete each word.

DAY 3 Discriminating Write the following words on the chalkboard: *chase, match, phone, race, math, back*. Invite children to indicate which words contain letter combinations *ch, ph,* or *tch*.

DAY 4 Words in Context Ask children working in small groups to create riddles containing *ch, tch,* and *ph* words. Have children take turns reading their riddles as the rest of the group guesses the word.

DAY 5 Writing Write the following list on the chalkboard: *peach, reach, beach, teach, match, patch, batch, catch*. Discuss meanings with children. Invite them to write a short rhyme using two or three of these words.

OBJECTIVES

Children will blend and read letter combinations *ph, tch,* and *ch*.

Apply ph, tch, and ch

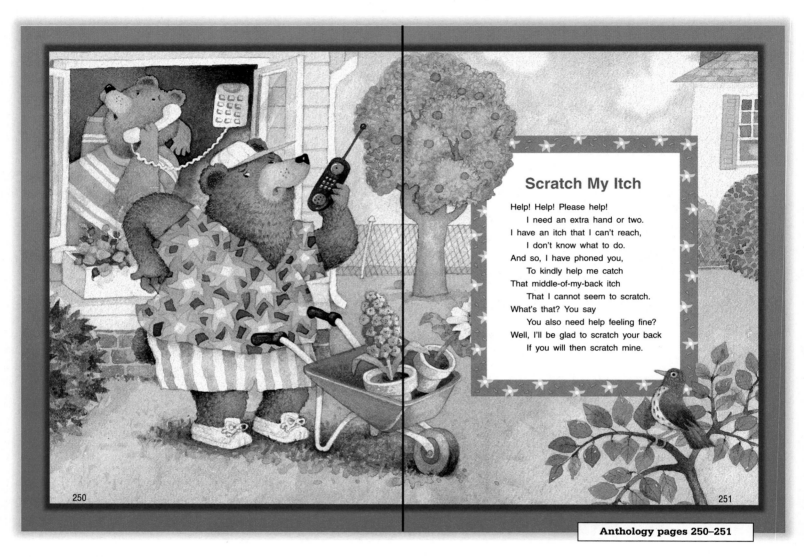

Scratch My Itch

Help! Help! Please help!
I need an extra hand or two.
I have an itch that I can't reach,
I don't know what to do.
And so, I have phoned you,
To kindly help me catch
That middle-of-my-back itch
That I cannot seem to scratch.
What's that? You say
You also need help feeling fine?
Well, I'll be glad to scratch your back
If you will then scratch mine.

250 251

Anthology pages 250–251

Read and Build Fluency

READ THE POEM Tell children to listen for the /ch/ and /f/ sounds as they listen and follow along while you read aloud "Scratch My Itch." Model fluent reading by expressively reading the poem, emphasizing periods, question marks, and exclamation points. Then, ask the class to echo your reading style as you read it once more.

PARTNERS **REREAD FOR FLUENCY** Have partners take turns reading the poem aloud to each other. Ask children to focus on punctuation and expression of emotion. Remind them to pause after commas, to add emphasis to sentences with exclamation points, and to vary the ending tone for questions.

Dictate and Spell

JOURNAL **DICTATE WORDS** Say the word *reach* aloud. Then segment it into its three individual sounds. Repeat the word and use it in a sentence, such as "I can reach the top of the board." Have children repeat the word and write the letters for each sound to make the whole word. Then repeat these steps with a *tch* word and a *ph* word. Ask them if they can find any other *tch, ch,* or *ph* words in the poem to segment. Continue the exercise with words not in the poem, such as *speech, watch,* and *graph.*

Intervention **Skills Intervention Guide,** for direct instruction and extra practice of *ph, tch, & ch*

Build Background

Science

Concept: Animals at Work

Evaluate Prior Knowledge

CONCEPT: ANIMALS AT WORK Ask children to share what they know about how animals help people work. Use the following activities if children need more information about the concept.

CREATE A WORD WEB FOR ANIMALS AT WORK Work with children to create a word web recording the different ways that animals help people work.

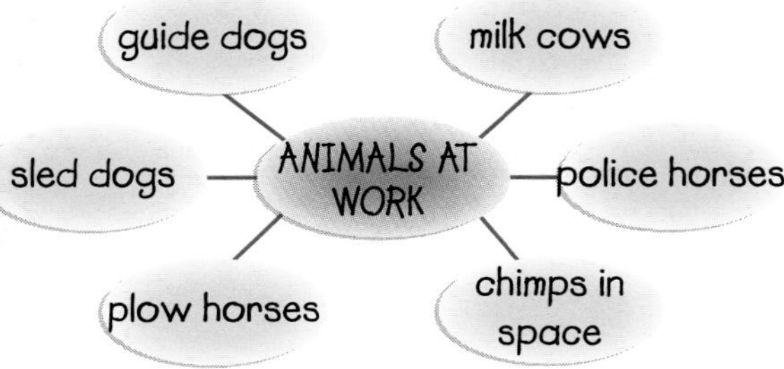

CREATE PICTURES OF ANIMALS AT WORK Encourage children to draw pictures of animals at work. Suggest that they refer to the word web for ideas. Invite children to write captions for their pictures.

Develop Oral Language

ROLEPLAY Have groups of children pretend to be animals engaged in the work activities listed in the word web. Encourage them to perform skits for the class in which they imagine a dialogue among a group of animals about the work they are performing.

ESL

Prompt children to include as much information as they can about the work, including:

- when it is performed
- how difficult it is
- what kinds of food the animals eat
- where the animals live
- what kind of training the animals might receive

▶ **Bodily/Kinesthetic**

Anthology and Leveled Books

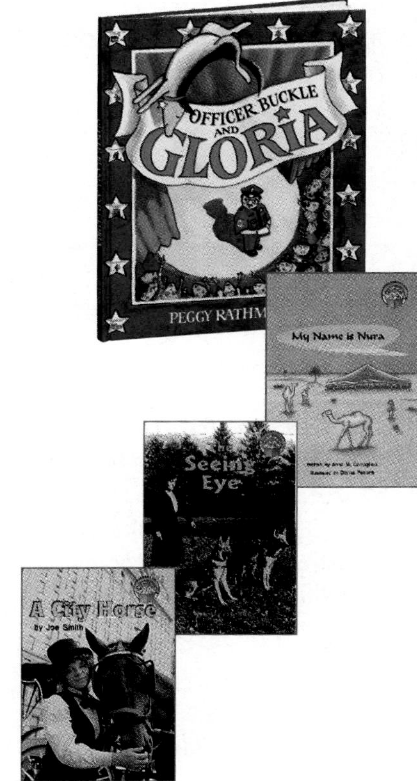

DAILY Phonics ROUTINES

DAY 2 **Segmenting** Write on the chalkboard the following list: *tea_, pa_, _one, _ange, _eck*. Call volunteers to the chalkboard to add the letter combination *ch, ph,* or *tch* to complete each word.

LANGUAGE SUPPORT

Use the Language Support Book, page 226–229 to help build background.

Children will use context and structural clues to determine the meanings of vocabulary words.

Definitions

accident (p. 263) a sad, unexpected event in which people may be hurt

audience (p. 262) a group of people gathered to hear or see something

cheered (p. 263) shouted with happiness or encouragement

slips (p. 261) moves suddenly from a position; slides

station (p. 264) a building or place used by an organization

wipe (p. 261) to clean or dry something by rubbing it

Story Words

These words from the selection may be unfamiliar. Before children read, have them check the meanings and pronunciations of the words in the Glossary, beginning on page 390, or in a dictionary.

- bulletin board, p. 255
- swivel chair, p. 255
- principal, p. 257
- thumbtack, p. 262
- auditorium, p. 268
- bravo, p. 269

accident
audience
cheered
slips
station
wipe

Vocabulary

Teach Vocabulary in Context

Identify Vocabulary Words Display **Teaching Chart 177** and read the passage with children. Have volunteers circle each vocabulary word and underline other words that are clues to its meaning.

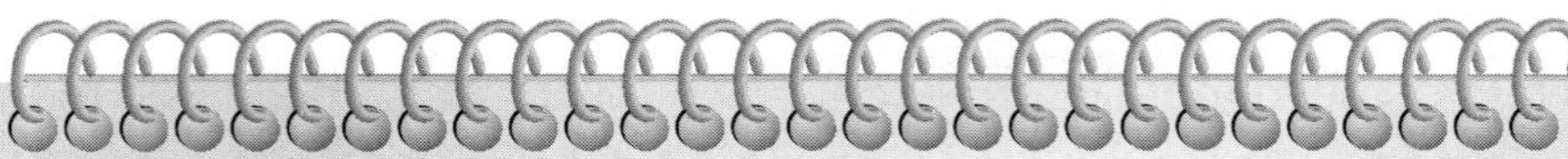

No Accidents, Please!

1. The school was near the police station where Officer Buckle worked. **2.** He could hear the large audience of students waiting inside to hear him speak. **3.** The students wanted Officer Buckle to know how excited they were to see him—they cheered when he and his dog walked in. **4.** Officer Buckle made sure to wipe his glasses, removing the dirt from them so he could see where the stage was. **5.** Sometimes Officer Buckle doesn't look where he is going, and he slips on something that has spilled and falls. **6.** Officer Buckle didn't want to have an accident, and fall down in front of so many people!

Teaching Chart 177

Discuss Meanings Ask questions like these to help clarify word meanings:

- Do you know where the nearest police station is located?
- Where are some places you might find an audience?
- When was the last time you cheered for something? What did it sound like?
- How might you wipe up something that is spilled? Show me.
- What might cause a person to slip and fall?
- What happens when two cars have an accident?

Practice

Pantomimes

PARTNERS

Have partners choose vocabulary cards from a pile and, without speaking, pantomime clues as a partner or small group tries to guess the word. ▶ **Kinesthetic**

Word Building Manipulative Cards

Context Sentences

PARTNERS

WRITING

Have partners write context sentences, leaving a blank for each vocabulary word. Encourage children to exchange papers and fill in the blanks or use vocabulary cards to show answers.

Assess Vocabulary

Identify Word Meaning in Context

PARTNERS

WRITING

Challenge children to write a short paragraph or story using as many of the vocabulary words as possible. Ask students to include clues that show each word's meaning. Partners can exchange papers and make sure the vocabulary words are used correctly.

Meeting Individual Needs for Vocabulary

EASY

Name________ Date______ Reteach 212

Vocabulary

Find a word in the box that matches each clue.
Write the word in the empty boxes.

accidents audience cheered slips station wipe

1. the people who watch a play
a u d i e n c e
2. the place where trains come and go
s t a t i o n
3. ways that people get hurt
a c c i d e n t s
4. what a pig does on the ice
s l i p s
5. what we did when we won
c h e e r e d
6. what you do to clean a table
w i p e

212 At Home: Have children draw a picture for two of the vocabulary words. Book 2.2/Unit 3 Officer Buckle and Gloria 6

Reteach, 212

ON-LEVEL

Name________ Date______ Practice 212

Vocabulary

Choose a word from the box to complete each sentence.
Write the words on the lines. Each word is used twice.

accidents audience cheered slips station wipe

1. The train came into the __station__ early.
Everyone shouted and __cheered__.
2. The children __cheered__ when the clown came out.
He said they were a good __audience__.
3. Jake __slips__ and falls every day.
He has too many __accidents__!
4. Please __wipe__ up the water that spilled.
Someone from the __audience__ might fall.
5. Many people had car __accidents__ yesterday.
Some of the people went to the police __station__.
6. Arthur forgets to __wipe__ the mud off his shoes.
He __slips__ on the floor.

212 At Home: Ask children to draw a picture to illustrate each sentence. Book 2.2/Unit 3 Officer Buckle and Gloria 12

Practice, 212

ON-LEVEL

Chad and the Horses

Chad's father phoned the vet. Then they all saw why the horse fell. There was water on the floor.

Mark said, "I spilled water. I forgot to wipe it up. I'm sorry."

Luckily the horse was fine. Everyone forgave Mark. From that day on he tried not to rush the horses.

At Home: Review with the children how the animals in this story danced for work. What are some other animals that work? What do they do?

4

212a

Practice, 212a
Take-Home Story

CHALLENGE

Name________ Date______ Extend 212

Vocabulary

Write a word from the box in each sentence.

audience accidents slips station wipe cheered

1. People get hurt in __accidents__.
2. The show had a big __audience__.
3. The fans __cheered__ at the big game.
4. Sometimes Joel __slips__ on icy sidewalks.
5. A police building is called a __station__ house.
6. If you __wipe__ up the spill, no one will slip and fall.

Choose two words from the box. Use them in your own sentences.

212 At Home: Have children draw a picture and write two sentences illustrating one of the vocabulary words. Book 2.2/Unit 3 Officer Buckle and Gloria

Extend, 212

SPELLING/VOCABULARY CONNECTIONS

See Spelling Challenge Words, page 281Q.

LANGUAGE SUPPORT

See the Language Support Book, pages 226–229, for teaching suggestions for Vocabulary.

Provides vocabulary activities.

Comprehension

Prereading Strategies

PREVIEW AND PREDICT Preview the story by taking a **picture walk** through the illustrations.

- What clues do the pictures give you about the story's main characters?
- What do you think the story is about?
- Will the story be nonfiction or will it be a funny story? How can you tell? (A funny story; the dog is doing unrealistic things in the picture.)

Have children record their predictions in a chart.

PREDICTIONS	WHAT HAPPENED
The story is about a policeman and a dog.	
The policeman talks to students.	

SET PURPOSES Ask children what they would like to learn as they read the story. For example:

- Does the dog work with the policeman?
- What will the policeman discuss with the students?

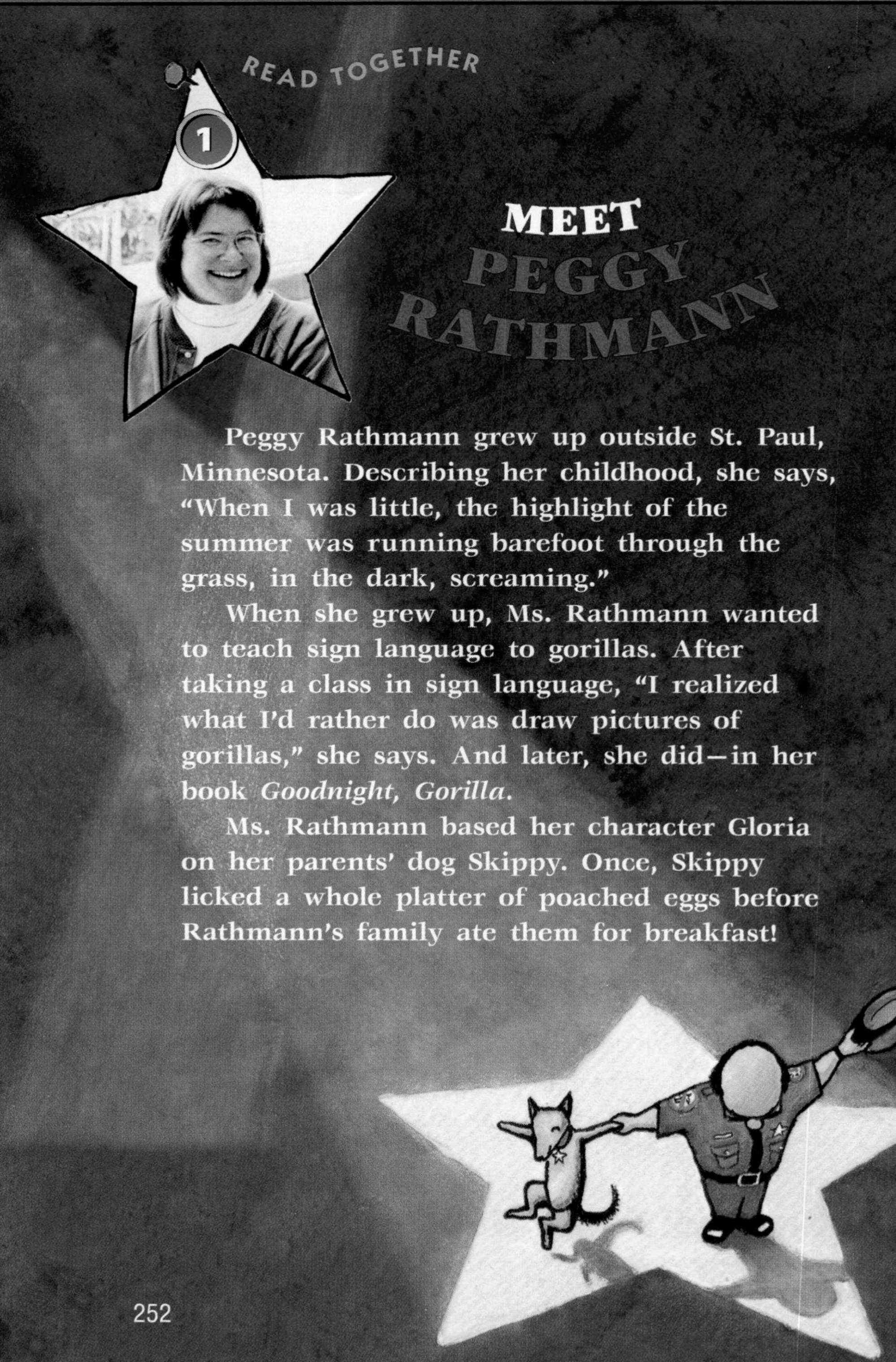

READ TOGETHER
1
MEET
PEGGY
RATHMANN
Peggy Rathmann grew up outside St. Paul, Minnesota. Describing her childhood, she says, "When I was little, the highlight of the summer was running barefoot through the grass, in the dark, screaming."
When she grew up, Ms. Rathmann wanted to teach sign language to gorillas. After taking a class in sign language, "I realized what I'd rather do was draw pictures of gorillas," she says. And later, she did—in her book *Goodnight, Gorilla*.
Ms. Rathmann based her character Gloria on her parents' dog Skippy. Once, Skippy licked a whole platter of poached eggs before Rathmann's family ate them for breakfast!
252

Meeting Individual Needs • Grouping Suggestions for Strategic Reading

EASY

Read Together Read the story aloud with children. Model using the strategy of noting cause and effect in order to better understand what is happening in the story. Comprehension and Intervention prompts offer additional help with decoding, vocabulary, and comprehension.

ON-LEVEL

Guided Instruction Read the story with the children using the Comprehension prompts. Monitor any difficulties children have in order to determine which prompts to emphasize. Afterward, have children reread the story on their own or have them use the **Listening Library.** You may want to have children read the story on their own first.

CHALLENGE

Read Independently Remind children to use their own experiences in order to better understand the causes and effects of actions in the story. After reading, have children retell the story, explaining whether they believe the story's events were realistic. Children can also use the questions on page 277 for a group discussion.

OFFICER BUCKLE AND GLORIA

PEGGY RATHMANN

253

Comprehension

Apply Digraphs *ph, tch, ch*

STRATEGIC READING Understanding what happens because of an event, action, or feeling will help you to better understand a story. Let's create some stick puppets of the story's characters and use them to act out things that happen in the story.

1 Look at the picture on page 252. This is Peggy Rathmann, the author. Why do you think she based the character of Gloria on a real-life dog? Let's read to find out what the made-up character of Gloria is like. *Author's Purpose*

LANGUAGE SUPPORT

Blackline masters of the stick puppets can be found in the **Language Support Book**.

LANGUAGE SUPPORT, 230

Genre

Fantasy

Explain that fantasies:

- include events and/or settings that could not happen in real life.
- may be set in imaginary worlds and have characters that may seem unreal.
- may be largely realistic stories with animals as main characters.

Activity After children read *Officer Buckle and Gloria,* brainstorm with them a list of Gloria's qualities that are imaginary. Have partners take turns being these two characters. Encourage them to create new imaginary situations in which Gloria mirrors Officer Buckle's words.

Comprehension

2 What is happening on these two pages? (Officer Buckle is falling off a chair.) What caused this to happen? (standing on a swivel chair) Act out the cause and effect with your stick puppet. *Cause and Effect/Story Props*

254

LANGUAGE SUPPORT

ESL Help students understand that visual clues are useful in figuring out what is happening in a story. Ask them to look carefully at this page. Then elicit descriptions by asking: What is happening to the chair? (It is sliding and is about to fall backward.) What does the chair have that makes it slide easily? (wheels) What else do you see that helps you think that the chair is moving? (flying paper)

Officer Buckle knew more safety tips than anyone else in Napville. 3

Every time he thought of a new one, he thumbtacked it to his bulletin board.

Safety Tip #77

NEVER stand on a SWIVEL CHAIR.

255

Comprehension

3 How might Officer Buckle come up with his safety tips? (He makes tips when he has an accident.) How does the picture help you to know? (It shows him having an accident while standing on a swivel chair.) ***Make Inferences***

MODEL I'm going to think about the events in the story that led up to Officer Buckle writing a new safety tip. First Officer Buckle fell off the swivel chair, and then he wrote the tip, "Never stand on a swivel chair." Maybe he writes a new tip every time he has an accident himself.

Comprehension

4 Imagine you are Officer Buckle. How do you feel while you are giving your speech? Why? (sad; nobody is listening) Why might you continue to give your speech even though nobody is listening to you? (you want to help; you believe in your safety tips) ***Make Inferences***

5 Why do you think there was sometimes snoring among the students? (Officer Buckle was so boring that sometimes students fell asleep.) ***Draw Conclusions***

6 What do you predict might happen to the students because they never listen to Officer Buckle's safety tips? (They might hurt themselves because they don't know how to be safe.) ***Make Predictions***

TEACHING TIP

MANAGEMENT **Read the story once with children using the Comprehension prompts before you have them do the Cross-Curricular activities.**

Officer Buckle shared his safety tips with the students at Napville School.

Nobody ever listened.

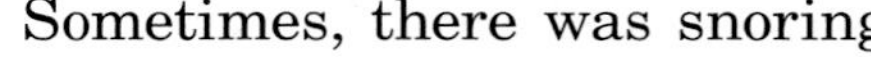

Sometimes, there was snoring.

4 5 6

LANGUAGE SUPPORT

ESL Point out the word *tips* and explain that *tip* has several meanings in English. Use the word in three sentences with different meanings. Say: *I'll give you a tip about how to get 100 on the quiz. I left a tip for the waiter in the restaurant. Don't tip the wastebasket; the papers will fall out.* Repeat each sentence and ask children to say in their own words what the word *tip* means in that context. (1. *advice* or *suggestion,* 2. *small amount of money you give someone who did something for you,* 3. *turn something partly on its side.)* Help children make up original sentences for each meaning.

Afterward, it was business as usual.

Mrs. Toppel, the principal, took down the welcome banner.

"NEVER stand on a SWIVEL CHAIR," said Officer Buckle, but Mrs. Toppel didn't hear him.

257

Comprehension

7 Look at the picture on this page. Do you think that your prediction from the last page came true? How do you know? (The picture shows students getting hurt because they didn't listen to Officer Buckle's safety tips.) ***Confirm Predictions***

8 What is Officer Buckle's biggest problem right now? (No one listens to him. His safety tips are not interesting.) Can you think of any possible solutions to that problem? (Possible answers: He could make his speeches funny; he could do demonstrations or show pictures.) ***Problem and Solution***

Minilesson

REVIEW/MAINTAIN

Review /ər/ and /əl/

Point out the /ər/ and /əl/ sounds as you read the words *never* and *swivel* on page 257. Ask children to:

- find one more word on page 257 that ends with the sound /ər/. (banner)
- say what sound Officer Buckle's name ends in. (/əl/)

Activity Invite volunteers to write a short poem using three words that have the /əl/ sound.

Comprehension

9 How do you think the children at school will feel about Gloria coming along with Officer Buckle? Why do you think that? (Possible answer: They will be happy; many children like animals.) Think about your own experience. How would you feel if you saw Gloria on stage with Officer Buckle? Why? (answers will vary) ***Make Predictions***

10 Phonics /ch/ Read the second sentence on page 258. What word in this sentence contains /ch/? (*speech*) Which letters stand for that sound? (*ch*) ***Graphophonic Cues***

Then one day, Napville's police department bought a police dog named Gloria.

When it was time for Officer Buckle to give the safety speech at the school, Gloria went along.

258

CULTURAL PERSPECTIVES

WORKING ANIMALS In different cultures, people use animals to help them do different kinds of work. Ask children if they know of work done by animals. Write responses on the board.

RESEARCH AND INQUIRY Have children work in small groups. Invite each group to choose a particular area of the world, and to research the different kinds of work that animals perform there. Have children present their findings to the class with pictures or photographs of animals at work. Create a bulletin-board display of animals at work around the world.

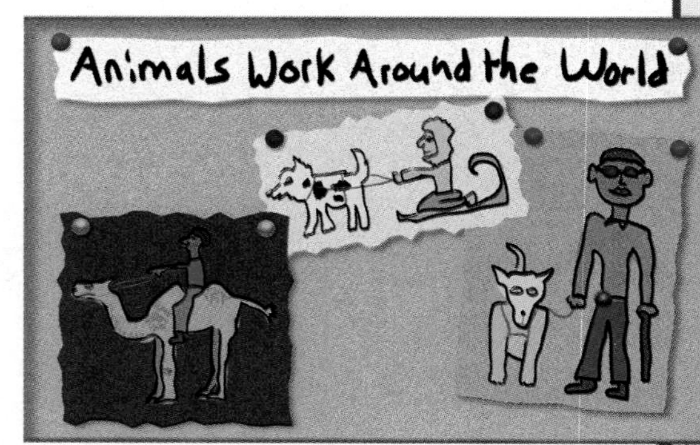

"Children, this is Gloria," announced Officer Buckle. "Gloria obeys my commands. Gloria, SIT!" And Gloria sat.

259

Comprehension

11 **Phonics** **/ch/** Point to the first word on this page. *(children)* Let's blend the sounds together to read it. Remember that *ch* together stand for the /ch/ sound. ch il dren children

Blending/Graphophonic Cues

TEACHING TIP

BACKGROUND INFORMATION Provide children with books and brochures on safety tips for home and school. Use the local fire and police departments as resources for these references. Allow children time to browse through these materials and discuss their findings.

Comprehension

12 What is Gloria doing in the illustration on the top of the page? (standing up like Officer Buckle) What is she doing in the illustration on the bottom of the page? (sitting like a dog) What is Officer Buckle doing in each picture? (In the first picture, Officer Buckle is looking out at the audience. In the second, he is looking at Gloria.) Let's use our puppets to show Officer Buckle looking away from Gloria and then looking back at her.
Story Props

13 How do you think children in the audience feel in this scene? (surprised) How do you know? (From their expressions; the story says they sat up and stared.) Show me what they did. Don't forget to consider what you have already read about the characters.
Character/Role-Play

Fluency

Read With Expression

PARTNERS Explain to children that authors sometimes use capital letters to show words with special emphasis. Point out the words *KEEP* and *SHOELACES* as examples. Have two students read aloud pages 260 and 261. One student can read the narration, and the other can read Officer Buckle's dialogue.

Remind students to:

- look for capital letters and exclamation points that indicate special emphasis.
- pause at the end of sentences.
- read with expression.

Officer Buckle gave Safety Tip Number One:

"KEEP your SHOELACES tied!"

The children sat up and stared.

Officer Buckle checked to see if Gloria was sitting at attention. She was.

260

"Safety Tip Number Two," said Officer Buckle. "ALWAYS wipe up spills BEFORE someone SLIPS AND FALLS!"

The children's eyes popped.

Officer Buckle checked on Gloria again.

"Good dog," he said.

Officer Buckle thought of a safety tip he had discovered that morning.

261

Comprehension

14 What does Officer Buckle say to Gloria? *(Good dog.)* Do you think Officer Buckle knows what Gloria is doing? Why? (No. In the picture, Gloria is standing on her head while Officer Buckle isn't looking.) How do you think Officer Buckle would feel if he knew what Gloria was doing? (annoyed; surprised) ***Make Inferences***

P/I **REVIEW LONG *a*** Read the first word in the second sentence on page 261. *(always)* What letters make the long *a* sound in this word? *(ay)*

P/I PREVENTION/INTERVENTION

VIEW LONG *a* Remind children t different letters and letter combi- ions can make the long *a* sound. view the letter combinations *ai, ay,* d the letters *a-e*. Write the following rds on the chalkboard: *sail, sway,* e, *acorn*. Say each word aloud as u emphasize the long *a* sound. Then e children blend the sounds in h word together and read each rd aloud.

Have children find the words on page 261 with the long *a* sound. (always, safety) Say the words with children. Have children brainstorm a list of words with /ā/. List children's words on the chalkboard. Then have volunteers come up to the chalkboard and circle the letters in each word that make the /ā/ sound. *Graphophonic Cues*

Comprehension

15 What did the children do on these pages? (roared, clapped, laughed, and cheered) Why did they do these things? (They liked Gloria's performance.) Let's use our stick puppets to act out what's causing the children's response. *Cause and Effect/Story Props*

16 **Phonics** /ch/ Look at the last word in the first sentence on page 263. Let's sound it out together.
/ch/ /îr/ /d/ cheered
Blending/Graphophonic Cues

"NEVER leave a THUMBTACK where you might SIT on it!"

The audience roared.

Officer Buckle grinned. He said the rest of the tips with *plenty* of expression.

262

Activity

Cross Curricular: Social Studies

SAFETY AWARENESS Ask students to invite a police officer to their school to offer safety tips. Brainstorm with children about all the important details the letter should contain. Then have students work as a group to write an invitation and send it to a local police station.

After the police officer's visit, have students write thank-you letters including information they learned from the speech.

Dear Officer,
Please visit our classroom. We would like information on safety tips. We are reading a story about a policeman who speaks to students about safety tips. Our School is located at

The children clapped their hands and cheered. Some of them laughed until they cried. 16

Officer Buckle was surprised. He had never noticed how funny safety tips could be. 17

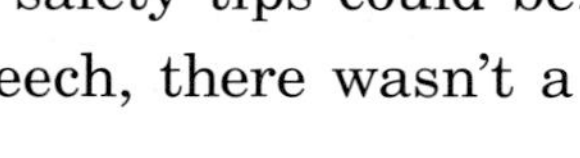

After *this* safety speech, there wasn't a single accident. 18

Comprehension

17 Officer Buckle thinks that his safety tips are funny. Do you think he is correct about this? Why or why not? (He does not know that Gloria is acting funny behind him, so he thinks that the safety tips are funny.) ***Draw Conclusions***

18 Why do you think there were no accidents after this speech? (The children paid attention to this speech because Gloria made it so funny.) ***Draw Conclusions***

Minilesson

REVIEW/MAINTAIN

Make Inferences

Remind children that even when an author doesn't tell you characters' feelings directly, you can infer, or make a good guess, about their feelings based on certain clues. Have children:

- look at page 262.
- infer how Officer Buckle might have thought of that safety tip.
- explain what information they used to make this inference.

Activity Have children look at the picture of Gloria on page 258 and write one sentence that describes how they think Gloria feels about riding with Officer Buckle.

Comprehension

Phonics Look at the last sentence on page 264. Point to the fifth word in the sentence. *(drawings)* Would someone like to read it aloud? ***Graphophonic Cues***

SELF-MONITORING STRATEGY

SEARCH FOR CLUES Searching for clues in the words and pictures of a story can help a reader to understand why characters think and feel as they do.

MODEL I'm not sure why Officer Buckle thought the students' drawings showed a lot of imagination. I'll search for clues. All the drawings show pictures of Gloria doing tricks. But Officer Buckle doesn't know that Gloria was doing tricks. So he must think that the students imagined her doing tricks!

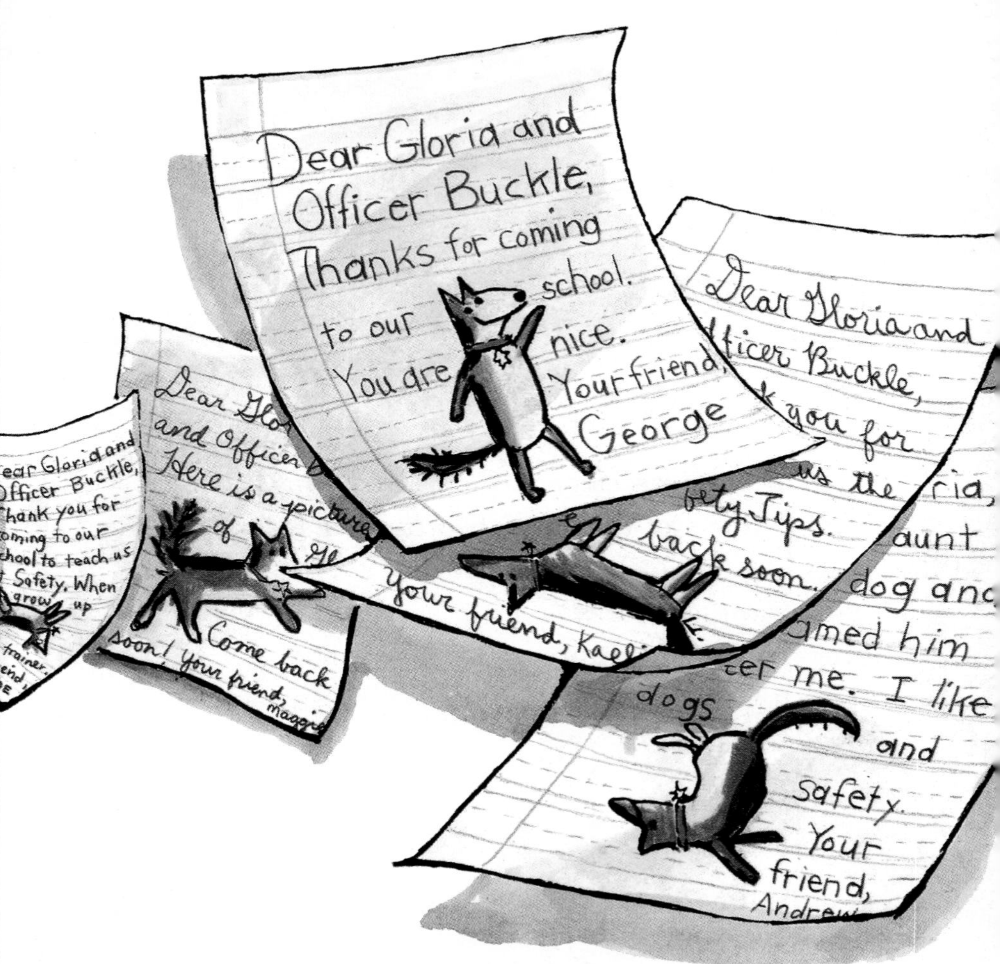

19 The next day, an enormous envelope arrived at the police station. It was stuffed with thank-you letters from the students at Napville School.

Every letter had a drawing of Gloria on it.

Officer Buckle thought the drawings showed a lot of imagination.

264

PREVENTION/INTERVENTION

Write the following words on a piece of chart paper: *lawn, hawk, drawn, awful.* Cover the consonants with self-stick notes, so that only the letters *aw* show. Ask children what sound is represented by the letter combination *aw*. (ô) Beginning with the first word on the chart paper, have a volunteer pull off the self-stick notes and blend the letters together to pronounce the word. Then have children read the word with you as you pass your hand beneath it. Repeat this activity with the rest of the words on the chart paper. ***Graphophonic Cues***

His favorite letter was written on a star-shaped piece of paper. It said:

You and Gloria make a good team.
Your friend,
Claire
P.S. I always wear
a crash helmet.
(Safety Tip #7)

265

Comprehension

19 How do you think Officer Buckle feels about receiving these letters from students? ***Character/Make Inferences***

MODEL If I were Officer Buckle, I'd feel really happy about all the thank-you notes. It makes me feel good to know that someone likes something I've done. And it says he had a favorite letter. My guess is that Officer Buckle feels very good.

LANGUAGE SUPPORT

ESL Help children figure out the meaning of the ...rase *a lot of imagination*. Ask: *What ...ifferent about these letters?* (They ...ve drawings on them. One is ...aped like a star.) Say: *Most letters don't have drawings. Most aren't shaped like stars. When you think of new ways of doing something, you are using your imagination.* Ask children to give other examples of things that take *a lot of imagination.*

Comprehension

20 Why do all the students now want to hear Officer Buckle's safety tips? How do you know? (People have heard about Gloria and want to see her perform. They tell Officer Buckle to bring along his dog.) ***Draw Conclusions***

21 **Phonics** /f/ Find the word with /f/ spelled *ph* in the first sentence on page 266. (*phones*) Read the word aloud. ***Graphophonic Cues***

20 Officer Buckle was thumbtacking Claire's
letter to his bulletin board when the phones
21 started ringing. Grade schools, high schools,
and day-care centers were calling about the
safety speech.

"Officer Buckle," they said, "our students want to hear your safety tips! And please, bring along that police dog."

Officer Buckle told his safety tips to 313 schools.

Everywhere he and Gloria went, children sat up and listened.

266

Activity

Cross Curricular: Math

ADD THE "THANK-YOU"S Officer Buckle and Gloria were sent many thank-you notes. Have children use the following word problems to figure out how many notes were sent by Hillside Elementary School.

- Every student in Mrs. Hagan's second-grade class sent a thank-you note. There were 14 boys and 11 girls. How many notes were sent? (25)
- The Hillside Elementary School sent 52 notes from the fifth grade and 75 from the sixth grade. How many fifth and sixth graders sent notes? (127)

After every speech, Officer Buckle took Gloria out for ice cream.

Officer Buckle loved having a buddy.

267

Comprehension

22 How would you describe the way Officer Buckle and Gloria are feeling now? (happy) Why do you think they feel this way? (They have become good friends. Everyone enjoys their speeches.) ***Make Inferences***

23 Look at the top picture on this page. What is Gloria doing? (signing autographs) What does this tell you about how the children feel about her? (The children love Gloria.) ***Draw Conclusions***

WORD STRUCTURE Read the last sentence on page 266. What did the children do? (*sat up and listened*) When did these actions take place: in the past, the present, or the future? (in the past) How do you know?(There is an *-ed* ending in the word *listened*.)

PREVENTION/INTERVENTION

ORD STRUCTURE Remind ildren that when the ending *-ed* added to a verb, it shows that the tion has already happened. Explain at the word *listened* indicates that e listening has already taken place. so remind children that some verbs ve irregular forms, such as *sit/sat* d *run/ran*.

Present children with the following verbs: *run, talk, brush, paint, cook, drive.* Have children write the past tense of these action verbs. Then ask children to use the past and present tenses of each word in a sentence. ***Semantic Cues***

Comprehension

24 How has Officer Buckle's safety speech changed from the beginning of the story? (He says the same thing in his speech, but Gloria performs now.) How have the feelings of the audiences changed? (The audiences used to get bored, but now they are entertained.) What caused the children to jump to their feet and applaud? Let's use our puppets to act out what happened on page 268. *Cause and Effect/Story Props*

MODEL I see that Gloria is jumping high in the air, as if she has been shocked by lightning. The audience must be impressed by her performance. I think Gloria's performance caused them to stand up and applaud.

Then one day, a television news team videotaped Officer Buckle in the state-college auditorium.

When he finished Safety Tip Number Ninety-nine, DO NOT GO SWIMMING DURING ELECTRICAL STORMS!, the students jumped to their feet and applauded.

24

268

"Bravo! Bravo!" they cheered.
Officer Buckle bowed again and again. 

269

Comprehension

25 Do you think that Officer Buckle will find out that Gloria is performing behind him? (Possible answer: Officer Buckle will probably find out about Gloria's performances.) ***Make Predictions***

Minilesson

REVIEW/MAINTAIN

Context Clues

Remind children that they can often figure out the meaning of an unfamiliar word by looking at context clues—the pictures and familiar words around the unfamiliar word. Ask:

- Can you figure out the meaning of the word *bravo* on page 269 using context clues?

Activity Using context clues from both words and pictures, have children figure out the meaning of the word *video-taped* on page 268. Have children tell the context clues they used.

Comprehension

26 How do you think Officer Buckle is feeling on this page? (very surprised) How can you tell? (by his expression; by the way he's spilling his popcorn) ***Make Inferences***

27 What do you think will happen now that Officer Buckle knows about Gloria? ***Make Predictions***

Visual Literacy

VIEWING AND REPRESENTING

Discuss the illustration on pages 270 and 271. Ask:

- What part of the television are we seeing on page 270? (the back)
- What is behind Officer Buckle? (a mirror)
- What is Officer Buckle seeing on television? How do you know? (Officer Buckle is seeing Gloria perform tricks behind him; we can see the reflection of the television screen in the mirror.)

Activity

Cross Curricular: Science

DOG BREEDS Tell children there are many different breeds of dogs and that, according to scientists, all dogs are members of the same species or group.

RESEARCH AND INQUIRY Have children choose a breed of dog to research. Suggest they find out the place of origin, size, color, type of fur, and classification.

For more information on dogs, have children visit ***www.mhschool.com/reading.***

A Collie is a herding dog with long black, brown, and white fur.

That night, Officer Buckle watched himself on the 10 o'clock news. 

271

Comprehension

28 Where is this part of the story taking place? (Officer Buckle's house) How can you tell? (Clues in the picture; text says they are watching the ten o'clock news.) ***Analyze Setting***

29 **Phonics** **/ch/** Let's read the fifth word in the sentence on this page. (*watched*) Which three letters together stand for /ch/? (*tch*) ***Graphophonic Cues***

Minilesson

REVIEW/MAINTAIN

Summarize

Explain to children that summarizing a story means telling the main parts, which include the main idea and the most important events in the story.

Ask children the following about summarizing *Officer Buckle and Gloria*:

- Would you tell about what Officer Buckle is wearing?
- Would you tell about Gloria performing behind Officer Buckle?

Activity In groups, have children summarize the story so far.

Comprehension

30 How do you think Officer Buckle feels now? What clues tell you he feels this way? What has caused Officer Buckle to feel different from the way he did before? (Officer Buckle is sad now because he has discovered that the audiences were cheering for Gloria, not him.) ***Analyze Character/Make Inferences***

31 Phonics /ph/ Find the word *tele-phoned* on this page. What letters in this word stand for /f/? ***Graphophonic Cues***

30 The next day, the principal of Napville School telephoned the police station.

31 "Good morning, Officer Buckle! It's time for our safety speech!"

Officer Buckle frowned.

"I'm not giving any more speeches! Nobody looks at me, anyway!"

"Oh," said Mrs. Toppel. "Well! How about Gloria? Could she come?"

272

Someone else from the police station gave Gloria a ride to the school.

Gloria sat onstage looking lonely. Then she fell asleep. So did the audience.

After Gloria left, Napville School had its biggest accident ever . . . .

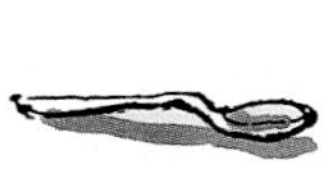

273

Comprehension

32 How do you think Gloria feels now? What clues tell you she feels this way? (She feels lonely without Officer Buckle. She no longer enjoys performing.) ***Analyze Character/Make Inferences***

33 Look at the people in this picture. Do they remind you of any people you saw earlier in this story? Why? ***Compare and Contrast***

MODEL They look like the people in the picture on page 260. Both pictures show people with their legs hanging over their chairs, falling asleep. The people in both audiences are bored by what they are seeing on stage, but this time it's Gloria.

LANGUAGE SUPPORT

ESL Have ESL children find the word *biggest* on ge 273. Help children identify the ot. Explain that the suffix *-est* means ne most." Therefore, *biggest* means ne most big."

ve children practice using superla- es by adding *-est* to the following root words: *fat, wide, small, tall, long.*

Then have them take turns drawing pictures to help illustrate word meaning (for example, fattest pig, tallest tree, and so on).

Comprehension

34 Would someone describe the events that caused this accident? Be sure to list the events in the order in which they took place. *Analyze Character/Sequence Events*

35 What do you think will happen to Officer Buckle and Gloria now? Do you think they will perform together again? Why or why not? (Possible answer: They will perform together so that there won't be another big accident.) *Make Predictions*

TEACHING TIP

TEXT FEATURES Direct children to page 274. Point out how the words *splat, splatter,* and *sploosh* are printed in increasingly larger and darker type for emphasis. Read them aloud, becoming louder and more dramatic with each word. Encourage children to read the words aloud with an emphasis that matches their appearance on the page.

34 It started with a puddle of banana pudding . . . .

35 **SPLAT!**

SPLATTER!

SPLOOSH!

36 Everyone slid smack into Mrs. Toppel, who screamed and let go of her hammer.

37

274

LANGUAGE SUPPORT

ESL Some children may not know that authors occasionally use special words that indicate sounds. Ask children which words on this page indicate sounds, and have them say the words aloud. Write on the chalkboard the words *screech, plop, creak, ding-dong, kaboom,* and *buzz.* Give children examples of how each word is used in a sentence. Say: *heard a loud screech just before the car accident; My ice cream cone dropped to the ground with a plop;* and so forth. Invite children to make up their own sentences using these words.

Comprehension

36 Why do you think the accident took place? (The students did not hear Officer Buckle's safety tips and so they did not know how to stay safe. This caused an accident.) ***Draw Conclusions***

37 What generalization can you make about following safety tips? (Following safety tips is always a good idea. It helps prevent accidents where you or someone else might get hurt.) ***Form Generalizations***

Comprehension

38 How do Officer Buckle and Gloria feel now? Make a face that shows Officer Buckle or Gloria's feelings now. *Role-Play/ Cause and Effect*

RETELL THE STORY Ask children to work in groups of three to retell the story. One child can "narrate" the story as the other two use their stick puppets to act out the events. *Summarize/Story Props*

STUDENT SELF-ASSESSMENT

Have children ask themselves the following questions to assess how they are reading:

- How did paying attention to the way one event effects or causes another help me to understand the plot?
- How did using what I know about letter sounds and word meanings help me to read and understand unfamiliar words?

TRANSFERRING THE STRATEGIES

- How can I use these strategies to help me read other stories?

The next morning, a pile of letters arrived at the police station. Every letter had a drawing of the accident.

Officer Buckle was shocked.

At the bottom of the pile was a note written on a paper star.

Officer Buckle smiled.

The note said:

Gloria gave Officer Buckle a big kiss on the nose. Officer Buckle gave Gloria a nice pat on the back. Then, Officer Buckle thought of his best safety tip yet . . .

276

REREADING FOR *Fluency*

PARTNERS

Have children read a favorite part of the story to a partner.

READING RATE When you evaluate reading rate, have children read aloud from the story for one minute. Place a stick-on note after the last word read. Count words read. To evaluate children's performance, see the Running Record in the **Fluency Assessment** book.

Intervention For leveled fluency lessons, passages, and norms charts, see **Skills Intervention Guide**, Part 5, Fluency.

Comprehension

Safety Tip #101

"ALWAYS STICK WITH YOUR BUDDY!"

277

Return to Predictions and Purposes

Reread children's predictions about the story. Discuss the predictions, noting which needed to be revised. Then ask children if the story answered the questions they had before they read it.

PREDICTIONS	WHAT HAPPENED
The story is about a policeman and a dog.	The story is about Officer Buckle and Gloria.
The policeman talks to students.	The policeman gives safety tips to students.

LITERARY RESPONSE

UICK-WRITE Invite children to use their journals to record their thoughts on what they did or idn't like about the story.

RAL RESPONSE Have children iscuss these questions:

- Which part of the story did you like best? Why?
- Why do you think Officer Buckle enjoyed giving safety speeches to students?
- Do you think someone should have told Officer Buckle that Gloria was performing behind him? Why?
- What did Officer Buckle and Gloria learn over the course of the story?

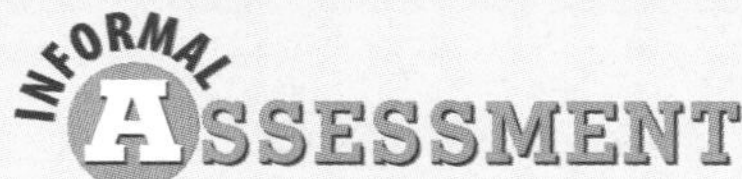

HOW TO ASSESS

DIGRAPHS *ph, tch, ch* Have children look at page 263. Invite them to find the three words in the sentence with /ch/ and then say those words aloud.

MAKE INFERENCES Have children make a chart with two columns. On one side, have children record the different feelings Officer Buckle had on pages 256, 262, 267, and 272. On the other side, have them write down the clues they used to understand his feelings each time.

FOLLOW UP

DIGRAPHS *ph, tch, ch* Continue to model the blending of sounds in words with *ph, ch,* and *tch* letter combinations for children who are having difficulty.

CAUSE AND EFFECT If children are having difficulty making inferences, suggest that they try to imagine themselves in Officer Buckle's situations.

Story Questions

Have children discuss or write answers to the questions on page 278.

Answers:

1. Safety tips *Literal/Plot*
2. They are interested in watching Gloria perform. *Inferential/Character*
3. Possible answer: Officer Buckle's speeches are helpful when people pay attention. *Critical/Judgments and Decisions*
4. A friendship between a policeman who likes to give safety tips and a dog who likes to perform *Critical/Summarize*
5. Answers may include that humans and dogs can be good friends. *Critical/Reading Across Texts*

Write a Gloria Story For a full writing process lesson related to this writing suggestion, see the lesson on Writing a Story, pages 281M–281N.

Story Questions & Activities

READ TOGETHER

1. What does Officer Buckle talk about when he visits schools?
2. Why do students start to pay attention to Officer Buckle's safety tips?
3. Do you think Officer Buckle's safety speeches are helpful? Explain.
4. What is this story mostly about?
5. If Gloria and Mudge could talk, what would they say about humans?

Write a Gloria Story

Gloria helps Officer Buckle see that making people laugh is a good way to get their attention. Write a funny story about a helpful friend. Tell the events in the order they happen.

Meeting Individual Needs

EASY

Name _____ Date _____ Reteach 213

Story Comprehension

Write **T** if the statement is true about "Officer Buckle and Gloria." Write **F** if the statement is false about the story.

F 1. Officer Buckle is a pilot.
T 2. Gloria is a dog.
T 3. Officer Buckle is a policeman.
T 4. This story is about safety.
T 5. Gloria was a talented dog.
T 6. Officer Buckle and Gloria gave speeches about safety.
F 7. The children did not like Gloria.
T 8. Gloria made the speeches exciting.
T 9. Gloria and Officer Buckle needed one another.
F 10. Gloria got her own TV show.

10 Book 2.2/Unit 3 **Officer Buckle and Gloria** **At Home:** Have children describe two other events that took place in the story. 213

Reteach, 213

ON-LEVEL

Name _____ Date _____ Practice 213

Story Comprehension

Answer each question about "Officer Buckle and Gloria."

1. In Napville, who knew more safety tips than anyone else?
   Officer Buckle
2. What was one of Officer Buckle's safety tips?
   Answers may vary. Never stand on a swivel chair; keep your shoelaces tied.
3. What did Gloria do while Officer Buckle gave speeches?
   She did tricks.
4. What did Officer Buckle think Gloria was doing while he was making speeches?
   He thought she was sitting at attention.
5. How did Officer Buckle find out what Gloria was doing?
   Officer Buckle found out about Gloria by watching himself on TV.
6. What was Officer Buckle's best safety tip?
   Always stick with your buddy.

6 Book 2.2/Unit 3 **Officer Buckle and Gloria** **At Home:** Have children tell which trick of Gloria's was their favorite. 213

Practice, 213

CHALLENGE

Name _____ Date _____ Extend 213

Story Comprehension

What makes Gloria a good partner for Officer Buckle? Write a sentence.

Officer Buckle is very serious. Gloria is funny and entertains the children.

What if your favorite animal was Officer Buckle's partner? Write two sentences that tell what might happen.

Answers will vary.

Draw a picture showing Officer Buckle and your favorite animal.

Book 2.2/Unit 3 **Officer Buckle and Gloria** **At Home:** Have children make up a safety rule and place it on a poster that they illustrate. 213

Extend, 213

Make Safety Tip Cards

Officer Buckle has lots of safety tips. Make up some of your own. Write three safety tips on index cards. Draw a picture to go with each one. Be original.

Draw Safety Signs

What safety signs have you seen in your neighborhood or near your school? Draw a picture of two safety signs. Then write one sentence about why these signs are important.

Find Out More

Gloria is a police dog who helps Officer Buckle. Find out more about working dogs. Name some other dogs that are specially trained to help humans? What do they do?

Story Activities

Make Safety Tip Cards

Materials: pens, felt-tipped markers, index cards

ONE Have children brainstorm a list of safety tips that they think would be helpful for other children to know. Prompt them by suggesting the following subjects: safety while playing; safety at school; and fire prevention. Bind children's cards together to create a class safety book.

Draw Safety Signs

Materials: felt-tipped markers, paint, poster board

PARTNERS Encourage partners to include signs they may have seen indoors as well as outdoors. Have them pay close attention to why they are placed there and their color or lettering.

Research and Inquiry Find Out More

GROUP Ask children what they think "A dog is man's best friend" means. With children, create a list on the chalkboard of different types of trained dogs (guard dogs, seeing-eye dogs and so forth). Invite groups to research a particular kind of trained dog. Have groups present their findings.

interNET CONNECTION Help children access links to various sites about working dogs by logging on to ***www.mhschool.com/reading.***

DAILY Phonics ROUTINES

DAY 3 **Discriminating** Write the following words on the chalkboard: *chase, match, phone, race, math, back*. Invite children to indicate which words contain letter combinations *ch, ph,* or *tch*.

CD-ROM

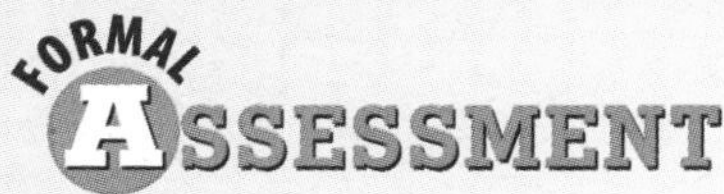

After page 279, see Selection Assessment.

Study Skills

LIBRARY/MEDIA CENTER

Children will use a computer display of a subject search to find information.

PREPARE Explain that using a library computer can help them to locate information. Display **Teaching Chart 178.**

TEACH Point to the call number and tell children that this number tells where a book or other material is located in the library. Ask: What is the call number for *The Bicycle Book*? (J629.22 G)

PRACTICE Have students answer questions 1–5. Review the following answers with them. **1.** bicycle safety **2.** *Bike on the Safe Side* **3.** Corrine J. Naden **4.** *The Bicycle Book* **5.** *Bicycling Safely*, because *Safely* is in the title.

ASSESS/CLOSE Have children explain how they would find books by Corrine J. Naden.

STUDY SKILLS

READ TOGETHER

Do a Library Subject Search

Enter the number of the search that you want:
1. Names **2.** Titles **3.** Subjects

Press number **3** for Subjects. Enter the subject that you want to search.

Type in BICYCLE SAFETY. Press ENTER.

Here are the results of your search.

Author and Title	Call Number and Format	Date
Bike on the Safe Side	J M16 2465 B [Movie]	1974
Gibbons, Gail *The Bicycle Book*	J 629.22 G	c 1995
Naden, Corrine J. *Bicycling Safely*	J 796.6 N	c 1979

Use the computer displays to answer the questions.

1. What subject are you researching?
2. The list has one movie. What is its title?
3. Who wrote *Bicycling Safely*?
4. Which book will have the newest information?
5. Which book will have the most information on bicycle safety? How do you know?

Meeting Individual Needs

EASY

Name________________ Date________ **Reteach 214**

Do a Subject Search at the Library

You can search for books on a computer by typing in the **title**, the **author**, or the **subject**.

For each of the following searches, choose the subject that you would type in to find books. Try to keep the subject simple—two or three words. Answers will vary.

Search #1 — Subject
You need a magic trick for show and tell. It has to be simple. What would you write in the search box? simple magic trick

Search #2 — Subject
You need to find out how a bridge is built. What would you write in the search box? bridge building

Search #3 — Subject
You want to learn how to become a clown. What would you write in the search box? clown school

Search #4 — Subject
You want a book about apples—how they're grown. apple growing

214 **At Home:** Bring children to the library and help them to research a topic of their choice using a computer. Book 2.2/Unit 3 **Officer Buckle and Gloria** 4

Reteach, 214

ON-LEVEL

Name________________ Date________ **Practice 214**

Do a Subject Search at the Library

When writing a report or looking for information, a computer **subject search** will give you a number of books to choose from.

Search of South Millford Library System

Search: Pumpkins

Items Found = 28
☒ First Ten ☐ Second Ten ☐ Third Ten

1. Title: *The Greatest Pumpkin Ever* Fiction
   Author: Hemsley Yorborough
   ■ See Full Record
   Pub. Date: ©1994
2. Title: *Pumpkin Pie Baking*
   Author: Nancy Edlands
   ■ See Full Record
   Pub Date: ©1999
3. Title: *Grow the Big Ones*
   Author: Ray Moncliff
   ■ See Full Record
   Pub. Date: ©1979
4. Title: *Pumping Iron for More Muscle*
   Author: Quincy Cummings
   ■ See Full Record
   Pub. Date: ©1989 Video recording

Use the results of the subject search shown above to answer the questions.

1. Which book would help you with baking a pumpkin pie? Pumpkin Pie Baking
2. Which book would help you with producing large pumpkins in your garden? Grow the Big Ones
3. Which book is fiction, or a made-up story? The Greatest Pumpkin Ever
4. Which book looks like it has nothing to do with pumpkins? (Hint: sometimes the computer confuses words that look alike. Pumpkin could be seen by the computer as Pump or kin.) Pumping Iron for More Muscle

214 **At Home:** Ask the children which of the books listed above was published most recently. Book 2.2/Unit 3 **Officer Buckle and Gloria** 4

Practice, 214

CHALLENGE

Name________________ Date________ **Extend 214**

Do a Subject Search at the Library

Officer Buckle is at the library to learn more about Gloria.

Look at his list. Help Officer Buckle think of subjects he can search for to get more information. Check ✔ the subjects on his list he can use. Cross out **X** the subjects on his list that won't work. Add new subjects to his list on the lines at the right.

Column 1	Column 2
✔ animal training	dog tricks
X wolves	pets
X zoos	pet training
✔ dogs	police dogs
X kittens	

Enter the name, title words, or subject words you want.

Dog Tricks

What will Officer Buckle see on the screen after he presses **enter?**

He will see a new screen that tells him the author, title, call number and format, and date of anything the library has on the subject of dog tricks.

214 **At Home:** Children can select a subject, then write directions on how to search for it at the library. Encourage them to use sequencing words: **first, next, then, last.** Book 2.2/Unit 3 **Officer Buckle and Gloria**

Extend, 214

Tell the story again to yourself in your own words to make sure you understand it.

DIRECTIONS:

Read the story. Then read each question about the story.

SAMPLE

What Is a Penny For?

Katie went for a walk to the ice cream store. As she walked, she looked down at the sidewalk. She walked carefully over the bumps and cracks. Katie saw something shiny on the sidewalk. She picked it up. It was a brand new penny.

"A penny is good luck," said Katie. She put the penny in her pocket. Katie felt lucky already. "I wish that a penny was enough money for ice cream," thought Katie.

It started to rain. Katie turned around to go home. She walked into the house and went into the kitchen. There on the table was a bowl of ice cream just for her!

1 What does Katie find in this story?

- ○ A rabbit's foot
- ● A penny
- ○ A friend's book
- ○ A raincoat

2 Which general statement can you make from this story?

- ○ Katie's house is like all other houses.
- ● Sometimes you get what you wish for.
- ○ A penny buys a lot of ice cream.
- ○ It's hard to eat ice cream in the rain.

281

Test Power

THE PRINCETON REVIEW

Read the Page

Explain to children that you will be reading this story as a group. You will read the story, and they will follow along in their books.

Request that children put pens, pencils, and markers away, since they will not be writing in their books.

Discuss the Questions

QUESTION 1: Instruct children to find the place in the story where Katie finds something. Ask them to read what she finds and compare that against the answer choices.

QUESTION 2: Remind children to look back to the story to find the choice that is discussed in the passage. In the last five sentences, Katie makes a wish and gets what she wished for.

Leveled Books

Intervention Skills
Intervention Guide, for direct instruction and extra practice of phonics and vocabulary

EASY

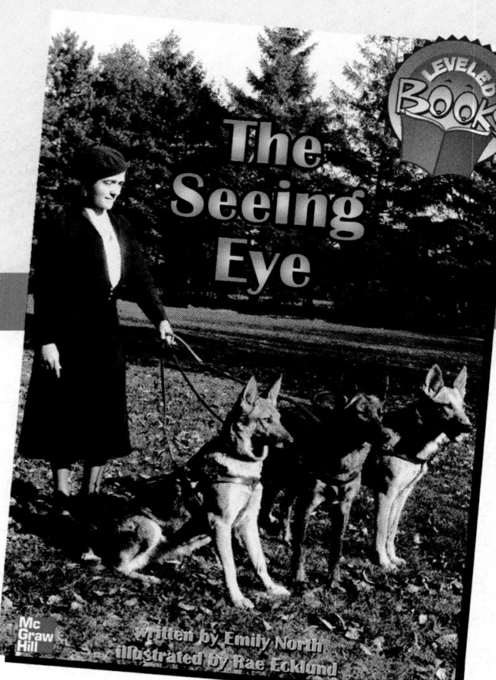

The Seeing Eye

- ☑ Phonics Digraphs *tch, ph, ch*
- ☑ Instructional Vocabulary: *accidents, audience, cheered, slips, station, wipe*

Guided Reading

PREVIEW AND PREDICT Take a **picture walk** through page 6 of the story with children. As children study the illustrations, see if they can predict what the story will be about. Chart their predictions.

SET PURPOSES Have children write why they want to read *The Seeing Eye*. For example: I want to learn about seeing-eye dogs.

READ THE BOOK Use questions like the following to guide children's reading or after they have read the story independently.

Page 4: How did the German shepherds help the men? (They helped the men "see") *Draw Conclusions*

Page 8: Find the word *slipped*. What would happen if a person *slipped*? Try to use the word *slipped* in a sentence. *Instructional Vocabulary*

Page 9: Point to the word that begins with *ch*. (cheered) What sound do the letters *ch* stand for? (/ch/) *Phonics and Decoding*

Pages 12–13: Why do the dogs learn on quiet streets before going to the city? (They can practice where it's safer until they are well-trained.) *Setting*

RETURN TO PREDICTIONS AND PURPOSES Discuss children's predictions. Ask which were close to the story and why. Have children review their purposes for reading. Did they find out what they wanted to know?

LITERARY RESPONSE Discuss these questions:

- What kind of person do you think Morris Frank was?
- In what other ways do you think dogs can help people?

Also see the story questions and activity in *The Seeing Eye*.

See the Phonics **CD-ROM** for practice using words with digraphs.

Answers to Story Questions

1. To get a dog that will help guide him.
2. So they will think a school for training more dogs would be a good idea.
3. So they can be independent.
4. To show how the Seeing Eye school started.
5. Probably yes because she's very smart and well-trained.

The Story Questions and Activity below appear in the Easy Book.

Story Questions and Writing Activity

1. Why does Morris Frank go to Germany?
2. Why does Morris show people how Buddy helps him?
3. Why do you think people want to get Seeing Eye dogs?
4. What is the main idea of this story?
5. Would Gloria make a good Seeing Eye dog? Why or why not?

Taking Care of Dogs

People who get Seeing Eye dogs must learn to take care of them. Draw a picture that shows something you need to do to take care of a dog. Write a few sentences explaining why what you chose is important.

from *The Seeing Eye*

Leveled Books

INDEPENDENT

A City Horse

☑ Phonics Digraphs *tch, ph, ch*

☑ Instructional Vocabulary: *accidents, audience, cheered, slips, station, wipe*

Guided Reading

PREVIEW AND PREDICT Discuss the illustrations through page 7 of the story. As you take the **picture walk**, have children predict what the story will be about. Chart children's ideas.

SET PURPOSES Have children write a question they want to answer by reading *A City Horse*. For example: Why does the horse live in a city?

READ THE BOOK Use questions like the following to guide children's reading or after they have read the story independently.

Page 3: Find a word with the /ch/ sound. (*stretch*) What letters make the /ch/ sound? (*tch*) ***Phonics and Decoding***

Page 7: Where do the horses work? (Central Park) What do they do there? (pull carriages that people ride in) ***Setting and Plot***

Page 11: Find the word *cheering*. What is its base word? (*cheer*) Show us what cheering sounds like. *Instructional Vocabulary*

Page 16: Do you think visitors to New York City would want to take a horse-and-carriage ride through Central Park? Why? *Draw Conclusions*

RETURN TO PREDICTIONS AND PURPOSES Discuss children's predictions. Have children review their purposes for reading. Did they find out what they wanted to know?

LITERARY RESPONSE Discuss these questions:

- Do you think having to pull a carriage is being cruel to a horse? Why or why not?
- What was your favorite part of the story?

Also see the story questions and activity in *A City Horse*.

See the Phonics **CD-ROM** for practice using words with digraphs.

Answers to Story Questions

1. They live in a stable.
2. It is warm and quiet and clean. They eat, sleep, and rest there.
3. Noise, people, cars, trucks
4. Horses work in Central Park pulling hansom cabs.
5. Answers will vary.

The Story Questions and Activity below appear in the Independent Book.

Story Questions and Writing Activity

1. Where do the horses of Central Park live?
2. Why do you think the horses love their stable?
3. Name some things that might frighten a new horse in the city.
4. What is the main idea of the book?
5. Both Gloria in *Officer Buckle and Gloria* and a Central Park horse help the people they work with. How are they different?

Where in the Park?

Look at the map on page 8. Find the zoo. What is the nearest street to the zoo? Now draw a picture of something you could find in Central Park. Write about it.

from *A City Horse*

Leveled Books

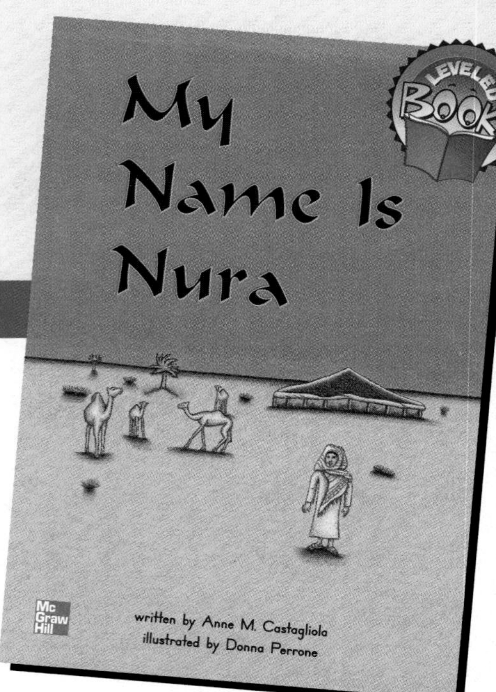

CHALLENGE

My Name Is Nura

- ☑ **Digraphs *tch, ph, ch***
- ☑ **Instructional vocabulary:** ***accidents, audience, cheered, slips, station, wipe***

Guided Reading

PREVIEW AND PREDICT Discuss the illustrations through page 5 of the story. As you take the **picture walk**, have children predict what the story will be about. Chart their ideas.

SET PURPOSES Have children write two or three sentences explaining what they hope to find out by reading *My Name Is Nura*. Have children share their reasons with the group.

READ THE BOOK Use questions like the following to guide children's reading or after they have read the story independently.

Page 3: Find two words with the /ch/ sound. (*chairs; children*) What letters stand for the sound in each word? (ch)

Page 5: What does Nura's family do after their camels eat all the grass (move) Why? (to find water and more grass) ***Cause and Effect***

Page 7: Find the word *wipe*. What kinds of things can you wipe away? (tears, dirt, water) ***Instructional Vocabulary***

Page 11: Why does Nura's family make the camels bend down low? (So they can load their supplies) ***Draw Conclusions.***

Page 13: What causes the camels to "spit and yell?" (when they are given too much to carry) ***Cause and Effect***

RETURN TO PREDICTIONS AND PURPOSES Discuss children's predictions. Ask which were close to the story and why. Have children review their purposes for reading. Did they find out what they wanted to know?

LITERARY RESPONSE Encourage children to share their thoughts about the book.

- How do you think a camel is like a horse?
- How do you think climate affects people who live in a desert?

Also see the story questions and activity in *My Name Is Nura*.

See the Phonics **CD-ROM** for practice using words with the /ph/ and /ch/ sounds.

Answers to Story Questions

1. In Arabia, in the desert.
2. To find food and water for their camels.
3. Camels can eat almost anything; they can close up their noses, ears, and eyes to keep sand out; they have wide feet to walk on the sand; they have humps filled with fat for energy.
4. A girl named Nura who lives in the desert and how important camels are to her way of life.
5. Answers will vary.

The Story Questions and Activity below appear in the Challenge Book.

Story Questions and Writing Activity

1. Where does Nura live?
2. Why does Nura's family move so much?
3. Name one way the camel is built for the desert.
4. What is this story mostly about?
5. What might Nura tell Officer Buckle about her life in the desert?

If I Were Nura

Look at the map of Saudi Arabia on page 4. This map shows the area where Nura and her family live. Draw a picture of something you would do if you lived where Nura does, or of something she and you would do if she lived near you.

from *My Name Is Nura*

Bringing Groups Together

Anthology and Leveled Books

Connecting Texts

HELPFUL ANIMALS CHART Write the story titles on a chart. Discuss with children the different ways animals were helpful to the people in each story. Have children from each reading level write their contributions on the chart.

Use the chart to help children learn about the ways animals help people.

Officer Buckle and Gloria	The Seeing Eye	A City Horse	My Name Is Nura
• Dogs are friends and true companions. • Dogs can do tricks to entertain people.	• German shepherds can help blind people by guiding them through streets and city traffic. • Dogs can keep people safe from hidden dangers.	• Horses can take people for rides by pulling them in carriages. • Horses can give people pleasure when they walk and parade.	• Camels help people by carrying their belongings. • People get milk and meat from camels. • Camel hair can be used for making clothes and blankets.

Viewing/Representing

GROUP PRESENTATIONS Divide the class into four groups, each group representing one of the stories in the lesson. Have children draw pictures showing the ways in which the animal in their story can be helpful to people. Then have children share their drawings with the class.

AUDIENCE RESPONSE Ask children to look carefully at the drawings of their classmates. Allow time for questions and discussion.

Research and Inquiry

MORE ABOUT HELPFUL ANIMALS Have children consider other animals and ways in which these animals might be helpful to people. Then invite them to:

- look at classroom and school library books that focus on helpful ways of animals.
- invite people who have been helped by animals to talk to the class.
- watch video tapes featuring helpful animals.

interNET CONNECTION Have children log on to ***www.mhschool.com/reading*** for links to web pages.

Children will:

- **identify digraphs *ph*, *tch*, and *ch*.**
- **blend and read words containing *ph*, *tch*, and *ch*.**

MATERIALS

- **Teaching Chart 179**
- **Word Building Manipulative Cards**

Skills Finder

Digraphs *ph, tch*

Introduce	B2: 92G-H
Review	B2: 115E-F, 116G-H, 250G-H, 281G-H
Test	B2: Unit 2

ALTERNATE TEACHING STRATEGY

REVIEW *ph, tch,* AND *ch*

For a different approach to teaching this skill, see page T65.

TEACHING TIP

DIGRAPHS Point out to children that the letter combinations *ch* and *ph* can be found at the beginning, middle, or end of a word. The letter combination *tch* can be found at the middle or end, but never at the beginning of a word.

Review Digraphs *ph, tch, ch*

PREPARE

Identify Words with Digraphs *ph, tch,* and *ch* Write the following sentence on the board. Ask volunteers to circle words with *ph*, underline words with *ch*, and double underline words with *tch*.

- The elephant eats his lunch, then stretches out for a nap.

TEACH

BLENDING Model and Guide Practice with *ph, ch,* and *tch* Words Display **Teaching Chart 179**. Explain to children that they can form words with *ph*, *tch*, and *ch* on the chart.

- Write the letters *ph* on the blank line in column 1. Then blend the sounds together and read the word *phone*. Repeat with the first words in columns 2 and 3, writing the letters *tch* in column 2, forming the word *watched;* and *ch* in column 3, forming the word *chair.*
- Read the words *phone, watched,* and *chair.* Then have children read the words aloud, emphasizing the digraphs.
- Invite volunteers to build words by writing the digraphs *ph*, *tch*, and *ch* on the blank lines.

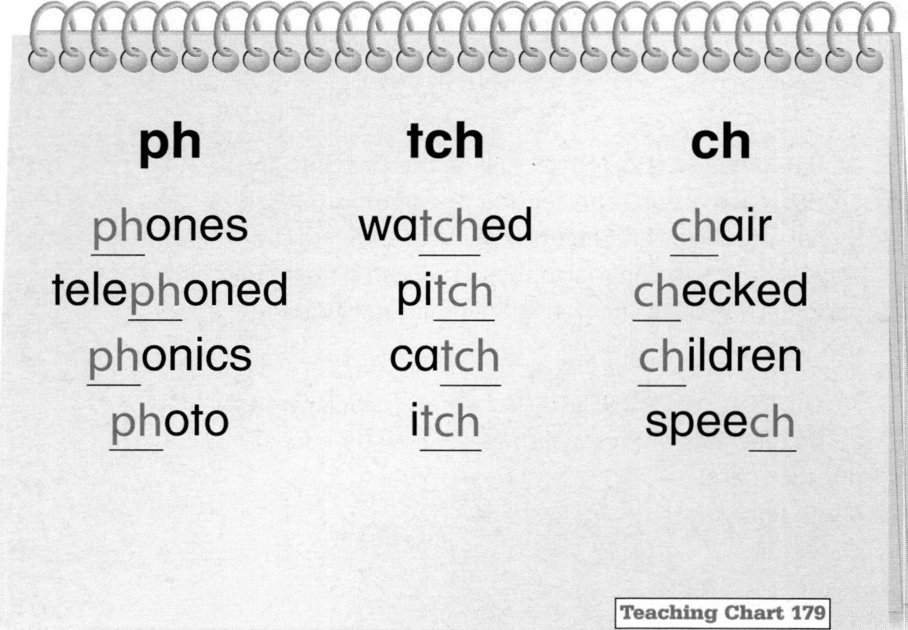

ph
tch
ch
phones
watched
chair
telephoned
pitch
checked
phonics
catch
children
photo
itch
speech
Teaching Chart 179

Use the Words in Context Have volunteers use each word in a sentence to reinforce its meaning. Example: *During the sale, the phones rang all day.*

Repeat the Procedure Follow the same procedure for each word on the chart.

PRACTICE

SEGMENTING
Build Words with *ch, tch,* and *ph*

Using the **Word Building Manipulative Cards**, have children work in pairs to build the following words that you say aloud: *hatch, graph, chair, cheer, match, phone, phonics*. Tell children to write their words on paper, circle the letter combination *ph, ch,* or *tch* in the word, and then read each word aloud. Then have children write the words in separate lists according to their word families. ▶**Linguistic/Visual**

ASSESS/CLOSE

Write a Story Using *ph, ch,* and *tch* Words

Invite children to choose three words from their list of *ch, ph,* and *tch* words and write a one-paragraph story including all three words. Have children read their stories aloud.

ADDITIONAL PHONICS RESOURCES

Phonics/Phonemic Awareness Practice Book, pages 135–138

activities for practice with Discriminating and Segmenting

DAY 4 **Words in Context** Ask children working in small groups to create riddles containing *ph, tch,* and *ch* words. Have children take turns reading their riddles as the rest of the group guesses the word.

SPELLING/PHONICS CONNECTIONS

See the 5-Day Spelling Plan, pages 281Q–281R.

Intervention **Skills Intervention Guide,** for direct instruction and extra practice of *ph, ch,* and *tch*

Meeting Individual Needs for Phonics

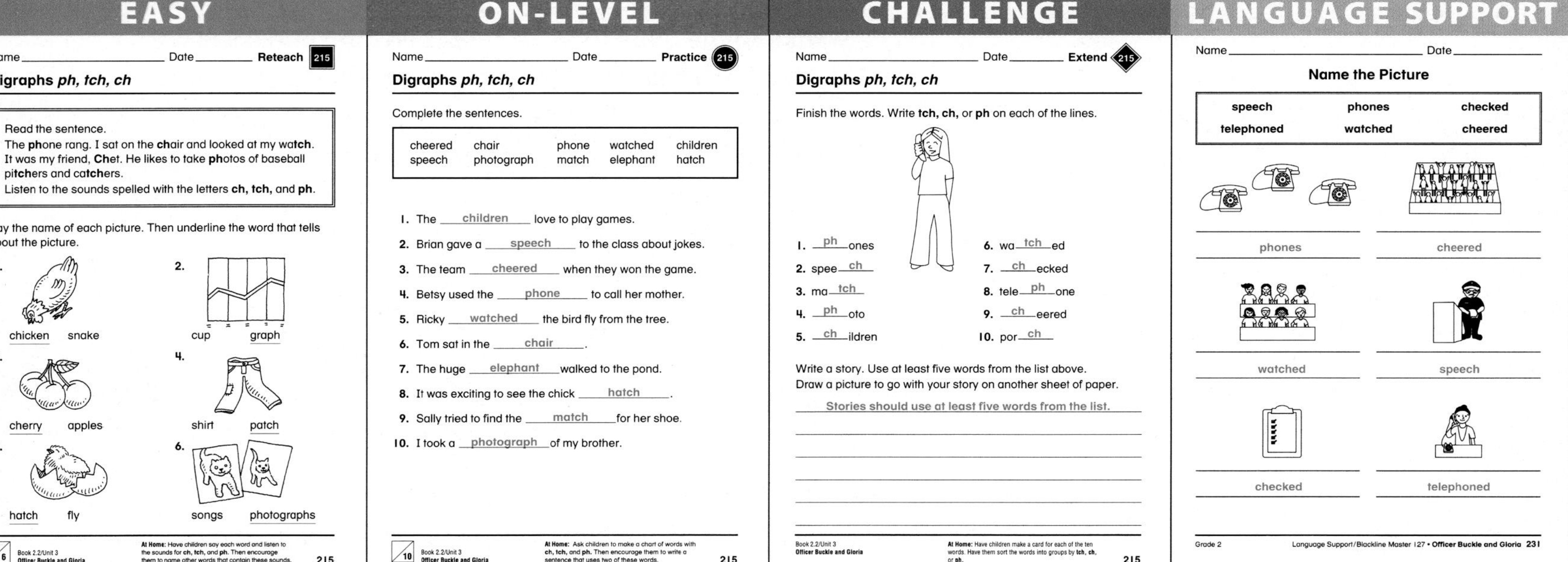

EASY

Name ____ Date ____ Reteach 215

Digraphs *ph, tch, ch*

Read the sentence.
The **ph**one rang. I sat on the **ch**air and looked at my wa**tch**. It was my friend, **Ch**et. He likes to take **ph**otos of baseball pi**tch**ers and ca**tch**ers.
Listen to the sounds spelled with the letters **ch, tch,** and **ph**.

Say the name of each picture. Then underline the word that tells about the picture.

1. chicken snake
2. cup graph
3. cherry apples
4. shirt patch
5. hatch fly
6. songs photographs

6 Book 2.2/Unit 3 **Officer Buckle and Gloria** **At Home:** Have children say each word and listen to the sounds for **ch, tch,** and **ph**. Then encourage them to name other words that contain these sounds. 215

ON-LEVEL

Name ____ Date ____ Practice 215

Digraphs *ph, tch, ch*

Complete the sentences.

cheered	chair	phone	watched	children
speech	photograph	match	elephant	hatch

1. The children love to play games.
2. Brian gave a speech to the class about jokes.
3. The team cheered when they won the game.
4. Betsy used the phone to call her mother.
5. Ricky watched the bird fly from the tree.
6. Tom sat in the chair.
7. The huge elephant walked to the pond.
8. It was exciting to see the chick hatch.
9. Sally tried to find the match for her shoe.
10. I took a photograph of my brother.

10 Book 2.2/Unit 3 **Officer Buckle and Gloria** **At Home:** Ask children to make a chart of words with **ch, tch,** and **ph**. Then encourage them to write a sentence that uses two of these words. 215

CHALLENGE

Name ____ Date ____ Extend 215

Digraphs *ph, tch, ch*

Finish the words. Write **tch, ch,** or **ph** on each of the lines.

1. ph ones
2. spee ch
3. ma tch
4. ph oto
5. ch ildren
6. wa tch ed
7. ch ecked
8. tele ph one
9. ch eered
10. por ch

Write a story. Use at least five words from the list above. Draw a picture to go with your story on another sheet of paper.

Stories should use at least five words from the list.

Book 2.2/Unit 3 **Officer Buckle and Gloria** **At Home:** Have children make a card for each of the ten words. Have them sort the words into groups by **tch, ch,** or **ph**. 215

LANGUAGE SUPPORT

Name ____ Date ____

Name the Picture

speech	phones	checked
telephoned	watched	cheered

phones
cheered
watched
speech
checked
telephoned

Grade 2 Language Support/Blackline Master 127 • **Officer Buckle and Gloria** 231

Reteach, 215 **Practice, 215** **Extend, 215** **Language Support, 231**

Review Digraphs *ph, tch, ch*

TESTED OBJECTIVES

Children will:

- **recognize digraphs *ph, tch,* and *ch*.**
- **identify and read words with digraphs *ph, tch,* and *ch*.**

MATERIALS

- **Teaching Chart 180**

Skills Finder

Digraphs *ph, tch*

Introduce	B2: 92G-H
Review	B2: 115E-F, 116G-H, 250G-H, 281E-F
Test	B2: Unit 2

PREPARE

Identify Words with *ph, tch, ch*

Write the following on the chalkboard:

- *speck, stretch, mesh*
- *home, phone, roam*
- *please, tease, cheese*

Invite children to circle the word in each group that contains the digraph *ph, tch, ch.* (stretch, phone, cheese)

TEACH

BLENDING Model and Guide Practice with *ph, ch,* and *tch* Words

- Display **Teaching Chart 180.** Have children read aloud the first sentence, pausing at the blanks.
- Invite a volunteer to fill in the blank with a word containing *ch, tch,* or *ph,* using the word in parentheses as a clue.
- Have children read the sentence aloud when it is complete.

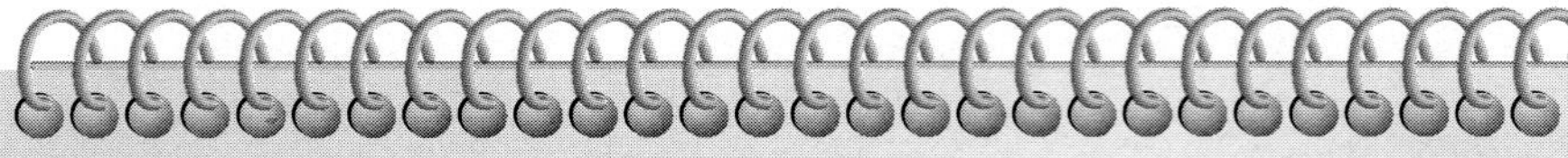

Yesterday I wanted to take a photo (picture) of my sister sitting in a chair (seat). I put my box of film on the ground and went into the other room to check (ask, find out) if she was ready. Then I heard a noise. When I came back, guess what I found? My dog had begun to chew (break down with his teeth) my box of film! I chased (ran after) him but I never did catch (capture) him.

Teaching Chart 180

Using the Words in Context

Have volunteers use the word they wrote in another sentence to further reinforce its meaning. Example: *The photo of the mountains made me feel like I was still there.*

Repeat the Procedure

Follow the same procedure for the remaining sentences on the chart.

PRACTICE

WORD BUILDING
Unscramble *ph*, *ch*, and *tch* Words

PARTNERS

Invite pairs of children to quietly brainstorm a list of ten words, at least five of which contain the /ch/ sound represented by *ch* or *tch*, or the /f/ sound represented by *ph*. On a piece of paper, have students create word scrambles, mixing up the letters in each word. Then have partners exchange papers and work to unscramble the letters. Have students circle the five words that contain the /ch/ or /f/ sounds. Invite children to read aloud the words they unscrambled. ▶ **Linguistic/Visual**

ASSESS/CLOSE

Read and Write a Paragraph Using Letter Combinations *ph*, *ch*, and *tch*

Observe children during the Practice activity to assess their abilities to decode and read letter combinations *ch, tch,* and *ph.* Then have children use the words with *ph, ch,* and *tch* that they unscrambled in a paragraph.

ADDITIONAL PHONICS RESOURCES

Phonics/Phonemic Awareness Practice Book, pages 135–138

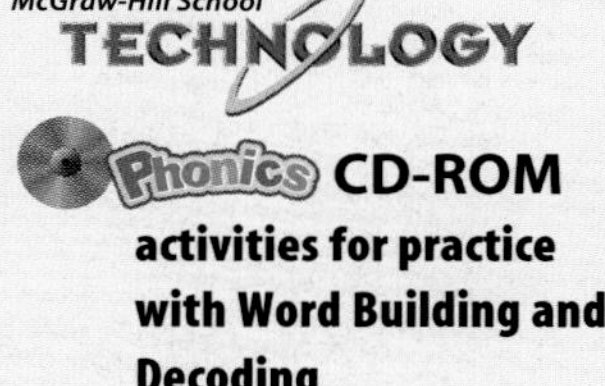

CD-ROM activities for practice with Word Building and Decoding

DAILY Phonics ROUTINES

DAY 5 **Writing** Write the following list on the chalkboard: *peach, reach, beach, teach, match, patch, batch, catch*. Discuss meanings with children. Invite them to write a short rhyme using two or three of these words.

CD-ROM

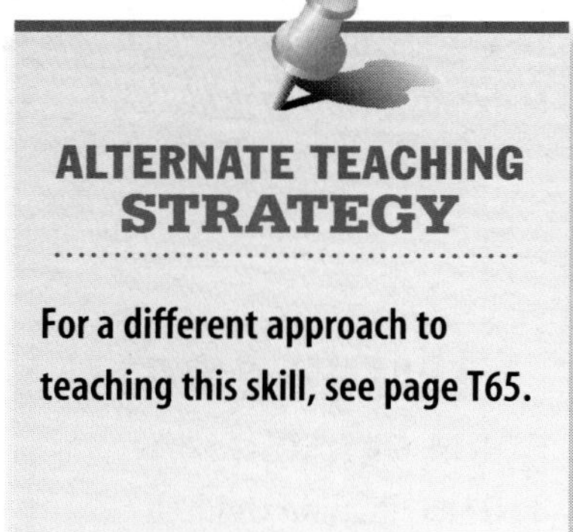

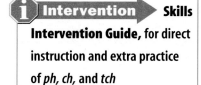

ALTERNATE TEACHING STRATEGY

For a different approach to teaching this skill, see page T65.

Intervention ▶ **Skills**

Intervention Guide, for direct instruction and extra practice of *ph, ch,* and *tch*

Meeting Individual Needs for Phonics

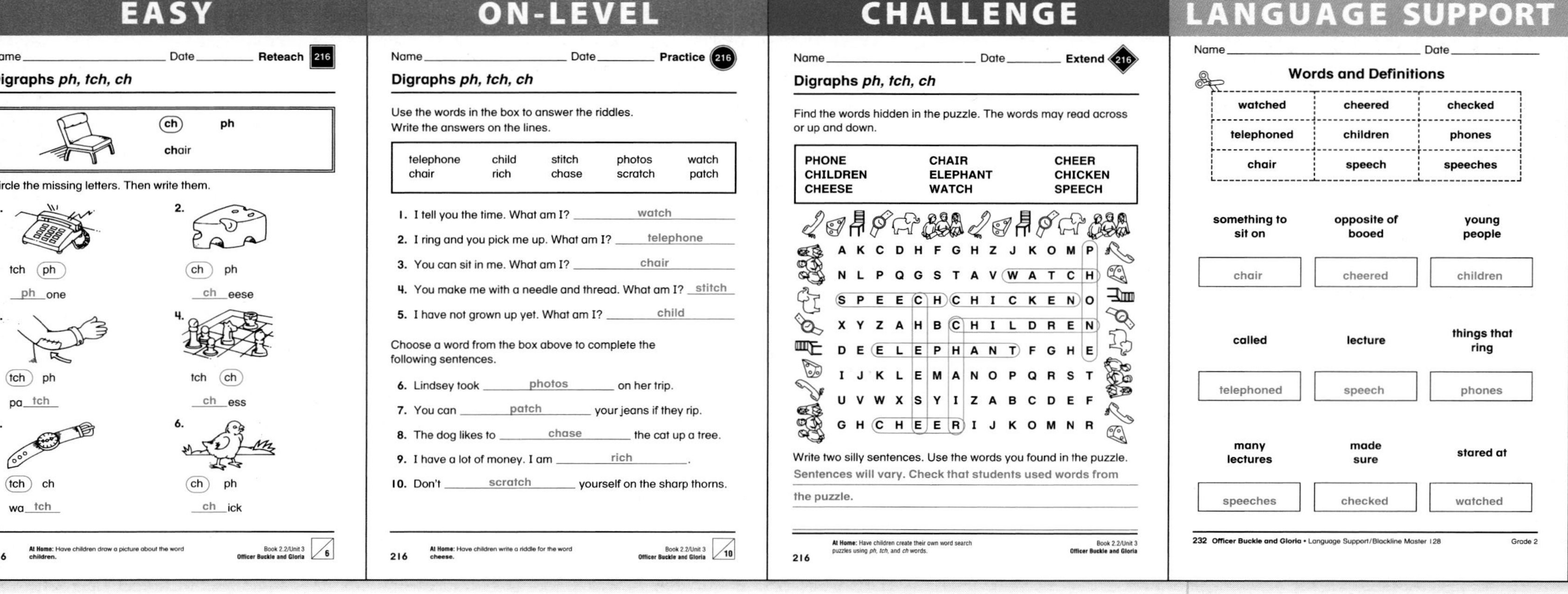

EASY

Name ____________ Date ________ **Reteach 216**

Digraphs *ph, tch, ch*

(ch) ph
chair

Circle the missing letters. Then write them.

1. tch (ph) — ph one
2. (ch) ph — ch eese
3. (tch) ph — pa tch
4. tch (ch) — ch ess
5. (tch) ch — wa tch
6. (ch) ph — ch ick

216 **At Home:** Have children draw a picture about the word children. Book 2.2/Unit 3 Officer Buckle and Gloria 6

ON-LEVEL

Name ____________ Date ________ **Practice 216**

Digraphs *ph, tch, ch*

Use the words in the box to answer the riddles.
Write the answers on the lines.

telephone	child	stitch	photos	watch
chair	rich	chase	scratch	patch

1. I tell you the time. What am I? watch
2. I ring and you pick me up. What am I? telephone
3. You can sit in me. What am I? chair
4. You make me with a needle and thread. What am I? stitch
5. I have not grown up yet. What am I? child

Choose a word from the box above to complete the following sentences.

6. Lindsey took photos on her trip.
7. You can patch your jeans if they rip.
8. The dog likes to chase the cat up a tree.
9. I have a lot of money. I am rich.
10. Don't scratch yourself on the sharp thorns.

216 **At Home:** Have children write a riddle for the word cheese. Book 2.2/Unit 3 Officer Buckle and Gloria 10

CHALLENGE

Name ____________ Date ________ **Extend 216**

Digraphs *ph, tch, ch*

Find the words hidden in the puzzle. The words may read across or up and down.

PHONE	CHAIR	CHEER
CHILDREN	ELEPHANT	CHICKEN
CHEESE	WATCH	SPEECH

A K C D H F G H Z J K O M P
N L P Q G S T A V W A T C H
S P E E C H C H I C K E N O
X Y Z A H B C H I L D R E N
D E E L E P H A N T F G H E
I J K L E M A N O P Q R S T
U V W X S Y I Z A B C D E F
G H C H E E R I J K O M N R

Write two silly sentences. Use the words you found in the puzzle.
Sentences will vary. Check that students used words from the puzzle.

216 **At Home:** Have children create their own word search puzzles using *ph, tch,* and *ch* words. Book 2.2/Unit 3 Officer Buckle and Gloria

LANGUAGE SUPPORT

Name ____________ Date ________

Words and Definitions

watched	cheered	checked
telephoned	children	phones
chair	speech	speeches

something to sit on	opposite of booed	young people
chair	cheered	children
called	lecture	things that ring
telephoned	speech	phones
many lectures	made sure	stared at
speeches	checked	watched

232 Officer Buckle and Gloria • Language Support/Blackline Master 128 Grade 2

Reteach, 216 **Practice, 216** **Extend, 216** **Language Support, 232**

OBJECTIVES

Children will form generalizations based on details given in a story.

Skills Finder

Form Generalizations

Introduce	B2: 281I-J
Review	B2: 339I-J, 371G-H
Test	B2: Unit 3
Maintain	B2: 107, 225

TEACHING TIP

FORM GENERALIZATIONS Remind children that not all generalizations are true. A generalization that is not true is called a *faulty generalization.*

SELF-SELECTED Reading

Children may choose from the following titles.

ANTHOLOGY

- *Officer Buckle and Gloria*

LEVELED BOOKS

- *The Seeing Eye*
- *A City Horse*
- *My Name is Nura*

Bibliography, pages T88–T89

Introduce Form Generalizations

PREPARE

Demonstrate a Generalization Ask children to raise their hands if they are seven years old. Then ask children to raise their hands if they are eight years old. Finally, have children who are nine years old raise their hands. Point out that *most* of the children in the class are eight years old. Explain to children that generalizations are broad statements about groups of things. Generalizations often use words such as *most, many, sometimes,* and *usually.*

TEACH

Form Generalizations About a Story Display **Teaching Chart 181**. Allow children to comment on the story.

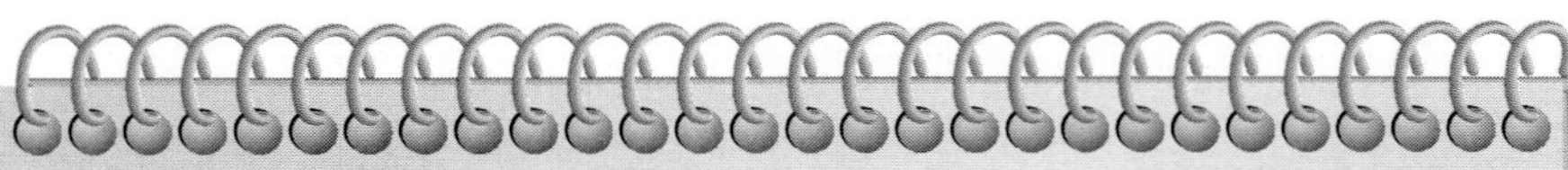

What a Team!

When Officer Buckle went to schools to give his safety tips, children usually did not listen. Many children slept, and some even snored! Often, after Officer Buckle spoke, an accident happened at school because no one had listened to him.

Then Gloria became Officer Buckle's partner. When Gloria and Officer Buckle worked together, everyone listened to the safety tips. Most children sent thank you notes to them. And there were less accidents at school!

Teaching Chart 181

MODEL I see clue words in the story—*usually, some, everyone, often, most,* and *many*—that show generalizations. I can make two generalizations about the story. Officer Buckle and Gloria worked better as a team, and less accidents happened at school when children listened to them.

PRACTICE

Ask children to underline words in the passage that indicate generalizations. Then ask them to make a generalization chart that shows what happened when Officer Buckle spoke by himself, and what happened when Officer Buckle and Gloria gave safety tips together.

OFFICER BUCKLE	OFFICER BUCKLE AND GLORIA
no one listened	everyone listened
children slept, some snored	most wrote thank-you notes
accidents happened	less accidents

Form Generalizations About Police Officers

Ask children to use the information in the story about Officer Buckle to form some generalizations about police officers. Invite them to look back through the story, to record details on a piece of paper, and to create one or two generalizations from the information. ▶ **Linguistic**

ASSESS/CLOSE

Encourage children to share their generalizations about police officers with the class. Have children share the details they used to form the generalizations in order to "prove" that the generalizations are correct.

ALTERNATE TEACHING STRATEGY

FORMING GENERALIZATIONS

For a different approach to teaching this skill, see page T67.

Skills Intervention Guide, for direct instruction and extra practice in forming generalizations

Meeting Individual Needs for Comprehension

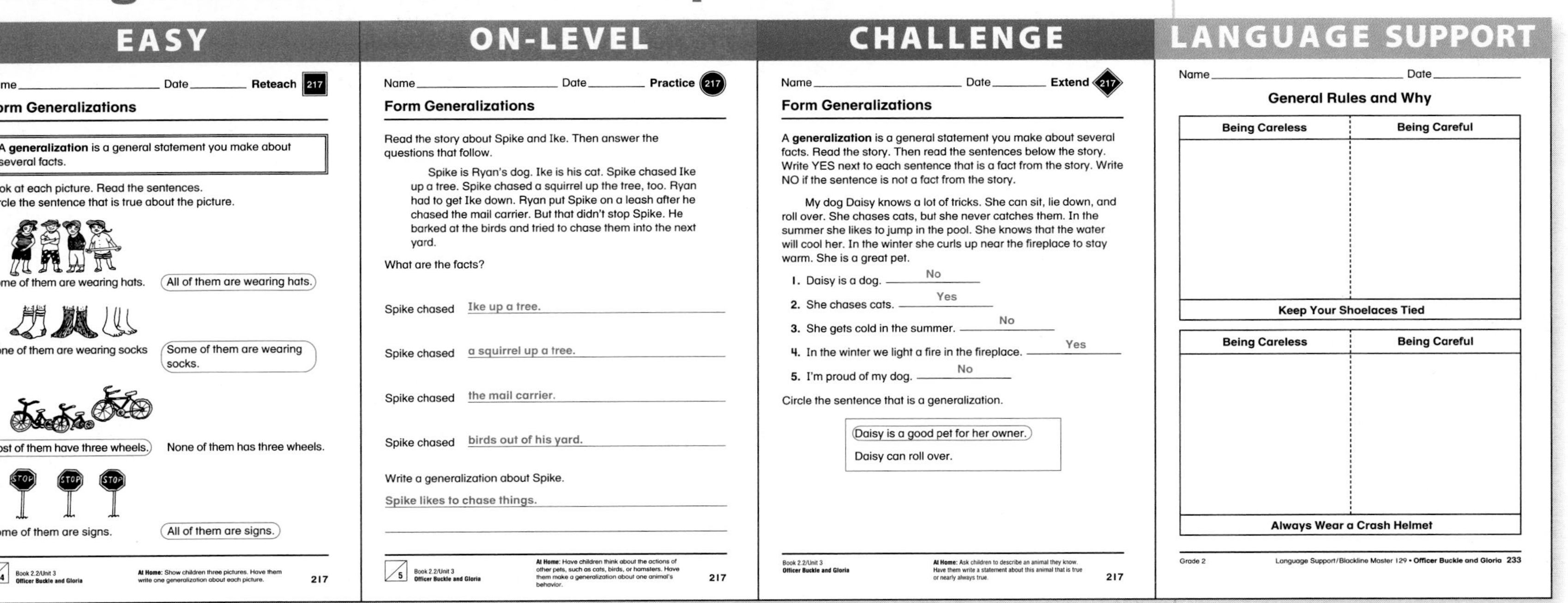

EASY

Name_______ Date_______ Reteach 217

Form Generalizations

A **generalization** is a general statement you make about several facts.

Look at each picture. Read the sentences.
Circle the sentence that is true about the picture.

1. Some of them are wearing hats. / (All of them are wearing hats.)
2. None of them are wearing socks / (Some of them are wearing socks.)
3. (Most of them have three wheels.) / None of them has three wheels.
4. Some of them are signs. / (All of them are signs.)

Book 2.2/Unit 3 Officer Buckle and Gloria — At Home: Show children three pictures. Have them write one generalization about each picture. 217

ON-LEVEL

Name_______ Date_______ Practice 217

Form Generalizations

Read the story about Spike and Ike. Then answer the questions that follow.

Spike is Ryan's dog. Ike is his cat. Spike chased Ike up a tree. Spike chased a squirrel up the tree, too. Ryan had to get Ike down. Ryan put Spike on a leash after he chased the mail carrier. But that didn't stop Spike. He barked at the birds and tried to chase them into the next yard.

What are the facts?

Spike chased Ike up a tree.

Spike chased a squirrel up a tree.

Spike chased the mail carrier.

Spike chased birds out of his yard.

Write a generalization about Spike.

Spike likes to chase things.

Book 2.2/Unit 3 Officer Buckle and Gloria — At Home: Have children think about the actions of other pets, such as cats, birds, or hamsters. Have them make a generalization about one animal's behavior. 217

CHALLENGE

Name_______ Date_______ Extend 217

Form Generalizations

A **generalization** is a general statement you make about several facts. Read the story. Then read the sentences below the story. Write YES next to each sentence that is a fact from the story. Write NO if the sentence is not a fact from the story.

My dog Daisy knows a lot of tricks. She can sit, lie down, and roll over. She chases cats, but she never catches them. In the summer she likes to jump in the pool. She knows that the water will cool her. In the winter she curls up near the fireplace to stay warm. She is a great pet.

1. Daisy is a dog. No
2. She chases cats. Yes
3. She gets cold in the summer. No
4. In the winter we light a fire in the fireplace. Yes
5. I'm proud of my dog. No

Circle the sentence that is a generalization.

(Daisy is a good pet for her owner.)
Daisy can roll over.

Book 2.2/Unit 3 Officer Buckle and Gloria — At Home: Ask children to describe an animal they know. Have them write a statement about this animal that is true or nearly always true. 217

LANGUAGE SUPPORT

Name_______ Date_______

General Rules and Why

Being Careless	Being Careful
Keep Your Shoelaces Tied	

Being Careless	Being Careful
Always Wear a Crash Helmet	

Grade 2 — Language Support/Blackline Master 129 • Officer Buckle and Gloria 233

Reteach, 217 — Practice, 217 — Extend, 217 — Language Support, 233

TESTED OBJECTIVES

Children will identify correct meanings for multiple-meaning words through the use of context clues.

MATERIALS
- **Teaching Chart 182**

Skills Finder

Multiple-Meaning Words

Introduce	B2: 281K-L
Review	B2: 309K-L, 371K-L
Test	B2: Unit 3

Introduce Multiple-Meaning Words

PREPARE

Define Multiple-Meaning Words

Write the word *fall* on the chalkboard. Invite a volunteer to use the word in a sentence. Ask children to write a sentence where *fall* has another meaning. *(to fall down, the fall season)* Explain that many words have more than one meaning. You can figure out which is the correct meaning in a specific sentence by looking for context clues. Make sure children understand the difference between multiple-meaning words, which *look* alike and have different meanings, and homophones, which *sound* alike and have different meanings. An example of a homophone is *too, two,* and *to.*

TEACH

Identify Multiple-Meaning Words Through Context Clues

Read **Teaching Chart 182** aloud with children. Model the skill beginning with the word *watch.*

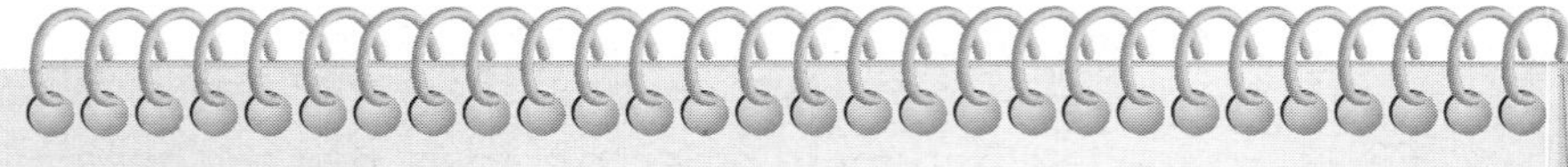

A Working Dog

The boy stopped to watch the dog bring the cows into the barn. He thought it must take a long time to train a dog to do that. The dog began to bark loudly at a cow. The cow thought the dog wanted to play.

Teaching Chart 182

MODEL When I am not sure of the correct meaning of a word, I can look at the other words in the sentence. I know that "a watch" tells the time, but "to watch" means to look at something. The other words in the sentence only make sense if I use the meaning "look at" for the word *watch*. This must be the correct meaning.

Have children locate and underline the remaining multiple-meaning words in the chart.

PRACTICE

Act It Out

PARTNERS

Have partners choose one multiple-meaning word from **Teaching Chart 182** and create a small scene in which they act out both meanings of the word. Encourage partners to perform their scenes for the class.

▶ **Kinesthetic**

ASSESS/CLOSE

Use Multiple-Meaning Words

Have children use the word they chose in the previous activity, and write a context sentence for each meaning.

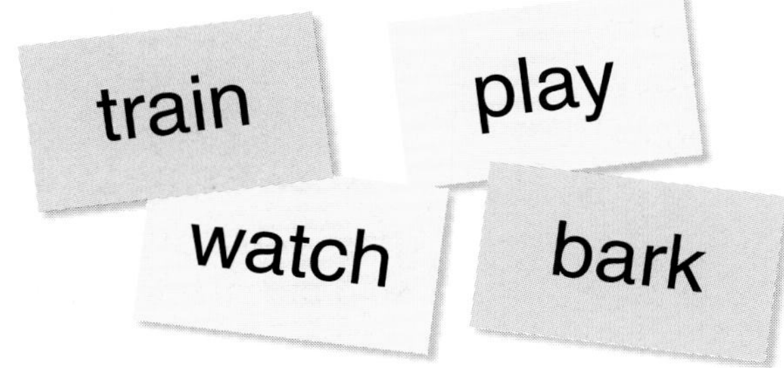

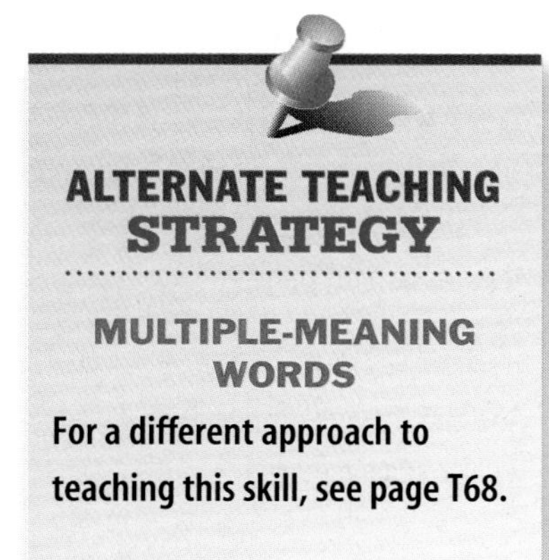

For a different approach to teaching this skill, see page T68.

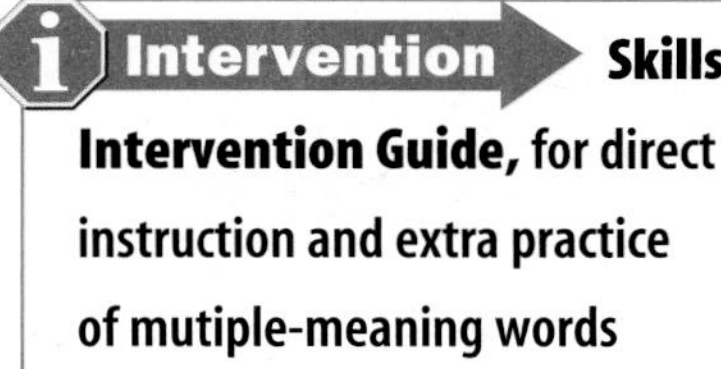

Intervention Guide, for direct instruction and extra practice of mutiple-meaning words

Meeting Individual Needs for Vocabulary

EASY

Name__________ Date______ **Reteach 218**

Multiple-Meaning Words

Some words have more than one meaning. Often you can tell which meaning is being used by looking for clues in the rest of the sentence.

Read each pair of sentences. Write the letter for the correct meaning of the underlined word.

1. One star shone bright in the night sky. a
2. Sammy was the star of the school show. b

a. a far-off light **b.** the most important person

3. It is always better to tell the truth than to lie. b
4. When I am tired, I lie down. a

a. to put your body flat **b.** say something that is not true

5. We always call my grandpa Pop. a
6. You can pop a balloon with a pin. b

a. a name for a father or grandfather **b.** to open with a bang

218 **At Home:** Challenge children to think up two meanings for the word **check.** Book 2.2/Unit 3 Officer Buckle and Gloria 6

Reteach, 218

ON-LEVEL

Name__________ Date______ **Practice 218**

Multiple-Meaning Words

The underlined words in the following sentences have more than one meaning. Read each sentence. Look for clues that tell you which meaning is being used. Fill in the circle next to the meaning of the underlined word.

1. The little dog can catch the stick.
   - ● a piece of wood
   - ⓑ to be held fast
2. His paws will stick in the mud.
   - ⓐ a piece of wood
   - ● to be held fast
3. The dog wore a checked shirt.
   - ⓐ tested to see if things were as they should be
   - ● marked with different-colored squares
4. He checked for food in his dish.
   - ● looked to see
   - ⓑ marked with different-colored squares
5. Please do not tip over the milk!
   - ● to turn over
   - ⓑ a round or pointed end
6. There is a fly on the tip of his nose.
   - ⓐ to turn over
   - ● a round or pointed end

218 **At Home:** Invite children to think of another word that has two meanings. Have them use each meaning in a sentence. Book 2.2/Unit 3 Officer Buckle and Gloria 6

Practice, 218

CHALLENGE

Name__________ Date______ **Extend 218**

Multiple-Meaning Words

Use a word from the box to take the place of the underlined words in the sentences.

watch	checks	tips	slip	fall

1. Officer Buckle is making a speech about safety hints. tips
2. He looks at the time on a small clock that he wears on his wrist. watch
3. He looks checks to see if his dog is ready to go.
4. The officer tells people to always wipe up spills before other people lose their balance slip and drop to the ground. fall

Now use a word from the box to answer these riddles.

1. When you look at someone, you also watch them.
2. I am a pattern of squares of different colors. I am called checks.
3. People who serve food sometimes get tips as a thank you.
4. I am a small piece of paper, or a slip.
5. I am known as autumn and also as fall.

218 **At Home:** Have children draw pictures showing both meanings of **coast.** Ask them to write sentences explaining their pictures. Book 2.2/Unit 3 Officer Buckle and Gloria

Extend, 218

LANGUAGE SUPPORT

Name__________ Date______

One Word, Two Meanings

1. Officer Buckle's telephone rings.
2. Claire wrote Officer Buckle two letters.

Q Z

Dear Officer Buckle, Dear Officer Buckle,

3. Wipe up your spill or you might fall.
4. Keep your shoelaces tied.

234 **Officer Buckle and Gloria** • Language Support/Blackline Master 130 Grade 2

Language Support, 234

GRAMMAR/SPELLING CONNECTIONS

See the 5-Day Grammar and Usage Plan on pages 281O–281P.

See the 5-Day Spelling Plan on pages 281Q–281R.

TEACHING TIP

Technology Encourage children to use any reference sources installed on the computer. A dictionary, thesaurus, or encyclopedia can be used for checking definitions, synonyms, and facts.

Proofreading Suggest that children use a reference source, such as a dictionary, to help them edit/proofread their writing.

Handwriting CD-ROM

Writing a Story

Prewrite

WRITE A GLORIA STORY Present this writing assignment: Think about a time when you needed someone to help you. Imagine that Gloria had been there. Write a story that tells what happened when Gloria tried to help you.

DEVELOP SEQUENCE OF EVENTS Have children brainstorm important events that they want to include in their story. They should consider why they needed someone to help them, how Gloria tried to help, and whether she was successful in helping.

Strategy: Create a Time Line Have children make a time line of important events in their stories. Suggest the following:

- Put the reason they needed help at the beginning of the time line.
- Put the story's conclusion at the end of the time line.
- Include the rest of the story's important events in the middle, in the order in which they take place.

Draft

FREE WRITE Encourage children to write their drafts without self-editing. Have them refer to their time line of events, and develop each event with details about main characters and the setting. Tell children they can enhance their story by imagining what the characters might say to one another, and create imaginative dialogue.

Revise

SELF-QUESTIONING Ask children to asses their drafts.

- Did I describe each event from my time line
- Did I use humor and detail to bring the story to life?

PARTNERS Have children trade stories with a peer to get another point of view.

Edit/Proofread

CHECK FOR ERRORS Children should reread their stories for spelling, grammar, and punctuation. Encourage them to check their time lines to be sure they included all the information in the correct order.

Publish

SHARE THE STORIES Collect children's stories in a class story collection. If possible, make a copy of the collection for each child.

HOW GLORIA HELPED ME
by Milton Rinaldo

One day Gloria and I went to the store to buy a turkey for my mother. It was windy outside, and I thought it might rain. I put my hand out to feel for raindrops, and the money I was holding blew out of my hand and on to a tree branch!

I didn't know what to do. But then I remembered how high Gloria could jump. "Can you help me, Gloria?" I asked. "Can you jump as high as that branch?"

Gloria wagged her tail. She jumped up, did a flip, and grabbed the money in her teeth! Then she gave it to me.

The next day, I made sure to give Gloria a nice big piece of turkey!

Presentation Ideas

LLUSTRATE THE STORY Have children llustrate a scene from their story. Create a lisplay of illustrations.
▶ Viewing/Representing

DO A READING Ask children to imagine they are writers giving a reading of their stories. Make a podium from a music stand or other object, and have children stand and read their stories to the class.
▶ Speaking/Listening

Consider children's creative efforts, possibly adding a plus (+) for originality, wit, and imagination.

Scoring Rubric

Excellent	Good	Fair	Unsatisfactory
4: The writer • crafts an imaginative story using Gloria the dog. • uses humor and elaborate details to enhance story events. • clearly and creatively resolves the problem.	**3:** The writer • presents a story using Gloria as a character. • attempts to enhance the story with some details and feelings. • clearly resolves the problem.	**2:** The writer • attempts to write a story. • may not follow the assignment model. • may have trouble resolving the story line.	**1:** The writer • may not grasp the assignment model. • may present vague or incomplete events. • does not resolve the problem.

ncomplete 0: The writer leaves the page blank or fails to respond to the writing task. The student does not address the topic or simply paraphrases the prompt. The response is illegible or incoherent.

Meeting Individual Needs for Writing

EASY

Make a Poster Have children draw a poster announcing a school safety speech by Officer Buckle. Remind them to include information about place, date, and time.

ON-LEVEL

Diary Entry Have children write a diary entry describing what happened the day they saw Gloria signing autographs. Encourage them to include what they saw, heard, thought, and felt.

CHALLENGE

Write a Scene Have children write a scene that tells what happened the next time Officer Buckle and Gloria did a safety speech together. Encourage children to think about the two characters and what they might really say and do. If they wish, children can also add illustrations of the scene.

Listening and Viewing

LISTENING Have children
- listen for the speaker's use of transition words.
- pay attention to the sequence of events that make up the story.
- write down questions to ask later.

VIEWING Encourage children to
- pay attention to the speaker's facial expressions and hand gestures.
- maintain eye contact with the speaker.

LANGUAGE SUPPORT

Suggest that ESL students and English-fluent partners read their first drafts together. Have them discuss any parts of each other's work that they don't understand. Encourage them to make suggestions for clarifying these parts. Also suggest that they think of ways to make both of their stories more interesting.

PORTFOLIO Invite children to include their stories or another writing project in their portfolios.

5 Day Grammar and Usage Plan

LANGUAGE SUPPORT

ESL **Write on the board some simple sentences containing adjectives. Ask a child to come to the board and underline the adjectives. Then ask children if the adjectives come before or after the thing they describe.** (before)

DAILY LANGUAGE ACTIVITIES

Write the Daily Language Activities on the chalkboard each day, or use **Transparency 26**. For each sentence, have children orally add an adjective. (Sample answers are given.)

Day 1

1. It was a ______ rule. new
2. She stood on the ______ chair. small
3. The policeman got a ______ dog. nice

Day 2

1. Gloria was a ______ dog. good
2. Gloria did ______ tricks. eight
3. ______ schools called about the speech. Three

Day 3

1. ______ children fell asleep. Some
2. Officer Buckle gave a ______ speech. great
3. The policeman gave ______ tips. smart

Day 4

1. Officer Buckle got ______ letters. friendly
2. He also got ______ calls. many
3. He made ______ speeches. three

Day 5

1. The school had a ______ accident. bad
2. Gloria gave him a ______ kiss. big
3. He and Gloria are ______ friends. good

Daily Language Transparency 26

DAY 1 Introduce the Concept

Oral Warm-Up Write this sentence and read it aloud: *The funny man gave a speech.* Ask children to tell what kind of man gave a speech.

Introduce Adjectives Tell children that the word *funny* is an adjective. Present:

Adjectives

- An **adjective** is a word that describes a noun.
- Some adjectives tell what kind.

Ask children which noun *funny* describes in the sentence above. (*man*)

Present the Daily Language Activity and have students add an adjective to each sentence. Then write the word *cookie* on the chalkboard. Ask children to write a list of adjectives that describe cookies. Model the first example.

Assign the daily Writing Prompt on page 250C.

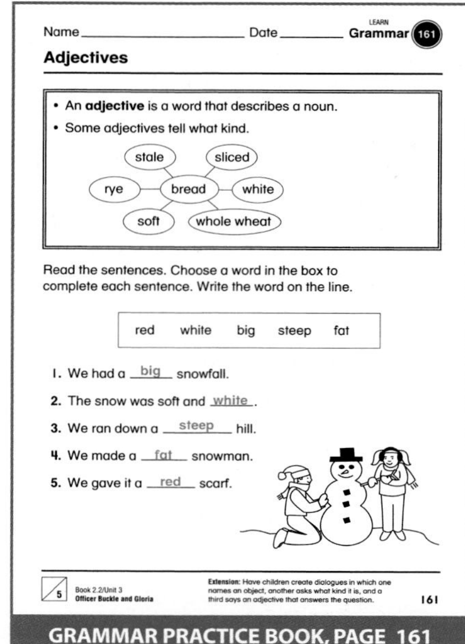

Name ____________ Date ________ LEARN Grammar 161

Adjectives

- An **adjective** is a word that describes a noun.
- Some adjectives tell what kind.

stale, sliced, rye, bread, white, soft, whole wheat

Read the sentences. Choose a word in the box to complete each sentence. Write the word on the line.

red white big steep fat

1. We had a big snowfall.
2. The snow was soft and white.
3. We ran down a steep hill.
4. We made a fat snowman.
5. We gave it a red scarf.

5 Book 2.2/Unit 3 Officer Buckle and Gloria

Extension: Have children create dialogues in which one names an object, another asks what kind it is, and a third says an adjective that answers the question.

161

GRAMMAR PRACTICE BOOK, PAGE 161

DAY 2 Teach the Concept

Review Adjectives that Tell *What Kind* Write this sentence: *That is a big dog.* Ask children what the word *big* tells. (what kind of dog.)

Adjectives that Tell *How Many* Some adjectives do not tell what kind. They describe numbers of things. Present:

Adjectives

Some adjectives tell how many.

Read the following sentences: *The dog did three tricks. The man had many friends.* Have children identify the adjectives that tell how many and the nouns they describe. (three tricks; many friends)

Present the Daily Language Activity. Then have children write a sentence including an adjective that tells how many. Ask them to underline the adjective they use.

Assign the daily Writing Prompt on page 250C.

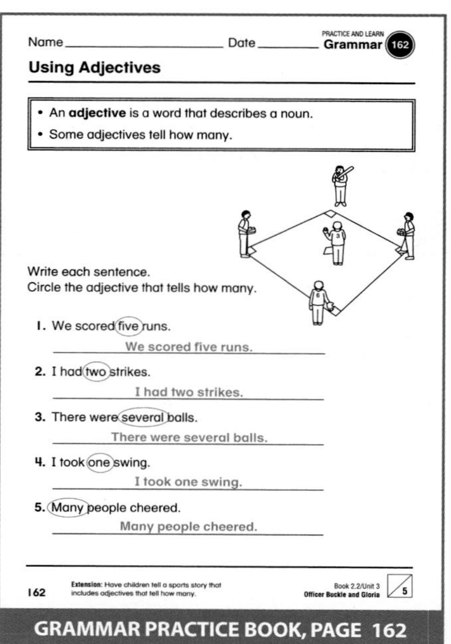

Name ____________ Date ________ PRACTICE AND LEARN Grammar 162

Using Adjectives

- An **adjective** is a word that describes a noun.
- Some adjectives tell how many.

Write each sentence.
Circle the adjective that tells how many.

1. We scored (five) runs.
   We scored five runs.
2. I had (two) strikes.
   I had two strikes.
3. There were (several) balls.
   There were several balls.
4. I took (one) swing.
   I took one swing.
5. (Many) people cheered.
   Many people cheered.

162

Extension: Have children tell a sports story that includes adjectives that tell how many.

Book 2.2/Unit 3 Officer Buckle and Gloria 5

GRAMMAR PRACTICE BOOK, PAGE 162

Adjectives

DAY 3 Review and Practice

earn from Literature Review adjec-ives. Read the sentences on page 276 of *)fficer Buckle and Gloria:*

> **Gloria gave Officer Buckle a big kiss on the nose. Officer Buckle gave Gloria a nice pat on the back.**

sk children to identify the adjectives in ne sentences, and to tell which noun ach adjective describes. (big *kiss*, nice *at*) What do the adjectives tell about ne nouns? (what kind)

dentify Adjectives Present the Daily anguage Activity. Then ask children to nd the adjective in the first sentence on age 258 of *Officer Buckle and Gloria.* one) Ask what this tells about the noun *ay.* (how many) Have children create ew sentences with *big, nice,* and *one.*

Assign the daily Writing Prompt on page 250D.

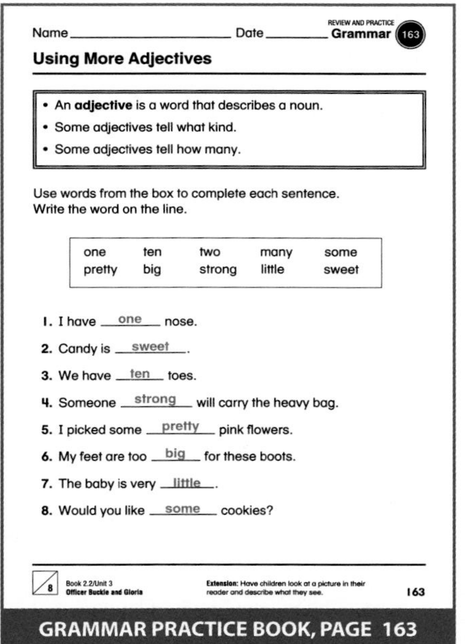

REVIEW AND PRACTICE

Name ______________ Date ________ Grammar 163

Using More Adjectives

- An **adjective** is a word that describes a noun.
- Some adjectives tell what kind.
- Some adjectives tell how many.

Use words from the box to complete each sentence.
Write the word on the line.

one	ten	two	many	some
pretty	big	strong	little	sweet

1. I have ___one___ nose.
2. Candy is ___sweet___.
3. We have ___ten___ toes.
4. Someone ___strong___ will carry the heavy bag.
5. I picked some ___pretty___ pink flowers.
6. My feet are too ___big___ for these boots.
7. The baby is very ___little___.
8. Would you like ___some___ cookies?

8 Book 2.2/Unit 3 **Officer Buckle and Gloria**

Extension: Have children look at a picture in their reader and describe what they see.

163

GRAMMAR PRACTICE BOOK, PAGE 163

Review and Practice

Review Adjectives Have each child write a sentence with an adjective in it. Ask volunteers to read aloud their sentences and have others identify the adjectives. Then present the Daily Language Activity.

Mechanics and Usage Review the use of commas in a series. Display and discuss:

> **Commas In Sentences**
>
> Use **commas** to separate three or more words in a series.

Tell students that some sentences may contain three or more adjectives. Write this sentence on the chalkboard: *The dog was big, white, and fluffy.* Have children identify the adjectives. Point out the commas and the word *and.*

Assign the daily Writing Prompt on page 250D.

MECHANICS

Name ______________ Date ________ Grammar 164

Using Commas

- Use commas to separate three or more words in a series.
  We made red, white, and blue flags.

yo-yo

Popcorn!

Read each sentence. Correct it.
Write the correct sentence on the line.

1. the fishing pole is long thin and brown
   The fishing pole is long, thin, and brown.
2. bud's wish list has a new TV a real basketball and a blue bike
   Bud's wish list has a new TV, a real basketball, and a blue bike.
3. sue's yo-yo is small round and red
   Sue's yo-yo is small, round, and red.
4. I'm happy with my yellow crunchy and tasty popcorn
   I'm happy with my yellow, crunchy, and tasty popcorn.

164

Extension: Have students write sentences with a series of words and punctuate the sentences with commas.

Book 2.2/Unit 3 **Officer Buckle and Gloria** 4

GRAMMAR PRACTICE BOOK, PAGE 164

DAY 5 Assess and Reteach

Assess Use the Daily Language Activity on page 165 of the **Grammar Practice Book** for assessment.

Reteach Review the rules about adjectives from the lesson grammar concepts. Then write several sentences similar to the Daily Language Activities on the board. After each, write a question to help children fill in an adjective. Examples: *I saw a ______ dog.* What kind of dog? ______ *dogs were barking.* How many dogs? Have children complete the sentences. Then list these nouns: *cat, girl, toys, people.* Have children write a sentence with an adjective that tells *what kind* or *how many* about each noun.

Use page 166 of the **Grammar Practice Book** for additional reteaching.

Assign the daily Writing Prompt on page 250D.

TEST

Name ______________ Date ________ Grammar 165

Adjectives

A. Circle the adjective in each sentence.

1. Jill took a (long) walk.
2. She passed an (old) house.
3. She saw a (new) mall.
4. She saw a (cute) baby.

B. Find the adjective in each sentence.
Write it on the line.

5. Let's go to a faraway place. ___faraway___
6. We can see little bugs. ___little___
7. We can hear strange music. ___strange___
8. We can feel soft winds. ___soft___

8 Book 2.2/Unit 3 **Officer Buckle and Gloria**

165

GRAMMAR PRACTICE BOOK, PAGE 165

GRAMMAR PRACTICE BOOK, PAGE 166

5 Day Spelling Plan

LANGUAGE SUPPORT

ESL **The letters *ll* represent the sound /y/ in Spanish. Write the words ending with *ll* on the chalkboard and pronounce them. Have children take turns underlining the double consonant and repeating the word.**

DICTATION SENTENCES

Spelling Words

1. I call her Mom.
2. I can add two and two.
3. He broke the egg.
4. He can sell the car.
5. She can give her father a kiss.
6. I can tell that you were here.
7. It is an odd story.
8. I fill it to the top.
9. She can press the leaves.
10. He is not well.

Challenge Words

11. Two accidents happened there.
12. The audience was happy.
13. They cheered for the boys.
14. The car is at the station.
15. I can wipe the cage.

DAY 1 Pretest

Assess Prior Knowledge Use the Dictation Sentences at left and **Spelling Practice Book** page 161 for the pretest. Allow children to correct their own papers. If children have trouble, have partners give each other a midweek test on Day 3. Children who require a modified list may be tested on the first five words.

Spelling Words		Challenge Words
1. call	6. tell	11. **accidents**
2. add	7. odd	12. **audience**
3. egg	8. fill	13. **cheered**
4. sell	9. press	14. **station**
5. **kiss**	10. **well**	15. **wipe**

*Note: Words in **dark type** are from the story.*

Word Study On page 162 of the **Spelling Practice Book** are word study steps and an at-home activity.

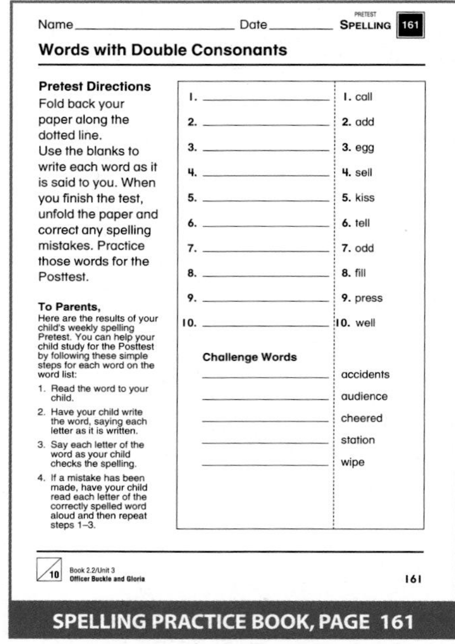
PRETEST SPELLING 161

Name_______________ Date_________

Words with Double Consonants

Pretest Directions
Fold back your paper along the dotted line. Use the blanks to write each word as it is said to you. When you finish the test, unfold the paper and correct any spelling mistakes. Practice those words for the Posttest.

To Parents,
Here are the results of your child's weekly spelling Pretest. You can help your child study for the Posttest by following these simple steps for each word on the word list:

1. Read the word to your child.
2. Have your child write the word, saying each letter as it is written.
3. Say each letter of the word as your child checks the spelling.
4. If a mistake has been made, have your child read each letter of the correctly spelled word aloud and then repeat steps 1–3.

1. ________ 1. call
2. ________ 2. add
3. ________ 3. egg
4. ________ 4. sell
5. ________ 5. kiss
6. ________ 6. tell
7. ________ 7. odd
8. ________ 8. fill
9. ________ 9. press
10. ________ 10. well

Challenge Words

________ accidents
________ audience
________ cheered
________ station
________ wipe

10 Book 2.2/Unit 3 **Officer Buckle and Gloria** 161

SPELLING PRACTICE BOOK, PAGE 161

WORD STUDY STEPS AND ACTIVITY, PAGE 162

DAY 2 Explore the Pattern

Sort and Spell Words Say *call, odd, press, egg*. Have children listen carefully and identify the ending sound in each word. Tell children that each word ends in a double consonant.

Ask children to read aloud the ten spelling words before sorting them according to spelling pattern.

Words ending with double consonants

ll	dd	ss
call	add	kiss
sell	odd	press
tell		
fill	**gg**	
well	egg	

Word Wall As children read other stories and texts, have them look for new words with double consonant endings *ll, dd, ss,* and *gg* and add them to the classroom word wall, underlining the spelling pattern in each word.

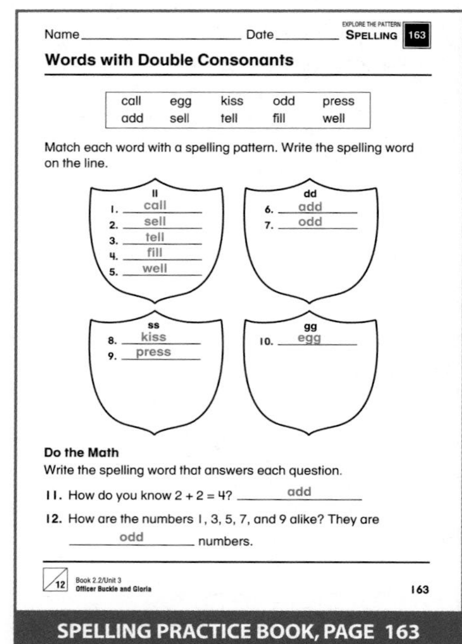
EXPLORE THE PATTERN SPELLING 163

Name_______________ Date_________

Words with Double Consonants

call	egg	kiss	odd	press
add	sell	tell	fill	well

Match each word with a spelling pattern. Write the spelling word on the line.

ll
1. call
2. sell
3. tell
4. fill
5. well

dd
6. add
7. odd

ss
8. kiss
9. press

gg
10. egg

Do the Math
Write the spelling word that answers each question.

11. How do you know $2 + 2 = 4$? add
12. How are the numbers 1, 3, 5, 7, and 9 alike? They are odd numbers.

12 Book 2.2/Unit 3 **Officer Buckle and Gloria** 163

SPELLING PRACTICE BOOK, PAGE 163

Words with Double Consonants

DAY 3 Practice and Extend

Vord Meaning: Prefixes Remind hildren that prefixes are letters added o the beginning of words that change he words' meaning. Tell them that the refix *re-* means *again*. Have children add he prefix *re–* to the words *fill, tell,* and *all*. Then have children write a context entence for each of these new words.

ilossary Have partners:

- write each Challenge Word.
- look up each Challenge Word and find the ones that have synonyms listed.
- write a synonym for each Challenge Word that has one listed.

Name________ Date______ PRACTICE AND EXTEND SPELLING 164

Words with Double Consonants

call	egg	kiss	odd	press
add	sell	tell	fill	well

Not the Same
In the space beside each word, write the spelling word that means the opposite.

1. buy __sell__ 3. empty __fill__
2. even __odd__ 4. subtract __add__

Again, please!
The prefix **re-** means **again**.
re + fill = refill
Refill means **to fill again**.

Add **re-** to these spelling words to make new words.

5. re + tell = __retell__
6. re + call = __recall__

Use spelling words to finish this phone message.

Hi. It's Amy. Can you __call__ me on the phone later? Please __tell__ me what time the play starts. I need to __press__ my pants before I go. __Well__, I'll see you soon.

164 **Challenge Extension:** Have students draw pictures to illustrate each word. They may exchange pictures with a partner to guess the illustrations. Book 2.2/Unit 3 **Officer Buckle and Gloria** 10

SPELLING PRACTICE BOOK, PAGE 164

DAY 4 Proofread and Write

Proofread Sentences Write these sentences on the chalkboard, including the misspelled words. Ask children to proofread, circling incorrect spellings and writing the correct spellings. There is one spelling error in each sentence.

Can you cook an eg? (egg)

Is the wel deep? (well)

Do you know how to adde? (add)

Did she tel a story? (tell)

Have children create additional sentences with errors for partners to correct.

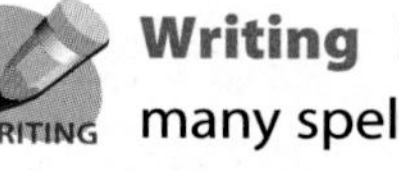

Writing Have children use as many spelling words as possible in the daily Writing Prompt on page 250D. Remind children to proofread their writing for errors in spelling, grammar, and punctuation.

Name________ Date______ PROOFREAD AND WRITE SPELLING 165

Words with Double Consonants

Proofreading Activity
There are five spelling mistakes in the poem below. Circle each misspelled word. Write the words correctly on the lines below.

I will not say, I cannot tel,
What I wished at the wishing weell.

1. __tell__ 2. __well__

I push and pres but it's a mess.
The cookie mix is not a success.

3. __press__

I add an eg and hope for the best.
I'll eat a few and selll the rest.

4. __egg__ 5. __sell__

Writing Activity
Imagine that you have an unusual pet. Write sentences about your pet. Use five spelling words in your sentences. Circle the spelling words you use.

10 Book 2.2/Unit 3 **Officer Buckle and Gloria** 165

SPELLING PRACTICE BOOK, PAGE 165

DAY 5 Assess and Reteach

Assess Children's Knowledge Use page 166 of the **Spelling Practice Book** or the Dictation Sentences on page 281Q for the posttest.

Personal Word List If children have trouble with any words in the lesson, have them create a personal list of troublesome words in their journals. Have children write a context sentence for each word.

Children should refer to their word lists during later writing activities.

Name________ Date______ POSTTEST SPELLING 166

Words with Double Consonants

Look at the words in each set. One word in each set is spelled correctly. Use a pencil to color in the circle in front of that word. Before you begin, look at the sample sets of words. Sample A has been done for you. Do Sample B by yourself. When you are sure you know what to do, you may go on with the rest of the page.

Sample A
(A) will
(B) whil
(C) wil
(D) wille

Sample B
(E) mis
(F) mmiss
(G) miss
(H) miis

1. (A) eeg (B) egg (C) eg (D) egge
2. (E) pres (F) prest (G) press (H) pess
3. (A) selle (B) sel (C) seel (D) sell
4. (E) tell (F) tel (G) telll (H) telle
5. (A) fiel (B) fiil (C) fill (D) fille
6. (E) call (F) kall (G) cahl (H) calle
7. (A) ade (B) add (C) aad (D) adde
8. (E) weil (F) well (G) whel (H) weel
9. (A) kisse (B) kis (C) kess (D) kiss
10. (E) ood (F) ohd (G) odd (H) odde

166 Book 2.2/Unit 3 **Officer Buckle and Gloria** 10

SPELLING PRACTICE BOOK, PAGE 166

Reaching All Learners

Concept
- On the Move

Comprehension
- Form Generalization

Phonics
- Long *e*; Long *i*

Vocabulary
- borrow
- desert
- evenings
- midnight
- package
- shoulder

Anthology

Tomás and the Library Lady

Selection Summary **With the help of the library lady, Tomás starts to find a new world of books and stories.**

Rhyme applies to phonics

Listening Library

INSTRUCTIONAL pages 284–309

About the Author Pat Mora has played an important role in preserving Mexican American culture. "I take pride in being a Hispanic author," she notes. Born and raised in Texas, she was a teacher for many years. She has written children's books in English and Spanish, as well as poetry and nonfiction.

About the Illustrator Raul Colón has not only illustrated children's books but has designed puppets and created short animated films for television. He was awarded the Society of Illustrators Gold Medal for *Always My Dad*, which was written by Sharon Dennis Wyeth.

Same Concept, Skills and Vocabulary!

Leveled Books

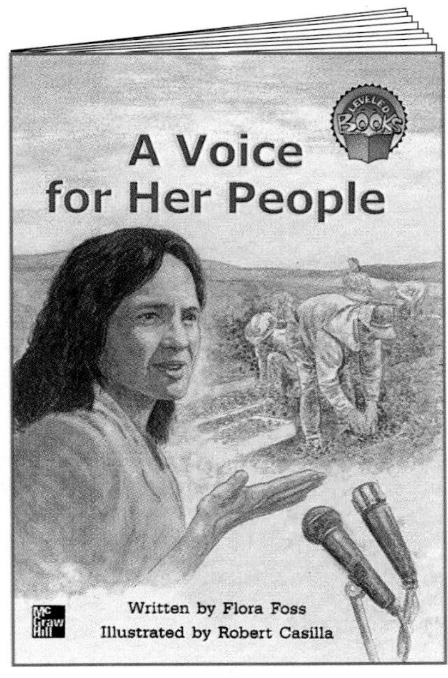

EASY
Lesson on pages 309A and 309D

DECODABLE

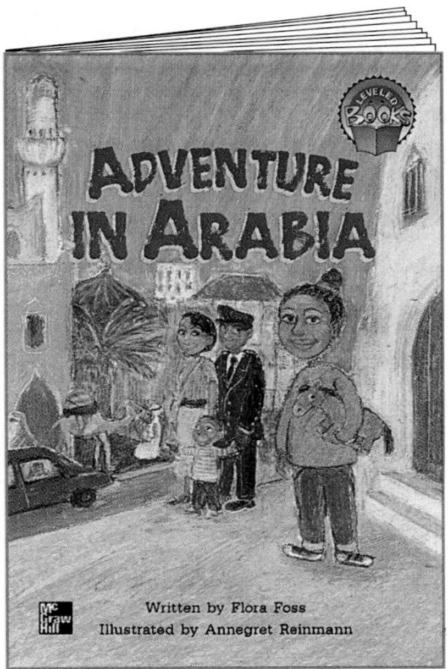

INDEPENDENT
Lesson on pages 309B and 309D

Take-Home version available

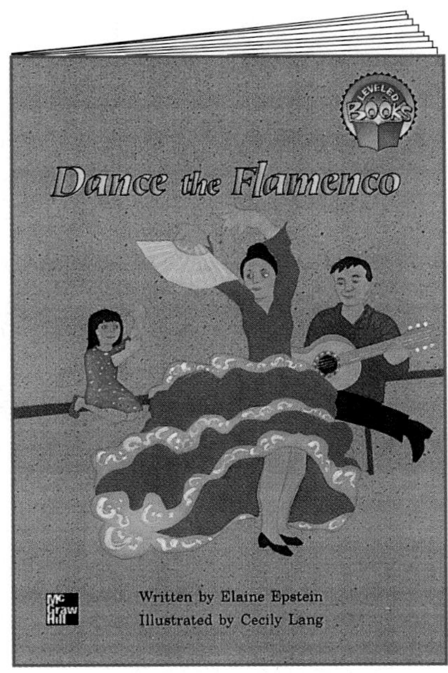

CHALLENGE
Lesson on pages 309C and 309D

Leveled Practice

EASY
Reteach, 219–226 Blackline masters with reteaching opportunities for each assessed skill

INDEPENDENT/ON-LEVEL
Practice, 219–226 Workbook with Take-Home stories and practice opportunities for each assessed skill and story comprehension

CHALLENGE
Extend, 219–226 Blackline masters that offer challenge activities for each assessed skill

Quizzes Prepared by  Accelerated Reader

Social Studies	America Working, *288*
Science	Recycling Matters, *296*
Math	Tiger Tips, *294*
Art	Be the Illustrator, *300*
Language Arts	Read Aloud, *282E*
Writing	Write an Adventure Story, *306*
Cultural Perspectives	Stories, *290*
Research and Inquiry	Find Out More, *307*
Internet Activities	www.mhschool.com/reading

Suggested Lesson Planner

READING AND LANGUAGE ARTS	 DAY 1 *Focus on Reading and Skills*	 DAY 2 *Read the Literature*
Phonics Daily Routines	**Daily Phonics Routine:** **Segmenting,** 282H Phonics **CD-ROM**	**Daily**  **Routine:** **Building,** 284A  **CD-ROM**
Phonological Awareness Phonics *Long e, i* Comprehension Vocabulary Study Skills Listening, Speaking, Viewing, Representing	 **Read Aloud: Poem,** 282E "The Library" ☑ **Develop Phonological Awareness,** 282F Long *e, i* ☑ **Review Long *e, i*,** 282G–282H **Teaching Chart 183** **Reteach, Practice, Extend,** 219 **Phonics/Phonemic Awareness Practice Book,** 139–142  **Apply Long *e, i*,** 282/283 "Magic Ticket" Intervention Program	**Build Background,** 284A Develop Oral Language **Vocabulary,** 284B–284C  ***borrow evenings package desert midnight shoulder*** **Word Building Manipulative Cards** **Teaching Chart 184** **Reteach, Practice, Extend,** 220 Read **Read the Selection,** 284–305 Comprehension ☑ Long *e, i* ☑ Form Generalizations **Genre:** Biographical Story, 285 **Writer's Craft:** Antonyms, 302 **Cultural Perspectives,** 290  Intervention Program
Curriculum Connections	 **Language Arts,** 282E	 **Social Studies,** 288
Writing	 **Writing Prompt:** Think about the first time you went to a library. Describe what you saw. Describe what you did.	 **Writing Prompt:** You are taking someone to the library for the first time. How will you help him or her learn about the library?  **Journal Writing** Quick-Write, 305
Grammar	**Introduce the Concept: Using *a* and *an*,** 309O Daily Language Activity: Use *a* and *an* correctly. **Grammar Practice Book,** 167	**Teach the Concept: Using *a* and *an*,** 309O Daily Language Activity: Use *a* and *an* correctly. **Grammar Practice Book,** 168
Spelling *sh, ch*	**Pretest: Words with Digraphs *sh, ch*,** 309Q **Spelling Practice Book,** 167, 168	**Explore the Pattern: Words with Digraphs *sh, ch*,** 309Q **Spelling Practice Book,** 169

 **Intervention Program Available**

Meeting Individual Needs

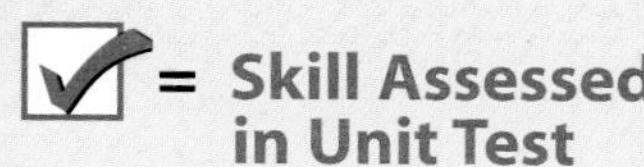
= Skill Assessed in Unit Test

Intervention Program Available

DAY 3 Read the Literature	DAY 4 Build Skills	DAY 5 Build Skills
 Daily Phonics Routine: **Letter Substitution,** 307 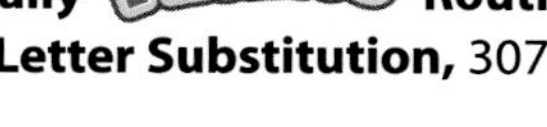 CD-ROM	Daily Phonics Routine: **Fluency,** 309F  CD-ROM	 Daily Phonics Routine: **Writing,** 309H  CD-ROM
Rereading for Fluency, 304 **Story Questions and Activities,** 306–307 **Reteach, Practice, Extend,** 221 **Study Skill,** 308 ☑ **Library/Media Center** **Teaching Chart 185** **Reteach, Practice, Extend,** 222 **Test Power,** 309 Read **Read the Leveled Books,** 309A–309D Guided Reading ☑ **Long *e*, *i*** ☑ **Form Generalizations** ☑ **Instructional Vocabulary** Intervention Program	 **Read the Leveled Books and the Self-Selected Books** ☑ **Review Long *e*, *i*,** 309E–309F **Teaching Chart 186** **Reteach, Practice, Extend,** 223 **Language Support,** 240 **Phonics/Phonemic Awareness Practice Book,** 139–142 ☑ **Long *e*; Long *i*; *tch*, *ch*,** 309G–309H **Teaching Chart 187** **Reteach, Practice, Extend,** 224 **Language Support,** 241 **Phonics/Phonemic Awareness Practice Book,** 139–142 **Minilessons,** 293, 295, 303  Intervention Program	 **Read Self-Selected Books** ☑ **Introduce Main Idea,** 309I–309J **Teaching Chart 188** **Reteach, Practice, Extend,** 225 **Language Support,** 242 ☑ **Review Multiple-Meaning Words,** 309K–309L **Teaching Chart 189** **Reteach, Practice, Extend,** 226 **Language Support,** 243 **Listening, Speaking, Viewing, Representing,** 309N Dioramas Stories on Tape **Minilessons,** 293, 295, 303 Intervention Program
Activity **Math,** 294	Activity **Science,** 296	Activity **Art,** 300
Writing Prompt: Compare reading a story yourself and listening to someone read a story. How is it the same? How is it different? **Writing a Story,** 309M Prewrite, Draft	**Writing Prompt:** Write a letter to your principal asking if your class can visit your public library. Give reasons why it's a good idea. **Writing a Story,** 309M Revise **Meeting Individual Needs for Writing,** 309N	**Writing Prompt:** Would you like to work in a library? Why or why not? **Writing a Story,** 309M Edit/Proofread, Publish
Review and Practice: Using *a* and *an*, 309P Daily Language Activity: Use *a* and *an* correctly. **Grammar Practice Book,** 169	**Review and Practice: Using *a* and *an*,** 309P Daily Language Activity: Use *a* and *an* correctly. **Grammar Practice Book,** 170	**Assess and Reteach: Using *a* and *an*,** 309P Daily Language Activity: Use *a* and *an* correctly. **Grammar Practice Book,** 171, 172
Practice and Extend: Words with Digraphs *sh*, *ch*, 309R **Spelling Practice Book,** 170	**Proofread and Write: Words with Digraphs *sh*, *ch*,** 309R **Spelling Practice Book,** 171	**Assess: Words with Digraphs *sh*, *ch*,** 309R **Spelling Practice Book,**172

Language Arts

Read Aloud

The Library

a poem by Barbara A. Huff

It looks like any building
When you pass it on the street,
Made of stone and glass and marble,
Made of iron and concrete.

But once inside you can ride
A camel or a train,
Visit Rome, Siam, or Nome,
Feel a hurricane,
Meet a king, learn to sing,
How to bake a pie,
Go to sea, plant a tree,
Find how airplanes fly,
Train a horse, and of course
Have all the dogs you'd like,
See the moon, a sandy dune,
Or catch a whopping pike.
Everything that books can bring
You'll find inside those walls.

Continued on page T2

Oral Comprehension

LISTENING AND SPEAKING Read the poem without stating the title, and ask children if they can guess what type of building is being described. When you have finished, ask, "Which clues in the text helped you guess what the building was?"

GENRE STUDY: POETRY Discuss the literary devices and techniques used in *The Library*.

- Reread the poem, asking children to raise their hands when they hear rhyming words. Remind children that rhymes can happen within a line as well as at the end.
- Discuss how the title of the poem relates to the poem's subject. Point out that the title is the only place in the poem where the word *library* is mentioned. Ask, *Can you think of another title for this poem that would still make sense?*
- Reread the poem, and show children where the three stanzas occur. Discuss why the poet may have chosen to break up the poem into three parts. Encourage children to think about how each stanza is different from one another.

Activity Invite children to think about the school library or a library in their community. Have them draw a picture of their favorite library and write a poem about it. Encourage children to include rhyming words in their poem.

Develop

Phonological Awareness

Blend Sounds

Phonemic Awareness

MATERIALS

- small colored bag or paper sack
- Phonics Picture Posters

Teach Tell children you have picture cards of some words in your bag. Say, */l/-/ē/-/f/. If we blend the sounds together, what word do we get?* (leaf) Pull the picture card of the leaf out of the bag and show it to the class. Have them blend the sounds again to say the word.

Practice Proceed with pictures of the following words: *queen, zebra, cheese, nine, bee, kite,* and *iron*.

Segment Sounds

Phonemic Awareness

MATERIALS

- colored blocks

Teach Say the word *deep*. Then say the sounds /d/-/ē/-/p/, placing a colored block for each sound. Count the blocks and tell children the word *deep* has three sounds.

Practice Distribute a set of colored blocks to each child. Have them continue to segment and count the sounds in the following words: *right, meet, read, met, fry, reach, batch,* and *piece*.

Delete Sounds

Phonemic Awareness

MATERIALS

- Photos or drawings of weather, colors, and insects

Teach Tell children you will say a word that has to do with weather. Then say: *If I take the /s/ sound away from the word snow, I get no.* Have children say both words with you: *snow, no*.

Practice Have children practice deleting the second sound of each of the following words: *sleet, sky, breeze, blow, bright*. You may wish to continue with the following color words: *green, black, blue, brown, gray*. Have children tell whether the new word is a real or nonsense word.

Observe children as they blend, segment, and delete sounds. If children have difficulty, see Alternate Teaching Strategies on p. T69.

Review Long *e, i*

OBJECTIVES

Children will:

- review /ē/: *ee, ea,* and *ie.*
- review /ī/: *i, y,* and *igh.*

MATERIALS

- cards and word building boxes from the **Word Building Manipulative Cards**
- **Teaching Chart 183**

Skills Finder

Long *i*	
Introduce	B1: 92G-H
Review	B1: 113E-F, 113G-H; B2: 309E-F, 309G-H
Test	B1: Unit 1
Maintain	B2: 21

SPELLING/PHONICS CONNECTIONS

Words with /ē/ and /ī/sounds: See the 5-Day Spelling Plan, pages 309Q–309R.

TEACHING TIP

LONG e AND LONG *i* Point out that the long *e* and long *i* sounds are sometimes represented by a single letter (long *i:y,i*), and sometimes represented by a letter combination (long *e: ee, ea, ie;* long *i: igh*).

PREPARE

Review the Symbols *ee, ea, ie* for the Sound /ē/ and the Symbols *i, y, igh* for the Sound /ī/

Tell children that they will review words in which the letters *e, ee, ie,* and *ea* stand for the long vowel sound /ē/. Tell children that they will also review words in which the letters *i, y,* and *igh* stand for the long /ī/ sound.

TEACH

BLENDING Model and Guide Practice with Long *e* and Long *i* Words

- Display **Teaching Chart 183**. Point to the letters *ee* at the top of column 1 and say /ē/.

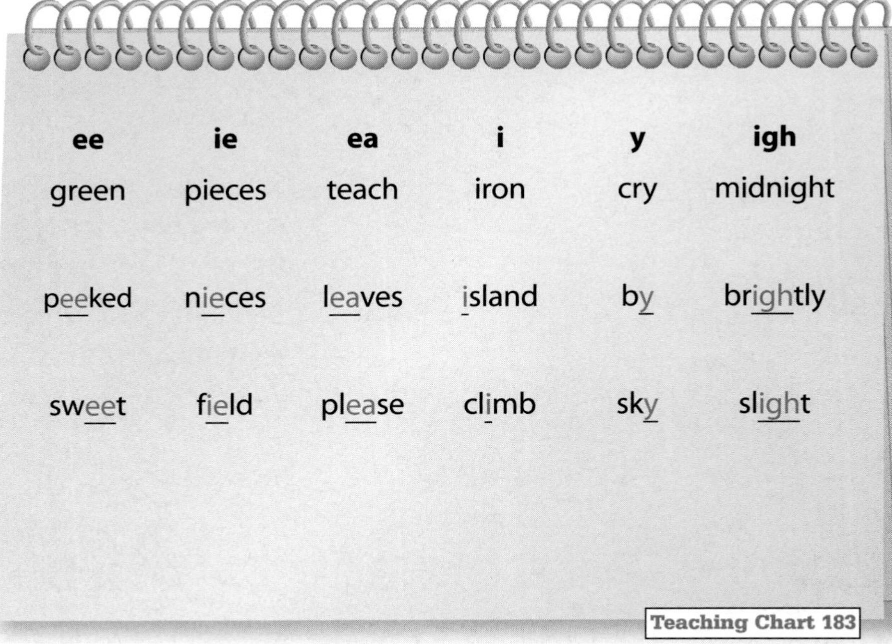

- Then point to the first word in column 1. Cover the letters *g, r,* and *n* and have children pronounce /ē/.
- Uncover the letters and use your hand to blend the sounds in *green*. Have children repeat after you. g r ee n green
- Continue with the procedure for all the words in the first column. Have children add the missing letters, blend and read the words.
- Point to the letters at the top of each of the other columns, say the sound, and then model the blending process for the first word in each column.

Use the Words in Context

- Ask children to use the words in sentences to reinforce their meanings. Examples: *That tree has tiny green leaves.*

Repeat the Procedure

- Have children complete the words in all the columns.

PRACTICE

WORD BUILDING
Build Long *e* and Long *i* Words

Using letter cards have children build the words *tree, tease, pieces, child, sly,* and *might.* Read aloud, and have children repeat. Ask children to identify the letter combinations in each word that make the sound /ē/. Repeat these steps for the long *i* sound, beginning by building the words *climb, by,* and *brightly.*

▶ **Linguistic/Intrapersonal**

ASSESS/CLOSE

Read and Sort Long *e* and Long *i* Words

To assess children's ability to build and decode long *e* and long *i* words, observe them as they complete the Practice activity. Have the class build a word wall representing each long-vowel sound. Encourage them to sort their words in the right column. Ask children to read aloud the phonics rhyme on page 283 in their books. Invite children to add words as they read to the appropriate column on the word wall.

ADDITIONAL PHONICS RESOURCES

Phonics/Phonemic Awareness Practice Book, pages 139–142

activities to practice Blending and Segmenting

Meeting Individual Needs for Phonics

EASY

Name ________ Date ______ **Reteach 219**

Long *e, i*

Say these words. All of them have the long **e** sound.
free piece leaves
Say these words. All of them have the long **i** sound.
sky high hi

Name the picture. Then circle the correct word for each picture. Write the word.

1. sweet (cry) — cry
2. (iron) fly — iron
3. sigh (tree) — tree
4. (leaves) piece — leaves
5. sky (field) — field
6. (light) see — light

6 Book 2.2/Unit 3 **Tomás and the Library Lady** **At Home:** Have children say each of the words they circled and listen to the vowel sound. 219

Reteach, 219

ON-LEVEL

Name ________ Date ______ **Practice 219**

Long *e, i*

Complete each sentence with a word from the box.

green	sweet	piece	trees
teaches	leader	climb	brightly
line	bike	fine	kite

1. The sun is shining very brightly.
2. The grass is green.
3. Ice cream is sweet.
4. Joe likes follow-the-leader.
5. Lucy loves to climb trees.
6. Karen teaches music.
7. Tim and Nora climb to the top.
8. Luis has a piece of apple.
9. Nancy drew a line on the paper.
10. Harold rode his bike to school.
11. He had to pay a fine for the late book.
12. They all wanted to fly the kite.

12 Book 2.2/Unit 3 **Tomás and the Library Lady** **At Home:** Have children write silly sentences using words from the box. 219

Practice, 219

CHALLENGE

Name ________ Date ______ **Extend 219**

Long *e, i*

Follow all the directions.

1. Color the top of the tree green.
2. Circle the leaves falling from the tree.
3. Draw a squirrel on the side of the tree.
4. Draw teeth on the eager beaver.
5. Draw the sun shining brightly.
6. Draw wings on the bird so it can fly.
7. Draw a piece of food to feed the squirrel.
8. Color the rest of the picture.

Sample sentences shown.
Write three sentences that tell what is happening in the picture.

The tree is green.
The bird is flying.
The sun shines brightly.

Book 2.2/Unit 3 **Tomás and the Library Lady** **At Home:** Ask children to write a short story using the following **long e** and **long i** words: **peeked, seen, sweet, teach, cry, midnight, by, brightly.** 219

Extend, 219

Daily Routines

DAY 1 Segmenting Have children use word building boxes to write the following words: *means, seen, pieces, climb, dry, light.* Have children point to the symbols for the /ē/, /ī/ sounds.

DAY 2 Word Building Write the following letters in a horizontal row on the chalkboard: *ee, ie, ea, i, g,* and *igh.* Then write the following list: *sl__p, dr__m, p__ce, fl_, sl___t, cl__mb.* Have volunteers fill in letters to make words with /ē/ or /ī/.

DAY 3 Letter Substitution Write the following words on the chalkboard: *meat, feet, yield, shy, fight, hind.* Have children substitute initial or final consonants to make new words.

DAY 4 Fluency Write the following words on the chalkboard: *teeth, eager, leader, iron, by,* and *midnight.* Ask a volunteer to blend the sounds silently and then read aloud each word.

DAY 5 Writing Have partners work together to write short, rhyming poems containing words with long *e* or long *i* vowel patterns.

Children will review long e: *ee, ea, ie*; and long i: *i, y, igh*.

Apply Long *e* and Long *i*

Magic Ticket

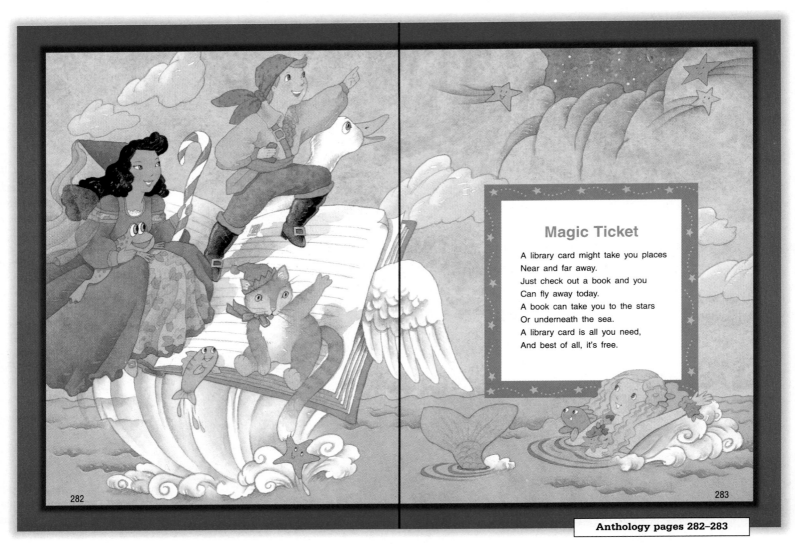

A library card might take you places
Near and far away.
Just check out a book and you
Can fly away today.
A book can take you to the stars
Or underneath the sea.
A library card is all you need,
And best of all, it's free.

282

283

Anthology pages 282–283

Read and Build Fluency

READ THE POEM Read aloud "Magic Ticket," modeling the smooth pause-and-restart between sentences. Have children listen for the long *e* and long *i* sounds as they follow along. For auditory modeling purposes, ask them to read the poem aloud in unison as you track the print.

GROUP **REREAD FOR FLUENCY** Encourage fluent reading by engaging in choral reading with the children. As you read the poem aloud together, gradually fade your voice as children become more fluent. Increase your volume if needed to keep the children on track.

Dictate and Spell

JOURNAL **DICTATE WORDS** Say the long *e* word *neat*. Segment it into its individual parts. Say *neat* again and use it in a sentence, for example, "I try to keep my room neat." Have children repeat the word. Then direct them to write down the letter or letter patterns for each sound until they make the entire word. Repeat these steps with the words *fly, sea*, and *library*. Then use words not from the poem, such as *sweet* and *climb*.

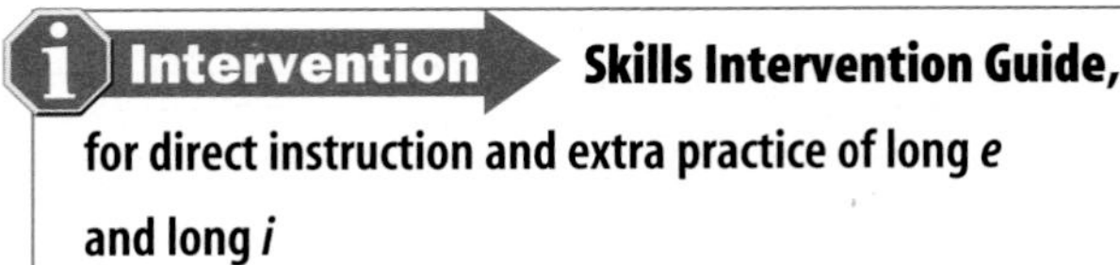

Build Background

ink
ial Studies

Concept: On the Move

Evaluate Prior Knowledge

ONCEPT: ON THE MOVE Ask children share what they know about the experience of moving from one place to another. xplain that different crops are harvested uring different seasons, so migrant workers e always moving to where work can be und.

REATE A WORD WEB Have children ake a word web recording their suggestions for why people might move om one place to another.
▶ **Linguistic/Logical**

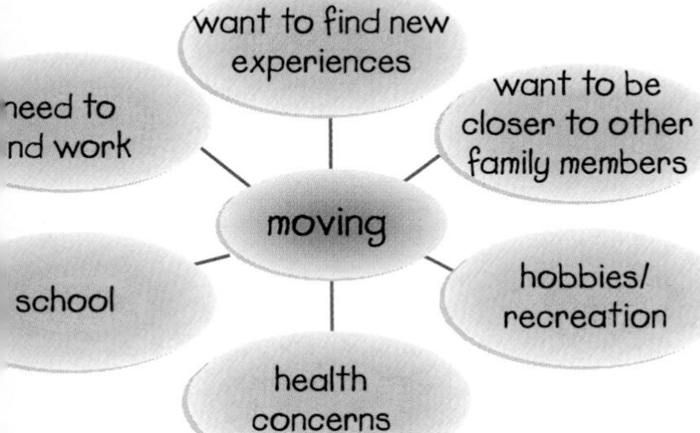

MAP A MOVE Invite children to look at a globe, map, or atlas, and to choose location where they ould like to live. Suggest at children use the ord web as a guide. ave each child write a few entences explaining what special about that articular location.

ONE

Develop Oral Language

ESL Have children brainstorm a list of words and activities related to moving such as:

- plane, car, moving van
- boxes, tape
- packing, driving, unpacking, lifting

Have children pantomime the different activities, such as packing, lifting boxes, and so on they might do when moving. Then ask:

- What are you doing?
- How might you feel while you were doing these things?
- Why are you moving?

▶ **Linguistic/Kinesthetic.**

Anthology and Leveled Books

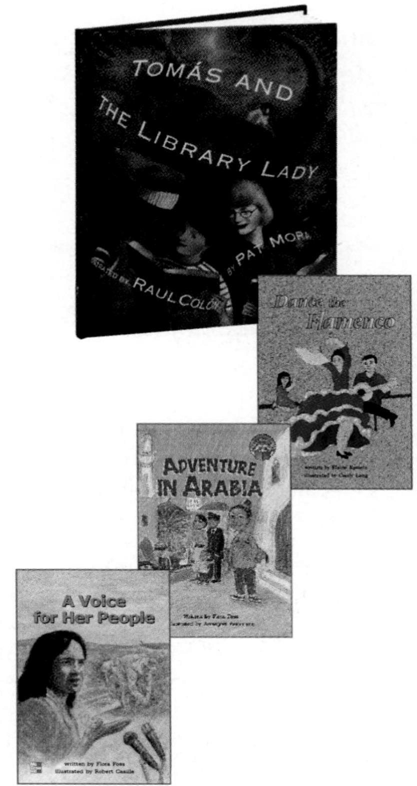

DAILY Phonics ROUTINES

DAY 2 **Building** Write on the chalkboard the following lists: *sl__p, dr__m, p__ce, fl__, sl__t, cl__mb*. Have volunteers fill in letters to make words with /e/ and /l/.

Phonics **CD-ROM**

LANGUAGE SUPPORT

See the **Language Support Book,** *pages 235–238* for teaching suggestions for Build Background.

TESTED OBJECTIVES

Children will use context and structural clues to determine the meanings of vocabulary words.

Definitions

borrow (p.296), to take something from someone with the agreement that it will be given back

desert (p.298), a dry area of land with little water or plant life

evenings (p.298), nights

midnight (p.287), twelve o' clock at night

package (p.300), thing or group of things packed together and wrapped up

shoulder (p.292), part of the body where the arm joins the torso

Story Words

These words from the selection may be unfamiliar. Before children read, have them check the meanings and pronunciations of the words in the Glossary, beginning on page 390, or in a dictionary.

- buenas noches, p. 288
- señor, p. 300
- señora, p. 300

borrow
desert
evenings
midnight
package
shoulder

Vocabulary

Teach Vocabulary in Context

Identify Vocabulary Words Display **Teaching Chart 184** and read the passage with children. Ask volunteers to circle each vocabulary word and to underline other words that are clues to its meaning.

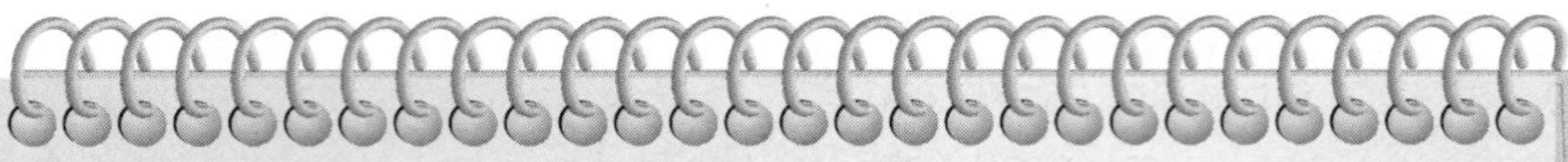

The Library Book

1. Tomás decides to borrow a book from the library so he can read it at home. **2.** He reads about camels in the hot, dry desert. **3.** In the evenings, Tomás and his family look at picture books. **4.** Enrique has to lean over Tomás's shoulder to see the wonderful pictures. **5.** They look at pictures of bats circling the sky at midnight. **6.** One day, Tomás would like to buy a whole package of books that he can keep forever.

Teaching Chart 184

Discuss Meanings Ask questions like these to help clarify word meanings:

- If you borrow something, do you intend to keep it or give it back?
- Would you want to live in the desert? Why?
- Do you eat dinner or breakfast in the evening?
- What does it look like outside at midnight?
- Which is probably bigger, a letter or a package?
- Can you point to your shoulders?

Practice

Relate Word Meanings

GROUP

Present each vocabulary card separately. Have children create a word web by brainstorming words related to the vocabulary card shown. ▶ **Linguistic/Visual**

Word Building Manipulative Cards

Write Riddles

PARTNERS

WRITING

Have partners write riddles that give clues to the meaning of each vocabulary word. Children can exchange papers and try to solve one another's riddles. Have children refer to their Glossary as needed.

▶ **Linguistic/Logical**

Assess Vocabulary

Identify Word Meaning in Context

PARTNERS

WRITING

Ask children to draw pictures that illustrate the vocabulary words. Then have them exchange their pictures with partners. Partners should write captions for the pictures. Each caption should include the word that is shown in the picture.

Meeting Individual Needs for Vocabulary

EASY

Name______________ Date________ **Reteach 220**

Vocabulary

Read the story. Circle the word that completes each sentence below.

borrow desert evenings midnight package shoulder

Pete is a pack rat. He has a dark spot on his shoulder. Pete lives in the desert. It is very hot there in the daytime. In the evenings, the desert cools off. It can be cold at midnight.

Pete likes to borrow things from other animals. He makes a little package of the things he finds. He hides the package in his nest.

1. Pete the pack rat lives in the ___ .
   forest ocean (desert)
2. Pete has a dark spot on his ___ .
   (shoulder) pocket nest
3. In the ___ , the desert cools off.
   summer days (evenings)
4. It can even be cold at ___ .
   daytime (midnight) noon
5. Pete likes to ___ stuff from other animals.
   drive read (borrow)
6. Pete makes a little ___ of the things he finds.
   (package) picture practice

220 At Home: Have children make up two more sentences using the vocabulary words they circled. Book 2.2/Unit 3 Tomás and the Library Lady 6

Reteach, 220

ON-LEVEL

Name______________ Date________ **Practice 220**

Vocabulary

Read the story. Choose a word from the box to complete each sentence. Write the word in the sentence. Then reread the story to check your answers.

borrow desert evenings midnight package shoulder

Larry wanted to __borrow__ a book from Tony. He walked up behind Tony and tapped him on the __shoulder__. "May I borrow your book?" he asked. Tony handed Larry a __package__. The book was inside.

The book was about life in the __desert__. It had pictures of plants and animals. A desert is very hot. Some animals sleep in the daytime. They come out in the __evenings__ when it is cool. Some even hunt as late as __midnight__. Larry liked the book. He hopes to visit a desert someday.

220 At Home: Have children write another story using the vocabulary words. Book 2.2/Unit 3 Tomás and the Library Lady 6

Practice, 220

ON-LEVEL

A Pet for My Pet

I asked my dad what he thought. He told me he had an idea. Then he left the hotel.

Later that night he returned with a brown package. It was about the size of my lizard. Quickly I opened the box. It was another lizard.

"I think your pet needs a pet," said Dad. I think he was right!

4 220a

Practice, 220a
Take-Home Story

CHALLENGE

Name______________ Date________ **Extend 220**

Vocabulary

borrow	desert	evenings
midnight	package	shoulder

Write words from the box to complete the story. Read the story over to check your answers.

The man carried a heavy __package__ on his __shoulder__. He wished that he could __borrow__ a wagon from a friend. The man was traveling through the hot, dry __desert__. It was after __midnight__ and the moon was bright. The man liked to travel when the sun was down because it was cooler in the __evenings__.

Write two or three sentences telling what the desert is like during the day.

220 At Home: Children can write the vocabulary words on cards. Divide the cards. Take turns "borrowing" a card and making a sentence with the word on it. Book 2.2/Unit 3 Tomás and the Library Lady

Extend, 220

SPELLING/VOCABULARY CONNECTIONS

See Spelling Challenge Words, page 309Q.

LANGUAGE SUPPORT

See the **Language Support Book, pages 235–238,** for teaching suggestions for Vocabulary.

Provides vocabulary activities.

Comprehension

Prereading Strategies

PREVIEW AND PREDICT Have students read the story title and take a **picture walk** through the illustrations. Discuss how pictures can give clues about characters and plot. Ask children:

- What clues do the title and pictures give you about the main character?
- Could this story be about a real person? How can you tell? *Genre*
- What will the story most likely be about?

Have children record in a chart their predictions about the story and the main character.

PREDICTIONS	WHAT HAPPENED
Tomás will meet a lady who works in the library.	
The lady will help Tomás find interesting books in the library.	

SET PURPOSES Ask children what they would like to learn as they read the story. For example:

- Will the story be about a trip to the library?
- Where is Tomás's family going in the car?

READ TOGETHER

MEET PAT MORA

Many of Pat Mora's ideas for stories come from her childhood days in the Texas desert. "I also like to write about my family, like my aunt who danced on her ninetieth birthday and my mother who wanted to be a rainbow tulip when she was in grade school," Ms. Mora says.

MEET RAUL COLÓN

Raul Colón likes to create many different kinds of art. He has illustrated several children's books, including *Always My Dad*, for which he won the Silver Medal from the Society of Illustrators.

A NOTE ABOUT THE STORY

Pat Mora based this story on Tomás Rivera, a real person. Rivera was a migrant farm worker. He was born in Crystal City, Texas, in 1935. Just like the boy in the story, Rivera felt education was very important. He grew up to be a writer, a teacher, and the leader of a university.

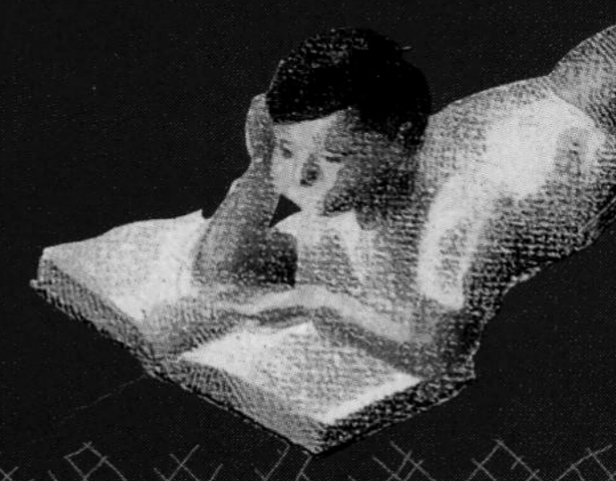

284

Meeting Individual Needs • Grouping Suggestions for Strategic Reading

EASY

Shared Reading Read the story with children, or have them use the **Listening Library.** Have children use their Generalization chart to record important information about the story. Model using the strategy of making generalizations in order to understand what is happening in the story.

ON-LEVEL

Guided Instruction Read the selection with children, using the Comprehension prompts. You may wish to have children read first on their own, while you monitor difficulties in order to determine which prompts to emphasize.

CHALLENGE

Read Independently Tell children that forming generalizations, general statements about a group of facts, can help them to understand a story's characters and main ideas. After reading, have children use their completed Generalization charts to summarize the story.

Comprehension

 **Apply Long *e* and Long *i***

 **Apply Form Generalizations**

STRATEGIC READING Forming generalizations—getting a broad understanding from a group of details—can help you to understand a story's characters and main ideas. Generalizations often contain words such as *most, all, every, often,* or *none.* Let's record in a chart the generalizations we form based on details we read about in the story.

WHAT HAPPENS	GENERALIZATION

1 Which two people do you think are pictured on this page? Based on the picture, what do you think the story will be about?

Genre

Biographical Story

Remind children that a biographical story:

- depicts events, settings, or characters that actually exist.
- may focus on only one or two incidents from the person's life.
- may include fictional elements, such as made-up dialogue or composite characters.

Activity Have children think of someone they know and recall a short incident which they can write about. Remind them they can include fictional elements, such as made-up dialogue.

LANGUAGE SUPPORT

A blackline master of the generalizations chart can be found in the **Language Support Book.**

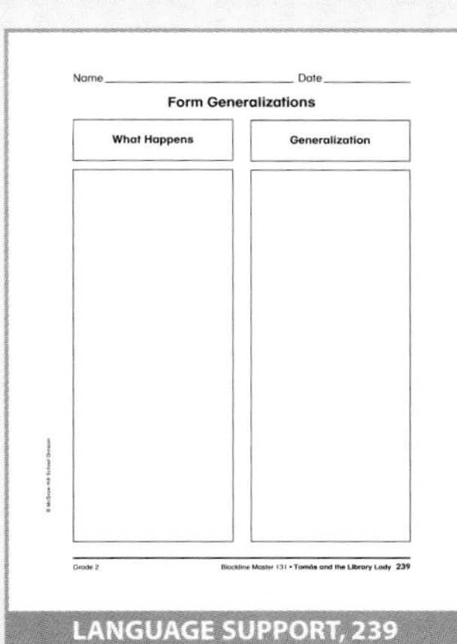
Name ______ Date ______

Form Generalizations

What Happens	Generalization

LANGUAGE SUPPORT, 239

Comprehension

2 **FORM GENERALIZATIONS** Let's begin reading the story, and look at the picture on page 286. How do you think Tomás is feeling right now? How do you think most children in Tomás's position would feel?

MODEL The story tells me that Tomás is hot and tired, and that he misses his own bed. It also says that he is on his way to Iowa again, so I know that Tomás and his family make this trip often. From the details the story gives me—that Tomás moves a lot, that he is hot and tired, and that he misses his bed at home—and from the picture, I am going to form the generalization that moving a lot is difficult.

Let's begin filling in our Generalization charts.

WHAT HAPPENS	GENERALIZATION
Tomás's family is moving again. He misses his bed in Texas.	Most people find moving from place to place difficult.

2

286

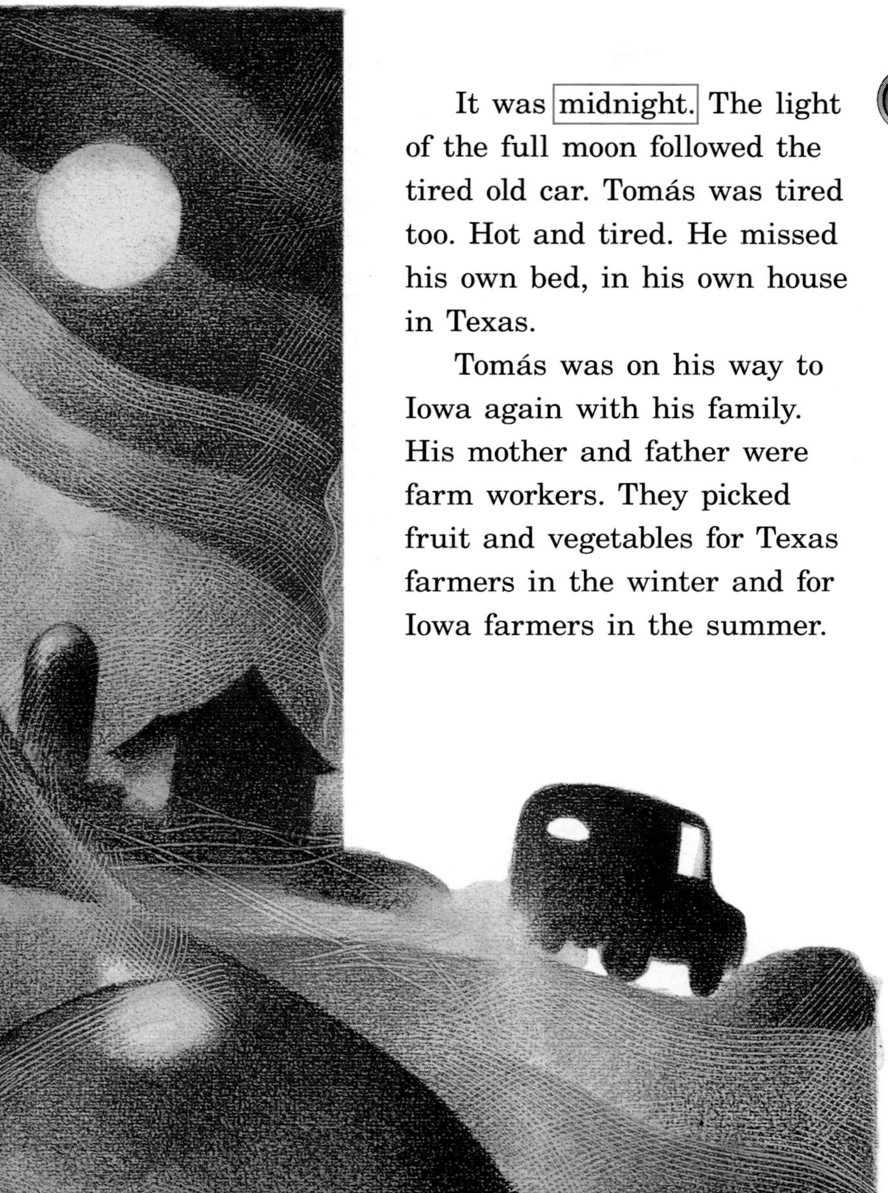

It was midnight. The light of the full moon followed the tired old car. Tomás was tired too. Hot and tired. He missed his own bed, in his own house in Texas. 3

Tomás was on his way to Iowa again with his family. His mother and father were farm workers. They picked fruit and vegetables for Texas farmers in the winter and for Iowa farmers in the summer.

287

Comprehension

3 Phonics **LONG *i*** Which word in the first sentence on page 287 contains the /ī/ sound? *(midnight)* The letters *igh* represent the /ī/ sound. Let's blend the sounds together and say the word: mid n igh t. Now, let's do the same thing to read the next word on this page that has the *igh* letter combination. *(light)* ***Blending/Graphophonic Cues***

TEACHING TIP

MAP SKILLS During the Language Support activity, some students may wish to figure out the actual distance in miles between Texas and Iowa, using the map's legend.

LANGUAGE SUPPORT

ESL Help students understand the length of Tomás's trip by showing the distance between Iowa and Texas. On a map of the United States, point out the locations of both states. Stretch a ruler or piece of string between the two. Now point to the children's home state. Using the ruler or string, show how far from home students would be traveling if they were going the same distance as Tomás and his family.

Comprehension

4 **Phonics** **LONG *i*** I'm going to read aloud the first sentence of the second paragraph. *Tomás was glad when the car . . .*

MODEL I don't know this word just by looking at it. I am going to blend together the sounds made by the letters so I can read the word: f i n a ll y *finally.* I know that the first vowel sound in this word is /ī/. I also know that the letter in this word that stands for the /ī/ sound is *i.* I'm going to use this information to read another word on this page that contains the letter *i.* (*climb*). ***Blending/Graphophonic Cues***

5 Tomás wishes he had a glass of cold water. During what time of year do you think the story is taking place? (summer) Do you think Tomás and his family have an easy time working in the summer? Why? (No. Their work is picking vegetables; if it is summer, they must be working outside in the hot sun.) ***Make Inferences***

Year after year they bump-bumped along in their rusty old car. "Mamá," whispered Tomás, "if I had a glass of cold water, I would drink it in large gulps. I would suck the ice. I would pour the last drops of water on my face."

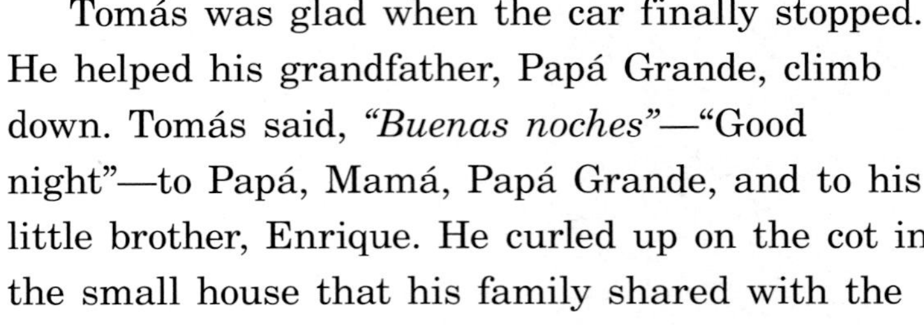

Tomás was glad when the car finally stopped. He helped his grandfather, Papá Grande, climb down. Tomás said, *"Buenas noches"*—"Good night"—to Papá, Mamá, Papá Grande, and to his little brother, Enrique. He curled up on the cot in the small house that his family shared with the other workers.

Early the next morning Mamá and Papá went out to pick corn in the green fields. All day they worked in the hot sun. Tomás and Enrique carried water to them. Then the boys played with a ball Mamá had sewn from an old teddy bear.

288

Cross Curricular: Social Studies

AMERICA WORKING Explain that some people live in particular places to find the jobs they want. Ask children: If you wanted to own a farm, where would you most likely need to live?

RESEARCH AND INQUIRY Have children create a list of jobs they find interesting. Have them discuss whether they would need to live somewhere in particular to do that job, and why. Add this information to the list, and display the list on a bulletin board.

▶ **Linguistic/Logical**

HELP WANTED
Work on fishing boat. Early riser!!

Comprehension

6 **Phonics** **LONG *e*** On page 288, let's read the last two words in the first sentence of the last paragraph. What vowel sound do you hear in these words? (long *e*) What letters make the /ē/ sound? (*ee, ie*) *Graphophonic Cues*

Minilesson

REVIEW/MAINTAIN

Make Inferences

Explain that the author doesn't always describe exactly what characters are feeling. However, the author will give clues that allow the reader to make a good guess, or inference, about a character's feelings or thoughts.

- Have children read the last paragraph on page 288.
- Ask children to brainstorm a list of words describing how Mamá and Papá might be feeling. Remind children of facts the author has given. (It is hot, they have been picking corn since dawn, and so on. Words might include *tired, thirsty, sleepy,* and *hungry.*)

Activity Have children draw pictures of Mamá and Papá that show how they might be feeling.

Comprehension

7 **Phonics** **LONG *e*** Do you see a word in the first sentence that contains the long *e* sound? *(tree)* Point to the word. Which letters in this word represent the /ē/ sound? *(ee)* There is another word on this page that has the long *e* sound. Point to this word. *(leaves)* Which letters in this word make the /ē/ sound? *(ea)* ***Graphophonic Cues***

290

CULTURAL PERSPECTIVES

STORIES Ask children if they know anyone who is a great storyteller. Ask what kinds of stories that person tells: folk tales, family stories, riddles, and so on. Explain that in many cultures, important lessons and family histories have been passed on through storytelling.

Activity Provide children with books containing stories and folk tales. Invite children to choose a story they would like to share with the rest of the class. ▶ **Linguistic/Interpersonal**

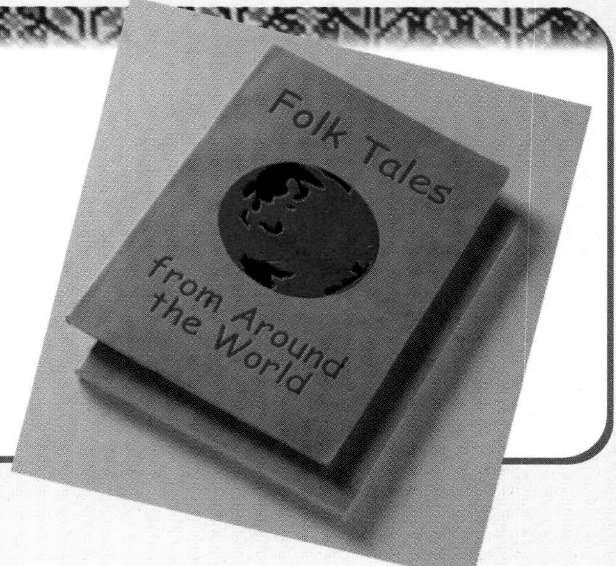

When they got hot, they sat under a tree with Papá Grande. "Tell us the story about the man in the forest," said Tomás. 

Tomás liked to listen to Papá Grande tell stories in Spanish. Papá Grande was the best storyteller in the family.

"*En un tiempo pasado*," Papá Grande began. "Once upon a time . . . on a windy night a man was riding a horse through a forest. The wind was howling, *whooooooooo*, and the leaves were blowing, *whish, whish* . . .

"All of a sudden something grabbed the man. He couldn't move. He was too scared to look around. All night long he wanted to ride away. But he couldn't.

"How the wind howled, *whooooooooo*. How the leaves blew. How his teeth chattered!

"Finally the sun came up. Slowly the man turned around. And who do you think was holding him?"

Tomás smiled and said, "A thorny tree." 

Comprehension

8 **FORM GENERALIZATIONS** Do you think Tomás has already heard the story that Papá Grande tells? How do you know? (Yes; he knows the ending.)

Let's fill in our Generalization charts.

WHAT HAPPENS	GENERALIZATION
Tomás moves again. He misses his bed in Texas.	Most people would find moving from place to place difficult.
Papá Grande is the family's best storyteller. Tomás has heard Papá Grande's stories before.	Good storytellers can make the same stories interesting over and over.

MODEL Even though Tomás and Enrique have heard Papá Grande's stories before, the story says they like to listen to him tell his tales. The generalization I can form from this detail is that good storytellers can make the same story interesting and exciting over and over again.

LANGUAGE SUPPORT

ESL Help children understand the meaning of the word *thorny*. Show them pictures and/or bring in an example of a plant or flower that has thorns. Point out the characteristics of something that is thorny. Ask children what it might feel like to bump into something thorny. Then discuss why the man in Papá Grande's story might have been frightened by a "thorny tree."

Comprehension

9 **Phonics** **LONG *e* AND LONG *i***
Let's look at the second sentence of the second paragraph. Point to the last word in the sentence. I'll read it, then you read it after me. Which letter in *library* represents the long *i* sound? (i) Which letter represents the long *e* sound? (y) *Decoding/Graphophonic Cues*

TEACHING TIP

MANAGEMENT You may want to read the story with children once before you do the minilessons and the cultural perspectives and cross-curricular activities.

Papá Grande laughed. "Tomás, you know all my stories," he said. "There are many more in the library. You are big enough to go by yourself. Then you can teach us new stories."

The next morning Tomás walked downtown. He looked at the big library. Its tall windows were like eyes glaring at him. Tomás walked around and around the big building. He saw children coming out carrying books. Slowly he started climbing up, up the steps. He counted them to himself in Spanish. *Uno, dos, tres, cuatro . . .* His mouth felt full of cotton.

Tomás stood in front of the library doors. He pressed his nose against the glass and peeked in. The library was huge!

A hand tapped his shoulder. Tomás jumped. A tall lady looked down at him. "It's a hot day," she said. "Come inside and have a drink of water. What's your name?" she asked.

"Tomás," he said.

"Come, Tomás," she said.

293

Comprehension

10 Why does Tomás think the library windows look like eyes glaring at him? How would you feel if you thought a building's windows were like glaring eyes? (He is scared of a new place.) ***Make Inferences***

11 When you read a story, you can use information the author gives you to help you figure out what will happen next. What do you think will happen next in this story? Will the lady help Tomás? Will Tomás enjoy being in the library? ***Make Predictions***

Minilesson

REVIEW/MAINTAIN

Long Vowel: /ū/

Read page 292, emphasizing the word *huge.* Ask children to:

- find the word on page 292 that has the /ū/ sound spelled *u-e.*

Activity Ask children to brainstorm a list of words containing the /ū/ sound. (*cute, few, music, use*) As children call out words, write them on the board. Then invite children to circle the letters that represent the /ū/ sound.

Phonics CD-ROM Have children use the interactive phonics activities on the CD-ROM for more reinforcement.

Comprehension

12 **Phonics** **LONG *e*** Are there any words on this page that contain the /ē/ sound? *(seen, leading, read)* Which letters in each word stand for the /ē/ sound? *(ee, ea)* ***Graphophonic Cues***

13 Authors often tell readers about a character's personality by describing the character's thoughts and actions. What do we learn about Tomás's personality on this page? (He is interested in animals; he is very imaginative.) From what you know about Tomás so far, does he seem like a person you might meet in real life, or does he seem like a character you would only find in a story? (He seems like a real person.) ***Character***

SELF-MONITORING STRATEGY

SEARCH FOR CLUES The details an author provides can be clues to a character's personality and feelings.

- What clues does the author give about the library lady?
- What clues does the author give about Tomás's favorite kinds of stories?

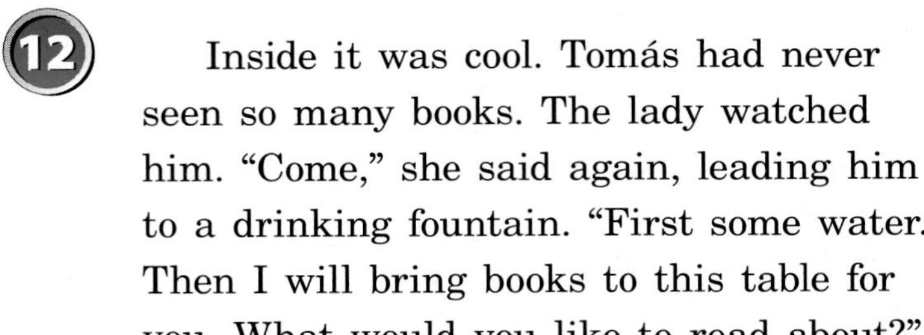

12 Inside it was cool. Tomás had never seen so many books. The lady watched him. "Come," she said again, leading him to a drinking fountain. "First some water. Then I will bring books to this table for you. What would you like to read about?"

13 "Tigers. Dinosaurs," said Tomás.

Tomás drank the cold water. He looked at the tall ceiling. He looked at all the books around the room. He watched the lady take some
14 books from the shelves and bring them to the table. "This chair is for you, Tomás," she said. Tomás sat down. Then very carefully he took a book from the pile and opened it.

Tomás saw dinosaurs bending their long necks to lap shiny water. He heard the cries of a wild snakebird. He felt the warm neck of the dinosaur as he held on tight for a ride. Tomás forgot about the library lady. He forgot about Iowa and Texas.

294

Activity

Cross Curricular: Math

TIGER TIPS Share these facts:

- An average male weighs 400-500 pounds and is between 7-10 feet in length.
- Female tigers are usually 100 pounds lighter than males, and a foot shorter.

Have children create graphs comparing male and female tigers.

▶ **Spatial/Mathematical**

RESEARCH AND INQUIRY Invite children to find out more about tigers.

interNET CONNECTION Children can learn more about tigers by visiting ***www.mhschool.com/reading.***

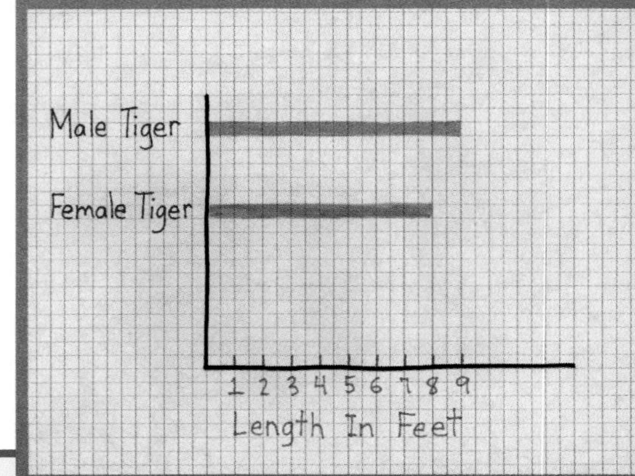

295

Comprehension

14 **FORM GENERALIZATIONS** The library lady probably found books for many children. Tomás enjoyed the books about animals that she chose. Can we make any generalizations from this information?

Let's fill in our Generalization charts.

WHAT HAPPENS	GENERALIZATION
Tomás moves again. He misses his bed in Texas.	Most people would find moving from place to place difficult.
Papá Grande is the family's best storyteller. Tomás has heard Papá Grande's stories before.	Good storytellers can make the same stories interesting over and over.
The library lady finds books for people. She chose books about animals for Tomás.	Many librarians know what books children like.

Minilesson

REVIEW/MAINTAIN

Context Clues

Explain to children that when they come across an unfamiliar word, they can use clues in nearby words or pictures.

- Have children read the first sentence of the last paragraph on page 294.
- Ask: Does the author use *lap* in this sentence to mean "a part of the body?"
- Help children use the rest of the sentence to see that here, *lap* means "drink."

Activity Have children figure out the meaning of the word *eager* in the third paragraph on page 296.

Comprehension

15 Why does the author tell us that the library is empty and the sun is setting? (to show us that Tomás has been there all day) ***Plot***

16 How do Papá Grande and the rest of Tomás's family seem to feel about the books Tomás is reading? (They enjoy the stories, and seem to enjoy Tomás being the storyteller.) What does this tell you about Tomás's family? (They enjoy learning and hearing stories; they are proud of Tomás.) ***Character, Plot***

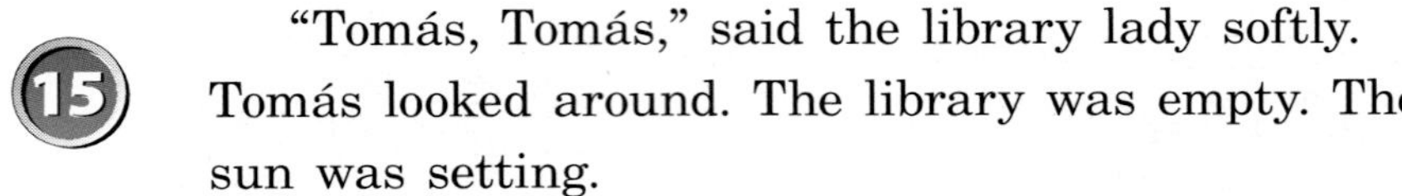

15 "Tomás, Tomás," said the library lady softly. Tomás looked around. The library was empty. The sun was setting.

The library lady looked at Tomás for a long time. She said, "Tomás, would you like to borrow two library books? I will check them out in my name."

Tomás walked out of the library carrying his books. He ran home, eager to show the new stories to his family.

16 Papá Grande looked at the library books. "Read to me," he said to Tomás. First Tomás showed him the pictures. He pointed to the tiger. *"¡Qué tigre tan grande!"* Tomás said first in Spanish and then in English, "What a big tiger!"

"Read to me in English," said Papá Grande. Tomás read about tiger eyes shining brightly in the jungle at night. He roared like a huge tiger. Papá, Mamá, and Enrique laughed. They came and sat near him to hear his story.

296

Cross Curricular: Science

RECYCLING MATTERS Share with children this information about recycling:

- Most articles made of metal, glass, or paper can be recycled.

Invite students to create a chart showing items that can be recycled.

▶ **Spatial/Interpersonal**

RESEARCH AND INQUIRY Have children obtain information on the recycling policies in your area.

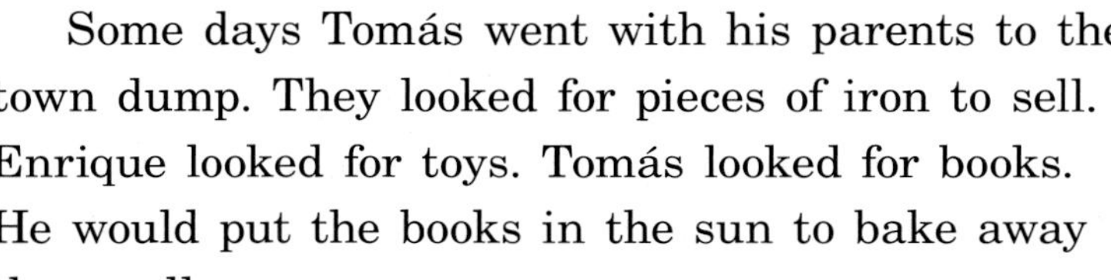

Some days Tomás went with his parents to the town dump. They looked for pieces of iron to sell. Enrique looked for toys. Tomás looked for books. He would put the books in the sun to bake away the smell.

All summer, whenever he could, Tomás went to the library. The library lady would say, "First a drink of water and then some new books, Tomás."

Comprehension

17 Make a face that shows how Tomás was feeling before entering the library. Now show how Tomás feels when he is leaving the library. *Role-Play*

18 **Phonics** **LONG *i*** Which word on this page begins with the letter *i*? *(iron)* Let's point to this word and say it together. *Graphophonic Cues*

LANGUAGE SUPPORT

ESL Have volunteers role-play the actions of omás and the librarian while you ead aloud from the story. Children an repeat the characters' lines of dia-ogue (or approximate the language) vhile they show the actions of drinking, getting books, sitting, and reading. Then call on children to help you list on the chalkboard the sequence of events that takes place when Tomás visits the library. Reread pages 294–297, encouraging students to follow the sequence of events as you read.

Comprehension

19 Did Tomás really smell smoke and ride a horse across the desert? Why does the author write that he did these things? (to show how powerful an experience Tomás had when he read those books, how imaginative he became) ***Author's Craft***

20 When you read about Tomás's first meeting with the library lady, you predicted, or guessed, what would happen next in the story. Was your prediction correct? ***Confirm Predictions***

21 Why do you think Tomás "likes being the teacher," and teaching words in Spanish to the library lady? (He enjoys being able to share what he knows.) ***Character***

P/i **CONTEXT CLUES** Look at the second sentence of the last paragraph. What is the fifth word? (pictures)

19

20 On quiet days the library lady said, "Come to my desk and read to me, Tomás." Then she would say, "Please teach me some new words in Spanish."

21 Tomás would smile. He liked being the teacher. The library lady pointed to a book. "Book is *libro*," said Tomás.

"Libro," said the library lady.

"Pájaro," said Tomás, flapping his arms.

The library lady laughed. "Bird," she said.

22 On days when the library was busy, Tomás read to himself. He'd look at the pictures for a long time. He smelled the smoke at an Indian camp. He rode a black horse across a hot, dusty desert. And in the evenings he would read the stories to Mamá, Papá, Papá Grande, and Enrique.

298

P/i PREVENTION/INTERVENTION

CONTEXT CLUES Read the first two sentences of the last paragraph aloud to children and emphasize the word *pictures*. Repeat the word as you write it on the chalkboard. Ask children what other words in the first two sentences they could use to figure out the meaning of *pictures*. (*library, read, look*) Remind children that looking for clues from surrounding words is a good strategy to use when having trouble identifying a word. *Semantic Cues*

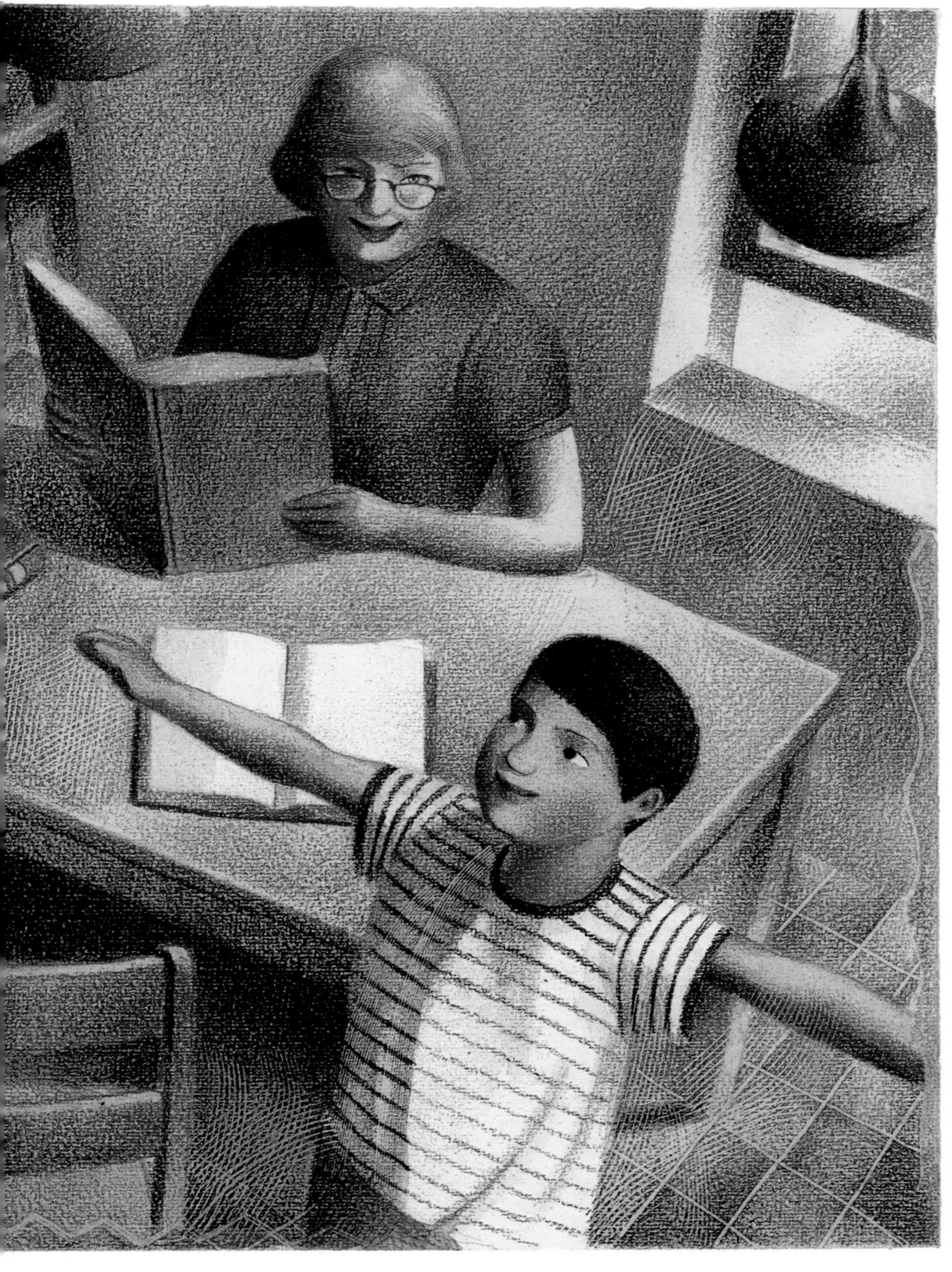

299

Comprehension

22 Remind students that some events in a story are the result, or effect, of other events. Ask: Why does Tomás read to himself some days? (The library is busy.) Why would this cause him to read to himself? (If the library is busy, the library lady is busy, so she does not have time to read with Tomás.) ***Cause and Effect***

23 Why does the library lady ask Tomás to help her learn words in Spanish? What does this tell you about the kind of person she is? (She enjoys learning new things.) ***Character***

LANGUAGE SUPPORT

ESL Read aloud the last paragraph on page 298. Ask ldren if Tomás really smells smoke ides a horse. (No) Ask why the author says he does these things if they aren't real. (She wants to show that the experiences are very real in Tomás's mind.)

Comprehension

 Remember that summarizing means retelling the main events that have taken place. Summarize what has happened since Papá Grande suggested that Tomás visit the library. (Tomás met the library lady, took books out for the first time, became a regular visitor to the library, and teaches Spanish to the library lady.) ***Summarize***

Fluency

READ DIALOGUE

GROUP Have students point out the punctuaution marks in the dialogue on page 300.

- Have groups of four read the dialogue on page 300, taking the parts of Tomás, Papá Grande, the library lady, and the narrator.
- Have each child read each part once.
- Remind children to use expression when reading dialogue, and to be sure that their reading reflects the selection's punctuation.

One August afternoon Tomás brought Papá Grande to the library.

The library lady said, *"Buenas tardes, señor."* Tomás smiled. He had taught the library lady how to say "Good afternoon, sir" in Spanish.

"Buenas tardes, señora," Papá Grande replied.

Softly Tomás said, "I have a sad word to teach you today. The word is *adiós.* It means good-bye."

Tomás was going back to Texas. He would miss this quiet place, the cool water, the many books. He would miss the library lady.

"My mother sent this to thank you," said Tomás, handing her a small package. "It is *pan dulce*, sweet bread. My mother makes the best *pan dulce* in Texas."

The library lady said, "How nice. How very nice. *Gracias*, Tomás. Thank you." She gave Tomás a big hug.

300

Activity

Cross Curricular: Art

BE THE ILLUSTRATOR With children, look back through the story's illustrations.

- Have children call out descriptions of the style of the illustrations. (sharp, looks like scratches, not photographs, and so on)
- Provide small groups with a familiar story or fairy tale to illustrate. Children should work together to determine the kind of illustrations they would use for the story. Would they use drawings or photographs? Would the art be realistic or more imaginary?
- Invite groups to share their illustrations.

▶ **Spatial/Interpersonal**

301

Comprehension

25 Why does Tomás describe *adios* as a sad word? What is causing Tomás to feel sad? (He is leaving the library and the library lady, and will miss both.) ***Cause and Effect***

P/I **COMPOUND WORDS** What two smaller words make up the word *afternoon?* (*after* and *noon*)

26 Why does the library lady say "thank you" to Tomás in Spanish? (She wants to show him that he was a good teacher, and she learned from him.) What does this tell you about the library lady? (She is caring; she respects Tomás.) ***Make Inferences***

PREVENTION/INTERVENTION

MPOUND WORDS Remind chil-
n that compound words are made
of two smaller words. Write the
rd *afternoon* on the chalkboard.
ite a volunteer to draw a circle
und each of the smaller words that
ke up the compound word, and to
each word aloud. (*after, noon*) Then
ite the following words in one col-
n on the chalkboard: *some, down, story*. In another column, write: *town, teller, thing*. Invite volunteers to draw lines connecting words from each column to form compound words. (*something, downtown, storyteller*) Remind children that knowing the meaning of the two smaller words will help them to understand the meaning of the compound word. *Semantic Cues*

Comprehension

27 **PHONICS: LONG *i*** Which words on this page contain the /ī/ sound? *(library, tired, night, shiny, smiled)* What are the letters in each word that stand for the long *i* sound? *(i, igh, i, i-e)* What other letters can stand for the/ī/ sound? *(y)* Can you name some words that are spelled that way? *(fly, cry, my)* ***Graphophonic Cues***

That night, bumping along
27 again in the tired old car,
Tomás held a shiny new book,
a present from the library
lady. Papá Grande smiled and
said, "More stories for the
new storyteller."

28

302

Writer's Craft

ANTONYMS

Explain: Antonyms are words that have opposite meanings.
Example: Point out the words *old* and *new* on page 302. Ask children for other examples of antonyms, such as *high, low; big, small; happy, sad.*

GROUP Ask children to create antonyms for some of the words that appear on page 302, such as *night (day); shiny (dull); smiled (frowned); more (fewer).*

Encourage children to look for antonyms throughout the story.

LANGUAGE SUPPORT

ESL Some children may have trouble decoding and pronouncing the long *i* sound. Have pairs of children find all the words on page 302 that contain the long *i* sound. *(night, tired, shiny, library, smiled)* Ask them to say the words ar write them on the board. Point to ar say each word aloud and have the children repeat them.

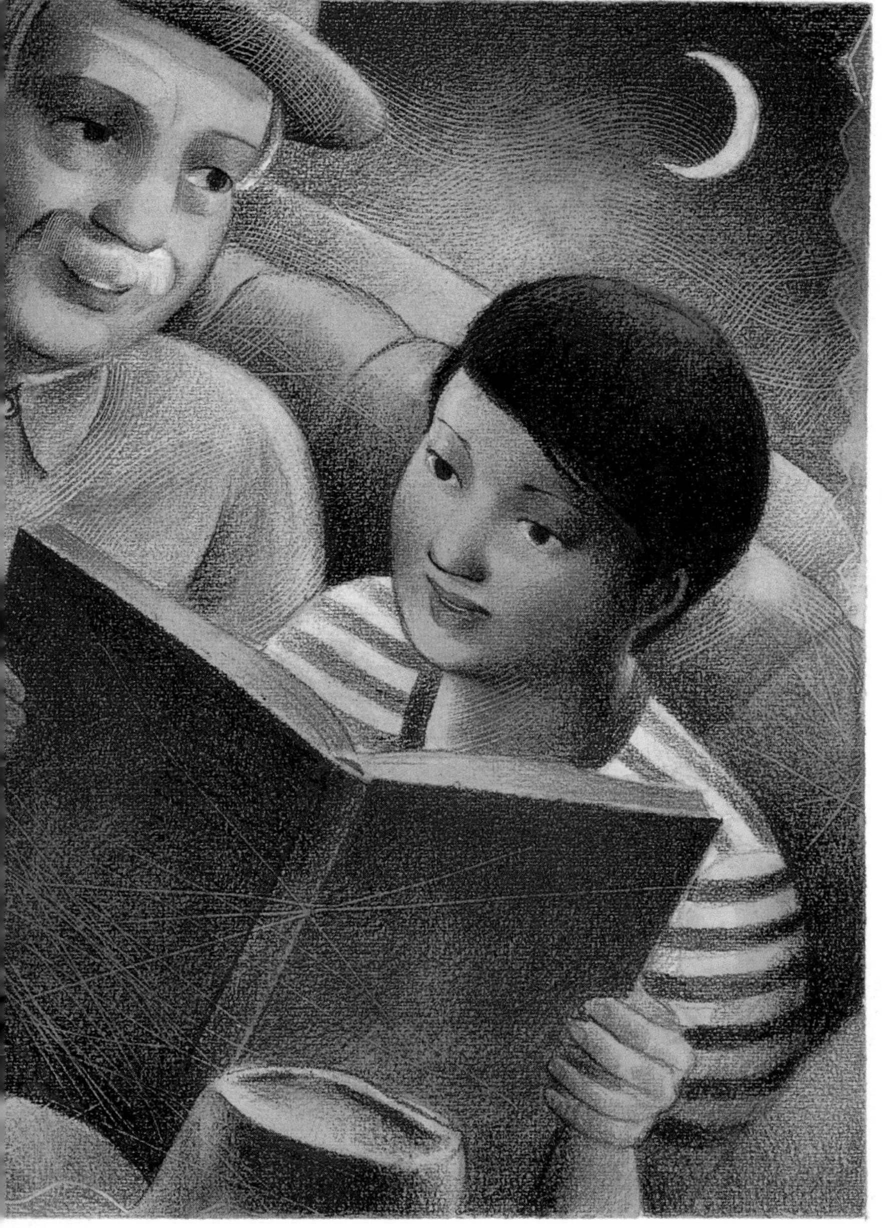

303

Comprehension

28 How is the ending of the story like the beginning? (Tomás and his family are on the road in their old car.) How is it different? (Tomás seems happier—he has a new book, and is using his imagination to make the car ride more interesting.) ***Compare and Contrast***

P/I **LONG *e*** Let's find the fourth word on the third line of page 302. Read it out loud. (*shiny*)

Minilesson

REVIEW/MAINTAIN

Summarize

Remind children that summarizing a story means telling about its main parts, including:

- the main idea of the story.
- important events and actions that take place.
- how the story ends.

Ask children the following about summarizing *Tomás and the Library Lady.*

- Would you include the part about Tomás meeting the library lady?
- Would you tell about when the library lady offered Tomás some water?

Activity Have children orally summarize the story. Help them to focus on the main points. Children may wish to create a list of the story's main points.

P/I PREVENTION/INTERVENTION

ONG *e* Write these words on the ıalkboard: *library, lady, very*. Say each ord aloud, emphasizing the long *e* ound at the end of the word and ave children repeat after you. Ask a olunteer to come to the board and oint out the letter that stands for /ē/ in each word.(*y*) Point out that the letters *ey* can also make the /ē/ sound as in the word *money*. Follow the same process using these words: *honey, key, donkey, valley*. *Graphophonic Cues*

Comprehension

29 **FORM GENERALIZATIONS** What effect has reading had on Tomás? (It has made his imagination very active; it will make moving less hard.) Do you think other people have this experience when they begin reading?

Let's fill in our Generalization charts.

WHAT HAPPENS	GENERALIZATION
Tomás moves again. He misses his bed in Texas.	Most people would find moving from place to place difficult.
Papá Grande is the family's best storyteller. Tomás has heard Papá Grande's stories before.	Good storytellers can make the same stories interesting over and over.
The library lady finds books for people. She chose books about animals for Tomás.	Many librarians know what books children like.
Reading interesting books made Tomás's imagination more active. He seemed happier after he began to read a lot.	Usually, reading a book is a good experience.

RETELL THE STORY Ask volunteers to retell the story. Encourage children to use their charts for help. *Summarize*

STUDENT SELF-ASSESSMENT

- How did using the details in the story to form generalizations help me?
- How did forming generalizations help me to better understand the story?

TRANSFERRING THE STRATEGIES

- How can I use these strategies to read other stories?

Tomás closed his eyes. He saw the dinosaurs drinking cool water long ago. He heard the cry of the wild snakebird. He felt the warm neck of the dinosaur as he held on tight for a bumpy ride.

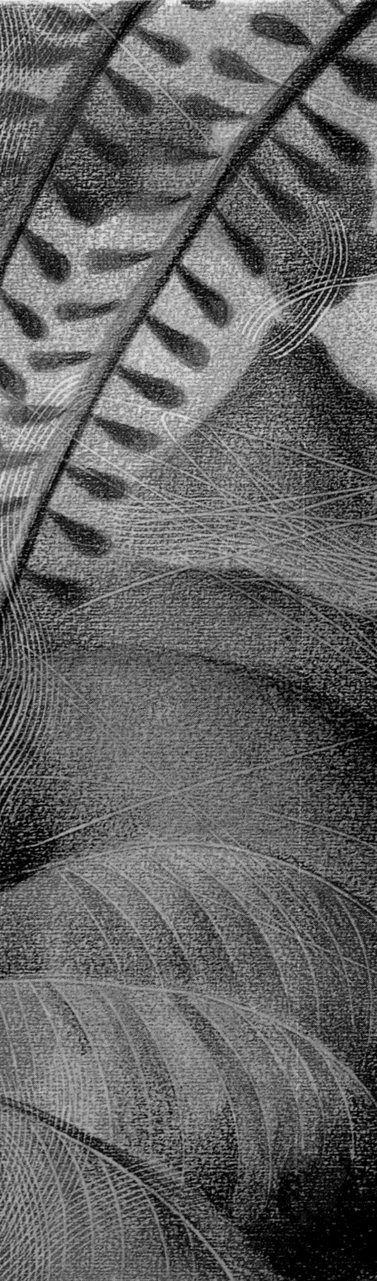

304

REREADING FOR *Fluency*

GROUP Children who need fluency practice can read along silently or aloud as they listen to the story on audiocassette.

READING RATE When you evaluate reading rate, have children read aloud from the story for one minute. Place a stick-on note after the last word read. Count words read. To evaluate children's performance, see the Running Record in the **Fluency Assessment** book.

For leveled fluency lessons, passages, and norms charts, see **Skills Intervention Guide,** Part 5, Fluency.

305

Comprehension

Return to Predictions and Purposes

Reread children's predictions about the story. Discuss the predictions, noting which needed to be revised.

PREDICTIONS	WHAT HAPPENED
Tomás will meet a lady who works in the library.	Tomás meets a kind librarian.
The lady will help Tomás find interesting books in the library.	The librarian helps Tomás to find books he enjoys.

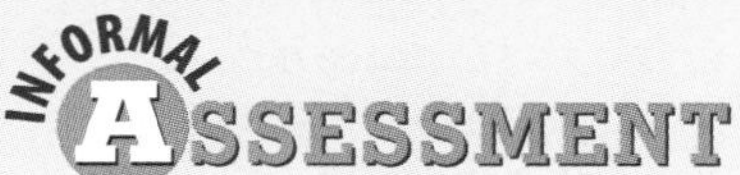

INFORMAL ASSESSMENT

HOW TO ASSESS

LONG *e* AND LONG *i* Have children turn to page 288 of the selection. Have them read the words *finally* and *green.*

FORM GENERALIZATIONS Remind students of a generalization they made, that moving a lot is difficult. Have them discuss how this generalization applies to Tomás.

FOLLOW UP

LONG *e* AND LONG *i* For children who are having difficulty, continue to model the blending words with long *e* and long *i*.

FORM GENERALIZATIONS Children who are having difficulty can use pictures from the story to help them form generalizations.

LITERARY RESPONSE

JICK-WRITE Invite children to use their journals to write a few sentences explaining why ey believe Tomás liked to spend so ıch time in the library.

URNAL

RAL RESPONSE Have children scuss these questions:

- What was special about the time Tomás spent in the library?
- How did his friendship with the library lady help Tomás to feel more comfortable in his temporary home?

Story Questions

Help children to read the questions on page 306. Have them discuss or write answers.

Answers:

1. His parents are farm workers, they must travel each season to find work. *Literal/Plot*
2. He wants to find new and exciting stories. *Inferential/Setting, Character*
3. He enjoys learning and loves to share what he learns with others. *Inferential/Judgments and Decisions*
4. A boy is befriended by a librarian, who provides him with books that activate his imagination. *Critical/Summarize*
5. Reading opened up a new world of knowledge and imagination for Tomás; reading changed Grandma's life in the same way. *Critical/Reading Across Texts*

Write an Adventure Story For a full writing process lesson related to this writing suggestion, see the lesson on pages 309M–309N.

Story Questions & Activities

READ TOGETHER

1. Why do Tomás and his family go back and forth between Texas and Iowa?
2. Why does Tomás go to the library?
3. How do you think Tomás feels about learning?
4. What is this story mainly about?
5. How do you think reading changed the lives of both Tomás and Grandma from "The Wednesday Surprise?"

Write an
Adventure Story
Write a story about yourself that takes place in a different land. Maybe it's under water, on the moon, or in the rain forest. Who do you meet there? What happens? Make sure you include a beginning, middle, and end.

Meeting Individual Needs

EASY

Name________ Date_____ **Reteach 221**

Story Comprehension

Think about "Tomás and the Library Lady." Then circle the word that best completes each sentence.

1. Tomás and his family must live near ___ so they can find work.
   roads (farms)
2. Tomás and Enrique carried___to their parents in the fields.
   (water) books
3. Papá Grande told Tomás to find more stories at the ___.
   store (library)
4. The library seemed very___to Tomás.
   (big) small
5. The library lady first gave Tomás some ___.
   (water) food
6. Tomás wanted to read books about tigers and ___.
   lions (dinosaurs)

6 Book 2.2/Unit 3 **Tomás and the Library Lady** **At Home:** Ask children to tell what happened after Tomás went into the library for the first time. 221

Reteach, 221

ON-LEVEL

Name________ Date_____ **Practice 221**

Story Comprehension

Think about "Tomás and the Library Lady." Finish each sentence by writing in the correct answer from the choices below.

1. Tomás moves from Texas to
   Iowa.
   a. Iowa
   b. Mexico
2. Tomás's parents work
   in the farm fields.
   a. in the farm fields
   b. in a school
3. Papá Grande is the best
   storyteller in the family.
   a. cook in the family
   b. storyteller in the family
4. Tomás goes to the library to find story books.
   a. story books
   b. a teacher
5. The library lady finds many
   books for Tomás.
   a. books for Tomás
   b. shells for Tomás
6. Tomás teaches
   Spanish words to the library lady.
   a. Spanish words to the library lady
   b. other children how to read
7. When Tomás must return to Texas,
   he brings sweet cake to the library lady.
   a. he is afraid to go to the library
   b. he brings sweet cake to the library lady
8. The library lady gives Tomás
   a shiny new book.
   a. a shiny new book
   b. a box of candy

8 Book 2.2/Unit 3 **Tomás and the Library Lady** **At Home:** Take children to a local library and have them choose a book to read. 221

Practice, 221

CHALLENGE

Name________ Date_____ **Extend 221**

Story Comprehension

Here are three changes to "Tomás and the Library Lady." How might the story you read been different if these changes had taken place? Write a sentence under each change.
Sample answers shown.

1. Tomás is old enough to work in the fields all day with his parents.
   Tomás might not have been able to go to the library.
2. Papa Grande is not a storyteller.
   Tomás might not have wanted to learn more stories.
3. The library lady is not friendly or helpful.
   Tomás might not have wanted to return to the library.

What if Tomás and his family had stayed in Iowa at the end of the summer? Draw a picture to show a new ending for the story.

Book 2.2/Unit 3 **Tomás and the Library Lady** **At Home:** Have children list what Tomás would have missed if he had never learned to read. Ask: What would you miss if you couldn't read? 221

Extend, 221

Make a Book Mark

is important to take care of library books. One way is to make book mark to hold your place. Fold a rectangle of waxed aper in half. Press leaves or flowers between the halves. Punch hole in the top and string yarn or ribbon through it.

Share a Story

Tomás and his grandfather enjoy sharing stories. What is your favorite story? Share it with the class. You can read the story aloud, tell about what happens in the story, or act out your favorite part.

Find Out More

Tomás learns how wonderful libraries can be. Find out more about your local library. When was it built? How many books does it have? Besides books, what else can you find in the library?

307

DAILY Phonics ROUTINES

DAY 3 **Letter Substitution** Write the following words on the chalkboard: *meet, feet, yield, shy, fight,* and *hind.* Have children substitute initial or final consonants to make new words.

 **CD-ROM**

Story Activities

Make a Book Mark

Materials: waxed paper, string, leaves or flowers, iron or hair dryer, hole punch

PARTNERS Tell children that bookmarks allow a reader to keep his or her place in a story without damaging the book. To seal children's bookmarks, blow hot air onto the folded waxed paper with a hair dryer, then place it between two heavy books.

Share a Story

GROUP Children can take turns acting as the "community storyteller." Have groups brainstorm a list of their favorite stories. Then, each day, have one child select a story to read, tell, or act out. Encourage listeners to pay attention to details and plot, so they can ask questions later.

Find Out More

RESEARCH AND INQUIRY As a group, or on their own with another adult, have children visit a local library. Remind children to record their findings about what kinds of resources can be found in the library. Encourage children to report back to the class on what resources they learned about at the library.

interNET CONNECTION Go to ***www.mhschool.com/reading*** for more information or activities on the topic.

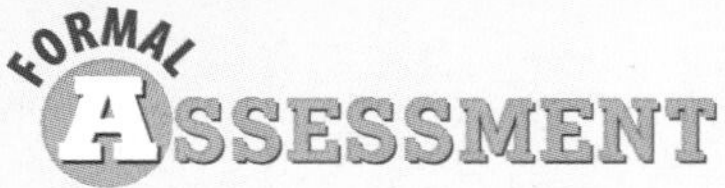

After page 307, see the Selection Assessment.

Study Skills

LIBRARY/MEDIA CENTER

BJECTIVES

Students will:

- read a library floor plan.
- learn where important library resources are located.

PREPARE Display **Teaching Chart 185.** Explain that a floor plan is a map of a building, showing where things can be found.

TEACH Study the floor plan with children. Have children point to the area that houses the card catalog. Have a volunteer explain how to get from the card catalog area to the fiction section.

PRACTICE Have students use the floor plan to answer questions 1–5. Review the following answers with them:

ANSWERS **1.** the left side **2.** the reference section; **3.** the circulation desk **4.** three **5.** non-fiction books about real stories or facts, not made-up stories

STUDY SKILLS

READ TOGETHER

Read a Library Floor Plan

Tomás spends a lot of time at a library. A floor plan can help you find what you're looking for in the library.

Library Floor Plan

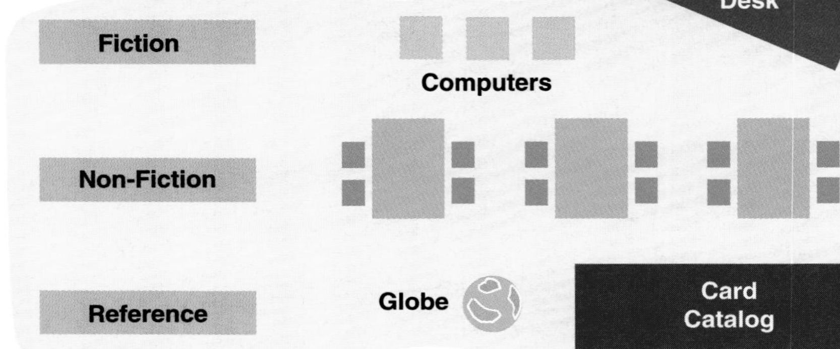

Use the floor plan to answer these questions.

1. On what side of the room are the fiction books?
2. In which section would you find encyclopedias?
3. Where would you go to check a book out?
4. Suppose six people want to use computers. How many people have to wait?
5. What books are closest to the reference books? What kind of books are these?

Meeting Individual Needs

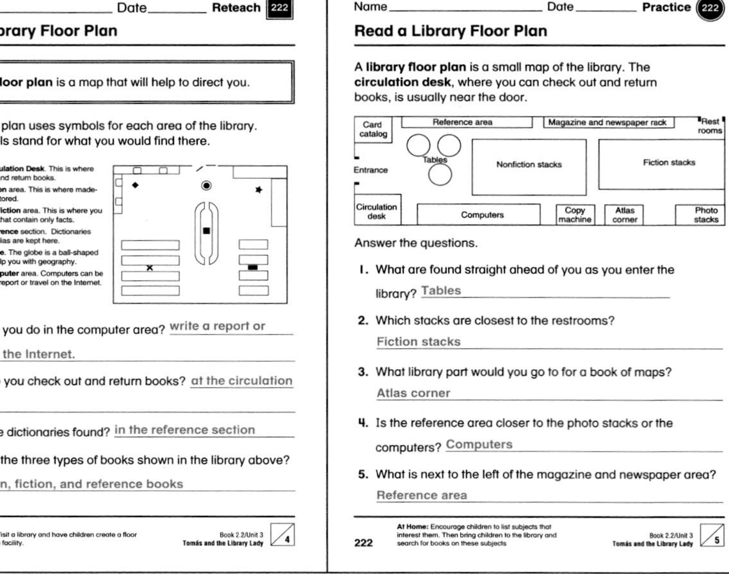

EASY

Name________ Date______ **Reteach 222**

Read a Library Floor Plan

A **library floor plan** is a map that will help to direct you.

A library floor plan uses symbols for each area of the library. These symbols stand for what you would find there.

- ■ This is the **Circulation Desk**. This is where you check out and return books.
- × This is the **fiction** area. This is where made-up stories are stored.
- ▬ This is the **nonfiction** area. This is where you can find books that contain only facts.
- ✱ This is the **reference** section. Dictionaries and encyclopedias are kept here.
- ● This is the **globe**. The globe is a ball-shaped map that will help you with geography.
- ◆ This is the **computer** area. Computers can be used to write a report or travel on the Internet.

1. What can you do in the computer area? write a report or travel on the Internet.
2. Where do you check out and return books? at the circulation desk
3. Where are dictionaries found? in the reference section
4. What are the three types of books shown in the library above? nonfiction, fiction, and reference books

222 **At Home:** Visit a library and have children create a floor plan of the facility. Book 2.2/Unit 3 **Tomás and the Library Lady** 4

Reteach, 222

ON-LEVEL

Name________ Date______ **Practice 222**

Read a Library Floor Plan

A **library floor plan** is a small map of the library. The **circulation desk**, where you can check out and return books, is usually near the door.

Answer the questions.

1. What are found straight ahead of you as you enter the library? Tables
2. Which stacks are closest to the restrooms? Fiction stacks
3. What library part would you go to for a book of maps? Atlas corner
4. Is the reference area closer to the photo stacks or the computers? Computers
5. What is next to the left of the magazine and newspaper area? Reference area

222 **At Home:** Encourage children to list subjects that interest them. Then bring children to the library and search for books on these subjects Book 2.2/Unit 3 **Tomás and the Library Lady** 5

Practice, 222

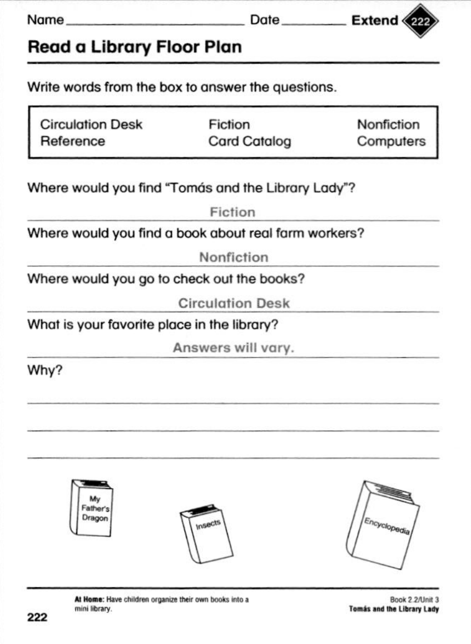

CHALLENGE

Name________ Date______ **Extend 222**

Read a Library Floor Plan

Write words from the box to answer the questions.

Circulation Desk	Fiction	Nonfiction
Reference	Card Catalog	Computers

Where would you find "Tomás and the Library Lady"? Fiction

Where would you find a book about real farm workers? Nonfiction

Where would you go to check out the books? Circulation Desk

What is your favorite place in the library? Answers will vary.

Why?

222 **At Home:** Have children organize their own books into a mini library. Book 2.2/Unit 3 **Tomás and the Library Lady**

Extend, 222

TEST POWER

Reading a story carefully will make it easier to answer the questions.

RECTIONS:

ead the story. Then read each question about the story.

AMPLE

Special Delivery

There are lots of people who ork at the post office. They lp us send and get letters. ese are very important jobs. Some people at the post office rt the mail. First, they read the dress on the envelope. Then, ey put the envelope in the bag at goes to the right place. A ferent bag goes to each city. me bags go by truck. Some gs go by airplane. New bags ive every day from other aces. These bags are full of ters that need to be delivered. Other people at the post office liver the mail. They are the ter carriers. They carry the ters from the post office to ur house. Everyone likes to get mail. That is why the people at the post office are so important.

1 Which general statement can you make from this story?

- ○ Many people get their mail on Tuesdays.
- ● It takes many people to make sure mail gets to the right place.
- ○ Most letter carriers fly planes.
- ○ Most mail has stamps on it.

2 In this story, some mail travels by—

- ○ bus
- ○ boat
- ● airplane
- ○ train

309

Test Power

THE PRINCETON REVIEW

Read the Page

Explain to children that you will be reading this story as a group. You will read the story, and they will follow along in their books.

Request that children put pens, pencils, and markers away, since they will not be writing in their books.

Discuss the Questions

QUESTION 1: Remind children that they should look for facts in the story to support a choice. The many people who deliver mail are mentioned at the beginning, middle, and end of the story.

QUESTION 2: Instruct children to find the place in the story where it describes the ways that mail travels. Ask them to read those lines of the story again.

Leveled Books

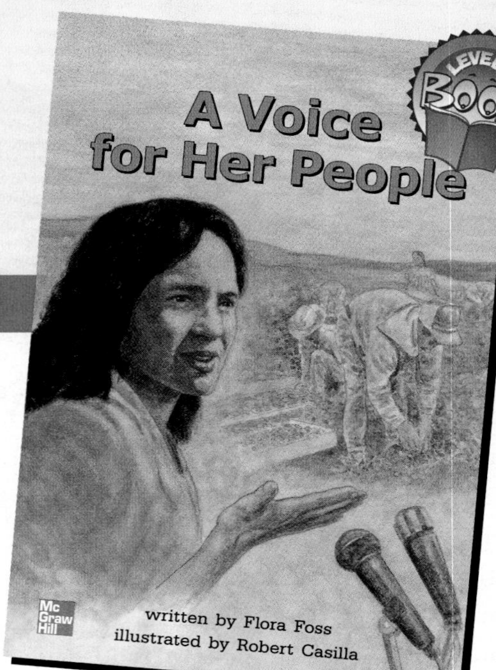

Intervention Skills

Intervention Guide, for direct instruction and extra practice in vocabulary and comprehension

Answers to Story Questions

1. New Mexico and California.
2. A migrant worker is a farm field worker who moves all over to pick crops; key words are "moved from school to school;" "picking fruits and vegetables."
3. They worked hard for what they wanted. They cared about other people and helped them.
4. How Dolores Huerta helped migrant workers get civil rights.
5. He could grow up to help people as Dolores did; he is alert and aware, and he loves to read and learn.

The Story Questions and Activity below appear in the Easy Book.

Story Questions and Writing Activity

1. In what two states did Dolores live?
2. Read page 9 of this book again. What is a migrant worker? What details tell you this?
3. Why, do you think, was Dolores so proud of her mother and father?
4. What is the main idea of this book?
5. Could Tomás from *Tomás and the Library Lady* grow up to be like Dolores?

Your Work for a Migrant Family

Draw a picture of one way you can help a new classmate whose relatives are migrant workers. Write one or two sentences about your drawing.

from *A Voice for Her People*

EASY

A Voice for Her People

- ☑ Phonics Long *e*; Long *i*
- ☑ Form Generalizations
- ☑ Instructional Vocabulary: ***borrow, desert, evenings, midnight, package, shoulder***

Guided Reading

PREVIEW AND PREDICT As you take the **picture walk**, have children predict what the story will be about.

SET PURPOSES Have children jot down why they want to read *A Voice for Her People*. For example, they may want to learn how Dolores Huerta helped her people.

READ THE BOOK Use the following questions to guide children's reading or after they have read the story independently.

Page 2: Find the word *liked*. What sound does the letter *i* make in the word? (long *i*) Can you think of other words that have the long *i* sound? ***Phonics and Decoding***

Page 4: What generalization can you make about the kind of people Dolores and her family are? (They are helpful and they care about others.) ***Form Generalizations***

Page 6: What is the main idea of the story? (Dolores wants to help her people.) What does Dolores do to be helpful? (teaches children of farm workers) ***Main Idea***

Page 9: Find the word *evening*. What part of the day is the evening? What words nearby help you figure this out? (*all day, after midnight*) ***Instructional Vocabulary***

Page 13: In what ways were Dolores Huerta and César Chavez alike? (Both tried to help people.) How are people like Dolores Huerta and César Chavez helpful to others? ***Form Generalizations***

RETURN TO PREDICTIONS AND PURPOSES Have children review their predictions and purposes for reading. Did they find out what they wanted to know?

LITERARY RESPONSE Discuss these questions:

- Can you describe another person you know about who was like Dolores Huerta?
- What do you think Dolores' children learned from her?

Also see the story questions and activity in *A Voice for Her People*.

See the Phonics **CD-ROM** for practice using words with long *e* and long *i* sounds.

Leveled Books

INDEPENDENT

Adventure in Arabia

 Long *e*; Long *i*

Form Generalizations

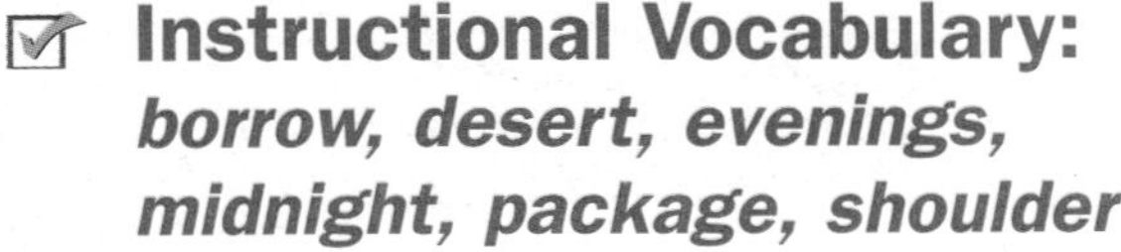
Instructional Vocabulary: *borrow, desert, evenings, midnight, package, shoulder*

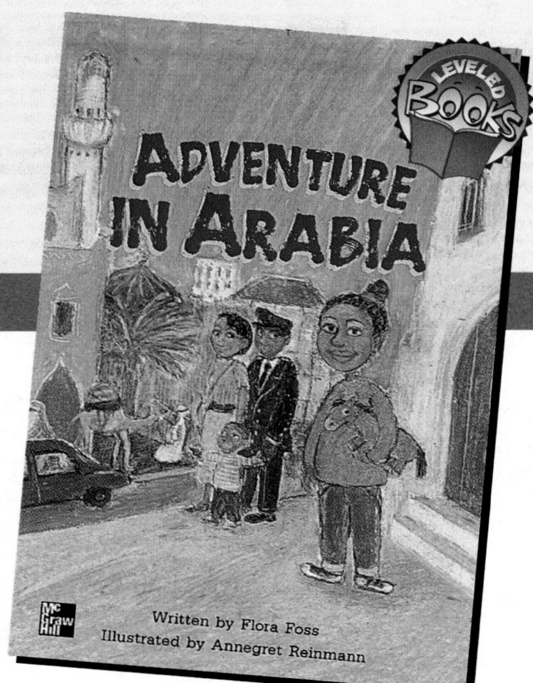

Guided Reading

PREVIEW AND PREDICT Take a **picture walk** with children through page 6 of the story. Have them predict what the story will be about.

SET PURPOSES Have children write or draw pictures showing what they want to find out as they read the story.

READ THE BOOK Use the following questions to guide children's reading or after they have read the story independently.

Page 2: Find the word *see* in the second sentence. Which two letters make the long *e* sound? *(ee)* Find another word on the page that has the long *e* sound spelled *ee*. (asleep) ***Phonics and Decoding***

Pages 4–5: What generalization can you form about the weather in Saudi Arabia? (It's like a desert–sunny and hot during the day, cool in the evenings.) ***Form Generalizations***

Pages 8–10: What kind of adult do you think someone like Jenna May, who travels around the world, will become? Why? ***Form Generalizations***

Page 15: When Jenna May says that Omar can *borrow* her cars and trucks, is she giving them to Omar or just letting him play with them for a while? ***Instructional Vocabulary***

Page 16: How do you think Jenna May is going to like living in Saudi Arabia? How can you tell? ***Make Predictions***

RETURN TO PREDICTIONS AND PURPOSES Discuss children's predictions. Then have children review their purposes for reading.

LITERARY RESPONSE Discuss these questions:

- How do you think that living in a foreign country can change a person?
- Would you enjoy living in any of the countries Jenna May has lived in–Germany, Japan, and Saudi Arabia? Why or why not?

Also see the story questions and activity in *Adventure in Arabia*.

See the Phonics **CD-ROM** for practice using words with the long *e* and long *i*.

Answers to Story Questions

1. Jenna May's father is in the army and is working there.
2. a muddy piece of land where rice grows
3. Possible response: He might help defend a friendly country.
4. moving to a different country
5. Answers will vary. Students may mention that the characters would talk about how they learned new things from new people; that it's hard at first to live in a new place with no friends.

The Story Questions and Activity below appear in the Independent Book.

Story Questions and Writing Activity

1. Why do Jenna May, Paul, and their mother move to Saudi Arabia?
2. Reread page 10 of this book. What is a rice paddy?
3. Why do you think Jenna May's father goes to work in other countries?
4. What is this story mostly about?
5. What if Tomás and Jenna May became friends? What are some things they'd tell one another about learning to live in a new and different place?

Use a Map

Locate the United States, Germany, Japan, and Saudi Arabia on a map of the world. Mark these spots with push pins or flags. Then write a short paragraph or draw a picture describing what it might be like to live in one of these countries.

from *Adventure in Arabia*

Leveled Books

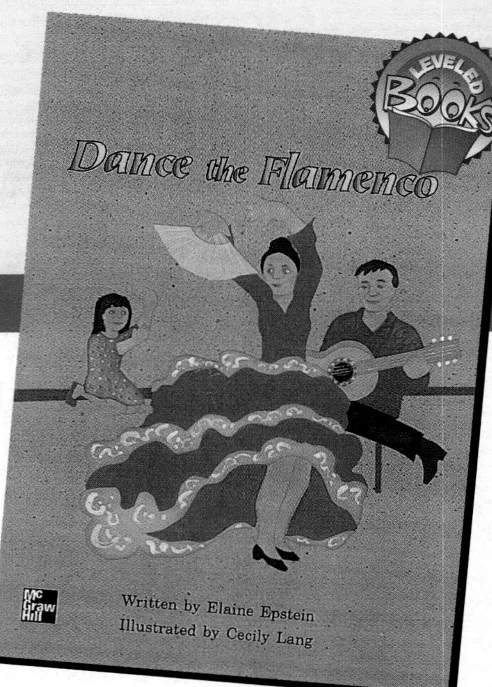

Leveled Books
Dance the Flamenco
Written by Elaine Epstein
Illustrated by Cecily Lang

CHALLENGE

Dance the Flamenco

 Long *e*; Long *i*

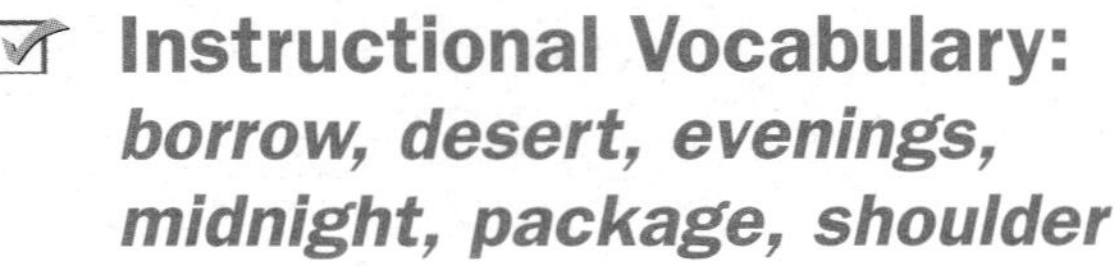

- Form Generalizations
- Instructional Vocabulary: *borrow, desert, evenings, midnight, package, shoulder*

Answers to Story Questions

1. A dance or music from Spain.
2. She could play number games on it, and she liked working with numbers the most.
3. They move from place to place; they don't stay in one place very long.
4. The life of a 7-year-old-girl whose parents perform the flamenco in various places in the United States.
5. Answers will vary. Possible answer: They both travel a lot with their families. They both have traditions. Anna's is flamenco, Tomás's is storytelling.

The Story Questions and Activity below appear in the Challenge Book.

Story Questions and Writing Activity

1. What is the flamenco?
2. Why do you think Anna enjoyed the computer so much?
3. From this story, what can you tell about the life of flamenco performers?
4. What is this story mostly about?
5. How are Tomás's and Anna's lives similar?

Be Strong!

Flamenco dancers must be very strong. What makes you and other children your age strong? Create a poster about how to be strong and healthy. Use pictures, words, and sentences to show your ideas.

from *Dance the Flamenco*

Guided Reading

PREVIEW AND PREDICT As you take the **picture walk**, have children predict what the story will be about. Chart their ideas.

SET PURPOSES Have children write several sentences about why they want to read *Dance the Flamenco*. Children may want to learn more about the dance or about other Spanish traditions.

READ THE BOOK Use the following questions to guide children's reading or after they have read the story independently.

Page 2: Find the word *feet*. Which letters make the long *e* sound? *(ee)* Find the word *midnight*. What sound do the letters *igh* make? (long *i*) ***Phonics and Decoding***

Page 6: Where did Anna rest her head when her father carried her out to the car? (on his shoulder) Point to your shoulder. Try to use the word *shoulder* in a sentence. ***Instructional Vocabulary***

Page 10: What is Anna excited about? (using a computer) What generalization can you form about Anna from reading this page? (She likes to learn new things.)

Page 13: What was the problem Anna's parents had? (They wanted Anna to stay in one school and learn the things she needed to learn.) How did they solve their problem? (Anna stayed with her grandparents for the school year.) ***Problem and Solution***

Page 16: What kind of work do you think Anna will do when she grows up? Why do you think so? ***Make Predictions***

RETURN TO PREDICTIONS AND PURPOSES Have children review their predictions and purposes for reading.

LITERARY RESPONSE Discuss these questions:

- Do you think Anna's parents made the right decision? Why?
- How do you think a good education can help a dancer?

Also see the story questions and activity in *Dance the Flamenco*.

See the Phonics **CD-ROM** for practice using words with long *e* and long *i*.

Bringing Groups Together

Anthology and Leveled Books

Connecting Texts

CLASS DISCUSSION
Discuss with children the concept of living in different places. Ask:

- Have you lived in a different city, state, or country? Where?
- How is where you live now different? How is it similar?

GRAPHIC ORGANIZER
Write the story titles on a graphic organizer. Write *Different Places* in the center. Have children name the places the character(s) in their story lived. Encourage children to talk about what they learned about those places from their reading.

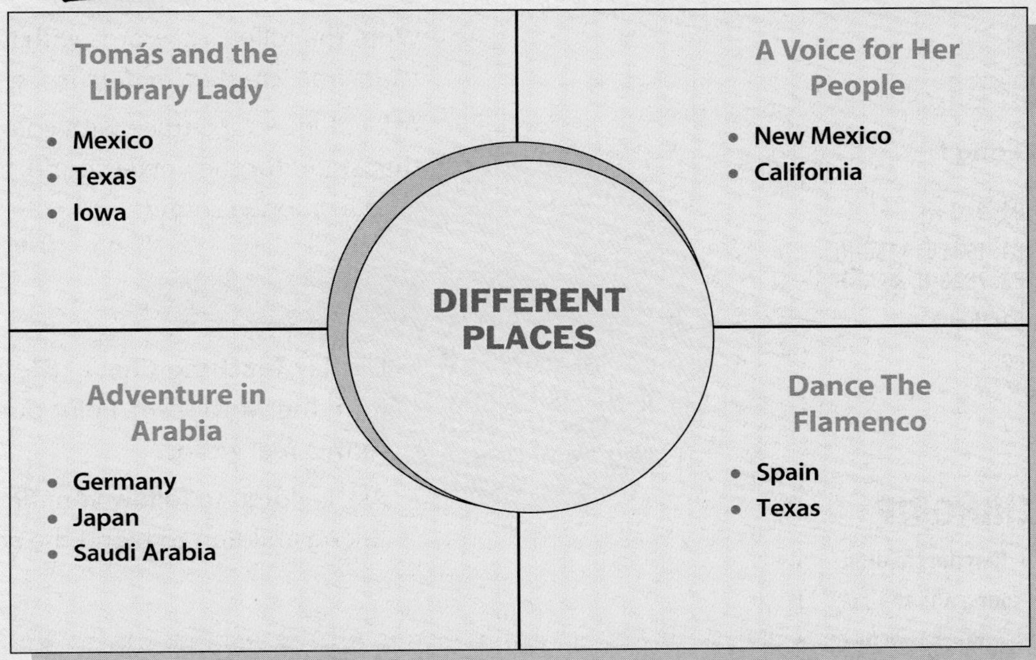

Viewing/Representing

VIEWING/REPRESENTING Divide the class into four groups, one for each of the four stories read in the lesson. Have each group work on a poster to advertise something about the country the story represents or something about the people of the country. Have each group share its poster with the rest of the class.

AUDIENCE RESPONSE
Have children look carefully at each group's posters and allow time for questions.

Research and Inquiry

MORE ABOUT SPAIN Invite children to learn more about Spain and Spanish traditions. Ask them to do the following:

- Look at classroom picture books and school-library reference books that feature Spain and its traditions.
- Invite a speaker with a Spanish background to talk to the class.
- Ask parents who can cook Spanish dishes to share one with the class.

Have children log on to ***www.mhschool.com/reading*** for links to Web pages.

Review Long e, i

TESTED OBJECTIVES

Children will:

- review/ē/, *ee, ea,* and /ī/, *y, igh.*
- decode and read words with long *e* and long *i* sounds.

MATERIALS

- Teaching Chart 186

Skills Finder

Long *i*	
Introduce	B1: 92G-H
Review	B1: 113E-F, 113G-H; B2: 282G-H, 309G-H
Test	B1: Unit 1
Maintain	B2: 21

TEACHING TIP

LONG *e, i* Remind children that the /ē/ sound and the /ī/ sound can be represented by many different letters and letter combinations.

ALTERNATE TEACHING STRATEGY

REVIEW LONG *e* AND LONG *i*

For a different approach to teaching this skill, see page T70.

PREPARE

Listen for Long *e* and Long *i* Sounds and Review Letter Combinations

Read the following sentences aloud. Tell children to raise their hands when they hear words with long *i* and long *e* sounds.

- The iron gate creaked open at midnight.
- The leaves high on the trees blew wildly in the breeze.

Write the following words with long *e* and long *i* on the chalkboard: *flight, iron, creaked, midnight, leaves, high, trees, wildly, breeze.*

Ask volunteers to trace with colored chalk the letters in each word that stand for the vowel sound, and to say whether the word makes a long *e* or long *i* sound.

TEACH

BLENDING Model and Guide Practice with Long *e* and Long *i* Words

- Display **Teaching Chart 186**. In the first example, write letters *ee* to form the word *seem*. Point out that the answer choice *ie* does not form a real word.
- Ask children to follow your finger as you blend the sounds. Repeat, asking children to blend the sounds with you.

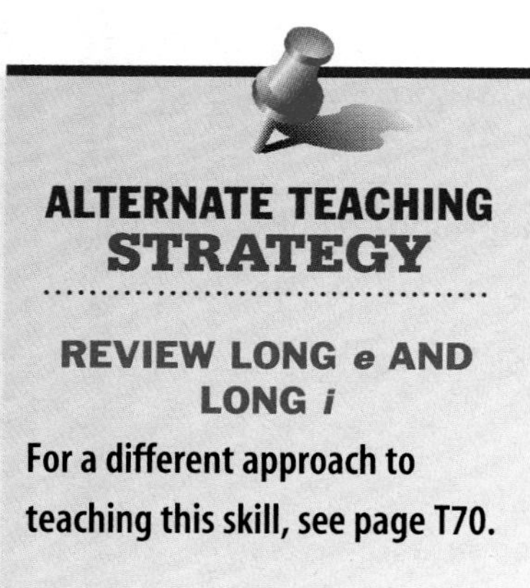

s ee m ee ie	i sland igh i	cl ea n ee ea
fr y igh y	sw ee t ee ea	p ie ce ee ie
h igh y igh	t ee th ea ee	f ie ld ee ie

Teaching Chart 186

Use the Words in Context

- Have volunteers use the word in a sentence to reinforce its meaning. Example: *My friends seem to know a lot about the library.*

Repeat the Procedure

- Repeat the procedure for the remaining words on the chart. Tell children that the letters they choose need to form a real word.

PRACTICE

BUILDING Words with Long *e* and Long *i* Sounds

Write the following letter banks on the chalkboard:

c	t	l
f	r	m

ee	ie	ea
i	y	igh

f	t	h
n	m	k

Encourage volunteers to form words by choosing a letter(s) from the letter banks. Then ask children to write the words they formed, blend the letters together, and read each word aloud. Have children separate their words into groups with common characteristics.

ASSESS/CLOSE

Read and Spell Long *e* and Long *i* Words

To assess children's ability to build and decode long vowel words, observe their work on the Practice activity. Ask each student to read and spell aloud words with each spelling of the /ē/ sound and /ī/ sound.

ADDITIONAL PHONICS RESOURCES

Phonics/ Phonemic Awareness Practice Book, pages 139–142

CD-ROM activities for practice with Decoding and Discriminating

DAILY 

ROUTINES

DAY 4 **Fluency** Write the following words on the chalkboard: *teeth, eager, leader, iron, by,* and *midnight.* Ask a volunteer to blend the sounds silently and then read aloud each word.

SPELLING/PHONICS CONNECTIONS

See the 5-Day Spelling Plan, pages 309Q–309R.

Intervention Skills

Intervention Guide, for direct instruction and extra practice of long *e, i*

Meeting Individual Needs for Phonics

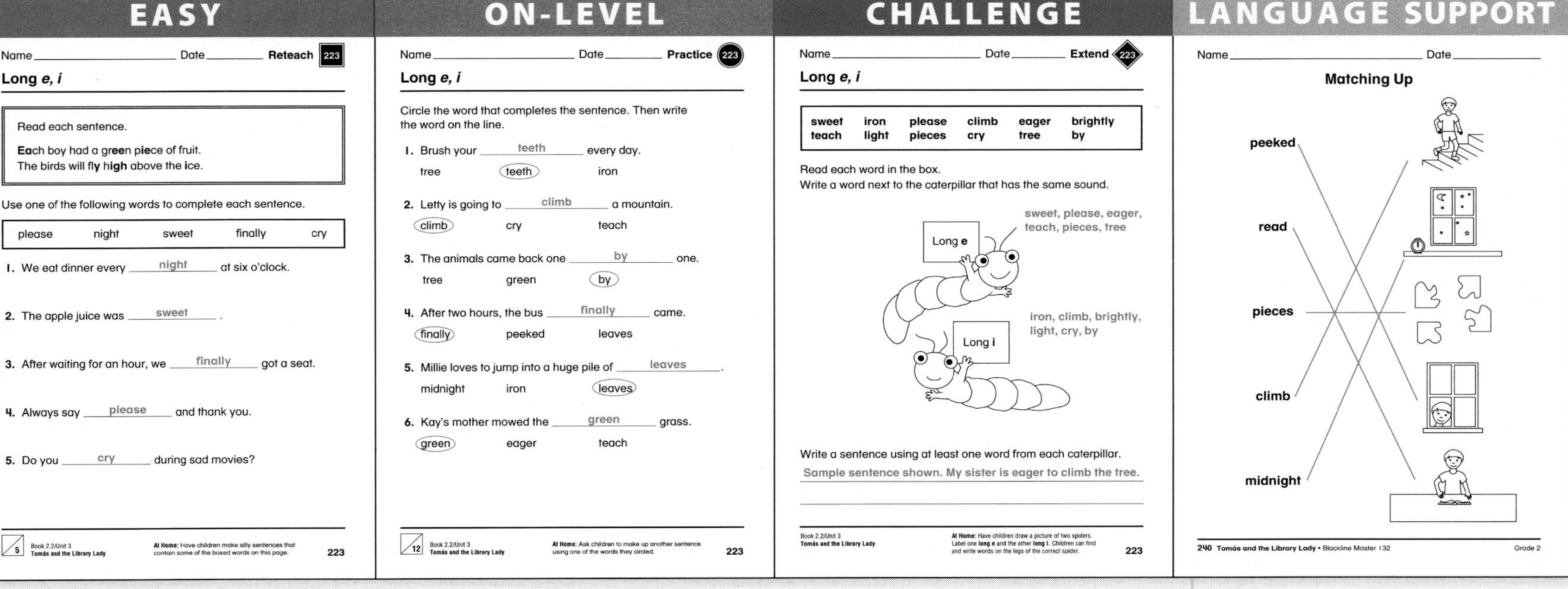

EASY

Name ______ Date ______ Reteach 223

Long *e, i*

Read each sentence.

Each boy had a green piece of fruit.
The birds will fly high above the ice.

Use one of the following words to complete each sentence.

please night sweet finally cry

1. We eat dinner every __night__ at six o'clock.
2. The apple juice was __sweet__.
3. After waiting for an hour, we __finally__ got a seat.
4. Always say __please__ and thank you.
5. Do you __cry__ during sad movies?

Book 2.2/Unit 3 Tomás and the Library Lady — At Home: Have children make silly sentences that contain some of the boxed words on this page. 223

ON-LEVEL

Name ______ Date ______ Practice 223

Long *e, i*

Circle the word that completes the sentence. Then write the word on the line.

1. Brush your __teeth__ every day. tree (teeth) iron
2. Letty is going to __climb__ a mountain. (climb) cry teach
3. The animals came back one __by__ one. tree green (by)
4. After two hours, the bus __finally__ came. (finally) peeked leaves
5. Millie loves to jump into a huge pile of __leaves__. midnight iron (leaves)
6. Kay's mother mowed the __green__ grass. (green) eager teach

Book 2.2/Unit 3 Tomás and the Library Lady — At Home: Ask children to make up another sentence using one of the words they circled. 223

CHALLENGE

Name ______ Date ______ Extend 223

Long *e, i*

sweet	iron	please	climb	eager	brightly
teach	light	pieces	cry	tree	by

Read each word in the box.
Write a word next to the caterpillar that has the same sound.

Long e: sweet, please, eager, teach, pieces, tree
Long i: iron, climb, brightly, light, cry, by

Write a sentence using at least one word from each caterpillar.
Sample sentence shown. My sister is eager to climb the tree.

Book 2.2/Unit 3 Tomás and the Library Lady — At Home: Have children draw a picture of two spiders. Label one long e and the other long i. Children can find and write words on the legs of the correct spider. 223

LANGUAGE SUPPORT

Name ______ Date ______

Matching Up

peeked
read
pieces
climb
midnight

240 Tomás and the Library Lady • Blackline Master 132 Grade 2

Reteach, 223 **Practice, 223** **Extend, 223** **Language Support Book, 240**

Children will:

- review long *e*: *ee, ie, ea*.
- review long *i*: *i, y, igh*.
- review /ch/: *tch* and *ch*.

MATERIALS

- **Word Building Manipulative Cards**
- **Teaching Chart 187**

Skills Finder

Long *i*	
Introduce	B1: 92G-H
Review	B1: 113E-F, 113G-H; B2: 282G-H, 309E-F
Test	B1: Unit 1
Maintain	B2: 21

Review Long *e*; Long *i*; *tch, ch*

PREPARE

Identify Long *e*, Long *i*, and /ch/ Sounds

Read the following sentences aloud. Have children say "e" when they hear the /ē/ sound, "i" when they hear the /ī/ sound, and "ch" when they hear the /ch/ sound.

- The dentist tried to teach me to eat fewer sweet foods, so my teeth don't chatter when he shines the light in my mouth!
- We put the chair under a tree where the sun shone less brightly.

TEACH

BLENDING Model and Guide Practice with Words Containing Long *e*, Long *i*, and /ch/ Sounds

ea ee ie i y igh ch tch

teach	cry	reach	dry
watch	light	batch	seat
pieces	iron	nieces	climb
seen		between	

* Other answers are possible

Teaching Chart 187

- Display **Teaching Chart 187**. Remind children of the different letters and letter combinations that stand for the long *e* sound, the long *i* sound, and the /ch/ sound.
- Point to the letter bank at the top of the chart. Write the letters *ea* on the blank in the first example. Run your fingers under the word as you blend the sounds to read *teach*. Have children blend after you.
- Have children tell whether the word contains a long *e* sound, a long *i* sound, or a /ch/ sound, and which letters represent the sound.

Use the Words in Context

Have volunteers use the word in a sentence to reinforce its meaning. Example: *I am going to teach my friend how to paint.*

Repeat the Procedure

Explain to the children that they can continue to make words by writing letters or letter combinations in the blank spaces. Have the children read each word aloud.

PRACTICE

WORD BUILDING
Build and Sort Long *e*, Long *i*, and /ch/ Words

PARTNERS

Have children work with a partner using **Word Building Manipulative Cards** to build as many words as possible containing letter combinations representing long *e*, long *i*, and /ch/. Create three columns on the chalkboard, one for each sound. Have partners build two words for each sound, and write them in the appropriate columns. Have children check their sorting by reading the words aloud.

▶ **Linguistic/Visual/Spatial**

ASSESS/CLOSE

Make a Word Train Using Words with Long *e*, Long *i*, /ch/ *ch, tch*

Use your observations from the Practice activity to determine if children need more reinforcement with long *e*, long *i*, or /ch/ words. Have children use the words they have sorted to make a word train, in which words with the same letter combinations are written in boxes that are joined together.

ADDITIONAL PHONICS RESOURCES

Phonics/ Phonemic Awareness Practice Book, pages 139–142

activities for practice with Decoding and Word Building

DAILY Phonics ROUTINES

Writing Have partners work together to write short, rhyming poems containing words with long *e* or long *i* vowel patterns.

ALTERNATE TEACHING STRATEGY

CUMULATIVE REVIEW

For a different approach to teaching this skill, see pages T65 and T70.

Intervention Skills

Intervention Guide, for direct instruction and extra practice of long *e*, long *i*; *tch, ch*

Meeting Individual Needs for Phonics

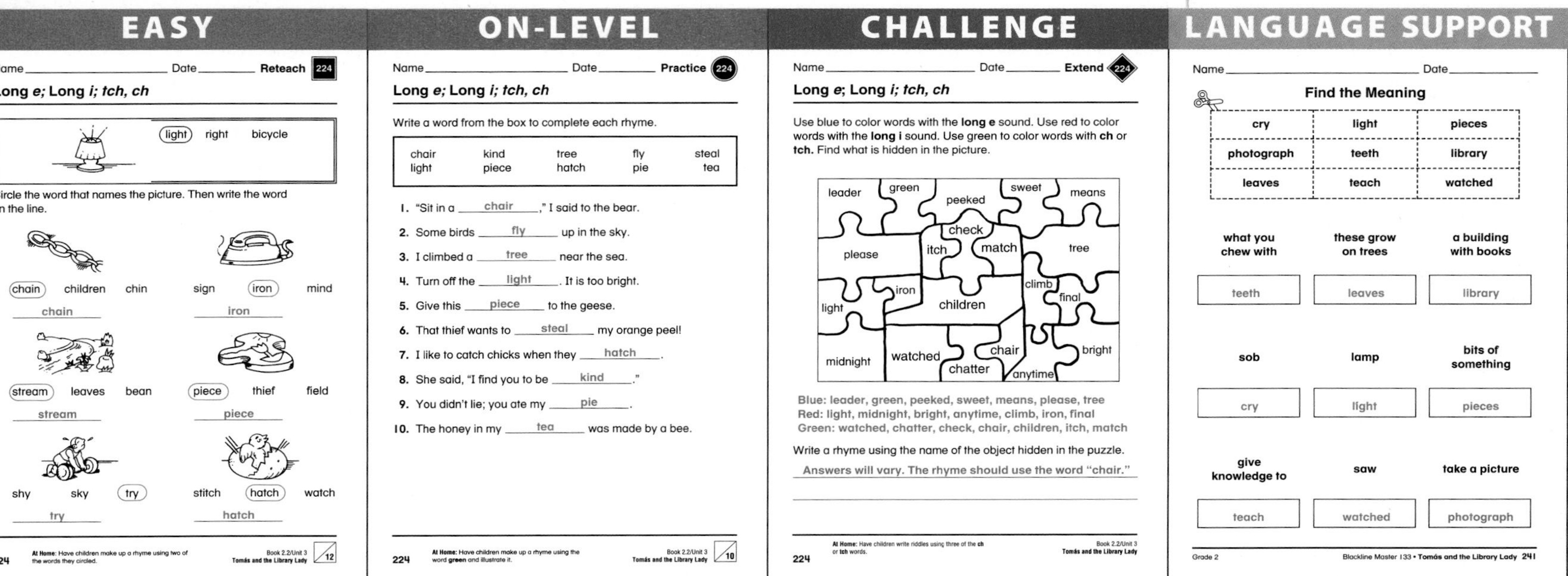

EASY

Name ________ Date ________ Reteach 224

Long *e*; Long *i*; *tch, ch*

(light) right bicycle

Circle the word that names the picture. Then write the word on the line.

(chain)	children	chin	sign	(iron)	mind
chain			iron		
(stream)	leaves	bean	(piece)	thief	field
stream			piece		
shy	sky	(try)	stitch	(hatch)	watch
try			hatch		

224 At Home: Have children make up a rhyme using two of the words they circled. Book 2.2/Unit 3 Tomás and the Library Lady 12

ON-LEVEL

Name ________ Date ________ Practice 224

Long *e*; Long *i*; *tch, ch*

Write a word from the box to complete each rhyme.

chair	kind	tree	fly	steal
light	piece	hatch	pie	tea

1. "Sit in a chair," I said to the bear.
2. Some birds fly up in the sky.
3. I climbed a tree near the sea.
4. Turn off the light. It is too bright.
5. Give this piece to the geese.
6. That thief wants to steal my orange peel!
7. I like to catch chicks when they hatch.
8. She said, "I find you to be kind."
9. You didn't lie; you ate my pie.
10. The honey in my tea was made by a bee.

224 At Home: Have children make up a rhyme using the word green and illustrate it. Book 2.2/Unit 3 Tomás and the Library Lady 10

CHALLENGE

Name ________ Date ________ Extend 224

Long *e*; Long *i*; *tch, ch*

Use blue to color words with the **long e** sound. Use red to color words with the **long i** sound. Use green to color words with **ch** or **tch**. Find what is hidden in the picture.

leader green peeked sweet means check please itch match tree light iron children climb final midnight watched chatter chair anytime bright

Blue: leader, green, peeked, sweet, means, please, tree
Red: light, midnight, bright, anytime, climb, iron, final
Green: watched, chatter, check, chair, children, itch, match

Write a rhyme using the name of the object hidden in the puzzle.

Answers will vary. The rhyme should use the word "chair."

224 At Home: Have children write riddles using three of the ch or tch words. Book 2.2/Unit 3 Tomás and the Library Lady

LANGUAGE SUPPORT

Name ________ Date ________

Find the Meaning

cry	light	pieces
photograph	teeth	library
leaves	teach	watched

what you chew with	these grow on trees	a building with books
teeth	leaves	library
sob	lamp	bits of something
cry	light	pieces
give knowledge to	saw	take a picture
teach	watched	photograph

Grade 2 Blackline Master 133 • Tomás and the Library Lady 241

Reteach, 224 **Practice, 224** **Extend, 224** **Language Support, 241**

Introduce Main Idea

TESTED OBJECTIVES

Children will connect main ideas with supporting details.

MATERIALS
- Teaching Chart 188

Skills Finder

Main Idea	
Introduce	B2: 309I-J
Review	B2: 361I-J, 371E-F
Test	B2: Unit 3
Maintain	B2: 109, 165, 229, 345

TEACHING TIP

DETAILS Remind children that details are little pieces of information. Sometimes they describe how something looks, sounds, smells, or feels. Details help the reader figure out the main idea when it is not stated directly.

SELF-SELECTED Reading

Children may choose from the following titles.

ANTHOLOGY
- *Tomás and the Library Lady*

LEVELED BOOKS
- *A Voice for Her People*
- *Adventure in Arabia*
- *Dance the Flamenco*

Bibliography, pages T88–T89

PREPARE

Introduce the Main Idea Explain to children that the main idea of a text tells what it will be about. Supporting details give extra information about the main idea.

TEACH

Infer the Main Idea in "Tomás Explores the Library" Display **Teaching Chart 188** and read the title aloud to children. Ask what they think the passage might be about. Then read the passage aloud.

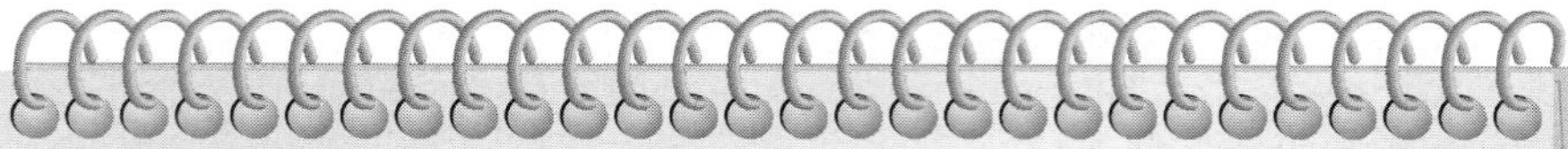

Tomás Explores the Library

The library lady showed Tomás many of the library's resources. She showed him the reference section, where he checked the encyclopedia for information about animals. She showed him the fiction section, where he found a book of stories. She showed him how to use the card catalog, so he could find the location of different books in the library. The card catalog showed that the library had books on thousands of subjects! The library lady even showed Tomás how to use the library's computers.

Teaching Chart 188

MODEL As I read about all the things the library lady showed Tomás—an encyclopedia, books of stories, a card catalog, and computers—I think I understand the main idea of the passage. The library has many resources. All the details helped me figure out the main idea.

Ask children to underline words in the passage that are details about the resources in the library.

Identify an Implied Main Idea

Explain: The main idea of a story is often implied. No single sentence states the main idea directly. Write on the chalkboard: *Libraries often have a special place where kids can read books. Many libraries bring in guest speakers for children and host children's activities.* Ask, *What is the main idea in our example?* (libraries are kid-friendly) *Is the main idea stated directly?* (no) *How can we know the main idea?* (by reading all of the details)

PRACTICE

Identify Supporting Details

Help children fill in a Main Idea and Supporting Details chart using words they underlined in the passage.

MAIN IDEA	SUPPORTING DETAILS
The library has many resources.	reference section
	fiction section
	card catalog
	computers

▶ **Linguistic/Visual/Spatial**

ASSESS/CLOSE

Main Idea and Details in *Going Batty for Bats*

Invite children to identify and discuss the main idea and supporting details of *Going Batty for Bats* on pages 118–121. Children may wish to create a Main idea and Supporting details flowchart. Have children work individually to fill in the chart, referring to the selection as needed.

ALTERNATE TEACHING STRATEGY

MAIN IDEA AND SUPPORTING DETAILS

For a different approach to teaching this skill, see page T71.

Skills

Intervention Guide, for direct instruction and extra practice of main idea

Meeting Individual Needs for Comprehension

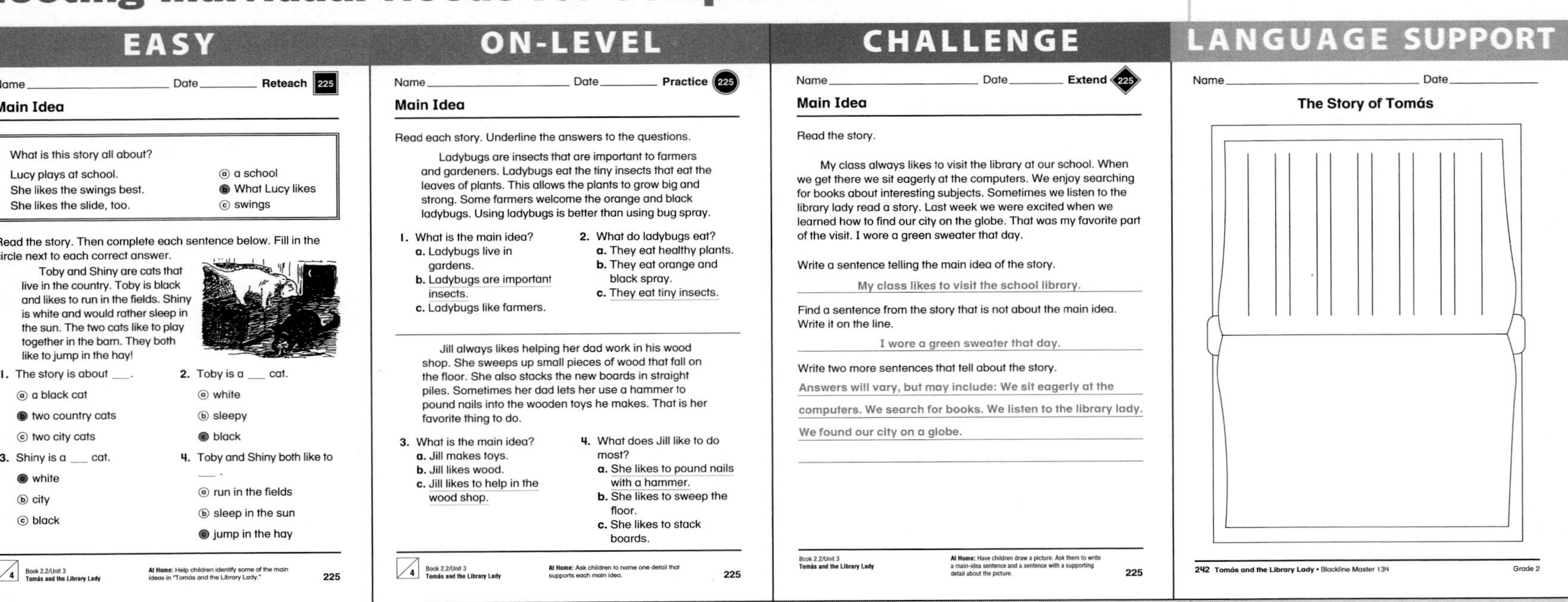

EASY

Name ______ Date ______ Reteach 225

Main Idea

What is this story all about?
Lucy plays at school.
She likes the swings best.
She likes the slide, too.
ⓐ a school
ⓑ What Lucy likes
ⓒ swings

Read the story. Then complete each sentence below. Fill in the circle next to each correct answer.

Toby and Shiny are cats that live in the country. Toby is black and likes to run in the fields. Shiny is white and would rather sleep in the sun. The two cats like to play together in the barn. They both like to jump in the hay!

1. The story is about ___.
 ⓐ a black cat
 ⓑ two country cats
 ⓒ two city cats
2. Toby is a ___ cat.
 ⓐ white
 ⓑ sleepy
 ⓒ black
3. Shiny is a ___ cat.
 ⓐ white
 ⓑ city
 ⓒ black
4. Toby and Shiny both like to ___.
 ⓐ run in the fields
 ⓑ sleep in the sun
 ⓒ jump in the hay

Book 2.2/Unit 3 Tomás and the Library Lady — At Home: Help children identify some of the main ideas in "Tomás and the Library Lady." 225

ON-LEVEL

Name ______ Date ______ Practice 225

Main Idea

Read each story. Underline the answers to the questions.

Ladybugs are insects that are important to farmers and gardeners. Ladybugs eat the tiny insects that eat the leaves of plants. This allows the plants to grow big and strong. Some farmers welcome the orange and black ladybugs. Using ladybugs is better than using bug spray.

1. What is the main idea?
 a. Ladybugs live in gardens.
 b. Ladybugs are important insects.
 c. Ladybugs like farmers.
2. What do ladybugs eat?
 a. They eat healthy plants.
 b. They eat orange and black spray.
 c. They eat tiny insects.

Jill always likes helping her dad work in his wood shop. She sweeps up small pieces of wood that fall on the floor. She also stacks the new boards in straight piles. Sometimes her dad lets her use a hammer to pound nails into the wooden toys he makes. That is her favorite thing to do.

3. What is the main idea?
 a. Jill makes toys.
 b. Jill likes wood.
 c. Jill likes to help in the wood shop.
4. What does Jill like to do most?
 a. She likes to pound nails with a hammer.
 b. She likes to sweep the floor.
 c. She likes to stack boards.

Book 2.2/Unit 3 Tomás and the Library Lady — At Home: Ask children to name one detail that supports each main idea. 225

CHALLENGE

Name ______ Date ______ Extend 225

Main Idea

Read the story.

My class always likes to visit the library at our school. When we get there we sit eagerly at the computers. We enjoy searching for books about interesting subjects. Sometimes we listen to the library lady read a story. Last week we were excited when we learned how to find our city on the globe. That was my favorite part of the visit. I wore a green sweater that day.

Write a sentence telling the main idea of the story.
My class likes to visit the school library.

Find a sentence from the story that is not about the main idea. Write it on the line.
I wore a green sweater that day.

Write two more sentences that tell about the story.
Answers will vary, but may include: We sit eagerly at the computers. We search for books. We listen to the library lady. We found our city on a globe.

Book 2.2/Unit 3 Tomás and the Library Lady — At Home: Have children draw a picture. Ask them to write a main-idea sentence and a sentence with a supporting detail about the picture. 225

LANGUAGE SUPPORT

Name ______ Date ______

The Story of Tomás

242 Tomás and the Library Lady • Blackline Master 134 — Grade 2

Reteach, 225 | Practice, 225 | Extend, 225 | Language Support, 242

OBJECTIVES

Children will review multiple meaning words.

MATERIALS

- **Teaching Chart 189**

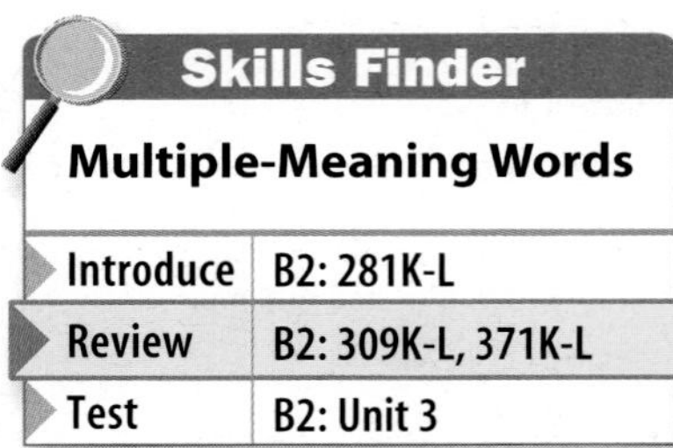

Skills Finder

Multiple-Meaning Words

Introduce	B2: 281K-L
Review	B2: 309K-L, 371K-L
Test	B2: Unit 3

TEACHING TIP

HOMOGRAPHS Remind children that homographs are different from synonyms, which are words that have the same meaning, but are spelled differently. Also, differentiate between homographs and homophones, which are words that sound alike but have different meanings. Write an example of homographs, synonyms, and homophones on the board and invite the class to talk about what makes them different from one another.

Review Multiple-Meaning Words

PREPARE

Pantomime Homographs Remind children that in some cases, two words are spelled the same although they have different meanings, and sometimes different pronunciations. Write the word *wind* on the chalkboard, but do not say it aloud. Ask children to pantomime the meaning of the word you have written on the board. Then ask children if they can think of and pantomime another meaning for the word.

TEACH

Identify Multiple Meanings With children, read aloud **Teaching Chart 189;** then model the skill beginning with the word *watch.*

Tomás and the Storm

Tomás is reading a very exciting story about a storm. First the wind blows so hard, it tears a row of trees out of the ground. All that is left of them are their roots. Then it begins to rain. It rains so hard that the streets are covered with water. People have to row boats to get home! Suddenly, Tomás looks at his watch and realizes he is late for dinner. He puts the book back on the shelf, and heads home. He will have a good story to tell his grandfather!

Teaching Chart 189

MODEL I see that the word *watch* is used in this paragraph. I know that this word has two different meanings. Tomás realizes he is late when he looks at his watch, so I know the word *watch* means *small clock* here. The other meaning of *watch* is *to look at.*

PRACTICE

Identify the Correct Meanings

Invite children to give the correct meaning for each word underlined in **Teaching Chart 189**. Have children circle clues they used to determine the meaning of each word.

▶ **Linguistic/Interpersonal**

ASSESS/CLOSE

Use Words with Multiple Meanings

Write on the chalkboard the words *rose, train,* and *pointed*. Invite children to write each word on a blank word card. Ask small groups to use each word in two sentences, using different meanings of each word in each sentence. Invite children to read their sentences aloud to the class.

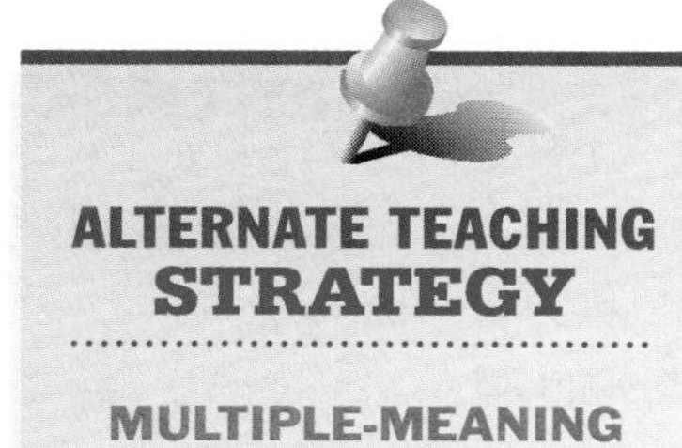

ALTERNATE TEACHING STRATEGY

MULTIPLE-MEANING WORDS

For a different approach to teaching this skill, see page T68.

Skills

Intervention Guide, for direct instruction and extra practice of multiple-meaning words

Meeting Individual Needs for Vocabulary

EASY

Name ____________ Date ________ **Reteach 226**

Multiple-Meaning Words

There are many words that have more than one meaning. Sometimes the different meanings are pronounced differently as well.

The singer was happy at the end of the show.

Sometimes he brought a toy to show everyone.

Draw a line from each underlined word to its meaning.

1. The singer will bow after her song.
2. Mr. Sands wore a bow tie.

to bend the body
a knot tied with loops

3. My backpack is light when it is empty.
4. It is getting light outside.

not dark
not heavy

5. Father leaves before I wake up.
6. In fall, the leaves turn colors.

parts of a tree
goes away

226 **At Home:** Challenge children to think of two meanings for the word **tie** and to use them in a sentence. Book 2.2/Unit 3 **Tomás and the Library Lady** 6

Reteach, 226

ON-LEVEL

Name ____________ Date ________ **Practice 226**

Multiple-Meaning Words

Read each sentence. Write the meaning of the underlined word on the line after each sentence. Answers may vary.

1. Dad always leaves early. goes away
2. The bus turned right at the corner. direction; not left
3. Burt can throw the ball across the field. a round toy
4. The light by her bed was off. lamp
5. We put the leaves in a big pile. parts of a tree
6. I got the right answer. not wrong; correct
7. A balloon floats because it is light. not heavy
8. The leaves turn brown every fall. the season after summer
9. Cinderella met a prince at the ball. a dance party
10. The children will watch the show. look at something
11. I always fall on the ice in the winter. drop to the ground
12. He was late, and he kept looking at his watch. a small clock, usually worn on the wrist

226 **At Home:** Ask children to think of another word that has two meanings. Have them draw a picture to illustrate each meaning. Book 2.2/Unit 3 **Tomás and the Library Lady** 12

Practice, 226

CHALLENGE

Name ____________ Date ________ **Extend 226**

Multiple-Meaning Words

Use these words to complete the sentences.

face	ball	glass	iron	wind

1. I drink milk out of a glass.
2. I like to throw a ball at the park.
3. The gate is made of iron.
4. I pat water on my face to cool it.
5. The wind blows leaves in the yard.

a. I can't face him.
b. I will wind up the string.
c. Please iron my shirt.
d. Who will dance at the ball?
e. The window is made of glass.

Which sentences use the same words? Write the number and the letter. The first one is done for you.

1, e
2, d
3, c
4, a
5, b

Which word sounds different when it has a different meaning?

wind

226 **At Home:** Have children write sentences for each meaning of these homographs: **bow, bow; read, read; does, does.** Book 2.2/Unit 3 **Tomás and the Library Lady**

Extend, 226

LANGUAGE SUPPORT

Name ____________ Date ________

Same Word, Different Meaning

ball	windy	leaves	bear

ball	windy
leaves	leaves
windy	ball
bear	bear

Grade 2 Blackline Master 135 • **Tomás and the Library Lady** 243

Language Support, 243

GRAMMAR/SPELLING CONNECTIONS

See the 5-Day Grammar and Usage Plan on pages 309O–309P.

See the 5-Day Spelling Plan on pages 309Q–309R.

TEACHING TIP

Technology Do children sometimes forget to indent paragraphs? Many word processing programs allow you to set margins so that the first line of a paragraph indents automatically.

Handwriting Remind children to print legibly. They should leave a little extra space between sentences and stay within the margins. See Handwriting pages T78–T79.

Handwriting CD-ROM

Writing a Story

Prewrite

WRITE AN ADVENTURE STORY Present the following: Tomás's imagination became very active when he read—he imagined himself in faraway places. Now, you are going to write a story where you have an adventure.

BRAINSTORM IDEAS Have children brainstorm individually about the places and people they might encounter on an adventure, and the things they might do.

Strategy: Make a Chart Have children create a three-column chart with the headings *Where I'll Go, Who I'll See,* and *What Will Happen*. Suggest that children:

- list in the *Where I'll Go* column some details of the setting.
- list in the *Who I'll See* column some details about the characters.
- list in the *What Will Happen* column some details about what the characters will do.

Draft

FREE WRITE Encourage children to write freely, using the idea from their charts. Remind them that a good story has a problem or conflict that the characters must solve, with a clear beginning, middle and end. Explain that using dialogue to tell the story can enliven the action and pace of the events.

Revise

SELF-QUESTIONING Ask children to assess their drafts.

- Does the reader know who the main characters are and where the story takes place?
- Is there a problem or conflict for the characters to solve?
- Is there a clear beginning, middle, and end?

Edit/Proofread

CHECK FOR ERRORS Children should reread their stories to check spelling, grammar, punctuation, and organization of information.

Publish

SHARE THE STORIES Children can draw pictures of their adventure stories.

Tracey's River Ride

I went rafting last weekend with my aunt and uncle. I had never done it before, and I had no idea what was in store for me. It's a good thing I don't mind getting wet! Everything started out smoothly enough. Suddenly, the wind began to blow. Big waves were crashing against our little boat. All three of us got soaked! Then the biggest wave of all hit the boat. The next thing I knew, the boat flipped over, and we were left standing in the river. Luckily, the water only came up to my waist. It was quite an adventure!

Presentation Ideas

IORAMA Using shoe boxes, have hildren create dioramas that represent a cene from their adventure story. Display the ompleted dioramas. ▶ **Viewing/Representing**

TORIES ON TAPE Have children read neir stories aloud to the class. Tell them they an use their pictures as they read to empha-ze important moments. Afterwards, each hild can set up a visual representation of his r her story, using the pictures and diorama.
▶ **Speaking/Listening**

Consider children's creative efforts, possibly adding a plus (+) for originality, wit, and imagination.

Scoring Rubric

Excellent	Good	Fair	Unsatisfactory
4: The writer: • presents an imaginative story where the characters creativly resolve a problem or conflict. • uses rich, expressive language to give details about the characters and setting. • has a clear beginning, middle, and end, with a strong conclusion for the story.	**3:** The writer: • presents a well-constructed story where the characters resolve a problem or conflict. • gives details about the characters and setting. • has a clear beginning, middle, and end.	**2:** The writer: • does not show characters clearly encountering or resolving a problem or conflict. • may give only a few details about the character and setting. • story has beginning, middle, and end, but it may be unclear or vague.	**1:** The writer: • does not show characters encountering or resolving a problem or conflict. • does not give details about character or setting. • does have a beginning, middle, or end for story.

complete 0: The writer leaves the page blank or fails to respond to the writing task. The student does not address the topic or simply paraphrases the prompt. The response is illegible or incoherent.

Meeting Individual Needs for Writing

EASY

Summary Have children recall the important events in the story and write a summary of Tomás and the Library Lady. Remind them to include key points and supporting details.

ON-LEVEL

Letter Have children write a letter from Tomás to his friends back in Texas. Remind them to include Tomás's feelings about some situations, and to recount the events Tomás experiences.

CHALLENGE

Newspaper Article Have children write a newspaper article about Tomás and the library lady. Ask them to focus on how the two characters help each other, and how they feel about the library's importance in their community.

Listening and Speaking

LISTENING Have children
- picture the characters and events the speaker is describing.
- imagine themselves in the place of the main character.
- maintain eye contact with the speaker.

SPEAKING Encourage children to
- speak slowly and loudly enough so that everyone can hear.
- show their feelings by varying the volume and tone of their voice.
- use appropriate hand gestures.

LANGUAGE SUPPORT

ESL Have ESL students work with native speakers to create captions for their pictures.

PORTFOLIO Invite children to include their stories or another writing project in their portfolios.

5 Day Grammar and Usage Plan

LANGUAGE SUPPORT

ESL Divide the class into small groups consisting of both ESL and English-proficient children. Give one child a book to hold, another an envelope, another an eraser. Ask children to make a statement beginning with: *He/She is holding a(n)*... Later, ask children to recall whether they used the word *a* or *an* in each case.

DAILY LANGUAGE ACTIVITIES

Write the Daily Language Activities on the chalkboard each day or use **Transparency 27**. Have children orally correct the article (*a, an*) in each sentence.

Day 1

1. Tomás was an boy. a
2. His father was an farmer. a
3. They rode in an car. a

Day 2

1. Tomás read about a animal. an
2. Papá Grande was a old man. an
3. He told an story. a

Day 3

1. The story was about an tree. a
2. The window was like a eye. an
3. They were in a empty library. an

Day 4

1. It was a interesting book. an
2. He met an nice lady. a
3. Tomás sat down with a open book. an

Day 5

1. The lady gave Tomás an hug. a
2. The ball was made from a old toy. an
3. They went on an long trip. a

Daily Language Transparency 27

DAY 1 Introduce the Concept

Oral Warm-Up Write the following on the chalkboard: *I have ____ cold. Does anyone have ____ pen?* Ask children to think of a very short word to put in both blanks.

Introduce Articles Tell children that the word *a* in each sentence is a special adjective called an article. Present:

Articles

- The words *a* and *an* are special adjectives called **articles**.
- Use *a* before a word that begins with a consonant sound.

Present the Daily Language Activity and have children correct the sentences orally. Then have children write a sentence using the article *a*.

WRITING

Assign the daily Writing Prompt on page 282C.

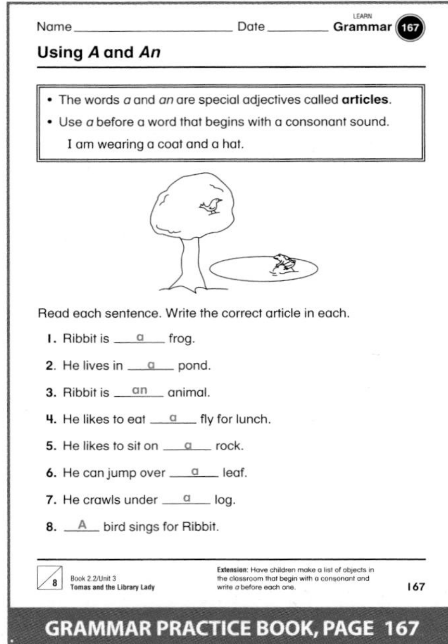
Name ____ Date ____ LEARN Grammar 167

Using *A* and *An*

- The words *a* and *an* are special adjectives called **articles**.
- Use *a* before a word that begins with a consonant sound.

I am wearing a coat and a hat.

Read each sentence. Write the correct article in each.

1. Ribbit is _a_ frog.
2. He lives in _a_ pond.
3. Ribbit is _an_ animal.
4. He likes to eat _a_ fly for lunch.
5. He likes to sit on _a_ rock.
6. He can jump over _a_ leaf.
7. He crawls under _a_ log.
8. _A_ bird sings for Ribbit.

8 Book 2.2/Unit 3 Tomás and the Library Lady

Extension: Have children make a list of objects in the classroom that begin with a consonant and write *a* before each one.

167

GRAMMAR PRACTICE BOOK, PAGE 167

DAY 2 Teach the Concept

Review Articles Remind children that articles are special adjectives and that the article *a* is used before words that begin with consonant sounds. Write the words *egg, book, act,* and *car* on the chalkboard. Have children identify which words begin with consonants and which with vowels.

Introduce *An* Write this sentence on the chalkboard: *I see an ant.* Ask children whether the word *ant* begins with a vowel or a consonant. Present:

Articles

Use *an* before a word that begins with a vowel sound.

Present the Daily Language Activity. Have children write a sentence using the article *an*.

WRITING

Assign the daily Writing Prompt on page 282C.

Name ____ Date ____ LEARN AND PRACTICE Grammar 168

Using Articles

- Use *an* before a word that begins with a vowel sound.

I saw **an** ape eat a banana.

Read the sentences. Write the article that completes each one.

1. The monkey ate (a, an) orange. _an_
2. I ate (a, an) pear. _a_
3. Two children shared (an, a) apple. _an_
4. We had (a, an) box of popcorn. _a_
5. (A, An) usher chewed gum. _An_
6. Jack ate (a, an) sandwich. _a_
7. I wanted (an, a) ice cream cone. _an_
8. Jan had (a, an) banana. _a_

168 **Extension:** Have children make up new sentences using *a* and *an*.

Book 2.2/Unit 3 Tomás and the Library Lady 8

GRAMMAR PRACTICE BOOK, PAGE 168

Using *A* and *An*

DAY 3 Review and Practice

earn from the Literature Review ar-
icles. Read the last sentence on page
88 of *Tomás and the Library Lady:*

> **Then the boys played with a ball Mamá had sewn from an old teddy bear.**

lave children find *a* and *an* in the sen-
ence. Ask: Why is the article *a* used be-
ore the word *ball* and the article *an* used
efore the word *old?*

Vriting Articles Present the Daily
anguage Activity and have children cor-
ect the sentences orally. Have children
ook for *a* and *an* in the sentences on
age 298 of *Tomás and the Library Lady.*
sk children to write each article and the
vord that follows it, circling the first let-
er of the following word.

Assign the daily Writing Prompt on page 282D.

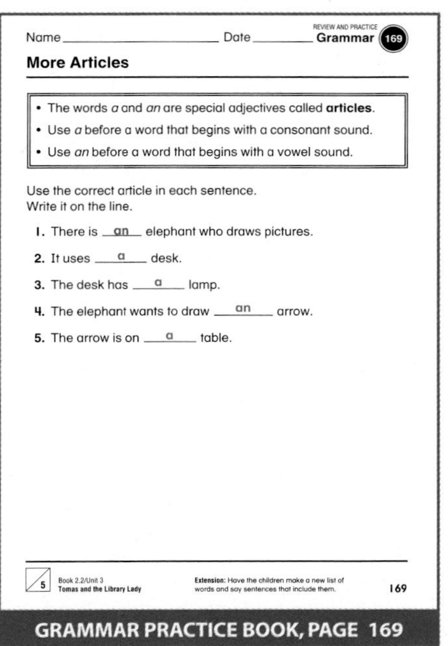
Name ______ Date ______ REVIEW AND PRACTICE Grammar 169

More Articles

- The words *a* and *an* are special adjectives called **articles**.
- Use *a* before a word that begins with a consonant sound.
- Use *an* before a word that begins with a vowel sound.

Use the correct article in each sentence.
Write it on the line.

1. There is __an__ elephant who draws pictures.
2. It uses __a__ desk.
3. The desk has __a__ lamp.
4. The elephant wants to draw __an__ arrow.
5. The arrow is on __a__ table.

5 Book 2.2/Unit 3 Tomas and the Library Lady — **Extension:** Have the children make a new list of words and say sentences that include them. 169

GRAMMAR PRACTICE BOOK, PAGE 169

DAY 4 Review and Practice

Review Articles Have a volunteer put a sentence using the article *a* or *an* on the chalkboard. Have another child identify the article used in the sentence and explain why that particular article was used. Then have children do the Daily Language Activity.

Mechanics and Usage Before children do the daily Writing Prompt on page 282D, review proper nouns. Display and discuss:

Proper Nouns

- A proper noun begins with a capital letter.
- An abbreviation of a person's title begins with a capital letter and ends with a period.

Assign the daily Writing Prompt on page 282D.

Name ______ Date ______ MECHANICS Grammar 170

Using Capital Letters

- A **proper noun** begins with a capital letter.
- An **abbreviation** of a person's title begins with a capital letter and ends with a period.

  Mr. James gave Tom a new basketball.

Read each sentence. Correct it.
Write the correct sentence on the line.

1. mr. and mrs kress live in a apartment next door to my sister jane
   Mr. and Mrs. Kress live in an apartment next door to my sister Jane.
2. mr. kress works with an friend of mine
   Mr. Kress works with a friend of mine.
3. dr. kress is an doctor
   Dr. Kress is a doctor.
4. it seems like the kress family is an part of my family!
   It seems like the Kress family is a part of my family!

170 — Book 2.2/Unit 3 Tomas and the Library Lady 4

GRAMMAR PRACTICE BOOK, PAGE 170

DAY 5 Assess and Reteach

Assess Use the Daily Language Activity and page 171 of the **Grammar Practice Book** for assessment.

Reteach Review the use of the articles *a* and *an* with children. Then collect a variety of objects and put them in a large bag. Include an earring, orange, apple, pen, pencil, and ruler in the bag. Have children take turns reaching into the bag and pulling out an object. Then have them say the sentence *I pulled out a(n)____.* Have children explain why they chose to use the article *a* or *an* in their sentences.

Use Page 172 of the **Grammar Practice Book** for additional reteaching.

Assign the daily Writing Prompt on page 282D.

Name ______ Date ______ TEST Grammar 171

Using *A* and *An*

Which sentence is correct? Mark your answer.

1. ⓐ I bought a ice cream cone.
   ● I bought an ice cream cone.
2. ⓐ I gave my cone to an little boy.
   ● I gave my cone to a little boy.
3. ● The boy had a monkey.
   ⓑ The boy had an monkey.
4. ● The boy had a taste.
   ⓑ The boy had an taste.
5. ⓐ The monkey had an bite.
   ● The monkey had a bite.
6. ● The monkey gave the cone to a zebra.
   ⓑ The monkey gave the cone to an zebra.
7. ⓐ The zebra tossed it to a elephant.
   ● The zebra tossed it to an elephant.
8. ● The elephant put it in a bird cage.
   ⓑ The elephant put it in an bird cage.

8 Book 2.2/Unit 3 Tomas and the Library Lady 171

GRAMMAR PRACTICE BOOK, PAGE 171

GRAMMAR PRACTICE BOOK, 172

5 Day Spelling Plan

LANGUAGE SUPPORT

ESL To help children distinguish between the *sh* and *ch* sounds at the beginning of words, play "Same or Different." Say some pairs of identical words which contain an initial digraph: *ship/ship, chair/chair,* etc. Then say other pairs of words in which the initial digraph is the only difference: *ship/chip, shin/chin,* etc. If the two words are identical, children call out, "Same!" If the words are different, they call out, "Different!"

DICTATION SENTENCES

Spelling Words

1. Can you shift your desk to the left?
2. The chair is broken.
3. I can give the check to her.
4. My shoe is white.
5. The children sleep here.
6. They shared the rice.
7. The star is shining.
8. A snake has a thin shape.
9. I can chase you.
10. My cheek is red.

Challenge Words

11. The desert is dry.
12. I like the evenings.
13. The bell rings at midnight.
14. I have a package for you.
15. The bird is on her shoulder.

DAY 1 Pretest

Assess Prior Knowledge Use the Dictation Sentences at left and **Spelling Practice Book** page 167 for the pretest. Allow children to correct their own papers. If children have trouble, have partners give each other a midweek test on Day 3. Children who require a modified list may be tested on the first five words.

Spelling Words		Challenge Words
1. shift	6. **shared**	11. **desert**
2. **chair**	7. **shining**	12. **evenings**
3. **check**	8. shape	13. **midnight**
4. shoe	9. chase	14. **package**
5. **children**	10. cheek	15. **shoulder**

*Note: Words in **dark type** are from the story.*

Word Study On page 168 of the **Spelling Practice Book** are word study steps and an at-home activity.

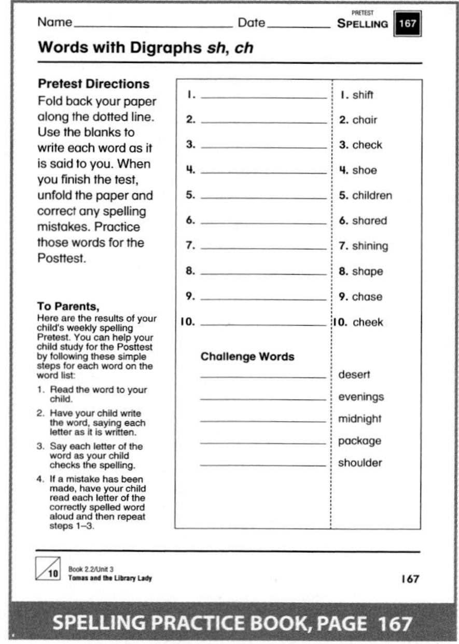

Name______ Date______ PRETEST SPELLING 167

Words with Digraphs *sh*, *ch*

Pretest Directions
Fold back your paper along the dotted line. Use the blanks to write each word as it is said to you. When you finish the test, unfold the paper and correct any spelling mistakes. Practice those words for the Posttest.

1. ______ 1. shift
2. ______ 2. chair
3. ______ 3. check
4. ______ 4. shoe
5. ______ 5. children
6. ______ 6. shared
7. ______ 7. shining
8. ______ 8. shape
9. ______ 9. chase
10. ______ 10. cheek

Challenge Words
______ desert
______ evenings
______ midnight
______ package
______ shoulder

To Parents,
Here are the results of your child's weekly spelling Pretest. You can help your child study for the Posttest by following these simple steps for each word on the word list:
1. Read the word to your child.
2. Have your child write the word, saying each letter as it is written.
3. Say each letter of the word as your child checks the spelling.
4. If a mistake has been made, have your child read each letter of the correctly spelled word aloud and then repeat steps 1–3.

10 Book 2.2/Unit 3 Tomas and the Library Lady 167

SPELLING PRACTICE BOOK, PAGE 167

WORD STUDY STEPS AND ACTIVITY, PAGE 168

DAY 2 Explore the Pattern

Sort and Spell Words Say *shift* and *chair*. Ask children what sound they hear at the beginning of each word. These words contain initial digraphs *sh* and *ch*.

Ask children to read aloud the ten spelling words before sorting them according to sound and spelling pattern.

Words beginning with	
sh	**ch**
shift	chair
shoe	check
shared	children
shining	chase
shape	cheek

Word Wall Have children look through their favorite books at home for new words that begin with the initial consonant sounds *sh* and *ch* and add them to the classroom word wall, underlining the spelling pattern in each word.

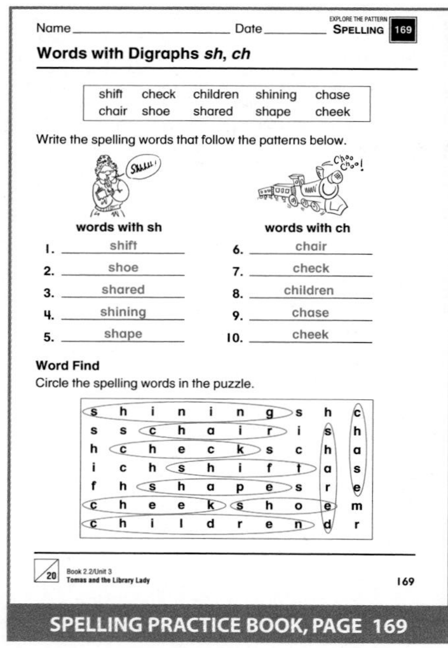

Name______ Date______ EXPLORE THE PATTERN SPELLING 169

Words with Digraphs *sh*, *ch*

shift	check	children	shining	chase
chair	shoe	shared	shape	cheek

Write the spelling words that follow the patterns below.

words with sh	words with ch
1. shift	6. chair
2. shoe	7. check
3. shared	8. children
4. shining	9. chase
5. shape	10. cheek

Word Find
Circle the spelling words in the puzzle.

s	h	i	n	i	n	g	s	h	c
s	s	c	h	a	i	r	i	s	h
h	c	h	e	c	k	s	c	h	a
i	c	h	s	h	i	f	t	a	s
f	h	s	h	a	p	e	s	r	e
c	h	e	e	k	s	h	o	e	m
c	h	i	l	d	r	e	n	d	r

20 Book 2.2/Unit 3 Tomas and the Library Lady 169

SPELLING PRACTICE BOOK, PAGE 169

Words with Digraphs *sh, ch*

DAY 3 Practice and Extend

Vord Meaning: Base Words Write he words *shared* and *shining* on the chalk-oard. Have children try to identify the ase word for each word. (*share, shine*) Ask hem how the spelling of the base word hanged when *-ed* or *-ing* was added. (The was dropped.) Give children other exam-les of inflected forms of verbs and have hem identify the base words.

lossary Have children:

- write each Challenge Word.
- look up the definition of each Challenge Word in the Glossary.
- write a sentence for each Challenge Word.

DAY 4 Proofread and Write

Proofread Sentences Write these sentences on the chalkboard, including the misspelled words. Ask children to proofread, crossing out incorrect spellings and writing the correct spellings. There are two spelling errors in each sentence.

He started to shyft in the chare.
(shift, chair)

The childwren chared the bread.
(children, shared)

Have children create additional sentences with errors for partners to correct.

WRITING **Writing** Have children use as many spelling words as possible in the daily Writing Prompt on page 282D. Remind children to proofread their writing for errors in spelling, grammar, and punctuation.

DAY 5 Assess

Assess Children's Knowledge Use page 172 of the **Spelling Practice Book** or the Dictation Sentences on page 309Q for the posttest.

Personal Word List If children have trouble with any words in the lesson, have them create a personal list of troublesome words in their journals. Have children write simple poems using the words on their lists.

JOURNAL

Name________ Date______ PRACTICE AND EXTEND SPELLING 170

Words with Digraphs *sh, ch*

shift	check	children	shining	chase
chair	shoe	shared	shape	cheek

Answer each question with a spelling word.

1. Who plays with toys? children
2. What can a person sit on? chair
3. What is a part of a face? cheek
4. What does a person wear on each foot? shoe

Action Words
Draw a line to connect each word with an action the word tells about.

5. check — move from place to place
6. chase — make sure
7. shift — build or create something
8. shape — run after

Word Meaning
Write the base word for each of these spelling words. Remember that some words change their spelling when adding **-ed** and **-ing**.

9. shared share
10. shining shine

170 **Challenge Extension:** Have students work in pairs and create riddles using the challenge words. Book 2.2/Unit 3 Tomas and the Library Lady 10

SPELLING PRACTICE BOOK, PAGE 170

Name________ Date______ PROOFREAD AND WRITE SPELLING 171

Words with Digraphs *sh, ch*

Proofreading Activity
There are six spelling mistakes in the report below. Circle each misspelled word. Write the words correctly on the lines below.

Our class took a trip to Noisy Brook. Erin tried to chaise a frog, but she fell and cut her cheak. At lunch, all the shildren shareed their snacks. Bobby lost a shoo in the river. He took it off to see how cold the water was. We were lucky that the sun was shyning.

1. chase 2. cheek 3. children
4. shared 5. shoe 6. shining

Writing Activity
Write sentences about a field trip you would like to take. Use four spelling words in your sentences. Circle the spelling words you use.

10 Book 2.2/Unit 3 Tomas and the Library Lady 171

SPELLING PRACTICE BOOK, PAGE 171

Name________ Date______ POSTTEST SPELLING 172

Words with Digraphs *sh, ch*

Look at the words in each set. One word in each set is spelled correctly. Use a pencil to color in the circle in front of that word. Before you begin, look at the sample sets of words. Sample A has been done for you. Do Sample B by yourself. When you are sure you know what to do, you may go on with the rest of the page.

Sample A
(A) chop
(B) chope
(C) choip
(D) schope

Sample B
(E) yoore
(F) yur
(G) your
(H) yure

1. (A) shayp (B) schape (C) shape (D) shaep
2. (E) children (F) childwrn (G) childrin (H) chilren
3. (A) shifft (B) shifit (C) chift (D) shift
4. (E) chare (F) chaar (G) chair (H) chere
5. (A) check (B) sheck (C) scheck (D) cheke
6. (E) sheek (F) cheek (G) cheak (H) cheke
7. (A) chas (B) chass (C) chase (D) chaes
8. (E) shue (F) schoo (G) shooe (H) shoe
9. (A) shineing (B) shining (C) schining (D) shiening
10. (E) scharred (F) shared (G) shaired (H) shered

172 Book 2.2/Unit 3 Tomas and the Library Lady 10

SPELLING PRACTICE BOOK, PAGE 172

Reaching All Learners

Concept
- Sibling Relationships

Comprehension
- Main Idea

Phonics
- Long *a*; Long *o*

Vocabulary
- cousins
- crowded
- golden
- princess
- restaurant
- world

Anthology

Princess Pooh

Selection Summary **Patty Jean is envious of all the attention her sister gets until she finds out what it's like to have a disability.**

Rhyme applies to phonics

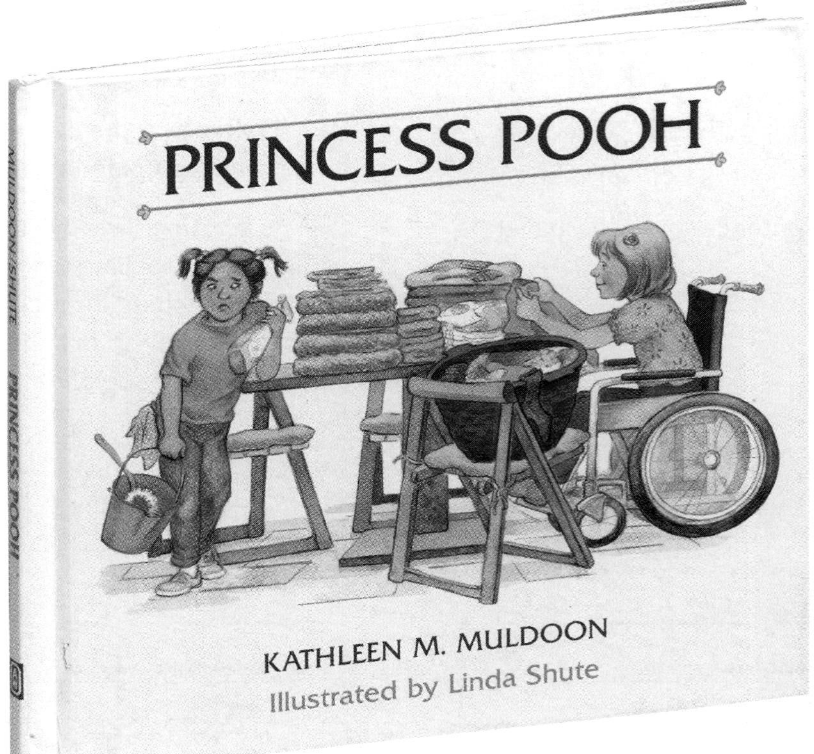

Listening Library

INSTRUCTIONAL pages 312–339

About the Author Kathleen M. Muldoon knows

what it is like to be physically challenged; she has an artificial leg and wears a brace on the other leg. She found that brothers or sisters of a challenged person sometimes felt pushed aside. She decided to write a story from the sister's point of view.

About the Illustrator Linda Shute says that the voice of Patty Jean made her want to create the pictures for *Princess Pooh*. "She sounded like a spunky, funny, and thoughtful person. I felt the story was as much about being sisters as about using a wheelchair, and I tried to show that in my pictures."

Same Concept, Skills and Vocabulary!

Leveled Books

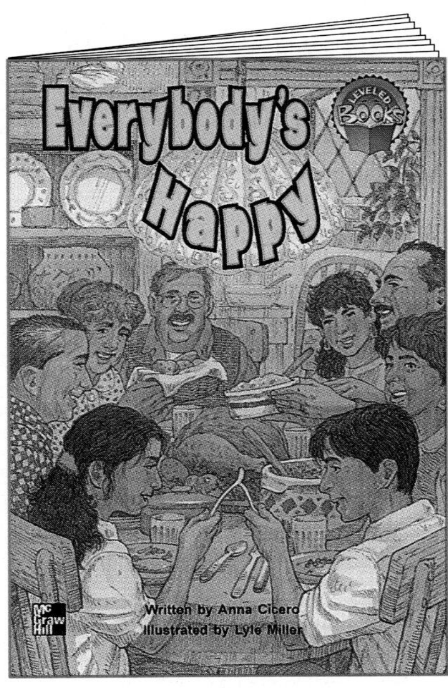

EASY
Lesson on pages 339A and 339D

DECODABLE

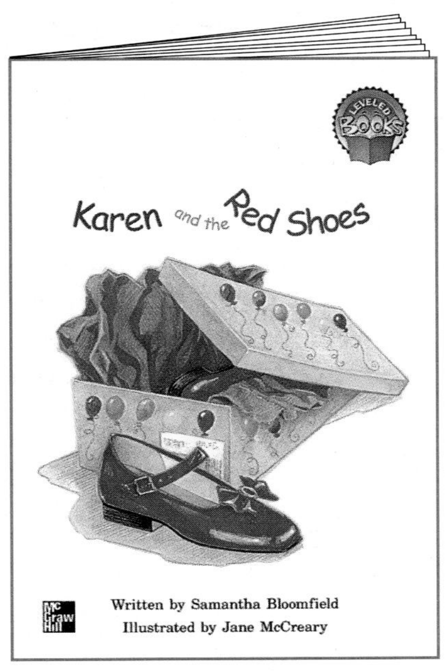

INDEPENDENT
Lesson on pages 339B and 339D

Take-Home version available

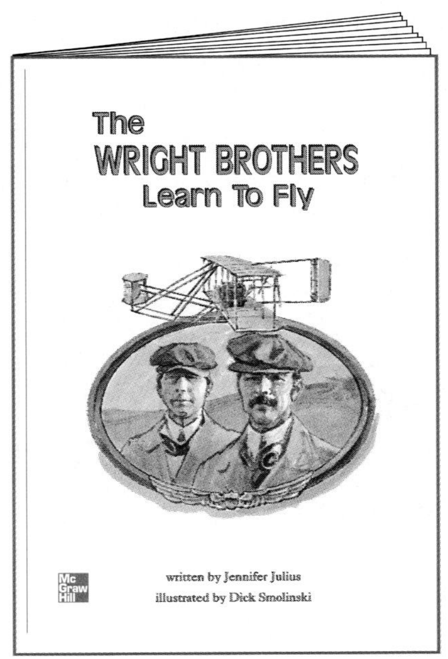

CHALLENGE
Lesson on pages 339C and 339D

Leveled Practice

EASY
Reteach, 227–234 Blackline masters with reteaching opportunities for each assessed skill

INDEPENDENT/ON-LEVEL
Practice, 227–234 Workbook with Take-Home stories and practice opportunities for each assessed skill and story comprehension

CHALLENGE
Extend, 227–234 Blackline masters that offer challenge activities for each assessed skill

Quizzes Prepared by 

WORKSTATION Activities

Social Studies . . . Who Helps?, *320*
Science . . . . An Inventor's Life, *330*
Math . . . . Finding the Space, *322*
Art . . . . Illustrate a Feeling, *314*
Language Arts . . Read Aloud, *310E*
Writing . . . . Write Penelope's Story, *336*
Cultural Perspectives . . . . . Going Far, *328*
Research and Inquiry . . . . . . Find Out More, *337*

Internet Activities . . . . www.mhschool.com/reading

Suggested Lesson Planner

READING AND LANGUAGE ARTS	DAY 1 Focus on Reading and Skills	DAY 2 Read the Literatur
Phonics Daily Routines	Daily Phonics Routine: **Segmenting,** 310H Phonics CD-ROM	Daily Phonics Routine: **Blending,** 312A Phonics CD-ROM
Phonological Awareness Phonics *Long a, o* Comprehension Vocabulary Study Skills Listening, Speaking, Viewing, Representing	**Read Aloud: Poem,** 310E "ME I AM!" ☑ **Develop Phonological Awareness,** 310F Long *a, o* ☑ **Review Long *a, o*,** 310G–310H **Teaching Chart 190** **Reteach, Practice, Extend,** 227 **Phonics/Phonemic Awareness Practice Book,** 143–146 Read **Apply Long *a, o*,** 310/311 "Little Sister" Intervention Program	**Build Background,** 312A Develop Oral Language **Vocabulary,** 312B–312C ***cousins*** ***golden*** ***restaurant*** ***crowded*** ***princess*** ***world*** **Word Building Manipulative Card** **Teaching Chart 191** **Reteach, Practice, Extend,** 228 Read **Read the Selection,** 312–335 Comprehension ☑ **Long *a, o*** ☑ **Main Idea** **Genre:** Realistic Fiction, 313 **Writer's Craft:** Figurative Language, 3 **Cultural Perspectives,** 328 Intervention Program
Curriculum Connections	Link **Language Arts,** 310E	Link **Social Studies,** 312A
Writing	**Writing Prompt:** Have you ever wanted to be someone else? What made you want to be like that person?	**Writing Prompt:** Everyone gets a little bit jealous sometimes. Describe a tim when you were jealous of a close friend or relative. What did he or she have or do that you didn't? **Journal Writing** Quick-Write, 335
Grammar	**Introduce the Concept: Adjectives That Compare,** 339O Daily Language Activity: Write adjectives that compare correctly. **Grammar Practice Book,** 173	**Teach the Concept: Adjectives That Compare,** 339O Daily Language Activity: Write adje tives that compare correctly. **Grammar Practice Book,** 174
Spelling *th, sh*	**Pretest: Words with Digraphs *th, sh*,** 339Q **Spelling Practice Book,** 173,174	**Explore the Pattern: Words with Digraphs *th, sh*,** 339Q **Spelling Practice Book,** 175

 **Intervention Program Available**

Meeting Individual Needs

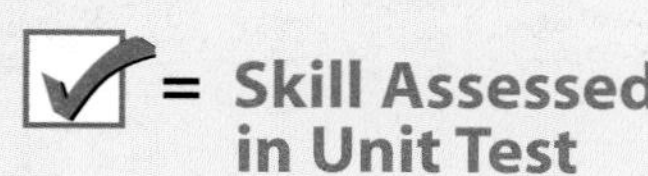
= Skill Assessed in Unit Test

Intervention Program Available

DAY 3 Read the Literature

Daily Phonics Routine:
Letter Substitution, 337

CD-ROM

Rereading for Fluency, 334

Story Questions and Activities, 336–337
Reteach, Practice, Extend, 229

Study Skill, 338
Library/Media Center
Teaching Chart 192
Reteach, Practice, Extend, 230

Test Power, 339

Read the Leveled Books, 339A–339D
Guided Reading
Long *a, o*
Main Idea
Instructional Vocabulary

Intervention Program

Art, 314; Social Studies, 320

Writing Prompt: What is the nicest thing you ever made or did for a relative? Tell what it was and why you did it.

Writing a Story, 339M
Prewrite, Draft

Review and Practice: Adjectives That Compare, 339P
Daily Language Activity: Write adjectives that compare correctly.
Grammar Practice Book, 175

Practice and Extend: Words with Digraphs *th, sh,* 339R
Spelling Practice Book, 176

DAY 4 Build Skills

Daily Phonics Routine:
Fluency, 339F

CD-ROM

Read the Leveled Books and the Self-Selected Books

Review Long *a, o,* 339E–339F
Teaching Chart 193
Reteach, Practice, Extend, 231
Language Support, 249
Phonics/Phonemic Awareness Practice Book, 143–146

Review Long *a, o, e, i; tch, ch,* 339G–339H
Teaching Chart 194
Reteach, Practice, Extend, 232
Language Support, 250
Phonics/Phonemic Awareness Practice Book, 143–146

Minilessons, 317, 323, 333

Intervention Program

Math, 322

Writing Prompt: Write a funny story about a brother and sister who always want what the other one has. Make sure to include a solution to their problem.

Writing a Story, 339M
Revise

Meeting Individual Needs for Writing, 339N

Review and Practice: Adjectives That Compare, 339P
Daily Language Activity: Write adjectives that compare correctly.
Grammar Practice Book, 176

Proofread and Write: Words with Digraphs *th, sh,* 339R
Spelling Practice Book, 177

DAY 5 Build Skills

Daily Phonics Routine:
Writing, 339H

CD-ROM

Read Self-Selected Books

Review Form Generalizations, 339I–339J
Teaching Chart 195
Reteach, Practice, Extend, 233
Language Support, 251

Introduce Figurative Language, 339K–339L
Teaching Chart 196
Reteach, Practice, Extend, 234
Language Support, 252

Listening, Speaking, Viewing, Representing, 339N

Minilessons, 317, 323, 333

Intervention Program

Science, 330

Writing Prompt: Your brother didn't want to play with you, now he does. Compare how you feel now with how you felt before.

Writing a Story, 339M
Edit/Proofread, Publish

Assess and Reteach: Adjectives That Compare, 371P
Daily Language Activity: Write adjectives that compare correctly.
Grammar Practice Book, 177, 178

Assess and Reteach: Words with Digraphs *th, sh,* 371R
Spelling Practice Book, 178

Language Arts

Read Aloud

ME I AM!

a poem by Jack Prelutsky

I am the only ME I AM
who qualifies as me;
no ME I AM has been before
and none will ever be.

No other ME I AM can feel
the feelings I've within;
no other ME I AM can fit
precisely in my skin.

There is no other ME I AM
who thinks the thoughts I do;
the world contains one ME I AM,
there is no room for two.

I am the only ME I AM
this earth shall ever see;
that ME I AM I always am
is no one else but ME!

Oral Comprehension

LISTENING AND SPEAKING Read aloud the poem. When you have finished, ask, *Did the author use a first-person or a third-person point of view?* Then ask, *Which words in the poem helped you understand this?* Remind children to look for the author's point-of-view in other poems and stories they read.

GENRE STUDY: POETRY Discuss the literary devices and techniques used in "ME I AM!"

- Remind children that many people write poems to express how they feel. Ask, *How does the author feel about himself? Does he think he is better than everyone else, or does he think everyone is special? How do you know?*
- Reread the poem and have children raise their hands when they hear rhyming words. Remind children that not all poems have a consistent rhyme scheme.
- Invite children to compare "ME I AM!" to last week's poem, "The Library." Ask children which poem they liked best. Invite children to share other poems that they know.

Activity Encourage children to create self-portraits. Have them use photographs of themselves or look into mirrors as references for their portraits. Then have them write a poem about themselves. They can paste the poem and the portrait together on a large piece of construction paper. ▶ **Visual/Linguistic**

Develop Phonological Awareness

Blend Sounds

Phonemic Awareness

MATERIALS
- models or photos of transportation

Teach Tell children they will play "Guess the Category." Say: /t/-/r/-/ā/-/n/. Have children guess the word by putting the sounds together. Do the same with *car* and *boat*. Then ask children if they can guess the category of words. (transportation)

Practice Use these categories and words to get started: weather: *rain, snow, wind*; body parts: *brain, toe, foot*; clothing: *coat, cap, shoe*.

Segment Sounds

Phonemic Awareness

Teach Invite children to listen closely as you say a rhyme. Say: *Listen, listen to this word; tell me all the sounds you heard: soak*. Say /s/-/ō/-/k/ and continue the rest of the rhyme: */s/ is one sound /ō/ is two /k/ is the last sound it is true. That's three!"*

Practice Say the rhyme again and have volunteers say the sounds for these words: *maid, chain, phone, fight, bye, grown, page, days,* and *black*.

Substitute Sounds

Phonemic Awareness

MATERIALS
- colored blocks

Teach Place a set of green blocks side by side and say: *These blocks show /b/-/ā/-/l/. Bail has three sounds. Now I want them to show /b/-/ā/-/t/.* (bait) Replace the third green block with a red one. Ask: *What sound changed?* (the last sound) Continue with *base/bake*.

Practice Have children use the colored blocks to substitute initial,middle, and final sounds for the following sets of words: *hail/tail, coal/coach, lean/loan, night/right, mean/mane, pail/pill, raid/read*.

Observe children as they blend, segment, and substitute sounds. If children have difficulty, see Alternate Teaching Strategies on p. T72.

Review Long *a, o*

OBJECTIVES

Children will:

- identify /ā/*ai, ay*.
- identify /ō/*oa, oe, ow*.
- decode and read words with long *a* and long *o* sounds.

MATERIALS

- **Teaching Chart 190**
- word building boxes from the **Word Building Manipulative Cards**

Long *o*

Introduce	B1: 92G-H
Review	B1: 113E-F, 113G-H; B2: 339E-F, 339G-H
Test	B1: Unit 1

SPELLING/PHONICS CONNECTIONS

See 5-Day Spelling Plan, pages 339Q–339R.

TEACHING TIP

PRONUNCIATION Point out that *ow* can represent either /ō/, as in *grow* and *follow*, or /ou/, as in *town* and *how*. In some words, like *bow*, the *ow* is pronounced /ō/ for one meaning and /ou/ for a different meaning.

PREPARE

Review *ai* and *ay* for the Sound /ā/ and *oa, oe,* and *ow* for the Sound /ō/

Remind children that they know several letter combinations that make the long *a* sound: *ai* and *ay*. They also know several letter combinations that make the long *o* sound: *oa, oe,* and *ow*.

TEACH

BLENDING Model and Guide Practice with Long *a* and Long *o* Words

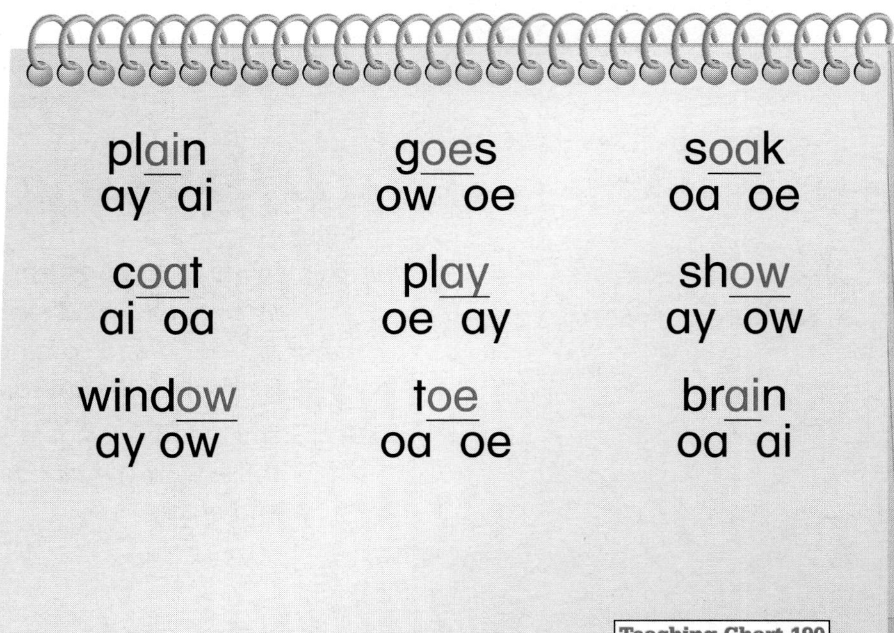

Display **Teaching Chart 190**, encouraging children to notice that there are two answer choices for each example.

Write the letters *ai* on the blank space in the first example. Blend the sounds together to read the word *plain*. Repeat, having children read the word with you.

Use the Word in Context

Have volunteers use the word in a sentence to reinforce its meaning. Example: *I want to eat something plain, not fancy.*

Repeat the Procedure

Repeat the same procedure for the rest of the words.

PRACTICE

WORD BUILDING
Building /ā/ Words and /ō/ Words

Have partners brainstorm other words with long *o* (*oe, oa, ow*) and long *a* (*ai, ay*). Have children choose two words for each vowel spelling to put on a word wall under long *a* and long *o*. Children should read the words they choose to check their sorting. ▶**Auditory/Linguistic**

ASSESS/CLOSE

Using /ā/ and /ō/ Words in Sentences

To assess children's ability to build and decode /ā/ and /ō/ words, observe their work on the Practice activity. Ask each child to write and read aloud a sentence using two to three words from the chart. Then have children read the phonics rhyme on page 311 in their books.

ADDITIONAL PHONICS RESOURCES

Phonics/ Phonemic Awareness Practice Book, pages 143–146

Phonics CD-ROM activities for practice with Discriminating and Word Building

Daily Routines

DAY 1 **Segmenting** Distribute word building boxes. Say an *ai, ay, oa, oe,* and *ow* word aloud. Have children write the spelling of each sound in the appropriate box. (Examples: *plain, stay, coat, toe,* and *snow*.)

DAY 2 **Blending** Write the spelling of each sound in *rainbow* as you say it. Have children repeat after you. Ask children to blend the sounds to read the word. Repeat using the words *sailboat* and *raincoat*.

DAY 3 **Letter Substitution** Have small groups pass around a paper, starting with the word *may* and changing the spelling of one sound to create new words such as *mow, bow, boat, coat.* (Save lists for Day 4 Activity.)

DAY 4 **Fluency** Using the lists the children made on Day 3, write the words on the chalkboard. Point to each word, asking children to blend the sounds silently. Ask a volunteer to read aloud each word.

DAY 5 **Writing** Have children write riddles using /ā/ and /ō/ words, then trade with partners to read aloud and answer. Ask children to underline letters that spell /ā/ and /ō/.

Meeting Individual Needs for Phonics

EASY

Name________ Date________ Reteach 227

Long *a*, *o*

Read the following sentences
It is **rainy** every **day**.
I caught my **toe** in the **window** on the **boat**.

Circle the words that have the same long **a** or long **o** sound in each sentence. Then write the words.

1. The man wears a coat in his boat. — coat, boat
2. Molly sees the rainbow through the window. — rainbow, window
3. I hit my toe with the hoe. — toe, hoe
4. There are rains on the plains. — rains, plains
5. Do you know the people in the show? — know, show
6. Every day in May was sunny. — day, May

6 Book 2.3/Unit 3 **Princess Pooh** **At Home:** Have children write a sentence that uses two of the words they circled. 227

Reteach, 227

ON-LEVEL

Name________ Date________ Practice 227

Long *a*, *o*

Complete each sentence with a word from the box below.

show yellow plain raincoat way day maid toes

1. Could you ___show___ me the picture?
2. Polly knows the ___way___ across the lake .
3. Henry colors the sun ___yellow___.
4. The ___maid___ cleaned the room.
5. I wear my ___raincoat___ when it rains.
6. May said that her fingers and ___toes___ were cold.
7. Sue wore a ___plain___ dress to the party.
8. Today is a sunny ___day___.

8 Book 2.2/Unit 3 **Princess Pooh** **At Home:** Ask children to think of more words that contain the sounds of long **a** spelled **ai**, **ay** and long **o**, spelled **oa**, **oe**, and **ow**. 227

Practice, 227

CHALLENGE

Name________ Date________ Extend 227

Long *a*, *o*

Read the story. Circle all the words with the **long a** sound. Underline all the words with the **long o** sound.

Play Today

There is no school today. I am ready to play. I look out the window and see the rain. I put on my plain yellow raincoat and run next door. My friend knows that I am on my way. We play a game.

Which word has both **long a** and **long o** sounds?
___raincoat___

Use the word in a sentence.
___Possible answer: The raincoat kept me dry.___

Book 2.2/Unit 3 **Princess Pooh** **At Home:** Have children draw a picture of a rainy day scene. Label the picture with two sentences using **long a** and **long o** words. 227

Extend, 227

OBJECTIVES

Children will decode and read words with long *a* and long *o* sounds.

Apply Long *a* and Long *o*

Little Sister

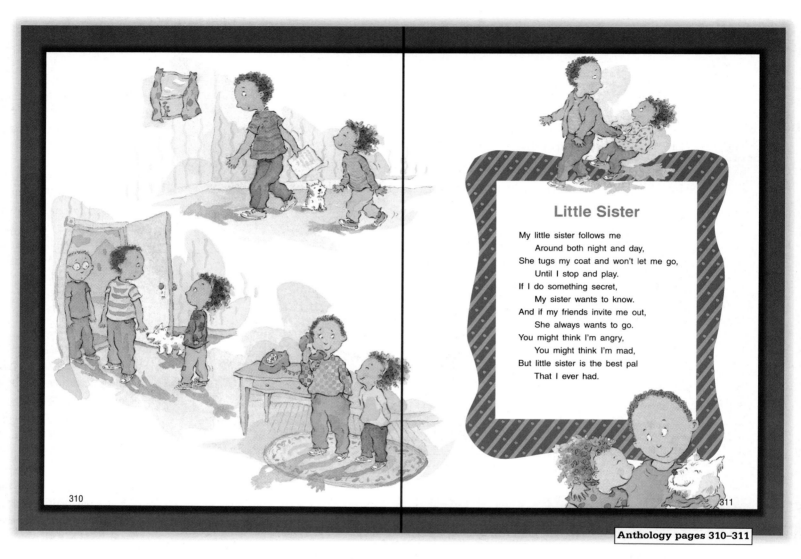

My little sister follows me
  Around both night and day,
She tugs my coat and won't let me go,
  Until I stop and play.
If I do something secret,
  My sister wants to know.
And if my friends invite me out,
  She always wants to go.
You might think I'm angry,
  You might think I'm mad,
But little sister is the best pal
  That I ever had.

310

311

Anthology pages 310–311

Read and Build Fluency

READ THE POEM Tell children they will now hear a poem called "Little Sister." Have them listen to an audio recording of the poem being read as they follow along in their books. Encourage children to listen for the long *a* and long *o* vowel sounds. As an auditory model, play the recording several times. Finally, invite children to engage in a shared reading with you.

PARTNERS **REREAD FOR FLUENCY** Have pairs of children take turns listening to the audio recording of the poem. One partner may track the print while the other uses gestures to simulate the action and emotion of the poem while reading.

Dictate and Spell

JOURNAL **DICTATE WORDS** Say the long *a* word *day*. Segment the word into its individual parts. Repeat the word and say it in a sentence, such as, "Every day I brush my teeth." After children repeat the word aloud, have them write the word, making sure they have a letter or letters for each sound. Continue with other long *a* and long *o* words, such as *play* and *coat*. Then use words not from the poem, such as *plain* and *toe*.

Intervention **Skills Intervention Guide,** for direct instruction and extra practice of long *a* and long *o*

Build Background

Concept: Sibling Relationships

Evaluate Prior Knowledge

CONCEPT: SIBLING RELATIONSHIPS
sk children to describe their relationships ith siblings. Are they friends with their rothers and sisters? Do they help each ther? What is fun about having siblings? /hat is frustrating? Children who do not ave siblings can discuss other family mem- ers or close friends, and share what it is like be an only child.

IAKE A SIBLING WORD WEB Work ith children to make a web of words that escribes siblings and expresses feelings bout having siblings, or being an only child. ncourage inclusion of a variety of feelings.
▸ Linguistic

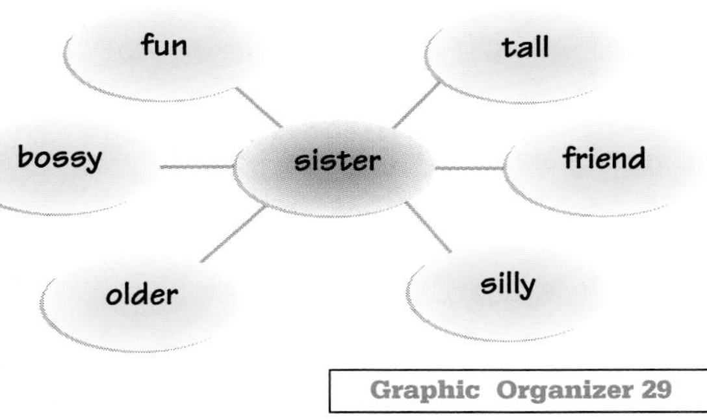

Graphic Organizer 29

RAW A PICTURE Invite children to draw pictures of themselves with a sibling or close friend, doing omething together. Have each child write entences describing who is in the picture nd what they are doing.
WRITING ONE

Develop Oral Language

CONNECT WORDS AND ACTIONS
ESL Have each child act out and describe an activity he or she has done with a sibling or close friend. Prompt childrens' descriptions with questions such as:

- Did you and your friend share something?
- Did you and your brother have fun that day?
- Did you and your sister help each other?

▶ Kinesthetic

Anthology and Leveled Books

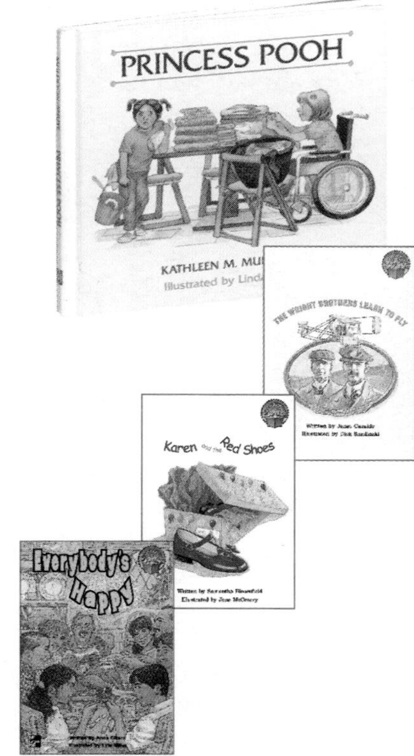

DAILY Phonics ROUTINES

DAY 2 **Blending** Write the spelling of each sound in *rainbow* as you say it. Have children repeat after you. Ask children to blend the sounds to read the word. Repeat using the words *sailboat* and *raincoat*.

 Phonics CD-ROM

LANGUAGE SUPPORT

Use the **Language Support Book, pages 244–247,** to help build background.

OBJECTIVES

Children will use context and structural clues to determine the meanings of vocabulary words.

Definitions

princess (p. 314) daughter of a king or queen

golden (p. 324) made of gold, gold-colored; bright or shining

world (p. 314) Earth

cousins (p. 317) children of one's aunt or uncle

restaurant (p. 322) a place where food is prepared and served to customers

crowded (p. 328) gathered closely, or in large numbers

Story Words

These words from the selection may be unfamiliar. Before children read, have them check the meanings and pronunciations of the words in the Glossary, beginning on page 390, or in a dictionary.

- throne, p. 314
- servant, p. 316
- hammock, p. 322
- therapy, p. 322
- wheelchair, p. 332

princess
golden
world
cousins
restaurant
crowded

Vocabulary

Teach Vocabulary in Context

Identify Vocabulary Words Display **Teaching Chart 191** and read passage with children. Have volunteers circle each vocabulary word and underline other words that are clues to its meaning.

Penny the Princess

1. Patty Jean calls her sister Penny a princess because she seems to rule over everyone like royalty. **2.** Their mom says Penny's hair is shining and golden like a crown, but Patty Jean thinks it is just brownish-yellow. **3.** Patty Jean feels that everybody treats her sister as if she were the most important girl in the whole world. **4.** Their aunts, uncles, cousins, and other family always make a fuss over Penny. **5.** Sometimes they take her out to eat at her favorite restaurant. **6.** Last time they went, there were many people crowded around the door waiting to get in.

Teaching Chart 191

Discuss Meanings Ask questions like these to help clarify word meanings:

- What would you call the daughter of a king and queen?
- If something is golden, is it silvery, or yellowish?
- Is someone famous if the whole world knows who he or she is?
- What do you call your aunts' and uncles' children?
- What do you call a business that makes and serves food?
- When people are all crowded together, do they have a lot of room?

Practice

Find the Word

GROUP

Instruct children to take out their vocabulary cards. Read aloud **Teaching Chart 191**, leaving out vocabulary words. Ask children to hold up the vocabulary card for the missing word in each sentence, and to say the word as they display the card.
▶ **Linguistic/Oral/Kinesthetic**

Word Building Manipulative Cards

Write Captions

PARTNERS

WRITING

Have children draw pictures to illustrate vocabulary words. Then, for each picture, have them write a caption that uses the vocabulary word depicted. ▶ **Linguistic/Spatial**

Assess Vocabulary

Identify Word Meaning in Context

PARTNERS

WRITING

Invite children to write sentences for four of the vocabulary words. Ask them to include and underline context clues for each vocabulary word, but to leave a blank space where the word would go. Then ask each child to trade sentences with a partner and determine the missing words.

SPELLING/PHONICS CONNECTIONS

See Spelling Challenge Words, pages 339Q–339R.

LANGUAGE SUPPORT

See the Language Support Book, pages 244–247, for teaching suggestions for Vocabulary.

Provides vocabulary activities.

Meeting Individual Needs for Vocabulary

EASY

Name_______________ Date_______ Reteach 228

Vocabulary

Read the sentences. The underlined words are definitions of the words in the box. Write the word under its definition.

cousins	crowded	golden	princess	restaurant	world

1. The room was full of people. — crowded
2. We saw a movie about the daughter of a king and queen. — princess
3. All the tables were taken at the place to eat. — restaurant
4. The sun was a yellow-colored ball. — golden
5. Two of my aunt and uncle's children came to see me. — cousins
6. Millions of people live around the Earth. — world

228 At Home: Have children draw a picture that illustrates two of the vocabulary words. Book 2.2/Unit 3 Princess Pooh 6

Reteach, 228

ON-LEVEL

Name_______________ Date_______ Practice 228

Vocabulary

Read the words in the box. Read the clues. Write the correct word on the line below each clue.

cousins	crowded	golden	princess	restaurant	world

1. This person might sit on a throne. — princess
2. We like to go here when we're hungry. — restaurant
3. These are people in your family you might visit. — cousins
4. During a big sale, a store might be like this. — crowded
5. A king might wear a crown this color. — golden
6. You might fly around this in a plane someday. — world

228 At Home: Have children make up new riddles for the vocabulary words. Book 2.2/Unit 3 Princess Pooh 6

Practice, 228

ON-LEVEL

The Princess With a Heart

Everyone asked the prince, "Why not Rita? She has long, beautiful hair." He said, "I want someone who can see outside her window."

"What could he mean?" asked Rita. One day she left the mirror and looked out her window. Since that day Rita stopped looking in the mirror.

One day she saw a prince below her window. Soon they were married!

At Home: Have children write the next page for this book. Suggest they begin by telling what happened next to Princess Rita.

4 228a

Practice, 228a
Take-Home Story

CHALLENGE

Name_______________ Date_______ Extend 228

Vocabulary

cousins	crowded	golden
princess	restaurant	world

Choose words to match each clue. Fill in the puzzle.

Across
1. The children of your uncle or aunt.
2. Yellow and bright.
5. A place where people pay to eat meals.

Down
1. Filled with a lot of people packed together.
3. The daughter of a king or queen.
4. The earth.

	[1]C	O	U	S	I	N	S		
	R								
[2]G	O	L	D	E	N			[3]P	
	W					[4]W		R	
	D					O		I	
[5]R	E	S	T	A	U	R	A	N	T
	D					L		C	
						D		E	
								S	
								S	

Write a sentence using three of the words from the box.
Answers could include: The restaurant was crowded with my cousins.

228 At Home: Challenge children to draw and label a picture that illustrates all the words from the puzzle. Book 2.2/Unit 3 Princess Pooh

Extend, 228

Comprehension

Prereading Strategies

PREVIEW AND PREDICT Have children take a **picture walk** through the illustrations, looking for clues about plot and characters.

- What might this story be about?
- What information do the pictures give about the two girls in the story?
- Is this a realistic story, or a fable? How can you tell? (The characters and surroundings look real.) ***Genre***

Have children record their predictions about the story's characters and plot.

PREDICTIONS	WHAT HAPPENED
The younger girl is jealous of the girl in the wheelchair.	
The younger girl takes the wheelchair.	

SET PURPOSES Ask children what they want to learn from reading the story. For example:

- Who is "Princess Pooh"?
- Why is the girl jealous of her sister?

Meeting Individual Needs • Grouping Suggestions for Strategic Reading

EASY

Read Together Read the story aloud with children or have them use the **Listening Library**. As you read, model for children the strategy of using their own experiences with siblings in order to understand the main idea of the story.

ON-LEVEL

Guided Instruction Before reading the story with the class, you may want to have children read the story first on their own. Monitor any difficulties in reading the children may have in order to determine which Comprehension prompts may be most useful.

CHALLENGE

Read Independently Remind children that identifying the main idea of the story and looking for supporting details will help them understand the story. After reading, have children sum up the story in their own words. Discuss the main ideas, and invite children to point out supporting details.

Princess Pooh

313

Comprehension

Phonics Apply Long *a, o*

Apply Main Idea

STRATEGIC READING The most important message of a story or passage is its main idea. Supporting details help us to understand the main idea. Before we begin reading, let's prepare a Main Idea/Supporting Details chart so we can write down story notes.

MAIN IDEA	SUPPORTING DETAILS

1 How would you describe the two characters pictured on these pages? (The younger girl looks angry. The girl folding laundry looks like she is enjoying herself.) *Make Inferences*

LANGUAGE SUPPORT

A blackline master of the Main Idea and Supporting Details chart is available in the **Language Support Book.**

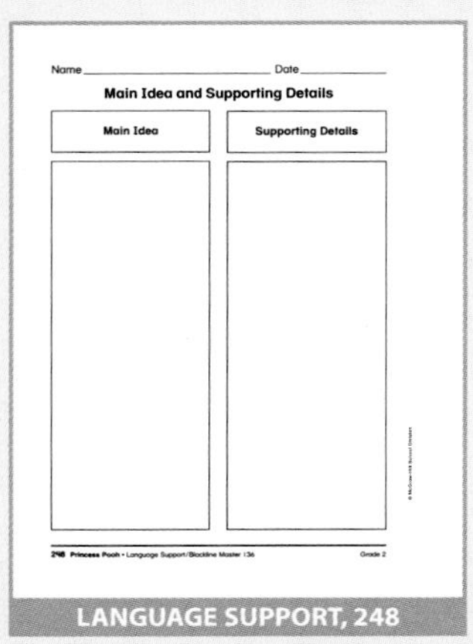

Name_______________ Date_______

Main Idea and Supporting Details

Main Idea	Supporting Details

LANGUAGE SUPPORT, 248

Genre

Realistic Fiction

Review with children that realistic fiction:

- depicts events, characters, and settings that could actually exist.
- has a setting that depends on the plot.
- has characters that experience believable emotions.

Activity After children read *Princess Pooh*, challenge them to compare this realistic fiction selection to the fictional fantasy *Best Wishes, Ed*. Encourage volunteers to compare and contrast animals and humans as main characters, and to analyze what plot events in both selections could and could not really happen.

Comprehension

2 **MAIN IDEA** What is the main idea, or most important point, on the story's first page?

MODEL I know from reading the first page that the girl thinks her sister tells everybody what to do. I think the main idea of this page is that the girl thinks her sister is bossy and spoiled.

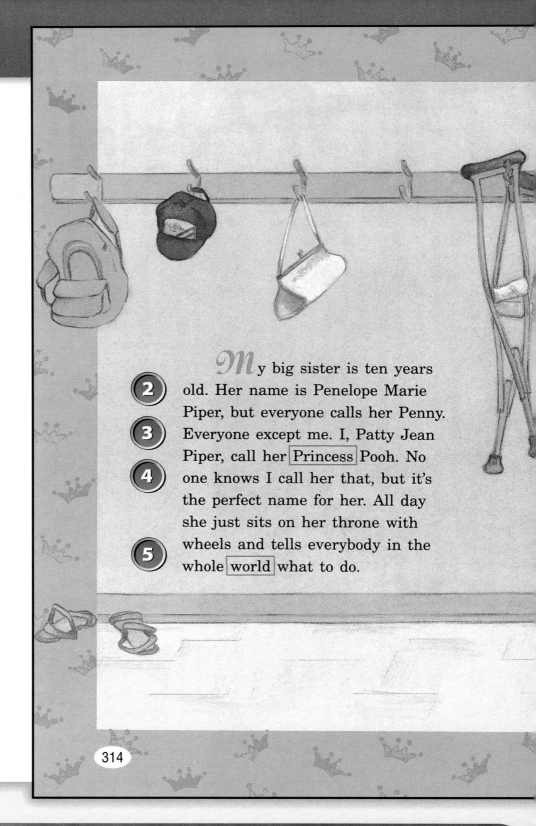

2 My big sister is ten years old. Her name is Penelope Marie Piper, but everyone calls her Penny.
3 Everyone except me. I, Patty Jean Piper, call her Princess Pooh. No
4 one knows I call her that, but it's the perfect name for her. All day she just sits on her throne with
5 wheels and tells everybody in the whole world what to do.

314

Cross Curricular: Art

ILLUSTRATE A FEELING Invite children to illustrate a situation or event that made them feel a strong emotion. For example, have they ever won a race or a contest? Encourage children to make a list of important events in their life and then choose one to draw. Ask them to put themselves into the picture. Ask children to describe their scenes and explain why they felt the way they did.

Comprehension

3 Patty Jean says she has a nickname for her sister, but she doesn't tell it to anyone. Why do you think she keeps it a secret? (The name makes fun of her sister.) ***Make Inferences***

4 Patty Jean says Penny sits on a throne with wheels. What does she mean? What are some clues that help you to figure this out? (The picture shows Penny sitting in a wheelchair.) ***Draw Conclusions***

5 **Phonics** **LONG *a*** Look at the word *day* on page 314. Let's read it aloud. What vowel sound do you hear? (long *a*) How is it spelled? (*ay*) ***Graphophonic Cues***

Comprehension

6 Does Patty Jean enjoy going to the mall with her family? (no) What bothers her about it? (Her sister gets wheeled around, while Patty Jean carries packages.)
Make Inferences

7 When Patty Jean compares her sister to a flower, she is using figurative language. Why might Patty Jean think of her sister as a flower and herself as a weed? (She feels Penny is more appreciated by her family like a flower would be more appreciated than a weed.) Imagine you are Patty Jean. Can you think of other ways to compare yourself to your sister using figurative language.
Figurative Language

TEACHING TIP

ANALYZE CHARACTER As students read, point out that one way to understand what a character is going through or feeling is to compare that character's life with their own lives. Like Patty Jean, have they been in a situation in which they felt like somebody else was getting all the attention? How did they feel? What did they decide to do to solve the problem?

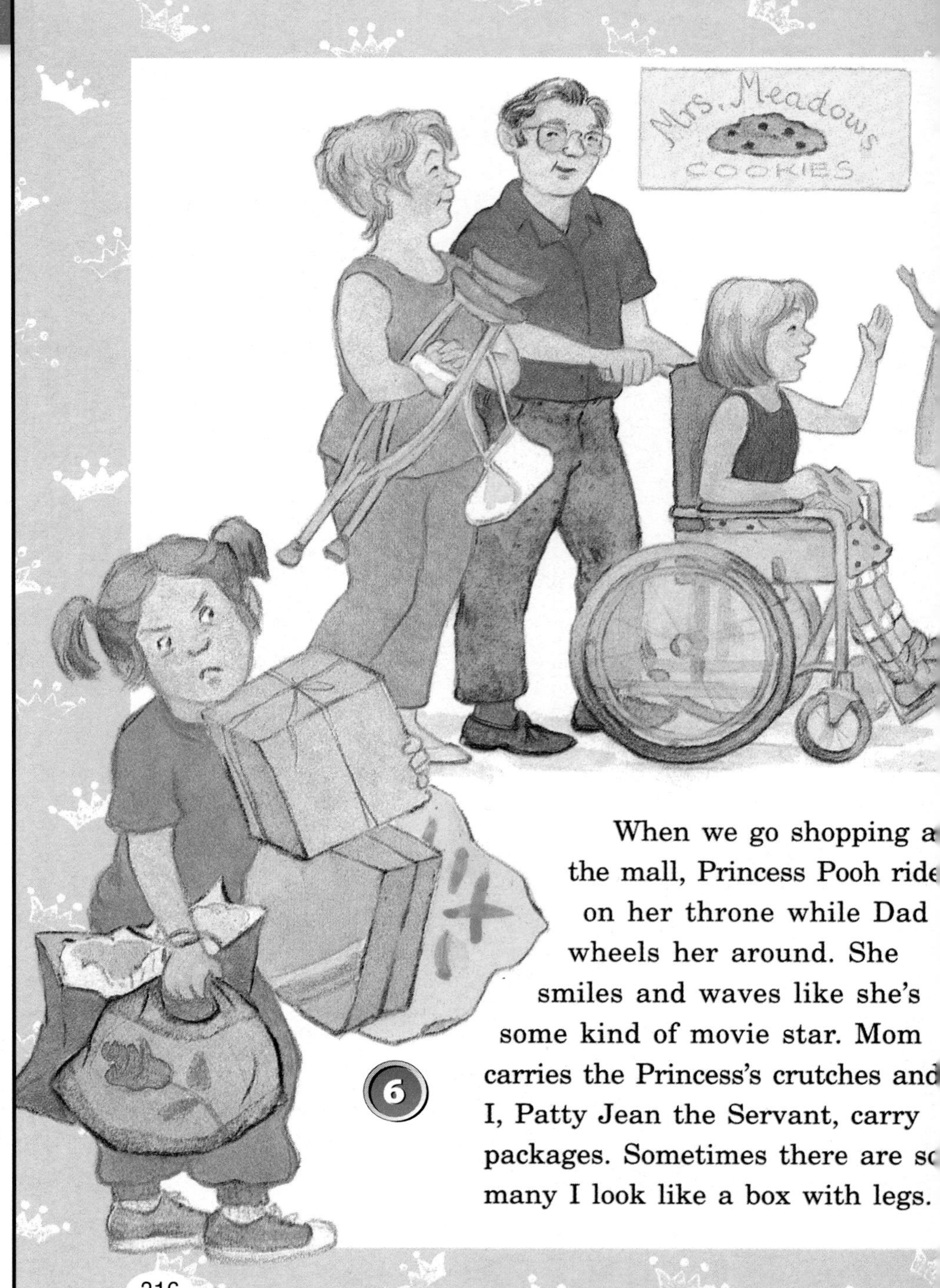

When we go shopping a
the mall, Princess Pooh ride
on her throne while Dad
wheels her around. She
smiles and waves like she's
some kind of movie star. Mom
6 carries the Princess's crutches and
I, Patty Jean the Servant, carry
packages. Sometimes there are so
many I look like a box with legs.

316

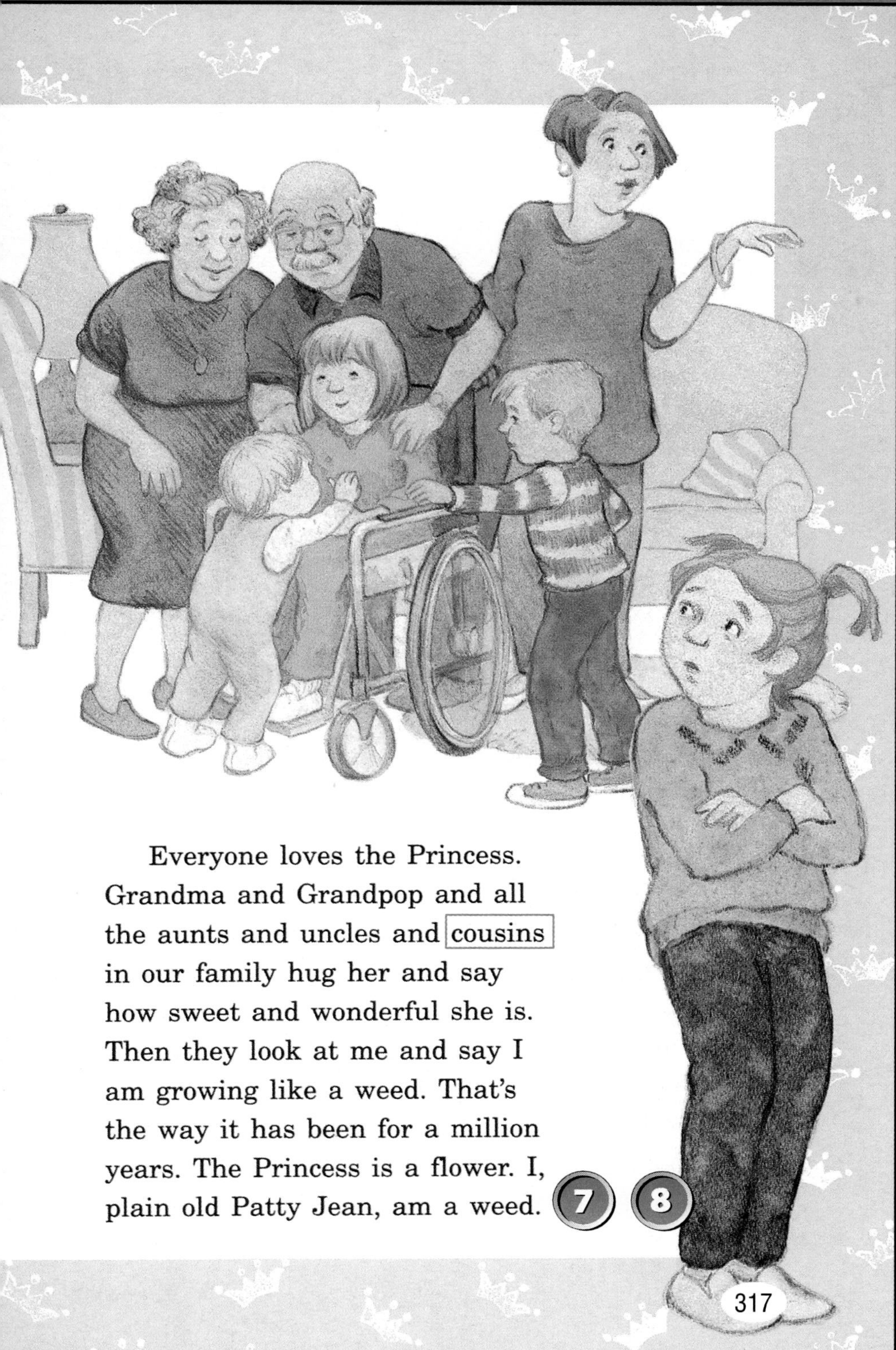

Everyone loves the Princess. Grandma and Grandpop and all the aunts and uncles and cousins in our family hug her and say how sweet and wonderful she is. Then they look at me and say I am growing like a weed. That's the way it has been for a million years. The Princess is a flower. I, plain old Patty Jean, am a weed. 7 8

317

LANGUAGE SUPPORT

ESL To help children who are English learners under-
and how Patty Jean feels about her
ter, invite them to role-play how
tty Jean might talk to her sister
hen they are at the mall. Invite children to work with a partner, one child playing the part of the older sister, the other playing the part of Patty Jean.

Comprehension

8 **MAIN IDEA** What do you think is the main idea of the story so far? (Patty Jean is jealous of her sister.) Let's add this idea to our charts, and look for some details to add, too.

MAIN IDEA	SUPPORTING DETAILS
Patty Jean is jealous of her sister.	Calls sister Princess Pooh; calls herself a weed and sister a flower.

Minilesson

REVIEW/MAINTAIN

Long *e*

Have children find *sweet* and *weed* on page 317. Write the words on the chalkboard and discuss how they are alike. (They both have the long *e* sound.)

- Ask children how the long *e* sound is spelled in both words. (*ee*)

Activity Have children brainstorm other words that have long *e* spelled *ee*. Then ask each child to write and illustrate a sentence using these words.

Phonics CD-ROM Have children use the interactive phonics activities on the CD-ROM for more reinforcement.

Comprehension

9 Why do you think Penny watches while Patty Jean rides the roller coaster alone? (She can't go on the roller coaster in a wheelchair.) Why do you think the man gives Penny a stuffed dog after Patty Jean spent her whole allowance trying to win something? (He probably feels bad that she is in a wheelchair and wants to make her feel better.) If you were Patty Jean, how would that make you feel? (Answers will vary.) ***Make Inferences***

Fluency

TONE OF VOICE

PARTNERS Point out that the way a passage is read can affect the meaning and feelings of the words. Model using tone of voice to express emotion as you read.

- Invite children to follow along as you read aloud page 318, first using an angry voice, and then using a sad voice. Discuss how this affects the main idea of the story. Which reading do children think comes closer to expressing how Patty Jean feels?
- Read aloud page 319 together with children. Then invite pairs of children to read the page to each other as they think Patty Jean would say it.

9 Once we went to a carnival. Princess Pooh watched me ride a hundred times on the roller coaster. It was fun, but it would have been better with a friend. I almost wished the Princess could ride with me. Then I tried to win a pink stuffed poodle. I spent all my allowance and threw a thousand balls, but I couldn't knock down the bottles. When we left, the man handed Princess Pooh a yellow stuffed poodle with a diamond collar! That's how it is. Everyone gives her things.

318

My school is a hundred years old. It is so far from my house I have to ride for hours on a school bus to get there. Princess Pooh goes to the new school right across the street. She can wheel herself there in one second.

If it rains, Dad carries her and her throne to his car and gives her a one-second ride. I, Patty Jean, wear an icky yellow raincoat and stand in mud puddles, (10) waiting for the bus. (11)

319

Comprehension

(10) Phonics **LONG *o*** Let's read the last sentence on this page aloud. Which two words have the long *o* sound? *(yellow, raincoat)* How is long *o* spelled in *yellow*? *(ow)* in raincoat? *(oa)* ***Graphophonic Cues***

(11) **MAIN IDEA** What is the main idea on these pages? What are some details that support this idea?

MODEL I think the main idea on these pages is that Patty Jean thinks that Penny gets special treatment. Some of the details that support this are that people give things to Penny. When it rains, their dad drives her across the street to school, but Patty Jean has to wait in the rain and then take a long bus ride.

LANGUAGE SUPPORT

ESL Help children understand the exaggerated nguage Patty Jean uses. *(hundred nes, thousand balls, ride for hours on a is, one-second ride)* Explain that peoe use words this way to make a oint, not to relay believable informaon. Explain that using exaggeration ows how Patty Jean is feeling.

Introduce and explain common hyperbolic expressions (for example: *starving to death, boiling hot, forever and a day,* and so on). Invite children who are English learners to share and explain such expressions from their languages.

Comprehension

12 Why does Patty Jean have to do Penny's chores? (Penny was too tired to do them because she went to therapy.) ***Cause and Effect***

13 Why can't Patty Jean go to summer camp? (There is no money for camp.) Why not? (because Penny needed new braces for her legs) Do you think this is a good reason? Why or why not? ***Judgments and Decisions***

Saturday is chore day. Mom mows the lawn.
Dad washes clothes and cleans the garage. Then
12 he brings the clean clothes to the Princess, and
she folds them into piles on the table. I, Patty
Jean the Maid, clean the bathroom.

One Saturday, Mom asked me to fold clothes
because Princess Pooh had therapy. I sat at the
table pretending I was the Princess. I folded the
13 clothes very fast and put them in perfect stacks.
When the Princess came home, I waited for Mom
to tell her to clean the bathroom. But Mom
put her right to bed because she was
14 tired. So I, exhausted Patty Jean,
had to clean the bathroom, too.

It is summer now. All
my friends have gone
15 to camp—everyone
except me. Mom
says there's no
money to send
me to camp
because the
Princess got
new braces
for her legs.

320

Activity

Cross Curricular: Social Studies

WHO HELPS? Invite children to discuss who does the chores in their households. What chores need to be done? Does each member have set chores, or do they take turns?

- Ask children to make a list of chores that are done in his or her home, and who does each one.
- Have children draw a picture of a household member doing a chore and write a caption describing it.

▶ **Linguistic/Spatial**

Comprehension

14 Do you think Penny feels lucky to have new braces? Do you think Patty Jean is the only one who feels bad that she wasn't able to go to camp? (probably not) ***Make Inferences***

15 Let's compare and contrast how the two sisters might feel about these events. (Patty Jean wishes she could go to camp. She probably envies Penny because she thinks Penny gets special treatment. Penny probably wishes she didn't need new braces. She probably envies her sister because Patty Jean doesn't need a wheelchair or braces.) ***Compare and Contrast***

P/I **CONTEXT CLUES** Read the first sentence on page 320. What do you think the word *chore* means? Can you find clues to the meaning in the rest of the paragraph?

P/I PREVENTION/INTERVENTION

ONTEXT CLUES Have children read the first paragraph on page 0. Ask them to point out words that ve clues about the meaning of the ord *chore*. (*mows, washes, cleans, lds*) Explain that the meaning of an unfamiliar word can often be guessed by looking at the words around it.

Have students use the word *chores* in a sentence. ***Semantic Cues***

Minilesson

REVIEW/MAINTAIN

Context Clues

Remind children that other words and pictures can help them figure out the meaning of an unfamiliar word. Have children read the last sentence on page 321. Then ask:

- What word is a clue to the meaning of the word *braces*? (*legs*)
- What clues does the picture provide? (*Penny has metal braces on her leg.*)

Activity Have students write context clues for the word *exhausted*.

Comprehension

16 Patty Jean seems upset, doesn't she? Who would like to be Patty Jean and read the first paragraph? How would you use your tone of voice to show your feelings? *Role-Play*

17 **Phonics** LONG *a* Which word in the first sentence has a long *a* sound? (*anyway*) Which pair of letters works together to make this sound? (*ay*) *Graphophonic Cues*

16 Princess Pooh doesn't need them anyway because all she does is sit. She only takes little tiny walks, like when she has to go to the bathroom at a restaurant and her wheelchair won't fit through
17 the door. Mom says she walks at therapy, too, but I've never seen her do it.

After dinner I go outside. The Princess is in the hammock reading a book.

"Do you want to make a puppet show?" I ask.

"No, thanks," she says in her princess voice. "I'm going to read lots of books so I can win a prize in the summer reading program."

322

Cross Curricular: Math

FINDING THE SPACE Tell children that a child's wheelchair is about 28 inches wide.

- Ask partners to measure and record the widths of doorways around school.
- Remind children to take into account doorknobs and other things that could get in the way.
- Help them to figure out whether a wheelchair could fit through each space.

▶ **Spatial/Logical**

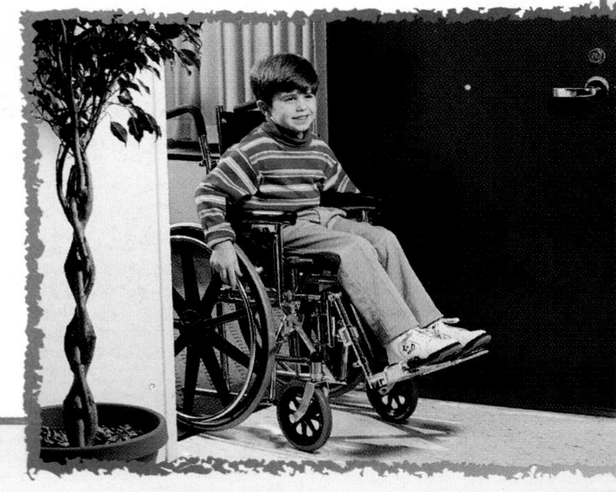

I don't feel like reading, but I get a book anyway and look at the pictures. I am finished in one minute. 18

"This book is boring," I say. "Let's play with puppets now." The Princess doesn't answer. I look over at the hammock—there she is, asleep.

Behind the tree is the throne. Seeing it empty gives me the best idea anyone in the whole world has ever had. Today I, Patty Jean, will be the Princess! 19

I sit on the throne. It is covered with cushions and feels like a cloud.

323

Comprehension

18 What happens when Patty Jean sees her sister's wheelchair behind the tree? (It gives her an idea. She will be the Princess.) ***Cause and Effect***

19 What does Patty Jean do to try to amuse herself? (She invites her sister to make a puppet show with her, reads a book, and tries out Penny's wheelchair.) ***Sequence of Events***

P/I **DIGRAPH sh:** Which word in the second sentence on page 323 has the /sh/ sound? (*finished*)

PREVENTION/INTERVENTION

DIGRAPH *sh* Write *finished* and *she* on the chalkboard. Ask children to read aloud each word. Ask volunteers to underline the letter pair that makes the /sh/ sound. Explain that when the letters *s* and *h* work as a pair, they make a single sound, /sh/, that is different from the sound each makes separately. Blend and read aloud each word and have children repeat. Have children look at the last sentence on page 323 and identify a word with the sound /sh/. (cushions) Write the word on the board and ask a volunteer to circle the letters that make the sound /sh/. ***Graphophonic Cues***

Minilesson

REVIEW/MAINTAIN

Summarize

Review with children that when they summarize a story, book, or article, they should tell the most important facts and leave out little details.

- Ask children to summarize the main ideas of the story so far. Encourage them to refer to their Main Idea/Supporting Details charts.

Activity Have children orally summarize ways in which being in a wheelchair affects Penny's daily activities.

Comprehension

20 Notice that Patty Jean predicts she will "rest" in the wheelchair. What does she discover when she tries to move it? (It is hard to wheel on the grass.) What happens next? (She falls out when she tries to ride down a hill.) ***Sequence of Events***

21 Look at the illustrations on these pages. How does the expression on Patty Jean's face change as she tries to use the wheelchair? Can you describe the three ways she looks here? (happy/excited; in pain; embarrassed) ***Compare and Contrast/Use Illustrations***

Writer's Craft

FIGURATIVE LANGUAGE

Explain: Writers use figurative language to describe objects and feelings in a colorful way. Figurative language does not literally mean what it says.

Example: Point out the last sentence on page 324, *Now I will spend every minute on the throne.* Discuss with children that Patty Jean does not mean exactly what she says. She is exaggerating to make her feelings clear.

Discuss the other examples of figurative language on the page, such as *throne, kingdom,* and *princess.*

WRITING Have partners write two sentences about Patty Jean, using figurative language.

"I will rest on my golden throne for the whole
20 evening," I say. I imagine all the people in my kingdom, looking at me and loving their beautiful new princess.

The throne is hard to wheel on the grass, so
21 I get up and pull it to the front yard. "Now I will spend *every minute* on the throne," I say.

324

I decide to ride to the Princess's school. There is a nice, steep little hill on the grass near the sidewalk. Maybe it would be fun to ride down it. I sit down and give the throne a good, hard push.

PLOP! The throne dumps me out on the sidewalk and lands upside down on top of me. My knee has a tiny cut on it, but it doesn't hurt much. Still, I'm glad no one is around to laugh. I wonder if Princess Pooh ever fell when she was learning. I put the throne rightside up and get back on it. Then I ride to the corner. I go down the low place on the curb so I can cross the street.

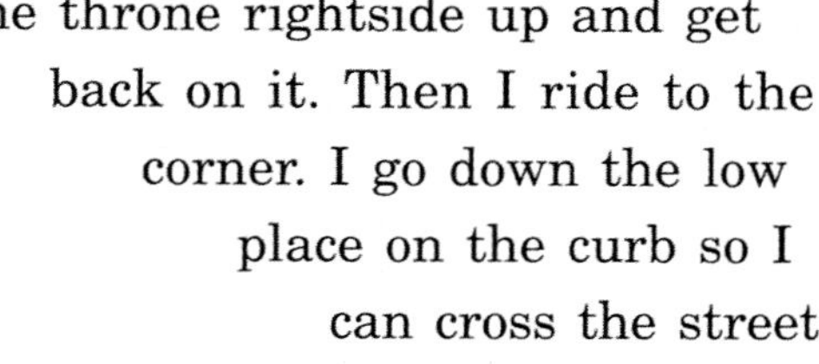

325

Comprehension

22 **MAIN IDEA** What is the main idea of these pages? What idea can you learn from everything you read and see on this page? (The wheelchair is harder to use than Patty Jean had thought.) Let's put this idea in our charts.

MAIN IDEA	SUPPORTING DETAILS
Patty Jean is jealous of her sister.	Calls sister Princess Pooh; calls herself a weed and her sister a flower.
The wheelchair is harder to use than Patty Jean had thought.	It is hard to wheel on the grass. She falls going down a hill.

23 **Phonics** **LONG *o*** Which word in the last sentence on page 325 has the long *o* sound? Which letters spell the long *o* sound in *low*? (*ow*) Can you find a different word in the same sentence that has the same pair of letters, but a different sound? (*down*)
Graphophonic Cues

LANGUAGE SUPPORT

ESL Point out the word *PLOP* in the second paragraph. plain that words like *PLOP*, *POW*, d *KABOOM* are meant to give an ea of a sound that happens in a ry; they are almost like sound ects. Ask: Why do you think the rd *PLOP* is capitalized? (to make it seem like a loud sound) Can you find a word like this on the next page? (*SPLAT*) Invite children to search through the story for other words that imitate sounds and to read them aloud, emphasizing the sound and action of the word as they say it.

Comprehension

24 What problems does Patty Jean have in using the wheelchair? (She finds it hard to cross a street, and her arms get tired.) How do you think she feels about the wheelchair now? (She probably thinks it is hard to use.) *Make Inferences*

SELF-MONITORING STRATEGY

ASK FOR HELP If you don't understand something you read, it can be helpful to ask someone else to discuss it with you or explain it to you.

MODEL I don't really understand why Patty Jean calls the wheelchair a throne. It doesn't look like one. I know we talked about this at the beginning of the story, but I don't remember. Probably some other kids don't remember either. I asked my neighbor and he said it was because Penny calls it a throne, but I think that's wrong. When my teacher finishes reading the next page with us, I'm going to ask her to remind me.

When the light turns green, I push the wheels as fast as I can. I make it to the island in the middle, but then the light turns red again.

Cars and trucks and buses rush by. I cover my face so I will not see myself go SPLAT.

24

326

Finally, the traffic stops and the light is green again. I finish crossing the street. I push the throne up the low place at the crosswalk. It is hard to go uphill, but I do it. I wheel down the sidewalk. I've been pushing so hard I feel like both my arms are broken.

327

Comprehension

25 Patty Jean got stuck in the middle of the street. How did she get there and why must she wait? (She couldn't make it across before the light changed.) ***Cause and Effect***

SILENT LETTERS Can you find a word in the first sentence on page 327 with a silent *gh*? (light)

PREVENTION/INTERVENTION

ILENT LETTERS Remind children ıat some words contain letters that re not pronounced, and that these re known as silent letters. Write the ollowing word pairs on the chalk-oard, and have children identify the ord in each pair that contains a silent letter. Ask volunteers to circle the silent letters in each word.

- knot/not
- write/winter

Graphophonic Cues

Comprehension

26 How do people react to Patty Jean when she is in the wheelchair? (The grown-ups turn away, and children make fun of her.) Do you think people ever treat Penny this way? (probably) ***Make Inferences***

27 This is the first time Patty Jean asks herself a question about her sister. What does this tell you? (Patty Jean is changing and thinking more about Penny's feelings.) ***Character***

28 Patty Jean says the rain is the worst thing in the world. Do you think she really means this? Why is she saying it? (She is exaggerating to show how she feels.) ***Draw Conclusions***

Some grown-ups are walking toward me. They look at me and my throne, and then they turn away fast, like I do when I'm watching a scary movie. Does this happen to Princess Pooh? **26**

Some boys are playing on the sidewalk and will not move out of my way. "Why don't you go over me, Wheel Legs?" says one of them. All his friends laugh. "I'll beat you up!" I yell, but they just laugh some more and run away. **27**

I see an ice-cream truck on the school playground. Lots of big kids are crowded around it. I make a shortcut across the baseball field, but by the time I get there and take some money out of my pocket, the worst thing in the world has happened. Great big raindrops have started falling over everything! SLAM goes the window on the truck. The children squeal and run away. **28** The man drives off and I'm alone on my wet throne.

328

CULTURAL PERSPECTIVES

GOING FAR Explain that many famous people have been physically challenged, yet still reached their goals.

RESEARCH AND INQUIRY Have children look for information about well-known people who are or were physically challenged. Have children share facts, such as what the people accomplished and what challenges they faced.

▶ **Interpersonal/Linguistic**

The rain comes faster and faster. I think about running home, too, but I can't leave the throne out in the rain. Besides, I am still the Princess. I'm spending every minute on my throne, even if I do get wet! So I push harder and harder. When I get back to the baseball field, I can see it's a muddy mess. The wheels of the throne sink down, down, down. They stop turning. My hands are covered with mud. I jump off the throne, and my new sandals sink, too. My feet go with them. By the time I pull the throne out, I am wetter and colder than I have ever been in my whole life. I, Princess Patty Jean, am a royal mess. It is definitely time to quit sitting on the throne.

29

30

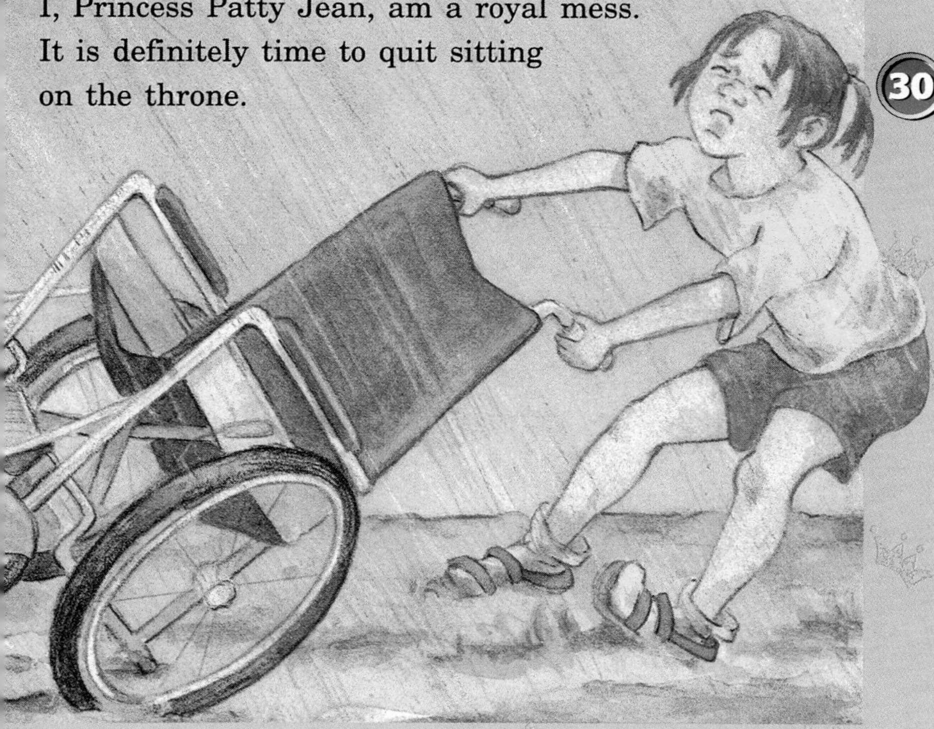

329

Comprehension

29 **MAIN IDEA** What is the main idea on these pages?

MODEL I read that grown-ups turn away from Patty Jean as she wheels toward them. Some boys call her names. Nobody helps her when it starts to rain. All these details point to one main idea: Using the wheelchair does not make Patty Jean feel like a princess.

30 Phonics **LONG *a*** Can you find a word in the first sentence on this page that has the long a sound? (rain) Which pair of letters works together to make the long *a* sound in rain? (*ai*) ***Graphophonic Cues***

Comprehension

31 When Patty Jean sees her parents again, what are they doing? (calling her name and looking for her) Do you think they have been worried about her? ***Make Inferences***

32 What does Patty Jean think her parents have been looking for? (the wheelchair) Are they happier to see Patty Jean or the wheelchair? (Patty Jean) How can you tell? (They run to her, hug her, and tell her they were looking for her.) ***Draw Conclusions***

31 The rain stops. Across the street there is a rainbow. I notice Dad standing in our front yard. He is calling and calling, but the cars and trucks are so noisy I can't hear him. Mom is walking up the street, looking around. I drag the muddy throne across the rest of the field to the sidewalk.

330

Activity

Cross Curricular: Science

AN INVENTOR'S LIFE Let children know that there are inventions to help people who have physical challenges.

RESEARCH AND INQUIRY

- Have children work in small groups to design an invention for a physically challenged person.
- Ask each group to draw the invention and label its parts.

▶ **Logical/Spatial**

Children can learn more about inventions at ***www.mhschool.com/reading***.

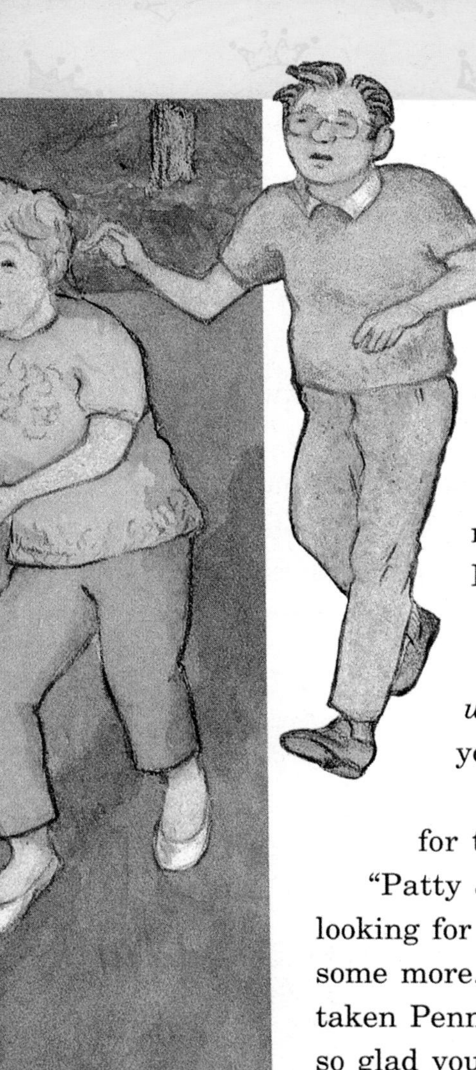

Then I cross the street. When Mom sees me, she runs and holds out her arms. Dad is right behind her. 32

"I didn't mean to mess up the throne. I'm sorry," I say.

"Throne?" says Mom. "Oh, the *wheelchair*. We thought you were lost!" 33

"You weren't looking for the chair?" I say.

"Patty Jean, we were looking for *you*." Mom hugs me some more. "You shouldn't have taken Penny's chair. But we're so glad you're back!" 34

Comprehension

33 If you were Patty Jean, how would you feel when you realized that your parents were looking for you and not the wheelchair? Why? (Possible answer: good; it meant they cared about you after all.) What has Patty Jean learned about her family? (Her parents love her as much as they love Penny.) ***Character***

34 Now that Patty Jean has experienced what it is like to be in a wheelchair, do you think she will still be jealous of her sister? Why or why not? ***Make Predictions***

Comprehension

35 The story says Patty Jean lies awake thinking. What might she be thinking about? (how it felt to spend time in the wheelchair, and what Penny's life might be like) ***Analyze/Make Inferences***

36 What does Patty Jean call her sister for the first time here? (Penny) What has she called her up until now? (Princess Pooh) Do you think her feelings about her sister have changed? How? (Yes. Spending time in the wheelchair has made Patty Jean understand that Penny may not be as lucky as she had thought.) ***Character***

TEACHING TIP

READ ALOUD SKILLS Invite children to read aloud Patty Jean's and Penny's dialogue. Encourage them to use tone of voice to show how the characters are feeling.

35 Mom washes me in the bathtub and puts me to bed just like she does for Penny. After Dad and Mom say good-night and turn out the lights, I lie there thinking.

"Penny," I whisper. "Are you awake?"

36 "Uh-huh."

"Do you like walking better than sitting?"

"Well," she says, "walking makes me awful tired, but so does pushing my wheelchair.

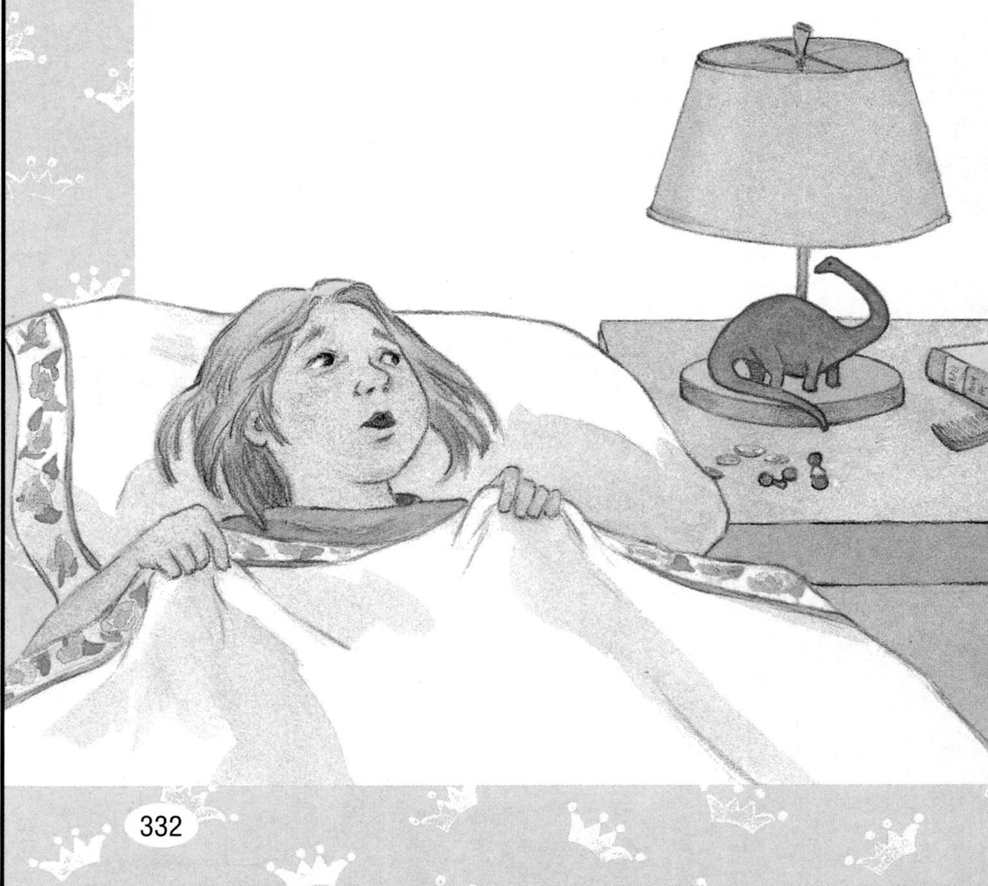

I guess I like the wheelchair best because I can do things with my hands while I sit. When I use my crutches, I can't."

"How can you smile all the time when you're in that yucky chair?"

"It's not yucky," says Penny. "It takes me places I can't go if I just have my crutches." 

That makes me think some more. "I'm sorry I took your chair," I say.

"That's all right. Just go to sleep now." 

333

Comprehension

37 Does Penny seem angry at Patty Jean for taking her wheelchair? (no) Why not? (She probably realizes that taking the wheelchair has helped Patty Jean understand Penny's own experience better.) ***Character/Make Inferences***

38 How have Patty Jean's feelings about the wheelchair changed from the beginning of the story? (She used to call it a *throne*. Now she says it is *yucky*.) ***Compare and Contrast***

LANGUAGE SUPPORT

ESL Ask children what they think the word *yucky* means. Review how to use context clues to figure out an unfamiliar word.

Explain that *yucky* is informal English. Ask children to brainstorm other words which are synonyms for *yucky*.

Minilesson

REVIEW/MAINTAIN

Make Inferences

Remind children that they can use their own experiences and what they have already read to help them to understand the story. Have children reread and study the illustration on pages 332–333. Then ask:

- Have you ever felt that a brother, sister, or friend was getting special treatment? How did this make you feel?
- Have you ever tried putting yourself in someone else's shoes? What did you learn?
- Do you think Patty Jean still resents Penny for getting extra attention?

Activity Invite children to role-play what Patty Jean is thinking before and after she talks with Penny.

Comprehension

 **MAIN IDEA AND DETAILS** What is the main idea of the past few pages? Let's add it to our charts, along with some details that support it.

MAIN IDEA	SUPPORTING DETAILS
Patty Jean is jealous of her sister.	Calls sister Princess Pooh; calls herself a weed and sister a flower.
The wheelchair is harder to use than Patty Jean had thought.	It is hard to wheel on the grass. She falls going down a hill.
Patty Jean understands more about her sister's life, so she doesn't resent Penny anymore.	She stops calling her a princess, says she's sorry, hopes Penny will be happy.

RETELL THE STORY Ask volunteers to retell the story in their own words. Guide them to use their charts to focus on the main ideas of the story. *Summarize*

STUDENT SELF-ASSESSMENT

- How did focusing on main ideas and details help me to understand the story?

TRANSFERRING THE STRATEGY

- Could I use this strategy to help me when I read other stories?

39 But I'm wide awake. I lie there and wish very hard that my sister will always be able to do things that make her happy. I think that maybe Princess isn't a good name for her, after all. Maybe it's nicer that she's just Penelope Marie and that I am her sister, Patty Jean Piper.

334

REREADING FOR *Fluency*

 ONE Children who need fluency practice can read along with a recording of the story.

READING RATE When you evaluate reading rate, have children read aloud from the story for one minute. Place a stick-on note after the last word read. Count words read. To evaluate children's performance, see the Running Record in the **Fluency Assessment** book.

 **Intervention** For leveled fluency passages, lessons, and norms charts, see **Skills Intervention Guide, Part 5, Fluency.**

READ TOGETHER

Meet KATHLEEN M. MULDOON

Kathleen M. Muldoon knows what it is like to be physically challenged—on one leg, she wears a brace, and on the other, an artificial leg. Talking to children, she began to realize what it's like to be a brother or sister of someone like herself. She found that these children often get pushed aside because their brother or sister needs so much attention. So Ms. Muldoon decided to write a story from the sister's point of view.

Children ask Ms. Muldoon how she came up with the name "Princess Pooh." She says, "I thought of the name 'Princess Pooh' because *pooh* is a word children love to say and hear. It's like saying 'you're not so great,' so I thought it'd be a perfect nickname for the sister."

Meet LINDA SHUTE

"What made me want to create the pictures for *Princess Pooh?* It was the voice of Patty Jean I heard speaking from the typewritten manuscript. She sounded like a spunky, funny, and thoughtful person I'd like to know. I felt the story is as much about being sisters as it is about using a wheelchair, and I tried to show that in my pictures."

335

LITERARY RESPONSE

QUICK-WRITE Invite children to record their reactions to the story in their journals. To help them get started, ask questions such as:

JOURNAL

- How would you describe Patty Jean and Penny?
- What are some of the problems each sister has? In what way is each sister lucky?
- How does Patty Jean come to understand more about her sister?
- If Penny were your sister, how would you feel about the special attention she received?

ORAL RESPONSE Have children share their journal entries and discuss what part of the story they enjoyed most.

Comprehension

Return to Predictions and Purposes

Ask children to reread the predictions they made about the story. Discuss their predictions, noting which ones needed to be revised.

PREDICTIONS	WHAT HAPPENED
The younger girl is jealous of the girl in the wheelchair.	Patty Jean is jealous at first, but she learns to understand her sister.
The younger girl takes the wheelchair.	Patty Jean realizes the wheelchair is harder to use than she had thought.

HOW TO ASSESS

LONG *a, o* Ask children to look through the story for words with the /ā/ sound spelled *ai* or *ay,* and the /ō/ sound spelled *oa, oe,* or *ow.* Ask volunteers to point to these words, and to spell and read them aloud.

MAIN IDEA Offer children examples of main ideas and details from the story. Ask them to identify each as a main idea or detail.

FOLLOW UP

LONG *a, o* For children who are having difficulty, model how to read words with long *a* and long *o* sounds.

MAIN IDEA Ask children who have difficulty distinguishing main ideas from details to sum up a familiar story, such as *The Three Little Pigs.*

Story Questions

Have children discuss or write answers to the questions on page 336.

Answers:

1. wheelchair *Literal/Supporting Detail*
2. She thinks Penny is bossy and spoiled. *Inferential/Character*
3. She learns that it is harder than she had thought. *Inferential /Summarize*
4. Patty Jean sees her sister in a new light when she discovers some of the challenges Penny faces. *Critical/Summarize*
5. Patty Jean understands her sister. Lizzie learns that it's better to work with people. They both learn from putting themselves in other peoples' shoes. *Critical Reading Across Texts*

Write Penelope's Story For a full lesson related to writing a story, see page 339M.

Story Questions & Activities

READ TOGETHER

1. What is Penelope's "throne with wheels"?
2. Why does Patty Jean call her sister "Princess"?
3. What does Patty Jean learn about using a wheelchair?
4. What is this story mainly about?
5. Both Patty Jean and Lizzie from "The Best Friends Club" learn important lessons that help them see people differently. Describe how you think each character changed.

Write Penelope's Story

What if this story was told by Penelope instead of Patty Jean? Imagine that you are Penelope, and you are writing in your journal about what happened the day your sister took your wheelchair. Tell the story of the day from beginning to end, and include how you felt about it.

Meeting Individual Needs

EASY

Name________ Date________ Reteach 229

Story Comprehension

Think about "Princess Pooh." Circle the word that best completes each sentence.

1. Everyone says that Patty Jean grows like a ___.
   flower (weed)
2. When they shop, Patty Jean carries so many packages, she looks like a ___ with legs.
   throne (box)
3. The carnival man gave a stuffed ___ to Penny.
   (poodle) chair
4. When it rains, Patty Jean must wait for the ___.
   throne (bus)
5. When she takes the wheelchair, Patty Jean learns how ___ it is for Penny.
   easy (hard)
6. In the end, Patty Jean just wants Penny to be ___.
   (happy) sad

6 Book 2.2/Unit 3 Princess Pooh
At Home: Ask children to talk about how Patty Jean felt about Penny at the end of the story. 229

Reteach, 229

ON-LEVEL

Name________ Date________ Practice 229

Story Comprehension

Think about "Princess Pooh." Draw a line to match the beginning of each sentence with the end.

1. Princess Pooh — says Penelope is wonderful.
2. Patty Jean Piper — cleans the bathroom on Saturdays.
3. Grandma — must sit in a wheelchair.
4. Dad — carries Princess Pooh's throne in his car.
5. Carnival Man — takes Princess Pooh to therapy.
6. Mom — gives Penelope a prize.

6 Book 2.2/Unit 3 Princess Pooh
At Home: Ask children to tell how Patty Jean felt about her sister at the beginning of the story and then at the end. What made her change her mind? 229

Practice, 229

CHALLENGE

Name________ Date________ Extend 229

Story Comprehension

Finish the letter from Patty Jean to her sister.

Dear Penny,

I am sorry that I took your chair. I learned that it is not always fun to sit in the chair. Answers will vary.

Your sister,
Patty Jean

Draw a picture illustrating how Penny might feel after reading the letter.

Book 2.2/Unit 3 Princess Pooh
At Home: Ask children to tell what happened in the story to change how Patty Jean felt about her sister. 229

Extend, 229

Find Information About Families

atty Jean has one sister. How many children e in your family? How many children are in ur classmates' families? Write the name of each child your family on a card. Don't forget yourself! Put the rds into different piles. Make one pile for families with ne child. Make another pile for families with two ildren. Make a different pile for every number.

A Special Event

Patty Jean and her family go to a carnival. What special event have you been to or would like to go to? Draw a picture of that event. Write the name of the event and three things that happen at this event.

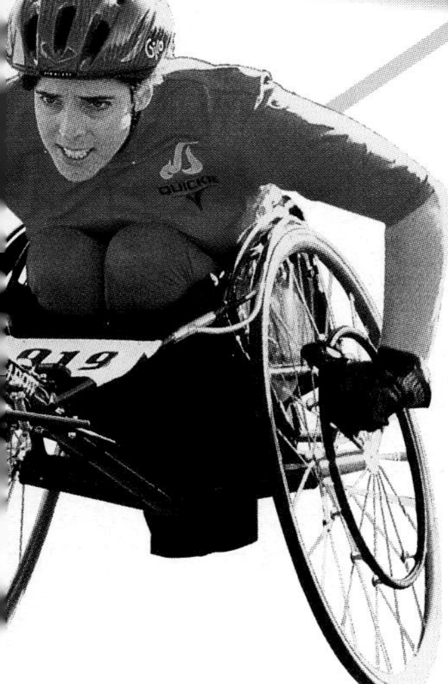

Find Out More

The Special Olympics is an international sporting event for the physically challenged. Find out more about the Special Olympics. When did they start? What are the events?

337

DAILY Phonics ROUTINES

DAY 3 **Letter Substitution** Have small groups pass around a paper, starting with the word *may* and changing the spelling of one sound to create new words such as *mow, bow, boat, coat*. (Save lists for Day 4 Activity.)

Phonics CD-ROM

Story Activities

Find Information About Families

Materials: index cards, pencils

GROUP Help children determine the following information about their class: How many one-child families are there? How many two- and three-child families? What is the largest number of children in one family?

A Special Event

Materials: paper, felt-tipped markers

ONE Help children to brainstorm a list of events they have attended such as weddings or fairs. Prompt discussion of things that happen at each event. Encourage children to include themselves in their drawings.

Find Out More

RESEARCH AND INQUIRY Direct children to appropriate resources such as encyclopedias, magazines, and the Internet. Encourage partners to pick one topic to focus on. Ask children to give a brief oral report.

PARTNERS

interNET CONNECTION Children can learn more about the Special Olympics at ***www.mhschool.com/reading***.

FORMAL ASSESSMENT

After page 337, see Selection Assessment.

LIBRARY/MEDIA CENTER

Children will read and get information from encyclopedias.

PREPARE Examine the sample entry with children. Display **Teaching Chart 192**.

TEACH Review what information can be found in an encyclopedia. Discuss subject titles, topic entries and guide words. Let children know that encyclopedias are divided alphabetically into several books called volumes. Then read aloud the entry on Stephen Hawking.

PRACTICE Have children answer questions 1–5. Review the answers with them.
1. the volume that has topics beginning with the letters *ha* **2.** *Hawking, Stephen* and *Hay* **3.** ALS **4.** with a computer **5.** He works for the rights of the disabled.

ASSESS/CLOSE Have children use encyclopedias to find information about other scientists.

STUDY SKILLS

READ TOGETHER

Use an Encyclopedia

112 Hawking, Stephen **Hay**

Hawking, Stephen William

(1942–) Stephen William Hawking is a British scientist. Hawking studies questions about the universe.

Stephen Hawking has a disease called ALS. He can't talk. He can only move a few muscles in his hands and face. But Hawking still is able to work. He uses a wheelchair, and a computer that talks for him. Besides studying science, he also works for the rights of disabled people.

Use the part of an encyclopedia page to answer the questions.

1. What volume would have this entry about Stephen Hawking? Explain.
2. What are the guide words on this page?
3. What is Stephen Hawking's disability?
4. How does he communicate?
5. What work besides science does Stephen Hawking do?

Meeting Individual Needs

EASY

Name__________ Date______ **Reteach 230**

Use an Encyclopedia

An **encyclopedia** provides general information on numerous topics.

Study the encyclopedia entry shown below.

Mercury–Mesa

MERRY-GO-ROUND is a machine that people ride for fun. It is often found at a fair or an amusement park. A merry-go-round is actually a platform that is in the shape of a circle. It turns slowly while music is played. Usually wooden horses are attached to poles for people to ride. Sometimes the poles go up and down. The horses are often brightly painted. The first merry-go-round was built in France in the late 1700s. It was called a *carrousel*. See also *rollercoaster*.

Use the encyclopedia entry to answer these questions.

1. What is the topic of this entry? a merry-go-round
2. Which guide words are found on this page? Mercury—Mesa
3. What was the name of the first merry-go-round? carousel
4. How do people use the wooden horses on the platform? they sit on them as the merry-go-round turns
5. What other topic does the encyclopedia suggest you see? roller coaster

At Home: Have children look up subjects that interest them in an encyclopedia and write reports about their findings.

230 Book 2.2/Unit 3 **Princess Pooh** 5

Reteach, 230

ON-LEVEL

Name__________ Date______ **Practice 230**

Use an Encyclopedia

One of the best ways to learn more about a subject is to look at more than one entry in an encyclopedia. Sometimes an entry will direct you to another entry that contains related information.

BUMBLEBEE is a large, hairy, black and yellow bee that is often seen in summer. Bumblebees live in almost every country. Some islands in the Pacific never had bumblebees until man brought them. They range in size from one half to one inch. Unlike honeybees, they do not die after they sting. Bumblebees can sting again and again. They make a loud buzzing noise as they fly, scaring many people. The enemies of the bumblebee are beetles, flies, ants, mites, and wasps. *See also: Bee, Clover*

BEE is an insect that lives everywhere in the world except near the North and South Poles. There are 10,000 kinds of bees but only the honeybee makes honey. Most people are afraid of bees, but they only sting when scared or hurt. Honeybees are social insects. They live and work in a huge group called a colony. They fly about 12 miles an hour. Bees have been found in amber that was fifty million years old. *See also: Clover, Honey, Pollen, Pupa*

Use the encyclopedia entries to answer the questions.

1. Which entry discusses one kind of bee only? bumblebee
2. What entry does both of these entries tell you to see? clover
3. What fact about bees do both entries mention? that bees live almost everywhere
4. What are the other entries that are suggested for you to read? honey, pollen, pupa

At Home: Have children illustrate one of the facts they have learned about bees from the entries above.

230 Book 2.2/Unit 3 **Princess Pooh** 4

Practice, 230

CHALLENGE

Name__________ Date______ **Extend 230**

Use an Encyclopedia

Read about Helen Keller in this encyclopedia entry. Write a report about Helen Keller using facts from the entry.

Keller, Helen Adams (1880–1968)
Helen Keller was an American writer. She became blind and deaf at eight months old. When she was almost seven, Anne Sullivan came to take care of her. Miss Sullivan became Helen Keller's friend and teacher. Helen Keller learned quickly. She graduated from Radcliffe College. She wrote many books. She also raised money so other blind people could learn new jobs and skills. **See also *Macy, Anne Sullivan***

HELEN KELLER

At Home: Help children to look up Helen Keller in an actual encyclopedia. Allow them to pick out the volume that has the entry about Keller. Have them point out the guide words on the page about Keller.

230 Book 2.2/Unit 3 **Princess Pooh**

Extend, 230

Pay attention to the details in the story.

RECTIONS:

ead the story. Then read each question about the story.

AMPLE

Which One Will Win?

Every October there is a mpkin contest. Many people ter their pumpkins in the ntest. There are many kinds of mpkins in the contest. Some e small. Some are big. Some e giant. When people enter the ntest, this is what they must . First, they must weigh their mpkin. Next, they must easure the pumpkin at its fattest int. Then, they must show their mpkins to the judges. The dges know everything about mpkins. The judges look at ch pumpkin. They look at its ape, its color, and its size. en, they choose a winner. ery winner gets a medal. The st winner gets the gold medal.

1 What is the main idea of this story?

- ● The best pumpkin is judged in many ways.
- ○ Growing pumpkins is easy.
- ○ My pumpkin is the best one.
- ○ Pumpkin pie tastes good.

2 Which is a general statement that you can make from this story?

- ○ Small pumpkins are best.
- ● Judges consider many things when choosing a winner of a contest.
- ○ All pumpkins are giant.
- ○ Pumpkin contests can only happen in October.

339

Read the Page

Explain to children that you will be reading this story as a group. You will read the story, and they will follow along in their books.

Request that children put pens, pencils, and markers away, since they will not be writing.

Discuss the Questions

QUESTION 1: Remind children that the title is a good clue to the main idea. This story is about which pumpkin will win the pumpkin contest. Ask: *What do judges look at in each pumpkin?* Answer: Shape, color, and size.

QUESTION 2: Remind children that they should look for facts in the story to support a choice. The twelfth sentence names things that judges look at when choosing a winner.

Leveled Books

Intervention Skills

Intervention Guide, for direct instruction and extra practice in vocabulary and comprehension

Answers to Story Questions

1. A dollhouse, a shelf for her books
2. They were trying to get ready for a big dinner and needed help. They probably didn't think that the other twin could do the work as well.
3. They finally get to do what they want. Their projects turn out well. They are talking again and doing their secret handshake.
4. A brother and sister. She wants to learn about wood; he wants to learn how to cook.
5. Lupe and Paco are jealous of each other and think that the other has all the fun. Patty Jean is jealous of Penny and thinks that Penny has it easy and gets to act like a princess.

The Story Questions and Activity below appear in the Easy Book.

Story Questions and Writing Activity

1. Name something Lupe wants to make with wood.
2. Why did Lupe and Paco's parents say no when the twins wanted to try each other's activities?
3. What happens at the end of the story that makes Lupe and Paco so happy? How do you know they are best friends again?
4. What is this story mostly about?
5. How is the misunderstanding between Lupe and Paco like the misunderstanding between Patty Jean and Penny in *Princess Pooh*?

Careful in the Kitchen!

When you cook, you have to be very careful. Draw a picture of something in the kitchen that can be dangerous. Then write a sentence telling how you can be careful.

from *Everybody's Happy*

EASY

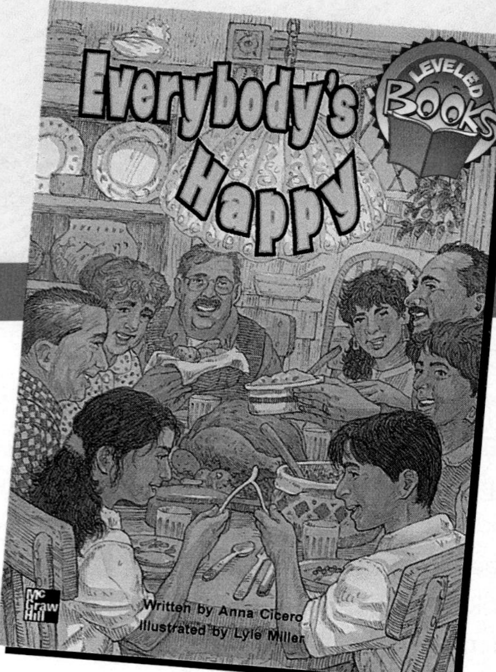

Everybody's Happy

- ☑ **Long *a*; Long *o***
- ☑ **Main Idea**
- ☑ **Instructional Vocabulary:** ***cousins, crowded, golden, princess, restaurant, world***

Guided Reading

PREVIEW AND PREDICT Discuss the illustrations through page 4. Can children predict what the story is about? Chart their ideas.

SET PURPOSES Have children write why they want to read *Everybody's Happy*.

READ THE BOOK Use questions like the following to guide children's reading or to ask after they read the story independently:

Page 3: Find the words that tell what Paco made out of wood. Hint: One word has the /ō/ sound. (*boat*) What letters spell /ō/? The other has the /ā/ sound. (*train*) What letters spell /ā/?

Page 4: Find the word *cousins*. What were Lupe's cousins' names? (Dona and Linda) How is a cousin related to you? ***Instructional Vocabulary***

Page 6: What is the main idea of this paragraph? (Paco wanted to know how to do more than one thing.)

Page 12: What happened the night before Paco and Lupe started talking to each another again? (They went to bed without saying goodnight.) ***Sequence of Events***

Page 16: What did Paco make at the end of the story? (*pan dulce*) What did Lupe make? (two chairs) What does this tell you about what boys can do and what girls can do? (Boys and girls can do the same kind of work.) ***Form Generalizations***

RETURN TO PREDICTIONS AND PURPOSES Have children review their purposes for reading. Did they find out what they wanted to know?

LITERARY RESPONSE Discuss this question:

- Do you think boys and girls should learn the same things? Why?

Also see the story questions and activity in *Everybody's Happy*.

See the Phonics **CD-ROM** for practice using long *a* and long *o*.

Leveled Books

INDEPENDENT

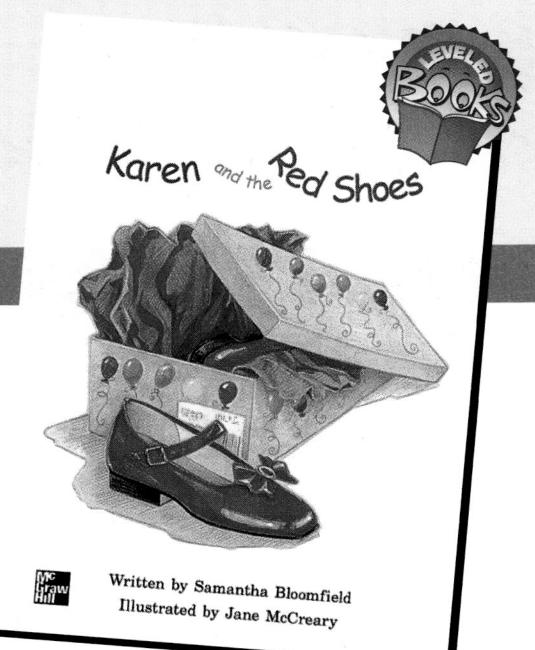

LEVELED BOOKS
Karen and the Red Shoes
Written by Samantha Bloomfield
Illustrated by Jane McCreary

Karen and the Red Shoes

- ☑ Long *a*; Long *o*
- ☑ Main Idea
- ☑ Instructional Vocabulary: *cousins, crowded, golden, princess, restaurant, world*

Guided Reading

PREVIEW AND PREDICT Look at the title of the story and take a **picture walk** with children through page 5. Encourage them to predict what the story is about.

SET PURPOSES Have children write a sentence explaining why they want to read *Karen and the Red Shoes*. Children might say, *I want to find out if Karen gives up the shoes or not.*

READ THE BOOK Ask questions like the following after children have read the story independently:

Page 2: What is the most important idea in the first paragraph on page 2? (Karen and her mom are shopping for shoes.) What other information does the paragraph give? (The store is crowded with many children.)

Page 3: Read the third word on page 3 aloud. (*know*) What vowel sound do you hear? (long *o*) What letters spell /ō/? (*ow*) ***Phonics and Decoding***

Pages 4–5: Find the word *princess*. Why do you think Karen said that the shoes were shoes for a princess? What kinds of clothes do you think princesses wear? ***Instructional Vocabulary***

Pages 14–15: What happened when Tracey and Karen arrived at the schoolyard? (Julie teased Karen about her shoes.) How did Tracey help Karen?(Tracey stood up to Julie and defended Karen's choice of shoes.) ***Sequence of Events***

RETURN TO PREDICTIONS AND PURPOSES Discuss children's predictions and purposes.

LITERARY RESPONSE Discuss these questions:

- Have you ever had a family member stand up for you? How did it feel?
- How do you feel about Tracey in the end?

Also see the story questions and activity in *Karen and the Red Shoes.*

See the Phonics **CD-ROM** for practice using long *a* and long *o*.

Answers to Story Questions

1. A clown
2. She was probably jealous. Also she just liked teasing her sister.
3. They fight a lot, but they do love each other.
4. It is about Karen who gets new shoes and is teased by her sister. When another girl teases Karen about the shoes, her sister stands up for her.
5. Answers will vary.

The Story Questions and Activity below appear in the Independent Book.

Story Questions and Writing Activity

1. What does Tracey think Karen's shoes make Karen look like?
2. What is probably the real reason Tracey teases Karen about her new shoes?
3. How do these sisters really feel about each other?
4. What is this story mainly about?
5. How is Patty Jean from "Princess Pooh" like Tracey in this story? How are they different?

My Favorite Thing

Draw a picture of something that you have that you really love. It could be a pair of shoes, an item of clothing, or a favorite toy. Write a sentence or two describing why you like this item.

from *Karen and the Red Shoes*

Leveled Books

The
WRIGHT BROTHE
Learn To Fly
LEVELED
Books
written by Jennifer Julius
illustrated by Dick Smolinski

CHALLENGE

The Wright Brothers Learn to Fly

- ☑ **Long *a*; Long *o***
- ☑ **Main Idea**
- ☑ **Instructional Vocabulary:** ***cousins, crowded, golden, princess, restaurant, world***

Guided Reading

PREVIEW AND PREDICT Have children look at the title page to predict what the story is about.

SET PURPOSES Have children write questions about what they hope to learn by reading the story.

READ THE BOOK Use questions like the following to guide children's reading or to ask after they read the story independently:

Page 4: Find and say a word with a long *a* spelled *ay.* (play) ***Phonics and Decoding***

Pages 4–5: What kinds of things did the Wright brothers do to earn money? (printing, sold and fixed bicycles) What does this tell you about the Wright brothers? (full of energy, interested in many things, and so on.) ***Form Generalizations***

Page 8: What is the last word on the page? *(restaurants)* What is your favorite restaurant? ***Instructional Vocabulary***

Page 16: What is the main idea of the second paragraph? (The Wright brothers became famous all over the world for their inventions.)

RETURN TO PREDICTIONS AND PURPOSES Discuss children's predictions. Ask which were close to the story and why. Have children review their purposes for reading. Did they find out what they wanted to know?

LITERARY RESPONSE Discuss these questions:

- What traits do you think inventors need?
- What do you think is the most important invention used in everyday life?

Also see the story questions and activity in *The Wright Brothers Learn to Fly.*

See the Phonics **CD-ROM** for practice using long *a* and long *e.*

Answers to Story Questions

1. It was a beach with soft sand, and the wind was not too fast and not too slow.
2. They liked to play with machines and build things. Bicycles were popular.
3. Because nobody had ever flown before.
4. The Wright brothers worked together to learn how to fly.
5. Answers will vary.

The Story Questions and Activity below appear in the Challenge Book.

Story Questions and Writing Activity

1. Why was Kitty Hawk a good place to fly a glider?
2. How did the Wright brothers know they could do well running a bicycle shop?
3. Reread page 15. Why was it amazing when Wilbur flew 852 feet in 59 seconds?
4. What is the main idea of the book?
5. What do you think Penny in *Princess Pooh* might ask the Wright brothers if she met them?

The First Airplane

Look at the diagram of the plane on page 13. Write a short paragraph describing it. Tell how you think this plane is different from the planes today.

from *The Wright Brothers Learn to Fly*

Bringing Groups Together

Anthology and Leveled Books

Connecting Texts

SIBLING CHART
Write the story titles on a chart. Discuss with children the relationships the siblings in each story have with each other and why. Call on volunteers from each reading level and write their suggestions on the chart.

Princess Pooh	Everybody's Happy	Karen and the Red Shoes	The Wright Brothers Learn to Fly
• Patty Jean is upset because her sister gets all the attention. • She finds that being in a wheelchair is not as easy as it looks.	• Paco is jealous of Lupe. • Lupe is jealous of Paco. • They each want to do what the other does, and when they do, they become friends again.	• Karen is upset at her sister Tracey because Tracey teases her about her shoes. • Tracey defends Karen in the schoolyard, and they become friends once again.	• Two brothers work and invent things together. • They become successful by sticking together.

Viewing/Representing

GROUP PRESENTATIONS Divide the class into four groups, one for each of the four books read in the lesson. Have each group dramatize a scene from the book they are representing.

AUDIENCE RESPONSE As children watch each dramatization, see if they can identify the story being dramatized. Allow time after each presentation for questions.

Research and Inquiry

MORE ABOUT INVENTIONS Remind children that the Wright brothers were always trying to invent new forms of air travel, and were first to fly an airplane with an engine. Invite children to learn more by:

- reading a biography of an inventor.
- planning a field trip to a museum where inventions are on display.
- holding an invention contest in the classroom.

Go to ***www.mhschool.com/reading*** for more information on this topic.

Children can write or draw what they learned about inventions and inventors in their journals.

TESTED OBJECTIVES

Children will:

- identify /ā/*ai, ay;* /ō/*oa, oe, ow.*
- decode and read words with long *a* and long *o.*

MATERIALS

- Teaching Chart 193

Skills Finder

Long *o*

Introduce	B1: 92G-H
Review	B1: 113E-F, 113G-H; B2: 310G-H, 339G-H
Test	B1: Unit 1

TEACHING TIP

LONG *O* When children are building /ō/ words, remind them to sound out each word so they don't include a word with *ow* that does not have the long *o* sound. For example, *fowl.*

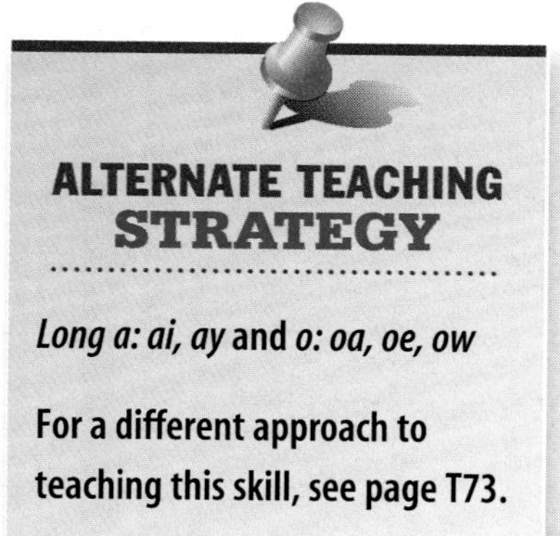

ALTERNATE TEACHING STRATEGY

Long a: ai, ay and *o: oa, oe, ow*

For a different approach to teaching this skill, see page T73.

Review Long *a, o*

PREPARE

Review Sound Symbol Relationships for Long *a: ai, ay;* Long *o: oa, oe, ow* Write the following words on the chalkboard. Read them aloud. Have volunteers underline the letters that spell /ā/ and circle the letters that spell /ō/.

- Today, that hat goes with my plain yellow raincoat.

TEACH

BLENDING Model and Guide Practice with Long *a, o* Words

- Display **Teaching Chart 193**. Tell children that they will use the letter combinations at the top of the chart to build words with long *a* and long *o* sounds.
- Introduce the first example. Model how to complete it by writing the letters *ai* in the blank space.
- Blend the sounds together to read the word *nail.* Have children read the word with you.

Challenge children to build more long *a* words by choosing letter combinations to complete each word.

ai/ay	oa oe ow
nail	coast
plain	slow
clay	float
play	toe*
braid	toad
snail	show

*another possible answer: tow.

Teaching Chart 193

Use Words in Context Ask each child to say a sentence using at least two words from the list. Example: *I like to play with clay.*

Repeat the Procedure Continue the activity, asking children to build long *o* words by choosing the appropriate long *o* letter combinations from the top of the second column.

PRACTICE

SEGMENTING
Write a Story with Long *a, o* Words

Have children work together to create a brief story, using as many long *a* and long *o* words as they can. Suggest that they use the words from the Teaching Chart for ideas. As children offer sentences, write them on the chalkboard. When the story is completed, ask volunteers to underline letter pairs that spell long *a* and long *o* sounds. Then write the letter pairs in a row on the chalkboard. Have children write words from their story under the row that contains the same letter pair. ▶**Visual/Linguistic**

ASSESS/CLOSE

Identify and Read Long *a, o* Words

To assess children's mastery of reading and segmenting long *a* and long *o* words, observe them as they create the story and underline letter pairs in the Practice activity. Ask each child to read aloud three or four long *a* and long *o* words from the story. Tell them to suggest other words with these letter pairs and sounds.

ADDITIONAL PHONICS RESOURCES

Phonics/ Phonemic Awareness Practice Book, pages 143–146

Phonics CD-ROM activities for practice with Blending and Segmenting

Fluency Using the lists the children made on Day 3, write the words on the chalkboard. Point to each word, asking children to blend the sounds silently. Ask a volunteer to read aloud each word.

Phonics CD-ROM

SPELLING/PHONICS CONNECTIONS

See the 5-Day Spelling Plan, pages 339Q–339R.

Skills Intervention Guide, for direct instruction and extra practice of long *a* and long *o*

Meeting Individual Needs for Phonics

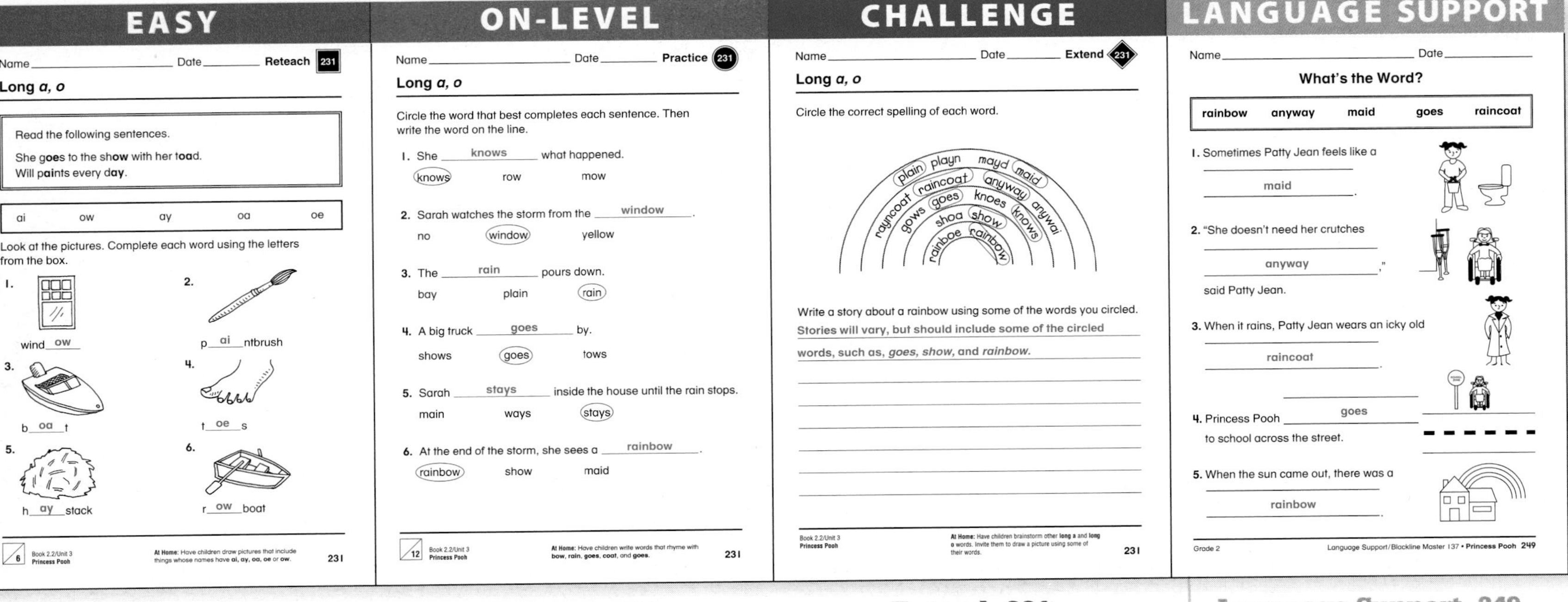

EASY

Name ____ Date ____ Reteach 231

Long *a, o*

Read the following sentences.
She **goes** to the **show** with her **toad**.
Will **paints** every **day**.

ai	ow	ay	oa	oe

Look at the pictures. Complete each word using the letters from the box.

1. wind_ow_
2. p_ai_ntbrush
3. b_oa_t
4. t_oe_s
5. h_ay_stack
6. r_ow_boat

6 Book 2.2/Unit 3 Princess Pooh — At Home: Have children draw pictures that include things whose names have ai, ay, oa, oe or ow. 231

ON-LEVEL

Name ____ Date ____ Practice 231

Long *a, o*

Circle the word that best completes each sentence. Then write the word on the line.

1. She _knows_ what happened.
(knows) row mow
2. Sarah watches the storm from the _window_.
no (window) yellow
3. The _rain_ pours down.
bay plain (rain)
4. A big truck _goes_ by.
shows (goes) tows
5. Sarah _stays_ inside the house until the rain stops.
main ways (stays)
6. At the end of the storm, she sees a _rainbow_.
(rainbow) show maid

12 Book 2.2/Unit 3 Princess Pooh — At Home: Have children write words that rhyme with bow, rain, goes, coat, and goes. 231

CHALLENGE

Name ____ Date ____ Extend 231

Long *a, o*

Circle the correct spelling of each word.

(plain) playn mayd (maid) raycoat (raincoat) (anyway) anywai gows (goes) knoes (knows) shoa (show) rainboe (rainbow)

Write a story about a rainbow using some of the words you circled.
Stories will vary, but should include some of the circled words, such as, goes, show, and rainbow.

Book 2.2/Unit 3 Princess Pooh — At Home: Have children brainstorm other long a and long o words. Invite them to draw a picture using some of their words. 231

LANGUAGE SUPPORT

Name ____ Date ____

What's the Word?

rainbow	anyway	maid	goes	raincoat

1. Sometimes Patty Jean feels like a _maid_.
2. "She doesn't need her crutches _anyway_," said Patty Jean.
3. When it rains, Patty Jean wears an icky old _raincoat_.
4. Princess Pooh _goes_ to school across the street.
5. When the sun came out, there was a _rainbow_.

Grade 2 — Language Support/Blackline Master 137 • Princess Pooh 249

Reteach, 231 — Practice, 231 — Extend, 231 — Language Support, 249

OBJECTIVES

Children will:

- review /ā/*ai, ay*; /ō/*oa, oe, ow*; /ē/*ee, ie, ea*; /ī/ *i, y, igh*; /ch/*tch, ch*.
- blend and read words with long *a, o, e, i*; and *tch, ch*.

MATERIALS

- **Teaching Chart 194**
- **Word Building Manipulative Cards**

Skills Finder

Long *o*	
Introduce	B1: 92G-H
Review	B1: 113E-F, 113G-H; B2: 310G-H, 339E-F
Test	B1: Unit 1

LANGUAGE SUPPORT

ESL Read aloud each word written on the chalkboard and have children repeat after you as you point to it. Ask volunteers to show the meaning of each word through drawing, pantomime, or verbal clues.

Review Long *a, o, e, i*; *tch, ch*

PREPARE

Review Long *a, o, e, i* Write the following words on the chalkboard: *maid, day, coaster, goes, mows, feet, chief, mean, library, myself, light*. Ask volunteers to read aloud each word, say the long vowel sound, and circle the letters that spell that sound.

Review *tch, ch* Write *watch* and *chair* on the chalkboard. Have a volunteer read the words and underline the letters that spell /ch/.

TEACH

BLENDING Model and Guide Practice with Long *a, o, e, i; tch, ch* Words

- Display **Teaching Chart 194.**
- In the first column, read the words *plain*, *play*, and *waited* with children, blending the sounds together.
- Ask children to say the vowel sound they hear in each word (/ā/) and underline the spelling for /ā/ in each word.

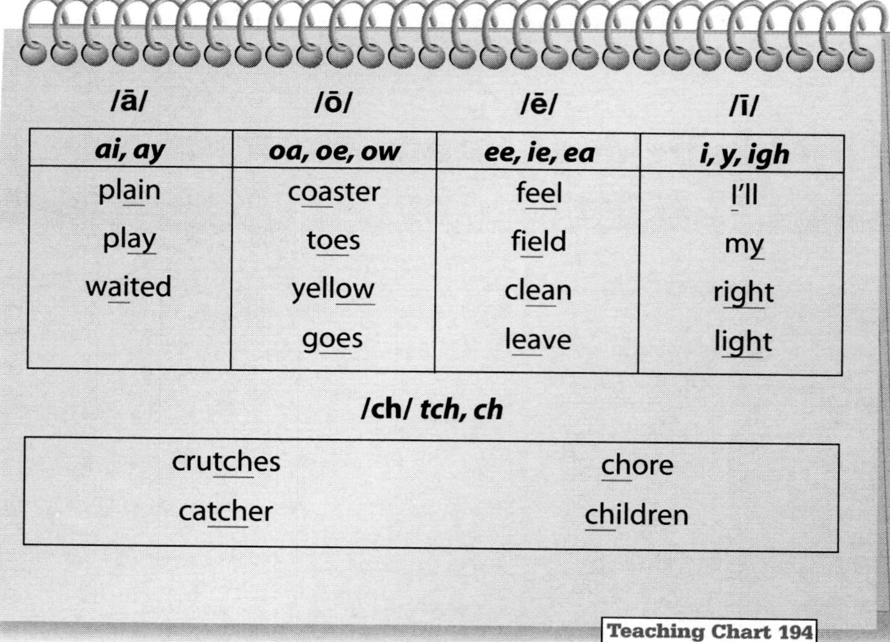

/ā/
ai, ay
plain
play
waited
/ō/
oa, oe, ow
coaster
toes
yellow
goes
/ē/
ee, ie, ea
feel
field
clean
leave
/ī/
i, y, igh
I'll
my
right
light
/ch/ tch, ch
crutches
catcher
chore
children

Teaching Chart 194

Use the Words in Context

- Have children use the words in oral sentences. Example: *I play soccer. Jen wore a plain blue shirt.*

Repeat the Procedure

- Repeat the procedure with the words in the other columns.

PRACTICE

WORD BUILDING
Sort and Read Long *a, o, e, i* and *tch, ch* Words

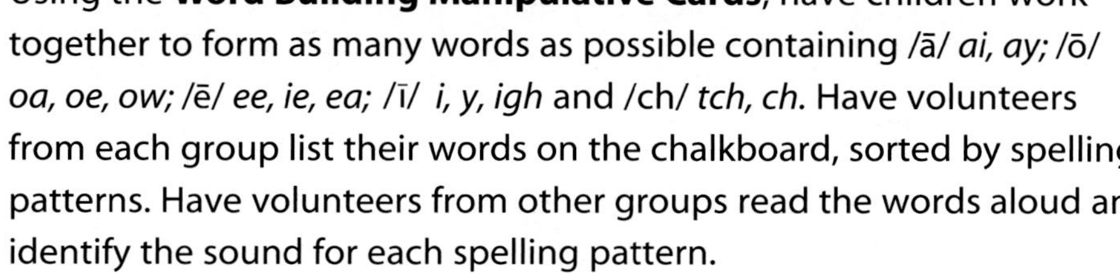

GROUP

Using the **Word Building Manipulative Cards**, have children work together to form as many words as possible containing /ā/ *ai, ay;* /ō/ *oa, oe, ow;* /ē/ *ee, ie, ea;* /ī/ *i, y, igh* and /ch/ *tch, ch.* Have volunteers from each group list their words on the chalkboard, sorted by spelling patterns. Have volunteers from other groups read the words aloud and identify the sound for each spelling pattern.

▶ **Interpersonal/Linguistic**

ASSESS/CLOSE

Read and Write Sentences Using Words with Long Vowels *a, o, e, i;* and *tch, ch*

To assess children's mastery of building, blending, and reading long *a, o, e, i;* and *tch, ch* words, observe their work in the Practice activity. Then encourage children to write sentences using two to three words from their lists.

ADDITIONAL PHONICS RESOURCES

Phonics/ Phonemic Awareness Practice Book, pages 143–146

CD-ROM activities for practice with Blending and Segmenting

DAILY Phonics ROUTINES

DAY 5 **Writing** Have children write riddles using /ā/ and /ō/ words, then trade with partners to read aloud and answer. Ask children to underline letters that spell /ā/ and /ō/.

Phonics CD-ROM

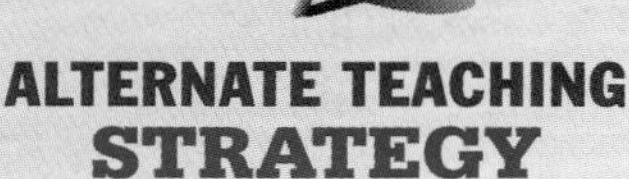

ALTERNATE TEACHING STRATEGY

LONG *a, o, e, i; tch, ch*

For a different approach to teaching this skill, see pages T65, T70, T73.

Intervention **Skills Intervention Guide**, for direct instruction and extra practice of long *a, o, e, i; tch, ch*

Meeting Individual Needs for Phonics

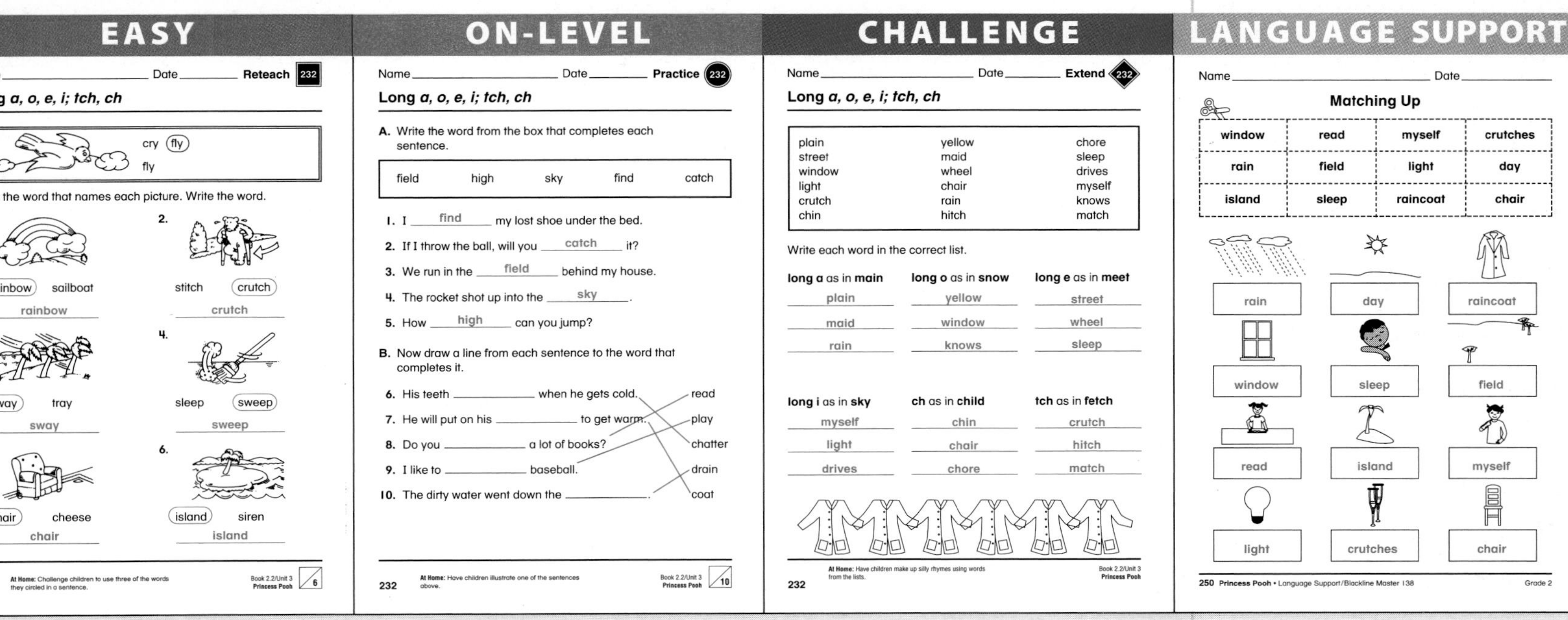

EASY

Name________ Date______ Reteach 232

Long *a, o, e, i; tch, ch*

cry (fly) fly

Circle the word that names each picture. Write the word.

1. (rainbow) sailboat — rainbow
2. stitch (crutch) — crutch
3. (sway) tray — sway
4. sleep (sweep) — sweep
5. (chair) cheese — chair
6. (island) siren — island

232 At Home: Challenge children to use three of the words they circled in a sentence. Book 2.2/Unit 3 Princess Pooh 6

ON-LEVEL

Name________ Date______ Practice 232

Long *a, o, e, i; tch, ch*

A. Write the word from the box that completes each sentence.

field high sky find catch

1. I find my lost shoe under the bed.
2. If I throw the ball, will you catch it?
3. We run in the field behind my house.
4. The rocket shot up into the sky.
5. How high can you jump?

B. Now draw a line from each sentence to the word that completes it.

6. His teeth _____ when he gets cold. — read
7. He will put on his _____ to get warm. — play
8. Do you _____ a lot of books? — chatter
9. I like to _____ baseball. — drain
10. The dirty water went down the _____. — coat

232 At Home: Have children illustrate one of the sentences above. Book 2.2/Unit 3 Princess Pooh 10

CHALLENGE

Name________ Date______ Extend 232

Long *a, o, e, i; tch, ch*

plain	yellow	chore
street	maid	sleep
window	wheel	drives
light	chair	myself
crutch	rain	knows
chin	hitch	match

Write each word in the correct list.

long a as in main	long o as in snow	long e as in meet
plain	yellow	street
maid	window	wheel
rain	knows	sleep

long i as in sky	ch as in child	tch as in fetch
myself	chin	crutch
light	chair	hitch
drives	chore	match

232 At Home: Have children make up silly rhymes using words from the lists. Book 2.2/Unit 3 Princess Pooh

LANGUAGE SUPPORT

Name________ Date______

Matching Up

window	read	myself	crutches
rain	field	light	day
island	sleep	raincoat	chair

rain, day, raincoat, window, sleep, field, read, island, myself, light, crutches, chair

250 Princess Pooh • Language Support/Blackline Master 138 Grade 2

Reteach, 232 **Practice, 232** **Extend, 232** **Language Support, 250**

OBJECTIVES

Children will form generalizations based on a reading passage.

MATERIALS

- Teaching Chart 195

Skills Finder

Form Generalizations	
Introduce	B2: 281I-J
Review	B2: 339I-J, 371G-H
Test	B2: Unit 3
Maintain	B2: 107, 225

TEACHING TIP

FORM GENERALIZATIONS Point out that a generalization can often be inaccurate. Example: *Maria was in a bad mood yesterday. Maria is an unhappy girl.* Discuss that Maria may be a happy girl, but there may have been a reason why she was in a bad mood. Invite children to form generalizations about people, places, and events. Explore how they may or may not be accurate.

SELF-SELECTED Reading

Children may choose from the following titles.

ANTHOLOGY

- *Princess Pooh*

LEVELED BOOKS

- *Everybody's Happy*
- *Karen and the Red Shoes*
- *The Wright Brothers Learn to Fly*

Bibliography, pages T82–T83

Review Form Generalizations

PREPARE

Discuss Making Generalizations Invite several children to finish this sentence orally: *Summer is always _________ than winter.* Discuss that this is a generalization.

TEACH

Read "My Sister the Princess" and Model the Skill Display **Teaching Chart 195**, and read the passage aloud. Ask a volunteer to circle the sentence that best sums up the general point of the passage. Explain that words like *always* and *everyone* are often clues that someone is making a general point.

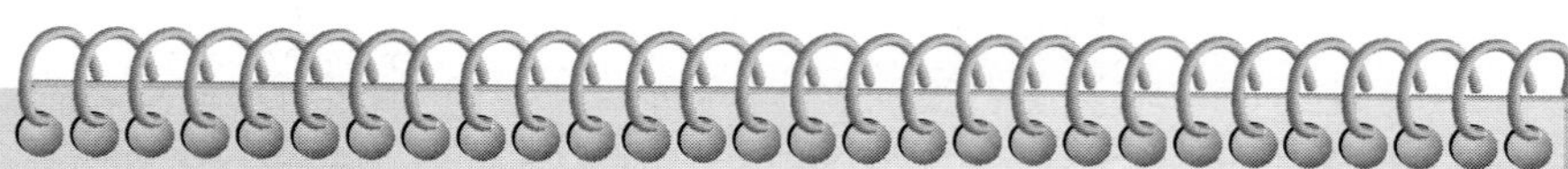

My Sister the Princess

My sister Penny is always treated as special by everyone. Penny does only the easiest chores and relaxes all the time. I, Patty Jean, have to do everything around our house. It must be fun to be treated like a princess every day. Everyone seems to love Penny best, and I don't think it's fair.

Teaching Chart 195

MODEL Patty Jean says Penny is treated better than she is. She uses words like *all the time* and *everybody,* so she is probably trying to make a general point. She says Penny is treated like a princess. Then she says she doesn't think it's fair. That sentence seems to sum up the general point best.

PRACTICE

Form Generalizations

PARTNERS

Invite children to work with a partner to make their own generalizations about the selection *Princess Pooh* or another familiar story. Have them write the general point in one sentence, and then orally give details and facts that support it.

ASSESS/CLOSE

Guide children to form generalizations about earlier selections in the book, and record them in a "What's the Big Idea?" chart. Have children explain orally how they formed these generalizations.

WHAT'S THE BIG IDEA?	
STORY	**GENERALIZATION**
The Best Friends Club	It's more important to work together with people than to boss everyone around.

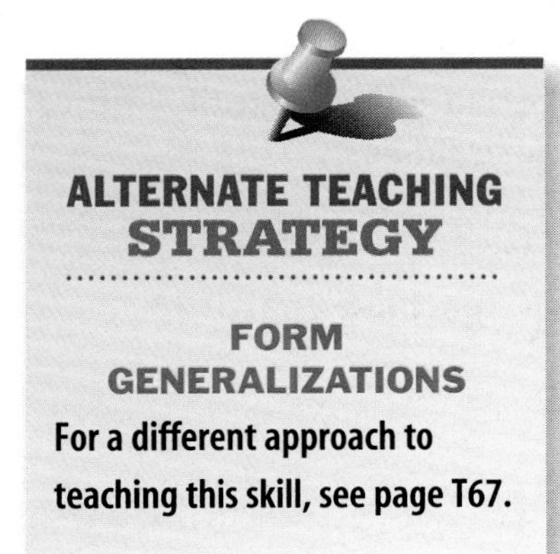

ALTERNATE TEACHING STRATEGY
FORM GENERALIZATIONS
For a different approach to teaching this skill, see page T67.

Intervention **Skills**

Intervention Guide, for direct instruction and extra practice in forming generalizations

leeting Individual Needs for Comprehension

EASY

Name__________ Date______ Reteach 233

Form Generalizations

A **generalization** is one statement you make about several facts.

Read the sentences about milk. Write four facts about milk. Then, write a sentence that states a generalization you can form based on the paragraph.

Do you like milk? Your body needs 2 to 3 servings of milk a day to stay healthy. Milk builds strong bones. It makes teeth whiter and harder. It is good for your hair and nails, too. Answers may vary.

Drink Milk

Milk __________

Milk __________

Milk __________

Milk __________

Generalization: __________

5 Book 2.2/Unit 3 **Princess Pooh**

At Home: Help children write four facts from "Princess Pooh." Then have them write a generalization based on those facts.

233

Reteach, 233

ON-LEVEL

Name__________ Date______ Practice 233

Form Generalizations

Think about the story "Princess Pooh." Then write the answer to each question on the line.

1. Why does Patty Jean call Penny Princess Pooh?
   She thinks Penny acts like and is treated as a princess; everyone does things for her and she tells everyone what to do.
2. How does Patty Jean feel about Penny at the beginning of the story?
   She doesn't like her because she thinks Penny always gets her way.
3. How does Patty Jean think that other people feel about Penny?
   She thinks that other people like her and think she is sweet and wonderful.
4. Does Patty Jean think she is treated as well as Penny?
   No. She thinks she is treated like a servant.
5. Is everyone nice to Patty Jean when she rides in the wheelchair? Give examples.
   No. Some people look away as if frightened; some boys are mean and won't get out of her way.

5 Book 2.2/Unit 3 **Princess Pooh**

At Home: Ask children to make another generalization about either Patty Jean or Penny.

233

Practice, 233

CHALLENGE

Name__________ Date______ Extend 233

Form Generalizations

Read these facts.

A lot of people were in the park on Saturday.
The family did not have room to play ball.
The family did not find an empty table when it was time for lunch.
The playground was full.
The family wanted to go home.

Write a generalization about the park on Saturday.

Possible answer: The park was crowded on Saturday.

Do you think the family had fun at the park? Why?

No, there were too many people at the park.

Draw a picture showing what the park might have looked like on Saturday.

Book 2.2/Unit 3 **Princess Pooh**

At Home: Have children write a generalization about playing in a crowded park.

233

Extend, 233

LANGUAGE SUPPORT

Name__________ Date______

In Someone Else's Shoes

① ② ③

Before	During	After
①	②	③

Grade 2

Language Support/Blackline Master 139 • **Princess Pooh** 251

Language Support, 251

Children will identify and use similes.

MATERIALS
- **Teaching Chart 196**

Skills Finder

Figurative Language

Introduce	B2: 339K-L
Review	B2: 361K-L, 371I-J
Test	B2: Unit 3

LANGUAGE SUPPORT

ESL Discuss with children examples of figurative language such as *That test was a piece of cake* and *Carlos was as mad as a wet hen.* Ask children to try to explain the meaning of each expression. (The test was easy. Carlos was very angry.) Explain that such expressions are used to emphasize a point. Ask children to give examples of figurative language translated from their first languages. Do any of the expressions mean the same thing in English?

Introduce Figurative Language

PREPARE

Discuss Figurative Language Write this sentence on the chalkboard: He is growing *as fast as* a weed.

Underline the figurative language in the sentence. Point out that comparing one thing to another helps the reader to see the thing in a new and different way.

TEACH

Define and Explain Simile Tell children that figurative language makes a comparison between two things. Explain that when the words *like* or *as* are used to make a comparison, it is called a *simile*. Have children read **Teaching Chart 196**.

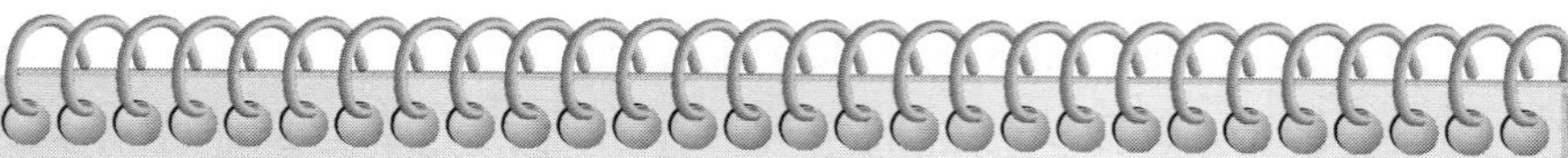

Patty Jean and Penny

Patty Jean did more chores than Penny did. Patty Jean was mad as a hornet. Penny just sat in her wheelchair like a lucky princess. After Patty Jean spent time in the wheelchair, she understood her sister's life better. She realized she was lucky, too. She may do more chores, but she is able to ride the roller coaster. Now, when people say Penny is as pretty as a flower and Patty Jean is growing like a weed, the sisters smile together like two peas in a pod.

Teaching Chart 196

Ask volunteers to underline examples of figurative language, and to explain their meaning.

MODEL Patty Jean was as mad as a hornet. The word *as* tells me that this is a simile. I can picture how mad Patty Jean is, since I know that hornets are wasps that get angry when they are bothered.

PRACTICE

Use Similes

Have each child make up a simple descriptive sentence and tell it to a partner. Examples: *He is tall. She was happy.* Have partners respond by writing a sentence that uses a simile to add color to the description. Examples: *He is tall as a goal post. She lit up like a cake full of birthday candles.* ▶ **Linguistic/Spatial**

ASSESS/CLOSE

Read and Define Figurative Expressions

Invite children to read aloud their sentences to the rest of the class. Ask volunteers to identify and explain the figurative language in their classmates' sentences.

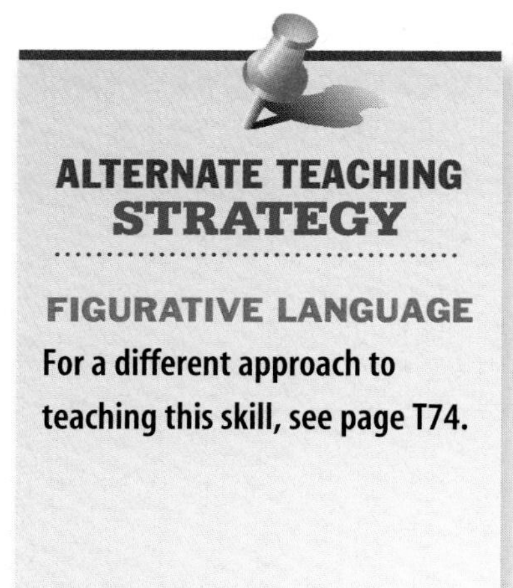

ALTERNATE TEACHING
STRATEGY
FIGURATIVE LANGUAGE
For a different approach to teaching this skill, see page T74.

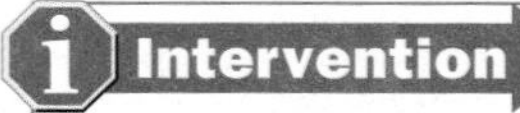

Skills

Intervention Guide, for direct instruction and extra practice of figurative language

eeting Individual Needs for Vocabulary

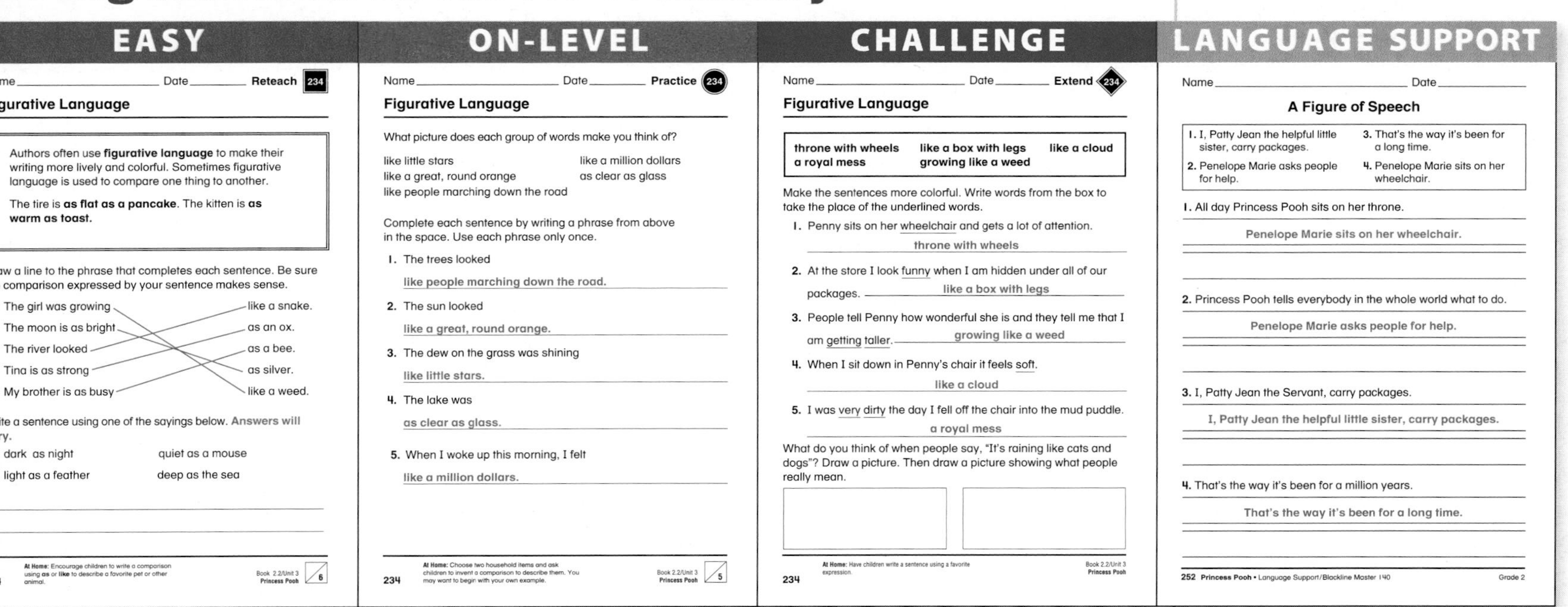

EASY

ame_______________ Date_______ Reteach 234

igurative Language

Authors often use **figurative language** to make their writing more lively and colorful. Sometimes figurative language is used to compare one thing to another.

The tire is **as flat as a pancake**. The kitten is **as warm as toast.**

'aw a line to the phrase that completes each sentence. Be sure e comparison expressed by your sentence makes sense.

. The girl was growing	like a snake.
. The moon is as bright	as an ox.
The river looked	as a bee.
. Tina is as strong	as silver.
My brother is as busy	like a weed.

rite a sentence using one of the sayings below. Answers will ıry.

dark as night	quiet as a mouse
light as a feather	deep as the sea

4 **At Home:** Encourage children to write a comparison using **as** or **like** to describe a favorite pet or other animal. Book 2.2/Unit 3 Princess Pooh 6

ON-LEVEL

Name_______________ Date_______ Practice 234

Figurative Language

What picture does each group of words make you think of?

like little stars	like a million dollars
like a great, round orange	as clear as glass
like people marching down the road	

Complete each sentence by writing a phrase from above in the space. Use each phrase only once.

1. The trees looked
   like people marching down the road.
2. The sun looked
   like a great, round orange.
3. The dew on the grass was shining
   like little stars.
4. The lake was
   as clear as glass.
5. When I woke up this morning, I felt
   like a million dollars.

234 **At Home:** Choose two household items and ask children to invent a comparison to describe them. You may want to begin with your own example. Book 2.2/Unit 3 Princess Pooh 5

CHALLENGE

Name_______________ Date_______ Extend 234

Figurative Language

throne with wheels	**like a box with legs**	**like a cloud**
a royal mess	**growing like a weed**	

Make the sentences more colorful. Write words from the box to take the place of the underlined words.

1. Penny sits on her wheelchair and gets a lot of attention.
   throne with wheels
2. At the store I look funny when I am hidden under all of our packages. like a box with legs
3. People tell Penny how wonderful she is and they tell me that I am getting taller. growing like a weed
4. When I sit down in Penny's chair it feels soft.
   like a cloud
5. I was very dirty the day I fell off the chair into the mud puddle.
   a royal mess

What do you think of when people say, "It's raining like cats and dogs"? Draw a picture. Then draw a picture showing what people really mean.

234 **At Home:** Have children write a sentence using a favorite expression. Book 2.2/Unit 3 Princess Pooh

LANGUAGE SUPPORT

Name_______________ Date_______

A Figure of Speech

1. I, Patty Jean the helpful little sister, carry packages.	3. That's the way it's been for a long time.
2. Penelope Marie asks people for help.	4. Penelope Marie sits on her wheelchair.

1. All day Princess Pooh sits on her throne.
   Penelope Marie sits on her wheelchair.
2. Princess Pooh tells everybody in the whole world what to do.
   Penelope Marie asks people for help.
3. I, Patty Jean the Servant, carry packages.
   I, Patty Jean the helpful little sister, carry packages.
4. That's the way it's been for a million years.
   That's the way it's been for a long time.

252 **Princess Pooh** • Language Support/Blackline Master 140 Grade 2

Reteach, 234 **Practice, 234** **Extend, 234** **Language Support, 252**

GRAMMAR/SPELLING CONNECTIONS

See the 5-Day Grammar and Usage Plan on pages *339O–339P*.

See the 5-Day Spelling Plan on pages *339Q–339R*.

TEACHING TIP

Technology Use your computer's *caps lock* key to capitalize all the letters in a word that describes a loud sound like *KABOOM* or *SPLAT*.

Handwriting CD-ROM

Writing a Story

Prewrite

WRITE A STORY Present this writing assignment: Imagine that you are Penelope, and you are writing in your journal about what happened the day Patty Jean took your wheelchair. Describe the day from beginning to end. Share how you felt about it.

VISUALIZING Review key events from *Princess Pooh*. Have children close their eyes and picture themselves as Penelope. Ask: *How would it feel to be Penelope at these moments?*

Strategy: Make a List Ask children to make a list of important moments from the story and the feelings they imagine Penelope might have. Have them describe what Penelope might say:

- at the moment she discovers that her sister took her wheelchair.
- when Patty Jean returns.
- during the talk the sisters have before they sleep.

Draft

FREE WRITE Guide children to write freely without self-editing. Encourage them to imagine how Penelope would express her feelings in a journal that no one else would read. Have them refer to their prewrite lists for details about story events and characters.

Revise

PARTNERS

WORK WITH A PARTNER Have partners share their work. As they give feedback, remind children to:

- be positive about their partner's work by sharing something they like in the story.
- ask questions about their partner's work i a polite way.
- explain their suggestions clearly.

Edit/Proofread

CHECK FOR ERRORS Children should re-read their stories to check spelling, punctuation, and grammar.

Publish

SHARE THE STORIES Have volunteers read their stories to the class. Discuss how Penelope's story differs from writer to write

Penelope's Day

Dear Diary,

Today something terrible happened! It was a beautiful day, with big, puffy clouds floating across the blue sky. I fell asleep outside in the hammock. When I woke up, my wheel-chair was gone! I was really scared. How would I get out of the hammock?

Then Mom came out and took me inside. Dad went to look for my chair. It turned out that Patty Jean had taken it just to see what it was like. I think she sometimes thinks I get too much attention. I just wish people wouldn't notice me as much. Patty Jean and I had a talk about it. I think we both feel better now.

Presentation Ideas

LUSTRATE A MOMENT Have children d drawings to their stories or make covers them. Encourage them to illustrate key oments that show what is happening and w Penelope feels. ▶ **Viewing/Representing**

ROLE-PLAY Have partners role-play scenes from their stories, including a dialogue between Penelope and Patty Jean. ▶ **Speaking/Listening**

nsider children's creative efforts, possibly adding a plus (+) for originality, wit, and imagination.

Scoring Rubric

Excellent	Good	Fair	Unsatisfactory
4: The writer • vividly reimagines the original story. • vividly describes both key events and characters' reactions. • uses figurative language and/or interesting dialogue to enrich the story.	**3:** The writer • clearly retells the story. • describes key events and characters' reactions. • includes some description and/or dialogue.	**2:** The writer • attempts to retell the story. • includes some description of characters' feelings. • includes no vivid description or dialogue.	**1:** The writer • does not tell a story. • does not develop characters at all. • does not write in clear or complete sentences.

complete 0: The writer leaves the page blank or fails to respond to the writing task. The student does not address the topic or simply paraphrases the prompt. The response is illegible or incoherent.

leeting Individual Needs for Writing

EASY

Picture This Have children draw a picture of Penelope and a friend playing a game or sport that both would enjoy. Have them write a sentence or two about why Penelope would enjoy this activity.

ON-LEVEL

A Day in the Life Have children write a paragraph describing a day in Penelope's life. Have them write about what she likes to do, where she likes to go, and who would go with her.

CHALLENGE

Penelope's Wish Have children discuss what Penelope might want to do when she grows up. Ask them to write about why she might want to do this and how she can prepare.

Listening and Speaking

LISTENING Remind children to
- imagine themselves in the situation the partners are role-playing.
- listen for story details that explain the characters' feelings and actions.

SPEAKING Have children
- speak slowly and loudly enough so that everyone can hear.
- change the tone of their voice while acting out their character.
- use appropriate tone of voice and gestures to indicate the feelings of their character.

LANGUAGE SUPPORT

ESL Invite a volunteer to pantomime key events in the story and ask children to write a sentence describing each event. Children can use some of these sentences as they write their stories.

PORTFOLIO Invite children to include their stories or another writing project in their portfolios.

5 Day Grammar and Usage Plan

LANGUAGE SUPPORT

Hold up two objects and have children compare them, saying which is bigger, smaller, thinner, wider, lighter, heavier, and so on.

DAILY LANGUAGE ACTIVITIES

Write the Daily Language Activities on the board each day or use **Transparency 28**. Have children correct the sentences orally, using the correct form of the adjective.

Day 1

1. Patty is tall than Penny. taller
2. Her chair is soft than mine. softer
3. Is Penny old than Patty? older

Day 2

1. That is the higher hill in town. highest
2. Penny had the bright smile in her class. brightest
3. Patty's was the colder day of all. coldest

Day 3

1. These clothes are the cleaner of all. cleanest
2. Mom is kindest than Penny. kinder
3. Patty does hard work than Penny. harder

Day 4

1. I was the fast girl in school. fastest
2. Her braces are newest than her crutches. newer
3. Penny was quietest than Patty. quieter

Day 5

1. The seat is softest than a cloud. softer
2. The cars were fastest than the wheelchair. faster
3. Her parents are the nicer ones on the block. nicest

Daily Language Transparency 28

DAY 1 Introduce the Concept

Oral Warm-Up Put two children back to back. Ask the class to make up a sentence about them using the word *tall* or *short*. Point out the *-er* ending in *taller* and *shorter*.

Introduce Adjectives That Compare Adjectives can tell how people, places, or things are different.

Adjectives That Compare

- You can use adjectives to compare people, places, or things.
- Add *-er* to an adjective to compare two nouns.

Present the Daily Language Activity and have children correct orally. Then have children pick two objects in the room and write a sentence comparing their sizes.

Assign the daily Writing Prompt on page 310C.

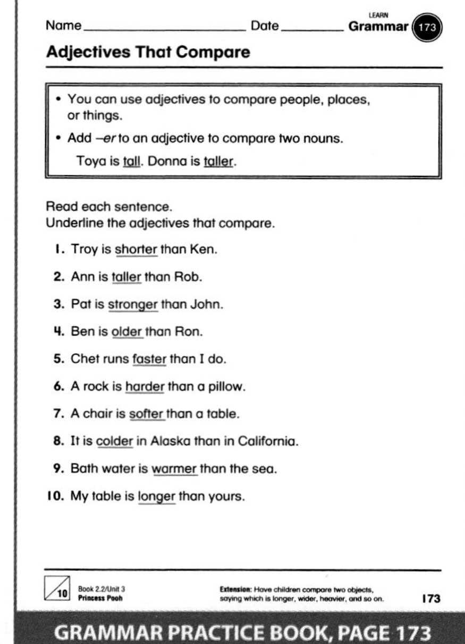

Name ________ Date ________ LEARN Grammar 173

Adjectives That Compare

- You can use adjectives to compare people, places, or things.
- Add *–er* to an adjective to compare two nouns.

  Toya is tall. Donna is taller.

Read each sentence.
Underline the adjectives that compare.

1. Troy is shorter than Ken.
2. Ann is taller than Rob.
3. Pat is stronger than John.
4. Ben is older than Ron.
5. Chet runs faster than I do.
6. A rock is harder than a pillow.
7. A chair is softer than a table.
8. It is colder in Alaska than in California.
9. Bath water is warmer than the sea.
10. My table is longer than yours.

10 Book 2.2/Unit 3 Princess Pooh

Extension: Have children compare two objects, saying which is longer, wider, heavier, and so on.

173

GRAMMAR PRACTICE BOOK, PAGE 173

DAY 2 Teach the Concept

Review Adjectives That Compare Ask children when they would add *-er* t an adjective.

Comparing More Than Two Tell chi dren that sometimes they may want to compare a person, place, or thing to many others or all the others.

Adjectives That Compare

Add *-est* to compare more than two nouns.

Present the Daily Language Activity. Th have children add *-est* to *strong, old,* an *long* and write sentences using the superlative forms.

Assign the daily Writing Prompt on page 310C.

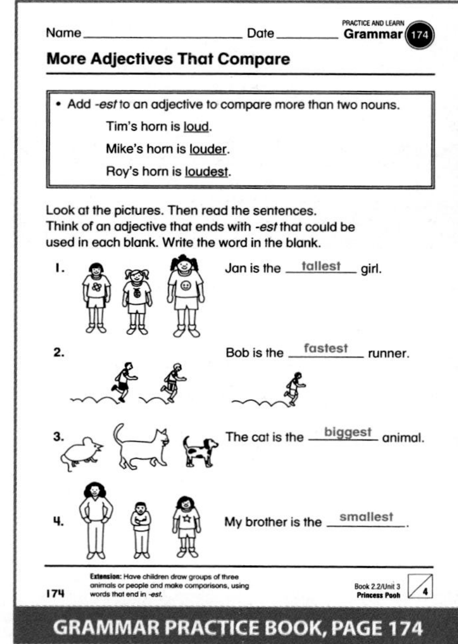

Name ________ Date ________ PRACTICE AND LEARN Grammar 174

More Adjectives That Compare

- Add *-est* to an adjective to compare more than two nouns.

  Tim's horn is loud.

  Mike's horn is louder.

  Roy's horn is loudest.

Look at the pictures. Then read the sentences.
Think of an adjective that ends with *-est* that could be used in each blank. Write the word in the blank.

1. Jan is the tallest girl.
2. Bob is the fastest runner.
3. The cat is the biggest animal.
4. My brother is the smallest.

174

Extension: Have children draw groups of three animals or people and make comparisons, using words that end in *-est*.

Book 2.2/Unit 3 Princess Pooh 4

GRAMMAR PRACTICE BOOK, PAGE 174

Adjectives That Compare

DAY 3 Review and Practice

earn from the Literature Review ljectives that end with *-er* and *-est.* ead the third sentence from the bottom page 329 of *Princess Pooh.*

By the time I pull the throne out, I am wetter and colder than I have ever been in my whole life.

k children to identify the adjectives at compare. You may point out that adctives that end in a consonant may uble the consonant before adding *-er* id *-est*. Ask children to add *-est* to *cold* id tell how it is spelled.

orm Adjectives That Compare esent the Daily Language Activity. Then rite this list of adjectives on the board: *nall, light, new, high, clean, old, short, fast, ow, hard, soft.* Have children rewrite the ljectives in their *-er* and *-est* forms.

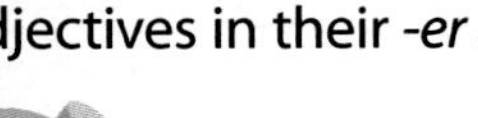

Assign the daily Writing Prompt on page 310D.

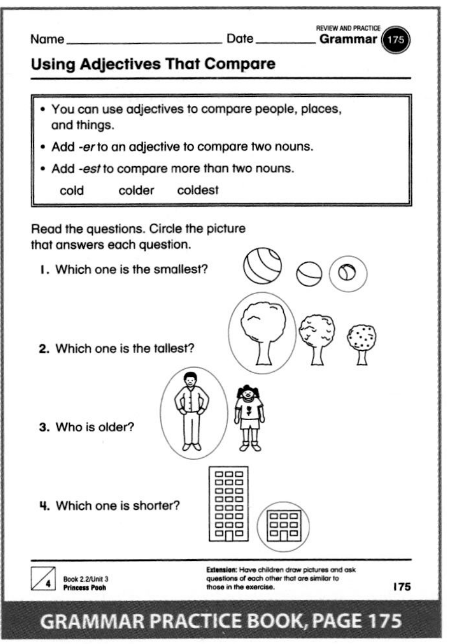

Name ______________ Date ________ REVIEW AND PRACTICE Grammar 175

Using Adjectives That Compare

- You can use adjectives to compare people, places, and things.
- Add *-er* to an adjective to compare two nouns.
- Add *-est* to compare more than two nouns.

cold colder coldest

Read the questions. Circle the picture that answers each question.

1. Which one is the smallest?
2. Which one is the tallest?
3. Who is older?
4. Which one is shorter?

4 Book 2.2/Unit 3 Princess Pooh

Extension: Have children draw pictures and ask questions of each other that are similar to those in the exercise.

175

GRAMMAR PRACTICE BOOK, PAGE 175

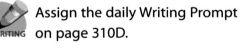

DAY 4 Review and Practice

Review Adjectives That Compare List corrected adjectives from the Daily Language Activities for Days 1 through 3. Have children use them in new sentences. Introduce the Daily Language Activity for Day 4.

Mechanics and Usage Before children begin the daily Writing Prompt on page 310D, review the rules for using an apostrophe. Display and discuss:

Apostrophes

- Add an apostrophe and *-s* to make a singular noun possessive.
- Add an apostrophe to make most plural nouns possessive.

Assign the daily Writing Prompt on page 310D.

Name ______________ Date ________ MECHANICS Grammar 176

Apostrophe

- Add an apostrophe and *-s* to make a singular noun possessive.
- Add an apostrophe to make most plural nouns possessive.

the girl's chair the girls' chairs

Write each sentence correctly on the line.

1. Two boys are in a doctors office.
   Two boys are in a doctor's office.
2. The taller boy coat is hanging in a closet
   The taller boy's coat is hanging in a closet.
3. the closets door has drawings of cats.
   The closet's door has drawings of cats.
4. the biggest cats whiskers makes it look like a monster
   The biggest cat's whiskers make it look like a monster.

176 Book 2.2/Unit 3 Princess Pooh 8

GRAMMAR PRACTICE BOOK, PAGE 176

DAY 5 Assess and Reteach

Assess Use the Daily Language Activity and page 177 of the **Grammar Practice Book** for assessment.

Have children write each rule about adjectives that compare on an index card.

List the corrected adjectives from the Daily Language Activities for Days 1 through 4 on the board. Have children take turns underlining the *-er* or *-est* endings in each word. Then write these two incomplete sentences next to each other on the board:

_____ is _____ than _____.
_____ is the _____ of all.

Under each model, have children write sentences following the same form, using adjectives ending with *-er* in the first set and those with *-est* in the second.

Use page 178 of the **Grammar Practice Book** for additional reteaching.

Assign the daily Writing Prompt on page 310D.

Name ______________ Date ________ TEST Grammar 177

Adjectives That Compare

A. Read each sentence. Add *-er* or *-est* to each adjective. Write the new adjective on the line.

1. That is the (tall) tree on the street. tallest
2. It has the (hard) wood of all. hardest
3. Wood is (strong) than paper. stronger

B. Read each pair of sentences. Mark the one that is correct.

4. ◎ My fingers are coldest than yours.
   ● My fingers are colder than yours.
5. ◎ Jane is shortest than Emily.
   ● Jane is shorter than Emily.

5 Book 2.2/Unit 3 Princess Pooh 177

GRAMMAR PRACTICE BOOK, PAGE 177

GRAMMAR PRACTICE BOOK, PAGE 178

5 Day Spelling Plan

LANGUAGE SUPPORT

ESL Write the spelling words on the chalkboard, but leave a space where the final consonant of each word would be. Point to each word and use it in a sentence. Then spell out each word letter by letter and have children call out the missing letter when you get to it. Write the missing letter in the space on the chalkboard. Then circle the digraph and say the word again.

DICTATION SENTENCES

Spelling Words

1. I can go with you.
2. She can push the toy duck.
3. They both have a cold.
4. My mother can rush to you.
5. The bath is for her.
6. My mouth is dry.
7. He has a new brush.
8. Her teeth are clean.
9. He made a dash for the car.
10. The fish is good to eat.

Challenge Words

11. My cousins came to my home.
12. The bike is golden.
13. The princess is very busy.
14. We can eat at the restaurant.
15. He can take a trip around the world.

DAY 1 Pretest

Assess Prior Knowledge Use the Dictation Sentences at left and **Spelling Practice Book** page 173 for the pretest. Allow children to correct their own papers. If children have trouble, have partners give each other a midweek test on Day 3. Children who require a modified list may be tested on the first five words.

Spelling Words		Challenge Words
1. **with**	6. mouth	11. **cousins**
2. **push**	7. brush	12. **golden**
3. **both**	8. teeth	13. **princess**
4. **rush**	9. dash	14. **restaurant**
5. bath	10. fish	15. **world**

*Note: Words in **dark type** are from the story.*

Word Study On page 174 of the **Spelling Practice Book** are word study steps and an at-home activity.

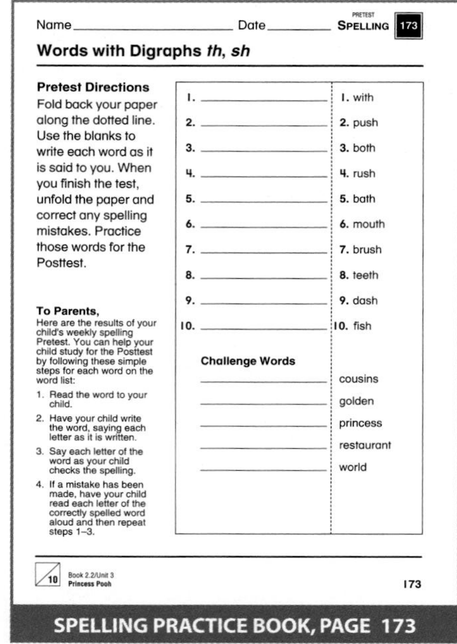

Name_______________ Date_______ PRETEST SPELLING 173

Words with Digraphs *th, sh*

Pretest Directions
Fold back your paper along the dotted line. Use the blanks to write each word as it is said to you. When you finish the test, unfold the paper and correct any spelling mistakes. Practice those words for the Posttest.

To Parents,
Here are the results of your child's weekly spelling Pretest. You can help your child study for the Posttest by following these simple steps for each word on the word list:
1. Read the word to your child.
2. Have your child write the word, saying each letter as it is written.
3. Say each letter of the word as your child checks the spelling.
4. If a mistake has been made, have your child read each letter of the correctly spelled word aloud and then repeat steps 1–3.

1. ______ 1. with
2. ______ 2. push
3. ______ 3. both
4. ______ 4. rush
5. ______ 5. bath
6. ______ 6. mouth
7. ______ 7. brush
8. ______ 8. teeth
9. ______ 9. dash
10. ______ 10. fish

Challenge Words
______ cousins
______ golden
______ princess
______ restaurant
______ world

10 Book 2.2/Unit 3 Princess Pooh 173

SPELLING PRACTICE BOOK, PAGE 173

WORD STUDY STEPS AND ACTIVITY, PAGE 174

DAY 2 Explore the Pattern

Sort and Spell Words Say the words *with* and *push*. Ask children what sound they hear at the end of each word. Tell children that these words end with the letters *th* and *sh*.

Ask children to read aloud the ten spelling words before sorting them according to sound and spelling pattern.

Words ending with	
th	**sh**
with	push
both	rush
bath	brush
mouth	dash
teeth	fish

Word Wall As children enjoy books from the school library, have them look for new words ending with final digraph *th* and *sh* and add them to the classroom word wall, underlining the spelling pattern in each word.

Name_______________ Date_______ EXPLORE THE PATTERN SPELLING 175

Words with Digraphs *th, sh*

with	both	bath	brush	dash
push	rush	mouth	teeth	fish

Write the spelling words that follow the patterns in the crowns below.

Words ending with th
1. with
2. both
3. bath
4. mouth
5. teeth

Words ending with sh
6. push
7. rush
8. brush
9. dash
10. fish

Scramble
Unscramble each set of letters to make a spelling word. Write the words. Then circle the two letters that are the same in each word.

11. eehtt teeth
12. tohb both
13. thba bath
14. oumht mouth
15. ithw with

15 Book 2.2/Unit 3 Princess Pooh 175

SPELLING PRACTICE BOOK, PAGE 175

Words with Digraphs *th, sh*

DAY 3 Practice and Extend

ord Meaning: Synonyms Remind ildren that a synonym is a word that as the same meaning as another word. sk children to think of synonyms for as any spelling words as they can. xamples: *rush/hurry, dash/run.*)

lossary Have children:

- write each Challenge Word.
- look up the Challenge Words in the Glossary and identify the nouns.
- write a context sentence for each noun.

Name ____________ Date ______ PRACTICE AND EXTEND SPELLING 176

Words with Digraphs *th, sh*

with	both	bath	brush	dash
push	rush	mouth	teeth	fish

Gone Fishing

Use spelling words to complete each sentence below.

1. A ___fish___ swims in water.
2. Be careful not to ___push___ me.
3. The fish has a wide ___mouth___.
4. Come ___with___ me in the boat.
5. We will have to ___rush___ if we want to be on time.
6. I'm late; now I'll have to ___dash___.
7. I'll take a quick ___bath___.
8. I'll brush my ___teeth___.
9. Then I will ___brush___ my hair.
10. When we are ready, we'll ___both___ go and dance.

Word Meaning

Synonyms are words that have the same or similar meaning. Write a spelling word that has the same meaning as each word below.

11. hurry ___rush___ 12. run ___dash___

Challenge Extension: Have students describe a new restaurant that opened and write a menu for it.

176 Book 2.2/Unit 3 Princess Pooh 12

SPELLING PRACTICE BOOK, PAGE 176

DAY 4 Proofread and Write

Proofread Sentences Write these sentences on the chalkboard, including the misspelled words. Ask children to proofread, circling incorrect spellings and writing the correct spellings. There are two spelling errors in each sentence.

I put a piece of fishe in my mout.
(fish, mouth)

He had to bruch his teath.
(brush, teeth)

Have children create additional sentences with errors for partners to correct.

Writing Have children use as many spelling words as possible in the daily Writing Prompt on page 310D. Remind children to proofread their writing for errors in spelling, grammar, and punctuation.

Name ____________ Date ______ PROOFREAD AND WRITE SPELLING 177

Words with Digraphs *th, sh*

Proofreading Activity

There are six spelling mistakes in the paragraph below. Circle each misspelled word. Write the words correctly on the lines below.

The big fishe began to rusch toward him. It wanted to bite him with its sharp teith. What could he do? He waited for the fish to close its big mout. Then he said, "Listen, I don't see why you want to pussh me. There's enough room for botth of us to swim here."

1. ___fish___ 2. ___rush___ 3. ___teeth___
4. ___mouth___ 5. ___push___ 6. ___both___

Writing Activity

What are the girls doing? Write sentences about the picture. Use four of your spelling words. Circle the spelling words you use.

10 Book 2.2/Unit 3 Princess Pooh 177

SPELLING PRACTICE BOOK, PAGE 177

DAY 5 Assess and Reteach

Assess Children's Knowledge Use page 178 of the **Spelling Practice Book** or the Dictation Sentences on page 339Q for the posttest.

Personal Word List If any children have trouble with any words in the lesson, have them create a personal word list of troublesome words in their journals. Have children write imaginary invitations to favorite book characters using these words.

Children should refer to their word lists during later writing activities.

Name ____________ Date ______ POSTTEST SPELLING 178

Words with Digraphs *th, sh*

Look at the words in each set. One word in each set is spelled correctly. Use a pencil to color in the circle in front of that word. Before you begin, look at the sample sets of words. Sample A has been done for you. Do Sample B by yourself. When you are sure you know what to do, you may go on with the rest of the page.

Sample A: (A) wich (B) wish (C) wisch (D) weish

Sample B: (E) nede (F) need (G) neede (H) neade

1. (A) dash (B) dach (C) desh (D) dassh
2. (E) wiht (F) withh (G) with (H) wiith
3. (A) boht (B) bothe (C) both (D) bohte
4. (E) mouthe (F) mouhte (G) mouht (H) mouth
5. (A) bresh (B) bruth (C) brush (D) brussh
6. (E) teth (F) teeh (G) teeht (H) teeth
7. (A) resh (B) rush (C) reshh (D) russh
8. (E) fish (F) fith (G) fiss (H) fissh
9. (A) baht (B) bah (C) bath (D) bahte
10. (E) pust (F) puhs (G) pusht (H) push

178 Book 2.2/Unit 3 Princess Pooh 10

SPELLING PRACTICE BOOK, PAGE 178

Concept

- Sea Creatures

Comprehension

- Form Generalizations

Phonics

- Soft *c* and Soft *g*

Vocabulary

- escaped
- fierce
- hidden
- machine
- swaying
- swift

Reaching All Learners

Anthology

Swimmy

Selection Summary **A little black fish named Swimmy meets many creatures that live in the sea and teaches them to solve problems by working together.**

Party Time

Change into your swimsuit,
Get your flippers, follow me.
We're going to a party
Underneath the deep, blue sea.
You're sure to have a nice time
In this strange and fishy place,
Where crab and lobster crawl about
And watch the seahorse race.
Have a slice of fishcake
And a bit of seafood stew.
Then shake hands with the octopus,
And say, "How do you do."

Rhyme applies to phonics

Listening Library

INSTRUCTIONAL pages 342–361

About the Author/Illustrator Leo Lionni is a four-time Caldecott Honor Book winner. Asked where he got the idea for *Swimmy*, he says: "I was watching the minnows swimming around in the harbor one day. Standing by the water, I didn't have an idea for a book. But later, as I began writing the book, I realized that seeing the fish gave me the idea and set the story off."

Same Concept, Skills and Vocabulary!

Leveled Books

EASY
Lesson on pages 361A and 361D
DECODABLE

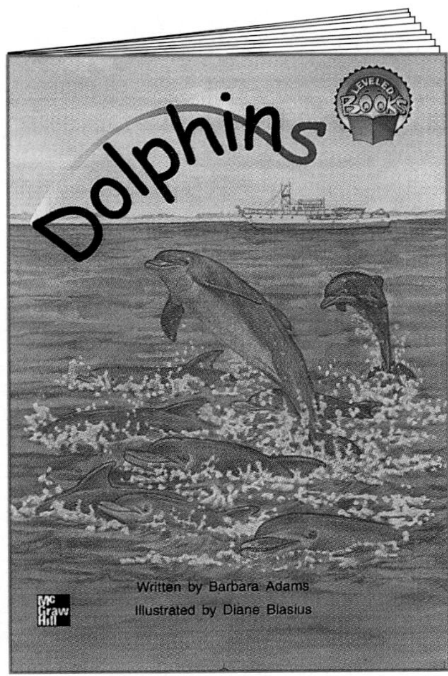

INDEPENDENT
Lesson on pages 361B and 361D

Take-Home version available

CHALLENGE
Lesson on pages 361C and 361D

Leveled Practice

EASY
Reteach, 235–242 Blackline masters with reteaching opportunities for each assessed skill

INDEPENDENT/ON-LEVEL
Practice, 235–242 Workbook with Take-Home stories and practice opportunities for each assessed skill and story comprehension

CHALLENGE
Extend, 235–242 Blackline masters that offer challenge activities for each assessed skill

Quizzes Prepared by  Accelerated Reader

WORKSTATION Activities

Social Studies . . . Oceans of the World, *348*
Science . . . . Learn About Food Chains, *344*
Math . . . . The Biggest and the Smallest, *346*
Art . . . . Sponge Painting, *354*
Language Arts . . Read Aloud, *340E*
Writing . . . . Write a Fairy Tale, *358*
Cultural Perspectives . . . . . Origami Fish, *350*
Research and Inquiry . . . . . . Find Out More, *359*
Internet Activities . . . . www.mhschool.com/reading

Suggested Lesson Planner

READING AND LANGUAGE ARTS	 DAY 1 Focus on Reading and Skills	 DAY 2 Read the Literature
Phonics Daily Routines	**Daily Phonics Routine: Segmenting,** 340H Phonics CD-ROM	 **Daily Phonics Routine: Blending,** 342A Phonics CD-ROM
Phonological Awareness Phonics *Soft c, g* Comprehension Vocabulary Study Skills Listening, Speaking, Viewing, Representing	 **Read Aloud: Folk Tale,** 340E "The Discontented Fish" ☑ **Develop Phonological Awareness,** 340F Soft *c, g* ☑ **Review Soft *c* and Soft *g*,** 340G–340H **Teaching Chart 197** **Reteach, Practice, Extend,** 235 **Phonics/Phonemic Awareness Practice Book,** 147–150 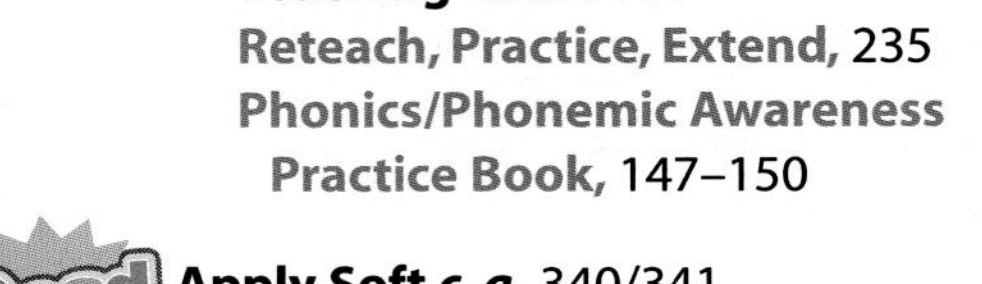 **Apply Soft *c, g*,** 340/341 "Party Time"  Intervention Program	**Build Background,** 342A Develop Oral Language **Vocabulary,** 342B–342C ***escaped*** ***hidden*** ***swaying*** ***fierce*** ***machine*** ***swift*** **Word Building Manipulative Card** **Teaching Chart 198** **Reteach, Practice, Extend,** 236  **Read the Selection,** 342–357 Comprehension ☑ **Soft *c, g*** ☑ **Form Generalizations** **Genre:** Fiction/Fantasy, 343 **Cultural Perspectives,** 350  Intervention Program
Curriculum Connections	 Link **Language Arts,** 340E	 Link **Science,** 342A
Writing	 **Writing Prompt:** What size fish would you rather be—big enough to scare other fish, or small enough to hide and be safe? Explain your choice.	 **Writing Prompt:** Is this statement tru or false: You have to be big to be smart. Explain your answer.  **Journal Writing** Quick-Write, 357
Grammar	**Introduce the Concept: Adverbs,** 361O Daily Language Activity: Identify adverbs. **Grammar Practice Book,** 179	**Teach the Concept: Adverbs,** 361O Daily Language Activity: Identify adverbs. **Grammar Practice Book,** 180
Spelling *th, wh*	**Pretest: Words with Digraphs *th, wh*,** 361Q **Spelling Practice Book,** 179, 180	**Explore the Pattern: Words with Digraphs *th, wh*,** 361Q **Spelling Practice Book,** 181

 **Intervention Program Available**

leeting
ndividual
eeds

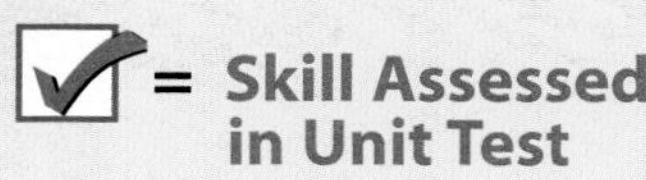
= Skill Assessed in Unit Test

Intervention Program Available

DAY 3 Read the Literature

Daily Phonics Routine:
Letter Substitution, 359

Phonics CD-ROM

Rereading for Fluency, 356

Story Questions and Activities, 358–359
Reteach, Practice, Extend, 237

Study Skill, 360
☑ Library/Media Center
Teaching Chart 199
Reteach, Practice, Extend, 238

Test Power, 361

Read the Leveled Books, 361A–361D
Guided Reading
☑ Soft *c, g*
☑ Form Generalizations
☑ Instructional Vocabulary

Intervention Program

Activity Science, 344 Math, 346

Writing Prompt: Think of a time when you wanted to do something that you couldn't do alone. What did you do?

Writing a Story, 361M
Prewrite, Draft

Review and Practice: Adverbs, 361P
Daily Language Activity: Identify adverbs.

Grammar Practice Book, 181

Practice and Extend: Words with Digraphs *th, wh,* 361R

Spelling Practice Book, 182

DAY 4 Build Skills

Daily Phonics Routine:
Fluency, 361F

Phonics CD-ROM

Read the Leveled Books and the Self-Selected Books

☑ Review Soft *c* and Soft *g*, 361E–361F
Teaching Chart 200
Reteach, Practice, Extend, 239
Language Support, 258
Phonics/Phonemic Awareness Practice Book, 147–150

☑ Review Soft *c, g;* Long *a, o, e, i,* 361G–361H
Teaching Chart 201
Reteach, Practice, Extend, 240
Language Support, 259
Phonics/Phonemic Awareness Practice Book, 147–150

Minilessons, 345, 347, 349, 351, 353, 355

Intervention Program

Activity Social Studies, 348

Writing Prompt: If you were Swimmy, how would you persuade the other fish to follow your plan?

Writing a Story, 361M
Revise

Meeting Individual Needs for Writing, 361N

Review and Practice: Adverbs, 361P
Daily Language Activity: Identify adverbs.

Grammar Practice Book, 182

Proofread and Write: Words with Digraphs *th, wh,* 361R

Spelling Practice Book, 183

DAY 5 Build Skills

Daily Phonics Routine:
Writing, 361H

Phonics CD-ROM

Read Self-Selected Books

☑ Review Main Idea, 361I–361J
Teaching Chart 202
Reteach, Practice, Extend, 241
Language Support, 260

☑ Review Figurative Language, 361K–361L
Teaching Chart 203
Reteach, Practice, Extend, 242
Language Support, 261

Listening, Speaking, Viewing, Representing, 361N
Make a Book
Act It Out

Minilessons, 345, 347, 349, 351, 353, 355

Intervention Program

Activity Art, 354

Writing Prompt: Write a short story about a fish that wants to learn to fly. Describe the fish and its movements.

Writing a Story, 361M
Edit/Proofread, Publish

Assess and Reteach: Adverbs, 361P
Daily Language Activity: Identify adverbs.

Grammar Practice Book, 183, 184

Assess and Reteach: Words with Digraphs *th, wh,* 361R

Spelling Practice Book, 184

Language Arts

Read Aloud

The Discontented Fish

an African folk tale retold by Kathleen Arnott

Once upon a time there was a colony of little fishes who lived together in their own small pool, isolated from the rest of the fish in the river. It was a still, gray pool, dotted with stone and clumps of weeds and surrounded by thorn bushes and a few palm trees.

Most of these fish were as happy and as friendly as they could be. But there was one fish, much bigger and stronger than all the others, who kept himself aloof, and who would draw himself up in a haughty manner whenever the others came near him.

"My good fellow," he would say, opening his eyes as wide as he could, and balancing himself erect on his handsome tail, "do stop making such a commotion in the water beside me. Can't you see I am having my afternoon siesta? Go away! And take that rabble away with you," he would add, sweeping one glistening fin towards a shoal of cheerful small fish darting in and out among the shadows.

Continued on pages T3–T4

Oral Comprehension

LISTENING AND SPEAKING Read aloud this story of a big fish in a little pond. Ask children to think about the sequence of events as you read. When you have finished, ask, "Did the fish meet the tiger-fish before or after he left the pond?"

GENRE STUDY: FOLK TALE Discuss some of the characteristics of a folk tale.

- Remind children that folk tales were not always written down but were told orally by storytellers to a group. Discuss how folk tales have changed over time because they were dependent on the memories of storytellers.
- Point out that characters in folk tales are often stereotypical characters who may be extremely good or extremely bad. Ask, *How would you describe the big fish at the beginning of the tale? Is he good or bad? What is he like by the story's end?*

Activity Help children make fish mobiles. Have each child cut a fish out of cardboard and paint it on both sides. Help them punch a hole in each fish; then invite them to make a mobile by hanging five fish from long sticks or wire hangers. Have them use the mobile as a prop while they take turns in groups retelling the folk tale, *The Discontented Fish*.

Develop Phonological Awareness

Blend Sounds

Phonemic Awareness

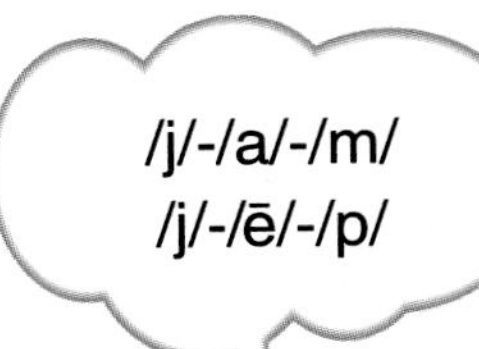

Teach Have children listen as you say the sounds: /j/-/a/-/m/. Then say the word *jam*. Tell them to listen as you say more sounds. Say: /j/-/ē/-/p/. *Let's put the sounds together: jeep.* What sound do you hear in both *jar* and *jeep*? (/j/)

Practice Have children blend the sounds to say the following word pairs. After blending each pair, have children tell which sound is in both words: *cage/huge; piece/trace; race/pain; dear/drive/; stage/huge.*

Segment Sounds

Phonemic Awareness

Teach Tell children you have two "Sound Friends," Madge and Grace. Explain that Madge only likes to hear words that have the /j/ sound. Grace only likes words with the /s/ sound. Say *badge* and have children say the word again, sound-by-sound. Hold up a picture for *badge* and say the word. Prompt them to say, "It's a Madge word."

Practice Proceed with the following words: *twice, face, age, large, strange, rice, cage,* and *spice.*

Substitute Sounds

Phonemic Awareness

Teach Play a sound game. Explain that you will say a word and then pick a child who will say the word again, but with a different sound. Demonstrate by saying the word *pig*. Have children repeat the word. Then choose a child and say: *Now say it again, but change the* /p/ to /j/. *What word is it now?* (jig)

Practice Have children substitute beginning, middle, and ending sounds in the following sets of words: *page/wage, rice/race, stage/stain, click/clock, spoke/spike, place/plate,* and *dice/mice.*

Observe children as they blend, segment, and substitute sounds. If children have difficulty, see Alternate Teaching Strategies on p. T75.

OBJECTIVES

Children will:

- identify /s/*ce* and /j/*ge*.
- decode and read words with /s/*ce* and /j/*ge*.

MATERIALS

- **Teaching Chart 197**
- **cards and word building boxes from the Word Building Manipulative Cards**

Skills Finder

Soft *c* and Soft *g*

Introduce	B2: 44G-H
Review	B2: 67E-F, 361E-F, 361G-H, 362G-H
Test	B2: Unit 1
Maintain	B2: 221

SPELLING/PHONICS CONNECTIONS

See 5-Day Spelling Plan, pages 361Q–361R.

TEACHING TIP

SOFT c AND SOFT g

After children have heard and repeated the soft sounds for *ce* and *ge*, ask them what other letter sounds the same as *ce*. (*s*) What other letter sounds the same as *ge*? (*j*) Brainstorm with children a list of words with the letters *s* and *j*.

Review Soft *c* and Soft *g*

PREPARE

Identify the /s/ and /j/ Sounds Review with children that the letters *ce* stand for the sound /s/ and the letters *ge* stand for the sound /j/.

TEACH

BLENDING Model and Guide Practice with Soft *c* and *g* Words

- Display **Teaching Chart 197**. Point to the top of the first column and say /s/. Have children repeat after you.
- Run your finger under the word *race*, blending the letters to read the word. Have children repeat after you. Do the same with the word *twice*.
- In the first incomplete word, write the letters *ce* in the underlined space to form the word *place*.
- Blend the sounds together with children.
- Have volunteers add *ce* to the other incomplete words in the first column and read the words.

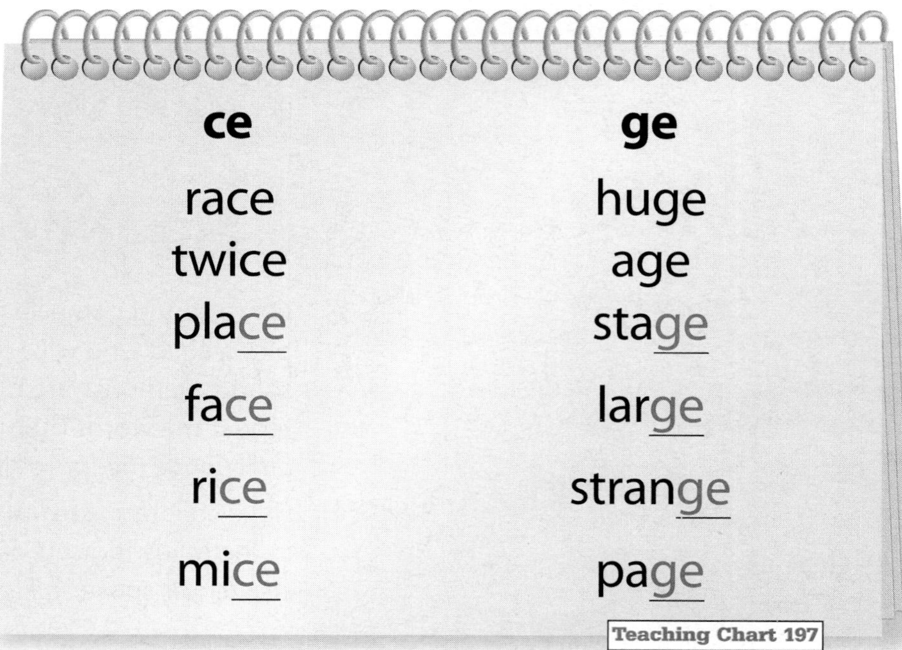

Use the Words in Context

- Have volunteers use the words in sentences to reinforce their meanings. Example: *I know a place where we can play soccer.*

Repeat the Procedure

- Follow the same procedure to complete the words in column 2 on the chart.

PRACTICE

LETTER SUBSTITUTION Use Letter Cards to Build Words with Soft *c* and *g* Sounds

Using the **Word Building Manipulative Cards**, have children build the word *trace*. Tell them to change the word to *lace* by replacing the *tr* with *l*. Have children repeat this new word after you. Next, ask children to build and write the following words, substituting the appropriate letters: *grace, race, rice, nice, price*. Repeat the procedure with the /j/ sound using the following words: *cage, stage, page*.

▶ **Kinesthetic/Linguistic**

ASSESS/CLOSE

Read and Use Soft *c* and *g* Words in Sentences

To assess children's ability to blend and read soft *c* and *g* words, observe them as they work on the Practice activity. Then have them write new words that contain soft *c* and soft *g* sounds. Ask children to use these words in sentences that show what they mean.

ADDITIONAL PHONICS RESOURCES

Phonics/Phonemic Awareness Practice Book, pages 147–150

Phonics CD-ROM activities for practice with Blending and Segmenting

Daily Routines

DAY 1 **Segmenting** Distribute word building boxes. Say aloud a word with soft *c*, such as *slice*. Have children write the spelling of each sound in the appropriate box. Repeat with *face, range,* and *hinge*.

DAY 2 **Blending** Say *ice* and write the letters that stand for each sound. Ask children to blend the sounds to read the word. Repeat with *rice, strange,* and *large*.

DAY 3 **Letter Substitution** Write these words on the board: *cage, dice, pace*. Read the words together. Ask volunteers to change the beginning letter in each word to make a new word.

DAY 4 **Fluency** Write these words on the board: *mice, nice, pace, face, stage, page, age*. Point to each word, asking children to blend the sounds silently. Then ask volunteers to use the words in sentences.

DAY 5 **Writing** Have partners use /s/ and /j/ words to create rhyming couplets. Have children read their rhymes to the class. Have listeners identify rhyming words and write them on the chalkboard.

Meeting Individual Needs for Phonics

EASY

Name ______ Date ______ **Reteach 235**

Soft *c* and Soft *g*

Read the words.
brace dance page huge

Complete each sentence with a word from the box.

fierce bridge face lace place change

1. The __fierce__ tiger is hungry.
2. Sammy needs to __change__ his wet socks.
3. Leslie drew a smiling __face__ .
4. This dress has __lace__ on it.
5. Loren walked over the __bridge__ .
6. Tom's favorite __place__ is the ocean.

6 Book 2.2/Unit 3 **Swimmy** — **At Home:** Have children make a drawing of one of the sentences. 235

Reteach, 235

ON-LEVEL

Name ______ Date ______ **Practice 235**

Soft *c* and Soft *g*

Complete the words that answer the riddles.

1. This is something that is cold and hard. You can also see through it.
   i_c_e
2. This is something that helps you cross over the water.
   brid_g_e
3. This is something you must run fast in to win.
   ra_c_e
4. These are small furry animals. Most of them like to eat cheese.
   mi_c_e
5. This is where small animals are kept.
   ca_g_e
6. Lions, tigers, and bears are this word.
   fier_c_e
7. This is what you turn in a book.
   pa_g_e
8. This is something you can cook on.
   ran_g_e

6 Book 2.2/Unit 3 **Swimmy** — **At Home:** Have children write a silly sentence using some of the answers on this page. 235

Practice, 235

CHALLENGE

Name ______ Date ______ **Extend 235**

Soft *c* and Soft *g*

The fish can only follow words with the same ending sound as **place** or **strange.** Color the fish's path blue.

Start, Finish
candy, cow, orange, goose, face, good, game, fierce, cage, race, range, coat, place, space, change, dragon, guess, car, carrot

shade in these words in maze: place, race, space, fierce, cage, change, range, face, orange.

Write a paragraph about a fierce orange fish.

______

Book 2.2/Unit 3 **Swimmy** — **At Home:** Have children draw a fish bowl. Ask them to brainstorm other *-ce* and *-ge* words. List the words inside the fish bowl. 235

Extend, 235

Children will decode and read words with /s/*ce* and /j/*ge*.

Apply Soft *c* and Soft *g*

Party Time

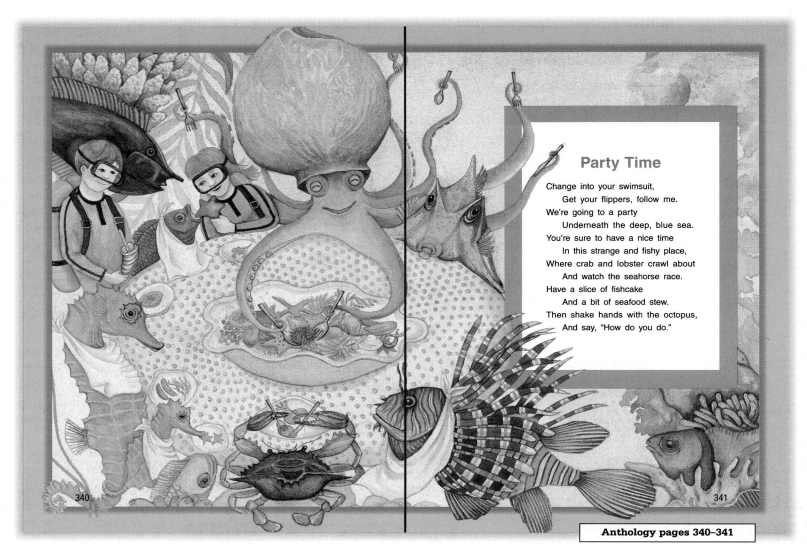

Change into your swimsuit,
  Get your flippers, follow me.
We're going to a party
  Underneath the deep, blue sea.
You're sure to have a nice time
  In this strange and fishy place,
Where crab and lobster crawl about
  And watch the seahorse race.
Have a slice of fishcake
  And a bit of seafood stew.
Then shake hands with the octopus,
  And say, "How do you do."

340 341

Anthology pages 340–341

Read and Build Fluency

READ THE POEM Tell children they will read a poem called "Party Time." Encourage children to listen for the /s/ and /j/ sounds as you read the poem aloud in a deliberate, humorous tone. Invite children to consider the author's point of view. Tell them to use expression as they engage in a shared reading with you for auditory modeling purposes.

PARTNERS **REREAD FOR FLUENCY** Encourage children to take turns rereading the poem with a partner. Suggest that children picture themselves at this underwater party. Have them ask themselves, "How should I say that?" Remind children they can change their voice to show the various characters in the poem.

Dictate and Spell

JOURNAL **DICTATE WORDS** Say the word *change* aloud, and segment it into its individual sounds. Use it in a sentence, such as, "At night, I change into my pajamas." Do the same for *nice* and *race.* Have children pronounce and then write each word, making sure they have a letter or letters for each sound. Continue the practice with other /s/ and /j/ words from the poem: *strange, place, slice.*

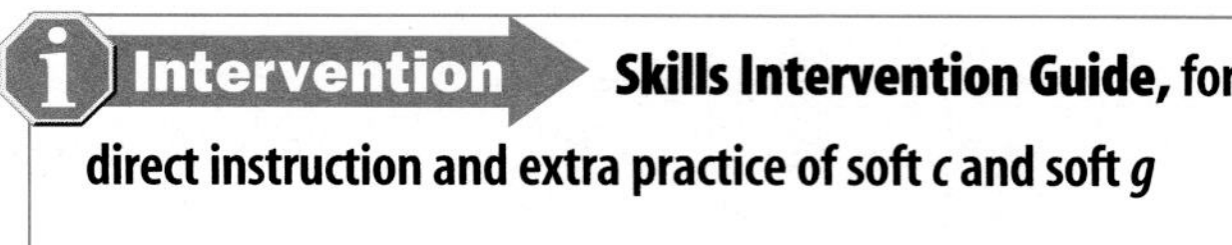

Build Background

Concept: Sea Creatures

Evaluate Prior Knowledge

CONCEPT: SEA CREATURES Ask children to tell about any visit they may have made to an aquarium. Ask them how the creatures there were different from land animals.

MAKE A WORD WEB Have children draw a fish. Have them think of parts of the fish, where they live, how they move, and so on.
Linguistic/Spatial

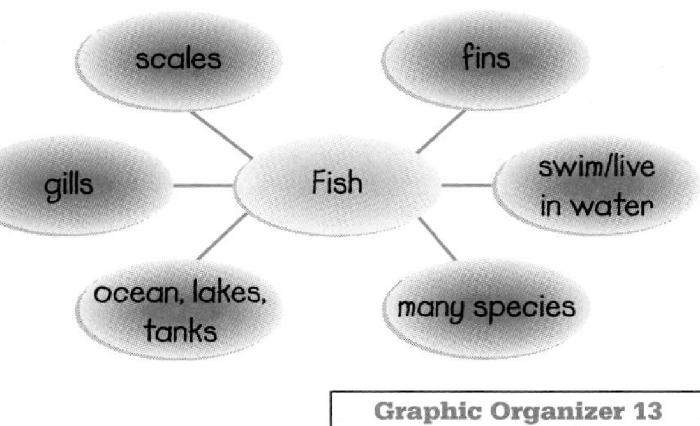

Graphic Organizer 13

WRITE A LIST Have children write a list of all the fish parts that are different from those of land animals, such as gills and fins. Then ask them to write a brief explanation of how sea creatures use those parts.

Develop Oral Language

CONNECT WORDS AND ACTIONS

ESL Have children pretend to be fish. Remind them that they have fins and tails instead of hands and feet and that they cannot talk. Let small groups take turns "swimming" around the classroom. Encourage them to picture things that they might see in the ocean. When they return to their seats, ask them:

- What did you like about being a fish?
- What did you miss about being a human?
- Name the kinds of things you saw underwater, such as: *seaweed, whales, seals, seashells,* and so on.

▶ **Linguistic/Kinesthetic**

Anthology and Leveled Books

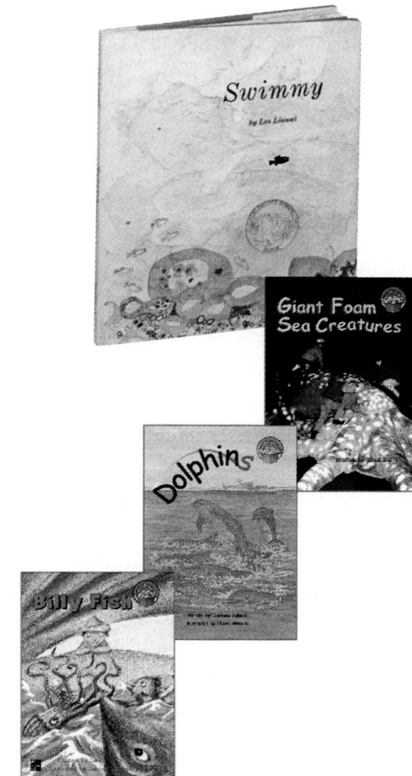

DAY 2 **Blending** Say *ice* and write the letters that stand for each sound. Ask children to blend the sounds to read the word. Repeat with *rice, strange,* and *large.*

LANGUAGE SUPPORT

Use the **Language Support Book, pages 253–256,** to help build background.

Children will use context and structural clues to determine the meanings of vocabulary words.

swift (p. 344) fast

escaped (p. 345) got away

hidden (p. 354) out of sight

machine (p. 349) something made by humans to do some kind of work

swaying (p. 352) bending slowly back and forth

fierce (p. 344) ready to fight or hurt something

Story Words

These words from the selection may be unfamiliar. Before children read, have them check the meanings and pronunciations of the words in the Glossary, beginning on page 390, or in a dictionary.

- mussel, p. 343
- marvel, p. 346
- medusa, p. 346
- seaweed, p. 352
- eel, p. 352

swift
escaped
hidden
machine
swaying
fierce

Vocabulary

Teach Vocabulary in Context

Identify Vocabulary Words Display **Teaching Chart 198** and read the passage with children. Have volunteers circle each vocabulary word and underline other words that are clues to its meaning.

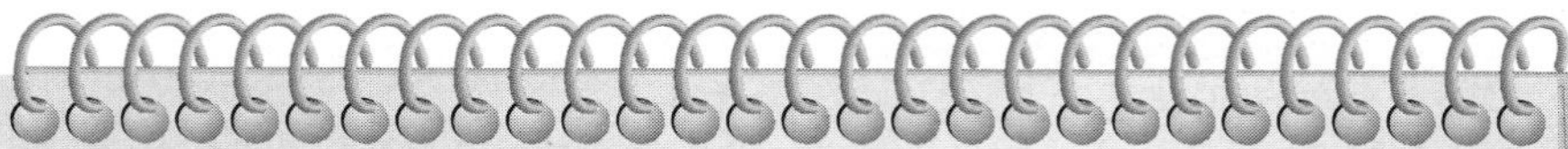

Just In Time!

1. One day Ellie the eel saw a swift shark coming toward her, like a streak of lightning. **2.** If she had had time, Ellie would have escaped his great jaws by swimming away. **3.** But on this day, she could only dart under a rock, where she hoped she would be well hidden. **4.** There Ellie saw a machine, a box with buttons and knobs that began to make music. **5.** Bending its body back and forth, the shark started swaying to the beat. **6.** The shark didn't seem so fierce and dangerous anymore.

Teaching Chart 198

Discuss Meanings Ask questions like these to help clarify word meanings:

- Is a swift movement fast or slow?
- If you have escaped from danger, are you safe?
- When you pull the covers over your head, are you hidden?
- Which is a machine, a car or a dog?
- Have you ever seen a tree swaying back and forth in the wind?
- Is a tiger fierce or gentle?

Practice

Ask Questions to Define Words

PARTNERS

Have partners take turns choosing vocabulary cards. One partner defines the word on the card, and the other identifies it.

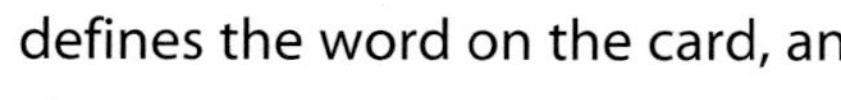

▶ Logical/Linguistic

Word Building Manipulative Cards

Illustrate Sentences

PARTNERS WRITING

Have each partner write sentences using three of the words at the bottom of a blank sheet of paper. Have them exchange papers and draw a picture to represent each sentence. Have children refer to their Glossary as needed. ▶ Linguistic/Visual

Assess Vocabulary

Identify Word Meaning in Context

PARTNERS WRITING

Have children write context sentences for four of the vocabulary words. Ask them to use a synonym or group of words for each vocabulary word, not the vocabulary word itself. Then have partners exchange papers and ask children to write the vocabulary word suggested by each sentence.

SPELLING/VOCABULARY CONNECTIONS

See Spelling Challenge Words, pages 361Q–361R.

LANGUAGE SUPPORT

See the **Language Support Book**, pages 353–356, for teaching suggestions for Vocabulary.

Vocabulary PuzzleMaker

Provides vocabulary activities.

Meeting Individual Needs for Vocabulary

EASY

Name________ Date________ Reteach 236

Vocabulary

Read each riddle. Circle the word that answers the riddle.

1. I am a monkey. I just got away from the zoo. I am very happy to be free. What did I do? — (escaped) sang jumped
2. I am not a person. But I do a lot of work. I make many things. I can lift heavy boxes. What am I? — ship (machine) artist
3. I am a wild lion. Don't come too close. If you try to catch me, watch out! What would you say I am? — friendly kind (fierce)
4. You can't see me. I'm not out in the open. I won't come out until you find me. What would you say I am? — (hidden) asleep hungry
5. I am a large tree. I am moving in the wind. I lean one way. Then I lean the other way. What am I doing? — walking running (swaying)
6. I am a bug. I can fly fast in the air. I fly so fast that you might not even see me. What might you say about me? — pretty (swift) slow

236 At Home: Have children write a sentence for each of the words they circled. Book 2.2/Unit 3 Swimmy 6

ON-LEVEL

Name________ Date________ Practice 236

Vocabulary

Read each sentence. Write T if the sentence is true. Write F if the sentence is false.

escaped fierce hidden machine swaying swift

T 1. If you are hidden, you can't be seen.
F 2. A swift deer moves slowly.
T 3. The fish that escaped is free.
F 4. If you are swaying, you are very still.
T 5. You should be careful around a fierce dog.
T 6. If you are a swift runner, you might win the race.
F 7. Most machines are very slow.
F 8. A fierce animal is friendly to people.
F 9. A monkey that has escaped is still in a cage.
F 10. If you are hidden, everyone can see you.
T 11. A machine can do a lot of work.
T 12. The swaying branches on a tree are moving.

236 At Home: Have children make up other true and false statements about the vocabulary words. Book 2.2/Unit 3 Swimmy 12

ON-LEVEL

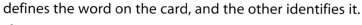

Going to School

I have escaped many scary things! Sometimes when I'm afraid I hide in strange places. I dig into the sand. I even hide behind a rock. My friends and I will stay hidden for hours. Life in the sea is dangerous and exciting!

236a

CHALLENGE

Name________ Date________ Extend 236

Vocabulary

machine	hidden	swaying
escaped	fierce	swift

The sentences tell what is happening in the picture. Write the words from the box that have nearly the same meaning as the underlined words.

1. The dog broke free and ran out the door. escaped
2. This dog looks mean and angry. fierce
3. The cat stays out of sight so the dog can't find it. hidden
4. A lawn mower is something with moving parts used to do a job. machine
5. The branches of the tree are moving back and forth in the wind. swaying
6. The cat will have to be fast when it comes down. swift

Will the dog find the cat? Will the cat escape? Write two sentences to tell what will happen next. Use words from the box.

Sample answers are shown.

The cat escaped by jumping over the dog.

The dog was not as swift as the cat.

236 At Home: Have children draw a picture illustrating the vocabulary words. Ask children to use the words to label their picture. Book 2.2/Unit 3 Swimmy

Reteach, 236 | Practice, 236 | Practice, 236a Take-Home Story | Extend, 236

Comprehension

Prereading Strategies

PREVIEW AND PREDICT Have children preview the story by taking a **picture walk** through the illustrations.

- Where does this story take place?
- What subject do all the pictures have in common? (life under the sea)
- Will the story be a realistic one or a fantasy? (fantasy; the pictures are not realistic) *Genre*
- What will the story most likely be about? (a little fish)

Have children record their predictions about the story in a chart.

PREDICTIONS	WHAT HAPPENED
The story takes place in the water.	
The story is about a little fish.	

SET PURPOSES What do children want to find out by reading this story? For example:

- How did the little black fish end up on his own?
- Why did all the little fish swim in a group shaped like a big fish?

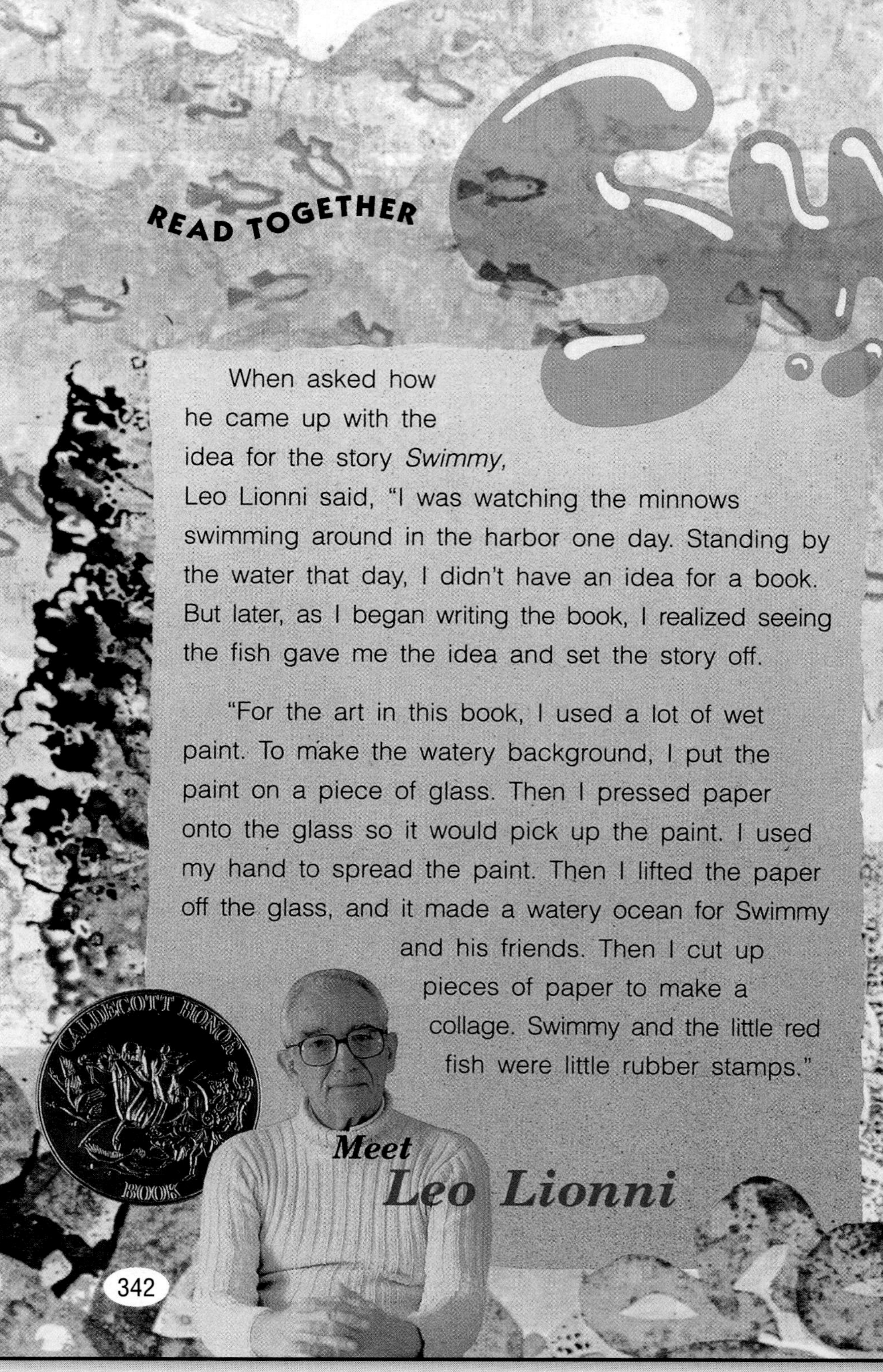

READ TOGETHER
When asked how he came up with the idea for the story *Swimmy*, Leo Lionni said, "I was watching the minnows swimming around in the harbor one day. Standing by the water that day, I didn't have an idea for a book. But later, as I began writing the book, I realized seeing the fish gave me the idea and set the story off.
"For the art in this book, I used a lot of wet paint. To make the watery background, I put the paint on a piece of glass. Then I pressed paper onto the glass so it would pick up the paint. I used my hand to spread the paint. Then I lifted the paper off the glass, and it made a watery ocean for Swimmy and his friends. Then I cut up pieces of paper to make a collage. Swimmy and the little red fish were little rubber stamps."
CALDECOTT HONOR BOOK
Meet
Leo Lionni
342

Meeting Individual Needs • Grouping Suggestions for Strategic Reading

EASY

Read Together Read the story together with children or have them use the **Listening Library.** Have children make a Form Generalizations chart and add to it when they make a generalization. Comprehension and Intervention prompts offer additional help with decoding and comprehension.

ON-LEVEL

Guided Instruction Ask children to read the story with you. Monitor any difficulties they may have in order to determine which parts of Comprehension to emphasize. After they have read the story, have children reread it using the rereading suggestions on page 356.

CHALLENGE

Read Independently Have children make and record predictions before reading. Then have them fill in the chart as they read and form generalizations about aspects of the story. After reading they can check their predictions.

by Leo Lionni

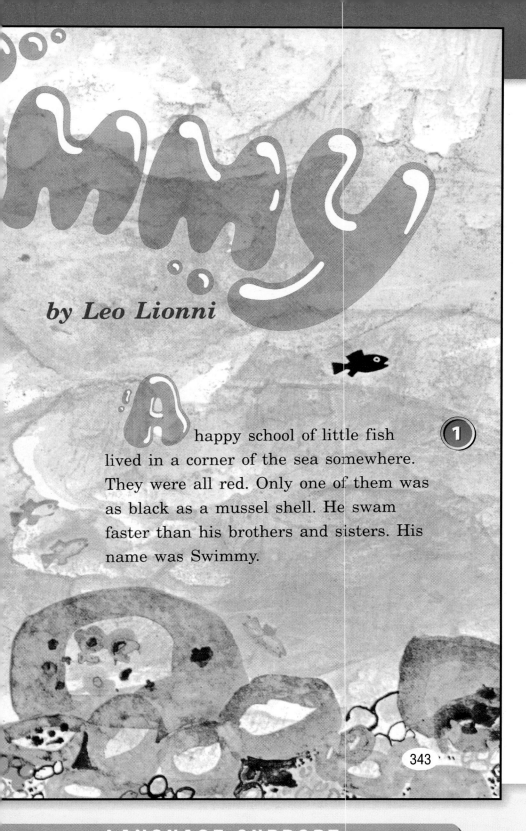

A happy school of little fish lived in a corner of the sea somewhere. They were all red. Only one of them was as black as a mussel shell. He swam faster than his brothers and sisters. His name was Swimmy. 1

343

Comprehension

  **Apply Soft *c* and *g***

Apply Form Generalizations

STRATEGIC READING Tell children that forming generalizations can help them understand parts of the story. They can make a chart of generalizations they form as they read.

CLUES FROM THE STORY	GENERALIZATIONS FORMED

1 **FORM GENERALIZATIONS** The author tells us that the little red fish lived together in a group called a *school*. What generalization might you make? (Groups of one kind of fish stay together.)

Genre

Fiction/Fantasy

Review with children that a fantasy:

- includes events and/or settings that could not happen in real life.
- may be largely realistic with animals as main characters.
- may have a theme that deals with the struggle between good and evil.

Activity After children read *Swimmy,* have them work in groups to come up with an idea for a short fantasy. Encourage them to create a good vs. evil situation, and to decide if they want animal or human characters. Have groups share their ideas with the class.

LANGUAGE SUPPORT

A blackline master of the generalization chart is available in the **Language Support Book.**

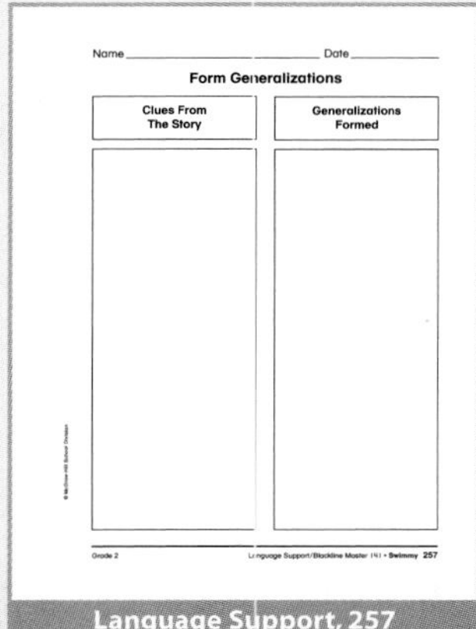
Name _______ Date _______

Form Generalizations

Clues From The Story	Generalizations Formed

Language Support, 257

Comprehension

2 Phonics **SOFT *c* WORDS** Look at the first sentence on this page and read it to yourselves. Point to the eighth word. What two sounds can the letter *c* stand for? Sometimes *c* can stand for /k/ as in *cat*. Sometimes *c* stands for /s/ as in *face*. Let's blend the sounds together. f ie r ce The word is *fierce*. *Blending/Graphophonic Cues*

MODEL This word begins with the sound /f/. The next three letters make the sound /îr/. So far I have /fîr/. Now comes the letter c. First I'll try the /k/ sound. /fîrk/. No, that doesn't sound like a word. How about /fîrs/? That's a word I've heard before.

TEACHING TIP

PRONUNCIATION Point out the letter that follows *c* in each word. (*a* in *cat*; *e* in *face*) Tell children that most of the time, when the letters *a, o,* or *u* come after the c, the *c* is pronounced /k/. When *c* is followed by *e*, it is usually pronounced /s/.

2 One bad day a tuna fish, swift, fierce and very hungry, came darting through the waves. In one gulp he swallowed all the little red fish.

344

Cross Curricular: Science

LEARN ABOUT FOOD CHAINS Explain to children that big fish eat little fish, little fish eat even smaller fish, and these smaller fish eat the tiniest of sea creatures. This is called a food chain.

RESEARCH AND INQUIRY Children can work in groups to learn which fish eat other fish and which fish eat plants. Each group can then make a poster showing the food chain in the ocean.

▶ **Logical/Interpersonal**

Only Swimmy escaped. He swam away in the deep wet world. He was scared, lonely and very sad.
3
4
345

Comprehension

3 Swimmy swims away from his corner in the sea. Do you wonder why? Did the author give you any information that helps you to understand why Swimmy leaves his home? (He wanted to get away from the tuna.) What effect did being alone in the world have on Swimmy? (It made him feel scared, lonely, and sad.) ***Cause and Effect***

4 How does knowing where Swimmy lives help you understand the story? How would the story be different if Swimmy lived in an aquarium or a lake instead of the sea? (An aquarium is too small for Swimmy to be alone; a lake has different sea life.) ***Character/Setting***

Minilesson

REVIEW/MAINTAIN

Main Idea and Details

Help children select the most important events on the last two pages. Ask questions such as:

- What did the tuna do?
- What did this cause Swimmy to do?
- How did Swimmy feel?

Help children construct a sentence that includes these main ideas. (After the tuna ate all the little red fish, Swimmy swam away feeling sad.)

Activity Ask children to write a main idea statement about what they did last night and read it to the class.

Comprehension

5 **FORM GENERALIZATIONS** On page 346, the author says that the sea was "full of wonderful creatures." Do you think this means that every creature in the sea is wonderful?

MODEL Well, Swimmy sees many interesting and pretty creatures. But he also saw the big hungry tuna eat all his brothers and sisters. So I can form the generalization that some of the animals in the sea are wonderful.

CLUES FROM THE STORY	GENERALIZATIONS FORMED
fierce tuna	Some sea animals are dangerous.
The sea was full of wonderful creatures.	Some sea animals are pretty and gentle.

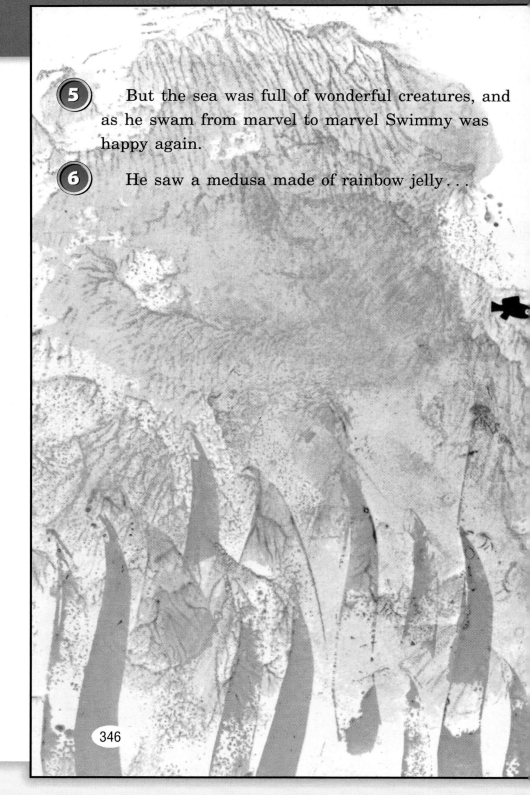

5 But the sea was full of wonderful creatures, and as he swam from marvel to marvel Swimmy was happy again.

6 He saw a medusa made of rainbow jelly . . .

346

Cross Curricular: Math

THE BIGGEST AND THE SMALLEST Have children compare the sizes of sea creatures.

- Have partners measure a piece of adding machine tape 90 feet long. Tape it to a wall and label it "blue whale."
- Have children make a dot on a piece of adding machine tape, tape it to the wall, and label the dot "plankton."
- Have children find out the sizes of other ocean animals and cut adding machine tape to the sizes of the new animals.

▶ **Logical/Visual**

Comprehension

6 How did seeing the wonderful creatures in the sea make Swimmy feel? (happy) ***Cause and Effect***

BLENDING CONSONANTS Find two words in the first sentence on page 346 that begin with the letters *sw*. (*swam* and *Swimmy*) Say each word.

PREVENTION/INTERVENTION

ENDING CONSONANTS Write e two letters *s* and *w* on the chalk- ard. Ask a volunteer to give the und for each letter. Model the nding of the two sounds. Have ldren blend the sounds as you derline them.

Write the following sentence on the chalkboard: *Sue sings sweetly as she swings*. Have children read the sentence and identify the words beginning with *sw*. Then ask volunteers to make up other sentences using two words that begin with *sw*. ***Graphophonic Cues***

Minilesson

REVIEW/MAINTAIN

/ē/ spelled *y*

Remind children that *y* can stand for the long *e* sound.

Have children find the three words on page 346 that end in *y*. (*Swimmy, happy, jelly*) Point out that these words end with the long *e* sound.

Activity Write these words on the chalkboard: *silly, cry, wiggly, shy*. Ask children whether the final *y* stands for the long *i* or long *e* sound in each word.

Phonics CD-ROM Have children use the interactive phonics activities on the CD-ROM for more reinforcement.

Comprehension

7 Name the main character in the story. (Swimmy) What changes has Swimmy had to face so far? (the loss of his school and home; seeing new creatures) How does Swimmy react to his changing circumstances? (He is sad at first, but begins to see wonderful things in the larger world.) ***Character***

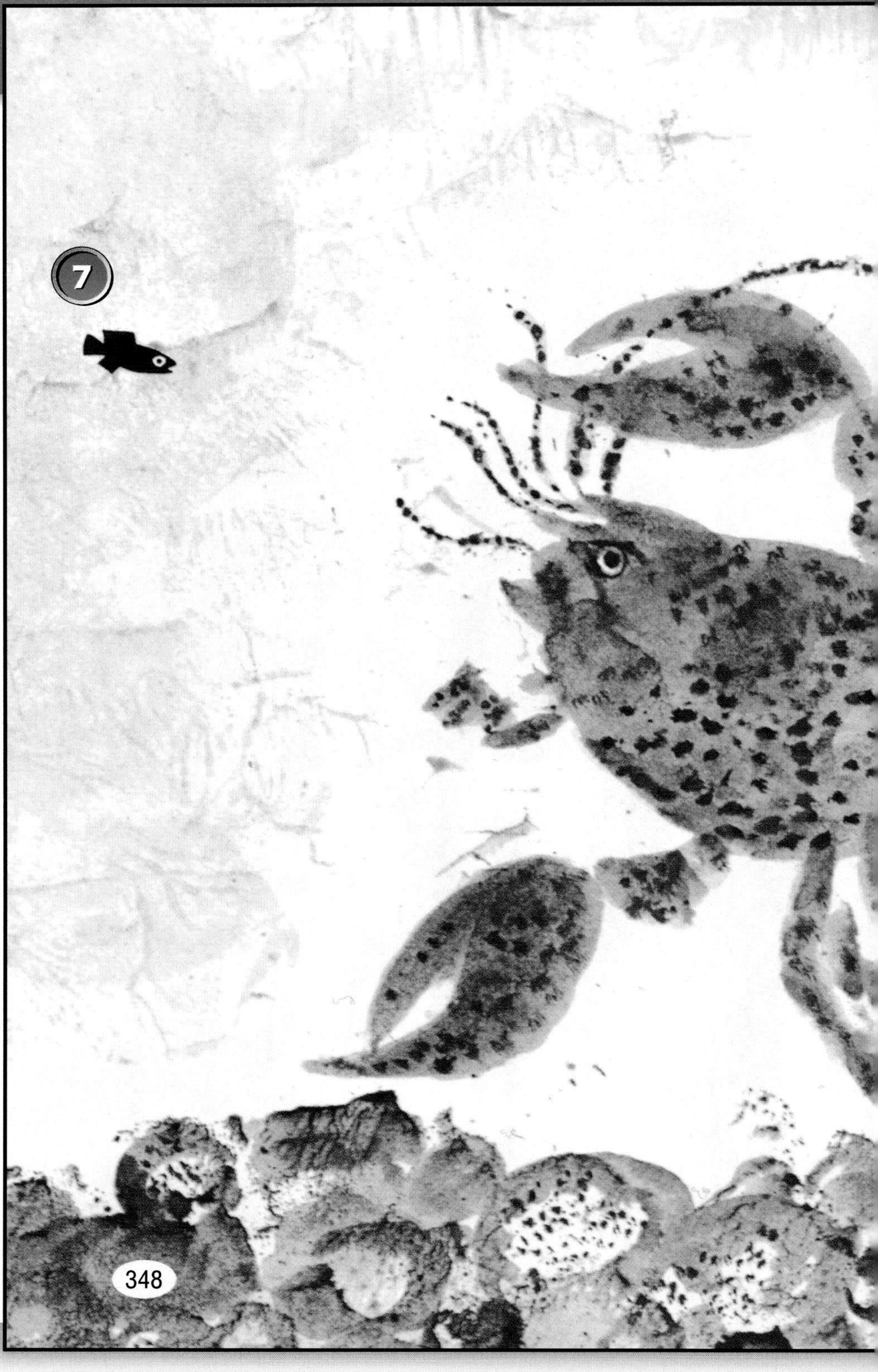

SELF-MONITORING STRATEGY

RELATE TO PERSONAL EXPERIENCES Ask children if they have ever seen a live lobster at a zoo, aquarium, or fish market. Then have them compare it to the lobster shown and described on pages 348–349.

MODEL The lobster I saw was shaped like the one in the picture. But it was a darker green. Its movements were jerky. Perhaps that's why the author says that Swimmy's lobster walked "like a water-moving machine." I think my lobster looked scarier than Swimmy's does.

Activity

Cross Curricular: Social Studies

OCEANS OF THE WORLD Invite partners to look at a globe of the world and find the name of each ocean. Then have them make a chart that lists the oceans from largest to smallest.

RESEARCH AND INQUIRY If children have trouble figuring out the relative sizes of the oceans from maps, help them find the information in an encyclopedia or atlas. ▶ **Visual/Logical**

Children can learn more about oceans by visiting ***www.mhschool.com/reading.***

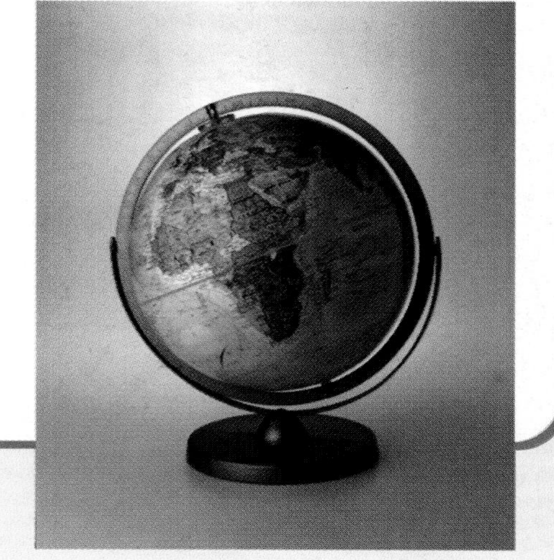

a lobster, who walked about like a water-moving machine . . .

8

9

Comprehension

8 What would you look like if you walked like a water-moving machine? Use your bodies to show how the lobster moves through the water. ***Pantomime***

9 When the author describes the lobster as a "water-moving machine," he is using language that paints a picture. What words might you use to say how the lobster looked to Swimmy? (*giant, moves stiffly, like a robot*) ***Figurative Language***

Minilesson

REVIEW/MAINTAIN

Make Inferences

Review with children the major events of the story so far. Have children discuss Swimmy's feelings and emotions about the events:

- How did Swimmy feel when the tuna ate all the little red fish?
- How does Swimmy feel now that he is seeing so many beautiful sights?

Activity Ask children to draw a picture of Swimmy alone and feeling sad and another picture of him surrounded by the sea creatures and feeling happy.

Comprehension

10 Phonics Point to the first word on the page. Let's sound out each part. I'll put my hand under each sound as we say it. str a nge Let's say the whole word together. strange Let's all say the word: *strange*.
Blending/Graphophonic Cues

Visual Literacy

VIEWING AND REPRESENTING

Have students turn back to pages 344–345. Ask what details the illustrator included to make the tuna appear swift and fierce. If necessary, point out the churning water around the tuna and its sharp teeth.

Compare the tuna with the fish on pages 350–351. Do these fish look fierce? Why or why not? (No, the fish don't seem to be rushing towards anything and they aren't showing sharp teeth.)

10 strange fish, pulled by an invisible thread . . .

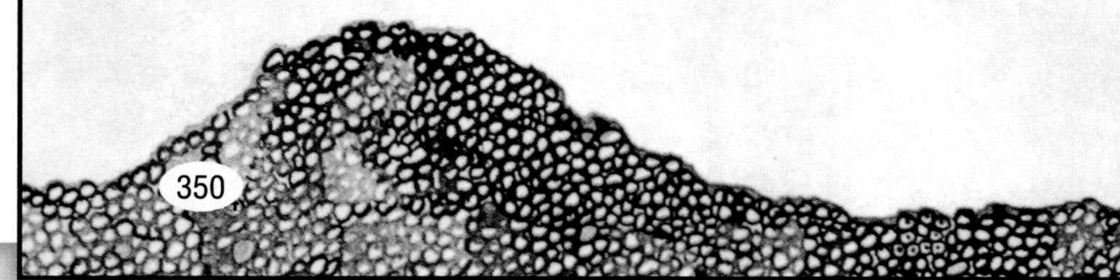

350

CULTURAL PERSPECTIVES

ORIGAMI FISH Give children squares of thin paper. Then have them follow your directions.

- Fold the paper in half twice to form a smaller square with four layers.
- Hold the square so the folds are on the top and on the right.
- Bring the bottom left corner of the first layer of the square to the right until a triangle is formed. Press in the folds.
- Turn over and repeat.
- The inside point is the fish's mouth. The long side of the triangle is the tail fin.

▶ **Visual/Kinesthetic**

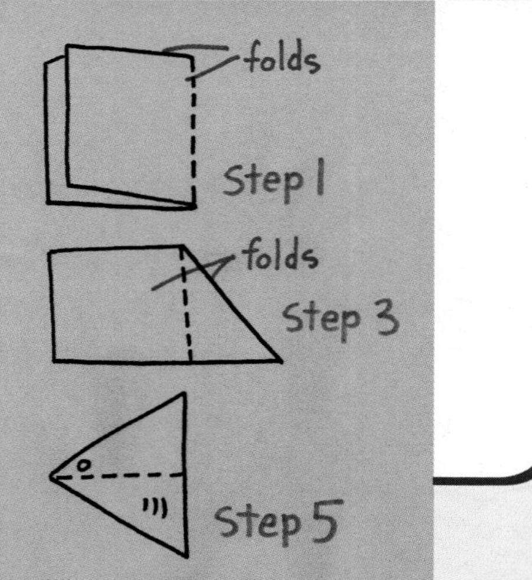

Comprehension

11 Do you think the strange fish are really being pulled by an invisible thread? Why or why not? (The fish are not really being pulled by thread. The author is helping us to picture the fish moving.) ***Figurative Language***

TEACHING TIP

MANAGEMENT You may want to divide the class into small groups to do the Cultural Perspectives activity. Visit each group separately and read the directions as you supervise and guide the children's work.

LANGUAGE SUPPORT

ESL Some children may need help with understanding e word *invisible* on page 350. Have ildren name some things that they n feel or hear but cannot see. (heat, ld, the wind, music) Tell them that ese things are invisible.

Show children an object hanging from a clear plastic thread. Point out that if they weren't looking carefully, they might think the fish was floating in midair. If you have an aquarium in the classroom, have students watch to see if some of the fish look as if they are being pulled along by a clear plastic thread.

Minilesson

REVIEW/MAINTAIN

Multiple-Meaning Words

Review with children that multiple-meaning words look and sound alike but have different meanings. Write the word *school* on the board and have children discuss the possible meanings. Then turn to page 343 and ask, *What does school mean in our story?* (a group of fish) Remind children that multiple-meaning words, which sound alike and are spelled alike, are different from homophones, which sound alike but are spelled differently. (in, inn)

Activity Ask children to look through the story for other multiple-meaning words. Remind them that the words must look alike and sound alike.

Comprehension

12 **FORM GENERALIZATIONS** Seaweed is a plant, but sea anemones are animals that look like plants. To what kind of plant does the author compare sea anemones? (palm trees) What else does the author write about the sea anemones? (They are pink.) Let's add some words from the story to the clues column. What generalizations can we make from these clues?

LONG *e* Locate the words *seaweed* and *eel*. What letters are used to represent the long *e* sound? (*ea*, *ee*)

CLUES FROM THE STORY	GENERALIZATIONS FORMED
fierce tuna	Some sea animals are dangerous.
The sea was full of wonderful creatures.	Some sea animals are pretty and gentle.
sugar-candy, pink palm trees swaying	Some of the plants and animals in the sea are very colorful.

Fluency

GROUP READING The sentence that began on page 346 ends on page 352.

- Note that the three dots after the group of words on each page shows that the sentence will continue on the next page.
- Model the reading of the long sentence, tracing the sentence's path with your finger as you read.
- Then have the children read the entire sentence together, showing continuity from phrase to phrase.

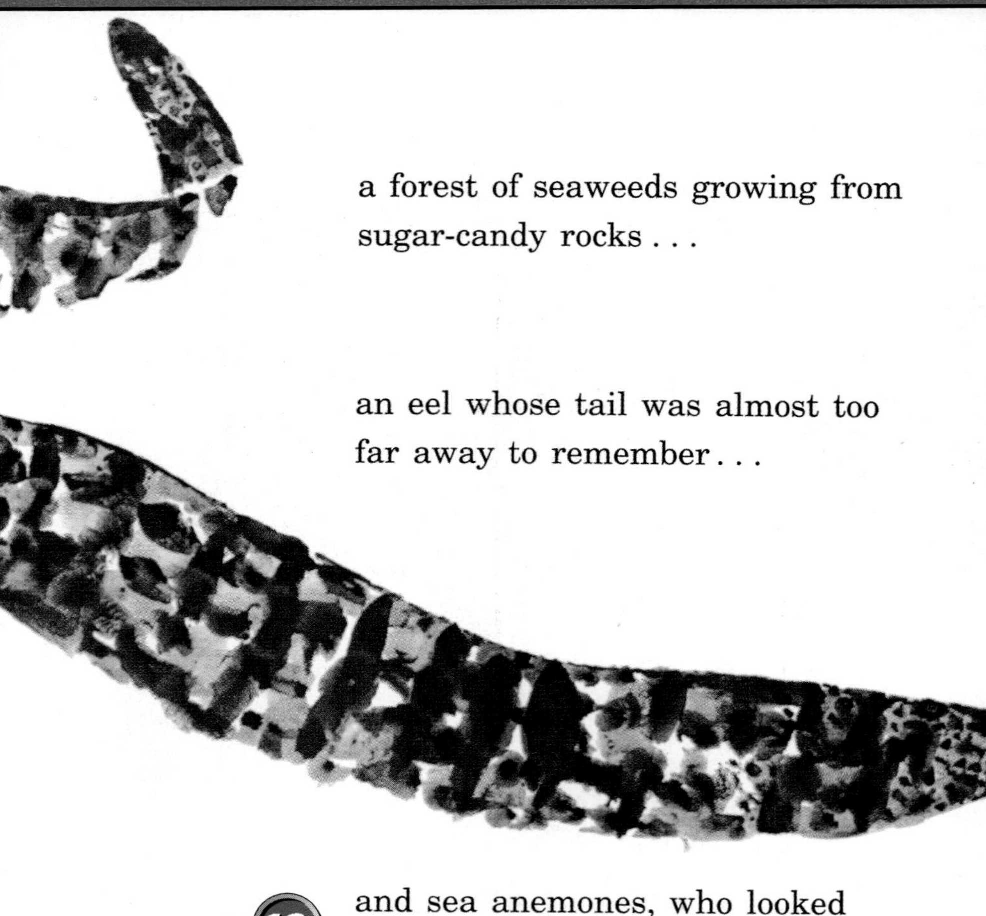

a forest of seaweeds growing from sugar-candy rocks . . .

an eel whose tail was almost too far away to remember . . .

12 and sea anemones, who looked like pink palm trees swaying in the wind.

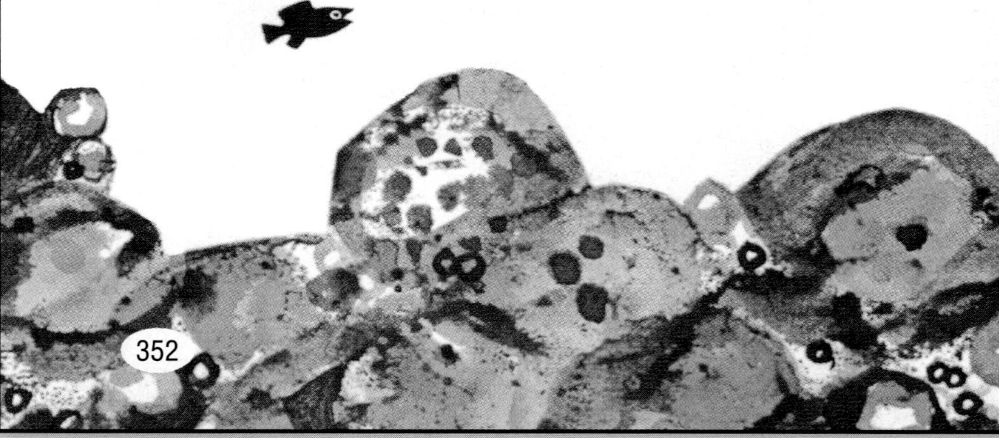

352

PREVENTION/INTERVENTION

LONG *e* Remind children that the letters *ee* and *ea* can make the long *e* sound. Write the following words on the chalkboard as you model the blending process: *meal, eat, weed, feel, seaweed*. Have children repeat the blending process with you and then underline the letter combination in each word that makes the long *e* sound. *Graphophonic Cues*

Comprehension

13 Look at the picture on page 353. Then read the first two lines on page 352. How does the picture help you understand the phrase "a forest of seaweeds"? (It looks like a group of trees or a forest.) How are the rocks like sugar candy? (They have candylike colors.) ***Using Picture Clues***

LANGUAGE SUPPORT

ESL Help children understand the colorful language on age 352.

emind children what it is like to wear long scarf. They must remember to eep its end from trailing on the floor r from getting caught in doors. Tell iem that the eel might have a similar roblem with its long tail. Perhaps that is what the author meant when he said the eel's tail "was almost too far away to remember." Have children pantomime the eel trying to keep track of its long tail.

Ask children to stand up, arms raised, and act like "palm trees swaying in the wind."

Minilesson

REVIEW/MAINTAIN

Context Clues

Have children look for clues to the meaning of *eel*. Remind them that clues can be found in pictures as well as words. (The words on page 352 describe the eel as having a long tail. In the picture, the creature with a long tail looks like a snake. An eel is a sea creature that looks like a snake.)

Activity Have students find picture clues for the phrase *forest of seaweeds*.

Comprehension

14 Imagine that you are Swimmy. Explain why you ask the little, red fish to swim with you. (Because fish swim in schools, Swimmy wanted to be with fish like himself while he swam around and saw marvels.) *Make Inferences*

15 **FORM GENERALIZATIONS** Let's look at the third paragraph. What are the little fish afraid of? (the big fish) At the bottom of the page, Swimmy has an idea.

MODEL Swimmy's idea is for all the little fish to swim together like one giant fish. This makes me think that sometimes little fish get eaten by big fish, and big fish get eaten by even bigger fish.

Then, hidden in the dark shade of rocks and weeds, he saw a school of little fish, just like his own.

14 "Let's go and swim and play and SEE things!" he said happily.

15 "We can't," said the little red fish. "The big fish will eat us all."

"But you can't just lie there," said Swimmy. "We must THINK of something."

Swimmy thought and thought and thought. Then suddenly he said, "I have it! We are going to swim all together like the biggest fish in the sea!"

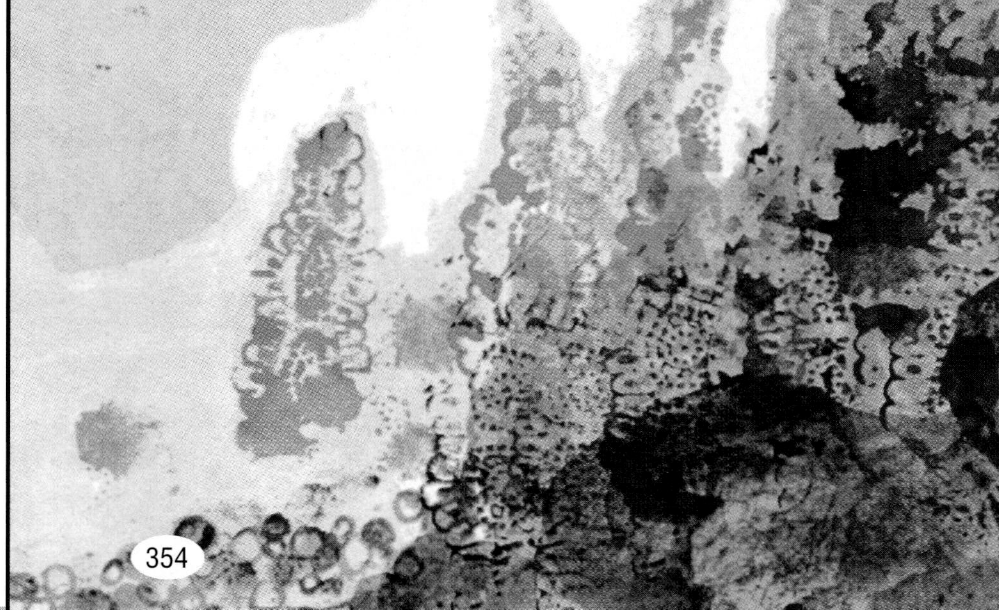

354

Cross Curricular: Art

SPONGE PAINTING Tell children that they are going to make a picture of the little fish swimming like one big fish.

- Give children a piece of blue construction paper.
- Children can pencil in the outline of a large fish on the blue background.
- Cut out small fish shapes from sponges. Children can dip the fish sponges in red poster paint, then stamp them inside the fish outline. One can be dipped in black paint for the eye.

▶ **Kinesthetic/Spatial**

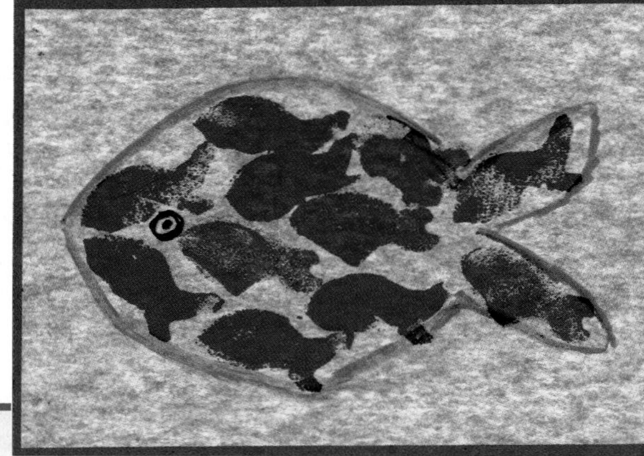

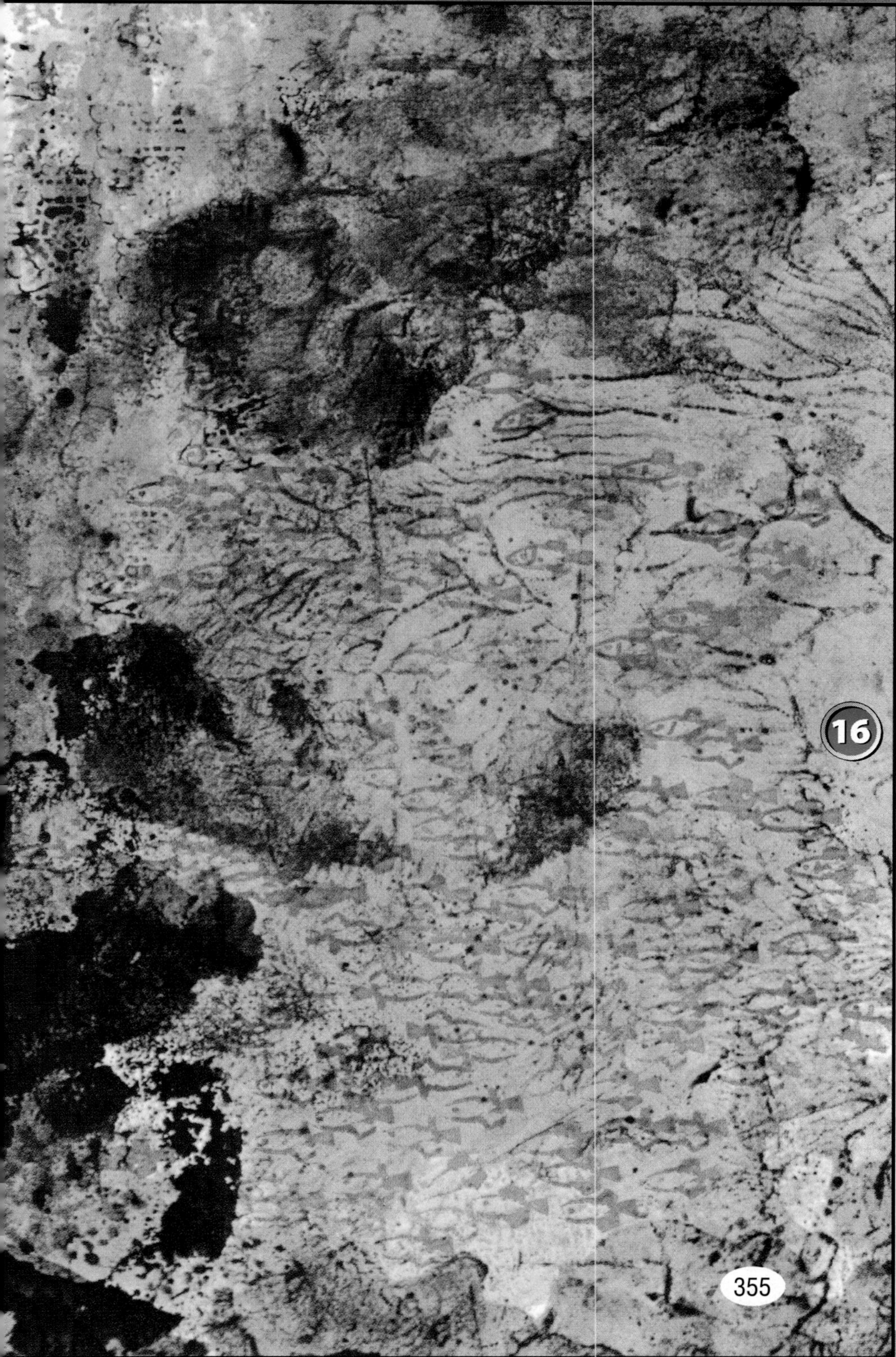

Comprehension

16 Why will it help the little red fish to swim together "like the biggest fish in the sea"? (Since the bigger fish eat the smaller fish, all the other fish will be afraid of them and leave them alone.) ***Draw Conclusions***

P/i **WORDS WITH /ü/*oo*** Find the word *school* on page 354. What sound do the letters *oo* make? (/ü/)

P/i PREVENTION/INTERVENTION

WORDS WITH /ü/*oo* Explain to children that the letters *oo* can make the /ü/ sound. Write the word *school* on the chalkboard. Model the blending process. s ch oo l school. Ask children to brainstorm words that rhyme with *school*. (tool, stool, spool) Be sure to include the word *cool* which children will read on page 357.

You may point out that the letters *oo* do not always make the /ü/ sound. Tell them that sometimes *oo* makes the /u̇/ sound as in the word *book*. Suggest that if they are unsure of the word, they should try saying the word with each sound and figure out which one sounds like a real word. ***Graphophonic Cues***

Minilesson

REVIEW/MAINTAIN

Suffixes

Remind children that adding letters to the end of a word can change its meaning.

- Have children find the word on page 354 that is similar to *happy*.
- Remind them that adding *ly* makes the word describe how something is done.
- Ask children what action *happily* describes (say).

Activity Ask children to think of three or more words they can add *ly* to. Have them use each in a sentence.

Comprehension

17 FORM GENERALIZATIONS Read the last sentence of the story. What generalization can you form about what animals are scared of?

CLUES FROM THE STORY	GENERALIZATIONS FORMED
fierce tuna	Some sea animals are dangerous.
The sea was full of wonderful creatures.	Some sea animals are pretty and gentle.
sugar-candy, pink palm trees swaying	Some of the plants and animals in the sea are very colorful.
Little fish swam together and chased the big fish away.	Sometimes animals are scared of bigger animals.

RETELL THE STORY Have children work in pairs to retell the story. They can draw pictures of each main event and write a sentence under each picture.

STUDENT SELF-ASSESSMENT

Have children ask themselves the following questions to assess how they are reading:

- How did making generalizations help me to understand parts of the story?
- How did I put together letters and sounds I know to help me read the words in the story?

TRANSFERRING THE STRATEGY

How might I use these strategies to help me read other stories?

He taught them to swim close together, each in his own place, and when they had learned to swim
17 like one giant fish, he said, "I'll be the eye."

356

REREADING FOR *Fluency*

PARTNERS Have children read a favorite section of the story to a partner with expression.

READING RATE When you evaluate reading rate, have children read aloud from the story for one minute. Place a stick-on note after the last word read. Count words read. To evaluate children's performance, see the Running Record in the **Fluency Assessment** book.

Intervention For leveled fluency lessons, passages, and norms charts, see **Skills Intervention Guide**, Part 5, Fluency.

And so they swam in the cool morning water and in the midday sun and chased the big fish away.

357

Comprehension

Return to Predictions and Purposes

Review with students their story predictions. Were their predictions correct?

PREDICTIONS	WHAT HAPPENED
The story takes place in the water.	The story starts in a little corner of the sea.
The story is about one little fish.	The story is about a fish named Swimmy who is alone after his brothers and sisters are eaten.

INFORMAL ASSESSMENT

HOW TO ASSESS

SOFT *c, g* Have children turn to page 350 and read the first word. *(strange)* Have them read the third word in the second line on page 356. *(place)*

FORM GENERALIZATIONS Ask children what they learned about the sea and its creatures. (There are both good and bad creatures in the sea. Little fish are scared of big fish. Some big fish eat small fish.)

FOLLOW UP

SOFT *c, g* Model the soft *c* and *g* sounds. Repeat together. Children can practice by using the words in context sentences.

FORM GENERALIZATIONS If students have trouble stating the generalizations, have them review their completed charts.

LITERARY RESPONSE

UICK-WRITE Have children draw the marvel that they thought was most beautiful in their urnals. Ask them to write a sentence nder their drawing.

OURNAL

RAL RESPONSE Have children are their journal entries with a part- er. Encourage them to

- use descriptive words to describe their marvels.
- explain why that particular marvel was most appealing to them.
- tell whether they had ever seen an example of that particular marvel.

Story Questions

Have children discuss or write answers to the questions on page 358.

Answers:

1. The tuna eats them. *Literal/Sequence*
2. The red fish scare it by swimming in the shape of a huge fish. *Inferential/Cause and Effect*
3. Swimmy thinks of a solution and teaches the red fish to work together. *Inferential/Character*
4. It is mainly about a fish who teaches the other little fish how to work together to face danger. *Critical/Summarize*
5. Characters from both stories need to work together to scare away enemies. *Critical/Reading Across Texts*

Write a Fairy Tale For a full writing process lesson on writing a story, see the lesson on page 361M–361N.

READ TOGETHER

Story Questions & Activities

1. At the beginning of the story, what happens to the little red fish?
2. At the end of the story, why does the big fish get chased away?
3. What makes Swimmy a good leader?
4. What is this story about?
5. The animals in "The Bremen Town Musicians" and the fish in "Swimmy" have the same problem. What is it? How do they solve it?

Write a Fairy Tale

Write a fairy tale about a group of small animals, insects, or birds who have a problem. Can they be stronger together than alone? Show how they work together to solve their problem.

Meeting Individual Needs

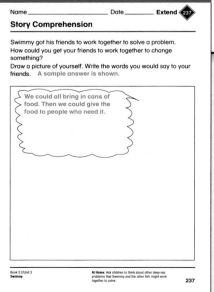

EASY

Name_____ Date_____ **Reteach 237**

Story Comprehension

Complete the chart. Answers may vary.

Main Character: Swimmy
Setting: The ocean
Beginning of the Story: All of Swimmy's brothers and sisters are eaten by a big tuna fish.
Middle of the Story: Swimmy sees all of the different creatures that live in the sea. He meets another school of fish that are hiding.
End of the Story: Swimmy teaches the other fish how to swim so that they will be safe from bigger fish.
Draw a picture of Swimmy and his friends swimming safely.

5 Book 2.2/Unit 3 Swimmy — **At Home:** Ask children to talk about why the school of little fish could scare away a big fish. 237

Reteach, 237

ON-LEVEL

Name_____ Date_____ **Practice 237**

Story Comprehension

Think about "Swimmy." Read this passage about "Swimmy."

Swimmy wanted to look all around. But the little red fish were afraid a large fish would eat them. Swimmy wanted to think of some way to have fun.

Write a complete sentence to answer each question.

1. What did Swimmy do right before this part of the story?
   He explored the deep wet world all by himself. Then he met a school of fish just like himself.
2. What did Swimmy do right after this part of the story?
   He organized the school of fish to look like one large fish moving through the water.
3. What is important about this part of the story?
   It shows that the little fish can solve a big problem if they all work together.
4. How do you think the little fish would describe Swimmy?
   Possible response: They would describe him as their leader.

4 Book 2.2/Unit 3 Swimmy — **At Home:** Ask children to name things that Swimmy and the fish will see as they travel the deep, wet world. 237

Practice, 237

CHALLENGE

Name_____ Date_____ **Extend 237**

Story Comprehension

Swimmy got his friends to work together to solve a problem. How could you get your friends to work together to change something?

Draw a picture of yourself. Write the words you would say to your friends. A sample answer is shown.

We could all bring in cans of food. Then we could give the food to people who need it.

Book 2.2/Unit 3 Swimmy — **At Home:** Ask children to think about other deep-sea problems that Swimmy and the other fish might work together to solve. 237

Extend, 237

Hide and Seek

By pretending to be one large fish, Swimmy and his friends were able to hide themselves. Draw a picture that shows how another animal hides itself. Describe it.

Make a Pet Graph

"Swimmy" tells the story of a small fish. Have you ever had a fish as a pet? What kinds of pets do you and your classmates have? Find out what pets your classmates have. Count the total number of each kind of pet. Show your results in a bar graph.

Find Out More

Swimmy sees all kinds of animals in the sea. Find out about one animal that lives in the ocean. Write down three facts about that animal.

359

Story Activities

Hide and Seek

Materials: paper, pencils, crayons or paints

ONE Discuss with children how different animals hide. Some lizards change color; tigers' stripes look like shadows in the grass; mother birds are the color of nests. Children can describe their drawings as they display them to the class.

Make a Pet Graph

Materials: paper large enough to cover the bulletin board, strips of paper, felt-tipped markers

GROUP Have children gather the information. Construct a graph on a bulletin board, with categories of pets across the bottom. Together, total the number of each kind of pet. Attach strips of paper to the graph vertically for a visual comparison of the information.

Find Out More

RESEARCH AND INQUIRY Suggest that ONE children consult an encyclopedia, nature magazines, or the Internet. Have children draw their animal, label it with its name, and write three facts under its picture.

interNET CONNECTION For more information or activities on the topic, go to ***www.mhschool.com/reading***.

DAILY Phonics ROUTINES

DAY 3 **Letter Substitution** Write these words on the board: *cage, dice, pace.* Read the words together. Ask volunteers to change the beginning letter in each word to make a new word.

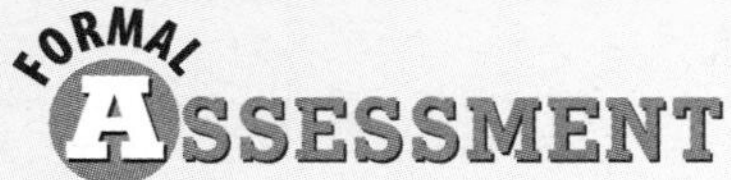

After page 359 see Selection Assessment.

Study Skills

LIBRARY/MEDIA CENTER

Children will interpret an author search screen.

PREPARE Look over the sample author search screen with children. Display **Teaching Chart 199.**

TEACH Point out the headings and abbreviations on the computer search screen and discuss each, using entries as examples.

PRACTICE Have children answer questions 1–5, then review the answers: **1.** fiction **2.** *The Biggest House in the World* **3.** J Fic L. **4.** *The Alphabet Tree*, copyright 1968 **5.** *Fiction Section*

ASSESS/CLOSE Have children write the title, call number, and copyright date for the Leo Lionni book they would most like to read.

READ TOGETHER

Do an Author Search at the Library

Here are the results of a search for books by Leo Lionni at a library.

Author and Title	Call number	Date
Lionni, Leo		
Alexander and the Wind-up Mouse	J Fic L	c 1969
The Alphabet Tree	J Fic L	c 1968
The Biggest House in the World	J Fic L	c 1969
An Extraordinary Egg	J Fic L	c 1994
Fish Is Fish	J Fic L	c 1970
Swimmy	J Fic L	c 1976

Use the search results to answer the questions.

1. Fic is short for something. What do you think it is?
2. Which book is about a house?
3. What is the call number of Leo Lionni's books?
4. What is the oldest book on this list?
5. In what section of the library will you find Leo Lionni's books?

Meeting Individual Needs

EASY

Name________ Date______ **Reteach 238**

Do an Author Search at the Library

If you want to find a list of books by a particular author, you can do an **author search** at the computer in your library.

Below is an author search of books by Michelle Miller.

Results of Search

Top 8 matches (*author, Michelle Miller*)

1. Title: **Car Cat Rides Again** Published 1996
2. Title: **Car Cat** Published 1993
3. Title: **I Want to Be a Queen** Published 1993
4. Title: **A Garden for Mr. Rat** Published 1992
5. Title: **Nursery Rhymes A-B-C** Published 1992
6. Title: **I Want to Be a Doctor** Published 1992
7. Title: **I Want to Be a Dancer** Published 1991
8. Title: **I Want to Be a Teacher** Published 1990

Use the above list to answer these questions.

1. Which of the above books was published first? I Want to Be a Teacher
2. In which year was the first book in the "Car Cat" series published? 1993
3. If you liked "Car Cat", which book here would be good to read next? Car Cat Rides Again
4. Which book has something about the alphabet in its title? Nursery Rhymes A-B-C

238 **At Home:** Have children go to the library and do a computer author search of a favorite writer. Book 2.2/Unit 3 **Swimmy** 4

Reteach, 238

ON-LEVEL

Name________ Date______ **Practice 238**

Do an Author Search at the Library

When you do an **author search,** it is important to look closely at the description of the books listed. If you click on the icon that says "Full Record," you will find more information about a specific book.

Look at this result list of an author search. Let's say you read *Take Joy: The Tasha Tudor Christmas Book.* Now you want another book about the holidays. What would be a good choice?

1. Title: Take Joy: The Magical World of Tasha Tudor (video recording) Pub. Date: 1996 ■ See Full Record
2. Title: A Time to Keep: The Tasha Tudor Book of Holidays Pub. Date: 1992 ■ See Full Record
3. Title: Take Joy: The Tasha Tudor Christmas Book Pub. Date: 1966 ■ See Full Record

1. A Time to Keep: The Tasha Tudor Book of Holidays

To further help you decide, click on the Full Record icon. This is what you'd see. Use this information to answer the questions that follow.

Title: A Time to Keep: The Tasha Tudor Book of Holidays
Author: Tudor, Tasha
Publisher: Chicago: Rand McNally, © 1977; 58 pages, illustrations
Subjects: holidays in old New England

Library Location	Call Number
Wilson	J 394 TUD
East Treamer	J/394.26974/T

2. What is the subject of this book? holidays in old New England
3. Which library locations have a copy? Wilson and East Treamer
4. What is the call number of this book at Wilson library? J 394 TUD

238 **At Home:** Ask children what, besides books, is available by Tasha Tudor. (a videotape) Book 2.2/Unit 3 **Swimmy** 4

Practice, 238

CHALLENGE

Name________ Date______ **Extend 238**

Do an Author Search at the Library

Choose your favorite author. Go to the library. Use the computer to do an author search. List the books the author has written below.

1. ________
2. ________
3. ________
4. ________
5. ________
6. ________

What kinds of books do you think your author likes to write? Answers will vary.

How can you tell? Answers will vary, but should be based on the list generated by the computer.

238 **At Home:** Have children make a list of all their favorite authors. Encourage children to look in the library for books by these authors. Book 2.2/Unit 3 **Swimmy**

Extend, 238

Take your time reading the story, the questions, and the answers.

DIRECTIONS:

Read the story. Then read each question about the story.

SAMPLE

Going on a Treasure Hunt

Tammy invited Pat over for a treasure hunt. When Pat arrived, Tammy gave her a list of things to find. Pat was very excited, since she had never been on a treasure hunt before. Pat had to look for or find out:

a green leaf, a dog hair, a bug, a flower, Tammy's mother's birthday, and the cat's name.

When Pat found all of the things on her list, she called to Tammy. Tammy checked that everything was there. She told Pat that she had done a great job in a short time. Pat thanked Tammy for all of the fun and asked if they could have another treasure hunt soon.

1 Which of these is a general statement you can make from this story?

- ○ Finding bugs is an easy thing to do.
- ● Spending time with a friend can be a lot of fun.
- ○ All friends like to look for things.
- ○ Most treasure hunts take a long time.

2 What is this story mostly about?

- ● Tammy and Pat's treasure hunt
- ○ Pat's house
- ○ Tammy's mother
- ○ What to look for when you have a treasure hunt

361

Test Power

THE PRINCETON REVIEW

Read the Page

Explain to children that you will be reading this story as a group. You will read the story, and they will follow along in their books.

Request that children put pens, pencils, and markers away, since they will not be writing in their books.

Discuss the Questions

QUESTION 1: Remind children that they should look for details in the story to support a choice. In the final sentence, it says that Pat thanked Tammy for the fun she had.

QUESTION 2: Remind children that the title often is a good clue to the main idea of the story. In this case, the story is about Pat and Tammy's treasure hunt.

Leveled Books

EASY

Billy Fish

- ☑ Phonics Soft *c* and Soft *g*
- ☑ Form Generalizations
- ☑ Instructional Vocabulary *escaped, fierce, hidden, machine, swaying, swift*

Guided Reading

PREVIEW AND PREDICT As you take the **picture walk**, see if children can predict what the story will be about. Chart children's ideas.

SET PURPOSES Have children discuss why they want to read *Billy Fish*. For example, children may want to find out more about sea life.

READ THE BOOK Use the following questions to guide children's reading or after they have read the story independently.

Page 2: Find the word *once*. What sound do the letters *ce* make in the word *once?* /s/ Can you find another word on this page where the letters *ce* make the /s/ sound? (chance) ***Phonics and Decoding***

Page 3: Read the last sentence. Why do you think the author described the shark as fierce? Can you think of any other creatures that are fierce? ***Instructional Vocabulary***

Page 6: What do you think might happen if the leak in the boat's engine was never fixed? ***Make Predictions***

Page 14: What generalizations can you make about Billy Fish? (He understands animals and is brave.) ***Form Generalizations***

Page 16: What generalizations can you make about the way some people treat the ocean? (Many people abuse and pollute oceans.) ***Form Generalizations***

RETURN TO PREDICTIONS AND PURPOSES Have children review their predictions and purposes for reading.

LITERARY RESPONSE Discuss these questions:

- What did you think about how the sea animals reacted to the pollution?
- Do you have a favorite sea creature?

Also see the story questions and activity in *Billy Fish*.

See the Phonics **CD-ROM** for practice using words with the /s/ and /j/ sounds.

Intervention Skills

Intervention Guide, for direct instruction and extra practice of vocabulary and comprehension

Answers to Story Questions

1. The boat had a leak.
2. He loved the sea more than anything and knew how to talk to sea animals.
3. Possible response: boats everywhere would have to be cleaner; people would have to stop polluting bodies of water.
4. A boy who can talk to animals goes on a boat and learns that animals are angry about pollution.
5. The other fish; he forms them into the shape of a giant fish to scare away the predator fish.

The Story Questions and Activity below appear in the Easy Book.

Story Questions and Writing Activity

1. Why was the water full of oil?
2. Why did Billy's parents take him on a big boat for his birthday?
3. In the story, the captain promises to keep the water clean. What are some things we can do to keep our ocean clean?
4. What is this story mostly about?
5. In this story, the sea animals fight to protect the ocean. What does Swimmy want to protect? How does he do it?

Sea Animal Math

There are some math problems hidden in this book. Reread page 10. How many giant sea horses swim up to the boat? What multiplication problem can you write to find the answer? Now reread page 12. How many cans of juice did the octopus throw at the boat? How did you find your answer?

from *Billy Fish*

Leveled Books

INDEPENDENT

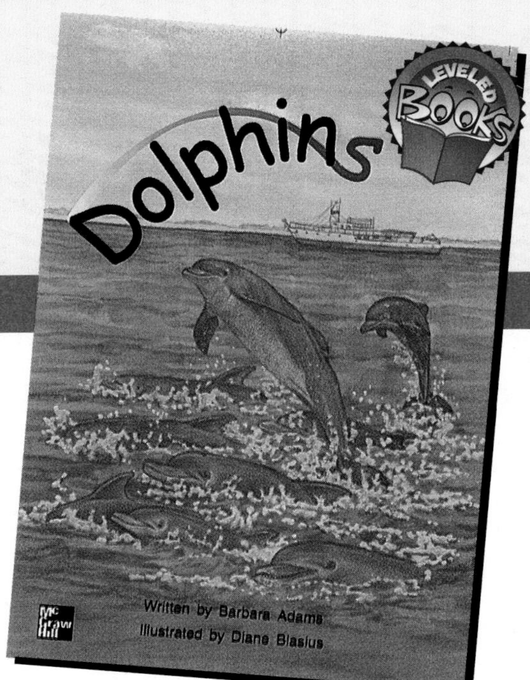

Dolphins

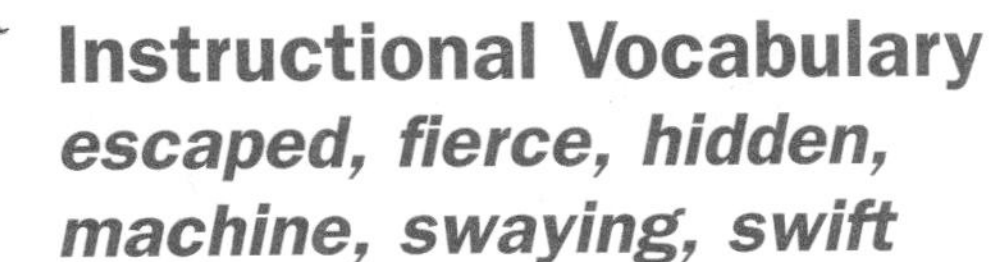

- Phonics Soft *c* and Soft *g*
- Form Generalizations
- Instructional Vocabulary *escaped, fierce, hidden, machine, swaying, swift*

Guided Reading

PREVIEW AND PREDICT Take a **picture walk** through page 5 of the story. Have children predict what the story will be about. Chart children's ideas.

SET PURPOSES Children should discuss what they want to learn by reading *Dolphins*. For example, they may want to know why dolphins are friendly creatures.

READ THE BOOK Use questions like the following to guide children's reading or after they have read the story independently.

Page 3: Based on reading this page, what generalization can you form about dolphins? (They are friendly and sometimes even help people.) *Form Generalizations*

Page 4: Read the last sentence. What word has the /j/sound? (messages) Which letter makes the /j/ sound? (*g*) *Phonics and Decoding*

Page 6: Which of the following is *not* a generalization you can make about all mammals: Mammals feed their babies milk. Mammals breathe with lungs. Mammals are friendly. *Form Generalization*

Page 7: Find the word *swaying*. Can you show what *swaying* looks like? Try to use the word *swaying* in a sentence. *Instructional Vocabulary*

Page 16: What kinds of things might we be able to do with dolphins in the future? What kinds of things might they help us learn? *Make Predictions*

RETURN TO PREDICTIONS AND PURPOSES Discuss children's predictions. Then have children review their purposes for reading. Did they find out what they wanted to know?

LITERARY RESPONSE Discuss these questions:

- How are dolphins similar to or different from other sea creatures that you've learned about?
- Did you learn any new things about dolphins from reading this story?

Also see the story questions and activity in *Dolphins*.

See the Phonics **CD-ROM** for practice using words with the /s/ and /j/ sounds.

Answers to Story Questions

1. A hydrophone
2. Dolphins and people are mammals, they breathe air, they take care of their babies and nurse them.
3. It is likely that dolphins communicate with each other using many different sounds, touch, and movements.
4. Scientists are trying to discover the meaning of the sounds and movements that dolphins use to communicate with each other.
5. This is based on fact; "Swimmy" is fantasy.

The Story Questions and Activity below appear in the Independent Book.

Story Questions and Writing Activity

1. What machine do scientists use to record a dolphin's clicks and whistles?
2. How are dolphins and people alike?
3. From reading this book and from what you know already about dolphins, what do you think about their ability to communicate with each other?
4. What is the main idea of the book?
5. How does the information about dolphins given here differ from the plot of *Swimmy*?

A Dolphin Friend

If people and dolphins do learn to communicate, what might they say to one another? Write an interview between you and a dolphin.

from *Dolphins*

Leveled Books

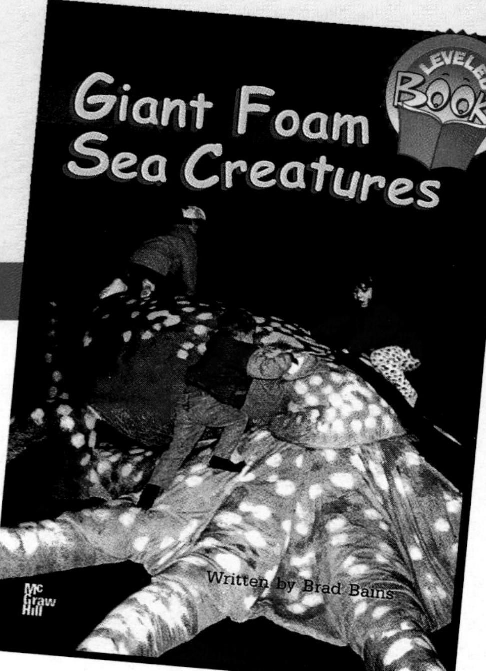

CHALLENGE

Giant Foam Sea Creatures

- ☑ Phonics Soft *c* and Soft *g*
- ☑ Form Generalizations
- ☑ Instructional Vocabulary
  escaped, fierce, hidden, machine, swaying, swift

Guided Reading

PREVIEW AND PREDICT Take a **picture walk** with children and have them predict what the story will be about. Chart children's predictions.

SET PURPOSES Have children write about why they want to read *Giant Foam Sea Creatures*. For example, children may want to find out about the different kinds of sea life represented in an aquarium.

READ THE BOOK Use questions like the following to guide children's reading or after they have read the story independently.

Pages 4–5: Find the word *placed*. What sound do the letters *ce* make in the word *placed*? (/s/) What other words can you think of that use the letters *ce* to make the /s/ sound? (*race, pace*) ***Phonics and Decoding***

Page 7: What generalization can you make about the ocean based on what you've read about the parts of the aquarium? (The ocean has very deep water that is dark; deep water that gets little light; and slightly deep water that receives lots of light.) ***Form Generalizations***

Pages 8–9: Find the word *machine*. What kind of machine is being used on these pages? What other kinds of machines can you think of? ***Instructional Vocabulary***

Pages 12–13: What generalizations can you make about sea creatures that live in deep water? (They are more difficult to see.) ***Form Generalizations***

Page 16: What do you think visitors to the aquarium will think of the sea sculptures? How will the sculptures be helpful to visitors? ***Make Predictions***

RETURN TO PREDICTIONS AND PURPOSES Have children review their predictions and purposes for reading.

LITERARY RESPONSE Discuss these questions:

- What fish would you most like to see as a sculpture?
- Which would you prefer to see in an aquarium—a real fish or a sculpture of that fish?

Also see the story questions and activity in *Giant Foam Sea Creatures*.

See the Phonics **CD-ROM** for practice in using words with the /s/ and /j/ sounds.

Answers to Story Questions

1. sculptures of sea creatures
2. to get an idea of how the exhibit would look
3. They thought they were interesting creatures.
4. It is about a group of artists who made big sculptures for an exhibit.
5. Answers will vary.

The Story Questions and Activity below appear in the Challenge Book.

Story Questions and Writing Activity

1. What do the artists in this story make?
2. Why did the artists make a model of the exhibit before they started?
3. Why, do you think, did the artists want to make sculptures of sea creatures?
4. What is this story mainly about?
5. What do you think Swimmy might tell artists about his life in the ocean?

Make a Sea Creature

Look up pictures of sea creatures in a science book or an encyclopedia. Choose one and draw an outline of it. Cut out the creature, and then color it in using markers or crayons.

from *Giant Foam Sea Creatures*

Bringing Groups Together

Anthology and Leveled Books

Connecting Texts

SEA CREATURE ORGANIZER Use the chart to talk about different kinds of sea creatures.

Write the story titles in the chart. Have children name the sea creatures featured in that story. Write children's contributions under each story title.

Swimmy	Billy Fish	Dolphins	Giant Foam Sea Creatures
• Tuna • Medusa • Lobster • Eel • Sea anemone • Seaweed	• Blue whale • Sea horse • Octopus	• Dolphin • Killer whales	• Lion fish • Moray eel • Jaw fish • Ghost anemone • Jellyfish • Giant octopus • Angelfish

Viewing/Representing

GROUP PRESENTATIONS Divide the class into four groups, one for each of the four stories read in the lesson. Have each group work on a diorama that includes the sea creatures highlighted in the story. When finished, have each group present its diorama to the class.

AUDIENCE RESPONSE Ask children to look carefully at the dioramas created by each group and to ask thoughtful questions about the sea creatures featured.

Research and Inquiry

MORE ABOUT SEA CREATURES Have children ask themselves what else they might like to know about sea creatures. Invite them to:

- look at classroom picture books and school library reference books that feature sea creatures.
- visit a local aquarium or museum exhibit that features sea life.
- invite a marine biologist or other person familiar with sea creatures and their environments to speak to the class.

interNET CONNECTION Have children log on to ***www.mhschool.com/reading*** for links to Web pages.

Review Soft *c* and Soft *g*

TESTED OBJECTIVES

Children will:

- Review /s/ *ce* and /j/ *ge*.
- Blend and read soft *c* and *g* words.

MATERIALS:

- Teaching Chart 200

Skills Finder

Soft *c* and Soft *g*

Introduce	B2: 44G-H
Review	B2: 67E-F, 340G-H, 361G-H, 362G-H
Test	B2: Unit 1
Maintain	B2: 221

TEACHING TIP

SOFT C AND G You may want to point out to children that when the letters *c* or *g* precede the letters *e*, *i*, or *u* in a word, the letters *c* and *g* make the soft sound /s/ and /j/ respectively.

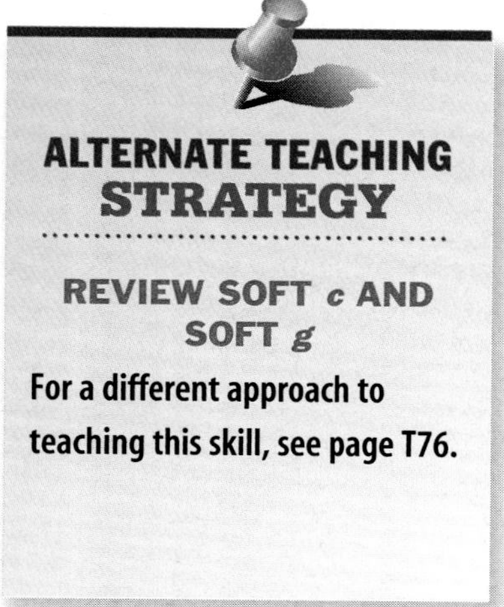

ALTERNATE TEACHING STRATEGY

REVIEW SOFT *c* AND SOFT *g*

For a different approach to teaching this skill, see page T76.

PREPARE

Review the Letters *ce* and *ge* as Symbols for /s/ and /j/

Read this sentence aloud and have children raise their hands whenever they hear a word with the soft *c* or *g* sound:

- The orange car won the race.
- Tell children that they will review the letters *ce* and *ge* and the sounds they make.
- Write the words *brace* and *barge* on the board. Ask volunteers to underline *ce* and *ge* in the words. Then have the class say the words in unison.

TEACH

BLENDING Model and Guide Practice with Soft *c* and *g* Words

- Display **Teaching Chart 200.** Write *ce* after the letter *i* in the first column. Then ask children to blend the sounds to read the word *ice.* i ce ice
- Have children complete the rest of the words in column 1. Ask volunteers to blend the sounds together to read the completed words.

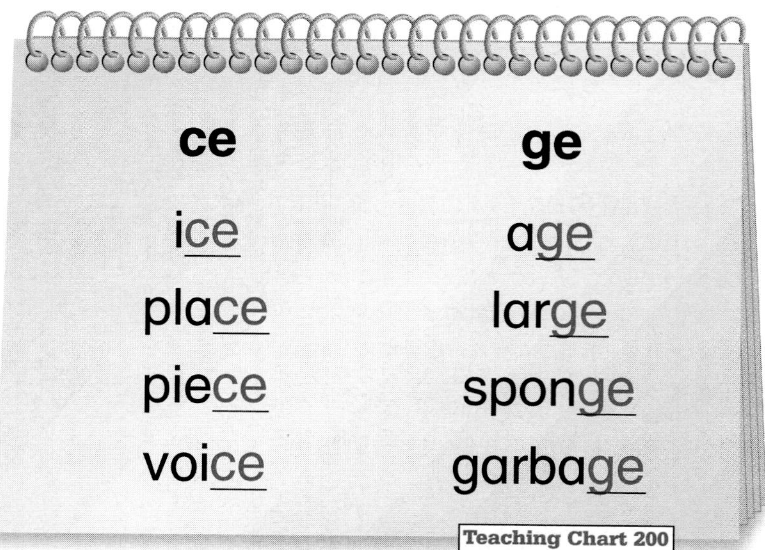

Teaching Chart 200

Use the Words in Context

Have children write sentences to reinforce the meanings of the words in column 1. Then have volunteers read their sentences aloud. Example: *My mom put the ice cream in the freezer.*

Repeat the Procedure

- Repeat the procedure to complete column 2 of the chart.

PRACTICE

BLENDING
Build Soft *c* and *g* Words with Letter Banks

Write the following letters in a letter bank on the chalkboard as shown.

sli__	**ce**	hu__	**ge**	twi__
ra__		tra__		mi__

Have volunteers make words by writing *ce* or *ge* after the letters in the letter bank. Have children write these words on slips of paper sorting them according to their word family. Tell children that they can add either *ce* or *ge* to the end of one of the examples to form two real words. ▶**Auditory/Linguistic**

ASSESS/CLOSE

Build and Read Soft *c* and *g* Words

To assess children's ability to blend and read soft *c* and *g* words, observe them building words during the Practice activity. Have them list any words from *Swimmy* that have soft *c* and soft *g*. Have each child read his or her list.

ADDITIONAL PHONICS RESOURCES

Phonics/Phonemic Awareness Practice Book, pages 147–150.

Phonics CD-ROM activities for practice with Blending and Segmenting

DAY 4 **Fluency** Write these words on the board: *mice, nice, pace, face, stage, page, age.* Point to each word, asking children to blend the sounds silently. Then ask volunteers to use the words in sentences.

SPELLING/PHONICS CONNECTIONS

See the 5-Day Spelling Plan, pages 361Q–361R.

Intervention Guide, for direct instruction and extra practice of soft *c* and soft *g*

Meeting Individual Needs for Phonics

EASY

Name________ Date______ **Reteach 239**

Soft *c* and Soft *g*

Say these words. Listen for each sound made by the letters in dark type.
fen**ce** twi**ce** ed**ge** ra**ge**

Use a word from the box to answer each riddle. Write the word on the line.

face nice cage ice stage rice

1. This is a place where a mouse might live. cage
2. This is someone who is kind. nice
3. This is something everyone has. face
4. This is very cold. ice
5. This is where a play happens. stage
6. This is something we eat. rice

6 Book 2.2/Unit 3 **Swimmy** **At Home:** Have children write two more words that contain the sounds /s/ spelled **ce** and /j/ spelled **ge**. 239

Reteach, 239

ON-LEVEL

Name________ Date______ **Practice 239**

Soft *c* and Soft *g*

Below are pairs of words. The second word is scrambled. Unscramble the second word to make it rhyme with the first word and write your word on the line.

1.	range	asgtrne	strange
2.	race	epalc	place
3.	rice	inec	nice
4.	face	lcea	lace
5.	cage	tsgae	stage
6.	mice	cei	ice
7.	page	gera	rage
8.	twice	cmei	mice
9.	brace	ctrae	trace
10.	wage	gea	age
11.	nice	lisce	slice
12.	juice	ecrtu	truce

12 Book 2.2/Unit 3 **Swimmy** **At Home:** Have children write a sentence for two of the words they formed. 239

Practice, 239

CHALLENGE

Name________ Date______ **Extend 239**

Soft *c* and Soft *g*

Put an **X** on words that are not spelled correctly. Use the words left in the box to answer the riddles.

fierse	strange	chanj	ras	place
fierce	stranj	change	race	plas

1. I am somewhere you can go. place
2. Some dangerous animals are like this. fierce
3. Something odd can also be this. strange
4. The runner at the finish line has just won this. race
5. This is what happens to the color of some trees in the fall. change

Write two or three sentences telling about your favorite place.

Book 2.2/Unit 3 **Swimmy** **At Home:** Have children write riddles for other **-ce** and **-ge** words. 239

Extend, 239

LANGUAGE SUPPORT

Name________ Date______

Circle the Picture

1. A fierce tuna fish came darting through the waves.
2. Swimmy saw strange fish, pulled by an invisible thread.
3. The fish swam together, each in his own place.

258 **Swimmy** • Language Support/Blackline Master 142 Grade 2

Language Support, 258

Review Soft *c*, *g*; Long *a*, *o*, *e*, *i*

TESTED OBJECTIVES

Children will:

- **review soft *c*, *g*.**
- **review /ā/*ai*, *ay*; /ō/ *oa*, *oe*, *ow*; /ē/ *ee*, *ie*, *ea*; /ī/ *i*, *y*, *igh*; /s/ *ce*, /j/ *ge*.**
- **blend and read words with long *a*, *o*, *e*, *i* and soft *c*, *g*.**

MATERIALS

- **Teaching Chart 201**

Skills Finder

Soft *c* and Soft *g*

Introduce	B2: 44G-H
Review	B2: 67E-F, 340G-H, 361E-F, 362G-H
Test	B2: Unit 1
Maintain	B2: 221

PREPARE

Identify the Letters *ai*, *ay*; *oa*, *oe*, *ow*; *ee*, *ie*, *ea*; *i*, *y*, *igh*; *ce*, *ge* as Symbols for Long *a*, *o*, *e*, *i*, /s/, /g/

- Write this sentence on the chalkboard: *I know a place where rainbow-colored creatures play in the sea.* Ask volunteers to underline the letters that represent the sounds: /ī/, /ā/, /ō/, /ē/.
- Write the following sentence on the chalkboard: *Once there was a prince who lived in a huge castle.* Have children circle the letters that represent /s/ and /j/.

TEACH

BLENDING Model and Guide Practice with Long *a*, *o*, *e*, *i* and Soft *c* and *g*

- Display **Teaching Chart 201.** Point to the first incomplete word and the two answer choices. Write the letters *ai* on the blank line. Blend the sounds together to read the word *tail.*
- Invite children to blend the sounds and read the word *tail* with you.

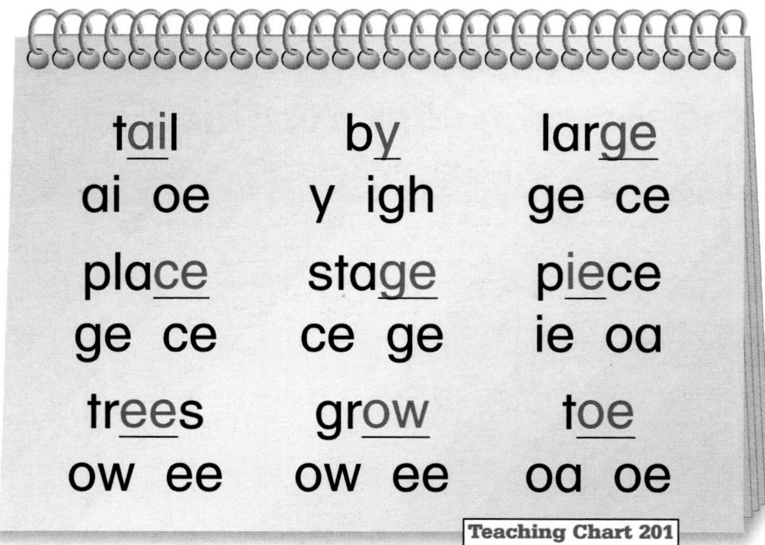

Use the Word in Context Ask a volunteer to use the word *tail* in context to reinforce its meaning. Example: *The fish moved its tail as it swam.*

Repeat the Procedure Continue with **Teaching Chart 201**. Have children the choose appropriate letter combination to complete the rest of the chart.

PRACTICE

SORTING
Build and Sort Words with /ā/, /ō/, /ē/, /ī/ and Soft *c* and Soft *g*

Have small groups of children brainstorm other words with each long vowel sound: /ā/, /ō/, /ē/, /ī/ and with /j/*ge* and /s/*ce*. Ask each group to sort their words in columns under the appropriate heading.
▶ **Interpersonal/Linguistic**

GROUP

ASSESS/CLOSE

Read and Use Words with /ā/, /ō/, /ē/, /ī/, Soft *c* and Soft *g* in Context

To assess children's ability to blend and read words with long *a, e, o, i* and soft *c* and soft *g*, observe children as they engage in the Practice activity. Encourage children to choose a word from each list, read it aloud, and then use the word in context.

ADDITIONAL PHONICS RESOURCES

Phonics/Phonemic Awareness Practice Book, pages 147–150.

Phonics CD-ROM activities for practice with Blending and Segmenting

DAILY Phonics ROUTINES

DAY 5 **Writing** Have partners use /s/ and /j/ words to create rhyming couplets. Have children read their rhymes to the class. Have listeners identify rhyming words and write them on the chalkboard.

Intervention ▶ **Skills**
Intervention Guide, for direct instruction and extra practice of soft *c, g;* Long *a, o, e, i*

Meeting Individual Needs for Phonics

EASY

Name ____ Date ____ Reteach 240

Soft *c, g;* Long *a, o, e, i*

I ____ an apple.
read mean (eat)

Read the sentence. Circle the word that completes the sentence. Then write the word on the line.

1. The children ___hide___ in the garden.
(hide) side high
2. I ___mow___ the lawn.
know low (mow)
3. The dog wags her ___tail___.
nail (tail) jail
4. What ___day___ of the week is it?
bay spray (day)
5. I bake a ___huge___ cake.
age (huge) page
6. The ___mice___ share some bread.
rice dice (mice)

240 **At Home:** Have children write three questions using some of the words they did not circle. Book 2.2/Unit 3 **Swimmy** 6

Reteach, 240

ON-LEVEL

Name ____ Date ____ Practice 240

Soft *c, g;* Long *a, o, e, i*

Circle, then write, the word that completes each sentence.

1. Can you ___blow___ out all the candles?
(blow) snow flow
2. I put ___ice___ in my drink.
(ice) mice dice
3. He made a pot with some ___clay___.
hay (clay) say
4. The leaves fell from the ___tree___.
(tree) bee sneeze
5. Pam had a ___dream___ that she could fly.
leap cream (dream)
6. I use my ___brain___ to think.
stain chain (brain)
7. I ___change___ into pajamas before I go to bed.
(change) strange page
8. Let's take the ___train___ to the beach.
hail (train) rain

240 **At Home:** Have children write a one-paragraph story based on one of the sentences above. Book 2.2/Unit 3 **Swimmy** 8

Practice, 240

CHALLENGE

Name ____ Date ____ Extend 240

Soft *c, g;* Long *a, o, e, i*

eel	deep	fierce	giant	place	sky
strange	sea	swaying	swallowed	weeds	

Unscramble the letters. Then write the words correctly. The first one is done for you.

caple	place
gsrtnae	strange
eeicrf	fierce
ele	eel
gwysnai	swaying
wdewlalso	swallowed
edep	deep
dwsee	weeds
esa	sea
ating	giant
ysk	sky

Use some of the words to write a sentence about what you might find in the sea.

Answers will vary.

240 **At Home:** Play a game of "Twenty Questions" in which you pick an object in the sea. Have children ask questions that can be answered with "yes" or "no." Book 2.2/Unit 3 **Swimmy**

Extend, 240

LANGUAGE SUPPORT

Name ____ Date ____

Word and Picture Match

place	strange	tail	day
rainbow	eel	eat	giant

Grade 2 Language Support/Blackline Master 143 • **Swimmy** 259

Language Support, 259

Children will:

- infer main ideas.
- identify supporting details.

MATERIALS

- Teaching Chart 202

Skills Finder

Main Idea	
Introduce	B2: 309I-J
Review	B2: 361I-J, 371E-F
Test	B2: Unit 3
Maintain	B2: 109, 165, 229, 345

TEACHING TIP

MAIN IDEA AND SUPPORTING DETAILS
If children have difficulty understanding the concepts, relate them to their experiences. Ask:

- What is the main reason for having schools? (To help children learn–this is a main idea.)
- What are some subjects we study in school? (Reading and Math–these are supporting details.)

SELF-SELECTED Reading

Children may choose from the following titles.

ANTHOLOGY

- *Swimmy*

LEVELED BOOKS

- *Billy Fish*
- *Dolphins*
- *Giant Foam Sea Creatures*

Bibliography, page T88–T89

Review Main Idea

PREPARE

Discuss Main Idea and Supporting Details Remind children that the main idea of a story is what the story is about, or the most important idea of the story. The main idea is supported by details. Sometimes the main idea is stated directly, and sometimes it is not.

TEACH

Read the Chart and Model the Skill Display **Teaching Chart 202**. Ask a volunteer to read the chart. Remind them to pay attention to details and to consider the main idea of the story.

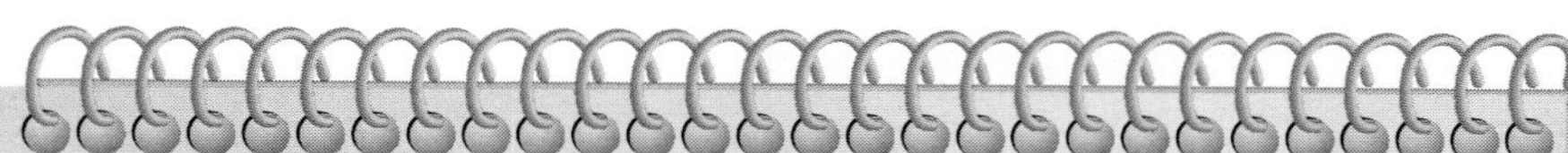

Hermie Hides Himself

Hermie the crab creeps along the ocean floor. Suddenly he sees a big fish swimming toward him. "I better hide," he thinks.

Hermie stops moving. He is as still as a rock or a seashell. His shell is the same color as the sand. The fish swims right by him. Hermie escapes by just being himself.

Teaching Chart 202

MODEL The details of the story tell me how Hermie hides from the fish. When he doesn't move, he looks like a rock or shell. He blends in with the sand. I think these details support the idea that Hermie uses what he looks like to escape the fish.

Ask a volunteer to underline the sentence that tells the main idea of the paragraph.

PRACTICE

Identify an Implicit Main Idea

Explain: Sometimes the main idea of a passage is not directly stated. Write on the chalkboard:

"Oh, no!" thought Fishie. "Here comes that big shark! He must be hungry for a little fish like me!" Fishie slipped into a cave in the rocks.

Then ask: *What is the main idea of these sentences? How do you know?* (Fishie is afraid; the details in the sentence reveal the main idea)

Create a Main Idea Chart

PARTNERS

Have children work in pairs to create a Main Idea chart. If necessary, prompt by asking, "How does Hermie escape the big fish?"

▶**Linguistic/Visual**

MAIN IDEA	SUPPORTING DETAILS
Hermie uses what he looks like to escape the fish.	He stops moving and looks like a rock. His tan shell blends in with the sand.

ASSESS/CLOSE

Illustrate Supporting Details and Infer Main Idea

Have children draw a picture that shows how Hermie hides from the fish. Ask them to add a main idea title to their drawing that would also be a good title for the **Teaching Chart**. Observe whether children use the details from the story in their pictures. Note whether their titles reflect the main idea of the picture and the story.

ALTERNATE TEACHING STRATEGY

MAIN IDEA

For a different approach to teaching this skill, see page T71.

Intervention **Skills**

Intervention Guide, for direct instruction and extra practice of main idea

Meeting Individual Needs for Comprehension

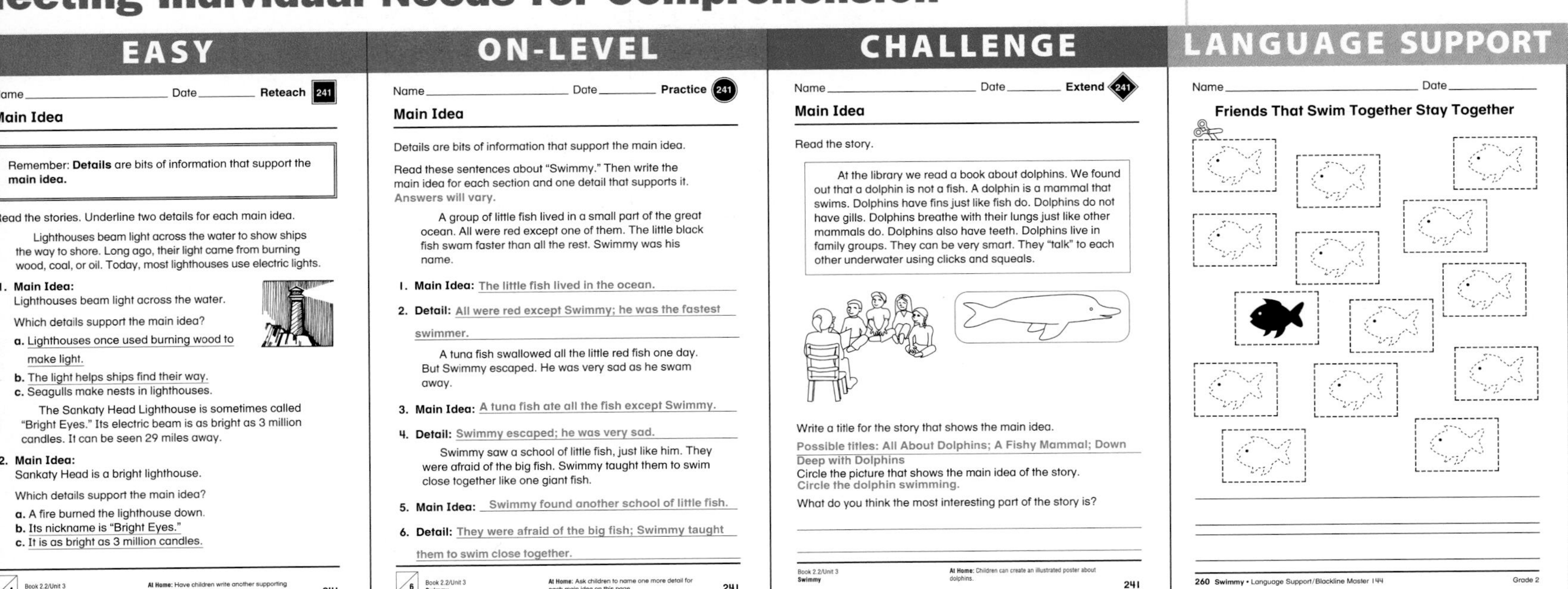

EASY

Name______ Date______ Reteach 241

Main Idea

Remember: **Details** are bits of information that support the **main idea.**

Read the stories. Underline two details for each main idea.

Lighthouses beam light across the water to show ships the way to shore. Long ago, their light came from burning wood, coal, or oil. Today, most lighthouses use electric lights.

1. **Main Idea:** Lighthouses beam light across the water.
   Which details support the main idea?
   a. Lighthouses once used burning wood to make light.
   b. The light helps ships find their way.
   c. Seagulls make nests in lighthouses.

The Sankaty Head Lighthouse is sometimes called "Bright Eyes." Its electric beam is as bright as 3 million candles. It can be seen 29 miles away.

2. **Main Idea:** Sankaty Head is a bright lighthouse.
   Which details support the main idea?
   a. A fire burned the lighthouse down.
   b. Its nickname is "Bright Eyes."
   c. It is as bright as 3 million candles.

4 Book 2.2/Unit 3 Swimmy — **At Home:** Have children write another supporting detail for each of the main ideas. 241

ON-LEVEL

Name______ Date______ Practice 241

Main Idea

Details are bits of information that support the main idea.

Read these sentences about "Swimmy." Then write the main idea for each section and one detail that supports it.
Answers will vary.

A group of little fish lived in a small part of the great ocean. All were red except one of them. The little black fish swam faster than all the rest. Swimmy was his name.

1. **Main Idea:** The little fish lived in the ocean.
2. **Detail:** All were red except Swimmy; he was the fastest swimmer.

A tuna fish swallowed all the little red fish one day. But Swimmy escaped. He was very sad as he swam away.

3. **Main Idea:** A tuna fish ate all the fish except Swimmy.
4. **Detail:** Swimmy escaped; he was very sad.

Swimmy saw a school of little fish, just like him. They were afraid of the big fish. Swimmy taught them to swim close together like one giant fish.

5. **Main Idea:** Swimmy found another school of little fish.
6. **Detail:** They were afraid of the big fish; Swimmy taught them to swim close together.

6 Book 2.2/Unit 3 Swimmy — **At Home:** Ask children to name one more detail for each main idea on this page. 241

CHALLENGE

Name______ Date______ Extend 241

Main Idea

Read the story.

At the library we read a book about dolphins. We found out that a dolphin is not a fish. A dolphin is a mammal that swims. Dolphins have fins just like fish do. Dolphins do not have gills. Dolphins breathe with their lungs just like other mammals do. Dolphins also have teeth. Dolphins live in family groups. They can be very smart. They "talk" to each other underwater using clicks and squeals.

Write a title for the story that shows the main idea.
Possible titles: All About Dolphins; A Fishy Mammal; Down Deep with Dolphins

Circle the picture that shows the main idea of the story.
Circle the dolphin swimming.

What do you think the most interesting part of the story is?

Book 2.2/Unit 3 Swimmy — **At Home:** Children can create an illustrated poster about dolphins. 241

LANGUAGE SUPPORT

Name______ Date______

Friends That Swim Together Stay Together

260 Swimmy • Language Support/Blackline Master 144 — Grade 2

Reteach, 241 **Practice, 241** **Extend, 241** **Language Support, 260**

Children will:

- **recognize simile.**
- **recognize metaphor.**

MATERIALS

- **Teaching Chart 203**

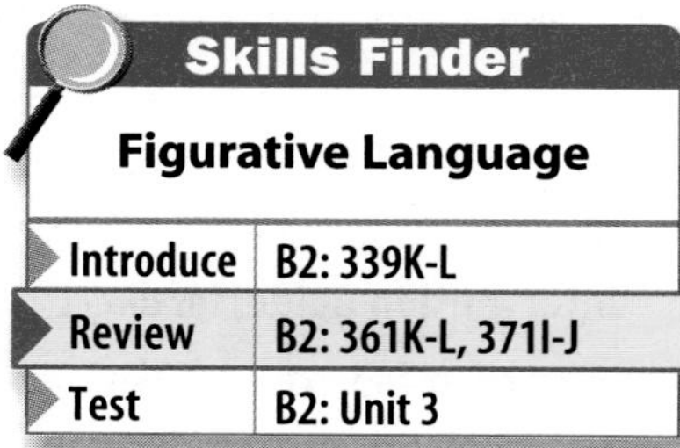

Figurative Language	
Introduce	B2: 339K-L
Review	B2: 361K-L, 371I-J
Test	B2: Unit 3

TEACHING TIP

MANAGEMENT While you work with children who have trouble with this concept, the rest of the class can draw pictures of sea creatures.

Review Figurative Language

PREPARE

Discuss Figurative Language Write these two sentences on the chalkboard. *Sarah was quiet. Sarah was quiet as a mouse.* Ask children to compare the two sentences. Ask them which sentence creates a picture in their mind. Discuss how comparing one thing to another can help children to see something in a new or unusual way.

TEACH

Define Simile and Metaphor Explain that when writers use the connecting words *like* or *as* to make a comparison, they are using a *simile.* For example, *quiet as a mouse.* When writers use a metaphor, they make a comparison by saying something *is* something else. For example, *Jorge is a wizard in math.*

Read "Hermie's Day on the Beach" and Model the Skill Ask children to pay close attention to comparisons or figurative language, as you read **Teaching Chart 203** with them.

Hermie's Day on the Beach

Hermie the crab crawls out of the ocean. Above the beach, the sun is a bright, orange ball. Its light makes the water sparkle like diamonds. Cotton-candy clouds float across the blue sky. The air is as hot as an oven. Hermie looks around for some shade, but he can't find any place on the beach that's as cool as the ocean.

Teaching Chart 203

MODEL When I read the words *the sun is a bright, orange ball,* I can picture how the sun looks above the beach. Comparing the sun to an orange ball makes me see it in a new, interesting way.

Have children discuss the comparison in the third sentence. How is it different from the comparison in the second sentence? Guide them to see the difference between a simile and a metaphor.

PRACTICE

Identify Similes and Metaphors

Have children find and circle the comparisons in "Hermie's Day on the Beach" that use *like* or *as*. Then have them find and underline the comparisons that say something *is* something else. Have volunteers read each comparison and say whether it is a simile or a metaphor.

▶ **Logical/Visual**

ASSESS/CLOSE

Recognize and Use Figurative Language

Have partners reread *Swimmy* and list all the examples of figurative language. Have volunteers write the examples on the chalkboard and then identify the similes and metaphors.

Encourage children to create their own similes and metaphors and use them in a story.

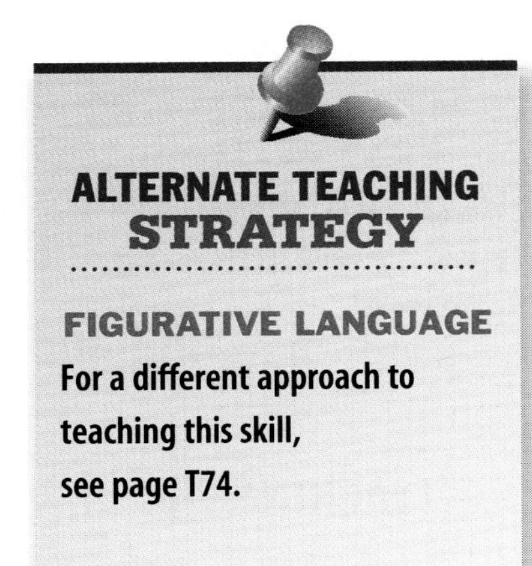

ALTERNATE TEACHING
STRATEGY
FIGURATIVE LANGUAGE
For a different approach to teaching this skill, see page T74.

Intervention ▶ **Skills**

Intervention Guide, for direct instruction and extra practice of figurative language

Meeting Individual Needs for Vocabulary

EASY

Name__________ Date______ **Reteach 242**

Figurative Language

To describe what something is like, a writer sometimes will compare it to something else.

That horse can race **like the wind.** My pet rabbit is **as soft as silk.**

Think about "Swimmy." Think about the things under the sea. Draw a line to the phrase that is a good comparison.

1. The sea is ______ as blue as the sky. / as red as a rose.
2. Sea anemones look ______ like a school of fish. / like pink palm trees.
3. The sea rocks look ______ like sugar candy. / as light as a feather.
4. An eel is ______ as long as a rope. / like a tooth
5. A clam is ______ as big as a house. / as hard as a rock.

242 **At Home:** Have children draw a picture for one of the comparisons above. Ask them to write the comparison as a caption. Book 2.2/Unit 3 **Swimmy** 5

Reteach, 242

ON-LEVEL

Name__________ Date______ **Practice 242**

Figurative Language

A writer will sometimes describe something by comparing it to something else.

Read the first sentence in each pair. Think about the picture the words bring to mind. Then complete the second statement to tell what the first sentence means.

1. My little dog can eat like a horse.
   My little dog can eat __a lot__.
2. The hailstones were the size of baseballs.
   The hailstones were __big__.
3. My sister is as light as a feather.
   My sister is not __heavy__.
4. His shirt looked like an old rag.
   His shirt was not __new or clean__.
5. Those deer can run like the wind.
   Those deer can run __fast__.
6. The forest fire spread like lightning.
   The forest fire spread __quickly__.

242 **At Home:** Point out that the last two sentences contain sayings that mean "quickly." Ask children to invent two more comparisons that mean the same thing. Book 2.2/Unit 3 **Swimmy** 6

Practice, 242

CHALLENGE

Name__________ Date______ **Extend 242**

Figurative Language

Draw a line under the words in each sentence that help you form a picture in your mind. Draw a picture to go with each sentence.

1. A creature as flat as a pancake creeps along the bottom of the sea.
2. It looks like a forest of seaweed is growing from sugar-candy rocks.
3. An eel almost too long to remember swam by.
4. The sea anemones looked like pink palm trees swaying in the wind.

Write two new sentences. Use words that form pictures in the reader's mind. Sample answers shown.

The man crushed the box as flat as a pancake.

Sam felt like he had a mountain of homework to do.

242 **At Home:** Work with children to make a list of favorite descriptive expressions. Invite children to choose one to illustrate. Book 2.2/Unit 3 **Swimmy**

Extend, 242

LANGUAGE SUPPORT

Name__________ Date______

Figuring Out What It Means

a very long eel	bright, shiny rocks	a lot of seaweed

a forest of seaweed — a lot of seaweed

an eel whose tail was almost too far away to remember — a very long eel

sugar-candy rocks — bright, shiny rocks

Grade 2 Language Support/Blackline Master 145 • **Swimmy** 261

Language Support, 261

Writing a Story

GRAMMAR/SPELLING CONNECTIONS

See the 5-Day Grammar and Usage Plan on Adverbs, pages 361O–361P.

TEACHING TIP

Technology
Does your school have a web site? Use your school's technology resources to publish the children's work on the Internet. Invite teams of children to help.

Handwriting
Remind children when making the final copy to leave space between the title and the rest of the story. They may want to print the title in all capital letters, especially on a cover page.

Handwriting CD-ROM

Prewrite

WRITE A STORY Present this writing assignment: Swimmy and the other little fish solved their problem by working together. Write a fairy tale about a group of animals who work together to solve their problem.

VISUALIZE Have children think of some animals and the problems they might have. Remind children that the animals in their story must find a solution that requires them to work together.

Strategy: Map out a Story Have children organize their thoughts by filling in the chart.

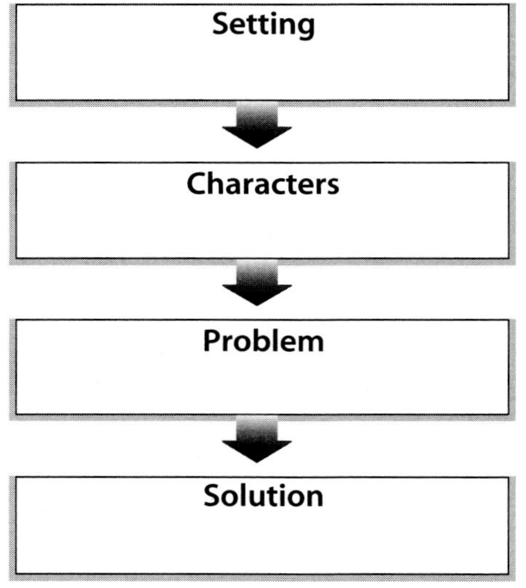

Graphic Organizer 10

Draft

BE CREATIVE Have the children use their charts to start writing their stories. Guide children to write freely without self-editing. Encourage them to be imaginative in creating the animals' personalities. Give each character a special part in resolving the story's problem.

Revise

SELF-QUESTIONING Ask children to assess their drafts.

- Have I solved the problem on my chart?
- Does each character have a personality?
- Do dialogue and descriptive detail help bring the story to life?

Have children trade stories with a peer to get another point of view.

Edit/Proofread

CHECK FOR ERRORS Children should check their stories for errors in spelling, grammar, and punctuation.

Publish

SHARE THE STORIES Have children rewrite their stories neatly. Display the stor where other classes can read them.

THE CATS GO ON VACATION

by Sarita Esposito

Five cats lived in the park in the center of the city. Their names were Kitty, Frisky, Midnight, Whiskers, and Tom. The cats loved living in the park. They drank from the fish pond and found plenty of food to eat. They were all happy until winter came.

The pond froze so that they couldn't drink. They found nothing to eat. But Frisky had an idea. "Nearly everyone's gone on winter vacation," he said. "We need one, too. Let's show what we want." The cats made signs that, when read all together, said: CATS NEED VACATIONS, TOO.

The cats took their signs and paraded up and down the street next to the park. The very first person who saw them said, "You must be smart cats. I'll take you all to my house for the winter!" The cats had a cozy winter with all the warm milk they could drink. The next spring, they moved back to the park.

Presentation Ideas

AKE A BOOK Have children arrange eir stories into booklets. Add illustrations d a heavy paper cover.
Viewing/Representing

T IT OUT Have children volunteer to act t stories. Use simple props. For example, the story "The Cats Go on Vacation" use avy paper for the signs.
Speaking/Listening

nsider children's creative efforts, possibly adding a plus (+) for originality, wit, and imagination.

Scoring Rubric

Excellent	Good	Fair	Unsatisfactory
4: The writer • crafts an entertaining story. • presents distinct characters. • presents original events in sequence. • resolves the story creatively. • has a good sense of audience.	**3:** The writer • attempts to devise an original story. • unfolds events in sequence. • creates characters with some special traits. • successfully resolves the story.	**2:** The writer • attempts to devise a story. • presents individual characters • may retell events from a book or film. • may not clearly resolve the story.	**1:** The writer • unsuccessfully tries to tell a story. • may not present characters. • may present disconnected events or descriptions. • does not resolve the story.

omplete 0: The writer leaves the page blank or fails to respond to the writing task. The student does not address the topic or simply paraphrases the prompt. The response is illegible or incoherent.

leeting Individual Needs for Writing

EASY

Let's Pretend Ask children to imagine what kind of animal they would like to be. Have them write a short paragraph that describes what their life would be like as this animal. Encourage use of descriptive detail. Children can make a drawing of their chosen animal.

ON-LEVEL

Plan a Day Ask children to choose a familiar animal and imagine how that animal spends its day. Have children make a chart showing each hour of the day and indicating what the animal might be doing at that time. Then have children write an interview with the animal about its day.

CHALLENGE

Conversation Ask children to imagine that their pet or some other animal is able to talk to them. Ask them what the animal would say and how they would respond. They can write the imagined conversation using quotation marks and indenting when someone new begins to speak.

Listening and Viewing

LISTENING Have children

- try to imagine themselves in the characters' situations.
- pay attention to the sequence of events in the story.
- listen for details that make one character different from another.

VIEWING Remind children to

- think about how the illustrations affect their understanding of story events.
- think about how the artist's feelings are shown in the pictures.

LANGUAGE SUPPORT

ESL When ESL students have chosen the animal they are going to write about, ask them to work with English-fluent partners to brainstorm lists of problems this animal might have. Then have them choose one problem from each of their lists and brainstorm possible solutions together.

PORTFOLIO

Invite children to include their stories or another writing project in their portfolios.

5 Day Grammar and Usage Plan

LANGUAGE SUPPORT

ESL **In a loud voice say: *I am talking loudly*. In a soft voice say: *I am talking softly*. Write these sentences on the chalkboard. Then ask, *What words in each sentence answer the question, "How am I talking?"*** (loudly, softly) **Explain that words that tell how you do something are adverbs.**

DAILY LANGUAGE ACTIVITIES

Write the Daily Language Activities on the chalkboard each day or use **Transparency 29**. Have children identify the adverb in each sentence.

Day 1

1. The fish swam slowly. slowly
2. Swimmy moved quickly. quickly
3. The big fish ate swiftly. swiftly

Day 2

1. Swimmy will go now. now
2. He saw the little fish there. there
3. The red fish came here. here

Day 3

1. The fish lived nearby. nearby
2. The school will move soon. soon
3. He happily went away. happily

Day 4

1. Swimmy went out early. early
2. The big fish quietly waited. quietly
3. The plants swayed softly. softly

Day 5

1. The fish could not find food today. today
2. Swimmy pushed them gently. gently
3. He proudly led the way. proudly

Daily Language Transparency 29

DAY 1 Introduce the Concept

Oral Warm-Up Write the following on the chalkboard: Jane talked quietly. Ask children to identify the action word, or verb *(talked)* Then have them find the word that tells how Jane talked. *(quietly)*

Introduce Adverbs Tell children that words that tell how something is done are called adverbs. Present:

Adverbs

- An **adverb** tells more about a verb.
- An adverb can tell **"how"**.

Introduce Adverbs Many adverbs end with *-ly*. Ask children to think of other adverbs that could describe how Jane talked. (examples: slowly, loudly)

Present the Daily Language Activity. Then have children write a sentence with an adverb that tells how something happened.

Assign the daily Writing Prompt on page 340C.

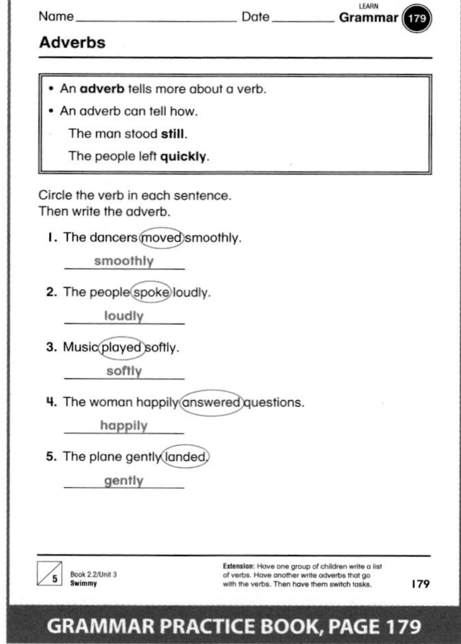
Name ______ Date ______ LEARN Grammar 179

Adverbs

- An **adverb** tells more about a verb.
- An adverb can tell how.

The man stood **still**.
The people left **quickly**.

Circle the verb in each sentence.
Then write the adverb.

1. The dancers (moved) smoothly. smoothly
2. The people (spoke) loudly. loudly
3. Music (played) softly. softly
4. The woman happily (answered) questions. happily
5. The plane gently (landed). gently

5 Book 2.2/Unit 3 **Swimmy**

Extension: Have one group of children write a list of verbs. Have another write adverbs that go with the verbs. Then have them switch tasks. 179

GRAMMAR PRACTICE BOOK, PAGE 179

DAY 2 Teach the Concept

Review Adverbs Remind children th[at] adverbs can tell how something is don[e].

More About Adverbs Write on the chalkboard: Stan is eating now. Ask chil[-] dren which word tells when Stan is eat- ing. now Then write: She sat there. Ask which word tells where she sat. Explain that these words are adverbs. Present:

Adverbs

An adverb can tell "when" or "where".

Give children other examples of adver[bs] that tell when *(then, early, soon, today, now, finally, later)* and where *(here, ther[e], nearby, around, up)*.

Present the Daily Language Activity. Have children point out which adverbs tell when and which tell where. Then have children write a sentence using a[n] adverb that tells when and another tha[t] tells where.

Assign the daily Writing Prompt on page 340C.

Name ______ Date ______ LEARN AND PRACTICE Grammar 180

Adverbs

- An adverb can tell when or where.

The bus leaves soon. (when)
It will roll away. (where)

Circle the adverb in each sentence.
Write **when** if it tells when.
Write **where** if it tells where.

1. (Now) we see the bus. when
2. We climb (inside). where
3. (Finally), the bus starts to move. when
4. We look (down). where
5. We stop (soon). when

180 **Extension:** Have the children underline the verb in each sentence.

Book 2.2/Unit 3 **Swimmy** 5

GRAMMAR PRACTICE BOOK, PAGE 180

Adverbs

DAY 3 Review and Practice

arn from the Literature Review verbs with children. Read the second ntence from page 354 of *Swimmy:*

"Let's go and swim and play and SEE things!" he said happily.

ve children identify the adverb in the ntence. Ask children what the adverb s. (how)

riting Adverbs Present the Daily nguage Activity and have children entify the adverb in each sentence. en write three sentences on the chalkard: Swimmy swam quickly. Swimmy am away. Swimmy swam yesterday. k children which adverb tells how, ich tells when, and which tells where. ve children write sentences using ch of the three adverbs.

Assign the daily Writing Prompt on page 340D.

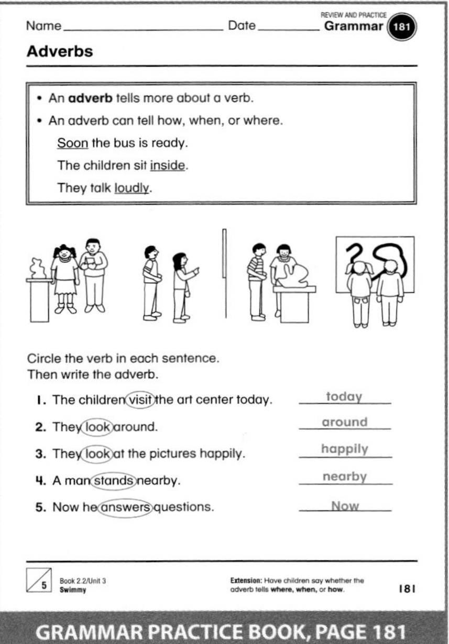

Name ________ Date ________ REVIEW AND PRACTICE Grammar 181

Adverbs

- An **adverb** tells more about a verb.
- An adverb can tell how, when, or where.

Soon the bus is ready.
The children sit inside.
They talk loudly.

Circle the verb in each sentence. Then write the adverb.

1. The children visit the art center today. today
2. They look around. around
3. They look at the pictures happily. happily
4. A man stands nearby. nearby
5. Now he answers questions. Now

5 Book 2.2/Unit 3 Swimmy — **Extension:** Have children say whether the adverb tells **where, when,** or **how.** 181

GRAMMAR PRACTICE BOOK, PAGE 181

DAY 4 Review and Practice

Review Adverbs Write the sentences from the Daily Language Activities for Days 2 and 3. Have children replace each adverb with another appropriate adverb. Then have children do the Daily Language Activity for Day 4.

Mechanics and Usage Before children do the daily Writing Prompt, review capitalization of nouns and pronouns. Display and discuss:

Capitalization

- The pronoun *I* is always a capital letter.
- A proper noun begins with a capital letter.

Assign the daily Writing Prompt on page 340D.

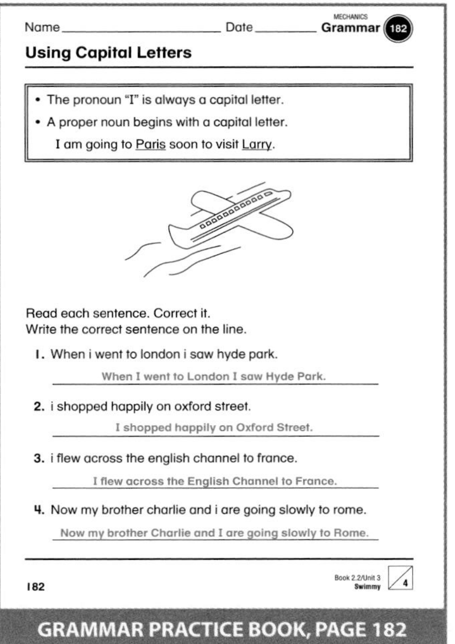

Name ________ Date ________ MECHANICS Grammar 182

Using Capital Letters

- The pronoun "I" is always a capital letter.
- A proper noun begins with a capital letter.

I am going to Paris soon to visit Larry.

Read each sentence. Correct it. Write the correct sentence on the line.

1. When i went to london i saw hyde park.
   When I went to London I saw Hyde Park.
2. i shopped happily on oxford street.
   I shopped happily on Oxford Street.
3. i flew across the english channel to france.
   I flew across the English Channel to France.
4. Now my brother charlie and i are going slowly to rome.
   Now my brother Charlie and I are going slowly to Rome.

182 — Book 2.2/Unit 3 Swimmy 4

GRAMMAR PRACTICE BOOK, PAGE 182

DAY 5 Assess and Reteach

Assess Use the Daily Language Activity and page 183 of the **Grammar Practice Book** for assessment.

Reteach Review adverbs with children. Write some of the adverbs from the lesson on the chalkboard. Ask children to identify the adverbs that tell how, when, or where.

Write incomplete sentences on individual slips of paper, leaving out the adverb. Pin the sentences on the bulletin board. Then write adverbs that can complete each sentence on individual index cards. Have children pin the cards on the sentences that can be completed with those particular adverbs.

Use page 184 of the **Grammar Practice Book** for additional reteaching.

Assign the daily Writing Prompt on page 340D.

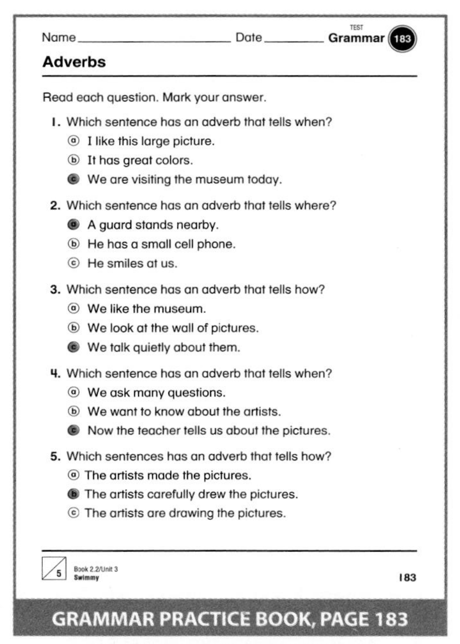

Name ________ Date ________ TEST Grammar 183

Adverbs

Read each question. Mark your answer.

1. Which sentence has an adverb that tells when?
   - ⓐ I like this large picture.
   - ⓑ It has great colors.
   - ● We are visiting the museum today.
2. Which sentence has an adverb that tells where?
   - ● A guard stands nearby.
   - ⓑ He has a small cell phone.
   - ⓒ He smiles at us.
3. Which sentence has an adverb that tells how?
   - ⓐ We like the museum.
   - ⓑ We look at the wall of pictures.
   - ● We talk quietly about them.
4. Which sentence has an adverb that tells when?
   - ⓐ We ask many questions.
   - ⓑ We want to know about the artists.
   - ● Now the teacher tells us about the pictures.
5. Which sentences has an adverb that tells how?
   - ⓐ The artists made the pictures.
   - ● The artists carefully drew the pictures.
   - ⓒ The artists are drawing the pictures.

5 Book 2.2/Unit 3 Swimmy — 183

GRAMMAR PRACTICE BOOK, PAGE 183

GRAMMAR PRACTICE BOOK, PAGE 184

5 Day Spelling Plan

LANGUAGE SUPPORT

ESL Demonstrate the two different ways the *th* digraph is pronounced. With voiceless *th*, the voice isn't used and air passes around the tongue as it is placed on the teeth. With voiced *th*, the voice box adds vibrations to the sound. Point out the voiceless *th* at the beginning of the words *thought* and *through*. Then demonstrate the voiced *th* at the beginning of the words *there* and *than*. Ask children to give other examples of each sound.

DICTATION SENTENCES

Spelling Words

1. I can take you there.
2. The wheel is broken.
3. I eat everything other than fish.
4. The whale went down into the ocean.
5. The baby made a whimper.
6. I thought about the speech.
7. The toy can whirl around.
8. He can whisper to me.
9. She went through the fields.
10. My sister took them to the zoo.

Challenge Words

11. The rat escaped from the cage.
12. The animals were fierce.
13. The boy was hidden under the tree.
14. The machine made a loud noise.
15. The bee was swift.

DAY 1 Pretest

Assess Prior Knowledge Use the Dictation Sentences at left and **Spelling Practice Book** page 179 for the pretest. Allow children to correct their own papers. If children have trouble, have partners give each other a midweek test on Day 3. Children who require a modified list may be tested on the first five words.

Spelling Words		Challenge Words
1. **there**	6. **thought**	11. **escaped**
2. wheel	7. whirl	12. **fierce**
3. **than**	8. whisper	13. **hidden**
4. whale	9. **through**	14. **machine**
5. whimper	10. **them**	15. **swift**

*Note: Words in **dark type** are from the story.*

Word Study On page 180 of the **Spelling Practice Book** are word study steps and an at-home activity.

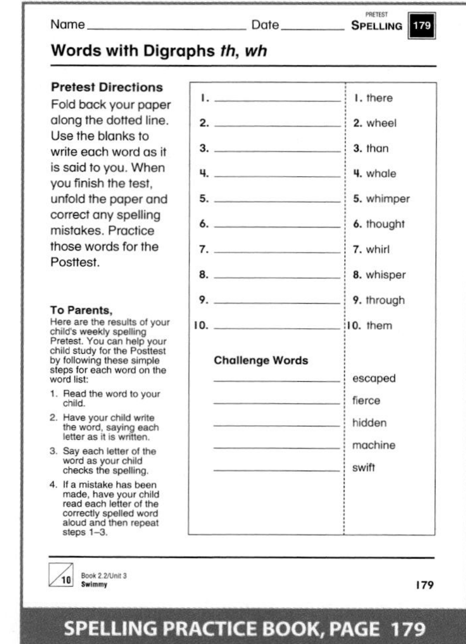

Name________ Date______ PRETEST SPELLING 179

Words with Digraphs *th*, *wh*

Pretest Directions
Fold back your paper along the dotted line. Use the blanks to write each word as it is said to you. When you finish the test, unfold the paper and correct any spelling mistakes. Practice those words for the Posttest.

1. ____ 1. there
2. ____ 2. wheel
3. ____ 3. than
4. ____ 4. whale
5. ____ 5. whimper
6. ____ 6. thought
7. ____ 7. whirl
8. ____ 8. whisper
9. ____ 9. through
10. ____ 10. them

Challenge Words
____ escaped
____ fierce
____ hidden
____ machine
____ swift

To Parents,
Here are the results of your child's weekly spelling Pretest. You can help your child study for the Posttest by following these simple steps for each word on the word list:
1. Read the word to your child.
2. Have your child write the word, saying each letter as it is written.
3. Say each letter of the word as your child checks the spelling.
4. If a mistake has been made, have your child read each letter of the correctly spelled word aloud and then repeat steps 1–3.

10 Book 2.2/Unit 3 Swimmy 179

SPELLING PRACTICE BOOK, PAGE 179

WORD STUDY STEPS AND ACTIVITY, PAGE 180

DAY 2 Explore the Pattern

Sort and Spell Words Say the words *there* and *wheel*. Ask children what sound they hear at the beginning of each word. Tell children that the words begin with the letters *th* and *wh*.

Ask children to read aloud the ten spelling words before sorting them according to sound and spelling pattern.

Words beginning with	
th	**wh**
there	wheel
than	whale
thought	whimper
through	whirl
them	whisper

Word Wall As children read other texts, have them look for new words with initial digraphs *th* and *wh*, and add them to the classroom word wall, underlining the spelling pattern in each word.

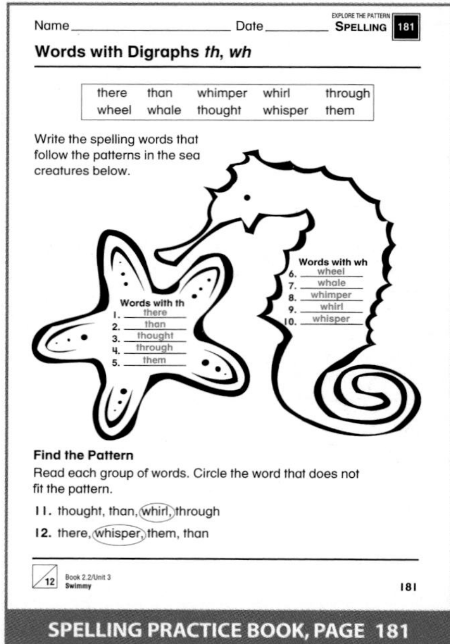

Name________ Date______ EXPLORE THE PATTERN SPELLING 181

Words with Digraphs *th*, *wh*

there	than	whimper	whirl	through
wheel	whale	thought	whisper	them

Write the spelling words that follow the patterns in the sea creatures below.

Find the Pattern
Read each group of words. Circle the word that does not fit the pattern.

11. thought, than, (whirl), through
12. there, (whisper), them, than

12 Book 2.2/Unit 3 Swimmy 181

SPELLING PRACTICE BOOK, PAGE 181

...... Words with Digraphs *th, wh*

DAY 3 Practice and Extend

ord Meaning: Context Write the ords *than, them, there,* and *through* on e chalkboard. Then have children write eir own context sentences. Provide ntences for children to complete. xample: She drove_____ the tunnel.)

lossary Have children:

- write each Challenge Word.
- look up the Challenge Words in the Glossary and locate those with synonyms listed.
- write a synonym for each Challenge Word that has one listed.

Name__________ Date______ PRACTICE AND EXTEND SPELLING 182

Words with Digraphs *th, wh*

there	than	whimper	whirl	through
wheel	whale	thought	whisper	them

A Whale of a Time

Complete each sentence with a spelling word.

1. A ___whale___ is a large animal that swims in the sea.
2. Do you see the whale over ___there___ by the boat?
3. Whales are bigger ___than___ any other animals.
4. People love whales and want to protect ___them___.
5. Whales swim ___through___ the sea.
6. She ___thought___ she saw a whale, but it was only a big wave.
7. The captain turned the ___wheel___ and headed home.

What's That Sound?

Choose the word below that tells about the sound in each sentence. Write the word.

whimper whisper

8. The dog was hurt and started to ___whimper___.
9. Susan began to ___whisper___ to Martin so no one else could hear her.
10. Which spelling word rhymes with **twirl**? ___whirl___

182 **Challenge Extension:** Have students draw cartoon characters speaking to each other. They should use the Challenge Words in the dialogue. Book 2.2/Unit 3 Swimmy 10

SPELLING PRACTICE BOOK, PAGE 182

DAY 4 Proofread and Write

Proofread Sentences Write these sentences on the chalkboard, including the misspelled words. Ask children to proofread, circling incorrect spellings and writing the correct spellings. There are two spelling errors in each sentence.

The (weele) is not (thair). (wheel, there)

I (thawt) I saw her (wisper). (thought, whisper)

Have children create additional sentences with errors for partners to correct.

WRITING **Writing** Have children use as many spelling words as possible in the daily Writing Prompt on page 340D. Remind children to proofread their writing for errors in spelling, grammar, and punctuation.

Name__________ Date______ PROOFREAD AND WRITE SPELLING 183

Words with Digraphs *th, wh*

Proofreading Activity

There are five spelling mistakes in these lines from a play. Circle each misspelled word. Write the words correctly on the lines below.

Ike: Turn the (weel)! We want to go over (thre) by the store.
Ann: I (thoght) the store was down this street.
Ike: Be careful not to go (throogh) the yellow light.
Ann: Of course I will. It is better to be safe (thaen) sorry.

1. ___wheel___ 2. ___there___ 3. ___thought___
4. ___through___ 5. ___than___

Writing Activity

Use some of the spelling words to add lines to the play. Tell what Ann and Ike see or say when they go into a store.

6. Ann: ______
7. Ike: ______
8. Ann: ______
9. Ike: ______
10. Ann: ______

10 Book 2.2/Unit 3 Swimmy 183

SPELLING PRACTICE BOOK, PAGE 183

DAY 5 Assess and Reteach

Assess Children's Knowledge Use page 184 of the **Spelling Practice Book** or the Dictation Sentences on page 361Q for the posttest.

Personal Word List If children have trouble with any words in the lesson, have them create a personal list of troublesome words in their journals. Have children write a context sentence for each word.

JOURNAL

Name__________ Date______ POSTTEST SPELLING 184

Words with Digraphs *th, wh*

Look at the words in each set. One word in each set is spelled correctly. Use a pencil to color in the circle in front of that word. Before you begin, look at the sample sets of words. Sample A has been done for you. Do Sample B by yourself. When you are sure you know what to do, you may go on with the rest of the page.

Sample A
(A) whath
(B) whot
● (C) what
(D) whate

Sample B
● (E) play
(F) plai
(G) plaie
(H) plae

1. (A) wheal ● (B) wheel (C) weel (D) whele
2. (E) thann (F) thane ● (G) than (H) tane
3. ● (A) whimper (B) wimper (C) wimpher (D) whimpur
4. (E) tought (F) thawht (G) thout ● (H) thought
5. (A) wharl ● (B) whirl (C) whurl (D) wherl
6. ● (E) through (F) thru (G) threugh (H) threwgh
7. (A) whail ● (B) whale (C) whal (D) whayl
8. (E) thier (F) tere (G) thair ● (H) there
9. ● (A) whisper (B) wisperr (C) wisper (D) wissper
10. (E) themm (F) thim (G) tem ● (H) them

184 Book 2.2/Unit 3 Swimmy 10

SPELLING PRACTICE BOOK, PAGE 184

Lesson Overview

Cumulative Review with Expository Text

Time to Review

Anthology

The World's Plants Are in Danger

Selection Summary **Children will read about some plants that are in danger of extinction, and why it is important to sta working now to save them for the future.**

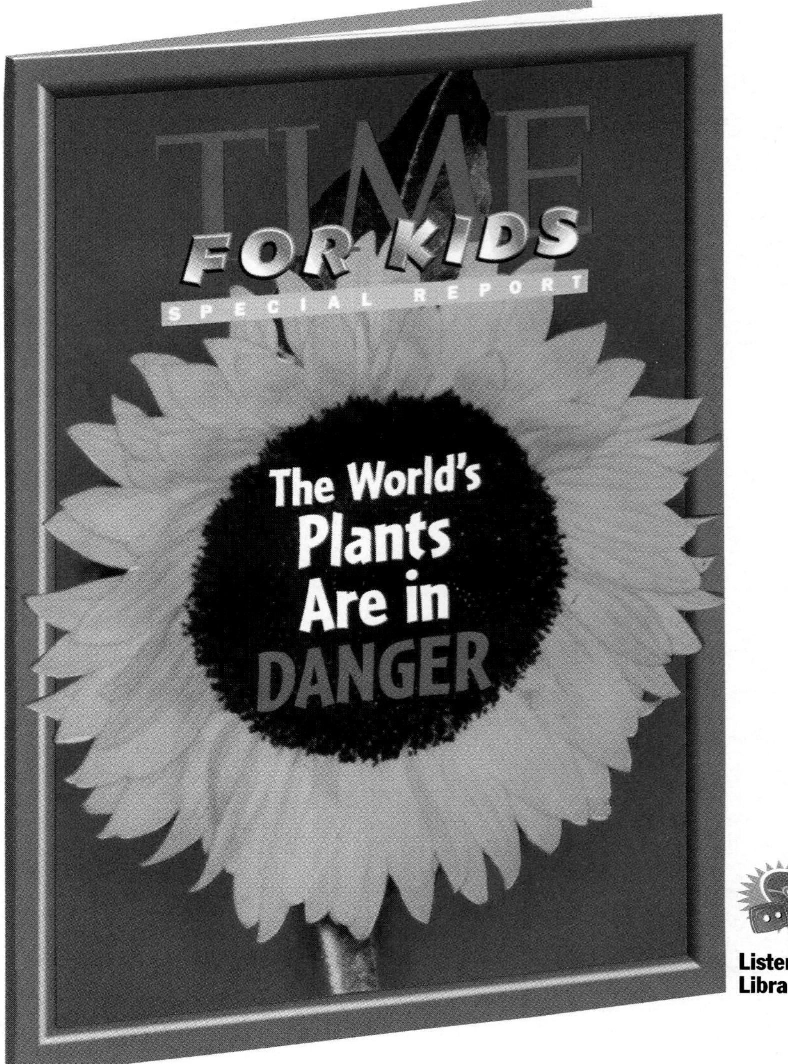

Listening Library

INSTRUCTIONAL pages 364–371

The Plan

Here's the plan. My friend began it.
Plant a plant to save the planet.
Every village, every place
Needs some green. So just in case
Your town is turning brown and bland,
Plant a seed right in the land.
Watch your plant grow every day
And soon your friends will see the way
To turn your town from brown to WOW.
So plan to plant a plant right now!

Rhyme applies to phonics

Time to Reread

Reread Leveled Books

EASY
Lesson on pages 371A and 371D

DECODABLE

INDEPENDENT
Lesson on pages 371B and 371D

Take-Home version available

CHALLENGE
Lesson on pages 371C and 371D

Leveled Practice

EASY

Reteach, 243–250 Blackline masters with reteaching opportunities for each assessed skill

INDEPENDENT/ON-LEVEL

Practice, 243–250 Workbook with Take-Home stories and practice opportunities for each assessed skill and story comprehension

CHALLENGE

Extend, 243–250 Blackline masters that offer challenge activities for each assessed skill

Quizzes Prepared by 

Social Studies	Create a Community Guide, *369*
	Prepare a Speech, *369*
Language Arts	Read Aloud, *362E*
Writing	Write a Story, *368*
Research and Inquiry	Find Out More, *369*
Internet Activities	www.mhschool.com/reading

Suggested Lesson Planner

READING AND LANGUAGE ARTS	DAY 1 Focus on Reading and Skills	DAY 2 Read the Literature
Phonics Daily Routines	**Daily Phonics Routine: Segmenting,** 362H Phonics CD-ROM	**Daily Phonics Routine: Letter Substitution,** 364A Phonics CD-ROM
Phonological Awareness Phonics *Review* Comprehension Vocabulary Study Skills Listening, Speaking, Viewing, Representing	**Read Aloud: Song,** 362E "All Living Things" ✓ **Develop Phonological Awareness,** 362F Review ✓ **Review Soft *c, g*; *ph, tch*; Long *a, o, e, i*,** 362G–362H **Teaching Chart 204** **Reteach, Practice, Extend,** 243 **Phonics/Phonemic Awareness Practice Book,** 151–154 Read **Apply:** *c, g; ph, tch;* Long *a, o, e, i*, 362/363 "The Plan" Intervention Program	**Build Background,** 364A Develop Oral Language **Vocabulary,** 364B–364C ***cleared*** ***forever*** ***save*** ***disappear*** ***problem*** ***warns*** **Word Building Manipulative Card** **Teaching Chart 205** **Reteach, Practice, Extend,** 244 Read **Read the Selection,** 364–367 Comprehension ✓ **Phonics Review** ✓ **Main Idea** **Genre:** Science Magazine Article, 365 Intervention Program
Curriculum Connections	Link **Language Arts,** 362E	Link **Science,** 364A
Writing	**Writing Prompt:** Do you think flowers are important to people? Why or why not? How do flowers make people feel?	**Writing Prompt:** What things in natu do you like to look at? Rivers, mountains, trees? Describe one. **Journal Writing** Quick-Write, 367
Grammar	**Introduce the Concept: Synonyms and Antonyms,** 371O Daily Language Activity: Replace words with synonyms. **Grammar Practice Book,** 185	**Teach the Concept: Synonyms and Antonyms,** 371O Daily Language Activity: Replace words with antonyms. **Grammar Practice Book,** 186
Spelling *Words from Science*	**Pretest: Words from Science,** 371Q **Spelling Practice Book,** 185, 186	**Explore the Pattern: Words from Science,** 371Q **Spelling Practice Book,** 187

  **Intervention Program Available**

eeting
dividual
eeds

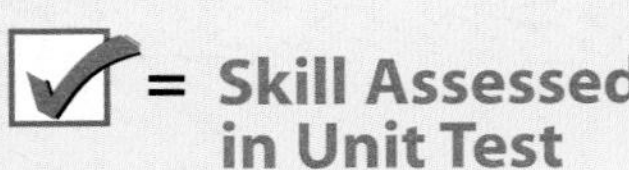
= Skill Assessed in Unit Test

Intervention Program Available

DAY 3 Read the Literature

Daily  Routine: **Blending,** 369

 CD-ROM

Rereading for Fluency, 366

Story Questions and Activities, 368–369
Reteach, Practice, Extend, 245

Study Skill, 370
- Library/Media Center

Teaching Chart 206
Reteach, Practice, Extend, 246

Test Power, 371

 **Read the Leveled Books,** 371A–371D
Guided Reading
- Cumulative Review
- Main Idea
- Instructional Vocabulary

Link Social Studies, 369

Writing Prompt: Write a poem about the way you feel when you see, touch, and smell beautiful flowers.

Writing a Story, 371M
Prewrite, Draft

Review and Practice: Synonyms and Antonyms, 371P
Daily Language Activity: Replace words with synonyms and antonyms.
Grammar Practice Book, 187

Practice and Extend: Words from Science, 371R
Spelling Practice Book, 188

DAY 4 Build Skills

Daily  Routine: **Fluency,** 371F

 CD-ROM

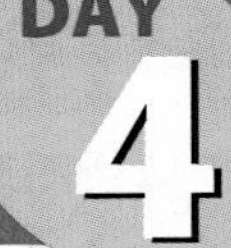 **Read the Leveled Books and the Self-Selected Books**

- Review Main Idea, 371E–371F

Teaching Chart 207
Reteach, Practice, Extend, 247
Language Support, 268

- Review Form Generalizations, 371G–371H

Teaching Chart 208
Reteach, Practice, Extend, 248
Language Support, 268

Writing Prompt: How would you feel if you woke up one day and there were no more flowers on Earth?

Writing a Story, 371M
Revise

Meeting Individual Needs for Writing, 371N

Review and Practice: Synonyms and Antonyms, 371P
Daily Language Activity: Replace words with synonyms and antonyms.
Grammar Practice Book, 188

Proofread and Write: Words from Science, 371R
Spelling Practice Book, 189

DAY 5 Build Skills

Daily  Routine: **Writing,** 371H

Phonics CD-ROM

 **Read Self-Selected Books**

- Review Figurative Language, 371I–371J

Teaching Chart 209
Reteach, Practice, Extend, 249
Language Support, 269

- Review Multiple-Meaning Words, 371K–371L

Teaching Chart 210
Reteach, Practice, Extend, 250
Language Support, 270

Listening, Speaking, Viewing, Representing, 371N

Intervention Program

Writing Prompt: Name some ways we could protect our flowers.

Writing a Story, 371M
Edit/Proofread, Publish

Assess and Reteach: Synonyms and Antonyms, 371P
Daily Language Activity: Replace words with synonyms and antonyms.
Grammar Practice Book, 189,190

Assess and Reteach: Words from Science, 371R
Spelling Practice Book, 190

Language Arts

Read Aloud

All Living Things

a song by W. Jay Cawley

All living things need air to breathe,

Need the sky up above, the earth beneath their feet.

For the fishes in the ocean and the birds that sing,

This world is the home of living things.

All living things need the warm sunshine,

Need the cool summer breeze, that blows on down the line.

For the apples in the orchards and the flowers in the spring,

This world is the home of living things.

Interlude

If we clear away the forest, strip the land, spoil the sea,

What will there be left for us to love in this world of living things?

Continued on page T5

Oral Comprehension

LISTENING AND SPEAKING Read the words to the song aloud to children. Invite them to join in as you repeat phrases, such as *All living things*. Ask: *What do you think is important to the songwriter?* and *How does the songwriter feel about all living things?* Have children name some of the living things listed in the song.

GENRE STUDY: SONG Discuss some of the characteristics of "All Living Things."

- Point out that some songs share similar characteristics to poems. Ask children to think of ways "All Living Things" is like a poem set to music. Discuss how the song expresses the author's feelings, and point out the song's rhyme scheme.
- Have children close their eyes while you sing the song again. Tell them to listen for specific words the songwriter uses to describe what living things need. When you are finished, ask children to describe some of the pictures the words helped create in their imaginations.

Activity Have children make posters to express how they feel about living things. Encourage children to devise slogans and to write them on their posters. Then have children work in small groups to compose a song about their feelings. Encourage them to perform their songs for the class.

▶ **Visual/Linguistic**

Develop **Phonological Awareness**

Blend Sounds

Phonemic Awareness

MATERIALS

- Phonics Picture Posters

Teach Display the Phonics Picture Posters showing animals on the chalkboard. Invite children to play "Zoo Sounds." Explain that you will say the sounds of an animal name. For example, say the sounds for the word *zebra*. Ask a volunteer to blend the sounds to say the word. Then have the child point to the zebra.

Practice Continue with these Phonics Picture Cards: *dog, seal, turtle, cat, fish, rabbit, pig, lion, duck, goat, bear, hen, zebra*.

Segment Sounds

Phonemic Awareness

MATERIALS

- drumstick and drum

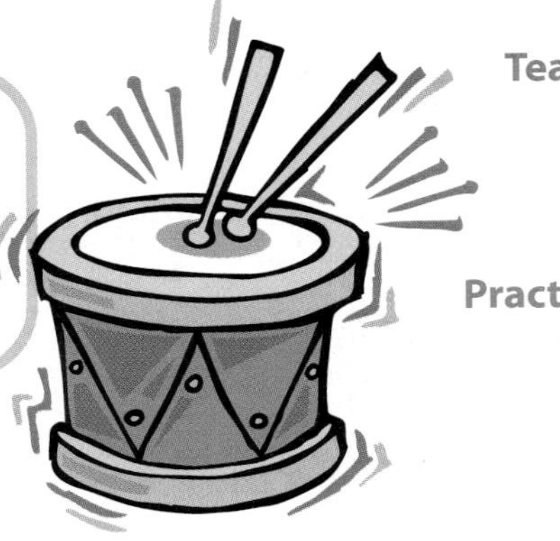

Teach Tell children you are going to say a word. Then you are going to tap the drum once for each sound in the word. For example, say: *Reach*.../r/-/ē/-/ch/ and tap the drum once for each sound. Have children clap out each sound with you.

Practice Have volunteers practice segmenting words by tapping the drum as they say each sound of these words: *peach, lace, graph, meat, cage, photo, watch, dice, field, claim, boat*.

Delete Sounds

Phonemic Awareness

Teach Tell children you are going to say a sentence. One word in the sentence will have a sound missing. Ask volunteers to tell what is missing. For example, say: *The grass is very geen*. Then ask: *What word has a missing sound?* (geen) *What is the missing sound?* (/r/)

Practice Create sentences for the words below and delete the second sound in the word. Have children identify the deleted sounds. Use the words: *speech, graph, blow, steam, stage, snail, bright*, and *float*.

Observe children as they blend, segment, and delete sounds. If children have difficulty, see Alternate Teaching Strategies on pp. T64–T69, T72 and T75.

TESTED OBJECTIVES

Children will:

- review soft *c, g; ph, tch;* long *a, o, e, i.*

MATERIALS

- **Teaching Chart 204**
- **Word Building Manipulative Cards**

Skills Finder

Soft *c* and Soft *g*

Introduce	B2: 44G-H
Review	B2: 67E-F, 340G-H 361E-F, 361G-H
Test	B2: Unit 1
Maintain	B2: 221

Review Soft *c, g; ph, tch;* Long *a, o, e, i*

PREPARE

Listen for Long *a, o, e, i; ph, tch;* Soft *c, g* Sounds

- Read the following sentence aloud. Tell children to raise their hands when they hear a word with a long vowel sound.
  May I eat a piece of that yellow cake?
- Repeat the same process with the following sentence and the sounds /ce/, /ge/, /f/, /ch/. *The children like to eat ice cream and sponge cake at the beach.*

TEACH

BLENDING Model and Guide Practice with Long *a, o, e, i; ph, tch;* Soft *c, g* Words

- Display **Teaching Chart 204**. Have a volunteer read the first sentence, and underline all the words with soft *c, g; ph, tch;* and long *a, o, e,* and *i.*
- Read the sentence aloud slowly, blending the sound of the letters in each word.

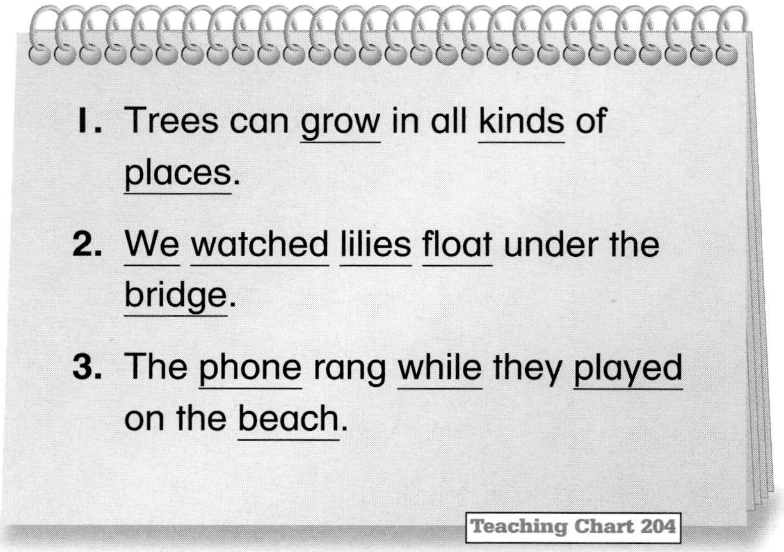

1. Trees can grow in all kinds of places.
2. We watched lilies float under the bridge.
3. The phone rang while they played on the beach.

Teaching Chart 204

Use the Word in Context

- Ask children to use each underlined word in another sentence to reinforce its meaning. For example: *The trees have green leaves.*

Repeat the Procedure

- Repeat the procedure for each sentence on **Teaching Chart 204**.

PRACTICE

SEGMENTING Sort Words with Soft *c, g; ph, tch;* Long *a, o, e, i*

PARTNERS

- Have children prepare a three-column chart with the following headings: Soft *c* and *g; ph* and *tch;* Long *a, o, e, i.*
- Tell children to write each underlined word in the sentence under the correct heading in their chart. ▶ **Linguistic/Interpersonal**

ASSESS/CLOSE

Write and Read Poems Using Words with Soft *c, g; ph, tch;* Long *a, o, e, i*

To assess children's ability to build and decode words with soft *c* and *g; ph* and *tch;* long *a, o, e,* and *i,* observe them as they work on the Practice activity. Ask partners to write poems made from their rhyming words, and read them to the class.

ADDITIONAL PHONICS RESOURCES

Phonics/Phonemic Awareness Practice Book, pages 151–154

CD-ROM activities for practice with Discriminating and Segmenting

Daily Routines

DAY 1 **Segmenting** Read the following words aloud: *sheep, place, huge, coat, tied.* Invite children to use their word building boxes to write the spelling of each sound in the appropriate box.

DAY 2 **Letter Substitution** Have partners use letter cards to build *beach.* Taking turns, one child changes a letter(s) to build a new word. The partner can then read it.

DAY 3 **Blending** Write *phone* on the chalkboard and have children blend the sounds. Call on volunteers to blend other words with soft *c, g; ph, tch;* long *a, o, e,* and *i.* Example: *circus, rage, graph, catch.*

DAY 4 **Fluency** Write the following words on the chalkboard: *ceiling, graph, judge, pitch, mow.* Point to each word, asking children to blend the sounds silently. Ask volunteers to read each word aloud.

DAY 5 **Writing** Have children work with partners to create shopping lists. Encourage them to use items whose names have soft *c, g; ph, tch;* long *a, o, e, i.* (For example: *rice, oats, jeans, watch*)

Meeting Individual Needs for Phonics

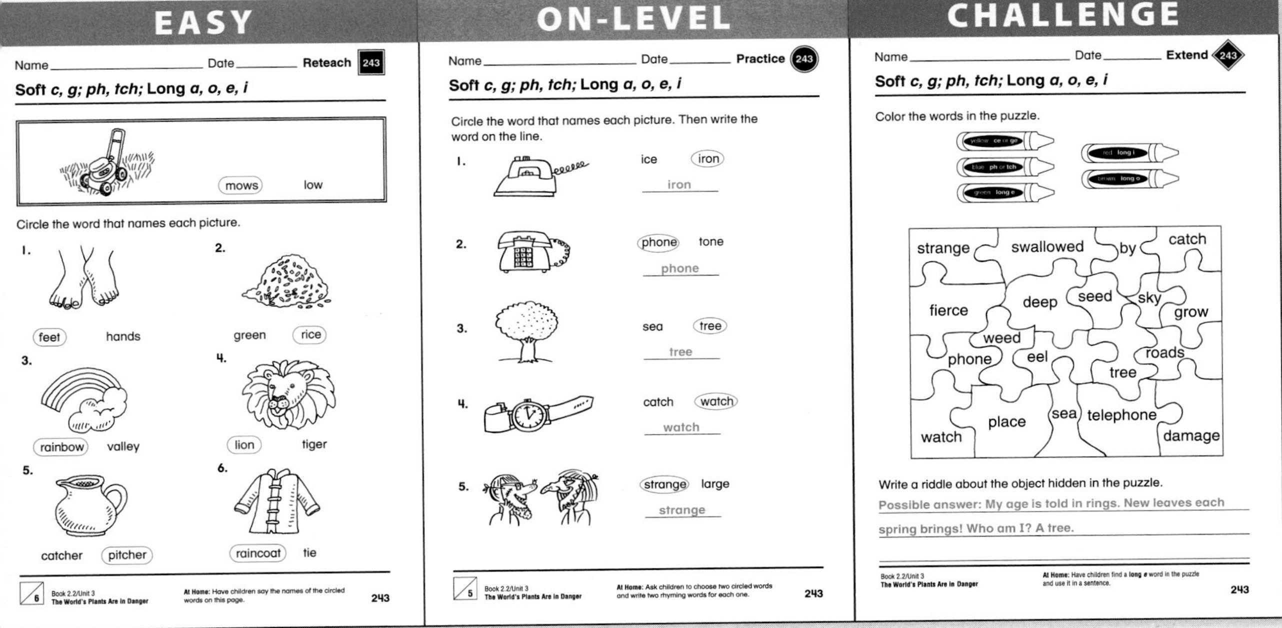

EASY

Name ______ Date ______ Reteach 243

Soft *c, g; ph, tch;* Long *a, o, e, i*

(mows) low

Circle the word that names each picture.

1. (feet) hands
2. green (rice)
3. (rainbow) valley
4. (lion) tiger
5. catcher (pitcher)
6. (raincoat) tie

6 Book 2.2/Unit 3 The World's Plants Are in Danger — At Home: Have children say the names of the circled words on this page. 243

ON-LEVEL

Name ______ Date ______ Practice 243

Soft *c, g; ph, tch;* Long *a, o, e, i*

Circle the word that names each picture. Then write the word on the line.

1. ice (iron) — iron
2. (phone) tone — phone
3. sea (tree) — tree
4. catch (watch) — watch
5. (strange) large — strange

5 Book 2.2/Unit 3 The World's Plants Are in Danger — At Home: Ask children to choose two circled words and write two rhyming words for each one. 243

CHALLENGE

Name ______ Date ______ Extend 243

Soft *c, g; ph, tch;* Long *a, o, e, i*

Color the words in the puzzle.

strange, swallowed, by, catch, fierce, deep, seed, sky, grow, weed, phone, eel, roads, tree, sea, telephone, watch, place, damage

Write a riddle about the object hidden in the puzzle.

Possible answer: My age is told in rings. New leaves each spring brings! Who am I? A tree.

Book 2.2/Unit 3 The World's Plants Are in Danger — At Home: Have children find a long e word in the puzzle and use it in a sentence. 243

Reteach, 243 **Practice, 243** **Extend, 243**

Children will review soft *c, g; ph, tch;* long *a, o, e, i.*

Apply Soft *c, g; ph, tch;* Long *a, o, e, i*

The Plan

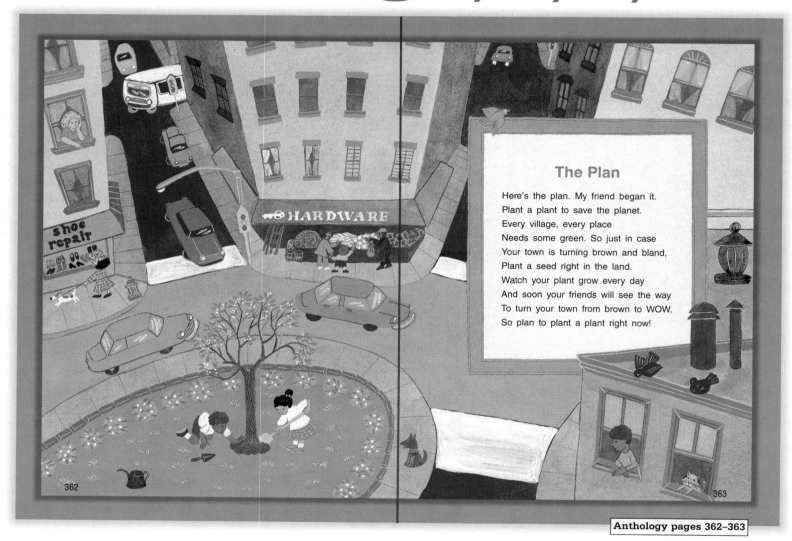

Here's the plan. My friend began it.
Plant a plant to save the planet.
Every village, every place
Needs some green. So just in case
Your town is turning brown and bland,
Plant a seed right in the land.
Watch your plant grow every day
And soon your friends will see the way
To turn your town from brown to WOW.
So plan to plant a plant right now!

shoe repair

HARDWARE

362 363

Anthology pages 362–363

Read and Build Fluency

READ THE POEM Tell children to listen for the /ch/, long *e* , long *i* and long *a* sounds as they listen and follow along while you read aloud "The Plan." Explain that authors sometimes use capital letters to emphasize words. Point out and say WOW from the poem. Then, for auditory modeling, ask children to read the poem aloud in unison as you track the print.

PARTNERS **REREAD FOR FLUENCY** Working in pairs, have one child read the poem aloud for one minute. Have the partner listen and then place a self-stick note after the last word read. Ask them to count the number of words read. Then have partners switch roles and continue.

Dictate and Spell

JOURNAL **DICTATE WORDS** Say the word *village* aloud and segment it into its individual sounds. Use it in a sentence, such as, "Our village is green in the summer." Do the same for *watch, place*, and *needs*. Have children say and then write each word, making sure they have a letter or letters for each sound. Continue to practice with words that have the following phonemic elements: soft *c, g; ph, tch*; long *a, o, e, i*.

Skills Intervention Guide, for direct instruction and extra practice of soft *c, g; ph, tch*; long *a, o, e, i*

Build Background

Concept: Some Plants are Endangered

valuate Prior Knowledge

ONCEPT: SOME PLANTS ARE ENDAN-ERED Ask children to discuss the concept things in nature disappearing or dying out. clude some of the reasons why plants and imals are in danger, as well as why it is portant to protect them from dying out.

AKE A WORD WEB FOR ENDAN-ERED PLANTS AND ANIMALS Work th children to create a word web to record ssible reasons why certain plants and ani-als are dying out. ▶ **Linguistic/Spatial**

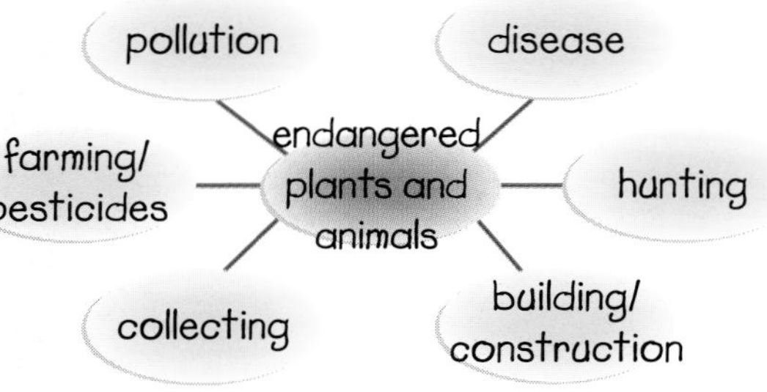

Graphic Organizer 29

RAW PICTURES OF FLOWERS

ONE WRITING Provide children with picture books, magazines, and seed talogs that show pictures of wild and rden flowers. Explain that wildflowers are dangered, while garden flowers are not. ve children draw pictures of each for bulletin board display. Then have em write a brief paragraph scribing their drawings.

Develop Oral Language

DRAW AND DISCUSS FLOWERS

ESL Display illustrations of wildflowers, telling children that one out of ten wildflowers in the United States is in danger of disappearing. Have children make "Don't Pick the Wildflowers" signs, to include drawings and sentences about wildflowers. Ask children to:

- write the names of the flowers on the chalkboard.
- brainstorm a list of words related to the topic, such as: *endangered, rare, few, extinct* and *protect*.
- refer to their word lists as they write sentences.
- read their completed sentences aloud to the class.

▶ **Interpersonal/Linguistic**

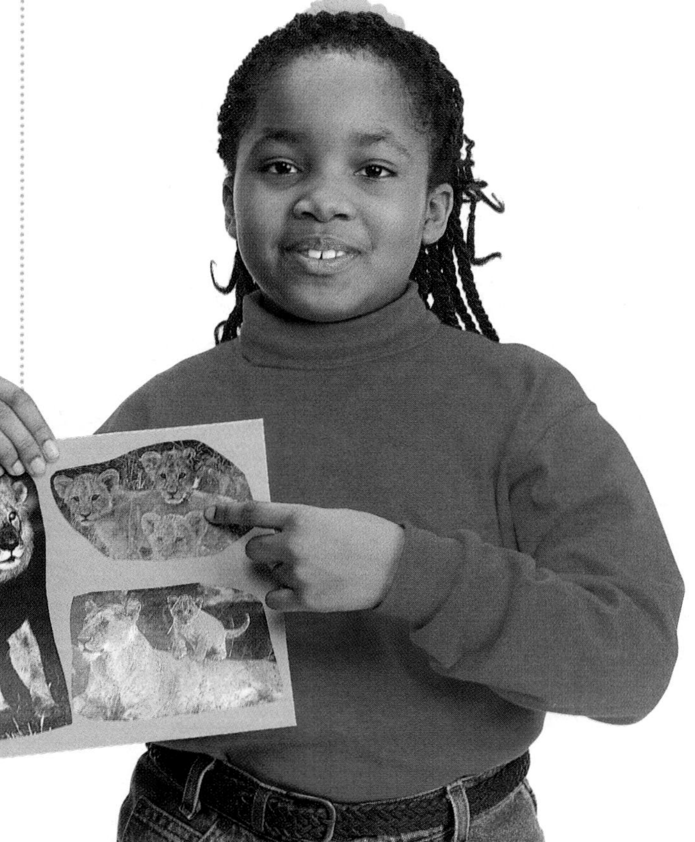

DAILY Phonics ROUTINES

DAY 2 **Letter Substitution** Have partners use letter cards to build *beach*. Taking turns, one child changes a letter(s) to build a new word. The partner can then read it.

Phonics CD-ROM

LANGUAGE SUPPORT

See **Language Support Book**, pages 262–265, for further suggestions on building background.

Children will use context and structural clues to determine the meanings of vocabulary words.

problem
disappear
cleared
warns
save
forever

Vocabulary

Teach Vocabulary in Context

Identify Vocabulary Words Display **Teaching Chart 205** and read the passage with children. Have volunteers circle each vocabulary word and underline other words that are clues to its meaning.

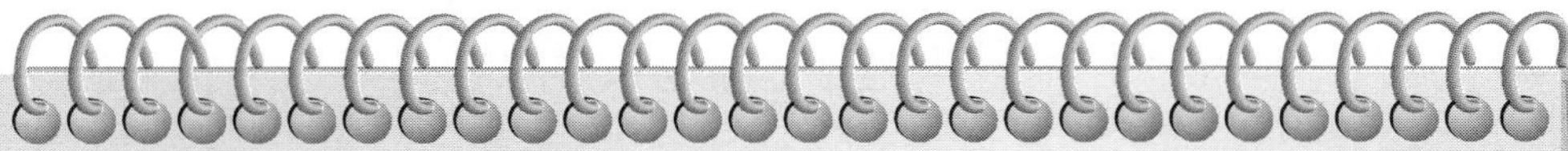

Vanishing Plants

1. We have a problem on our hands that we need to solve. **2.** Many kinds of plants may disappear, vanishing from our world **3.** When factories are built, land is cleared of all plants and trees to make room for the new buildings. **4.** Conservation groups warn or alert us that this destroys plants. **5.** It is important to save and protect plants. **6.** What if wildflowers disappeared forever, never again to be seen?

Teaching Chart 205

Definitions

problem (p. 366) a condition or fact that causes trouble and must be dealt with

disappear (p. 366) to go out of sight

cleared (p. 366) removed things from

warns (p. 367) tells beforehand about something that may happen; alerts

save (p. 367) to keep from harm; make safe

forever (p. 365) throughout time; without ever coming to an end

Story Words

These words from the selection may be unfamiliar. Before children read, have them check the meanings and pronunciations of the words in the Glossary, beginning on page 390, or in a dictionary.

- lilies, p. 365
- alyssum, p. 366
- coral, p. 366
- marigold, p. 366
- zinnias, p. 366

Discuss Meanings Ask questions like these to help clarify word meanings:

- Is it a good thing or a bad thing to have a problem?
- If something disappears, can you see it?
- If your desktop has been cleared, is it full of papers and pencils?
- Why would you warn someone about a very hot cup of cocoa?
- Can you name a plant or an animal that people want to save from disappearing forever?
- Is forever a long time or a short time?

Practice

Scramble the Letters

 PARTNERS  WRITING

Have partners take turns choosing vocabulary cards from a pile and scrambling the letters. The partner must write and pronounce the word correctly. ▶ **Linguistic**

Word Building Manipulative Cards

Write a Story

 PARTNERS  WRITING

Have partners take turns writing a sentence or two, using at least one vocabulary word each time. The sentences should tell a short story. Have students refer to their Glossary as needed.
▶ **Linguistic/Interpersonal**

Assess Vocabulary

Identify Word Meaning in Context

 GROUP  WRITING

Ask children to form small groups. Invite each group to write six questions, one for each of the vocabulary words. Encourage children to include context clues in their questions. Then have groups exchange papers and write answers to the questions they receive.

SPELLING/VOCABULARY CONNECTIONS

See Spelling Challenge Words, pages 371Q–371R.

LANGUAGE SUPPORT

See the **Language Support Book**, pages 262–265, for teaching suggestions for Vocabulary.

Vocabulary PuzzleMaker

Provides vocabulary activities.

Meeting Individual Needs for Vocabulary

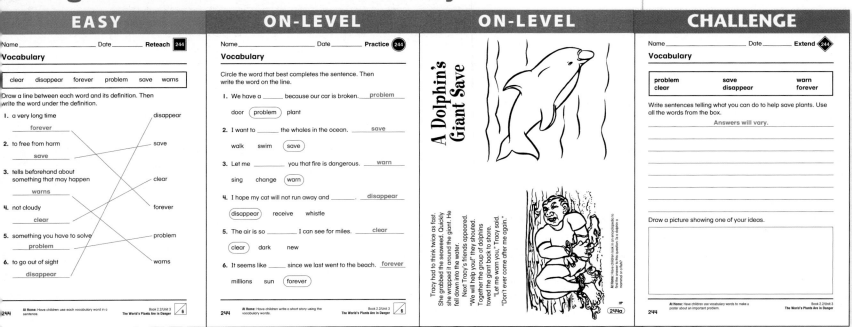

EASY	ON-LEVEL	ON-LEVEL	CHALLENGE

EASY

Name ______ Date ______ Reteach 244

Vocabulary

clear disappear forever problem save warns

Draw a line between each word and its definition. Then write the word under the definition.

1. a very long time — forever
2. to free from harm — save
3. tells beforehand about something that may happen — warns
4. not cloudy — clear
5. something you have to solve — problem
6. to go out of sight — disappear

(disappear, save, clear, forever, problem, warns)

244 At Home: Have children use each vocabulary word in a sentence. Book 2.2/Unit 3 The World's Plants Are in Danger 6

Reteach, 244

ON-LEVEL

Name ______ Date ______ Practice 244

Vocabulary

Circle the word that best completes the sentence. Then write the word on the line.

1. We have a ____ because our car is broken. problem
   door (problem) plant
2. I want to ____ the whales in the ocean. save
   walk swim (save)
3. Let me ____ you that fire is dangerous. warn
   sing change (warn)
4. I hope my cat will not run away and ____. disappear
   (disappear) receive whistle
5. The air is so ____ I can see for miles. clear
   (clear) dark new
6. It seems like ____ since we last went to the beach. forever
   millions sun (forever)

244 At Home: Have children write a short story using the vocabulary words. Book 2.2/Unit 3 The World's Plants Are in Danger 6

Practice, 244

ON-LEVEL

A Dolphin's Giant Save

Tracy had to think twice as fast. She grabbed the seaweed. Quickly she wrapped it around the giant. He fell down into the water.
Next Tracy's friends appeared. "We will help you!" they shouted. Together the group of dolphins towed the giant back to shore.
"Let me warn you," Tracy said. "Don't ever come after me again."

At Home: Have children look in an encyclopedia to find the answer to this question: Is a dolphin a mammal or a fish?

4 244a

Practice, 244a
Take-Home Story

CHALLENGE

Name ______ Date ______ Extend 244

Vocabulary

problem save warn
clear disappear forever

Write sentences telling what you can do to help save plants. Use all the words from the box.

Answers will vary.

Draw a picture showing one of your ideas.

244 At Home: Have children use vocabulary words to make a poster about an important problem. Book 2.2/Unit 3 The World's Plants Are in Danger

Extend, 244

Comprehension

Prereading Strategies

PREVIEW AND PREDICT Have children read the title and take a **picture walk** through the article. What clues about the article do the title and pictures give?

- Is the article nonfiction, or is it a fable? How can you tell? (Nonfiction; the photographs are all of real plants and flowers.) ***Genre***
- From looking at the pictures, what is this article most likely about?
- What might the main idea of the article be?

Have children record their predictions about the article.

PREDICTIONS	WHAT HAPPENED
The article is about plants.	
Plants are in some kind of danger.	

SET PURPOSES What do children want to find out by reading the article? For example:

- Why are plants in danger?
- Why is it important to save plants?

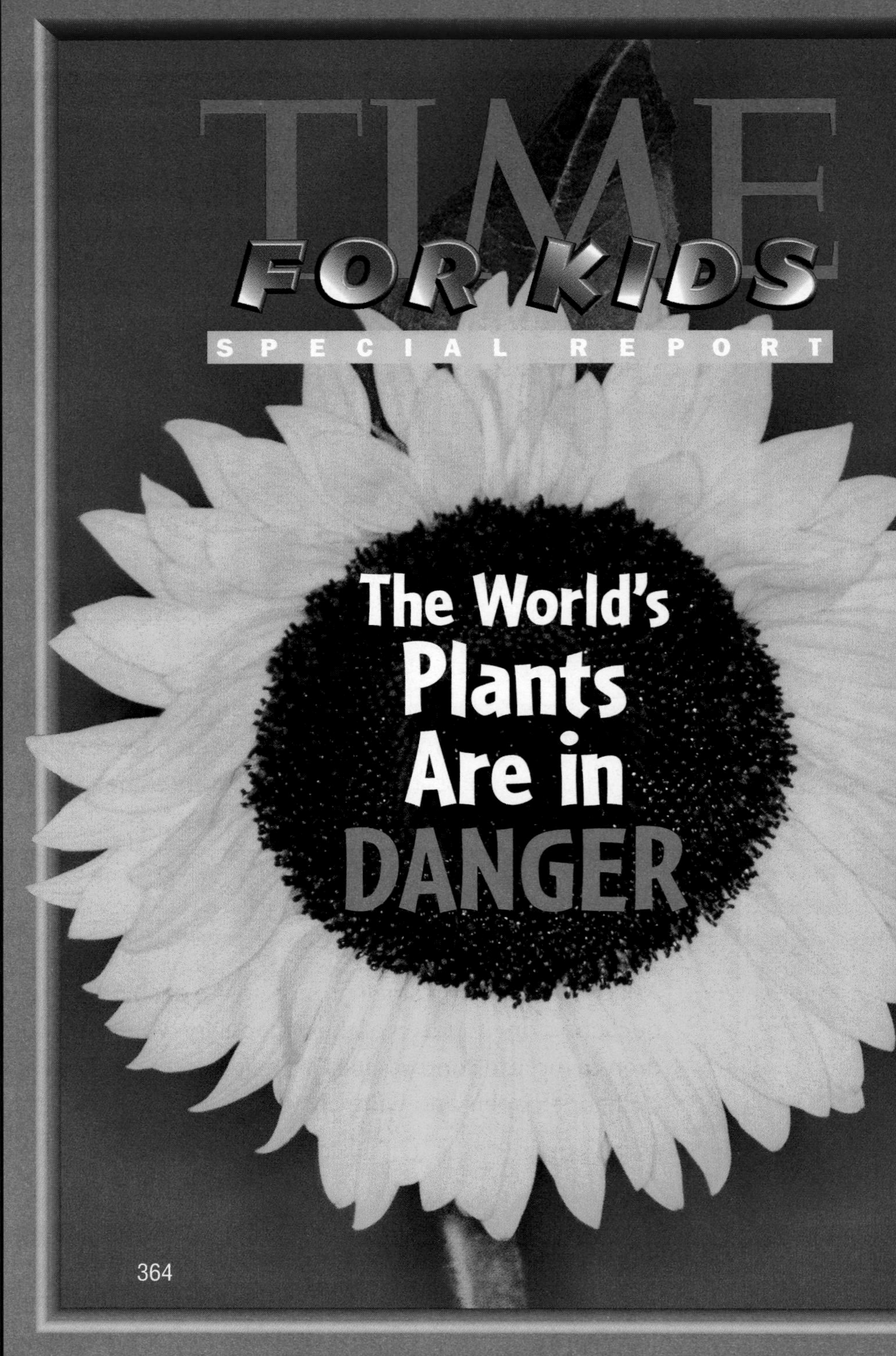

Meeting Individual Needs • Grouping Suggestions for Strategic Reading

EASY

Read Together Read the article with children. Invite them to keep a list of important information. Model the strategy of focusing on the main idea and supporting details to help them understand the article.

ON-LEVEL

Guided Instruction Review the story words listed on page 365. Then read the article with the children using the Comprehension Prompts. Monitor any difficulties in reading the children may have in order to determine which parts of Comprehension to emphasize.

CHALLENGE

Read Independently Have children set purposes before they read the article. Remind them that understanding the main idea as they read will help them understand the story. Have children use the Main Idea chart as they read.

TIME FOR KIDS

Vhere Are All he Flowers Going?

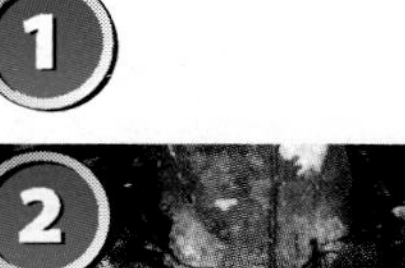

e careful next time you think of :king a pretty wildflower. It may in danger of disappearing forever. at's the bad news from the World nservation Union. The group ent 20 years coming up with a t of plants in trouble. The list mes about 34,000 types of plants, es, bushes, and flowers. Some ıds of palm trees, roses, lilies, d wildflowers are on the list.

JOHN HOLMES, FRANK LANE PICTURE AGENCY/CORBIS

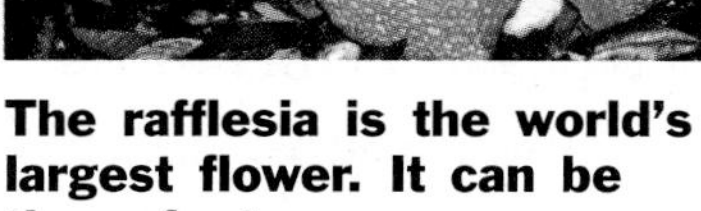

The rafflesia is the world's largest flower. It can be three feet across.

dflowers cover these California hills.

365

Comprehension

  **Apply /ē/**

 **Apply Main Idea**

STRATEGIC READING By figuring out the main idea of an article, you will be able to keep track of important information and have a better understanding of what you are reading. Let's set up a Main Idea chart to help organize the information you read.

1 **MAIN IDEA** What is the main idea found on page 365? (Some plants are in danger of disappearing forever.) What are some of the supporting details? (34,000 types of plants, trees, bushes, and flowers are in danger, including palm trees, roses, lilies, and wildflowers.) Let's add these details to our charts.

2 Why do you think the article tells you to think twice about picking a wildflower? (Wildflowers should be left for all to enjoy, since they are endangered.) ***Make Inferences***

Genre

Science Magazine Article

Explain that magazine articles:

- often include sidebars and other text features.
- use headings, captions, diagrams, and different typefaces.
- give information in short, detailed descriptions.

Activity Once children read *The World's Plants Are in Danger*, help them to identify examples of various text features such as sidebars and informational boxes. Prompt them to locate headings and captions, as well as variations in typeface. Encourage them to compare this selection with another *Time For Kids* selection in a previous unit.

LANGUAGE SUPPORT

'his chart is available as a blackline naster in the **Language Support ook**.

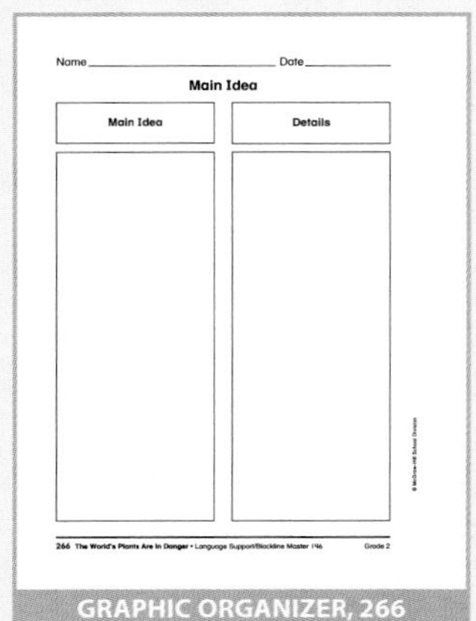

Name ________ Date ________

Main Idea

Main Idea	Details

GRAPHIC ORGANIZER, 266

Comprehension

3 What are two causes of plants' disappearing? (People use land to build factories or homes; new plants crowd out older plants.) *Cause and Effect*

4 **MAIN IDEA** Tell the most important information that the author writes in the article. (Unless we protect them, many plants we use and need will disappear forever.) How does the author develop this fact? (The author supports his/her main ideas with several details on each page.) Add this information to your chart.

Details
34,000 types of plants are in danger.

Details
One in eight types of plants may die out.

Details
Destroying plants' homes kills them.

Details
Plants provide us with medicine.

Details
Governments need to protect nature soon.

Main Idea
Unless we protect nature, many plants we use and need will disappear forever.

ORGANIZE INFORMATION Model how the main idea is developed by the supporting details. Explain to children that defining the main idea of an article will help them keep track of what they are reading. Invite children to use the chart to write one main idea of the article and a short list of supporting details. *Summarize*

(1) MARK HEIFNER/NATURAL SELECTION; (2) ORION PRESS/NATURAL SELECTION; (3) KAREN TWEEDY-HOLMES/CORBIS; (4) HORTICULTURE PHOTOGRAPHY; (5) DAVID CARRIERE/TONY STONE IMAGES

TOP 5 MOST PLANTED GARDEN FLOWERS

Here are the most popular garden flowers in the United States. None of them are in danger of dying out.

1 Zinnias

2 Marigolds

3 Alyssum

4 Sunflowers

5 Morning Glories

The Union's report warns that one out of eight types of plants in the world may die out. In the United States, nearly one out of three plants is in danger of disappearing. Many kinds of plants in danger can only be found in one part of the world. Some coral plants, for example, are found only in Chile.

Plants disappear when humans destroy the places where plants live. This problem can happen when people build new roads,
3 factories, or homes. Plants and trees can also disappear as land is cleared for other uses.

Sometimes, plants from one part of the world are brought to another part of the world.

STEPHANIE MAZE/CORBIS

Plants die when rain fore are cleared.

366

REREADING FOR *Fluency*

Children who need fluency practice can read the article aloud or silently.

READING RATE When you evaluate reading rate, have children read aloud from the story for one minute. Place a stick-on note after the last word read. Count words read. To evaluate children's performance, see the Running Record in the **Fluency Assessment** book

For leveled fluency passages, lessons, and norms charts, see **Skills Intervention Guide,** Part 5, Fluency.

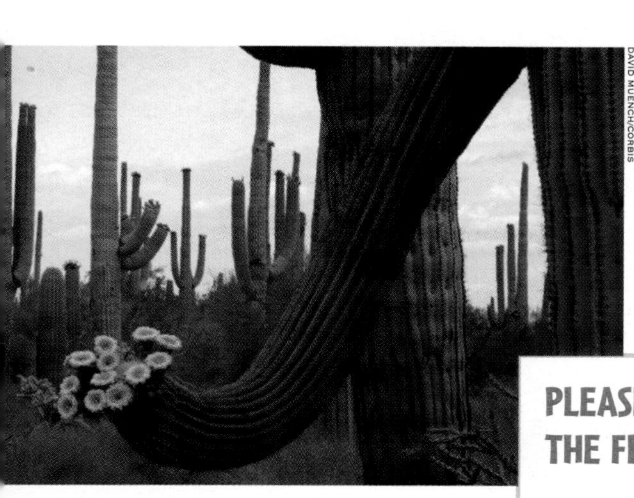

e saguaro cactus
protected in Arizona.

ıe new plants may crowd out
ıer plants that have been in that
ot for hundreds of years.

Why is it so important to save
ınts? "Plants clothe us, feed us,
d provide us with most of our
edicines," says David Brackett.
e is with the World Conservation
ıion. Brackett warns that people
ıst pay attention to the world's
ınts and help keep them safe.
we don't, some of nature's
auty may disappear forever.

4

PLEASE, DON'T PICK THE FLOWERS

About one out of every 10 kinds of U.S. wildflowers is in danger of disappearing. The U.S. doesn't want to lose these flowers. So it is against the law to pick wildflowers in U.S. parks and forests. In many states, it is against the law to pick wildflowers anywhere. These laws help save the flowers, so people will be able to enjoy them for years to come.

FIND OUT MORE
Visit our website:
www.mhschool.com/reading

interNET CONNECTION

on an article in *TIME FOR KIDS.* 367

LITERARY RESPONSE

ICK-WRITE Have children record their thoughts and feelings about the importance of plants.

RNAL

AL RESPONSE Have children
ıre their journal entries and discuss
v what they learned from the arti-
may change the way they act.

RESEARCH AND INQUIRY In groups, have children research other endangered plants or animals. Display their findings.

interNET CONNECTION For more information on this topic, go to ***www.mhschool.com/reading***.

Comprehension

Return to Predictions and Purposes

Discuss children's predictions, noting which ones need to be revised. Then ask children if the article answered their questions.

PREDICTIONS	WHAT HAPPENED
The article is about plants.	The article is about endangered plants.
Plants are in some kind of danger.	Some plants are in danger of disappearing forever due to human actions.

INFORMAL ASSESSMENT

MAIN IDEA

HOW TO ASSESS

- Have children write the main idea of the whole article.
- Ask children to tell some of the supporting details found in the article.

Children should recognize that the main idea of this article is that some plants are in danger of disappearing forever. They should also recognize the important supporting details that develop this concept. (For example, plants disappear when humans destroy the places where they live.)

FOLLOW UP If children have difficulty understanding the main idea of the article, ask questions such as: What is the author telling us about plants? Is there a problem with plants? What is the problem?

PART 2

Read the Literature

Story Questions

Have children discuss the questions about the story on page 368.

Answers:

1. 34,000 types of endangered plants, trees, bushes, and flowers. *Literal/Detail*
2. Plants clothe us, feed us, and provide us with medicines. *Literal/Summarize*
3. One out of every ten kinds of U.S. wildflowers is endangered. *Literal/Detail*
4. Some plants are in danger of disappearing. *Inferential/Summarize*
5. Answers will vary. People can help by not picking wildflowers. They can avoid destroying the places where endangered plants or animals live. *Inferential/Reading Across Texts*

Write a Story For a full writing process lesson, see the lesson on pages 371M–371N.

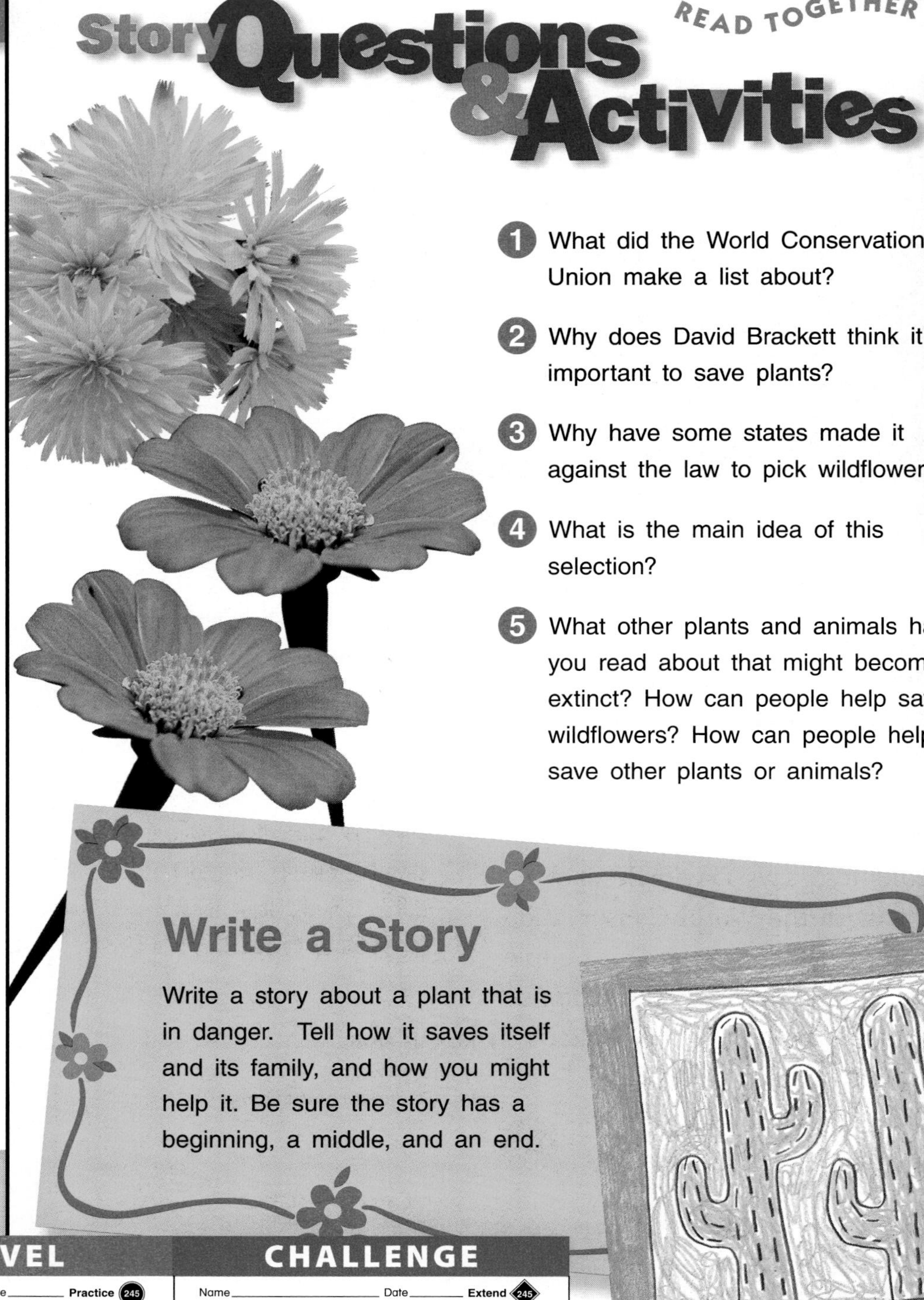

READ TOGETHER

Story Questions & Activities

1. What did the World Conservation Union make a list about?
2. Why does David Brackett think it important to save plants?
3. Why have some states made it against the law to pick wildflower
4. What is the main idea of this selection?
5. What other plants and animals ha you read about that might becom extinct? How can people help sa wildflowers? How can people help save other plants or animals?

Write a Story

Write a story about a plant that is in danger. Tell how it saves itself and its family, and how you might help it. Be sure the story has a beginning, a middle, and an end.

Meeting Individual Needs

EASY

Name________ Date______ Reteach 245

Story Comprehension

Circle the correct word to complete each sentence about "The World's Plants Are in Danger."

1. Wildflowers may be in danger of ____ forever.
   growing **(disappearing)**
2. There are about 34,000 types of plants, trees, ____, and flowers in danger.
   (bushes) animals
3. Some of the plants in danger are certain kinds of roses, lilies, and ____ .
   (wildflowers) sunflowers
4. In the U.S., nearly one out of ____ plants is in danger of dying out.
   ten **(three)**
5. New plants can ____ out other plants that have lived in a place for years.
   throw **(crowd)**
6. Some plants that are not in danger are zinnias, sunflowers, marigolds, alyssums, and ____ .
   (morning glories) roses

6 Book 2.2/Unit 3 **The World's Plants Are in Danger**

At Home: Have children make a drawing of a flower garden. Encourage them to include at least one kind of flower that grows where you live. 245

Reteach, 245

ON-LEVEL

Name________ Date______ Practice 245

Story Comprehension

Think about "The World's Plants Are in Danger." Circle the correct answer to each question.

1. Why should you not pick wildflowers?
   (They may be in danger of disappearing forever.)
   They may belong to someone else.
2. About how many types of plants are in trouble?
   about 1,000
   (about 34,000)
3. What is true about nearly all of the plants in danger?
   Each kind grows all around the world.
   (Each kind grows in only one part of the world.)
4. How do humans destroy plants?
   (Humans destroy the places where plants live.)
   Humans make animal parks.
5. Why is it so important to save plants?
   Plants live longer than humans.
   (Plants clothe us, feed us, and provide us with medicines.)

5 Book 2.2/Unit 3 **The World's Plants Are in Danger**

At Home: Have children name three favorite plants found where they live. 245

Practice, 245

CHALLENGE

Name________ Date______ Extend 245

Story Comprehension

What would a world without plants be like? Write a sentence answering each question. Sample answers are shown.

1. What would your favorite park look like if there were no plants?
   It might look like a desert with nothing green growing.
2. What are some foods that we would no longer be able to eat?
   We wouldn't have any vegetables or meat since animals eat plants, too.
3. What might happen if the plants that medicines are made of were no longer around?
   People might find a way to make the medicines from chemicals or they might not have those medicines anymore.

Draw a picture to show one of the reasons plants disappear.

Book 2.2/Unit 3 **The World's Plants Are in Danger**

At Home: Have children talk and write sentences about the importance of plants in their lives. 245

Extend, 245

Create a Community Guide

Where are the green places in your community? List the places in your neighborhood where you can go to see and smell flowers and other plants. Include parks, flower stores, and plant stores. Tell a little about each place. You might want to draw a map to show where these places are.

Prepare a Speech

Prepare a speech giving some reasons why it is important to protect flowers and plants. Include ways that you could help protect endangered plants in your community.

Find Out More

Every state has a state flower. What is your state's flower? Why was it chosen? What does it look like? Is it an endangered plant?

369

Story Activities

Create a Community Guide

Materials: Paper, pencil, crayons or felt-tipped markers.

GROUP Have children work in small groups as they make their guide. All the guides can be bound into a booklet titled: *A Guide to Our Community*.

▶ **Visual/Logical**

Prepare a Speech

PARTNERS Have each child make an outline of the speech. Remind them to think about the main idea and the supporting details. Then have them present their speech to a partner for practice before presenting it to the class. Encourage partners to ask questions.

▶ **Linguistic/Interpersonal**

Find Out More

ONE Children may use the Internet, an encyclopedia, and/or nonfiction books from the library to research their state flower.

interNET CONNECTION Have children visit ***www.mhschool.com/reading*** for more information on state flowers.

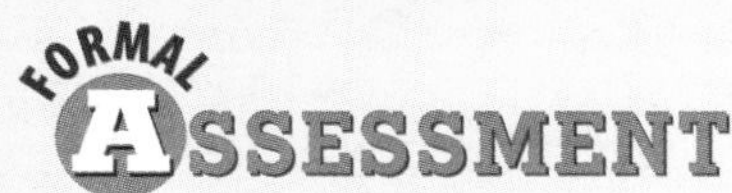

After p. 369, see Selection and Unit Assessment.

DAILY Phonics ROUTINES

DAY 3 **Blending** Write *phone* on the chalkboard and have children blend the sounds. Call on volunteers to blend other words with soft *c, g; ph, tch;* long *a, o, e,* and *i*. Example: *circus, rage, graph, catch.*

CD-ROM

LIBRARY/MEDIA CENTER

Children will learn when to use a dictionary, an encyclopedia, a nonfiction book, and a telephone directory.

PREPARE Display **Teaching Chart 206.** Preview the chart with children.

TEACH Read through the entries with children. Review when to use each kind of reference book.

PRACTICE Have children answer questions 1–5, and review their answers.

1. dictionary **2.** 718-4049 **3.** nonfiction book, *How to Care for Your Flowers* **4.** Answers may include: roses, tulips, violets, buttercups, and dandelions. **5.** Answers will vary.

ASSESS/CLOSE Ask children to find three reference sources from the library that they would use to write a research paper on the saguaro cactus. Have them write what type of sources they are and why they chose them.

STUDY SKILLS

READ TOGETHER

Choose a Reference Source

Dictionary

flower 1. A plant grown for its brightly colored petals. The garden was full of red and yellow *flowers. Noun.* **2.** To produce flowers; blossom. Cherry trees *flower* in early spring. *Verb.*
flow·er (flou´ər) *noun, plural* **flowers**; *verb* **flowered**, **flowering**.

Encyclopedia

flower A flower is a plant that has colorful blossoms. Examples of pop flowers are buttercups, dandelions, tulips, and violets. There are hundr other garden flowers and wildflowe

Nonfiction Book

How to Care for Your Flowers
by Daisy Littlefield

Telephone Directo

Flower Stores
Anne's Flowers..............525-678
Flowers by Ellen..........490-383
Mostly Orchids.............718-404

Choose a reference source to answer each question.

1. Which source would you use to find out all of the different meanings of the word *flower*?
2. What is the phone number for Mostly Orchids?
3. Which book would tell you the best time of year to plant roses?
4. Name three kinds of flowers.
5. When would you choose the book *How to Care for Your Flowers* instead of the encyclopedia?

Meeting Individual Needs

EASY

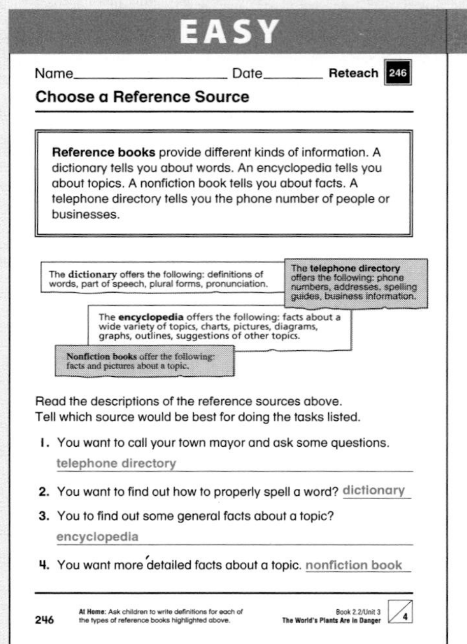

Name__________ Date______ Reteach 246

Choose a Reference Source

Reference books provide different kinds of information. A dictionary tells you about words. An encyclopedia tells you about topics. A nonfiction book tells you about facts. A telephone directory tells you the phone number of people or businesses.

The **dictionary** offers the following: definitions of words, part of speech, plural forms, pronunciation.

The **telephone directory** offers the following: phone numbers, addresses, spelling guides, business information.

The **encyclopedia** offers the following: facts about a wide variety of topics, charts, pictures, diagrams, graphs, outlines, suggestions of other topics.

Nonfiction books offer the following: facts and pictures about a topic.

Read the descriptions of the reference sources above. Tell which source would be best for doing the tasks listed.

1. You want to call your town mayor and ask some questions. telephone directory
2. You want to find out how to properly spell a word? dictionary
3. You to find out some general facts about a topic? encyclopedia
4. You want more detailed facts about a topic. nonfiction book

246 **At Home:** Ask children to write definitions for each of the types of reference books highlighted above. Book 2.2/Unit 3 The World's Plants Are in Danger 4

Reteach, 246

ON-LEVEL

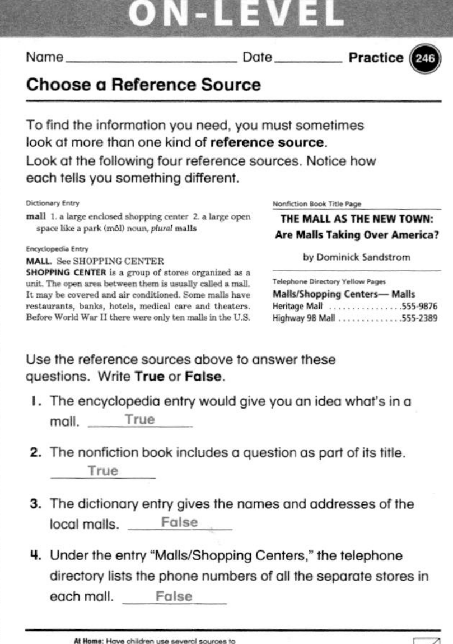

Name__________ Date______ Practice 246

Choose a Reference Source

To find the information you need, you must sometimes look at more than one kind of **reference source.** Look at the following four reference sources. Notice how each tells you something different.

Dictionary Entry
mall 1. a large enclosed shopping center 2. a large open space like a park (môl) noun, *plural* **malls**

Encyclopedia Entry
MALL. See SHOPPING CENTER
SHOPPING CENTER is a group of stores organized as a unit. The open area between them is usually called a mall. It may be covered and air conditioned. Some malls have restaurants, banks, hotels, medical care and theaters. Before World War II there were only ten malls in the U.S.

Nonfiction Book Title Page
THE MALL AS THE NEW TOWN: Are Malls Taking Over America?
by Dominick Sandstrom

Telephone Directory Yellow Pages
Malls/Shopping Centers— Malls
Heritage Mall 555-9876
Highway 98 Mall 555-2389

Use the reference sources above to answer these questions. Write **True** or **False**.

1. The encyclopedia entry would give you an idea what's in a mall. True
2. The nonfiction book includes a question as part of its title. True
3. The dictionary entry gives the names and addresses of the local malls. False
4. Under the entry "Malls/Shopping Centers," the telephone directory lists the phone numbers of all the separate stores in each mall. False

246 **At Home:** Have children use several sources to investigate a subject that interests them. Then compare the different reference sources. Book 2.2/Unit 3 The World's Plants Are in Danger 4

Practice, 246

CHALLENGE

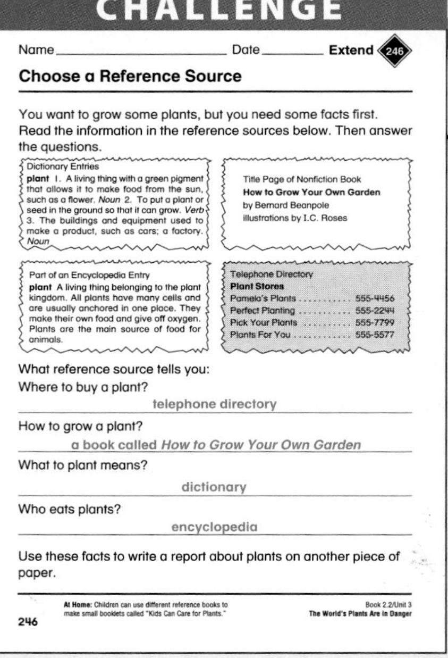

Name__________ Date______ Extend 246

Choose a Reference Source

You want to grow some plants, but you need some facts first. Read the information in the reference sources below. Then answer the questions.

Dictionary Entries
plant 1. A living thing with a green pigment that allows it to make food from the sun, such as a flower. *Noun* 2. To put a plant or seed in the ground so that it can grow. *Verb* 3. The buildings and equipment used to make a product, such as cars; a factory. *Noun*

Title Page of Nonfiction Book
How to Grow Your Own Garden
by Bernard Beanpole
illustrations by I.C. Roses

Part of an Encyclopedia Entry
plant A living thing belonging to the plant kingdom. All plants have many cells and are usually anchored in one place. They make their own food and give off oxygen. Plants are the main source of food for animals.

Telephone Directory
Plant Stores
Pamela's Plants 555-4456
Perfect Planting 555-2244
Pick Your Plants 555-7799
Plants For You 555-5577

What reference source tells you:
Where to buy a plant? telephone directory
How to grow a plant? a book called *How to Grow Your Own Garden*
What to plant means? dictionary
Who eats plants? encyclopedia

Use these facts to write a report about plants on another piece of paper.

246 **At Home:** Children can use different reference books to make small booklets called "Kids Can Care for Plants." Book 2.2/Unit 3 The World's Plants Are in Danger

Extend, 246

Ask yourself the questions again, but use your own words.

ɪRECTIONS:

ad the story. Then read each question about the story.

ɪMPLE

Ron and Liz's Adventure

Ron and Liz and their mom ɴt fishing. Liz carried the es, and Ron carried the jar worms. They all fished for a ɪple of hours. Ron caught a ɪfish. His mother showed him ɪ to carefully remove the hook that the fish would not be t. Then, she gently put the ɪ back into the water. Ron ɪched it swim away. Liz ɪught that she had caught a ɪ, but it turned out to be eds. Even though Liz was appointed, she still laughed. ɪr a while, they were all ɴgry for lunch. They carefully ɪked up their things and went ne.

1 What is the main idea of this story?
- ● Ron and Liz enjoy fishing with their mother.
- ○ Ron and Liz learned how to cook a fish.
- ○ Ron and Liz know where to go to catch fish.
- ○ Catching a bunch of weeds is disappointing.

2 What does Ron's mother do with the fish that Ron caught?
- ○ Takes it home to put in the fish pond.
- ● Takes the hook out and puts it back in the water.
- ○ Shows the fish's tail to Ron and Liz.
- ○ Takes a picture of it.

371

Read the Page

Explain to children that you will be reading this story as a group. You will read the story, and they will follow along in their books.

Request that children put pens, pencils, and markers away, since they will not be writing in their books.

Discuss the Questions

QUESTION 1: Remind children that the title often is a good clue to the main idea. The story is about Ron and Liz's adventure. What kind of adventure did they have? Have them reread the first line, "Ron and Liz go fishing."

QUESTION 2: Remind children to look back to the story to find where Ron caught a fish. Have them read what follows, which describes what his mother does with the fish.

Self-Selected Reading
Leveled Books

Intervention ▶ **Skills**

Intervention Guide, for direct instruction and extra practice in phonics and comprehension

- Digraphs *tch, ph*
- Long *e: ee, ie, ea*; Long *i: i, y, igh*
- Long *a: ai, ay*; Long *o: oa, oe, ow*
- /s/ *ce*; /j/ *ge*

Comprehension

- Form Generalizations
- Main Idea and Supporting Details
- Answers will vary. Have children cite examples from the story to support their answers.

EASY

Story Questions for Selected Reading

1. What did you learn first as you read the story?
2. What decisions did these characters have to make?
3. How did the illustrations help you imagine the characters and setting?
4. What do you remember most about the story?
5. What questions would you ask the author?

Draw a Picture

Draw a picture of you and your favorite character from the story.

EASY

UNIT SKILLS REVIEW

Comprehension

Help children self-select an Easy Book to read and apply phonics and comprehension skills.

Guided Reading

PREVIEW AND PREDICT Discuss the illustrations in the beginning of the book. As you take the **picture walk**, have children predict what the story will be about. List their ideas.

SET PURPOSES Have children write or draw why they want to read the book. Have them share their purposes.

READ THE BOOK Use questions like the following to guide children's reading, or to prompt discussion after they have read the story independently.

- MODEL: Look for words in your story that contain the letter blends *tch* or *ph*. What sound do each of these letter blends make in the words? *Phonics and Decoding*
- What is the story about? Why do you think that? Be specific. *Main Idea and Supporting Details*
- How would you describe the main character? Do you think you could say the same about the other characters? *Form Generalizations*

RETURN TO PREDICTIONS AND PURPOSES Discuss children's predictions. Ask which were correct and why. Have children review their purposes for reading. Did they find out what they wanted to know?

LITERARY RESPONSE Have children discuss questions like the following:

- What parts of the book were the most interesting to you?
- What would be another good title for the book?
- What kind of person do you think the author of the book is? Why do you think so?

See the Phonics **CD-ROM** for practice with reviewing digraphs *tch* and *ph*; long *e*; long *i*; long *a*; long *o*; and /s/ *ce*; /j/ *ge*.

Self-Selected Reading Leveled Books

INDEPENDENT

UNIT SKILLS REVIEW

 Comprehension

Help students self-select an Independent Book to read and apply phonics and comprehension skills.

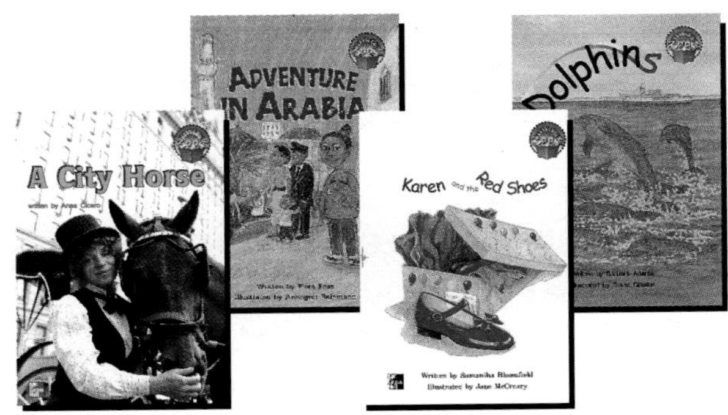

Guided Reading

PREVIEW AND PREDICT Discuss the illustrations in the beginning of the book. As you take the **picture walk**, have children predict what the story will be about. List their ideas.

SET PURPOSES Have children write or draw why they want to read the book. Have them share their purposes.

READ THE BOOK Use items like the following to guide children's reading, or to prompt discussion after they have read the story independently:

- Look for words in this book that contain the letters *ai* or *ay*. Do they sound like long *a*? What about words with *oa, oe,* or *ow*? Do they sound like long *o*? *Phonics and Decoding*
- If you had to find one word to describe the main character in this book, what would that word be? Why? *Forming Generalizations*
- Would you recommend this book to a friend? Why or why not? How would you describe the story to your friend? *Main Idea and Supporting Details*
- What small parts of the book helped you understand what it was really all about? How did these details help you? *Main Idea and Supporting Details*

RETURN TO PREDICTIONS AND PURPOSES Have children review their predictions. Children can talk about whether their purposes were met, and if they have any questions the story left unanswered. For books with chapter headings, were the headings useful? How?

LITERARY RESPONSE The following questions will help focus children's responses:

- What unexpected event happened in the book?
- How did that event lead to a new decision?
- Did the characters in this book change at all? How?

See the Phonics **CD-ROM** for practice with reviewing digraphs *tch* and *ph*; long *e*; long *i*; long *a*; long *o*; and /s/ *ce*; /j/ *ge*.

- Digraphs *tch, ph*
- Long *e: ee, ie, ea*; long *i: i, y, igh*
- Long *a: ai, ay*; long *o: oa, oe, ow*
- /s/ *ce*; /j/ *ge*

Comprehension

- Form Generalizations
- Main Idea and Supporting Details
- Answers will vary. Have children cite examples from the story to support their answers.

INDEPENDENT

Story Questions for Selected Reading

1. Did you learn anything from this book? What?
2. What are some of the words the author used to describe the people, objects, or places in the story?
3. Did these words give you a better idea of what these people, places, and things were like? How?
4. Do you think the illustrations helped this story?
5. If you had written this book, what would you have done differently?

Write a Review

Write a review of this book. Tell why people should or shouldn't read this book.

Self-Selected Reading
Leveled Books

CHALLENGE

UNIT SKILLS REVIEW

Comprehension

Help students self-select a Challenge Book to read and apply phonics and comprehension skills.

Guided Reading

PREVIEW AND PREDICT Have children predict what the story will be about as you take a **picture walk** through the beginning of the book. List their ideas. If the book has chapter headings, ask children to use the first heading to predict what will happen in Chapter One.

SET PURPOSES Have children write or draw why they want to read the book. Have them share their purposes.

READ THE BOOK Use questions like the following to guide children's reading, or to prompt discussion after they have read the story independently:

- Look for words in your story that contain the letters *ee*, *ie*, or *ea*. Do any of them sound like long *e*? How about words with *i*, *y*, or *igh*? Do they have a long *i* sound? *Phonics and Decoding*
- What is the main idea of this book? What specifics in the book make you think this? *Main idea and Supporting Details*
- What kind of book would you say this is? Have you read any other books like this one? *Forming Generalizations*
- If all the events described in the book changed, would that change the main idea? Why or why not? *Main Idea and Supporting Details*

RETURN TO PREDICTIONS AND PURPOSES Discuss children's predictions. Ask which were close to the story and why. Have children review their purposes for reading. Did they find out what they wanted to know? For books with chapter headings, were the headings useful? How?

LITERARY RESPONSE Have children discuss questions like the following:

- Were you able to guess the kinds of things that happened in the story? What clues were you given?
- Did this book make you want to read others like it? Why? Why not?
- What did you like about the main character in this book? What didn't you like?

See the Phonics **CD-ROM** for practice with reviewing digraphs *tch* and *ph*; long *e*; long *i*; long *a*; long *o*; and /s/ *ce*; /j/ *ge*.

Phonics

- Digraphs *tch, ph*
- Long *e: ee, ie, ea*; long *i: i, y, igh*
- Long *a: ai, ay*; long *o: oa, oe, ow*
- /s/ *ce*; /j/ *ge*

Comprehension

- Form Generalizations
- Main Idea and Supporting Details
- Answers will vary. Have children cite examples from the story to support their answers.

CHALLENGE

Story Questions for Selected Reading

1. Would you like to learn more about something in the book? What would you like to know?
2. How did the illustrations help to create a feeling for the topic?
3. What questions would you ask the author?
4. What was the most interesting thing about this book?
5. What would be another good title for the book?

Write about Another Character

Write a story about a character other than the main character of this book.

Bringing Groups Together

Anthology and Leveled Books

Connecting Texts

DECISION CHARTS
Write these story titles horizontally across the top of a chart: *The Seeing Eye, A Voice for Her People, The Wright Brothers Learn to Fly*, and *Karen and the Red Shoes*. Have children discuss the characters and the decisions that had to be made in each story. Have children list their contributions under the story titles.

The World's Plants Are in Danger	The Seeing Eye	A Voice for Her People	Karen and the Red Shoes
• People have to decide how they can save endangered plants.	• Morris Frank had to decide to leave his home and learn how to work with the Seeing Eye dogs.	• Dolores Huerta had to decide to speak up and fight for the rights of migrant workers.	• Karen had to decide whether to wear her shoes to school or not.

Viewing/Representing

GROUP PRESENTATIONS Divide the class into groups according to the stories they have read. Have each group choose one story to summarize and describe to the rest of the class. Children can accompany their story summaries with drawings. Have each group make a presentation to the rest of the class.

AUDIENCE RESPONSE Ask children to watch and listen carefully to each group's presentation. Allow time for questions after each presentation.

Research and Inquiry

INVESTIGATE Have children further investigate topics that interest them. Invite them to do this by:

- Using classroom picture books and school library reference books to begin their research.
- Keeping a simple notebook filled with facts and information they have gathered.
- Sharing what they learn with classmates as they gather new information.

Have children log on to ***www.mhschool.com/reading*** for links to Web pages.

Children can write or draw what they learned in their journals.

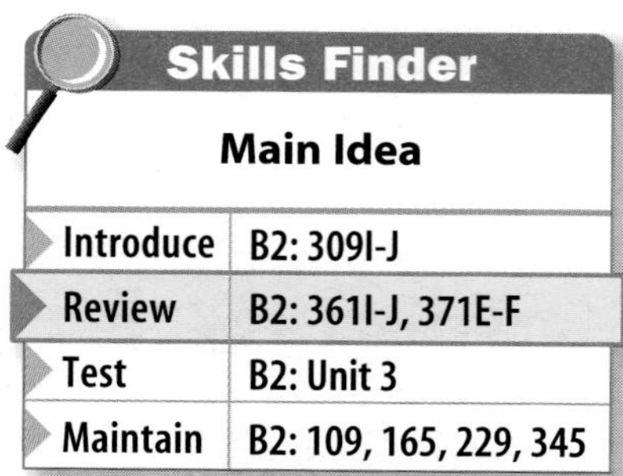

Children will identify main idea and supporting details.

Skills Finder

Main Idea

Introduce	B2: 309I-J
Review	B2: 361I-J, 371E-F
Test	B2: Unit 3
Maintain	B2: 109, 165, 229, 345

TEACHING TIP

MAIN IDEA Have children make main idea charts for one of the articles they previously read and present it to the class.

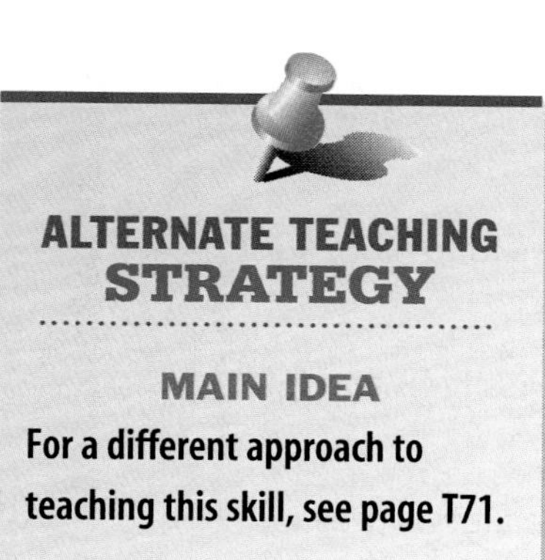

MAIN IDEA

For a different approach to teaching this skill, see page T71.

Review Main Idea

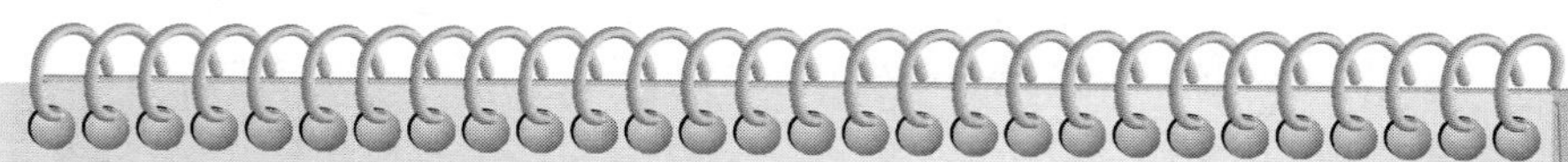

Discuss Main Idea Remind children that identifying the main idea of a selection will help them understand what they read. Supporting details help make the main idea clearer.

TEACH

Read "Nature at Risk" and Model the Skill Tell children to listen for the main idea as you read **Teaching Chart 207**.

Nature at Risk

Scientists put plants and animals in danger of dying out into three groups. The "endangered species" group is made up of plants and animals that are found in very small numbers and in very few places. The second group is called the "threatened species" group. These live in large numbers in some places, but their numbers are going down. The "rare species" group includes plants and animals that live in protected areas in small numbers that don't get larger. These groupings help scientists keep track of the plants and animals that need the most protection.

Teaching Chart 207

Discuss the clues that help readers find the main idea in the passage.

MODEL The first sentence tells me that scientists put plants and animals at risk of dying out into three groups. This must be the main idea of the passage.

DAILY Phonics ROUTINES

DAY 4 **Fluency** Write the following words on the chalkboard: *ceiling, graph, judge, pitch, mow.* Point to each word, asking children to blend the sounds silently. Ask volunteers to read each word aloud.

CD-ROM

Skills

Intervention Guide, for direct instruction and extra practice of main idea

Identify an Implied Main Idea Explain: Sometimes the main idea is not directly stated. Write on the chalkboard: *Plants can disappear when people build roads, factories, or homes. They can also disappear when land is cleared for other uses.* Then ask: *What is the main idea of these sentences?* (plants disappear when people destroy the places they live) *How do you know?* (by reading the details in the sentence)

PRACTICE

Identify Main Idea and Supporting Details Have children read the passage again and circle the sentence that tells the main idea. Have them underline any supporting details. Then ask children how these details supported the main idea.

▶ **Logical/Interpersonal**

ASSESS/CLOSE

Write a Paragraph with a Main Idea and Supporting Details Have children write a short paragraph about an animal or plant, clearly stating a main idea with at least two supporting details. Observe them as they explain to a partner how each supporting detail further develops the main idea.

Meeting Individual Needs for Comprehension

EASY

Name________ Date______ **Reteach 247**

Main Idea

Remember: **Details** are bits of information that support the **main idea.**

Read the paragraphs. Underline two details for each main idea.

Many flowers are in danger of disappearing forever. There are about 34,000 types of plants in danger. Some of these are types of palm trees, roses, lilies, and wildflowers.

1. Main Idea:
   Many flowers are in danger.
   Which details support the main idea?
   a. There are about 34,000 plants in danger.
   b. Be careful when you plant flowers.
   c. Roses and lilies are in danger.

Humans have a lot to do with plants dying out. Humans destroy places where plants live. This happens when humans build roads, factories, and homes. Humans bring new plants to places. New plants can crowd out other plants that have been in that spot for hundreds of years.

2. Main Idea:
   Humans have a lot to do with plants dying out.
   Which details support the main idea?
   a. Humans protect plants.
   b. Humans build roads, factories, and homes.
   c. Humans bring new plants to places.

4 Book 2.2/Unit 3 **The World's Plants Are in Danger** **At Home:** Have children write a poem or story about why it is important to keep plants from disappearing. 247

Reteach, 247

ON-LEVEL

Name________ Date______ **Practice 247**

Main Idea

Read each story. Then read each main idea. Write two details from each story that support the main idea.

A traffic light tells you to stop and go.
A flashing light warns of danger ahead.
Holiday lights are red and green.

Main idea: A light can be a safety signal.

Detail: A traffic light tells you to stop and go.

Detail: A flashing light warns of danger ahead.

An ant has a pair of antennas on its head.
Ants work hard to build their nests.
Ants carry heavy loads of food to their nests.

Main idea: Ants are busy insects.

Detail: Ants work hard to build their nests.

Detail: Ants carry heavy loads of food to their nests.

4 Book 2.2/Unit 3 **The World's Plants Are in Danger** **At Home:** Ask children to draw a picture about one detail from each story. 247

Practice, 247

CHALLENGE

Name________ Date______ **Extend 247**

Main Idea

Make a list of five ideas you have for helping the earth.
Sample answers are shown.

1. We can plant more trees.
2. (We can reuse and recycle paper.)
3. ________
4. ________
5. ________

Circle the one idea that you think is most important.
Write four details that help support that idea.

1. When we reuse paper, we can save trees.
2. There will be less garbage in dumps if we use less paper.
3. ________
4. ________

Write a speech on a piece of recycled paper. Let people know what you think about helping the earth.

Use your main idea and supporting details in your speech. Read your speech to the class.

Book 2.2/Unit 3 **The World's Plants Are in Danger** **At Home:** Ask children to think of supporting details for another one of their ideas. 247

Extend, 247

LANGUAGE SUPPORT

Name________ Date______

Picture This

a sea of sunflowers	an army of bulldozers
a city of cacti	the jewel of the garden

Grade 2 Language Support/Blackline Master 147 • **The World's Plants Are in Danger** 267

Language Support, 267

Children will recognize and form generalizations.

Skills Finder

Form Generalizations

Introduce	B2: 281I-J
Review	B2: 339I-J, 371G-H
Test	B2: Unit 3
Maintain	B2: 107, 225

TEACHING TIP

FORM GENERALIZATIONS Remind children that generalizations often begin with words such as *most*, *usually*, *some*, and *many*.

SELF-SELECTED Reading

Children may choose from the following titles for independent reading:

ANTHOLOGY

- *The World's Plants Are in Danger*

LEVELED BOOKS

- All 12 Selections
- Bookshelf Library

Bibliography, pages T82–T83

Review Form Generalizations

PREPARE

Discuss Form Generalizations Remind children that they can form generalizations when the author of a selection presents related details or facts. Review that generalizations are valid when there are enough examples.

TEACH

Read "Save the Tropical Rain Forests" and Model the Skill

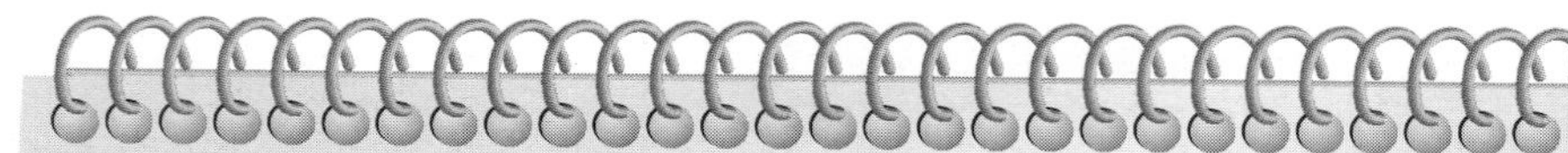

Save the Tropical Rain Forests

The covering formed by the tops of trees in the rain forest is called the canopy. Squirrels, parrots, and certain monkeys eat the nuts and fruit that grow there. Other kinds of monkeys feed on the leaves in the canopy. Tiny birds called hummingbirds drink out of the flowers growing near the tops of the trees. The ground under the trees is called the floor of the rain forest. Deer and rodents live on the floor of the forest, away from the sunlight. They eat roots, seeds, and leaves that grow on the ground.

Teaching Chart 208

Help children understand the generalizations they can form after reading the passage about animals that live in tropical rain forests.

MODEL The passage tells about many animals that live in the rain forest. It says that squirrels, parrots, and some monkeys eat fruits and nuts from the canopy. It mentions other animals that get food from the canopy, too. I think I can form a generalization: Many animals in the rain forest get their food from the canopy.

PRACTICE

Use a Chart

Tell children to underline the facts in the passage that help the reader form a generalization about animals in the rainforests. Then help children set up a Generalization chart to organize these facts. Remind them that a generalization needs to be supported by two or more facts. ▶ **Linguistic/Interpersonal**

Generalization Chart

GENERALIZATION	SUPPORTING FACTS
Many animals of the rainforest eat food from the canopy.	Squirrels, parrots, and monkeys eat fruit and nuts that grow in the canopy. Some monkeys eat leaves that grow in the canopy. Hummingbirds drink out of flowers that grow in the canopy.

ASSESS/CLOSE

Form a Generalization

Have children make a second chart to help them form another generalization based on the passage.

DAILY Phonics ROUTINES

DAY 5 **Writing** Have children work with partners to create shopping lists. Encourage them to use items whose names have soft *c, g; ph, tch;* long *a, o, e, i.* (For example: *rice, oats, jeans, watch*)

Phonics CD-ROM

ALTERNATE TEACHING STRATEGY

FORM GENERALIZATIONS

For a different approach to teaching this skill, see page T67.

Intervention **Skills**

Intervention Guide, for direct instruction and extra practice in forming generalizations

Meeting Individual Needs for Comprehension

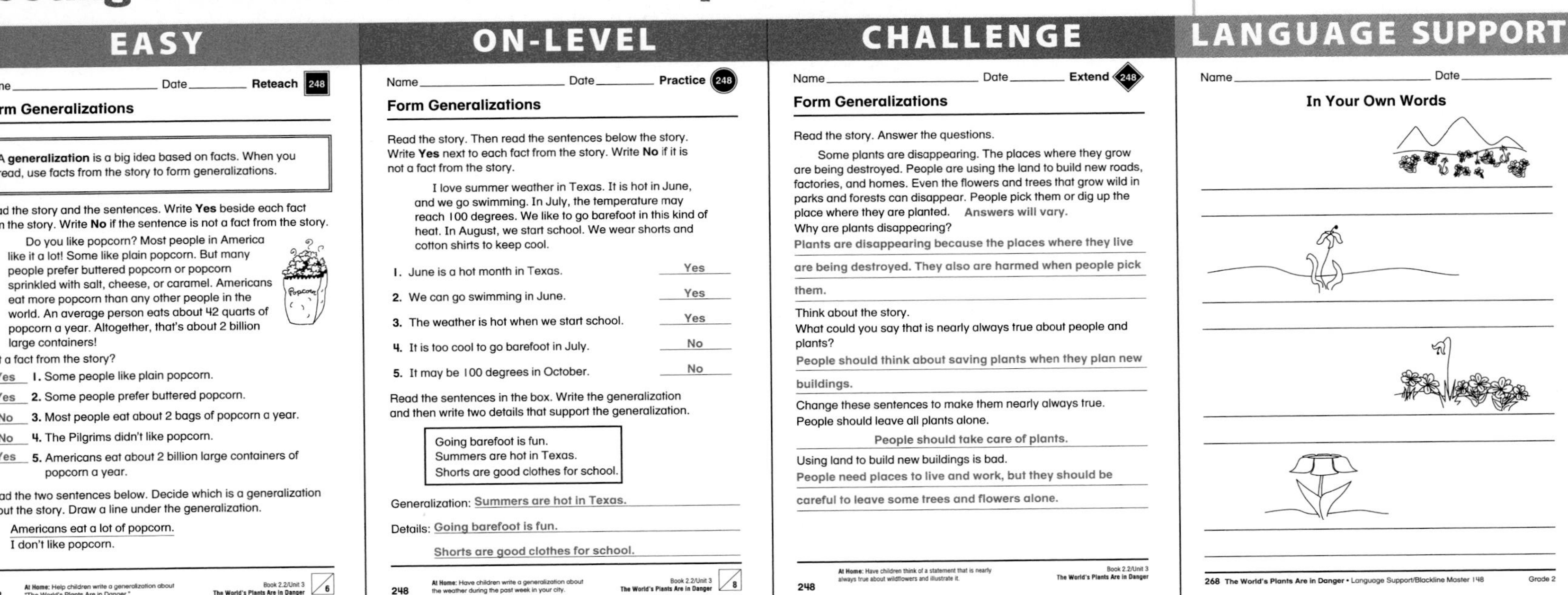

EASY

Name______ Date______ Reteach 248

Form Generalizations

A **generalization** is a big idea based on facts. When you read, use facts from the story to form generalizations.

Read the story and the sentences. Write **Yes** beside each fact from the story. Write **No** if the sentence is not a fact from the story.

Do you like popcorn? Most people in America like it a lot! Some like plain popcorn. But many people prefer buttered popcorn or popcorn sprinkled with salt, cheese, or caramel. Americans eat more popcorn than any other people in the world. An average person eats about 42 quarts of popcorn a year. Altogether, that's about 2 billion large containers!

Is it a fact from the story?

Yes 1. Some people like plain popcorn.
Yes 2. Some people prefer buttered popcorn.
No 3. Most people eat about 2 bags of popcorn a year.
No 4. The Pilgrims didn't like popcorn.
Yes 5. Americans eat about 2 billion large containers of popcorn a year.

Read the two sentences below. Decide which is a generalization about the story. Draw a line under the generalization.

Americans eat a lot of popcorn.
I don't like popcorn.

248 At Home: Help children write a generalization about "The World's Plants Are in Danger." Book 2.2/Unit 3 The World's Plants Are in Danger 6

ON-LEVEL

Name______ Date______ Practice 248

Form Generalizations

Read the story. Then read the sentences below the story. Write **Yes** next to each fact from the story. Write **No** if it is not a fact from the story.

I love summer weather in Texas. It is hot in June, and we go swimming. In July, the temperature may reach 100 degrees. We like to go barefoot in this kind of heat. In August, we start school. We wear shorts and cotton shirts to keep cool.

1. June is a hot month in Texas. Yes
2. We can go swimming in June. Yes
3. The weather is hot when we start school. Yes
4. It is too cool to go barefoot in July. No
5. It may be 100 degrees in October. No

Read the sentences in the box. Write the generalization and then write two details that support the generalization.

Going barefoot is fun.
Summers are hot in Texas.
Shorts are good clothes for school.

Generalization: Summers are hot in Texas.
Details: Going barefoot is fun.
Shorts are good clothes for school.

248 At Home: Have children write a generalization about the weather during the past week in your city. Book 2.2/Unit 3 The World's Plants Are in Danger 8

CHALLENGE

Name______ Date______ Extend 248

Form Generalizations

Read the story. Answer the questions.

Some plants are disappearing. The places where they grow are being destroyed. People are using the land to build new roads, factories, and homes. Even the flowers and trees that grow wild in parks and forests can disappear. People pick them or dig up the place where they are planted. Answers will vary.

Why are plants disappearing?
Plants are disappearing because the places where they live are being destroyed. They also are harmed when people pick them.

Think about the story.
What could you say that is nearly always true about people and plants?
People should think about saving plants when they plan new buildings.

Change these sentences to make them nearly always true.
People should leave all plants alone.
People should take care of plants.
Using land to build new buildings is bad.
People need places to live and work, but they should be careful to leave some trees and flowers alone.

248 At Home: Have children think of a statement that is nearly always true about wildflowers and illustrate it. Book 2.2/Unit 3 The World's Plants Are in Danger

LANGUAGE SUPPORT

Name______ Date______

In Your Own Words

268 The World's Plants Are in Danger • Language Support/Blackline Master 148 Grade 2

Reteach, 248 Practice, 248 Extend, 248 Language Support, 268

Children will:

- **review figurative language.**
- **review simile and metaphor.**

MATERIALS:

- **Teaching Chart 209**

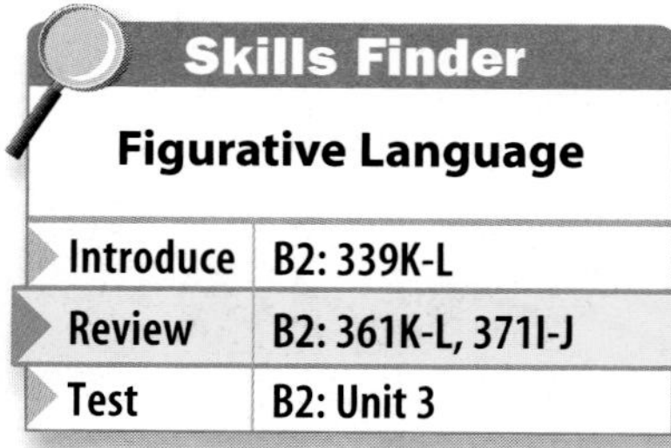

Skills Finder

Figurative Language	
Introduce	B2: 339K-L
Review	B2: 361K-L, 371I-J
Test	B2: Unit 3

TEACHING TIP

SIMILES Write the following sentence on the board: *Marta walked as ____ as a ____.*

Ask children how Marta might walk if she were going somewhere she didn't want to go. Then ask how she might walk if she were excited or interested.

Review Figurative Language

PREPARE

Discuss Figurative Language

Explain to children that figurative language uses colorful comparisons to help the reader picture what is happening. For example, "Her smile lit up the room" compares her smile to a light. It is a colorful way to show that she was very happy.

TEACH

Read "Spring Is Here" and Model the Skill

Ask children to listen carefully for the figurative language as you read the **Teaching Chart 209** passage.

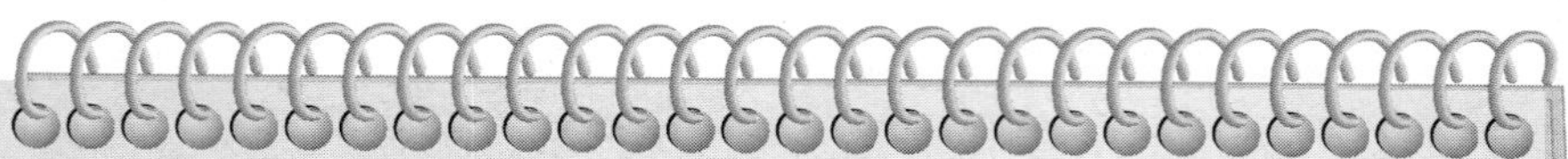

Spring Is Here

The sky was as blue as a bluejay. Fluffy white clouds danced by. A gentle breeze, soft as a whisper, made the leaves wave at the sun. It was the first day of Spring, and the flowers underground were dreaming of summer.

Teaching Chart 209

MODEL I know what a bluejay looks like, so that helps me to picture what color the sky is. I know that clouds can't really dance, but it helps me imagine how the clouds move.

PRACTICE

Identify Figurative Language

Work with children to underline other examples of figurative language on the **Teaching Chart**. ▶ **Linguistic/Interpersonal**

ASSESS/CLOSE

Use Figurative Language

Have each child write a simple story of five or six sentences, using no colorful language. Then have partners exchange stories and add two or three examples of figurative language to make the story more descriptive and interesting.

ALTERNATE TEACHING STRATEGY

FIGURATIVE LANGUAGE

For a different approach to teaching this skill, see page T74.

Skills

Intervention Guide, for direct instruction and extra practice of figurative language

Meeting Individual Needs for Vocabulary

EASY

Name__________ Date______ **Reteach 249**

Figurative Language

Sometimes an author will describe something by comparing it to something else.

The sea looks **like a big blue blanket**.

The waves sound **like the beat of a drum**.

Read each sentence. Fill in the circle next to the saying that matches the underlined word or words.

1. The garden looks beautiful. It looks ________.
   ● as pretty as a picture.
   ○ as happy as a lark.
2. The air smells nice. It smells ________.
   ○ as dark as the night.
   ● as sweet as a rose.
3. Under the ground there is no light. It is ________.
   ○ as sweet as a rose.
   ● as dark as the night.
4. The popped balloon was very flat. It was ________.
   ● as flat as a pancake.
   ○ as big as a house.
5. My uncle Irv is big and wide. He is ________.
   ○ as quiet as a mouse.
   ● as big as a bear.
6. We will have to keep still. We will be ________.
   ○ as big as a barn.
   ● as quiet as mice.

6 Book 2.2/Unit 3 The World's Plants Are in Danger — **At Home:** Ask children to make up two comparisons that describe how they get ready for school. 249

Reteach, 249

ON-LEVEL

Name__________ Date______ **Practice 249**

Figurative Language

Draw a line from each phrase to a saying that describes the underlined word.

1. The road turns and twists. The road is	as quick as a fox.
2. Jerry is a fast runner. He is	like a snake.
3. Our car is very big. It is	as big as a house.
4. That man is very smart. He is	as light as air.
5. The skater glided on the ice. She seemed	as mad as a hornet.
6. The bear became angry. He was	like a wise old owl.
7. The girl hasn't eaten all day. She is	as quiet as a mouse.
8. Sinbad makes very little noise. He is	as hungry as a wolf.

8 Book 2.2/Unit 3 The World's Plants Are in Danger — **At Home:** Have children choose three animals. Ask them to compare some characteristic of each to something else. 249

Practice, 249

CHALLENGE

Name__________ Date______ **Extend 249**

Figurative Language

The words in the box can help make your writing more interesting. Use the words to write four sentences. Sample sentences shown.

like two peas in a pod	**fork in the road**
turn over a new leaf	**has a green thumb**

1. My sister and I are like two peas in a pod.
2. She has a green thumb.
3. I am going to turn over a new leaf.
4. The truck came to a fork in the road.

Draw a picture to show what you think of when you hear **fork in the road.**

What does **fork in the road** really mean? Draw a picture.

Book 2.2/Unit 3 The World's Plants Are in Danger — **At Home:** Have children list other favorite expressions. Let children tell what pictures they think of when they hear these words. 249

Extend, 249

LANGUAGE SUPPORT

Name__________ Date______

Same Word, Different Meaning

plant	**rose**	**types**	**safe**

plant	rose
types	plant
safe	types
rose	safe

Grade 2 Language Support/Blackline Master 149 • **The World's Plants Are in Danger** 269

Language Support, 269

Review Multiple-Meaning Words

OBJECTIVES

Children will review multiple-meaning words.

MATERIALS:
- **Teaching Chart 210**

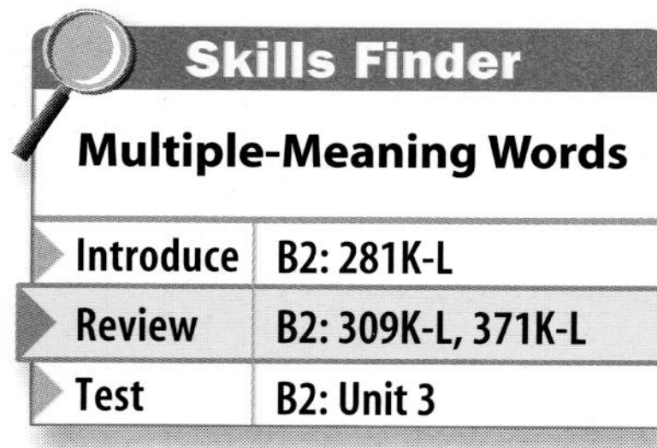

Skills Finder

Multiple-Meaning Words

Introduce	B2: 281K-L
Review	B2: 309K-L, 371K-L
Test	B2: Unit 3

TEACHING TIP

MULTIPLE-MEANING WORDS Children should refer to a dictionary when they cannot figure out the correct meaning of a multiple-meaning word with context clues.

PREPARE

Discuss Multiple-Meaning Words Review with children that some words have more than one meaning. Write the word *sharp* on the chalkboard. Call on children to define the different meanings of *sharp*. Review with children that when they come across a multiple-meaning word in a sentence, they can figure out its meaning by using the context clues.

TEACH

Read "A Good Deed" and Model the Skill Read the passage on **Teaching Chart 210** with the children. Then model the skill beginning with the word *kind.*

A Good Deed

Ingrid thought about all the trees that are cut down in forests every year. Since she was a kind, caring person, she decided to help the tree population. She volunteered at a tree farm to plant seedlings. Each day, she rose early, excited to start. The farmer told her that they mainly grew one type of tree called a blue spruce. When she left, she started thinking about other ways to help preserve nature. Maybe next year she would fly to Florida to protect the coral.

Teaching Chart 210

MODEL I know the word *kind* can mean a type or group of similar things. In this sentence it means something different. As I read the sentence, the surrounding words help me understand that *kind* is an adjective that describes Ingrid. I think that here *kind* means "nice."

Ask children to write down all of the meanings they know for the word *plant*. Then have them choose the meaning that fits in the passage.

PRACTICE

Define Multiple-Meaning Words

Have partners look at the rest of the circled words on **Teaching Chart 210**. Have them write each word's definitions and circle the one that is appropriate for the passage. Discuss the words when all partners have completed the activity. ▶ **Linguistic/Logical**

ASSESS/CLOSE

Draw or Write to Show Multiple Meanings

Have children draw pictures or write sentences to show two meanings for each word:

bat **ring** **point** **well**

ALTERNATE TEACHING STRATEGY

MULTIPLE-MEANING WORDS

For another approach to teaching this skill, see page T68.

Intervention Guide, for direct instruction and extra practice of multiple-meaning words

Meeting Individual Needs for Vocabulary

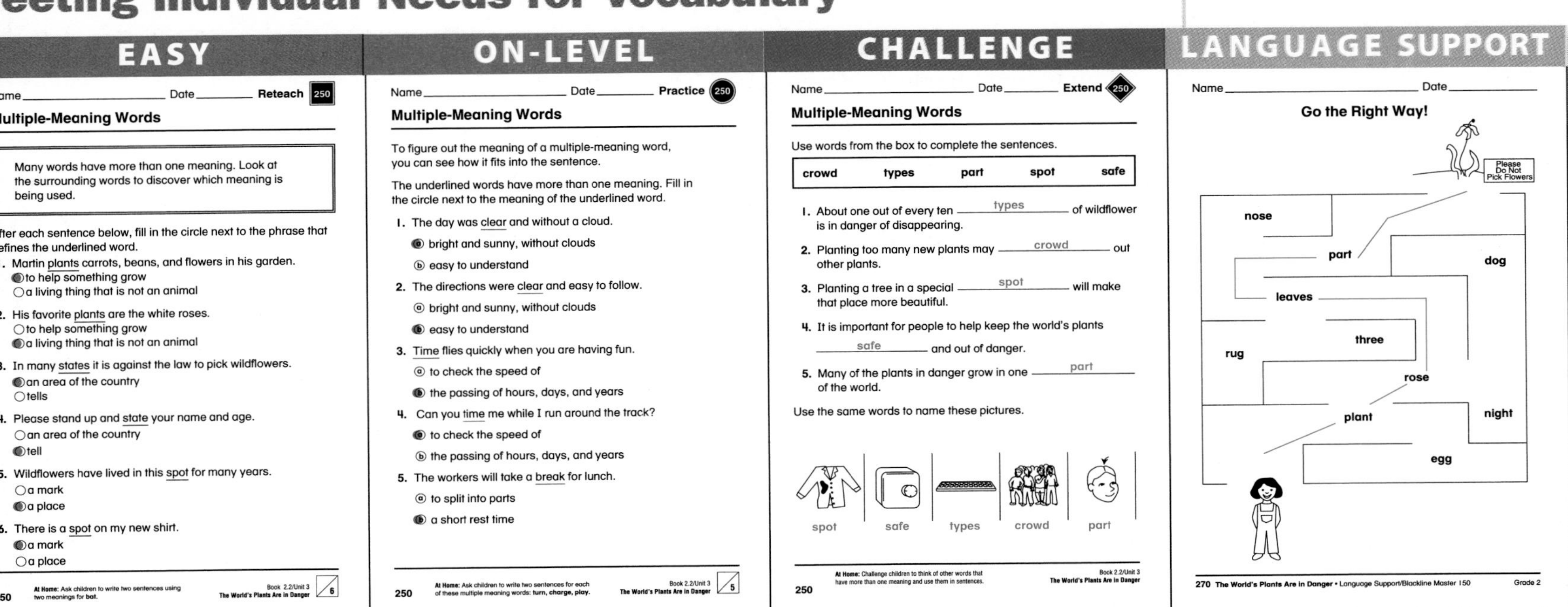

EASY

Name ________ Date ________ Reteach 250

Multiple-Meaning Words

Many words have more than one meaning. Look at the surrounding words to discover which meaning is being used.

After each sentence below, fill in the circle next to the phrase that defines the underlined word.

1. Martin plants carrots, beans, and flowers in his garden.
   - ● to help something grow
   - ○ a living thing that is not an animal
2. His favorite plants are the white roses.
   - ○ to help something grow
   - ● a living thing that is not an animal
3. In many states it is against the law to pick wildflowers.
   - ● an area of the country
   - ○ tells
4. Please stand up and state your name and age.
   - ○ an area of the country
   - ● tell
5. Wildflowers have lived in this spot for many years.
   - ○ a mark
   - ● a place
6. There is a spot on my new shirt.
   - ● a mark
   - ○ a place

250 **At Home:** Ask children to write two sentences using two meanings for **bat**. Book 2.2/Unit 3 **The World's Plants Are in Danger** 6

ON-LEVEL

Name ________ Date ________ Practice 250

Multiple-Meaning Words

To figure out the meaning of a multiple-meaning word, you can see how it fits into the sentence.

The underlined words have more than one meaning. Fill in the circle next to the meaning of the underlined word.

1. The day was clear and without a cloud.
   - ● bright and sunny, without clouds
   - ⓑ easy to understand
2. The directions were clear and easy to follow.
   - ⓐ bright and sunny, without clouds
   - ● easy to understand
3. Time flies quickly when you are having fun.
   - ⓐ to check the speed of
   - ● the passing of hours, days, and years
4. Can you time me while I run around the track?
   - ● to check the speed of
   - ⓑ the passing of hours, days, and years
5. The workers will take a break for lunch.
   - ⓐ to split into parts
   - ● a short rest time

250 **At Home:** Ask children to write two sentences for each of these multiple meaning words: **turn, charge, play.** Book 2.2/Unit 3 **The World's Plants Are in Danger** 5

CHALLENGE

Name ________ Date ________ Extend 250

Multiple-Meaning Words

Use words from the box to complete the sentences.

crowd	types	part	spot	safe

1. About one out of every ten ___types___ of wildflower is in danger of disappearing.
2. Planting too many new plants may ___crowd___ out other plants.
3. Planting a tree in a special ___spot___ will make that place more beautiful.
4. It is important for people to help keep the world's plants ___safe___ and out of danger.
5. Many of the plants in danger grow in one ___part___ of the world.

Use the same words to name these pictures.

spot safe types crowd part

250 **At Home:** Challenge children to think of other words that have more than one meaning and use them in sentences. Book 2.2/Unit 3 **The World's Plants Are in Danger**

LANGUAGE SUPPORT

Name ________ Date ________

Go the Right Way!

Please Do Not Pick Flowers

nose part dog leaves three rug rose plant night egg

270 **The World's Plants Are in Danger** • Language Support/Blackline Master 150 Grade 2

Reteach, 250 **Practice, 250** **Extend, 250** **Language Support, 270**

GRAMMAR/SPELLING CONNECTIONS

See the 5-Day Grammar and Usage Plan, pages 371O–371P.

See the 5-Day Spelling Plan on pages 371Q–371R.

TEACHING TIP

Technology

The Thesaurus feature lists words and their synonyms. It will help you find new words or new ways of saying something.

Writing a Story

Prewrite

WRITE A STORY Present this writing assignment: Write a story about a plant that is in danger. Tell how it is saved and if you helped it. Be sure the story has a beginning, middle, and end.

TALK ABOUT PURPOSE Have children think about what the purpose of their stories will be. Do they want to teach about plants in danger? Do they want to make the readers laugh?

Strategy: Ask Questions Have children think of questions that will help organize their ideas. For example:

- What kind of plant is it?
- Why is the plant in danger?
- Who is telling this story?
- How will it be saved?

Draft

USE THE QUESTIONS Encourage the children to write freely, using the ideas from their list. Ask them to think about who is telling the story, and remind them that a good story should have a beginning, middle, and end. Invite children to further develop their ideas with creative descriptions and dialogue.

Revise

SELF-QUESTIONING Ask children to asse their drafts:

- Do I clearly describe the plant's situation?
- Does my story have a beginning, middle, and end?
- Do I use rich, descriptive language to bring my story to life?

Edit/Proofread

CHECK FOR ERRORS Children should reread their stories for spelling, grammar, and punctuation.

Publish

SHARE THE STORIES Have children fin photographs or draw pictures of the plants their stories. Bind the pictures and stories together to create a "Plant Rescue!" storybo

WEEPING WILLOW
By Elvira Lopez
A big old Weeping Willow Tree lives in our yard. It helps makes the summer feel cool. One day, when it was very hot, I overheard the super of our buildinc say, "We're going to build a pool." "Great," said Mrs Garcia. "Where will you put it?" "Here in the yard. W can chop down some of the trees," he answered. I loved swimming, but wanted to save our tree. Later that day, the tree spoke to me, "Psst, Elvira! Do you know how to help me?" Willow asked. After a long talk, I went to my dad. He explained to the super that the tree would keep the building–and the pool–shady and cool. He helped the super buy and set up an above-ground pool right under the tree. Willow has been my friend ever since.

Presentation Ideas

ELL A STORY Have children sit in small ʼoups and present their stories orally. ɪcourage speakers to tell their stories with-ɪt looking at their papers. Invite them to act ɪt their story or use different voices for each ɪaracter. ▶ **Speaking/Listening**

AKE A STORYBOARD Have children ɔse their eyes to visualize their stories. Invite em to draw pictures that show the action in ɪch scene. ▶ **Viewing/Representing**

Consider children's creative efforts, possibly adding a (+) for originality, wit, and imagination.

Scoring Rubric

Excellent	Good	Fair	Unsatisfactory
4: The writer • creates an interesting problem and solves it. • clearly presents a beginning, middle, and end. • presents vivid descriptions of characters and events and makes creative comparisons.	**3:** The writer • creates a problem and solves it. • presents the events of the story in an easy-to-follow manner. • presents clear descriptions of characters and events.	**2:** The writer • presents a vague or confusing problem and solution. • does not provide a clear beginning, middle, or end. • does not present clear descriptions of characters and events.	**1:** The writer • does not attempt to create a central problem for the story. • does not present a beginning, middle, or end. • has not described his or her ideas.

complete 0: The writer leaves the page blank or fails to respond to the writing task. The student does not address the topic or simply paraphrases the prompt. The response is illegible or incoherent.

leeting Individual Needs for Writing

EASY

Make a Poster Have children make a poster of a plant that is at risk of extinction. Have them describe their plant, including details such as where the plant lives, what kind of weather it likes, and why we should save it.

ON-LEVEL

Make a Comic Strip Have children draw a series of illustrations to tell a story about a person and a plant having a conversation. Encourage them to make the dialogue humorous.

CHALLENGE

Write an Editorial Have children write a brief editorial for their local or school paper stating their opinion about whether plants should be protected and why.

Listening and Speaking

LISTENING Have children

- try to picture the characters and events the speaker is describing.
- be alert to different tones of voice that indicate different characters.

SPEAKING Encourage children to

- speak slowly and loudly enough so that everyone can hear.
- vary volume and tone of voice to match different characters and their emotions.

LANGUAGE SUPPORT

ESL Ask each ESL student to work with an English-fluent partner. Have them describe their plants to each other and discuss the stories they plan to write. As they talk, suggest that they write down any new ideas they come up with, as well as useful words and phrases to use in their stories.

Invite children to include their stories in their portfolios.

5 Day Grammar and Usage Plan

LANGUAGE SUPPORT

ESL Write *big* on the chalkboard. Have children name words that mean the same thing. List them on the board. Point to the list and say: *These words are synonyms for "big." They mean the same thing as "big."*

DAILY LANGUAGE ACTIVITIES

Write each day's activities or use **Transparency 30.** Have children choose the best synonym or antonym for the underlined word, and identify it as a synonym or antonym.

Day 1

nice **quickly** **large**

1. The leaf is big. large; synonym
2. Plants need help fast. quickly; synonym
3. The kind people helped me. nice; synonym

Day 2

happy **slowly** **small**

1. The leaf is big. small; antonym
2. Are the plants sad? happy; antonym
3. The plant grew quickly. slowly; antonym

Day 3

tiny **old** **hot**

1. The weather is cold. hot; antonym
2. A little flower bloomed. tiny; synonym
3. That plant is new. old; antonym

Day 4

always **shining** **good**

1. We never saw a bright star. shining; synonym
2. I never pick wildflowers. always; antonym
3. It is bad to pick them. good; antonym

Day 5

always **fat** **low**

1. The stem is thin. fat; antonym
2. The plants are high. low; antonym
3. Will they last forever? always; synonym

Daily Language Transparency 30

DAY 1 Introduce the Concept

Oral Warm-Up Point out and describe things and people in the classroom. For each description, challenge children to think of other ways to say the same thing. (Example: *The air is chilly./The air is cold. This chair is little./This chair is small.*)

Introduce Synonyms Explain that words that say the same thing as other words are called *synonyms*. Present:

> **Synonyms**
>
> **Synonyms** are words that have the same or almost the same meanings.

Present the Daily Language Activity and have children find the synonym for each underlined word. Then have them rewrite the sentences with the synonyms.

WRITING

Assign the daily Writing Prompt on page 362C.

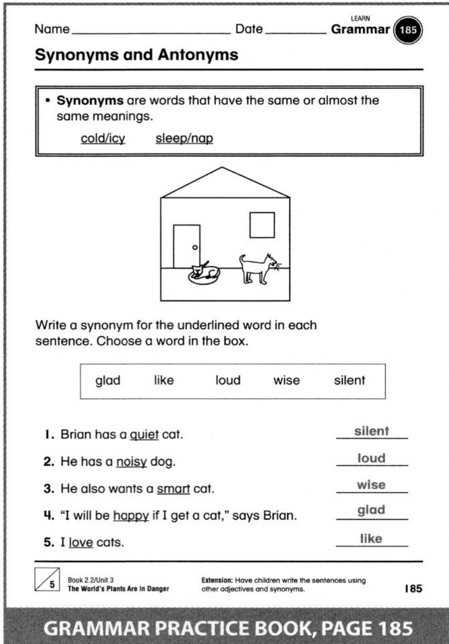

Name ________ Date ______ LEARN Grammar 185

Synonyms and Antonyms

- **Synonyms** are words that have the same or almost the same meanings.
  cold/icy sleep/nap

Write a synonym for the underlined word in each sentence. Choose a word in the box.

glad like loud wise silent

1. Brian has a quiet cat. silent
2. He has a noisy dog. loud
3. He also wants a smart cat. wise
4. "I will be happy if I get a cat," says Brian. glad
5. I love cats. like

5 Book 2.2/Unit 3 The World's Plants Are in Danger — Extension: Have children write the sentences using other adjectives and synonyms. 185

GRAMMAR PRACTICE BOOK, PAGE 185

DAY 2 Teach the Concept

Review Synonyms Ask children to ex- plain what a synonym is. Write on the chalkboard these words: *large, fast, loud* Invite volunteers to supply synonyms. (*big, quick, noisy*)

Introduce Antonyms Ask children to think of words that mean the opposite o the words on the chalkboard. (Examples *large/small; fast/slow; loud/quiet.*) Presen

> **Antonyms**
>
> **Antonyms** are words with opposite meanings.

Present the Daily Language Activity and have children find the antonym for each underlined word. Then have them rewrite the sentences, using the antonyms.

WRITING

Assign the daily Writing Prompt on page 362C.

Name ________ Date ______ PRACTICE AND LEARN Grammar 186

Synonyms and Antonyms

- **Antonyms** are words with opposite meanings.
  dark/light cold/hot

Write an antonym for the underlined word in each sentence. Use the words in the box.

dirty bad small short stop

1. I want the big piece of pie. small
2. It's on the clean plate. dirty
3. I'll eat it with my long fingers. short
4. May I start eating now? stop
5. This cake tastes good! bad

186 Extension: Have children write the sentences using other adjectives and other antonyms. Book 2.2/Unit 3 The World's Plants Are in Danger 5

GRAMMAR PRACTICE BOOK, PAGE 186

Synonyms and Antonyms

DAY 3 Review and Practice

earn from the Literature Review ʼnonyms and antonyms. Read aloud the ıllowing sentence from page 365 of *The ʼorld's Plants Are in Danger.*

The rafflesia is the world's largest flower.

ʼrite *largest* on the chalkboard, and ıvite children to think of synonyms and ıtonyms for it. (Examples: *biggest, nallest*)

ʼrite Synonyms and Antonyms ʼresent the Daily Language Activity. Then ırite the following sentences from the ʼticle on the chalkboard: *That's the bad ɜws from the World Conservation Group. ʼVe need to move quickly," Brackett warns.* ave children identify the adjective in ıe first sentence and the adverb in the ɜcond. (*bad, quickly*) Have them think of synonym and an antonym for each ord and use them in sentences.

Assign the daily Writing Prompt on page 362.

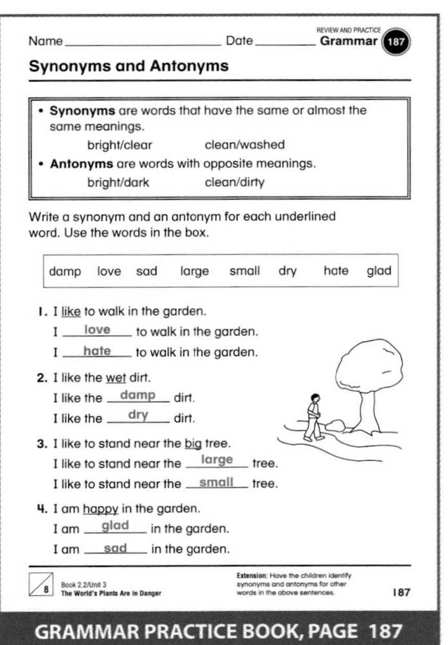

Name ________ Date ________ REVIEW AND PRACTICE Grammar 187

Synonyms and Antonyms

- **Synonyms** are words that have the same or almost the same meanings.
  bright/clear clean/washed
- **Antonyms** are words with opposite meanings.
  bright/dark clean/dirty

Write a synonym and an antonym for each underlined word. Use the words in the box.

damp love sad large small dry hate glad

1. I like to walk in the garden.
   I love to walk in the garden.
   I hate to walk in the garden.
2. I like the wet dirt.
   I like the damp dirt.
   I like the dry dirt.
3. I like to stand near the big tree.
   I like to stand near the large tree.
   I like to stand near the small tree.
4. I am happy in the garden.
   I am glad in the garden.
   I am sad in the garden.

8 Book 2.2/Unit 3 The World's Plants Are in Danger

Extension: Have the children identify synonyms and antonyms for other words in the above sentences.

187

GRAMMAR PRACTICE BOOK, PAGE 187

DAY 4 Review and Practice

Review Synonyms and Antonyms Write the underlined words from the Daily Language Activity for Days 1 through 3 on the chalkboard. Ask children to try to think of a synonym and an antonym for each. Then present the Daily Language Activity for Day 4.

Mechanics and Usage Before presenting the daily Writing Prompt, review:

Sentence Punctuation

- Begin every sentence with a capital letter.
- End statements and commands with a period.
- End a question with a question mark.
- End an exclamation with an exclamation point.

Assign the daily Writing Prompt on page 362D.

Name ________ Date ________ MECHANICS Grammar 188

Correcting Sentences

- Begin every sentence with a capital letter.
- End a statement and a command with a period.
- End a question with a question mark.
- End an exclamation with an exclamation point.

Read each sentence. Correct it.
Write the correct sentence on the line.

1. i am looking for my pet snake, goldie.
   I am looking for my pet snake, Goldie.
2. have you seen her
   Have you seen her?
3. there she is
   There she is!
4. please grab her
   Please grab her.

188

Extension: Have students write more sentences about a snake and exchange sentences with a partner to check the punctuation.

Book 2.2/Unit 3 The World's Plants Are in Danger 4

GRAMMAR PRACTICE BOOK, PAGE 188

DAY 5 Assess and Reteach

Assess Use the Daily Language Activity and page 189 of the **Grammar Practice Book** for assessment.

Reteach Write the synonyms and antonyms from the Daily Language Activities on the chalkboard. Then have children find pictures in magazines or draw their own pictures to illustrate antonyms and synonyms. For example, children can find a picture of an elephant and a picture of a mouse to illustrate *big* and *small*. Have children label their pictures with the synonyms or antonyms.

Have children hang their pictures on a word wall, under the heading "Synonyms and Antonyms."

Use page 190 of the **Grammar Practice Book** for additional reteaching.

Assign the daily Writing Prompt on page 362D.

Name ________ Date ________ TEST Grammar 189

Synonyms and Antonyms

Write synonyms for the underlined words.

1. I have a large dog. big
2. She is very noisy. loud
3. She runs quickly. fast
4. Her bark sounds joyful. happy

Write the antonyms for the underlined words.

5. My cat is very large. small
6. He is always very good. bad
7. He plays quietly. loudly
8. He walks carefully. carelessly

8 Book 2.2/Unit 3 The World's Plants Are in Danger

189

GRAMMAR PRACTICE BOOK, PAGE 189

GRAMMAR PRACTICE BOOK, PAGE 190

5 Day Spelling Plan

LANGUAGE SUPPORT

ESL Help children hear the difference between one-syllable words and two-syllable words by clapping on each syllable as you say the list of spelling words. Next ask them to clap on the syllables as they say each word. Then say a word and ask them to call out "one" or "two" to indicate how many syllables the word has.

DICTATION SENTENCES

Spelling Words

1. The seed is tiny.
2. The roses are red.
3. The bird went into the bushes.
4. The flower is white.
5. A bloom is on the plant.
6. The cactus is green.
7. The root is under the soil.
8. I can hold the stem.
9. The petal is soft.
10. The bud can grow.

Challenge Words

11. The water is clear.
12. The road could disappear in the dark.
13. Does this speech go on forever?
14. That problem is not hard.
15. I have to warn you.

DAY 1 Pretest

Assess Prior Knowledge Use the Dictation Sentences at left and **Spelling Practice Book** page 185 for the pretest. Allow children to correct their own papers. If children have trouble, have partners give each other a midweek test on Day 3. Children who require a modified list may be tested on the first ten words.

Spelling Words		Challenge Words
1. seed	6. **cactus**	11. **clear**
2. **roses**	7. root	12. **disappear**
3. **bushes**	8. stem	13. **forever**
4. **flower**	9. petal	14. **problem**
5. bloom	10. bud	15. **warn**

*Note: Words in **dark type** are from the story.*

Word Study On page 186 of the **Spelling Practice Book** are word study steps and an at-home activity.

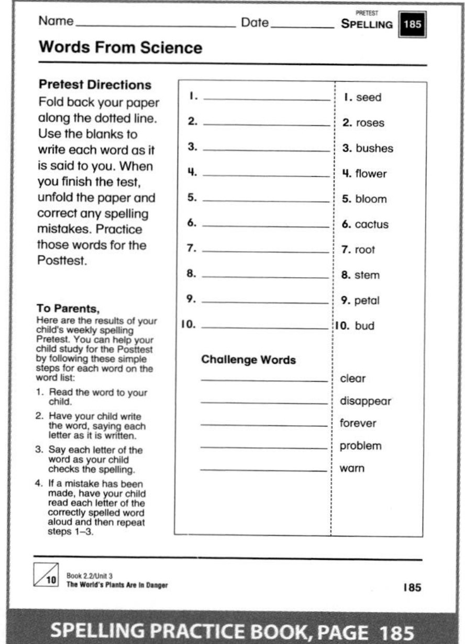

Name ______ Date ______ PRETEST SPELLING 185

Words From Science

Pretest Directions
Fold back your paper along the dotted line. Use the blanks to write each word as it is said to you. When you finish the test, unfold the paper and correct any spelling mistakes. Practice those words for the Posttest.

1. ______ 1. seed
2. ______ 2. roses
3. ______ 3. bushes
4. ______ 4. flower
5. ______ 5. bloom
6. ______ 6. cactus
7. ______ 7. root
8. ______ 8. stem
9. ______ 9. petal
10. ______ 10. bud

Challenge Words
______ clear
______ disappear
______ forever
______ problem
______ warn

To Parents,
Here are the results of your child's weekly spelling Pretest. You can help your child study for the Posttest by following these simple steps for each word on the word list:
1. Read the word to your child.
2. Have your child write the word, saying each letter as it is written.
3. Say each letter of the word as your child checks the spelling.
4. If a mistake has been made, have your child read each letter of the correctly spelled word aloud and then repeat steps 1–3.

10 Book 2.2/Unit 3 The World's Plants Are in Danger 185

SPELLING PRACTICE BOOK, PAGE 185

WORD STUDY STEPS AND ACTIVITY, PAGE 186

DAY 2 Explore the Pattern

Sort and Spell Words Say the words *seed* and *cactus*. Have children listen carefully for the number of syllables in each word pair. As you repeat the words tell children that the words in the first word pair contain one syllable, the words in the second pair contain two.

Ask children to read aloud the ten spelling words before sorting them according to the number of syllables.

Words with one syllable	Words with two syllables
seed	roses
bloom	bushes
root	flower
stem	cactus
bud	petal

Word Wall Have children write letters to classmates, look for new words with one and two syllables in the letters they receive, and add them to the classroom word wall, identifying the one- and two-syllable words.

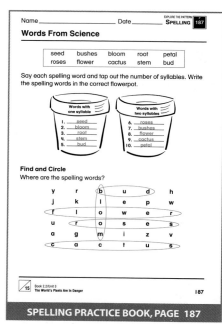

Name ______ Date ______ EXPLORE THE PATTERN SPELLING 187

Words From Science

seed	bushes	bloom	root	petal
roses	flower	cactus	stem	bud

Say each spelling word and tap out the number of syllables. Write the spelling words in the correct flowerpot.

Words with one syllable: 1. seed 2. bloom 3. root 4. stem 5. bud

Words with two syllables: 6. roses 7. bushes 8. flower 9. cactus 10. petal

Find and Circle
Where are the spelling words?

y	r	b	u	d	h
j	k	l	e	p	w
f	l	o	w	e	r
u	r	o	s	e	s
a	g	m	i	z	v
c	a	c	t	u	s

15 Book 2.2/Unit 3 The World's Plants Are in Danger 187

SPELLING PRACTICE BOOK, PAGE 187

Words from Science

DAY 3 Practice and Extend

ord Meaning: Base Words Write e words *roses* and *bushes* on the chalk-oard. Have children identify the base ord for each of these words. Then have ildren use both the singular and plural rsions of each word in a sentence.

lossary Review the pronunciation key the Glossary. Have partners:

write each Challenge Word.

look up the pronunciation in the Glossary.

say each Challenge Word aloud and use it in a sentence.

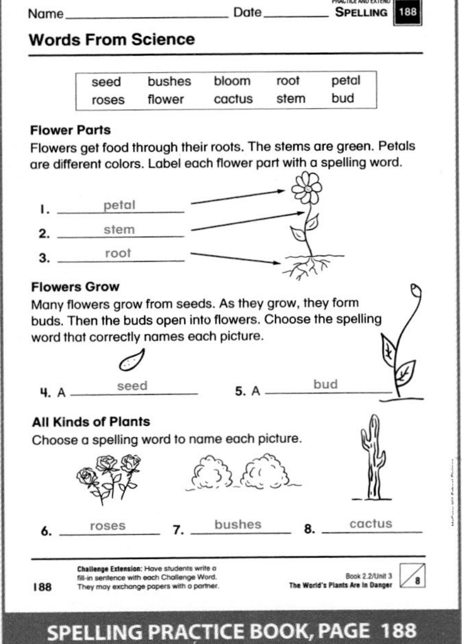
Name_____ Date_____ PRACTICE AND EXTEND SPELLING 188

Words From Science

seed	bushes	bloom	root	petal
roses	flower	cactus	stem	bud

Flower Parts

Flowers get food through their roots. The stems are green. Petals are different colors. Label each flower part with a spelling word.

1. petal
2. stem
3. root

Flowers Grow

Many flowers grow from seeds. As they grow, they form buds. Then the buds open into flowers. Choose the spelling word that correctly names each picture.

4. A seed 5. A bud

All Kinds of Plants

Choose a spelling word to name each picture.

6. roses 7. bushes 8. cactus

188 **Challenge Extension:** Have students write a fill-in sentence with each Challenge Word. They may exchange papers with a partner.

Book 2.2/Unit 3 The World's Plants Are in Danger 8

SPELLING PRACTICE BOOK, PAGE 188

DAY 4 Proofread and Write

Proofread Sentences Write these sentences on the chalkboard, including the misspelled words. Ask children to proofread, circling incorrect spellings and writing the correct spellings. There are two spelling errors in each sentence.

The rozes have pretty petels. (roses, petals)

The floer is a budd. (flower, bud)

Have children create additional sentences with errors for partners to correct.

WRITING **Writing** Have children use as many spelling words as possible in the daily Writing Prompt on page 362D. Remind children to proofread their writing for errors in spelling, grammar, and punctuation.

Name_____ Date_____ PROOFREAD AND WRITE SPELLING 189

Words From Science

Proofreading Activity

There are six spelling mistakes in the journal below. Circle each misspelled word. Write the words correctly on the lines below.

July 7 Today, there are many budes on the rose bushis. The rowzis will be in blum by next week, I think. I will be able to cut some pretty flowrs for the house.

July 15 Two weeks ago I planted two new plants. The wind last night broke the steme on one of the plants.

1. buds 2. bushes 3. roses
4. bloom 5. flowers 6. stem

Writing Activity

Pretend that you have a garden. Write a paragraph about how your garden grows. Use four spelling words to describe what happens.

10 Book 2.2/Unit 3 The World's Plants Are in Danger 189

SPELLING PRACTICE BOOK, PAGE 189

DAY 5 Assess and Reteach

Assess Children's Knowledge Use page 190 of the **Spelling Practice Book** or the Dictation Sentences on page 371Q for the posttest.

Personal Word List If children have JOURNAL trouble with any words in the lesson, have them create a personal list of troublesome words in their journals. Have children write their own stories, using words from their list.

Name_____ Date_____ POSTTEST SPELLING 190

Words From Science

Look at the words in each set. One word in each set is spelled correctly. Use a pencil to color in the circle in front of that word. Before you begin, look at the sample sets of words. Sample A has been done for you. Do Sample B by yourself. When you are sure you know what to do, you may go on with the rest of the page.

Sample A
- Ⓐ need
- Ⓑ nead
- Ⓒ nede
- Ⓓ neede

Sample B
- Ⓔ meny
- Ⓕ miny
- Ⓖ meney
- Ⓗ many

1. Ⓐ petl Ⓑ petel Ⓒ petal Ⓓ petul
2. Ⓔ cactus Ⓕ caktus Ⓖ cactez Ⓗ cactuz
3. Ⓐ blum Ⓑ blume Ⓒ bluhm Ⓓ bloom
4. Ⓔ seed Ⓕ sead Ⓖ ceed Ⓗ seede
5. Ⓐ bede Ⓑ bud Ⓒ budd Ⓓ beud
6. Ⓔ bushs Ⓕ bushes Ⓖ bushiz Ⓗ bushis
7. Ⓐ rute Ⓑ rhute Ⓒ root Ⓓ ruute
8. Ⓔ stem Ⓕ stam Ⓖ stehm Ⓗ steme
9. Ⓐ rozes Ⓑ rosis Ⓒ rosez Ⓓ roses
10. Ⓔ flower Ⓕ flowr Ⓖ fower Ⓗ flouer

190 Book 2.2/Unit 3 The World's Plants Are in Danger 10

SPELLING PRACTICE BOOK, PAGE 190

UNIT 3 Unit Closer

Wrap Up the Theme

Starting Now

Unexpected events can lead to new decisions.

REVIEW THE THEME Remind children that all the selections in this unit relate to the theme Starting Now. Ask children to tell how the theme relates to one of the selections they read. Encourage them to name other stories, movies, or television shows that have the same theme.

READ THE POEM Read aloud the poem "If You Ever Meet a Whale." Point out that this is a humorous poem, and the poet is giving advice about a situation that will never happen. After reading, discuss how this poem relates to the theme Starting Now. Invite children to give advice about other imaginary situations, such as how to feed a dragon.

LISTENING LIBRARY Children can listen to an audio recording of the poem.

GROUP **MAKE CONNECTIONS** Have children work in small groups to brainstorm a list of ways that the stories, poems, and the *Time for Kids* magazine article relate to the theme Starting Now. Groups can then compare their lists as they share them with the class.

Have children listened to an audio recording of any selection or poetry? If so, ask them to explain what they liked or disliked about experiencing the literature in that way.

372

LOOKING AT GENRE

Have children review *Officer Buckle and Gloria* and *Tomás and the Library Lady*. What makes *Officer Buckle* humorous fiction? What makes *Tomás* biographical?

Help children list the key characteristics of each genre. Can they name other stories that have the same characteristics?

HUMOROUS FICTION *Officer Buckle and Gloria*	BIOGRAPHICAL FICT *Tomás and the Library Lady*
• Some characters seem real, but others do not.	• Characters are re people.
• Settings look and sound real.	• Settings are real.
• Characters' problems and actions make you laugh.	• Characters' prob lems are based o real events.

EAD TOGETHER

IF YOU EVER MEET A WHALE

Traditional Rhyme

If you ever, ever, ever, ever,
ever meet a whale,
You must never, never, never, never
grab him by his tail.
If you ever, ever, ever, ever
grab him by his tail—
You will never, never, never, never
meet another whale.

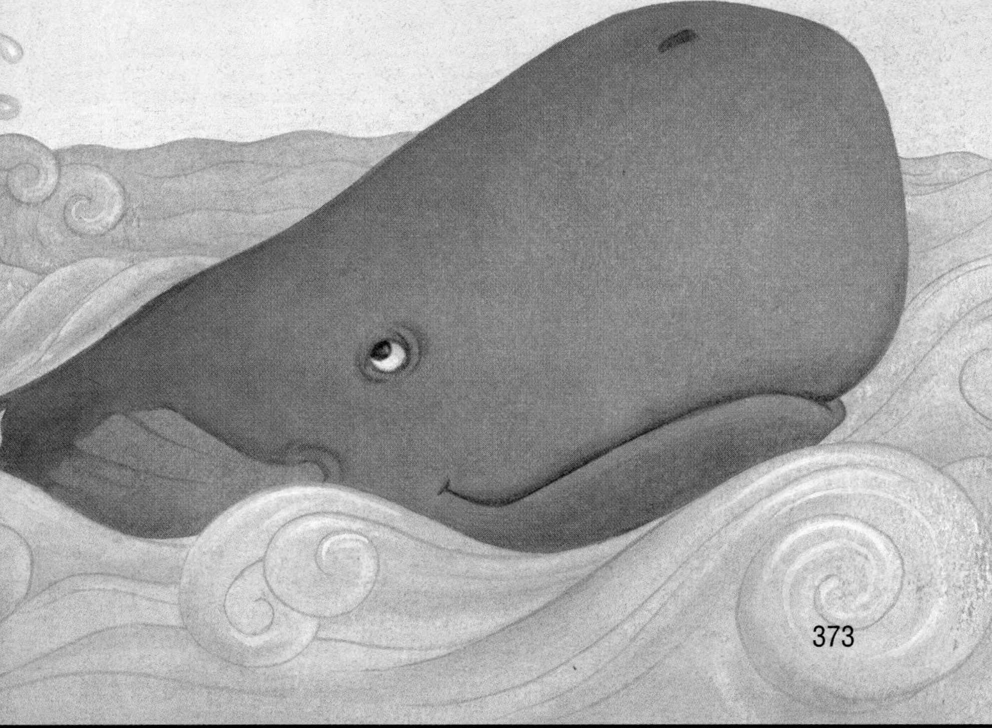

373

LEARNING ABOUT POETRY

erary Devices: Repetition Point how many times the words *ever* never are repeated. Discuss with dren why this is or is not effective. d the poem again and have chil- n chime in on the words *ever* and er.

WRITING

Poetry Activity Invite children to write a poem that they think would fit with the theme Starting Now. Encourage them to make use of repetition in their poems.

Children can use the same format as "If You Ever Meet a Whale," or you may choose to model another poem for them to follow.

Activity

Research and Inquiry

GROUP **Complete the Theme Project** Have each team complete its part of the class project. Encourage children to share making visuals or scenery, or writing the scripts so that each team member can contribute to the project.

Make a Classroom Presentation Have teams take turns presenting their projects. Remind children that the purpose of the presentation is to convince their classmates to visit the destination each team has selected. Be sure to include time for questions from the audience.

Draw Conclusions Have children draw conclusions about what they learned from researching and preparing their projects. Was the resource chart they made helpful? What other resources, such as the Internet, did they use? Did they make the best possible vacation choice? Why or why not? Did the most effective presentations include visuals? How were they used? In what way did they enhance the presentation?

Ask More Questions What additional questions do children have about the vacation places they have heard about? You might encourage them to prepare a report on another place very different from their first choice. For example, if they wrote about a warm place, they could research a very cold place.

Reading Online Resources

E-mail, or electronic mail, lets you write and send letters on the computer. Your reader will get the letter just minutes after you send it. You can write to someone next door or many miles away.

Use a Computer

1. **Type the e-mail address** in the box marked **To:**
2. **Type what your letter is about** in the **Subject** box.
3. **Type your letter** on the screen.
4. **Reread your letter.** Does it make sense? Did you leave out any words?
5. **Click on Send** to "mail" your letter.

Our New Puppy!

Writing an E-mail

1. **Type the e-mail address.** This tells who the letter will go to. I'm sending this to Jan Calhoun.
2. **Type the subject.** My letter is about our new puppy.

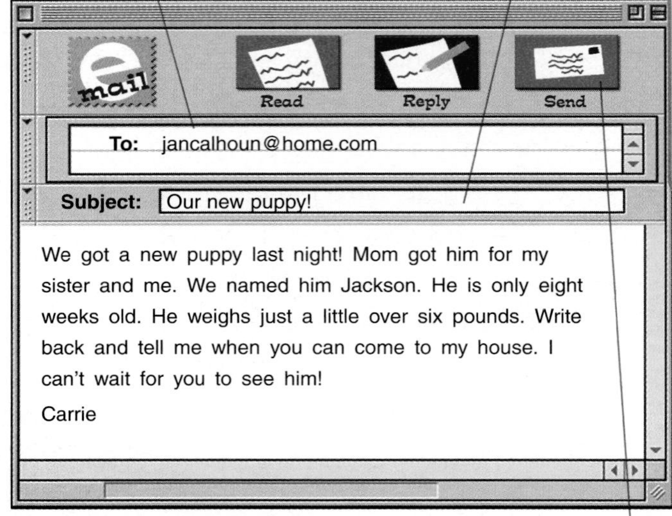

mail
Read
Reply
Send
To: jancalhoun@home.com
Subject: Our new puppy!
We got a new puppy last night! Mom got him for my sister and me. We named him Jackson. He is only eight weeks old. He weighs just a little over six pounds. Write back and tell me when you can come to my house. I can't wait for you to see him!
Carrie

3. **Type your letter.** My letter can be long or short.
4. **Reread your letter.** Make sure you said everything you wanted to say.
5. **Click on Send.**

Anthology pages 386–387

Reading Online Resources

OBJECTIVES Children will:

- use online resources, such as e-mail
- learn an effective strategy to use in reading and writing an e-mail message.

INTRODUCE Have children **preview** page 386. Explain that this lesson will help them learn how to write and send a clear e-mail message. ***(Set Purposes)***

MODEL One step says, "Reread your letter." I've gotten e-mail that I couldn't understand because the sender didn't reread it. Then I had to e-mail the person back and ask questions. I will remember to reread my messages so they are clear.

PRACTICE/APPLY Have children preview, read, and discuss page 387, including the callouts. Explain that most people use a simple font and do not use **text features** such as boldface or italic in e-mails because they won't appear to the sender. After they read pages 388 and 389 and see how the steps apply, *ask:*

- What kinds of mistakes might be in an e-mail message? (Possible answers: words left out, words repeated, misspellings, unclear ideas)
- What kinds of mistakes does a computer spell-checker miss? (Possible answers: words left out; misused words, such as *do* for *to* or *hour* for *our*)
- What can happen if you send e-mail with mistakes in it? (Possible answers: confusion, misunderstandings)

Have children answer the questions on page 389.

E-mail to a Friend

Kevin wrote an e-mail to his friend Kesha. He wanted to tell her about a book that he had read.

Read Reply Send

To: keshaallen@school.com

Subject: Great book!

I just read an exciting book! You would like it, too. In the story, a cat lives with a boy in his house. She jumps out a window and runs away. The boy looks everywhere for her but cannot find her.

It has a great ending. The cat comes back and they are both happy. You should read the book!

Kevin

The Friend's Reply

Here is Kesha's answer to Kevin. To write back to him, first she clicked on the **Reply** button. Then she wrote her letter, reread it, and sent it.

Read Reply Send

To: kevinsimpson@casa.com

Subject: re: Great Book!

Wow, I can't wait to read the book! You didn't tell me the name of the book or who wrote it. Please write and tell me the title and author as soon as you can. Also, where did you find the book? Did you borrow it from the school library?

Kesha

Review Questions

1. Why should you reread your message before you send it?
2. What button did Kesha click on to send her message?
3. Why is it important to learn how to send an e-mail?

Anthology pages 388–389

ANSWERS TO REVIEW QUESTIONS

1. Rereading is important because it allows you to find and fix mistakes and clarify your ideas.
2. Kesha clicked on the Send button.
3. It's important to know how to send e-mail because e-mail is used more and more every day. Also, you can keep in touch with people who live far away.

TRANSFER THE STRATEGY

Ask: How can the five steps on page 386 help you write an e-mail message?

Explain: E-mail is a quick, easy way for people to communicate with each other. Being able to send a clear, polite e-mail message is a necessary skill for everyone.

Discuss: What could happen if you sent a "sloppy" e-mail to someone you don't know very well?

Enjoying E-Mail

Complete one of these activities:

- Use a computer to send an e-mail message to a classmate. Follow the steps on page 386. Then reply to a classmate's e-mail. Afterward, talk about any mistakes in your messages or any ideas that were not clear.
- On a sheet of paper, write an e-mail message to a classmate. Follow the steps on page 386, except for clicking on *send,* of course. You will also need to check your own spelling. Exchange messages with a classmate. Talk about any changes that might improve your messages.

Writing a Story

CONNECT TO LITERATURE In *Officer Buckle and Gloria,* Officer Buckle must make some decisions. Engage children in a discussion of Officer Buckle's problems and how he decides to solve them. Ask how his decisions affect his work and his relationship with Gloria. Have students make a list of their classmates' responses.

GROUP

A Rescue in Fuzz and Fur

There's a town called Fuzz and Fur where only animals can live. All the animals have different jobs. They help each other any way they can.

Once Sammy Kitten got stuck up a tree. Mrs. Mouse, the baker, called the Monkey Fire Department. The monkeys held on to each other's tails and formed a chain that reached all the way up to the kitten. Sammy slid down the chain of Monkey Firefighters, all the way to the ground. "Thank you!" said Mother Cat "I don't know what we'd do without the monkeys' help!" "You're all heroes!" barked Mayor Mutt. Sammy agreed.

Prewrite

PURPOSE AND AUDIENCE Explain to students that they will write a story about characters who work together to solve a problem. Tell students that the purpose of the story is to entertain. Ask them to think about who will be reading their stories as they write.

STRATEGY: BRAINSTORM Help students explore original ideas for characters, settings, and actions. Have them jot down notes about what traits an interesting character might have. Have them discuss ideas for characters' appearance, attitude, and ways of moving and talking. Then show them how to use a story map to sketch out a plot.

Use **Writing Process Transparency 6A** as a model.

STORY-WRITING FEATURES

- unfolds a sequence of original narrative events
- has a beginning, middle, and end
- explores character, events, and location

PREWRITE TRANSPARENCY

"A Rescue in Fuzz and Fur"

My Characters:
Sammy Kitten Mrs. Mouse
Mayor Mutt Monkey Firefighters

Where They Live:
Fuzz and Fur Only animals live there.

Problem:
Sammy Kitten is stuck in a tree.

Event 1:
Sammy Kitten gets stuck up a tree.
Mayor Mutt tries to reach him but can't.

Event 2:
Mrs. Mouse calls the Monkey Fire Department.
The Monkey Fire Department comes.

Event 3:
The monkeys hang onto each other's tails to form a chain.
Sammy Kitten slides down the monkey chain.

Event 4:
Mayor Mutt says they are heroes.
Sammy Kitten promises to stay out of tall trees.

Book 2.2/Unit 3: Writing a Story / Prewriting 6A

TEACHING TIP

ORGANIZATION Help students to use their story maps effectively to plot out their stories. Show them how to use the map to unfold the events in a narrative order. Have them list the important traits of characters and places. Encourage them to give each character a specific role that moves the story along.

Writing a Story

Draft

STRATEGY: FREEWRITING Have students exchange stories with a partner. Model how to make constructive, creative suggestions that wi help them improve their work. Encourage them to comment on what they like about a story.

Use Writing Process Transparency 6B for classroom discussion on the drafting process.

WORD CHOICE Have children review adjectives and adverbs. Ask chi dren to look for places in their drafts which need more details. Instruct them to choose a sentence from their drafts and add an adjective and adverb to make it more descriptive.

LANGUAGE SUPPORT

Children who need help getting started can adapt a familiar storybook character for their own story. Help them to develop new physical and personality traits to expand the character. Encourage them to create unexpected ways for their familiar character to think and behave. Ask them to think of a dilemma for the character to solve and use that to build a story.

DRAFT TRANSPARENCY

There's a town called Fuzz and fur. All of the animals have diffrent jobs. They help each other any way they can. Once Sammy Kitten got stuck up a tree. Mayor Mutt heard him and rushed over to the tree. He jumped, but he couldn't reach Sammy. Mayor Mutt barks loudly.

Mrs. Mouse, the baker, and called the Monkey Fire Department. The monkeys held onto each other's tails and reached all the way up to the kitten. Sammy slid down the chain of Monkey Firefighters, all the way to the grond. "You're all heroes" barked Mayor Mutt. Sammy agreed and promised never to climb tall trees again.

Book 2.2/Unit 3: Writing a Story / Drafting 6B

Revise

Have students exchange stories with a partner. Model how to make constructive, creative suggestions that will help them improve their work. They can make individual comment sheets for partners, noting what they liked best about their characters, actions, and descriptions.

Use **Writing Process Transparency 6C** for classroom discussion on the revision process. Ask students to comment on how revisions may have improved this writing example.

STRATEGY: ELABORATION Discuss with the class various ways to expand on their drafts. Ask them to consider what could bring more feeling or excitement to their stories. Write these questions on the board for students to think about as they revise:

- Do each of my characters play their own special role?
- Are my story events funny, sad, or exciting? How do I want the reader to feel?
- Does each scene move the story forward?

REVISE TRANSPARENCY

A Rescue in Fuzz and Fur

There's a town called Fuzz and fur where only animals can live. All of the animals have diffrent jobs. They help each other any way they can. Once Sammy Kitten got stuck up a tree. Mayor Mutt heard him and rushed over to the tree. He jumped as high as he could, but he couldn't reach Sammy. Mayor Mutt barks loudly.

Mrs. Mouse, the baker, heard Mayor Mutt and called the Monkey Fire Department. The monkeys held onto each other's tails and made a chain that reached all the way up to the kitten. Sammy slid down the chain of Monkey Firefighters, all the way to the grond. "You're all heroes" barked Mayor Mutt. Sammy agreed and promised never to climb tall trees again.

Book 2.2/Unit 3: Writing a Story / Revising 6C

TEACHING TIP

TEACHER CONFERENCE
While students are revising, circulate and conference with them individually. You may use these questions for a conferencing checklist:

- **Do your characters feel alive to you? Why?**
- **How do they play different roles ?**
- **Do your descriptions bring the story to life? How?**
- **What's the best part of your story? How do you want it to end?**

Writing a Story

Edit/Proofread

After students finish revising their stories, have them proofread for fin. corrections and additions.

GRAMMAR/SPELLING CONNECTIONS

See the 5-Day Grammar and Usage Plans, pp. 281O–281P, 309O–309P, 339O–339P, 361O–361P, 371O–P, and 5-Day Spelling Plans, pp. 281Q–281R, 309Q–309R, 339Q–339R, 361Q–361R, 371Q–371R

GRAMMAR, MECHANICS, USAGE

- Use adjectives and adverbs correctly.
- Begin proper nouns with a capital letter.
- Use quotation marks at the beginning and end of what a person says.
- Use commas to separate three or more words in a series.

Publish

Have children share their stories with parents and other classes.

Use **Writing Process Transparency 6D** as a proofreading model and to discuss presentation ideas.

PROOFREAD TRANSPARENCY

A Rescue in Fuzz and Fur

There's a town called Fuzz and fur. where only animals can live All of the animals have diffrent jobs. They help each other any way they can. Once Sammy Kitten got stuck up a tree. Mayor Mutt heard him and rushed over to the tree. He jumped, as high as he could but he couldn't reach Sammy. Mayor Mutt barks ed loudly.

Mrs. Mouse, the baker, heard Mayor Mutt and called the Monkey Fire Department. The monkeys held onto each other's tails and made a chain that reached all the way up to the kitten. Sammy slid down the chain of Monkey Firefighters, all the way to the grond. u

¶"You're all heroes," barked Mayor Mutt. Sammy agreed and promised never to climb tall trees again.

McGraw-Hill School Division

Book 2.2/Unit 3: Writing a Story / Proofreading 6D

PUBLISH TRANSPARENCY

A Rescue in Fuzz and Fur

There's a town called Fuzz and Fur where only animals can live. All of the animals have different jobs. They help each other any way they can. Once Sammy Kitten got stuck up a tree. Mayor Mutt heard him and rushed over to the tree. He jumped as high as he could, but he couldn't reach Sammy. Mayor Mutt barked loudly.

Mrs. Mouse, the baker, heard Mayor Mutt and called the Monkey Fire Department. The monkeys held onto each other's tails and made a chain that reached all the way up to the kitten. Sammy slid down the chain of Monkey Firefighters, all the way to the ground.

"You're all heroes!" barked Mayor Mutt. Sammy agreed and promised never to climb tall trees again.

McGraw-Hill School Division

Book 2.2/Unit 3: Writing a Story / Publishing 6E

Presentation Ideas

RECORD THE STORIES Record children reading their own stories. Play the tapes for the class and record their comments. Give children their own copies to take home, and put copies in the library.
▶ **Listening/Speaking**

DRAW THE CHARACTERS Have students make illustrations of their story characters. They can write captions or word bubbles that express something about each character. Display the drawings and have the class discuss them. ▶ **Representing/Speaking**

Assessment

SCORING RUBRIC When using the rubric, please consider students' creative efforts, possibly adding a plus (+) for originality, wit, and imagination.

SELF-ASSESSMENT Present the Story Writing Features from page 373B in question form. Have students use these questions to self-assess their writing.

Listening and Speaking

LISTENING STRATEGIES

- Watch speaker's expressions to better understand dialogue.
- Make a list of story details, including characters, setting and plot.
- Listen closely to how the story ends.

SPEAKING STRATEGIES

- Change sound of voice to represent different characters.
- Adjust volume of voice to convey various emotions.
- Use hand gestures to emphasize important words.

Scoring Rubric: 6-Trait Writing

4 Excellent

Ideas & Content
- crafts an entertaining, fully-detailed original story; each characters play its own special role.

Organization
- consistent, well-organized sequence moves the reader smoothly through the story events, from an inviting beginning to a satisfying ending.

Voice
- shows originality, imagination, and has a strong personal message that speaks directly to the reader.

Word Choice
- makes creative use of vocabulary that paints a memorable picture of characters and events.

Sentence Fluency
- fluid, effective, easy-to-read sentences enhance and strengthen the story line.

Conventions
- is skilled in most writing conventions; proper use of the rules of English enhances clarity and narrative style.

3 Good

Ideas & Content
- presents a focused, clear story with a beginning, middle, and end.

Organization
- carefully-planned narrative is easy to follow; ideas are smoothly connected from beginning to ending.

Voice
- attempts to share an authentic personal message with the reader.

Word Choice
- has overall clarity of expression, and a control of new and everyday words that help bring the story to life.

Sentence Fluency
- crafts careful, easy-to-follow sentences; may effectively use fragments and/or dialogue to strengthen and enhance the story.

Conventions
- has some errors in spelling, capitalization, punctuation or usage, which do not interfere with understanding the story; some editing may be needed.

2 Fair

Ideas & Content
- attempts to write a story; may not elaborate clearly; may lose control of the narrative after a good beginning.

Organization
- may not have a clear story line, or may have trouble connecting ideas; events or characters may be incomplete or unclear.

Voice
- may get the basic story across, without a sense of connection to the main idea.

Word Choice
- may not explore words that express a strong feeling; may not choose words that create striking pictures for the reader.

Sentence Fluency
- sentences are understandable, but may be choppy or awkward.

Conventions
- makes enough noticeable mistakes which may interfere with a smooth reading of the story.

1 Unsatisfactory

Ideas & Content
- does not grasp the task to tell a story; narrative may go off in several directions, without a sense of purpose.

Organization
- extreme lack of organization interferes with understanding the story; sequence may be disorganized or incomplete; characters are vague or indistinct.

Voice
- does not attempt to make sense or connect with a reader.

Word Choice
- does not choose words that express clear feelings or images.

Sentence Fluency
- incomplete, rambling, or confusing sentences.

Conventions
- repeated errors in spelling, word choice, punctuation and usage make some parts impossible to follow.

Incomplete This piece is either blank, or fails to respond to the writing task. The topic is not addressed, or the child simply paraphrases the prompt. The response may be illegible or incoherent.

UNIT 3

Unit Assessment

VOCABULARY

GROUP Divide the class into two teams. Write the review words on cards and divide them between the two teams. A player on Team A calls out a word, a player on Team B defines it. If the definition is correct the card is taken out, if not it is kept. The team that finishes the other team's cards first wins.

Unit Review

Officer Buckle and Gloria

accidents	cheered	station
audience	slips	wipe

Tomás and the Library Lady

borrow	evenings	package
desert	midnight	shoulder

Princess Pooh

cousins	golden	restaurant
crowded	princess	world

Swimmy

escaped	hidden	swaying
fierce	machine	swift

The World's Plants Are in Danger

clear	forever	save
disappear	problem	warn

Name______ Date______ Practice 251

Unit 3 Vocabulary Review

A. Find a word that means almost the same thing. Write the matching word on the line.

fast	1. swift	always
rescue	2. save	fast
ran off	3. escaped	rescue
twelve A.M.	4. midnight	wild
always	5. forever	twelve A.M.
wild	6. fierce	ran off

B. Use the words in the box to complete the questions. Write the words on the lines.

hidden	restaurant	wipe	audience

1. When the play ended, what did the audience do?
2. Did you wipe up the milk you spilled?
3. Would you rather go to a restaurant or eat at home?
4. Where is the gift hidden?

10 Book 2.2/Unit 3 Unit 3 Vocabulary Review   At Home: Have children make up questions and answers for some of the words in Exercise A.   251

PRACTICE BOOK, 251–252

GRAMMAR

PARTNERS Partners find two treasure chests. Each treasure chest contains six objects. First the partners list the objects. Then each partner selects three objects in each treasure chest and writes three sentences comparing them.

Unit Review

Officer Buckle and Gloria
Adjectives

Tomás and the Library Lady
Using *a* and *an*

Princess Pooh
Adjectives That Compare

Swimmy
Adverbs

The World's Plants Are in Danger
Synonyms and Antonyms

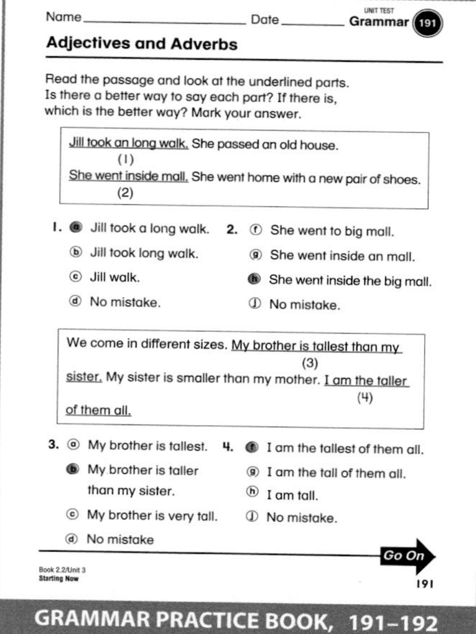

Name______ Date______ UNIT TEST Grammar 191

Adjectives and Adverbs

Read the passage and look at the underlined parts. Is there a better way to say each part? If there is, which is the better way? Mark your answer.

Jill took an long walk. (1) She passed an old house. She went inside mall. (2) She went home with a new pair of shoes.

1. ⓐ Jill took a long walk. ⓑ Jill took long walk. ⓒ Jill walk. ⓓ No mistake.
2. ⓕ She went to big mall. ⓖ She went inside an mall. ⓗ She went inside the big mall. ⓙ No mistake.

We come in different sizes. My brother is tallest than my sister. (3) My sister is smaller than my mother. I am the taller of them all. (4)

3. ⓐ My brother is tallest. ⓑ My brother is taller than my sister. ⓒ My brother is very tall. ⓓ No mistake
4. ⓕ I am the tallest of them all. ⓖ I am the tall of them all. ⓗ I am tall. ⓙ No mistake.

Go On

Book 2.2/Unit 3 Starting Now   191

GRAMMAR PRACTICE BOOK, 191–192

SPELLING

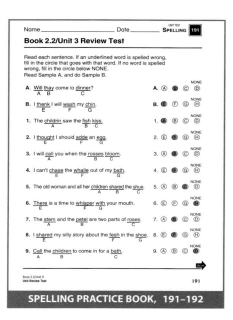

GROUP Partners choose a spelling word and spell it out letter by letter, using their hands and bodies. The other children try to guess the letters and then the word.

Unit Review

Double Consonants
call
add
egg
kiss

Digraphs *th, wh*
there
whale
thought
whisper

Digraphs *sh, ch*
shoe
children
shared
chase

Science Words
roses
bloom
stem
petal

Digraphs *th, sh*
bath
mouth
brush
fish

Name ________ Date ______ UNIT TEST SPELLING 191

Book 2.2/Unit 3 Review Test

Read each sentence. If an underlined word is spelled wrong, fill in the circle that goes with that word. If no word is spelled wrong, fill in the circle below NONE.
Read Sample A, and do Sample B.

A. Will thay come to dinner? — A. Ⓐ Ⓑ Ⓒ Ⓓ NONE
B. I thenk I will wash my chin. — B. Ⓔ Ⓕ Ⓖ Ⓗ NONE
1. The childrin saw the fish kiss. — 1. Ⓐ Ⓑ Ⓒ Ⓓ NONE
2. I thought I should adde an egg. — 2. Ⓔ Ⓕ Ⓖ Ⓗ NONE
3. I will call you when the rosses bloom. — 3. Ⓐ Ⓑ Ⓒ Ⓓ NONE
4. I can't chase the whaile out of my bath. — 4. Ⓔ Ⓕ Ⓖ Ⓗ NONE
5. The old woman and all her children shared the shue. — 5. Ⓐ Ⓑ Ⓒ Ⓓ NONE
6. There is a time to whisper with your mouth. — 6. Ⓔ Ⓕ Ⓖ Ⓗ NONE
7. The stem and the petel are two parts of roses. — 7. Ⓐ Ⓑ Ⓒ Ⓓ NONE
8. I shared my silly story about the fesh in the shoe. — 8. Ⓔ Ⓕ Ⓖ Ⓗ NONE
9. Call the children to come in for a bath. — 9. Ⓐ Ⓑ Ⓒ Ⓓ NONE

Go on

Book 2.2/Unit 3
Unit Review Test 191

SPELLING PRACTICE BOOK, 191–192

SKILLS & STRATEGIES

Phonics and Decoding

- ☑ Digraphs *ph, tch, ch*
- ☑ Long *e, i*
- ☑ Long *a, o*
- ☑ Soft *c* and Soft *g*

Comprehension

- ☑ Form Generalizations
- ☑ Main Idea

Vocabulary Strategies

- ☑ Multiple-Meaning Words
- ☑ Figurative Language

Study Skills

- ☑ Library/Media Center

Writing

- ☑ Writing a Story

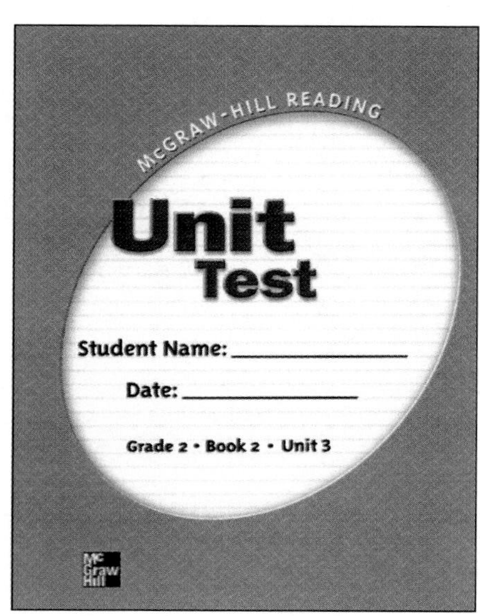

Assessment Follow-Up

Use the results of the informal and formal assessment opportunities in the unit to help you make decisions about future instruction.

SKILLS AND STRATEGIES	Reteaching Blackline Masters	Alternate Teaching Strategies	Skills Intervention Guide
Phonics and Decoding			
Digraphs *ph, tch, ch*	211, 215, 216, 224, 232, 243	T65	✓
Long *e, i*	219, 223, 224, 232, 240, 243	T70	✓
Long *a, o*	227, 231, 232, 240, 243	T73	✓
Soft *c* and Soft *g*	235, 239, 240, 243	T76	✓
Comprehension			
Form Generalizations	217, 233, 248	T67	✓
Main Idea	225, 241, 247	T71	✓
Vocabulary Strategies			
Multiple Meaning Words	218, 219, 250	T68	✓
Figurative Language	234, 242, 249	T74	✓
Study Skills			
Library/Media Center	214, 222, 230, 238, 246	T66	✓

Writing	Alternate Writing Project–Easy	Unit Writing Process Lesson
Writing a Story	281N, 309N, 339N, 361N, 371N	373C-373H

CD-ROM Provides extra phonics support.

Research & Inquiry ideas. Visit ***www.mhschool.com/reading.***

Glossary

Introduce children to the Glossary by reading through the introduction and looking over the pages with them. Encourage the class to talk about what they see.

Words in a glossary, like words in a dictionary, are listed in **alphabetical order.** Point out the **guide words** at the top of each page that tell the first and last words appearing on that page.

Point out examples of **entries** and **main entries.** Read through a simple entry with the class, identifying each part. Have children note the order in which information is given: entry word(s), definition(s), example sentence(s), syllable division, pronunciation respelling, part of speech, plural/verb/adjective forms.

Note that if more than one definition is given for a word, the definitions are numbered. Note also the format used for a word that is more than one part of speech.

Review the parts of speech by identifying each in a sentence:

inter.	*adj.*	*n.*	*conj.*	*adj.*	*n.*
Wow!	**A**	**dictionary**	**and**	**a**	**glossary**
v.	*adv.*	*pron.*	*prep.*	*n.*	
tell	**almost**	**everything**	**about**	**words!**	

Explain the use of the **pronunciation key** (either the **short key,** at the bottom of every other page, or the **long key,** at the beginning of the Glossary). Demonstrate the difference between **primary** stress and **secondary** stress by pronouncing a word with both.

Point out an example of the small triangle signaling a homophone. **Homophones** are words with different spellings and meanings but with the same pronunciation. Explain that a pair of words with the superscripts **1** and **2** are **homographs**—words that have the same spelling, but different origins and meanings, and in some cases, different pronunciations.

The **Word History** feature tells what language a word comes from and what changes have occurred in its spelling and/or meaning. Many everyday words have interesting and surprising stories behind them. Note that word histories can help us remember the meanings of difficult words.

Allow time for children to further explore the Glossary and make their own discoveries.

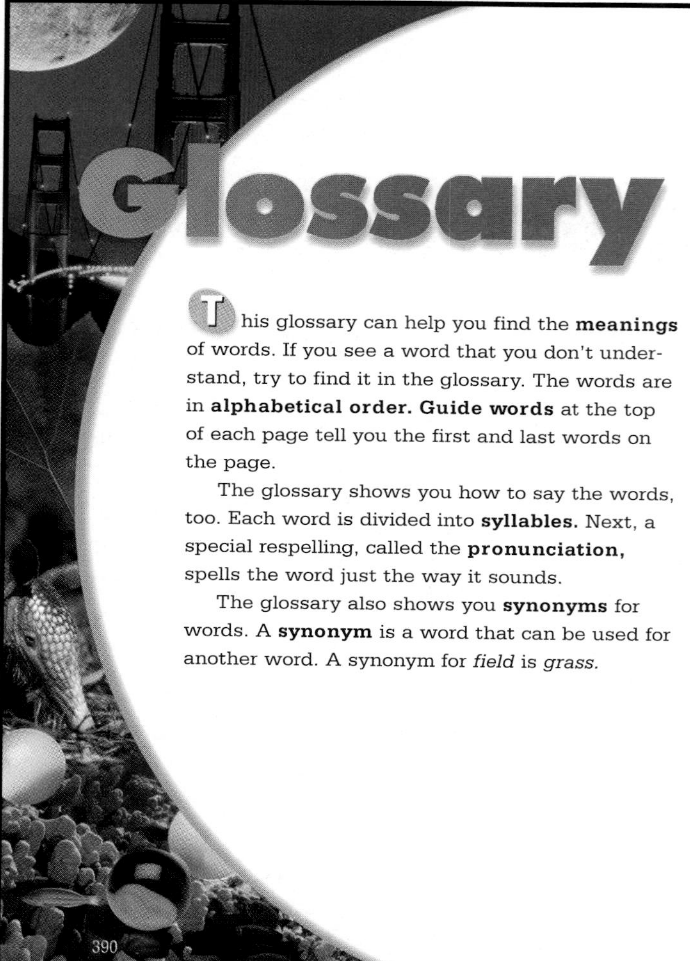

Glossary

This glossary can help you find the **meanings** of words. If you see a word that you don't understand, try to find it in the glossary. The words are in **alphabetical order. Guide words** at the top of each page tell you the first and last words on the page.

The glossary shows you how to say the words, too. Each word is divided into **syllables.** Next, a special respelling, called the **pronunciation,** spells the word just the way it sounds.

The glossary also shows you **synonyms** for words. A **synonym** is a word that can be used for another word. A synonym for *field* is *grass.*

Guide Words

accident / binoculars

First word on the page — Last word on the page

Sample Entry

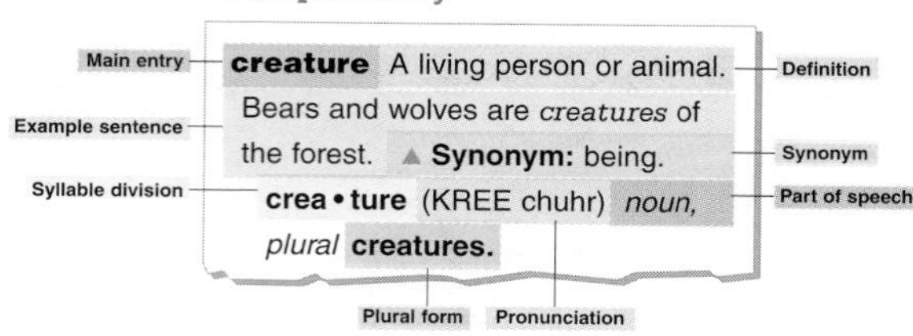

Use the **Pronunciation Key** below to find examples for the sounds you see in the **pronunciation** spellings.

Phonetic Spelling	Examples	Phonetic Spelling	Examples
a	cat	oh	go, home
ah	father	aw	saw, fall
ay	late, day	or	more, four
air	there, hair	oo	too, do
b	bit, rabbit	oy	toy
ch	chin	ow	out, cow
d	dog	p	pig
e	met	r	run, carry
ee	he, see	s	song, mess
f	fine, off	sh	shout, fish
g	go, bag, bigger	t	ten, better
h	hat	th	thin
hw	wheel	thh	them
ih	sit	u	sun
ī	fine, tiger, my	u̇	look, should
ihr	near, deer, here	yoo	music, new
j	jump, page	ur	turn, learn
k	cat, back	v	very, of
l	line, hill	w	we
m	mine, hammer	y	yes
n	nice, funny	z	has, zoo
ng	sing	zh	treasure, division
o	top	uh	about, happen, lemon

Aa

accident Something unlucky that happens without warning. There were many *accidents* the day of the snowstorm. ▲ **Synonym:** mishap.
ac•ci•dent (AK sih duhnt) *noun, plural* **accidents.**

afraid Feeling fear; frightened. There is no reason to be *afraid* of bats. ▲ **Synonym:** scared.
a•fraid (uh FRAYD) *adjective.*

Alamo (AL uh moh)

alyssum A plant of the mustard family that bears small white or yellow flowers.
a•lys•sum (uh LIHS um) *noun, plural* **alyssum.**

audience A group of people gathered to hear and see something. My family was in the *audience* to watch my school play ▲ **Synonyms:** spectators, listeners.
au•di•ence (AW dee uhns) *noun, plural* **audiences.**

auditorium A large room or building where people can gather. The concert will be in the school *auditorium.*
au•di•to•ri•um (aw dih TOR ee uhm) *noun, plural* **auditoriums.**

Bb

binoculars A device that makes distant objects look larger and closer, made up of two small telescopes joined together. We needed *binoculars* to see the ship on the horizon.
bi•noc•u•lars (buh NAHK yoo luhrz) *plural noun.*

borrow To take something to use for a while. Hector let me *borrow* his roller skates.
bor•row (BAHR oh) *verb,* **borrowed, borrowing.**

brachiopod Any of a large group of sea animals having a shell with a top and bottom half. We saw several different *brachiopods* while scuba diving.
bra•chi•o•pod (BRAY kee uh pahd) *noun, plural* **brachiopods.**

brave Having courage. The *brave* lifeguard jumped into the water to save the child.
brave (BRAYV) *adjective,* **braver, bravest.**

bravo Well done! Good! Excellent! The grateful audience clapped and cried *"Bravo!"*
bra•vo (BRAH voh) *interjection, plural* **bravos** or **bravoes.**

breath Air drawn into and forced out of the lungs; respiration. The doctor asked me to take a big *breath.*
breath (BRETH) *noun, plural* **breaths.**

Buenas noches Spanish for "good night." (BWAY nuhs NOH chez)

bulletin board A board for putting up notices, announcements, and pictures. She pinned the advertisement on the *bulletin board.*
bul•le•tin board (BÜL ih tihn bord) *noun, plural* **bulletin boards.**

bumblebee A large bee with a thick, hairy body. Most *bumblebees* have yellow and black stripes.
bum•ble•bee (BUHM buhl bee) *noun, plural* **bumblebees.**

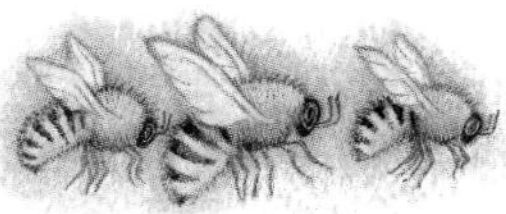

burrito A Mexican food made of a tortilla wrapped around a filling. We had a choice of *burritos* or pizza for dinner.
bur•ri•to (bur EE toh) *noun, plural* **burritos.**

bury To cover up; hide. The letter was *buried* in a pile of papers.
▲ **Synonyms:** conceal, hide.
bur•y (BER ee) *verb,* **buried, burying.**

Cc

chance 1. A turn to do something. Each child will have a *chance* to ride the pony. **2.** The possibility that something might happen. There is a *chance* that it may snow tomorrow.
▲ **Synonym:** opportunity.
chance (CHANS) *noun, plural* **chances.**

change 1. To make or become different. I will *change* the way I sign my name. *Verb.* **2.** The money that is given back when something costs less than the amount paid for it. I gave the ice cream man a dollar and got back twenty cents in *change. Noun.*
change (CHAYNJ) *verb,* **changed, changing;** *noun, plural* **changes.**

cheer The shout you make to give someone hope or courage.
cheer (CHIHR) *noun, plural* **cheers.**

chocolate A food used in making sweet things to eat. Billy unwrapped the bar of *chocolate.*
choc•o•late (CHAWK liht) *noun, plural* **chocolates.**

clear 1. To remove things from. I *cleared* the dishes after supper. *Verb.* **2.** Free from anything that darkens; bright. The sky is *clear* today. *Adjective.*
clear (KLIHR) *verb,* **cleared, clearing;** *adjective,* **clearer, clearest.**

clothes Things worn to cover the body. Coats, dresses, pants, and jackets are kinds of *clothes.*
▲ **Synonym:** clothing.
clothes (KLOHZ *or* KLOHTHHZ) *plural noun.*

coach A person who trains athletes. The *coach* made the team practice every day.
▲ **Synonym:** trainer.
coach (KOHCH) *noun, plural* **coaches.**

collide To crash against each other. The two players *collided* as they chased the ball.
col•lide (kuh LĪD) *verb,* **collided, colliding.**

colony 1. A group of animals of the same kind that live together. Ants live in *colonies.* **2.** A territory ruled by another country. The British *colonies* became the United States.
col•ony (KOL uh nee) *noun, plural* **colonies.**

coral 1. A hard, stony substance found in tropical seas. We saw huge pieces of *coral* while scuba-diving. *Noun.* **2.** A pinkish red color. Her nail polish matched her *coral* sweater. *Adjective.*
cor•al (KOR uhl) *noun, plural* **corals.**

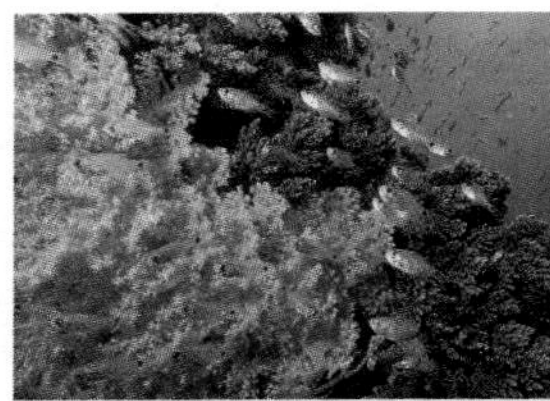

Costa Rica A country in Central America. (KOH stuh REE kuh)

cousin The child of an aunt or uncle. My *cousin* and I have the same grandfather.
cou•sin (KUZ ihn) *noun, plural* **cousins.**

cover 1. To put something on or over. *Cover* your head with a hat in cold weather. *Verb.* **2.** Something that is put on or over something else. The *cover* will keep the juice from spilling. *Noun.*
cov•er (KUV uhr) *verb,* **covered, covering;** *noun, plural* **covers.**

creature A living person or animal. Bears and wolves are *creatures* of the forest.
▲ **Synonym:** being.
crea•ture (KREE chuhr) *noun, plural* **creatures.**

crinoid Any of a group of colorful, flower-shaped saltwater animals. Crinoids are usually found in deep tropical waters. The glass-bottom boat let us see the colorful *crinoids* and coral on the ocean floor.
cri•noid (KRĪ noyd) *noun, plural* **crinoids.**

Cristobal (KRIHS tuh bahl)

crocodile A long animal with short legs, thick, scaly skin, and a long, powerful tail. *Crocodiles* have longer heads than alligators.
croc•o•dile (KROK uh dil) *noun, plural* **crocodiles.**

crop Plants grown to be used as food. I grew my own *crop* of tomatoes in our garden.
crop (KROP) *noun, plural* **crops.**

crowd 1. To put or force too many people or things into too small a space. My cousin *crowded* the shelf with books. *Verb.* **2.** A large group of people in one place. The *crowd* waited for the game to start. *Noun.*
▲ **Synonyms:** swarm, flock, assembly.
crowd (KROWD) *verb,* **crowded, crowding;** *noun, plural* **crowds.**

Dd

darkness Little or no light. *Darkness* comes earlier in the winter.
dark•ness (DAHRK nihss) *noun.*

daughter The female child of a mother and a father. Claire is the *daughter* of her mother and father. Claire's mother is the *daughter* of Claire's grandmother and grandfather.
daugh•ter (DAW tuhr) *noun, plural* **daughters.**

desert A hot, dry, sandy area of land. It can be hard to find water in the *desert.*
des•ert (DEZ uhrt) *noun, plural* **deserts.**

disappear 1. To go out of sight. We watched the moon *disappear* behind the clouds. **2.** To become extinct. The dinosaurs *disappeared* from the earth millions of years ago.
dis•ap•pear (dihs uh PIHR) *verb,* **disappeared, disappearing.**

disturb To break in on; to interrupt. The telephone call *disturbed* everyone's sleep.
▲ **Synonym:** bother.
dis•turb (dihs TURB) *verb,* **disturbed, disturbing.**

dive To go into the water with your head first. When Maria and Carlos took swimming lessons, they learned how to *dive.*
▲ **Synonym:** plunge.
dive (DĪV) *verb,* **dived** or **dove, dived, diving.**

dribble To move a ball along by bouncing or kicking it. Players *dribble* the basketball.
drib•ble (DRIHB uhl) *verb,* **dribbled, dribbling.**

Ee

echolocation A method of determining the location of objects by bouncing sound waves off the objects.
ech•o•lo•ca•tion (EK oh loh KAY shun) *noun.*

eel A long, thin fish that looks like a snake. The *eel* darted swiftly through the water.
eel (EEL) *noun, plural* **eels.**

endanger To threaten with becoming extinct. Pollution *endangers* many species.
en•dan•ger (en DAYN juhr) *verb,* **endangered, endangering.**

envy 1. A feeling of disliking or desiring another person's good luck or belongings. I felt *envy* for your new toy. *Noun.*
▲ **Synonym:** jealousy.
2. To feel envy toward. Everyone in our class *envies* you because of your good grades. *Verb.*
en•vy (EN vee) *noun, plural* **envies;** *verb,* **envied, envying.**

escape To get away from something. People knew a storm was coming and could *escape* before it started.
es•cape (es KAYP) *verb,* **escaped, escaping.**

evening The time of day when it starts to get dark, between afternoon and night. We eat dinner at 6 o'clock in the *evening.*
▲ **Synonyms:** dusk, nightfall, twilight.
eve•ning (EEV ning) *noun, plural* **evenings.**

explain To give a reason for. *Explain* why you were late.
▲ **Synonyms:** make clear, say.
ex•plain (ek SPLAYN) *verb,* **explained, explaining.**

explore To look around a place and discover new things. Nancy and Robert couldn't wait to *explore* their new neighborhood.
▲ **Synonym:** search.
ex•plore (ek SPLOR) *verb,* **explored, exploring.**

extinct No longer existing. The dodo bird became *extinct* because people hunted it.
ex•tinct (ek STINGKT) *adjective;* **extinction** *noun.*

Ff

fact Something that is real or true. It is a *fact* that there are 50 states in the United States.
▲ **Synonym:** truth.
fact (FAKT) *noun, plural* **facts.**

favorite Liked best. I always wear my *favorite* cap.
▲ **Synonym:** preferred.
fa•vor•ite (FAY vuhr iht) *adjective.*

Fernando (fur NAN doh)

field 1. An area of land where some games are played. Football is played on a football *field.* **2.** An area of land that has no trees, used for growing grass or food. We planted corn in this *field.*
▲ **Synonym:** grass. **field** (FEELD) *noun, plural* **fields.**

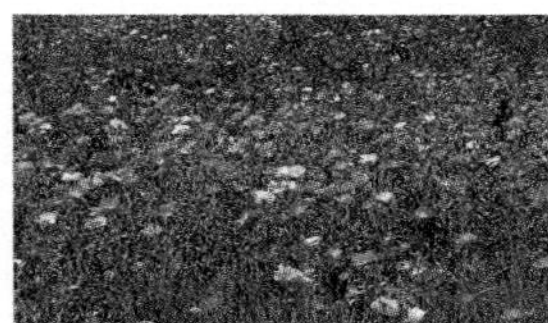

fierce Wild and dangerous. A hungry lion is *fierce.*
▲ **Synonyms:** ferocious, savage. **fierce** (FIHRS) *adjective,* **fiercer, fiercest.**

forest A large area of land covered by trees and plants. They camped in the *forest.*
▲ **Synonym:** woods.
for•est (FOR ist) *noun, plural* **forests.**

forever 1. For all time; without ever coming to an end. Things cannot stay the same *forever.* **2.** Always; on and on. That grouch is *forever* complaining.
for•ev•er (for EV uhr) *adverb.*

fossil What is left of an animal or plant that lived a long time ago. Fossils are found in rocks, earth, or clay. The bones and footprints of dinosaurs are *fossils.*
▲ **Synonyms:** relic, remains
fos•sil (FOS uhl) *noun, plural* **fossils.**

fresh Newly made, done, or gathered. We ate *fresh* tomatoes from June's garden.
▲ **Synonyms:** sweet, new, unused. **fresh** (FRESH) *adjective,* **fresher, freshest.**

Gg

glue 1. A material used for sticking things together. I used *glue* to stick the magazine pictures on the paper. *Noun.* **2.** To stick things together with glue. Please *glue* the pieces of the vase together. *Verb.*
glue (GLOO) *noun, plural* **glues;** *verb,* **glued, gluing.**

goalie The player who defends the goal in soccer, hockey, and some other games. The *goalie* stopped the puck.
goal•ie (GOHL ee) *noun, plural* **goalies.**

golden 1. Made of or containing gold. My mother has a pair of *golden* earrings. **2.** Having the color or shine of gold; bright or shining. The field of *golden* wheat swayed in the wind.
gol•den (GOHL duhn) *adjective.*

guess 1. To form an opinion without sure knowledge. Did you *guess* how much that would cost? *Verb.* **2.** An opinion formed without enough information. My *guess* is that the trip will take four hours. *Noun*
guess (GES) *verb,* **guessed, guessing;** *noun, plural* **guesses.**

Hh

halftime A rest period in the middle of some games. The players had a chance to cool off at *halftime.*
half•time (HAF tim) *noun, plural* **halftimes.**

hammock A swinging bed made from a long piece of canvas or netting. She fell asleep in the *hammock.*
ham•mock (HAM uhk) *noun, plural* **hammocks.**

harm An injury. She put the baby where he would be safe from *harm. Noun.*
▲ **Synonyms:** hurt, wrong.
harm (HAHRM) *noun, plural* **harms;** *verb,* **harmed, harming.**

heavy Hard to lift or move. The bag of groceries was too *heavy* for Derek to lift.
▲ **Synonyms:** hefty, weighty.
heav•y (HEV ee) *adjective,* **heavier, heaviest.**

hibernate To spend the winter sleeping. Some bears, woodchucks, frogs, and snakes *hibernate* all winter.
hi•ber•nate (HĪ buhr nayt) *verb,* **hibernated, hibernating;** *noun,* **hibernation.**

hidden Past participle of **hide.** To put yourself or something else in a place where it cannot be seen. My cat likes to stay *hidden* under my bed.
▲ **Synonym:** unseen.
hide (HĪD) *verb,* **hid, hidden** (HIHD uhn) or **hid, hiding.**

hunt 1. To look hard to find something or someone. I will *hunt* all over my room until I find my watch. *Verb.* **2.** A search to try to find something or someone. We went on a *hunt* through all the stores to find the toy he wanted. *Noun.*
hunt (HUNT) *verb,* **hunted, hunting;** *noun, plural* **hunts.**

Ii

ichthyosaur Any of an extinct group of porpoise-like marine reptiles. **ich•thy•o•saur** (IHK thee oh sor) *noun.*

iguanodon (ih GWAH nuh don)

insect Any of a large group of small animals without a backbone. Insects have a body divided into three parts, with three pairs of legs and usually two pairs of wings. Flies, ants, grasshoppers, and beetles are *insects.*
in•sect (IN sekt) *noun, plural* **insects.**

intercept To stop or take something on its way from one person or place to another. I tried to pass the ball to a teammate, but a player on the other team *intercepted* it.
in•ter•cept (IHN tuhr sept) *verb,* **intercepted, intercepting.**

Ll

La Brea (lah BRAY uh)

layer One thickness of something. A *layer* of dust covered the table. **lay•er** (LAY uhr) *noun, plural* **layers.**

lily A large flower shaped like a trumpet. **lil•y** (LIHL ee) *noun, plural* **lilies.**

Mm

machine A thing invented to do a particular job. Airplanes are *machines* that fly.
▲ **Synonyms:** device, mechanism. **ma•chine** (muh SHEEN) *noun, plural* **machines.**

magazine A printed collection of stories, articles, and pictures usually bound in a paper cover. I read that article about fossils in a nature *magazine.*
mag•a•zine (MAG uh zeen) *noun, plural* **magazines.**

marigold A garden plant that bears yellow, orange, or red flowers in the summer.
mar•i•gold (MAR ih gohld) *noun, plural* **marigolds.**

marvel 1. A wonderful or amazing thing. Space travel is one of the *marvels* of modern science. *Noun.* **2.** To feel wonder and astonishment. We *marveled* at the acrobat's skill. *Verb.*
mar•vel (MAHR vuhl) *noun, plural* **marvels;** *verb,* **marveled, marveling.**

medusa A jellyfish.
me•du•sa (muh DOO suh) *noun, plural* **medusas** or **medusae.**

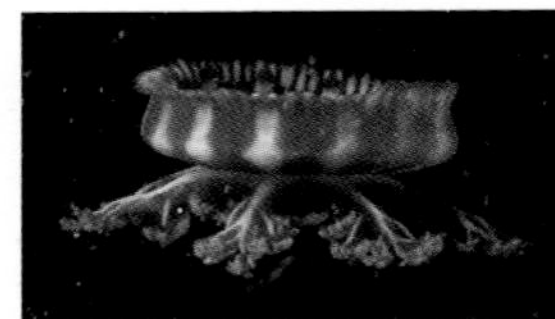
medusa

membrane A thin, flexible layer of skin or tissue that lines parts of the body. The skin that connects a bat's wing bones to its body is called a *membrane.*
mem•brane (MEM brayn) *noun, plural* **membranes.**

middle A place halfway between two points or sides. Noon is in the *middle* of the day.
▲ **Synonym:** center.
mid•dle (MIHD uhl) *noun, plural* **middles.**

midnight Twelve o'clock at night; the middle of the night. Cinderella's coach turned into a pumpkin at *midnight.*
mid•night (MIHD nīt) *noun.*

miller A person who owns or operates a mill, especially one for grinding grain. The *miller* sold the wheat to the baker.
mill•er (MIHL uhr) *noun, plural* **millers.**

million 1. One thousand times one thousand; 1,000,000. *Noun.* **2.** Having a very large number. It looks like a *million* stars in the sky. *Adjective.*
mil•lion (MIHL yuhn) *noun, plural* **millions;** *adjective.*

mine A large area dug out in or under the ground. Coal and gold are dug out of *mines.*
mine (MĪN) *noun, plural* **mines.**

mosquito A small insect with two wings. The female gives a sting or bite that itches. There were hundreds of *mosquitoes* near the swamp.
mos•qui•to (muh SKEE toh) *noun, plural* **mosquitoes** or **mosquitos.**

museum A building where pieces of art, science displays, or objects from history are kept for people to see. I saw one of George Washington's hats at the history *museum.*
mu•se•um (myoo ZEE uhm) *noun, plural* **museums.**

music A beautiful combination of sounds. When you sing or play an instrument, you are making *music.*
mu•sic (MYOO zihk) *noun.*

musician A person who is skilled in playing a musical instrument, writing music, or singing. The *musician* prepared to play for the audience.
mu•si•cian (myoo ZIHSH uhn) *noun, plural* **musicians.**

mussel An animal that looks like a clam. Saltwater *mussels* have bluish-black shells.
▲ Another word that sounds like this is *muscle*. **mus•sel** (MUS uhl) *noun, plural* **mussels.**

Nn

nature All things in the world that are not made by people. Plants, animals, mountains, and oceans are all part of *nature*.
na•ture (NAY chuhr) *noun.*

nervous 1. Not able to relax. Loud noises make me *nervous*. **2.** Fearful or timid. I am very *nervous* about taking the test.
▲ **Synonym:** anxious.
nerv•ous (NUR vuhs) *adjective.*

noisy Making harsh or loud sounds. It is *noisy* at the airport.
▲ **Synonym:** loud.
nois•y (NOY zee) *adjective,* **noisier, noisiest.**

Oo

object Anything that can be seen and touched. Is that large, round *object* an orange?
▲ **Synonym:** thing.
ob•ject (OB jihkt) *noun, plural* **objects.**

offer To present for someone to take or refuse. Mom *offered* to pick us up if it gets dark before the game ends.
▲ **Synonym:** volunteer, give.
of•fer (AHF uhr) *verb,* **offered, offering.**

office A place where people work. The principal's *office* is at the end of the hall.
▲ **Synonym:** workplace.
of•fice (AHF ihs) *noun, plural* **offices.**

out-of-bounds In sports, outside the area of play allowed. I kicked the ball *out-of-bounds*, so the other team was given the ball.
out•of•bounds (OWT uv BOWNDZ) *adverb, adjective.*

Pp

package A thing or group of things that are packed in a box, wrapped up, or tied in a bundle. We sent a *package* of treats to my sister at camp.
▲ **Synonyms:** bundle, parcel.
pack•age (PAK ihj) *noun, plural* **packages.**

Parthenon (PAHR thuh nahn)

piece A part that has been broken, cut, or torn from something. There are *pieces* of broken glass on the floor.
piece (PEES) *noun, plural* **pieces.**

practice To do something over and over to gain skill. I *practice* playing guitar every day.
prac•tice (PRAK tihs) *verb,* **practiced, practicing.**

preserve To keep from being damaged, decayed, or lost; protect. You can *preserve* the wood of the table by waxing it.
pre•serve (prih ZURV) *verb,* **preserved, preserving.**

princess The daughter of a king or queen; a female member of a royal family other than a queen; the wife of a prince. The people of the kingdom bowed to the *princess*.
prin•cess (PRIHN sihs *or* PRIHN ses) *noun, plural* **princesses.**

principal The person who is the head of a school. The *principal* gave a speech.
▲ Another word that sounds like this is *principle*. **prin•ci•pal** (PRIHN suh puhl) *noun, plural* **principals.**

problem Anything that causes trouble and must be dealt with. A barking dog can be a *problem*.
prob•lem (PRAHB luhm) *noun, plural* **problems.**

prowl To move or roam quietly or secretly. The tiger *prowled* through the forest.
prowl (PROWL) *verb,* **prowled, prowling.**

Rr

reptile One of a class of cold-blooded animals with a backbone and dry, scaly skin. Lizards are *reptiles*.
rep•tile (REP til) *noun, plural* **reptiles.**

restaurant A place where food is prepared and served. We ate at the *restaurant*.
res•tau•rant (RES tuh ruhnt *or* RES tuh rahnt) *noun, plural* **restaurants.**

roof The top part of a building. There was a leak in the *roof*.
roof (ROOF *or* RU̇F) *noun, plural* **roofs.**

Ss

save 1. To keep from harm; to make safe. The cat *saved* her kittens from the fire. **2.** To set aside for future use. I will *save* some cookies to eat later.
save (SAYV) *verb,* **saved, saving.**

scare To make afraid. Loud noises always *scare* the puppy.
▲ **Synonyms:** alarm, frighten.
scare (SKAIR) *verb,* **scared, scaring.**

scary Causing alarm or fear; frightening. Your monster costume is very *scary*.
scar•y (SKAIR ee) *adjective,* **scarier, scariest.**

score 1. To get a point or points in a game or on a test. The baseball team *scored* five runs in one inning. *Verb.* **2.** The points gotten in a game or on a test. The final *score* was 5 to 4. *Noun.*
▲ **Synonym:** tally. **score** (SKOR) *verb,* **scored, scoring;** *noun, plural* **scores.**

sea anemone A sea animal shaped like a tube that attaches itself to rocks and to other objects.
sea a•nem•o•ne (SEE uh NEM uh nee) *noun, plural* **sea anemones.**

seaweed Any plant or plants that grows in the sea, especially certain kinds of algae.
sea•weed (SEE weed) *noun.*

señor Sir; mister. Spanish form of respectful or polite address for a man. **se•ñor** (sen YOR)

señora Mistress; madam. Spanish form of respectful or polite address for a woman.
se•ño•ra (sen YOR uh)

servant A person hired to work for the comfort or protection of others. The *servant* brought in their dinner.
serv•ant (SUR vuhnt) *noun, plural* **servants.**

several More than two, but not many. We saw *several* of our friends at the parade.
▲ **Synonym:** various.
sev•er•al (SEV uhr ul *or* SEV ruhl) *adjective; noun.*

shoulder The part on either side of the body from the neck to where the arm joins. I carry the sack over my *shoulder.*
shoul•der (SHOHL duhr) *noun, plural* **shoulders.**

skeleton A framework that supports and protects the body. Birds, fish, and humans have *skeletons* made of bones.
skel•e•ton (SKEL uh tuhn) *noun, plural* **skeletons.**

slip To slide and fall down. Be careful not to *slip* on the wet floor.
▲ **Synonyms:** slide, skid.
slip (SLIHP) *verb,* **slipped, slipping.**

soil The top part of the ground in which plants grow. There is sandy *soil* near the coast.
▲ **Synonyms:** dirt, earth.
soil (SOYL) *noun, plural* **soils.**

station A place of business where something specific is done. We get gas for a car at a gas *station.* Police officers work in a police *station.*
▲ **Synonym:** precinct.
sta•tion (STAY shuhn) *noun, plural* **stations.**

stepmother A woman who has married a person's father after the death or divorce of the natural mother. Dan's *stepmother* came to his school play.
step•moth•er (STEP muthh uhr) *noun, plural* **stepmothers.**

storyteller A person who tells or writes stories.
sto•ry•tell•er (STOR ee tel uhr) *noun, plural* **storytellers.**

stretch To spread out to full length. The lazy cat *stretched* and then went back to sleep.
▲ **Synonym:** extend. **stretch** (STRECH) *verb,* **stretched, stretching.**

study To try to learn by reading, thinking about, or looking; examine closely. A detective *studies* clues carefully.
stud•y (STUD ee) *verb,* **studied, studying.**

sway To move back and forth. The tree branches *swayed.*
▲ **Synonyms:** swing, wave, lean.
sway (SWAY) *verb,* **swayed, swaying.**

swift Moving or able to move very quickly. The rider had a *swift* horse.
▲ **Synonyms:** speedy, fast.
swift (SWIHFT) *adjective,* **swifter, swiftest.**

swivel chair A chair with a seat that spins. She spun around on the *swivel chair.*
swi•vel chair (SWIHV uhl chair) *noun, plural* **swivel chairs.**

teenager A person who is between the ages of thirteen and nineteen.
teen•a•ger (TEEN ay juhr) *noun, plural* **teenagers.**

termite An insect that eats wood, paper, and other materials. The *termites* ate through the floor of the old house.
ter•mite (TUR mit) *noun, plural* **termites.**

therapy Treatment for a disability, injury, psychological problem, or illness. He needed physical *therapy* to help heal his broken leg.
ther•a•py (THER uh pee) *noun, plural* **therapies.**

third Next after the second one. We had seats in the *third* row of the theater.
third (THURD) *adjective.*

throne 1. The chair that a king or queen sits on during ceremonies and other special occasions. **2.** The power or authority of a king or queen.
throne (THROHN) *noun, plural* **thrones.**

throw To send something through the air. *Throw* the ball to the dog, and she will bring it back to you.
▲ **Synonyms:** toss, fling, pitch.
throw (THROH) *verb,* **threw, thrown, throwing.**

thumbtack A tack with a flat, round head that can be pressed into a wall or board with the thumb. Notices are often pinned to bulletin boards with *thumbtacks.*
thumb•tack (THUM tak) *noun, plural* **thumbtacks.**

ton A measure of weight equal to 2,000 pounds in the United States and Canada, and 2,240 pounds in Great Britain.
ton (tun) *noun, plural* **tons.**

tooth One of the hard, white, bony parts in the mouth used for biting and chewing. I got a filling in my front *tooth.*
tooth (TOOTH) *noun, plural* **teeth.**

touch To put your hand on or against something. If you *touch* the stove, you will get burned.
▲ **Synonym:** feel.
touch (TUCH) *verb,* **touched, touching.**

trilobite An extinct sea animal that lived hundreds of millions of years ago.
tri•lo•bite (TRĪ loh bit) *noun, plural* **trilobites.**

upstairs 1. On or to a higher floor. My bedroom is *upstairs.* *Adverb.* **2.** On an upper floor. The *upstairs* bathroom was just cleaned. *Adjective.*
up•stairs (UP stairz) *adverb; adjective.*

Vv

vacation A period of rest or freedom. Summer *vacation* begins next week.
va•ca•tion (vay KAY shuhn) *noun, plural* **vacations.**

village A small town. The streets of the *village* were paved with stones.
▲ **Synonym:** community.
vil•lage (VIHL ihj) *noun, plural* **villages.**

voice The sound you make through your mouth. You use your *voice* when you sing.
voice (VOYS) *noun, plural* **voices.**

warn alert; To tell about something before it happens.
warn (WORN) *verb,* **warned, warning.**

waterfall A natural stream of water falling from a high place. We had a picnic by the *waterfall.* **wa•ter•fall** (WAH tuhr fawl) *noun, plural* **waterfalls.**

wheelchair A chair on wheels that is used by someone who cannot walk to get from one place to another. He needed a *wheelchair* until his leg healed. **wheel•chair** (HWEEL chair *or* WEEL chair) *noun, plural* **wheelchairs.**

whistle 1. To make a sound by pushing air out through your lips or teeth. My dog comes when I *whistle. Verb.* **2.** Something you blow into that makes a whistling sound. The police officer blew his *whistle. Noun.* **whis•tle** (HWIS uhl *or* WIS uhl) *verb,* **whistled, whistling;** *noun, plural* **whistles.**

wipe To clean or dry by rubbing. ▲ **Synonym:** clean. **wipe** (WĪP) *verb,* **wiped, wiping.**

wonder 1. To want to know or learn; be curious about. I *wonder* why the sky is blue. *Verb.* **2.** A surprising or impressive thing. *Noun.* **won•der** (WUN duhr) *verb,* **wondered, wondering;** *noun, plural* **wonders.**

world Place where all things live. **world** (WURLD) *noun, plural* **worlds.**

wrap To cover something by putting something else around it. We will *wrap* the package. **wrap** (RAP) *verb,* **wrapped, wrapping.**

xiphactinus (zee FAK ti nus)

zinnia A garden flower. **zin•ni•a** (ZIHN nee uh) *noun, plural* **zinnias.**

414

ACKNOWLEDGMENTS

The publisher gratefully acknowledges permission to reprint the following copyrighted material:

"Charlie Anderson" by Barbara Abercrombie, illustrated by Mark Graham. Text copyright © 1990 by Barbara Abercrombie. Illustrations copyright © 1990 by Mark Graham. Reprinted with permission of Margaret K. McElderry Books, Simon & Schuster Children's Publishing Division.

"Fernando's Gift" by Douglas Keister. Copyright © 1995 by Douglas Keister. Reprinted by permission of Sierra Club Books For Children.

"Fossils Tell of Long Ago" by Aliki. Copyright © 1972, 1990 by Aliki Brandenberg. Used by permission of HarperCollins Publishers.

"Neighbors" by Marchette Chute from RHYMES ABOUT US. by Marchette Chute. Published 1974 by E.P. Dutton. Reprinted with permission of Elizabeth Hauser.

"Officer Buckle and Gloria" by Peggy Rathmann. Copyright ©, Peggy Rathmann, 1995. Published by arrangement with Penguin Putnam Books for Young Readers, a division of Penguin Putnam Inc.

"Our Soccer League" from OUR SOCCER LEAGUE by Chuck Solomon. Text copyright © 1988 by Chuck Solomon. Reprinted by arrangement with Random House Children's Books, a division of Random House, Inc.

"Princess Pooh" is the entire text from PRINCESS POOH by Kathleen M. Muldoon with illustrations by Linda Shute. Text copyright © 1989 by Kathleen M. Muldoon. Illustrations copyright © 1989 by Linda Shute. Originally published in hardcover by Albert Whitman & Company. All rights reserved. Used with permission.

"River Winding" from RIVER WINDING by Charlotte Zolotow. Copyright © 1970 by Charlotte Zolotow. Reprinted by permission of Scott Treimel New York.

"Swimmy" from SWIMMY by Leo Lionni. Copyright © 1963 by Leo Lionni. Copyright renewed 1991 by Leo Lionni. Reprinted by arrangement with Random House Children's Books, a division of Random House, Inc.

"To Catch a Fish" by Eloise Greenfield from UNDER THE SUNDAY TREE. Text copyright © 1988 by Eloise Greenfield. Paintings copyright © 1988 by Amos Ferguson. Reprinted by permission of HarperTrophy, a division of HarperCollins Publishers.

"Tomás and the Library Lady" by Pat Mora. Text copyright © 1977 by Pat Mora. Illustrations copyright © 1997 by Raul Colón. Reprinted by permission of Alfred A. Knopf.

"The Wednesday Surprise" from THE WEDNESDAY SURPRISE by Eve Bunting with illustrations by Donald Carrick. Text copyright © 1989 by Eve Bunting. Illustrations copyright © 1989 by Donald Carrick. Reprinted by permission of Clarion Books, a Houghton Mifflin Co. imprint.

"What Is It?" by Eve Merriam from HIGGLE WIGGLE (MORROW JR BOOKS). Text copyright © 1994 by the Estate of Eve Merriam by Marian Reiner, Literary Executor. Used by permission of Marian Reiner.

"Which?" from CRICKETY CRICKET! THE BEST LOVED POEMS OF JAMES S. TIPPETT. Text copyright © 1933, copyright renewed © 1973 by Martha K. Tippett. Illustrations copyright © 1973 by Mary Chalmers. Reprinted by permission of HarperCollins Publishers.

"Zipping, Zapping, Zooming Bats" by Ann Earle. Text copyright © 1995 by Ann Earle. Illustrations copyright © 1995 by Henry Cole. Reprinted by permission of HarperCollins Children's Books, a division of HarperCollins Publishers.

Illustration
Matt Straub, 12–13; Leonor Glynn, 42; Claude Martinot, 43; Cuenhee Lee, 44–45; Myron Grossman, 67; Annette Cable, 68–69; Cecily Lang, 70–87; Claude Martinot, 91; Tim Raglin, 92–93; Claude Martinot, 115; Melinda Levine, 130–131; Mary GrandPre, 132–145; Julia Gorton, 149; Tom Barrett, 150–151; Myron Grossman, 179; Joe Cepeda, 180–181; Leonor Glynn, 210; Julia Gorton, 211; Suling Wang, 212–213; Vilma Ortiz–Dillon, 234; Myron Grossman, 235; Anne Lunsford, 282–283; Myron Grossman, 309; Jerry Smath, 250–251; Julia Gorton, 281; Abby Carter, 310–311; Claude Martinot, 339; Carol Inouye, 340–341; Claude Martinot, 361; Robert Crawford, 10–11; Taylor Bruce, 126–127; Russ Willms, 128–129; Marina Thompson, 248–249; Sonja Lamut, 372–373; Tom Leonard, 116–117; Myron Grossman, 125, 371; Michael Welch, 236–237; Claude Martinot, 245; Alexandra Wallner, 362–363; John Carozza, 410; Holly Jones, 394, 403; Miles Parnell, 398, 407, 412.

Photography
4: b. Douglas Keister; 5: b. Merline Tuttle/Photo Researchers; 7: b, John Cancalosis/Peter Arnold; 9: b. David Muench/Corbis; 41: r. Renee Lynn/Photo Researchers/l. Renee Lynn/Photo Researchers/Dough Plummer/Photonica; 42: b.r. Renee Lynn/Photo Researchers; 65: b. Andrea Pistolesi/The Image Bank; 70: b.r. Courtesy of Cecily Lang Studio/t.l. Courtesy of Diane Hoyt–Goldsmith; 75: t. Roy Morsch/The Stock Market/b. Brown Brothers; 77: r. Wernher Kruten/Liaison International/l. Chad Ehlers/Tony Stone Images; 79: Zigy Kalunzy/Tony Stone Images; 81: Merlin D. Tuttle/Bat Conservation International; 83: t. Wesley Hitt/Liaison International/b. Superstock; 84: Howard Grey/Tony Stone Images; 85: Robert Landau/Westlight; 87: t.r. Hiroyuki Matsumoto/Tony Stone Images/b.r. Marc Biggins/Liaison International/b.l. Tom Bean/Tony Stone/t.l. Superstock; 89: b. Merlin D. Tuttle/Bat Conservation International/t. Wesley Hitt/Liaison International; 94: t.l. Courtesy of HarperCollins Publishers; 113: b. T. Sawada/Photonica; 114: m.l. Merlin D. Tuttle/Bat Conservation International/t.r. Merlin D. Tuttle/Bat Conservation International/t.l. Merlin D. Tuttle/Bat Conservation International/b.r. Stephen Dalton/Photo Researchers; 122: t. Merlin D. Tuttle/Photo Researchers/m. Joe Mcdonald/Animals Animals/b. Merlin Tuttle/Bat Conservation International; 123 b. PhotoDisc; 132: Courtesy of the artist; 176-177: David Madison/Tony Stone Images; 214: T. Carolina Ambida. 233: b. Jeffrey Sylvester/FPG International; 242: t.l. PhotoDisc/b.r. Howard Grey/Tony Stone Images/m.l. PhotoDisc; 244: l. PhotoDisc/r. Howard Grey/Tony Stone Images; 252: t. Courtesy of Penguin Putnam Inc.; 279: m.r. Jonathan Nourok/Photo Edit/b. Tom Nebbia/Corbis-Bettman/m.c. David Young-Wolff/Photo Edit/m.l. Spencer Grant/Photo Edit; 284: t.l. Courtesy Random House/b.r. Courtesy of Raul Colon/t.l. Courtesy Alfred A. Knopf Inc.; 306-307: Tony Freeman/Photo Edit; 337: b. Jim Cummins/FPG International/m.r. PhotoDisc; 360: t. PhotoDisc/b. PhotoDisc; 368; m. Kit Latham/FPG.

Reading for Information
All photographs are by Macmillan/McGraw-Hill (MMH); Michael Groen for MMH; Ken Karp for MMH; and Chuck Solomon for MMH, except as noted below.

Table of Contents, pp. 374–375
Chess pieces, tl, Wides + Hall/FPG; Earth, mcl, M. Burns/Picture Perfect; CD's, mcl, Michael Simpson/FPG; Newspapers, bl, Craig Orsini/Index Stock/PictureQuest; Clock, tc, Steve McAlister/The Image Bank; Kids circle, bc, Daniel Pangbourne Media/FPG; Pencils, tr, W. Cody/Corbis; Starfish, tc, Darryl Torckler/Stone; Keys, cr, Randy Faris/Corbis; Cells, br, Spike Walker/Stone; Stamps, tr, Michael W. Thomas/Focus Group/PictureQuest; Books, cr, Siede Preis/PhotoDisc; Sunflower, cr, Jeff LePore/Natural Selection; Mouse, br, Andrew Hall/Stone; Apples, tr, Siede Preis/PhotoDisc; Watermelons, br, Neil Beer/PhotoDisc; Butterfly, br, Stockbyte

377: t.r. George Godfrey/Earth Scenes/b.r. Leonard Lee Rue/Stock Boston; 378-379: bkgd. Tom Walker/Stock Boston; 380: m.l. George Bernard/Animals Animals/m.r. M. MC. Chamberlain/DRK Photo/b.l. David Baron/Animals Animals: 380-381 bkgd. William Johnson/Stock Boston; 381: t.l. Fritz Polking/Dembinsky Photo Assoc./b.l. E. R. Dergginger/Dembinsky Photo Assoc.; 390: l. PhotoDisc; 392: Ron Chapple/FPG International; 393: Jose Azel/Aurora/PNI; 395: David Stockein/The Stock Market; 396: Mark A. Johnson/The Stock Market; 397: Tom Dean/The Stock Market; 398: Wayne Levin/FPG International; 400: Eric Meola/The Image Bank; 401: David Brooks/The Stock Market; 402: Michel Renaudeau/Liaison; 405: Don Perdue/Liaison; 406: Richard H. Johnston/FPG International; 408: Rick Rusing/Tony Stone Images; 409: Darryl Torchker/Tony Stone Images; 411: Hank de Lespinasse/Image Bank; 412: Adam Woolfitt/Woodfin Camp, Inc.

t/Illustration
nda Weller, 44F; Richard Kolding, 180F

otography
5A: M. Burns, Picture Perfect; Daniel gbourne, Media/FPG; 127A: Jeff Pore/Natural Selection; Stockbyte

Acknowledgments

Cover Illustration: Kenneth Spengler

The publisher gratefully acknowledges permission to reprint the following copyrighted material:

"All Living Things" by W. Jay Cawley. Words and music copyright © 1992 by W. Jay Cawley.

"The Bat" from BEAST FEAST by Douglas Florian. Copyright © 1984 by Douglas Florian. Used by permission of Voyager Books, Harcourt Brace & Company.

"Behind the Museum Door" from GOOD RHYMES, GOOD TIMES by Lee Bennett Hopkins. Copyright © 1973, 1995 by Lee Bennett Hopkins. Used by permission of Curtis Brown Ltd.

"Brothers" from SNIPPETS by Charlotte Zolotow. Copyright © 1993 by Charlotte Zolotow. Illustrations copyright © 1993 by Melissa Sweet. Used by permission of HarperCollins Publishers.

"The Bundle of Sticks" from THE CHILDREN'S AESOP: SELECTED FABLES retold by Stephanie Calmenson. Used by permission of Caroline House, Boyds Mills Press, Inc.

"The Cat Came Back" arranged by Mary Goetze. Copyright © 1984 MMB Music, Inc.

"Covers" from VACATION TIME: POEMS FOR CHILDREN by Nikki Giovanni. Copyright © 1980 by Nikki Giovanni. Used by permission of William Morrow & Company, Inc.

"The Day the Sun Hid" from MICHAEL FOREMAN'S WORLD OF FAIRY TALES. Copyright © 1991 by Pavilion Books Limited. Used by permission of Arcade Publishing, Inc.

"The Dinosaur Who Lived in My Backyard" by B. G. Hennessey. Copyright © 1988 by B. G. Hennessey. Used by permission of Viking Books, a division of Penguin Books USA Inc.

"The Discontented Fish" from Tales from Africa by Kathleen Arnott. Copyright © 1962 by Kathleen Arnott. Used by permission of Oxford University Press.

"The Golden Touch" retold by Margaret H. Lippert from TEACHER'S READ ALOUD ANTHOLOGY. Copyright © 1993 by Macmillan/McGraw-Hill School Publishing Company.

"Gotta Find a Footprint" from BONE POEMS by Jeff Moss. Text copyright © 1997 by Jeff Moss. Illustrations copyright © 1997 by Tom Leigh. Used by permission of Workman Publishing Company, Inc.

"The Great Ball Game: A Muskogee Story" by Joseph Bruchac. Copyright © 1994 by Joseph Bruchac. Used by permission of Dial Books.

"Lemonade Stand" reprinted with the permission of Margaret K. McElderry Books, an imprint of Simon & Schuster Children's Publishing Division from WORLDS I KNOW and Other Poems by Myra Cohn Livingston. Text copyright © 1985 by Myra Cohn Livingston.

"The Letter" from FROG AND TOAD ARE FRIENDS by Arnold Lobel. Copyright © 1970 by Arnold Lobel. Used by permission of HarperCollins Publishers.

"The Library" by Barbara A. Huff from THE RANDOM HOUSE BOOK OF POETRY FOR CHILDREN. Copyright © 1983 by Barbara A. Huff.

"The Lion and the Mouse" from ONCE IN A WOOD: TEN TALES FROM AESOP adapted and illustrated by Eve Rice. Copyright © 1979 by Eve Rice. Used by permission of Greenwillow Books, a division of William Morrow & Company, Inc.

"Me I Am!" copyright © 1983 by Jack Prelutsky from THE RANDOM HOUSE BOOK OF POETRY FOR CHILDREN by Jack Prelutsky. Used by permission of Random House Children's Books, a division of Random House, Inc.

"Penguins" from A HIPPOPOTAMUSN'T AND OTHER ANIMAL VERSES by J. Patrick Lewis. Text copyright © 1990 by J. Patrick Lewis. Pictures copyright © 1990 by Victoria Chess. Used by permission of Dial Books for Young Readers, a division of Penguin Books USA Inc.

"Reading to Me" from THE OTHER SIDE OF THE DOOR by Jeff Moss. Text copyright © 1991 by Jeff Moss. Illustrations copyright © 1991 by Chris Demarest. Used by permission of Bantam Books, a division of Bantam Doubleday Dell Publishing Group, Inc.

"The Sharks" from IN THE SWIM by Douglas Florian. Copyright © 1997 by Douglas Florian. Used by permission of Harcourt Brace & Company.

"Summer Goes" from EGG THOUGHTS AND OTHER FRANCES SONGS by Russell Hoban. Copyright © 1964, 1974 by Russell Hoban. Used by permission of HarperCollins Publishers.

"A Superduper Pet" from SUPERDUPER TEDDY by Johanna Hurwitz. Text copyright © 1980 by Johanna Hurwitz. Illustrations copyright © 1990 by Lillian Hoban. Used by permission of William Morrow and Company, Inc.

"The Tall Tales," "The Tiger Story," and "Two Foolish Friends" by Tanya Lee, from FLOATING CLOUDS, FLOATING DREAMS: FAVORITE ASIAN FOLKTALES by I.K. Junne. Copyright © 1974 by I.K. Junne. Used by permission of Doubleday & Company, Inc.

"Thinking Green" from 50 SIMPLE THINGS KIDS CAN DO TO SAVE THE EARTH by The EarthWorks Group. Copyright © 1989 by John Javna, The EarthWorks Group. Used by permission of Andrew McMeel Publishers.

Untitled from A CHINESE ZOO: FABLES AND PROVERBS by Demi. Copyright © 1987. Used by permission of Harcourt Brace Jovanovich Publishers.

"Vacation" from FATHERS, MOTHERS, SISTERS, BROTHERS by Mary Ann Hoberman. Text copyright © 1991 by Mary Ann Hoberman. Illustrations copyright © 1991 by Marylin Hafner. Used by permission of Little, Brown and Company.

ZB Font Method Copyright © 1996 Zaner-Bloser. Handwriting Models, Manuscript and Cursive. Used by permission.

Backmatter Contents

The Lion and the Mouse

a fable by Aesop
adapted by Eve Rice

One day, a mighty Lion was
fast asleep in the woods.
Thinking he was just a rock,
a little Mouse ran up his back.
The Lion woke at once
and took the poor Mouse
by the tail.
"How dare you wake me up?"
he roared.
"I am going to eat you!"
"Oh, please," the Mouse said.
"Let me go, and someday
I will repay you."
"Don't be silly!" Lion roared.
"How will you repay me?
You are just a little Mouse—
too small to be
much use to me."
But then he laughed.
"All right. Go on."
He put the Mouse down and
she ran off into the woods.

When many days had passed,
the Mouse ran by that place again.
And hearing an awful roar,
she soon found Lion,
caught in a trap made of rope.
Quickly Mouse ran to the trap.
She took the rope in her teeth
and chewed and chewed until
she chewed right through the rope
and set the Lion free.
▶ "Thank you!" roared Lion.
"You are welcome," said the Mouse.
"And now I hope that you can see
how big a help
small friends can be."

The Library

Barbara A. Huff

It looks like any building
When you pass it on the street,
Made of stone and glass and marble,
Made of iron and concrete.

But once inside you can ride
A camel or a train,
Visit Rome, Siam, or Nome,
Feel a hurricane,
Meet a king, learn to sing,
How to bake a pie,
Go to sea, plant a tree,
Find how airplanes fly,
Train a horse, and of course
Have all the dogs you'd like,
See the moon, a sandy dune,
Or catch a whopping pike.
Everything that books can bring
You'll find inside those walls.
▶ A world is there for you to share
When adventure calls.

You cannot tell its magic
By the way the building looks,
But there's wonderment within it,
The wonderment of books.

ME I AM!

ck Prelutsky

m the only ME I AM
ho qualifies as me;
ME I AM has been before,
d none will ever be.

other ME I AM can feel
e feelings I've within;
other ME I AM can fit
ecisely in my skin.

ere is no other ME I AM
ho thinks the thoughts I do;
e world contains one ME I AM,
ere is no room for two.

m the only ME I AM
is earth shall ever see;
at ME I AM I always am
no one else but ME!

The Discontented Fish

an African folk tale
retold by Kathleen Arnott

Once upon a time there was a colony of little fishes who lived together in their own small pool, isolated from the rest of the fish in the river. It was a still, gray pool, dotted with stones and clumps of weed, and surrounded by thorn bushes and a few palm trees.

Most of these fish were as happy and as friendly as they could be. But there was one fish, much bigger and stronger than all the others, who kept himself aloof, and who would draw himself up in a haughty manner whenever the others came near him.

"My good fellow," he would say, opening his eyes as wide as he could, and balancing himself erect on his handsome tail, "do stop making such a commotion in the water beside me. Can't you see I am having my afternoon siesta? Go away! And take that rabble away with you," he would add, sweeping one glistening fin towards a shoal of cheerful small fish darting in and out among the shadows.

▶ This sort of thing happened so often that one day one of the older fish said sarcastically:

"I wonder you don't leave this tiny pool and go off to the big river. A fish as large and important as you should surely mix with others of his own size and excellent breeding."

The big fish thought things over for several days, and puffed himself even bigger with pride when at last he decided to leave his home and search for a better one.

"My friend is quite right," he said to himself. "I should be happier if I lived among fish of my own size. How tired I am of these stupid little creatures! With all the rain we've been having lately the time must be near when the big river overflows its banks, and the flood-water will soon be coming up into our pool. When it arrives, I'll go with it and let myself be swept down into the big river, and get away from all this."

▶ Continue reading here.

He told his companions what he had in mind. The older fish congratulated him on his enterprise with solemn faces, but the younger ones could not conceal their delight at the thought of being free from the big fish's criticisms, and they swam backwards and forwards, talking about it among themselves.

After a few more days of heavy rain the floods arrived. They covered the little pool, and the big fish rose to the top of the water and allowed himself to be swept downstream to the river. Once between the banks in the depths of the river itself, he noticed how different the water tasted, and how much larger the rocks and the weeds were. Then he sighed with relief and anticipation, thinking of the good life that lay ahead.

He was resting for a few moments beside a large stone when he felt the water swirling behind him. Suddenly four or five fish, much bigger than he, passed over his head. One of them looked down and exclaimed harshly:

"Out of our way, little fish! Don't you know this is *our* hunting ground?"

Then the others turned on him too and drove him away.

The poor fish hid beneath a large clump of weeds, and peered out anxiously from time to time. Presently two large black and white fish came rushing towards him, with fearsome jaws wide open. They would surely have eaten him up had he not managed to wedge himself in a crevice in the bank, just out of their reach.

"O dear!" he gasped, when the two monsters had at last tired of waiting about for him. "I do hope there aren't any more fish like that in this river. How am I to live if I have to spend the whole day in hiding, with no chance to search for food?"

All day long he stayed in his hiding-place, but when night came he slipped out and began swimming freely in the black water, looking for some supper.

Suddenly he felt a sharp nip in his tail, and turning swiftly he saw the bewhiskered face of a large tiger-fish. He was just about to give himself up for lost when a huge dark object passed overhead. It was a canoe, although the fish did not know this, and it disturbed the water so much that he was able to streak away from the tiger-fish and hide in the mud.

"Alas!" he said to himself. "Why did I come to thi terrible place? If only I could get back to my own little pool, I would never grumble again."

At last he determined to find the point where h had first entered the river, and then make his way back to the pool before the last of the flood-water receded.

He wriggled slowly along the muddy bottom of the river, until he recognized the spot where he had first arrived. Then with a leap he was out of th river and into the large expanse of flood-water which was surging past him.

How he struggled as he tried to force his way against the swirling water, until at last, when his strength was almost gone, he found himself back the pool again.

There he lay panting on the bottom, too tired to move, and as he turned his eyes this way and that and saw the old familiar landmarks, he said to him self:

"If I had only known what the river was really lik I would never have left the safety of our pool."

After that the tiny fish played undisturbed wher ever they pleased, and never again did the big fis say he was too grand to live among them, even though sometimes he may have thought so!

And so we see that every man should be contented with what he has.

ll Living Things

song by W. Jay Cawley

ll living things need the air to breathe,
eed the sky up above, the earth beneath their
feet.
or the fishes in the ocean and the birds that sing,
his word is the home of living things.

ll living things need the warm sunshine,
eed the cool summer breeze, that blows on down
the line.
or the apples in the orchards and the flowers in
the spring,
his world is the home of living things.

we clear away the forest,
trip the land, spoil the sea,
Vhat will there be left for us to love
ı this world of living things?

ll living things need to have a home,
Jeed a place to rest their heads, a purpose of their
own.
Ve must live together so let us dance and sing,
his world is the home of living things.

▶ Continue reading here.

Officer Buckle and Gloria • PRACTICE

Name____________________ Date________ **Practice 211**

Digraphs *ph, tch, ch*

Read the following words.

phone	wa**tch**	spee**ch**

Circle the word that answers each clue. Then write the word.

1. This is something you talk into.
   chair (telephone) watch
   telephone
2. This means to shout for joy.
   (cheer) children match
   cheer
3. This is something you can sit on.
   (chair) speeches catch
   chair
4. This is a talk given to a group.
   telephone checked (speech)
   speech
5. This is what you do at the movies.
   latch chicken (watch)
   watch
6. This is what you get with a camera.
   phone (photo) bench
   photo
7. This is when you grab something.
   (catch) cheered watch
   catch
8. This is a very large animal.
   chicken patch (elephant)
   elephant

At Home: Have children find pictures of words that have **ch, tch,** or **ph** in them.

Name____________________ Date________ **Practice 212**

Vocabulary

Choose a word from the box to complete each sentence. Write the words on the lines. Each word is used twice.

accidents	**audience**	**cheered**	**slips**	**station**	**wipe**

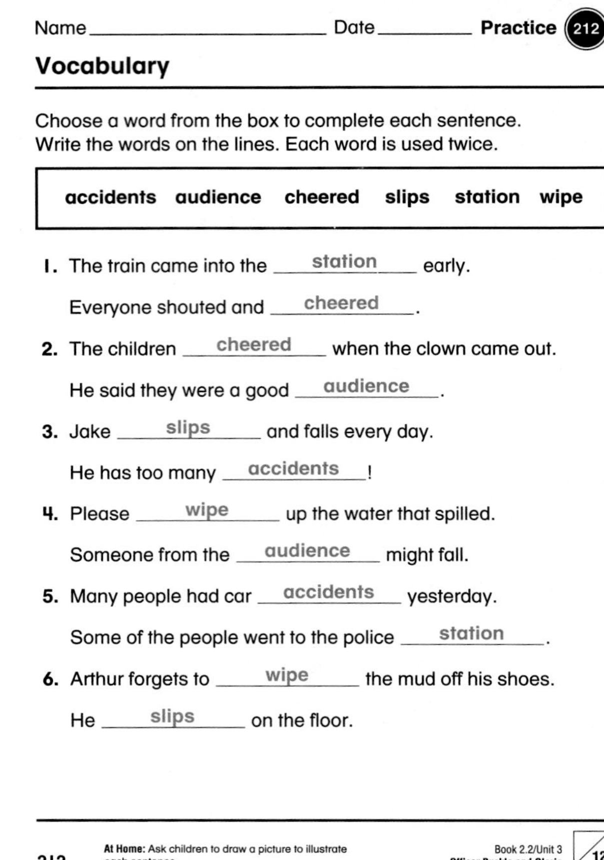

1. The train came into the __station__ early.
   Everyone shouted and __cheered__.
2. The children __cheered__ when the clown came out.
   He said they were a good __audience__.
3. Jake __slips__ and falls every day.
   He has too many __accidents__!
4. Please __wipe__ up the water that spilled.
   Someone from the __audience__ might fall.
5. Many people had car __accidents__ yesterday.
   Some of the people went to the police __station__.
6. Arthur forgets to __wipe__ the mud off his shoes.
   He __slips__ on the floor.

At Home: Ask children to draw a picture to illustrate each sentence.

Chad and the Horses

Chad's father phoned the vet. Then they all saw why the horse fell. There was water on the floor.
Mark said, "I spilled water. I forgot to wipe it up. I'm sorry."
Luckily the horse was fine. Everyone forgave Mark. From that day on he tried not to rush the horses.

At Home: Review with the children how the animals in this story danced for work. What are some other animals that work? What do they do?

Chad's father had beautiful horses. Every summer, the horses would perform in shows. The audience loved the shows.
Chad liked it when the children cheered for the horses. He also loved the speeches his father would make.
Chad and his brother Mark helped their father by bringing the horses water.

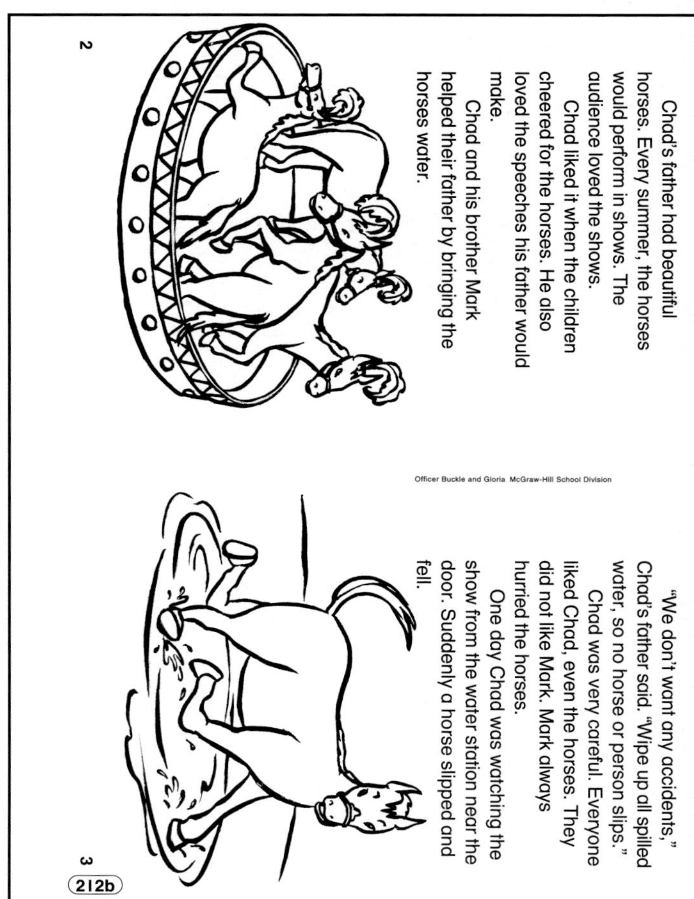

"We don't want any accidents," Chad's father said. "Wipe up all spilled water, so no horse or person slips."
Chad was very careful. Everyone liked Chad, even the horses. They did not like Mark. Mark always hurried the horses.
One day Chad was watching the show from the water station near the door. Suddenly a horse slipped and fell.

Officer Buckle and Gloria • PRACTICE

Name ______________ Date ________ **Practice 213**

Story Comprehension

Answer each question about "Officer Buckle and Gloria."

1. In Napville, who knew more safety tips than anyone else?

   Officer Buckle

2. What was one of Officer Buckle's safety tips?

   Answers may vary. Never stand on a swivel chair; keep your shoelaces tied.

3. What did Gloria do while Officer Buckle gave speeches?

   She did tricks.

4. What did Officer Buckle think Gloria was doing while he was making speeches?

   He thought she was sitting at attention.

5. How did Officer Buckle find out what Gloria was doing?

   Officer Buckle found out about Gloria by watching himself on TV.

6. What was Officer Buckle's best safety tip?

   Always stick with your buddy.

At Home: Have children tell which trick of Gloria's was their favorite.

Name ______________ Date ________ **Practice 214**

Do a Subject Search at the Library

When writing a report or looking for information, a computer **subject search** will give you a number of books to choose from.

Search of South Millford Library System

Search: Pumpkins

Items Found = 28

☒ First Ten ☐ Second Ten ☐ Third Ten

1. Title: *The Greatest Pumpkin Ever* Fiction — ■ See Full Record
   Author: Hemsley Yorborough — Pub. Date: ©1994
2. Title: *Pumpkin Pie Baking* — ■ See Full Record
   Author: Nancy Edlands — Pub Date: ©1999
3. Title: *Grow the Big Ones* — ■ See Full Record
   Author: Ray Moncliff — Pub. Date: ©1979
4. Title: *Pumping Iron for More Muscle* — ■ See Full Record
   Author: Quincy Cummings — Pub. Date: ©1989 Video recording

Use the results of the subject search shown above to answer the questions.

1. Which book would help you with baking a pumpkin pie?

   Pumpkin Pie Baking

2. Which book would help you with producing large pumpkins in your garden? Grow the Big Ones

3. Which book is fiction, or a made-up story? The Greatest Pumpkin Ever

4. Which book looks like it has nothing to do with pumpkins? (Hint: sometimes the computer confuses words that look alike. Pumpkin could be seen by the computer as Pump or kin.)

   Pumping Iron for More Muscle

At Home: Ask the children which of the books listed above was published most recently.

Name ______________ Date ________ **Practice 215**

Digraphs *ph, tch, ch*

Complete the sentences.

cheered	chair	phone	watched	children
speech	photograph	match	elephant	hatch

1. The children love to play games.
2. Brian gave a speech to the class about jokes.
3. The team cheered when they won the game.
4. Betsy used the phone to call her mother.
5. Ricky watched the bird fly from the tree.
6. Tom sat in the chair.
7. The huge elephant walked to the pond.
8. It was exciting to see the chick hatch.
9. Sally tried to find the match for her shoe.
10. I took a photograph of my brother.

At Home: Ask children to make a chart of words with **ch, tch,** and **ph.** Then encourage them to write a sentence that uses two of these words.

Name ______________ Date ________ **Practice 216**

Digraphs *ph, tch, ch*

Use the words in the box to answer the riddles.
Write the answers on the lines.

telephone	child	stitch	photos	watch
chair	rich	chase	scratch	patch

1. I tell you the time. What am I? watch
2. I ring and you pick me up. What am I? telephone
3. You can sit in me. What am I? chair
4. You make me with a needle and thread. What am I? stitch
5. I have not grown up yet. What am I? child

Choose a word from the box above to complete the following sentences.

6. Lindsey took photos on her trip.
7. You can patch your jeans if they rip.
8. The dog likes to chase the cat up a tree.
9. I have a lot of money. I am rich.
10. Don't scratch yourself on the sharp thorns.

At Home: Have children write a riddle for the word **cheese.**

Name________________________ Date__________ **Practice 217**

Form Generalizations

Read the story about Spike and Ike. Then answer the questions that follow.

Spike is Ryan's dog. Ike is his cat. Spike chased Ike up a tree. Spike chased a squirrel up the tree, too. Ryan had to get Ike down. Ryan put Spike on a leash after he chased the mail carrier. But that didn't stop Spike. He barked at the birds and tried to chase them into the next yard.

What are the facts?

Spike chased **Ike up a tree.**

Spike chased **a squirrel up a tree.**

Spike chased **the mail carrier.**

Spike chased **birds out of his yard.**

Write a generalization about Spike.

Spike likes to chase things.

At Home: Have children think about the actions of other pets, such as cats, birds, or hamsters. Have them make a generalization about one animal's behavior.

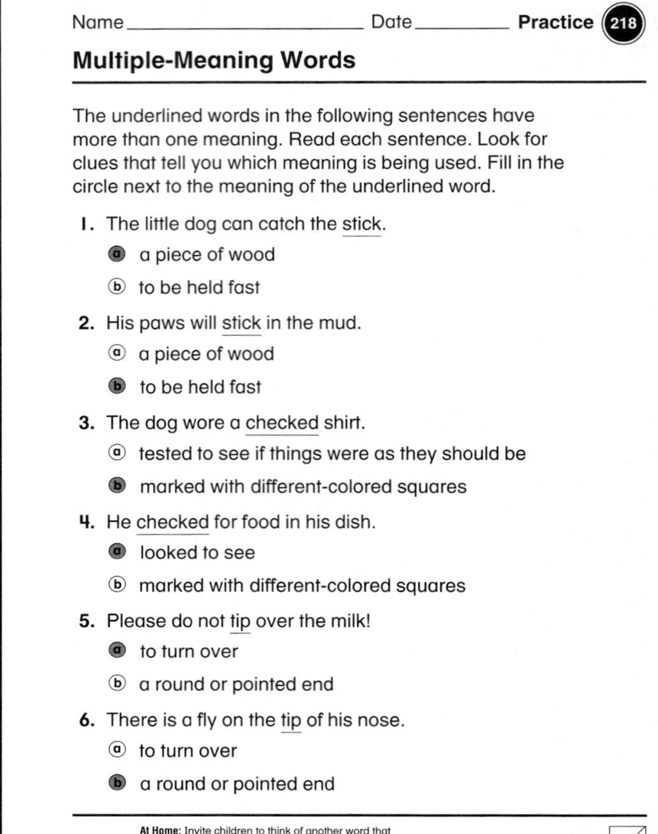

Name________________________ Date__________ **Practice 218**

Multiple-Meaning Words

The underlined words in the following sentences have more than one meaning. Read each sentence. Look for clues that tell you which meaning is being used. Fill in the circle next to the meaning of the underlined word.

1. The little dog can catch the stick.
   - ● a piece of wood
   - ⓑ to be held fast
2. His paws will stick in the mud.
   - ⓐ a piece of wood
   - ● to be held fast
3. The dog wore a checked shirt.
   - ⓐ tested to see if things were as they should be
   - ● marked with different-colored squares
4. He checked for food in his dish.
   - ● looked to see
   - ⓑ marked with different-colored squares
5. Please do not tip over the milk!
   - ● to turn over
   - ⓑ a round or pointed end
6. There is a fly on the tip of his nose.
   - ⓐ to turn over
   - ● a round or pointed end

At Home: Invite children to think of another word that has two meanings. Have them use each meaning in a sentence.

Officer Buckle and Gloria • RETEACH

Name______________________ Date__________ **Reteach 211**

Digraphs *ph, tch, ch*

Say these words. Listen for each sound made by the letters in dark type.

check pa**tch** ele**ph**ant

Circle the word that names each picture. Color each picture that contains the letters **ph, ch,** or **tch**.

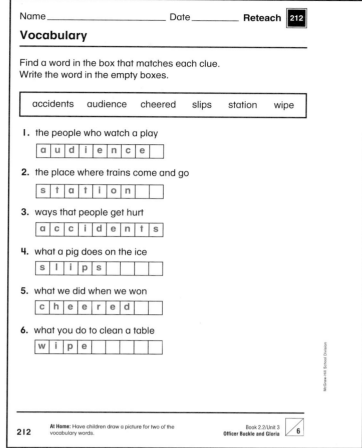

1. (chair) house
2. (seal) cat
3. (phone) car
4. goose (pitcher)
5. (boat) bus
6. (watch) head

At Home: Ask children to say the words for the pictures they colored.

Name______________________ Date__________ **Reteach 212**

Vocabulary

Find a word in the box that matches each clue.
Write the word in the empty boxes.

accidents	audience	cheered	slips	station	wipe

1. the people who watch a play
   audience
2. the place where trains come and go
   station
3. ways that people get hurt
   accidents
4. what a pig does on the ice
   slips
5. what we did when we won
   cheered
6. what you do to clean a table
   wipe

At Home: Have children draw a picture for two of the vocabulary words.

Name______________________ Date__________ **Reteach 213**

Story Comprehension

Write **T** if the statement is true about "Officer Buckle and Gloria."
Write **F** if the statement is false about the story.

F 1. Officer Buckle is a pilot.

T 2. Gloria is a dog.

T 3. Officer Buckle is a policeman.

T 4. This story is about safety.

T 5. Gloria was a talented dog.

T 6. Officer Buckle and Gloria gave speeches about safety.

F 7. The children did not like Gloria.

T 8. Gloria made the speeches exciting.

T 9. Gloria and Officer Buckle needed one another.

F 10. Gloria got her own TV show.

At Home: Have children describe two other events that took place in the story.

Name______________________ Date__________ **Reteach 214**

Do a Subject Search at the Library

You can search for books on a computer by typing in the **title**, the **author**, or the **subject**.

For each of the following searches, choose the subject that you would type in to find books. Try to keep the subject simple—two or three words. **Answers will vary.**

Search #1 — Subject

You need a magic trick for show and tell. It has to be simple. What would you write in the search box? **simple magic trick**

Search #2 — Subject

You need to find out how a bridge is built. What would you write in the search box? **bridge building**

Search #3 — Subject

You want to learn how to become a clown. What would you write in the search box? **clown school**

Search #4 — Subject

You want a book about apples—how they're grown. **apple growing**

At Home: Bring children to the library and help them to research a topic of their choice using a computer.

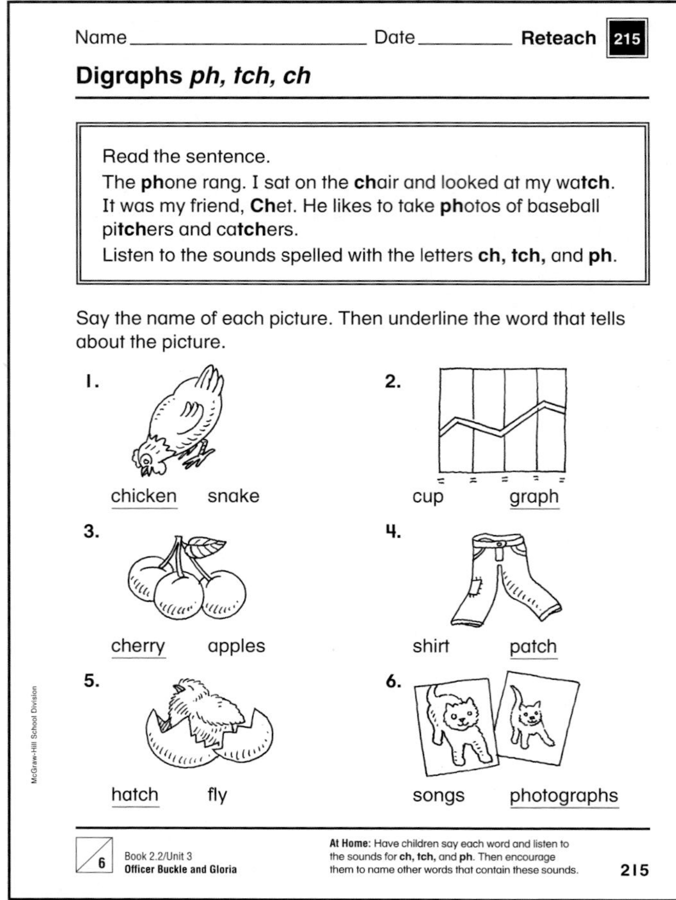

Name____________________ Date_________ **Reteach 215**

Digraphs *ph, tch, ch*

Read the sentence.
The **ph**one rang. I sat on the **ch**air and looked at my wa**tch**. It was my friend, **Ch**et. He likes to take **ph**otos of baseball pi**tch**ers and ca**tch**ers.
Listen to the sounds spelled with the letters **ch, tch,** and **ph**.

Say the name of each picture. Then underline the word that tells about the picture.

1. chicken snake
2. cup graph
3. cherry apples
4. shirt patch
5. hatch fly
6. songs photographs

McGraw-Hill School Division

6 Book 2.2/Unit 3 **Officer Buckle and Gloria**

At Home: Have children say each word and listen to the sounds for **ch, tch,** and **ph**. Then encourage them to name other words that contain these sounds.

215

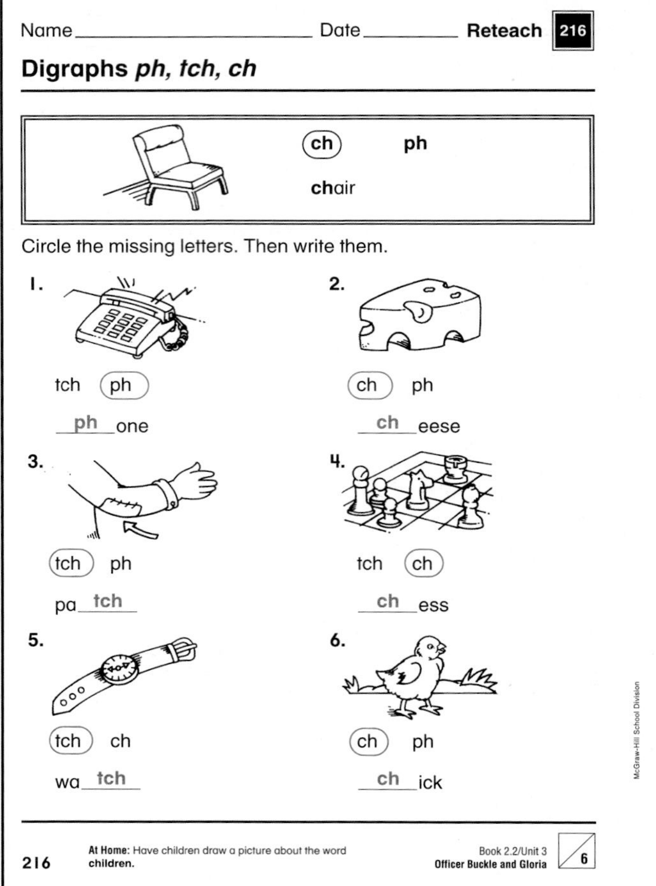

Name____________________ Date_________ **Reteach 216**

Digraphs *ph, tch, ch*

(ch) ph
chair

Circle the missing letters. Then write them.

1. tch (ph) — ph one
2. (ch) ph — ch eese
3. (tch) ph — pa tch
4. tch (ch) — ch ess
5. (tch) ch — wa tch
6. (ch) ph — ch ick

McGraw-Hill School Division

216

At Home: Have children draw a picture about the word **children.**

Book 2.2/Unit 3 **Officer Buckle and Gloria** 6

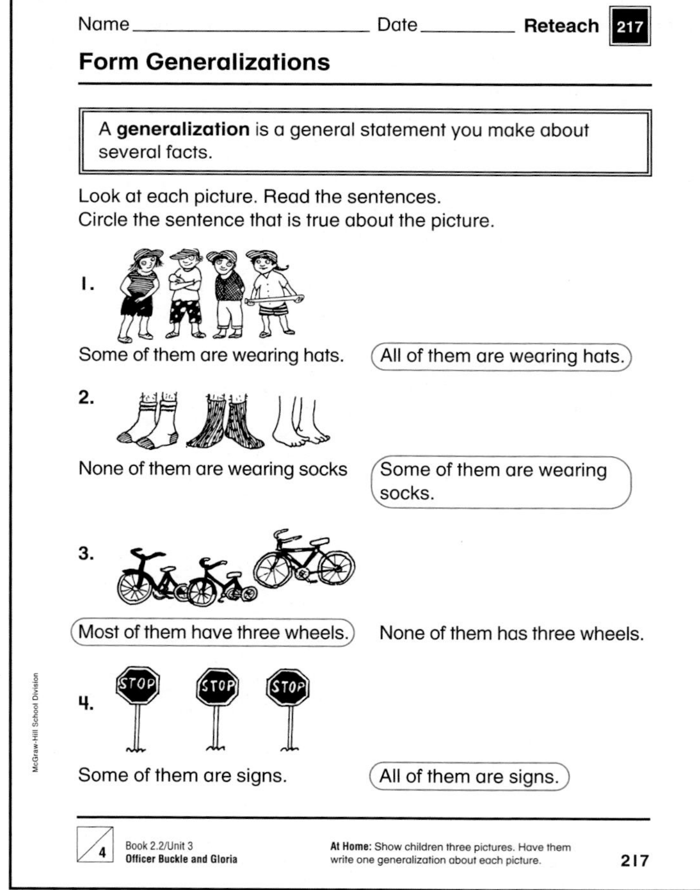

Name____________________ Date_________ **Reteach 217**

Form Generalizations

A **generalization** is a general statement you make about several facts.

Look at each picture. Read the sentences.
Circle the sentence that is true about the picture.

1. Some of them are wearing hats. (All of them are wearing hats.)
2. None of them are wearing socks (Some of them are wearing socks.)
3. (Most of them have three wheels.) None of them has three wheels.
4. Some of them are signs. (All of them are signs.)

McGraw-Hill School Division

4 Book 2.2/Unit 3 **Officer Buckle and Gloria**

At Home: Show children three pictures. Have them write one generalization about each picture.

217

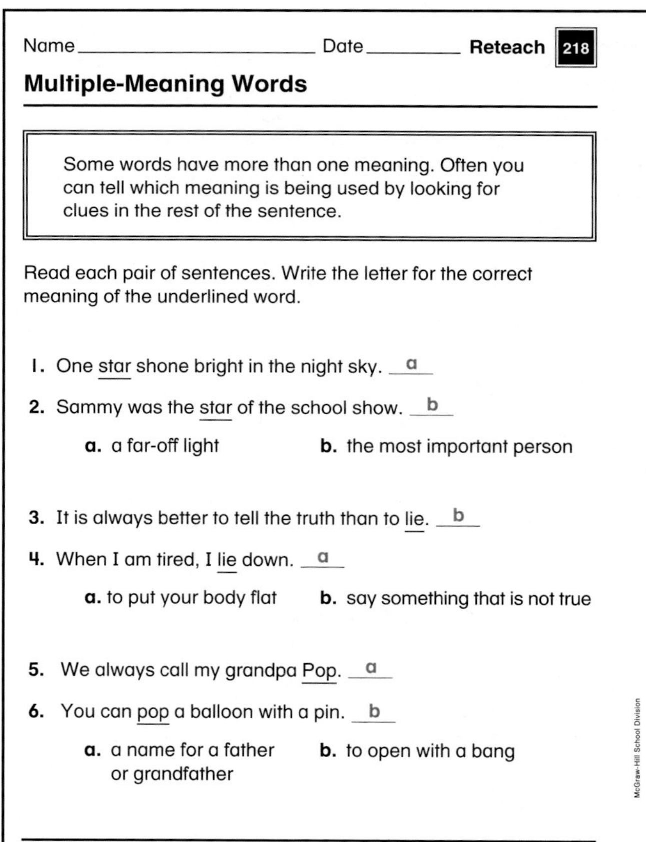

Name____________________ Date_________ **Reteach 218**

Multiple-Meaning Words

Some words have more than one meaning. Often you can tell which meaning is being used by looking for clues in the rest of the sentence.

Read each pair of sentences. Write the letter for the correct meaning of the underlined word.

1. One star shone bright in the night sky. a
2. Sammy was the star of the school show. b

a. a far-off light **b.** the most important person

3. It is always better to tell the truth than to lie. b
4. When I am tired, I lie down. a

a. to put your body flat **b.** say something that is not true

5. We always call my grandpa Pop. a
6. You can pop a balloon with a pin. b

a. a name for a father or grandfather **b.** to open with a bang

McGraw-Hill School Division

218

At Home: Challenge children to think up two meanings for the word **check.**

Book 2.2/Unit 3 **Officer Buckle and Gloria** 6

Name________________ Date________ Extend 211

Digraphs *ph, tch, ch*

The elephant follows words that have the same sound of **f** as in **phone.** Use green to color the elephant's path to the finish line.

The chicken follows words that have the same ending sound as **catch.** Use yellow to color the chicken's path to the finish line.

graph photo phase fetch match phantom elephant telephone alphabet catch pitch ditch itch watch FINISH!

Write a sentence to tell what happens when the elephant and the chicken finish the race.

____

____

The path from the elephant to the finish line should have the following words: graph, photo, phase, telephone, alphabet, phantom, elephant. The path from the chicken to the finish line should have the following words: watch, hitch, ditch, fetch, match, catch, pitch.

At Home: Have children make up rhymes using words that contain **ch**, **ph**, and **tch**.

Name________________ Date________ Extend 212

Vocabulary

Write a word from the box in each sentence.

audience	accidents	slips	station	wipe	cheered

1. People get hurt in ___accidents___.
2. The show had a big ___audience___.
3. The fans ___cheered___ at the big game.
4. Sometimes Joel ___slips___ on icy sidewalks.
5. A police building is called a ___station___ house.
6. If you ___wipe___ up the spill, no one will slip and fall.

Choose two words from the box. Use them in your own sentences.

____

____

____

____

At Home: Have children draw a picture and write two sentences illustrating one of the vocabulary words.

Name________________ Date________ Extend 213

Story Comprehension

What makes Gloria a good partner for Officer Buckle? Write a sentence.

Officer Buckle is very serious. Gloria is funny and entertains the children.

What if your favorite animal was Officer Buckle's partner? Write two sentences that tell what might happen.

Answers will vary.

____

Draw a picture showing Officer Buckle and your favorite animal.

At Home: Have children make up a safety rule and place it on a poster that they illustrate.

Name________________ Date________ Extend 214

Do a Subject Search at the Library

Officer Buckle is at the library to learn more about Gloria.

Look at his list. Help Officer Buckle think of subjects he can search for to get more information. Check ✔ the subjects on his list he can use. Cross out **X** the subjects on his list that won't work. Add new subjects to his list on the lines at the right.

Column 1	Column 2
✔ animal training	dog tricks
X wolves	pets
X zoos	pet training
✔ dogs	police dogs
X kittens	

Enter the name, title words, or subject words you want.

Dog Tricks

What will Officer Buckle see on the screen after he presses **enter?**

He will see a new screen that tells him the author, title, call number and format, and date of anything the library has on the subject of dog tricks.

At Home: Children can select a subject, then write directions on how to search for it at the library. Encourage them to use sequencing words: **first, next, then, last.**

Name____________________ Date________ **Extend 215**

Digraphs *ph, tch, ch*

Finish the words. Write **tch, ch,** or **ph** on each of the lines.

1. ph ones
2. spee ch
3. ma tch
4. ph oto
5. ch ildren
6. wa tch ed
7. ch ecked
8. tele ph one
9. ch eered
10. por ch

Write a story. Use at least five words from the list above. Draw a picture to go with your story on another sheet of paper.

Stories should use at least five words from the list.

At Home: Have children make a card for each of the ten words. Have them sort the words into groups by **tch, ch,** or **ph.**

Name____________________ Date________ **Extend 216**

Digraphs *ph, tch, ch*

Find the words hidden in the puzzle. The words may read across or up and down.

PHONE	**CHAIR**	**CHEER**
CHILDREN	**ELEPHANT**	**CHICKEN**
CHEESE	**WATCH**	**SPEECH**

A	K	C	D	H	F	G	H	Z	J	K	O	M	P
N	L	P	Q	G	S	T	A	V	W	A	T	C	H
S	P	E	E	C	H	C	H	I	C	K	E	N	O
X	Y	Z	A	H	B	C	H	I	L	D	R	E	N
D	E	E	L	E	P	H	A	N	T	F	G	H	E
I	J	K	L	E	M	A	N	O	P	Q	R	S	T
U	V	W	X	S	Y	I	Z	A	B	C	D	E	F
G	H	C	H	E	E	R	I	J	K	O	M	N	R

Write two silly sentences. Use the words you found in the puzzle.

Sentences will vary. Check that students used words from the puzzle.

At Home: Have children create their own word search puzzles using *ph, tch,* and *ch* words.

Name____________________ Date________ **Extend 217**

Form Generalizations

A **generalization** is a general statement you make about several facts. Read the story. Then read the sentences below the story. Write YES next to each sentence that is a fact from the story. Write NO if the sentence is not a fact from the story.

My dog Daisy knows a lot of tricks. She can sit, lie down, and roll over. She chases cats, but she never catches them. In the summer she likes to jump in the pool. She knows that the water will cool her. In the winter she curls up near the fireplace to stay warm. She is a great pet.

1. Daisy is a dog. No
2. She chases cats. Yes
3. She gets cold in the summer. No
4. In the winter we light a fire in the fireplace. Yes
5. I'm proud of my dog. No

Circle the sentence that is a generalization.

Daisy is a good pet for her owner. (circled)

Daisy can roll over.

At Home: Ask children to describe an animal they know. Have them write a statement about this animal that is true or nearly always true.

Name____________________ Date________ **Extend 218**

Multiple-Meaning Words

Use a word from the box to take the place of the underlined words in the sentences.

watch	**checks**	**tips**	**slip**	**fall**

1. Officer Buckle is making a speech about safety hints. tips
2. He looks at the time on a small clock that he wears on his wrist. watch
3. He looks checks to see if his dog is ready to go.
4. The officer tells people to always wipe up spills before other people lose their balance slip and drop to the ground. fall

Now use a word from the box to answer these riddles.

1. When you look at someone, you also watch them.
2. I am a pattern of squares of different colors. I am called checks.
3. People who serve food sometimes get tips as a thank you.
4. I am a small piece of paper, or a slip.
5. I am known as autumn and also as fall.

At Home: Have children draw pictures showing both meanings of **coast.** Ask them to write sentences explaining their pictures.

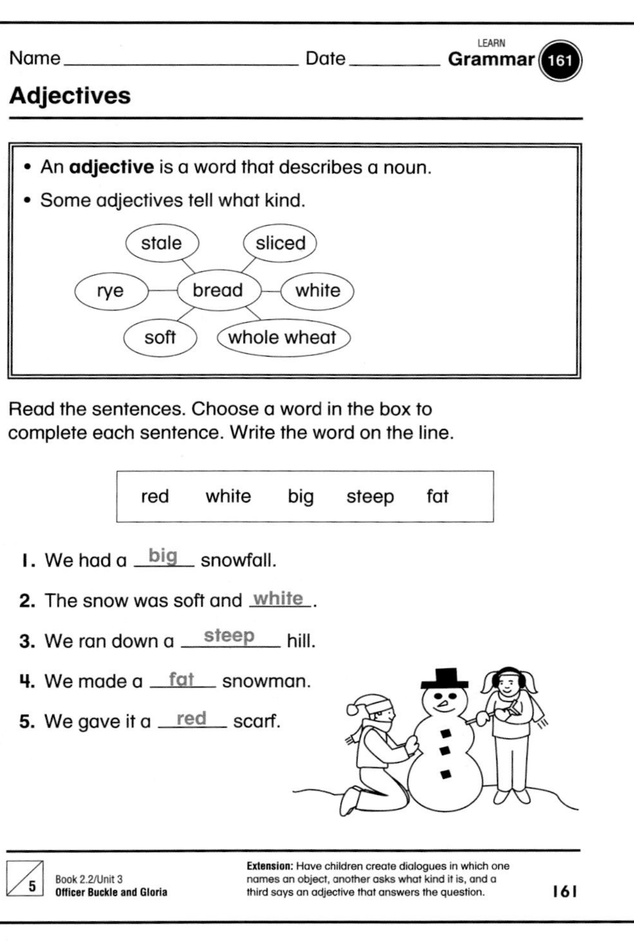

Name______________________ Date________ LEARN Grammar 161

Adjectives

- An **adjective** is a word that describes a noun.
- Some adjectives tell what kind.

Read the sentences. Choose a word in the box to complete each sentence. Write the word on the line.

red	white	big	steep	fat

1. We had a __big__ snowfall.
2. The snow was soft and __white__.
3. We ran down a __steep__ hill.
4. We made a __fat__ snowman.
5. We gave it a __red__ scarf.

5 Book 2.2/Unit 3 **Officer Buckle and Gloria**

Extension: Have children create dialogues in which one names an object, another asks what kind it is, and a third says an adjective that answers the question.

161

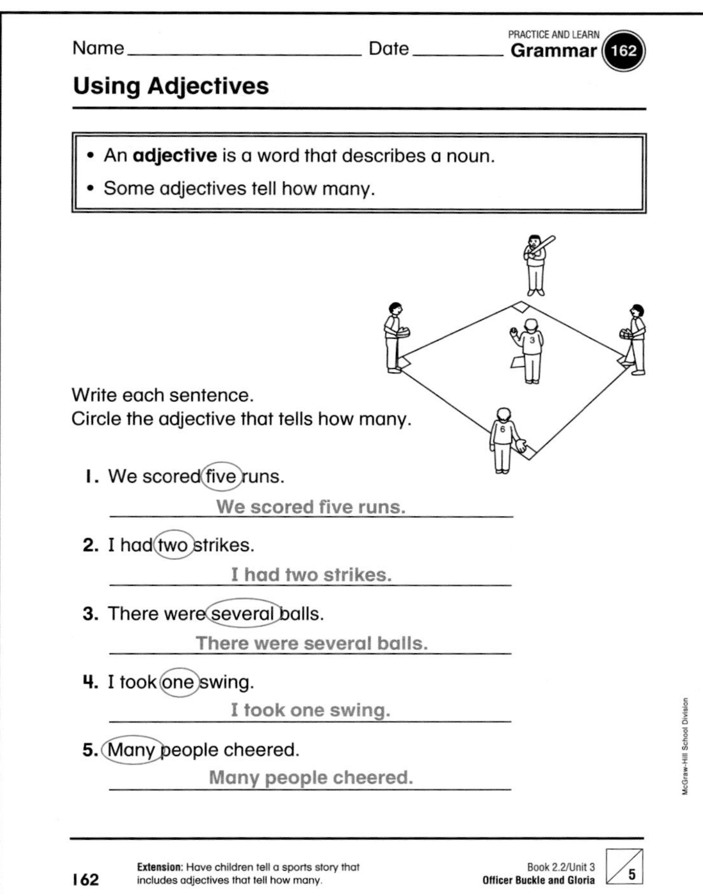

Name______________________ Date________ PRACTICE AND LEARN Grammar 162

Using Adjectives

- An **adjective** is a word that describes a noun.
- Some adjectives tell how many.

Write each sentence.
Circle the adjective that tells how many.

1. We scored (five) runs.
   We scored five runs.
2. I had (two) strikes.
   I had two strikes.
3. There were (several) balls.
   There were several balls.
4. I took (one) swing.
   I took one swing.
5. (Many) people cheered.
   Many people cheered.

162 **Extension:** Have children tell a sports story that includes adjectives that tell how many.

Book 2.2/Unit 3 **Officer Buckle and Gloria** 5

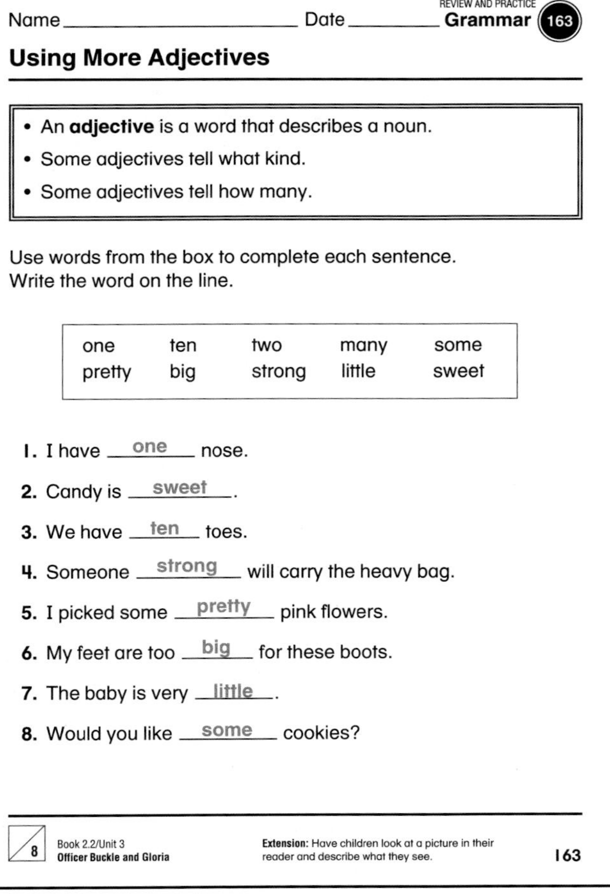

Name______________________ Date________ REVIEW AND PRACTICE Grammar 163

Using More Adjectives

- An **adjective** is a word that describes a noun.
- Some adjectives tell what kind.
- Some adjectives tell how many.

Use words from the box to complete each sentence.
Write the word on the line.

one	ten	two	many	some
pretty	big	strong	little	sweet

1. I have __one__ nose.
2. Candy is __sweet__.
3. We have __ten__ toes.
4. Someone __strong__ will carry the heavy bag.
5. I picked some __pretty__ pink flowers.
6. My feet are too __big__ for these boots.
7. The baby is very __little__.
8. Would you like __some__ cookies?

8 Book 2.2/Unit 3 **Officer Buckle and Gloria**

Extension: Have children look at a picture in their reader and describe what they see.

163

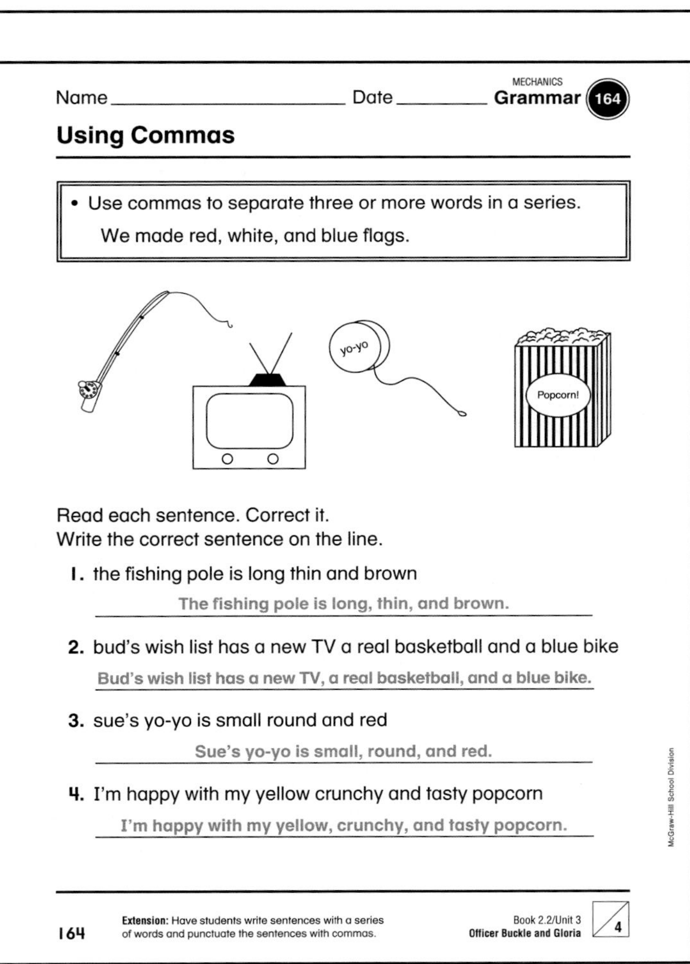

Name______________________ Date________ MECHANICS Grammar 164

Using Commas

- Use commas to separate three or more words in a series.
  We made red, white, and blue flags.

Read each sentence. Correct it.
Write the correct sentence on the line.

1. the fishing pole is long thin and brown
   The fishing pole is long, thin, and brown.
2. bud's wish list has a new TV a real basketball and a blue bike
   Bud's wish list has a new TV, a real basketball, and a blue bike.
3. sue's yo-yo is small round and red
   Sue's yo-yo is small, round, and red.
4. I'm happy with my yellow crunchy and tasty popcorn
   I'm happy with my yellow, crunchy, and tasty popcorn.

164 **Extension:** Have students write sentences with a series of words and punctuate the sentences with commas.

Book 2.2/Unit 3 **Officer Buckle and Gloria** 4

Name ____________ Date ________ TEST **Grammar 165**

Adjectives

A. Circle the adjective in each sentence.

1. Jill took a (long) walk.

2. She passed an (old) house.

3. She saw a (new) mall.

4. She saw a (cute) baby.

B. Find the adjective in each sentence. Write it on the line.

5. Let's go to a faraway place. faraway

6. We can see little bugs. little

7. We can hear strange music. strange

8. We can feel soft winds. soft

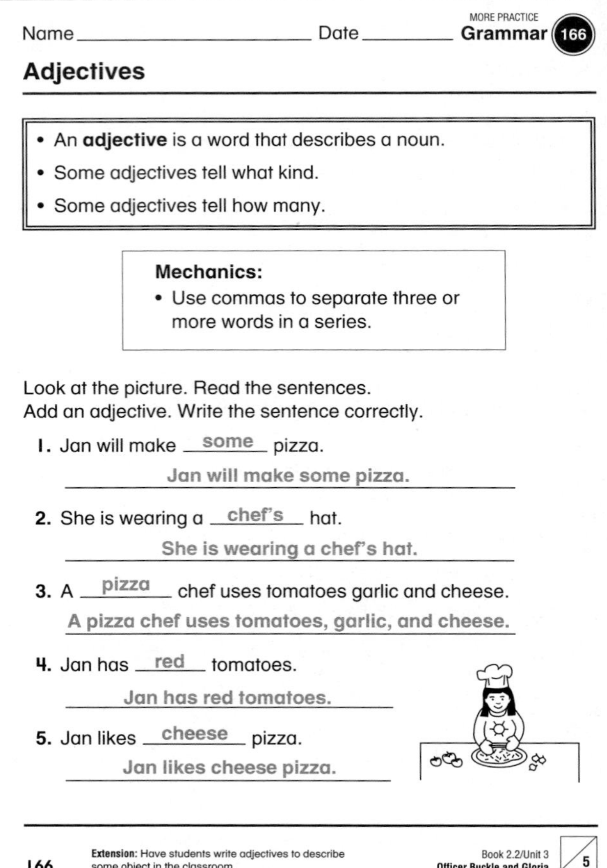

Name ____________ Date ________ MORE PRACTICE **Grammar 166**

Adjectives

- An **adjective** is a word that describes a noun.
- Some adjectives tell what kind.
- Some adjectives tell how many.

Mechanics:
- Use commas to separate three or more words in a series.

Look at the picture. Read the sentences. Add an adjective. Write the sentence correctly.

1. Jan will make some pizza.
Jan will make some pizza.

2. She is wearing a chef's hat.
She is wearing a chef's hat.

3. A pizza chef uses tomatoes garlic and cheese.
A pizza chef uses tomatoes, garlic, and cheese.

4. Jan has red tomatoes.
Jan has red tomatoes.

5. Jan likes cheese pizza.
Jan likes cheese pizza.

 Extension: Have students write adjectives to describe some object in the classroom.

Officer Buckle and Gloria • SPELLING

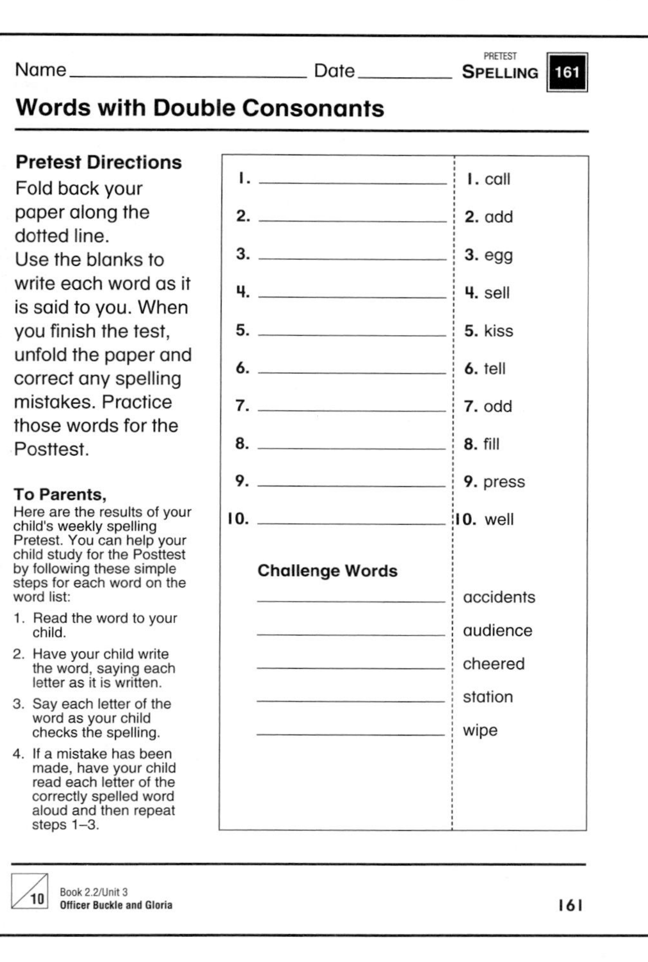

Name ____________________ Date __________ PRETEST SPELLING **161**

Words with Double Consonants

Pretest Directions

Fold back your paper along the dotted line. Use the blanks to write each word as it is said to you. When you finish the test, unfold the paper and correct any spelling mistakes. Practice those words for the Posttest.

To Parents,

Here are the results of your child's weekly spelling Pretest. You can help your child study for the Posttest by following these simple steps for each word on the word list:

1. Read the word to your child.
2. Have your child write the word, saying each letter as it is written.
3. Say each letter of the word as your child checks the spelling.
4. If a mistake has been made, have your child read each letter of the correctly spelled word aloud and then repeat steps 1–3.

1. ________	1. call
2. ________	2. add
3. ________	3. egg
4. ________	4. sell
5. ________	5. kiss
6. ________	6. tell
7. ________	7. odd
8. ________	8. fill
9. ________	9. press
10. ________	10. well

Challenge Words

________	accidents
________	audience
________	cheered
________	station
________	wipe

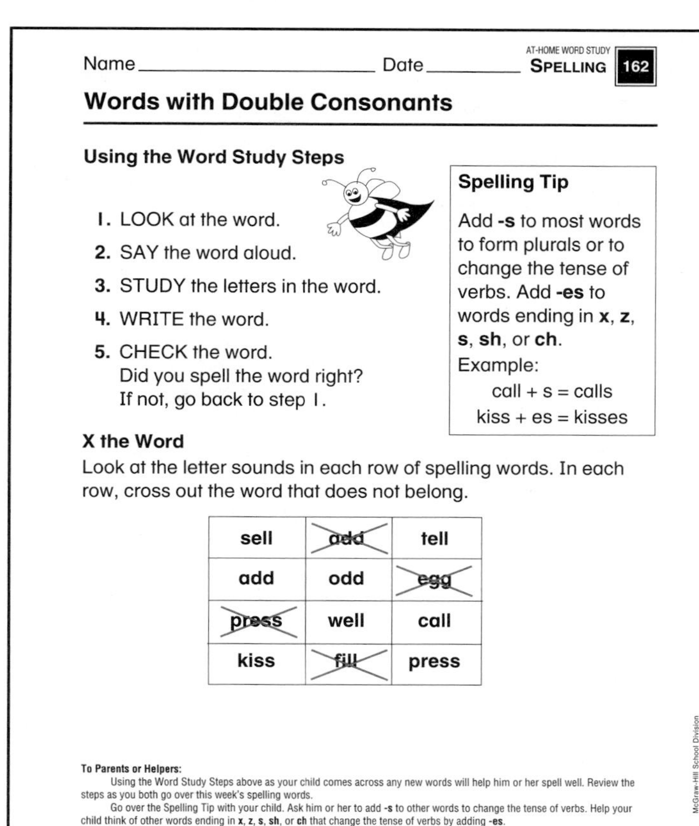

Name ____________________ Date __________ AT-HOME WORD STUDY SPELLING **162**

Words with Double Consonants

Using the Word Study Steps

1. LOOK at the word.
2. SAY the word aloud.
3. STUDY the letters in the word.
4. WRITE the word.
5. CHECK the word. Did you spell the word right? If not, go back to step 1.

Spelling Tip

Add **-s** to most words to form plurals or to change the tense of verbs. Add **-es** to words ending in **x**, **z**, **s**, **sh**, or **ch**.

Example:

call + s = calls

kiss + es = kisses

X the Word

Look at the letter sounds in each row of spelling words. In each row, cross out the word that does not belong.

sell	~~add~~	tell
add	odd	~~egg~~
~~press~~	well	call
kiss	~~fill~~	press

To Parents or Helpers:

Using the Word Study Steps above as your child comes across any new words will help him or her spell well. Review the steps as you both go over this week's spelling words.

Go over the Spelling Tip with your child. Ask him or her to add **-s** to other words to change the tense of verbs. Help your child think of other words ending in **x**, **z**, **s**, **sh**, or **ch** that change the tense of verbs by adding **-es**.

Help your child cross out the word that does not belong.

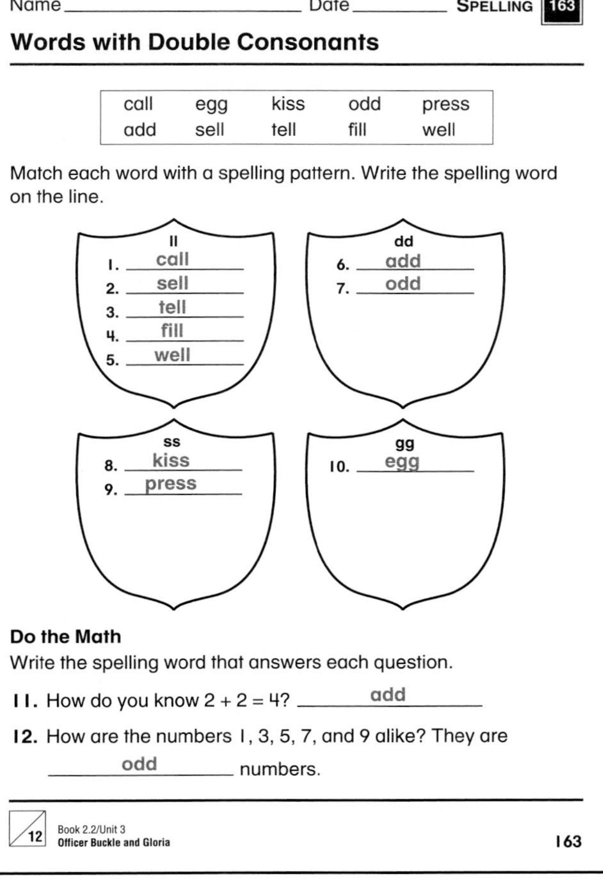

Name ____________________ Date __________ EXPLORE THE PATTERN SPELLING **163**

Words with Double Consonants

call	egg	kiss	odd	press
add	sell	tell	fill	well

Match each word with a spelling pattern. Write the spelling word on the line.

ll
1. call
2. sell
3. tell
4. fill
5. well

dd
6. add
7. odd

ss
8. kiss
9. press

gg
10. egg

Do the Math

Write the spelling word that answers each question.

11. How do you know 2 + 2 = 4? ___add___
12. How are the numbers 1, 3, 5, 7, and 9 alike? They are ___odd___ numbers.

Name ____________________ Date __________ PRACTICE AND EXTEND SPELLING **164**

Words with Double Consonants

call	egg	kiss	odd	press
add	sell	tell	fill	well

Not the Same

In the space beside each word, write the spelling word that means the opposite.

1. buy ___sell___
2. even ___odd___
3. empty ___fill___
4. subtract ___add___

Again, please!

The prefix **re-** means **again**.

re + fill = refill

Refill means **to fill again**.

Add **re-** to these spelling words to make new words.

5. re + tell = ___retell___
6. re + call = ___recall___

Use spelling words to finish this phone message.

Hi. It's Amy. Can you ___call___ me on the phone later? Please ___tell___ me what time the play starts. I need to ___press___ my pants before I go. ___Well___, I'll see you soon.

Challenge Extension: Have students draw pictures to illustrate each word. They may exchange pictures with a partner to guess the illustrations.

Name______________ Date__________ PROOFREAD AND WRITE SPELLING 165

Words with Double Consonants

Proofreading Activity

There are five spelling mistakes in the poem below. Circle each misspelled word. Write the words correctly on the lines below.

I will not say, I cannot (tel,)
What I wished at the wishing (weell.)

1. tell 2. well

I push and (pres) but it's a mess.
The cookie mix is not a success.

3. press

I add an (eg) and hope for the best.
I'll eat a few and (selll) the rest.

4. egg 5. sell

Writing Activity

Imagine that you have an unusual pet. Write sentences about your pet. Use five spelling words in your sentences. Circle the spelling words you use.

____
____
____
____
____

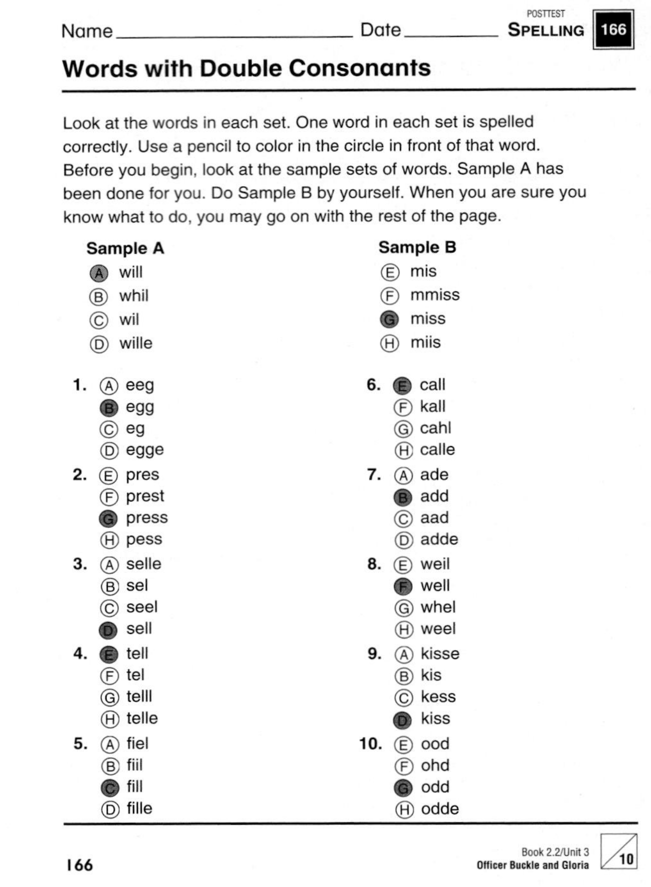

Name______________ Date__________ POSTTEST SPELLING 166

Words with Double Consonants

Look at the words in each set. One word in each set is spelled correctly. Use a pencil to color in the circle in front of that word. Before you begin, look at the sample sets of words. Sample A has been done for you. Do Sample B by yourself. When you are sure you know what to do, you may go on with the rest of the page.

Sample A
- **(A) will**
- (B) whil
- (C) wil
- (D) wille

Sample B
- (E) mis
- (F) mmiss
- **(G) miss**
- (H) miis

1. (A) eeg **(B) egg** (C) eg (D) egge
2. (E) pres (F) prest **(G) press** (H) pess
3. (A) selle (B) sel (C) seel **(D) sell**
4. **(E) tell** (F) tel (G) telll (H) telle
5. (A) fiel (B) fiil **(C) fill** (D) fille
6. **(E) call** (F) kall (G) cahl (H) calle
7. (A) ade **(B) add** (C) aad (D) adde
8. (E) weil **(F) well** (G) whel (H) weel
9. (A) kisse (B) kis (C) kess **(D) kiss**
10. (E) ood (F) ohd **(G) odd** (H) odde

Tomás and the Library Lady • PRACTICE

Name________________ Date________ **Practice 219**

Long *e, i*

Complete each sentence with a word from the box.

green	sweet	piece	trees
teaches	leader	climb	brightly
line	bike	fine	kite

1. The sun is shining very **brightly**.
2. The grass is **green**.
3. Ice cream is **sweet**.
4. Joe likes follow-the-**leader**.
5. Lucy loves to climb **trees**.
6. Karen **teaches** music.
7. Tim and Nora **climb** to the top.
8. Luis has a **piece** of apple.
9. Nancy drew a **line** on the paper.
10. Harold rode his **bike** to school.
11. He had to pay a **fine** for the late book.
12. They all wanted to fly the **kite**.

At Home: Have children write silly sentences using words from the box.

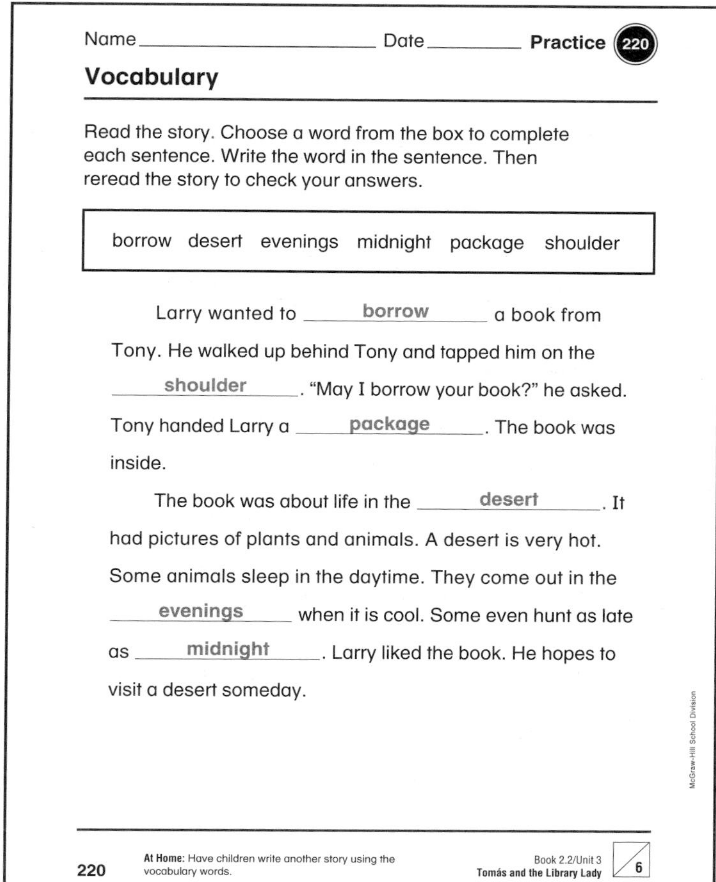

Name________________ Date________ **Practice 220**

Vocabulary

Read the story. Choose a word from the box to complete each sentence. Write the word in the sentence. Then reread the story to check your answers.

borrow	desert	evenings	midnight	package	shoulder

Larry wanted to **borrow** a book from Tony. He walked up behind Tony and tapped him on the **shoulder**. "May I borrow your book?" he asked. Tony handed Larry a **package**. The book was inside.

The book was about life in the **desert**. It had pictures of plants and animals. A desert is very hot. Some animals sleep in the daytime. They come out in the **evenings** when it is cool. Some even hunt as late as **midnight**. Larry liked the book. He hopes to visit a desert someday.

At Home: Have children write another story using the vocabulary words.

A Pet for My Pet

I asked my dad what he thought. He told me he had an idea. Then he left the hotel.

Later that night he returned with a brown package. It was about the size of my lizard. Quickly I opened the box. It was another lizard.

"I think your pet needs a pet," said Dad. I think he was right!

At Home: Have children talk about jobs or chores they have at home. What jobs would they like to have when they are older?

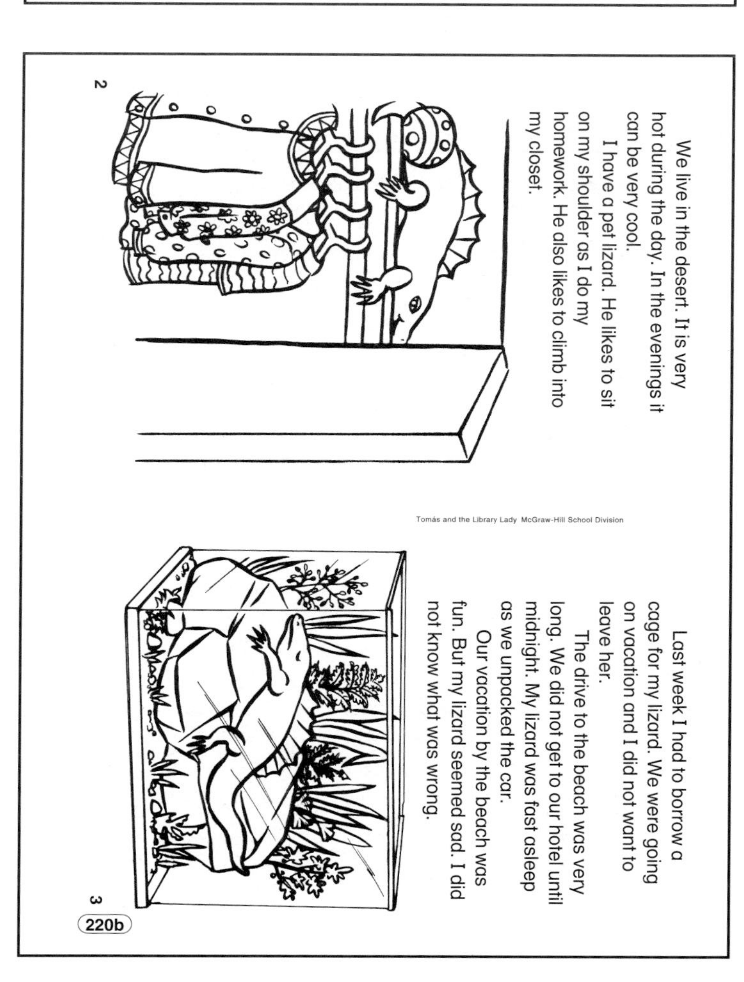

We live in the desert. It is very hot during the day. In the evenings it can be very cool.

I have a pet lizard. He likes to sit on my shoulder as I do my homework. He also likes to climb into my closet.

Last week I had to borrow a cage for my lizard. We were going on vacation and I did not want to leave her.

The drive to the beach was very long. We did not get to our hotel until midnight. My lizard was fast asleep as we unpacked the car.

Our vacation by the beach was fun. But my lizard seemed sad. I did not know what was wrong.

Name________________ Date________ **Practice 221**

Story Comprehension

Think about "Tomás and the Library Lady." Finish each sentence by writing in the correct answer from the choices below.

1. Tomás moves from Texas to Iowa.
   a. Iowa
   b. Mexico
2. Tomás's parents work in the farm fields.
   a. in the farm fields
   b. in a school
3. Papá Grande is the best storyteller in the family.
   a. cook in the family
   b. storyteller in the family
4. Tomás goes to the library to find story books.
   a. story books
   b. a teacher
5. The library lady finds many books for Tomás.
   a. books for Tomás
   b. shells for Tomás
6. Tomás teaches Spanish words to the library lady.
   a. Spanish words to the library lady
   b. other children how to read
7. When Tomás must return to Texas, he brings sweet cake to the library lady.
   a. he is afraid to go to the library
   b. he brings sweet cake to the library lady
8. The library lady gives Tomás a shiny new book.
   a. a shiny new book
   b. a box of candy

At Home: Take children to a local library and have them choose a book to read.

Name________________ Date________ **Practice 222**

Read a Library Floor Plan

A **library floor plan** is a small map of the library. The **circulation desk**, where you can check out and return books, is usually near the door.

Answer the questions.

1. What are found straight ahead of you as you enter the library? Tables
2. Which stacks are closest to the restrooms? Fiction stacks
3. What library part would you go to for a book of maps? Atlas corner
4. Is the reference area closer to the photo stacks or the computers? Computers
5. What is next to the left of the magazine and newspaper area? Reference area

At Home: Encourage children to list subjects that interest them. Then bring children to the library and search for books on these subjects

Name________________ Date________ **Practice 223**

Long *e, i*

Circle the word that completes the sentence. Then write the word on the line.

1. Brush your teeth every day.
   tree (teeth) iron
2. Letty is going to climb a mountain.
   (climb) cry teach
3. The animals came back one by one.
   tree green (by)
4. After two hours, the bus finally came.
   (finally) peeked leaves
5. Millie loves to jump into a huge pile of leaves.
   midnight iron (leaves)
6. Kay's mother mowed the green grass.
   (green) eager teach

At Home: Ask children to make up another sentence using one of the words they circled.

Name________________ Date________ **Practice 224**

Long *e;* Long *i; tch, ch*

Write a word from the box to complete each rhyme.

chair	kind	tree	fly	steal
light	piece	hatch	pie	tea

1. "Sit in a chair," I said to the bear.
2. Some birds fly up in the sky.
3. I climbed a tree near the sea.
4. Turn off the light. It is too bright.
5. Give this piece to the geese.
6. That thief wants to steal my orange peel!
7. I like to catch chicks when they hatch.
8. She said, "I find you to be kind."
9. You didn't lie; you ate my pie.
10. The honey in my tea was made by a bee.

At Home: Have children make up a rhyme using the word **green** and illustrate it.

Name______________________ Date________ **Practice 225**

Main Idea

Read each story. Underline the answers to the questions.

Ladybugs are insects that are important to farmers and gardeners. Ladybugs eat the tiny insects that eat the leaves of plants. This allows the plants to grow big and strong. Some farmers welcome the orange and black ladybugs. Using ladybugs is better than using bug spray.

1. What is the main idea?
- **a.** Ladybugs live in gardens.
- **b.** Ladybugs are important insects.
- **c.** Ladybugs like farmers.

2. What do ladybugs eat?
- **a.** They eat healthy plants.
- **b.** They eat orange and black spray.
- **c.** They eat tiny insects.

Jill always likes helping her dad work in his wood shop. She sweeps up small pieces of wood that fall on the floor. She also stacks the new boards in straight piles. Sometimes her dad lets her use a hammer to pound nails into the wooden toys he makes. That is her favorite thing to do.

3. What is the main idea?
- **a.** Jill makes toys.
- **b.** Jill likes wood.
- **c.** Jill likes to help in the wood shop.

4. What does Jill like to do most?
- **a.** She likes to pound nails with a hammer.
- **b.** She likes to sweep the floor.
- **c.** She likes to stack boards.

At Home: Ask children to name one detail that supports each main idea.

Name______________________ Date________ **Practice 226**

Multiple-Meaning Words

Read each sentence. Write the meaning of the underlined word on the line after each sentence. Answers may vary.

1. Dad always leaves early. goes away
2. The bus turned right at the corner. direction; not left
3. Burt can throw the ball across the field. a round toy
4. The light by her bed was off. lamp
5. We put the leaves in a big pile. parts of a tree
6. I got the right answer. not wrong; correct
7. A balloon floats because it is light. not heavy
8. The leaves turn brown every fall. the season after summer
9. Cinderella met a prince at the ball. a dance party
10. The children will watch the show. look at something
11. I always fall on the ice in the winter. drop to the ground
12. He was late, and he kept looking at his watch. a small clock, usually worn on the wrist

At Home: Ask children to think of another word that has two meanings. Have them draw a picture to illustrate each meaning.

Name____________________ Date________ **Reteach 219**

Long *e, i*

Say these words. All of them have the long **e** sound.
free pi**e**ce l**ea**ves
Say these words. All of them have the long **i** sound.
sk**y** h**igh** h**i**

Name the picture. Then circle the correct word for each picture. Write the word.

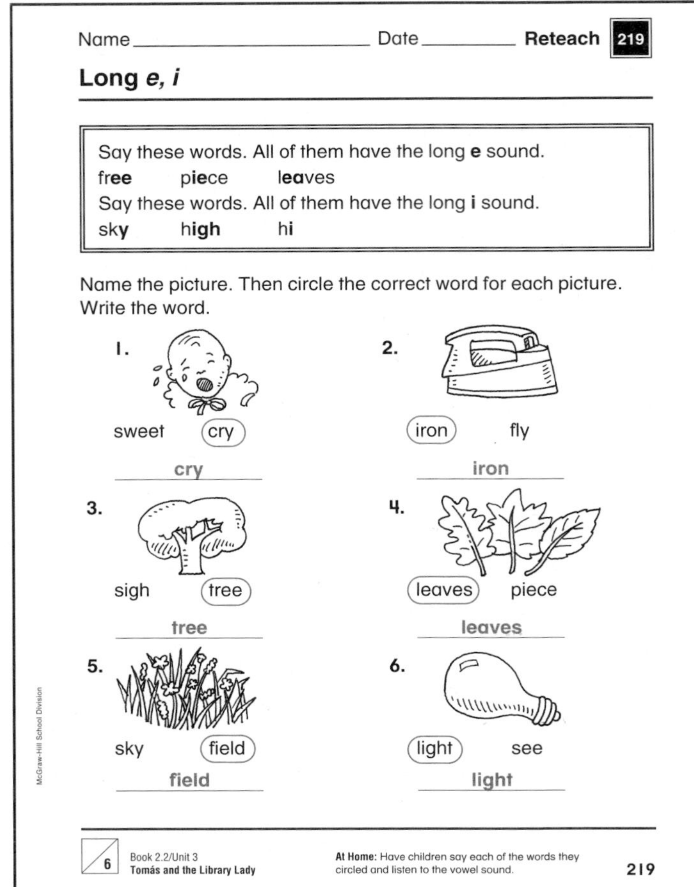

1. sweet (cry) — cry
2. (iron) fly — iron
3. sigh (tree) — tree
4. (leaves) piece — leaves
5. sky (field) — field
6. (light) see — light

Name____________________ Date________ **Reteach 220**

Vocabulary

Read the story. Circle the word that completes each sentence below.

borrow desert evenings midnight package shoulder

Pete is a pack rat. He has a dark spot on his shoulder. Pete lives in the desert. It is very hot there in the daytime. In the evenings, the desert cools off. It can be cold at midnight.

Pete likes to borrow things from other animals. He makes a little package of the things he finds. He hides the package in his nest.

1. Pete the pack rat lives in the ___ .
   forest ocean (desert)
2. Pete has a dark spot on his ___ .
   (shoulder) pocket nest
3. In the ___ , the desert cools off.
   summer days (evenings)
4. It can even be cold at ___ .
   daytime (midnight) noon
5. Pete likes to ___ stuff from other animals.
   drive read (borrow)
6. Pete makes a little ___ of the things he finds.
   (package) picture practice

Name____________________ Date________ **Reteach 221**

Story Comprehension

Think about "Tomás and the Library Lady." Then circle the word that best completes each sentence.

1. Tomás and his family must live near ___ so they can find work.
   roads (farms)
2. Tomás and Enrique carried___to their parents in the fields.
   (water) books
3. Papá Grande told Tomás to find more stories at the ___.
   store (library)
4. The library seemed very___to Tomás.
   (big) small
5. The library lady first gave Tomás some ___.
   (water) food
6. Tomás wanted to read books about tigers and ___.
   lions (dinosaurs)

Name____________________ Date________ **Reteach 222**

Read a Library Floor Plan

A **library floor plan** is a map that will help to direct you.

A library floor plan uses symbols for each area of the library. These symbols stand for what you would find there.

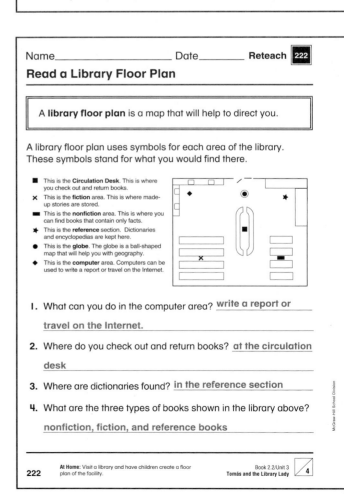

- ■ This is the **Circulation Desk**. This is where you check out and return books.
- × This is the **fiction** area. This is where made-up stories are stored.
- ▬ This is the **nonfiction** area. This is where you can find books that contain only facts.
- ★ This is the **reference** section. Dictionaries and encyclopedias are kept here.
- ● This is the **globe**. The globe is a ball-shaped map that will help you with geography.
- ◆ This is the **computer** area. Computers can be used to write a report or travel on the Internet.

1. What can you do in the computer area? write a report or travel on the Internet.
2. Where do you check out and return books? at the circulation desk
3. Where are dictionaries found? in the reference section
4. What are the three types of books shown in the library above?
   nonfiction, fiction, and reference books

Tomás and the Library Lady • RETEACH

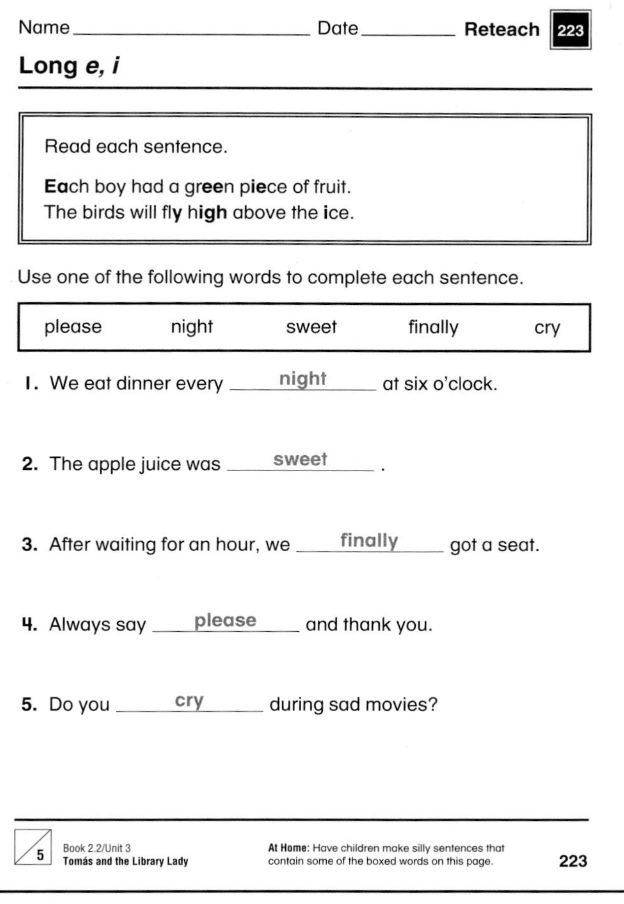

Name ______________ Date ________ **Reteach 223**

Long *e, i*

Read each sentence.

Each boy had a gr**ee**n p**ie**ce of fruit.
The birds will fly h**igh** above the **i**ce.

Use one of the following words to complete each sentence.

please	night	sweet	finally	cry

1. We eat dinner every ___night___ at six o'clock.
2. The apple juice was ___sweet___ .
3. After waiting for an hour, we ___finally___ got a seat.
4. Always say ___please___ and thank you.
5. Do you ___cry___ during sad movies?

5 Book 2.2/Unit 3 **Tomás and the Library Lady**

At Home: Have children make silly sentences that contain some of the boxed words on this page.

223

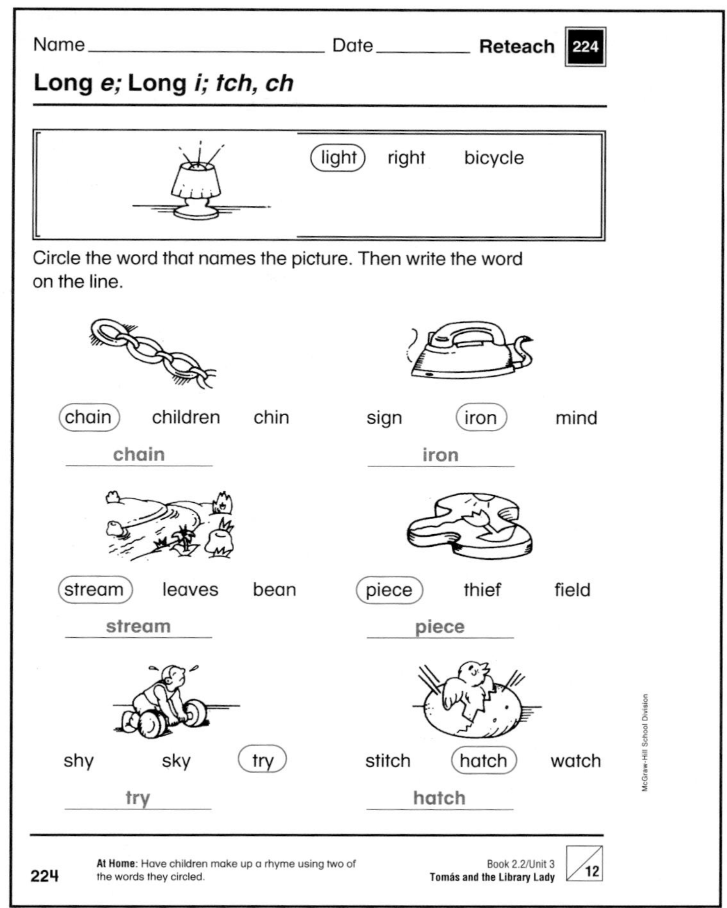

Name ______________ Date ________ **Reteach 224**

Long *e;* Long *i; tch, ch*

(light) right bicycle

Circle the word that names the picture. Then write the word on the line.

(chain) children chin — ___chain___

sign (iron) mind — ___iron___

(stream) leaves bean — ___stream___

(piece) thief field — ___piece___

shy sky (try) — ___try___

stitch (hatch) watch — ___hatch___

224

At Home: Have children make up a rhyme using two of the words they circled.

Book 2.2/Unit 3 **Tomás and the Library Lady** 12

McGraw-Hill School Division

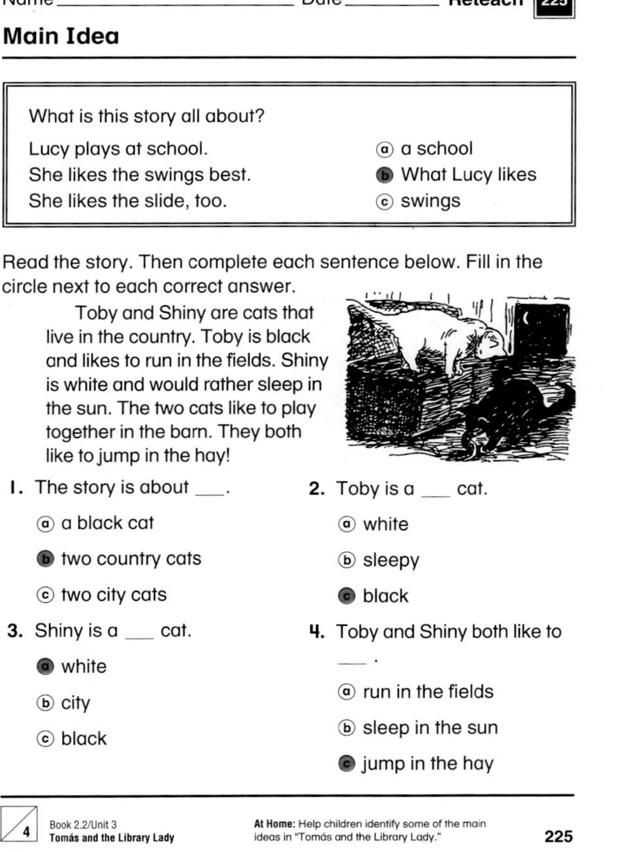

Name ______________ Date ________ **Reteach 225**

Main Idea

What is this story all about?

Lucy plays at school.
She likes the swings best.
She likes the slide, too.

ⓐ a school
● What Lucy likes
ⓒ swings

Read the story. Then complete each sentence below. Fill in the circle next to each correct answer.

Toby and Shiny are cats that live in the country. Toby is black and likes to run in the fields. Shiny is white and would rather sleep in the sun. The two cats like to play together in the barn. They both like to jump in the hay!

1. The story is about ___.
   - ⓐ a black cat
   - ● two country cats
   - ⓒ two city cats
2. Toby is a ___ cat.
   - ⓐ white
   - ⓑ sleepy
   - ● black
3. Shiny is a ___ cat.
   - ● white
   - ⓑ city
   - ⓒ black
4. Toby and Shiny both like to ___ .
   - ⓐ run in the fields
   - ⓑ sleep in the sun
   - ● jump in the hay

4 Book 2.2/Unit 3 **Tomás and the Library Lady**

At Home: Help children identify some of the main ideas in "Tomás and the Library Lady."

225

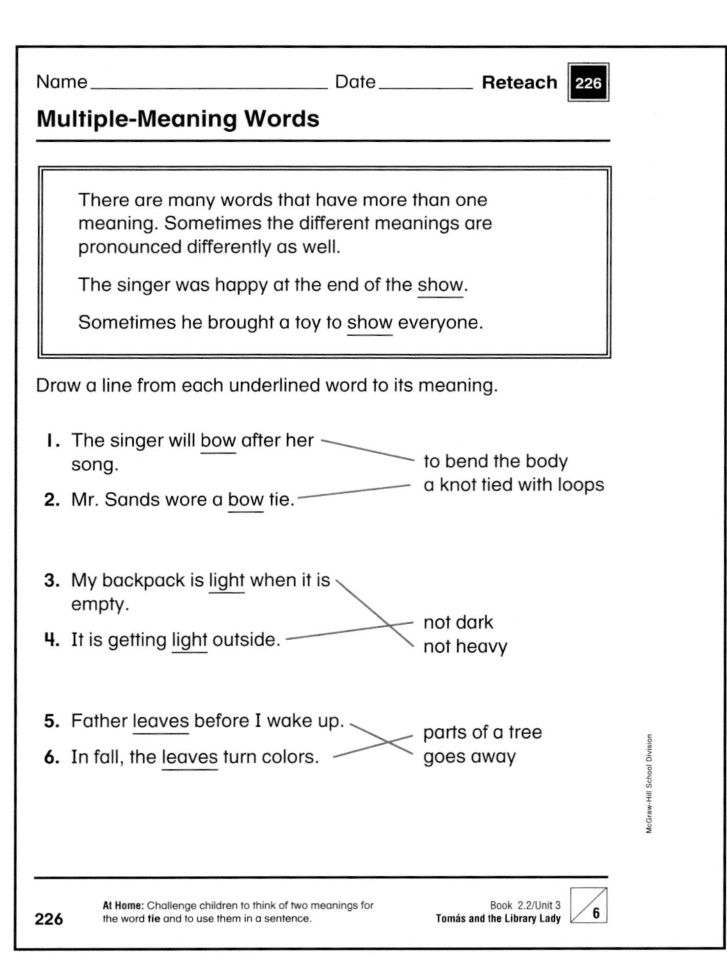

Name ______________ Date ________ **Reteach 226**

Multiple-Meaning Words

There are many words that have more than one meaning. Sometimes the different meanings are pronounced differently as well.

The singer was happy at the end of the show.

Sometimes he brought a toy to show everyone.

Draw a line from each underlined word to its meaning.

1. The singer will bow after her song. — to bend the body
2. Mr. Sands wore a bow tie. — a knot tied with loops
3. My backpack is light when it is empty. — not heavy
4. It is getting light outside. — not dark
5. Father leaves before I wake up. — goes away
6. In fall, the leaves turn colors. — parts of a tree

226

At Home: Challenge children to think of two meanings for the word **tie** and to use them in a sentence.

Book 2.2/Unit 3 **Tomás and the Library Lady** 6

McGraw-Hill School Division

Name ______________ Date ________ **Extend 219**

Long *e, i*

Follow all the directions.

1. Color the top of the tree green.
2. Circle the leaves falling from the tree.
3. Draw a squirrel on the side of the tree.
4. Draw teeth on the eager beaver.
5. Draw the sun shining brightly.
6. Draw wings on the bird so it can fly.
7. Draw a piece of food to feed the squirrel.
8. Color the rest of the picture.

Sample sentences shown.

Write three sentences that tell what is happening in the picture.

The tree is green.

The bird is flying.

The sun shines brightly.

At Home: Ask children to write a short story using the following **long e** and **long i** words: **peeked, seen, sweet, teach, cry, midnight, by, brightly.**

Name ______________ Date ________ **Extend 220**

Vocabulary

borrow	desert	evenings
midnight	package	shoulder

Write words from the box to complete the story.
Read the story over to check your answers.

The man carried a heavy **package** on his **shoulder**. He wished that he could **borrow** a wagon from a friend. The man was traveling through the hot, dry **desert**. It was after **midnight** and the moon was bright. The man liked to travel when the sun was down because it was cooler in the **evenings**.

Write two or three sentences telling what the desert is like during the day.

At Home: Children can write the vocabulary words on cards. Divide the cards. Take turns "borrowing" a card and making a sentence with the word on it.

Name ______________ Date ________ **Extend 221**

Story Comprehension

Here are three changes to "Tomás and the Library Lady." How might the story you read been different if these changes had taken place? Write a sentence under each change.

Sample answers shown.

1. Tomás is old enough to work in the fields all day with his parents.

   Tomás might not have been able to go to the library.

2. Papa Grande is not a storyteller.

   Tomás might not have wanted to learn more stories.

3. The library lady is not friendly or helpful.

   Tomás might not have wanted to return to the library.

What if Tomás and his family had stayed in Iowa at the end of the summer? Draw a picture to show a new ending for the story.

At Home: Have children list what Tomás would have missed if he had never learned to read. Ask: What would you miss if you couldn't read?

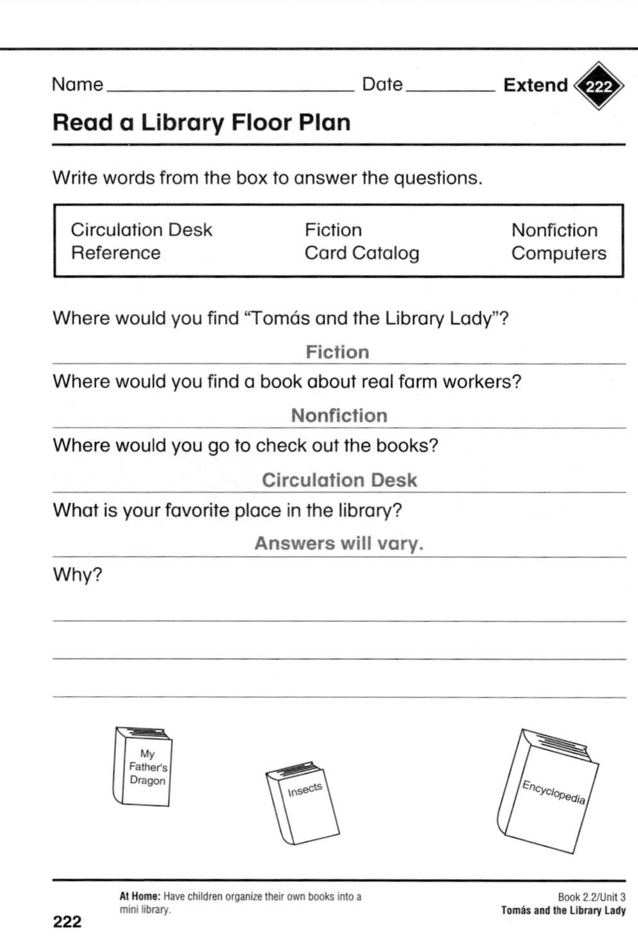

Name ______________ Date ________ **Extend 222**

Read a Library Floor Plan

Write words from the box to answer the questions.

Circulation Desk	Fiction	Nonfiction
Reference	Card Catalog	Computers

Where would you find "Tomás and the Library Lady"?

Fiction

Where would you find a book about real farm workers?

Nonfiction

Where would you go to check out the books?

Circulation Desk

What is your favorite place in the library?

Answers will vary.

Why?

At Home: Have children organize their own books into a mini library.

Name________________________ Date_________ **Extend 223**

Long *e, i*

sweet	iron	please	climb	eager	brightly
teach	light	pieces	cry	tree	by

Read each word in the box.
Write a word next to the caterpillar that has the same sound.

Long **e** — sweet, please, eager, teach, pieces, tree

Long **i** — iron, climb, brightly, light, cry, by

Write a sentence using at least one word from each caterpillar.

Sample sentence shown. My sister is eager to climb the tree.

At Home: Have children draw a picture of two spiders. Label one **long e** and the other **long i**. Children can find and write words on the legs of the correct spider.

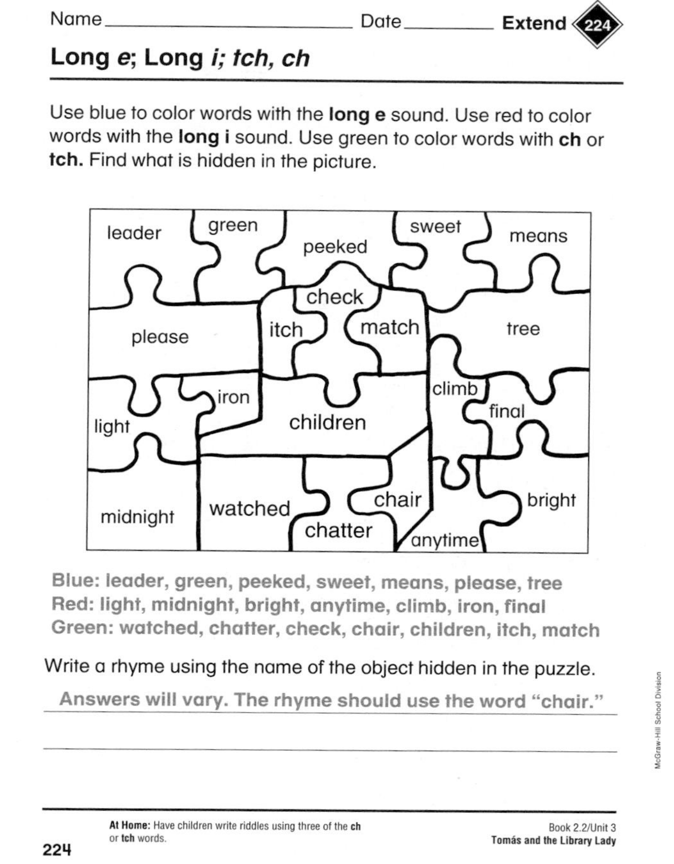

Name________________________ Date_________ **Extend 224**

Long *e*; Long *i; tch, ch*

Use blue to color words with the **long e** sound. Use red to color words with the **long i** sound. Use green to color words with **ch** or **tch.** Find what is hidden in the picture.

Blue: leader, green, peeked, sweet, means, please, tree
Red: light, midnight, bright, anytime, climb, iron, final
Green: watched, chatter, check, chair, children, itch, match

Write a rhyme using the name of the object hidden in the puzzle.

Answers will vary. The rhyme should use the word "chair."

At Home: Have children write riddles using three of the **ch** or **tch** words.

Name________________________ Date_________ **Extend 225**

Main Idea

Read the story.

My class always likes to visit the library at our school. When we get there we sit eagerly at the computers. We enjoy searching for books about interesting subjects. Sometimes we listen to the library lady read a story. Last week we were excited when we learned how to find our city on the globe. That was my favorite part of the visit. I wore a green sweater that day.

Write a sentence telling the main idea of the story.

My class likes to visit the school library.

Find a sentence from the story that is not about the main idea. Write it on the line.

I wore a green sweater that day.

Write two more sentences that tell about the story.

Answers will vary, but may include: We sit eagerly at the computers. We search for books. We listen to the library lady. We found our city on a globe.

At Home: Have children draw a picture. Ask them to write a main-idea sentence and a sentence with a supporting detail about the picture.

Name________________________ Date_________ **Extend 226**

Multiple-Meaning Words

Use these words to complete the sentences.

face	ball	glass	iron	wind

1. I drink milk out of a ___glass___.
2. I like to throw a ___ball___ at the park.
3. The gate is made of ___iron___.
4. I pat water on my ___face___ to cool it.
5. The ___wind___ blows leaves in the yard.
a. I can't ___face___ him.
b. I will ___wind___ up the string.
c. Please ___iron___ my shirt.
d. Who will dance at the ___ball___?
e. The window is made of ___glass___.

Which sentences use the same words? Write the number and the letter. The first one is done for you.

1, e — 4, a
2, d — 5, b
3, c

Which word sounds different when it has a different meaning?

wind

At Home: Have children write sentences for each meaning of these homographs: **bow, bow; read, read; does, does.**

Name________ Date______ LEARN Grammar 167

Using *A* and *An*

- The words *a* and *an* are special adjectives called **articles**.
- Use *a* before a word that begins with a consonant sound.

  I am wearing a coat and a hat.

Read each sentence. Write the correct article in each.

1. Ribbit is __a__ frog.
2. He lives in __a__ pond.
3. Ribbit is __an__ animal.
4. He likes to eat __a__ fly for lunch.
5. He likes to sit on __a__ rock.
6. He can jump over __a__ leaf.
7. He crawls under __a__ log.
8. __A__ bird sings for Ribbit.

Extension: Have children make a list of objects in the classroom that begin with a consonant and write *a* before each one.

Name________ Date______ LEARN AND PRACTICE Grammar 168

Using Articles

- Use *an* before a word that begins with a vowel sound.

  I saw **an** ape eat a banana.

Read the sentences. Write the article that completes each one.

1. The monkey ate (a, an) orange. __an__
2. I ate (a, an) pear. __a__
3. Two children shared (an, a) apple. __an__
4. We had (a, an) box of popcorn. __a__
5. (A, An) usher chewed gum. __An__
6. Jack ate (a, an) sandwich. __a__
7. I wanted (an, a) ice cream cone. __an__
8. Jan had (a, an) banana. __a__

Extension: Have children make up new sentences using *a* and *an*.

Name________ Date______ REVIEW AND PRACTICE Grammar 169

More Articles

- The words *a* and *an* are special adjectives called **articles**.
- Use *a* before a word that begins with a consonant sound.
- Use *an* before a word that begins with a vowel sound.

Use the correct article in each sentence. Write it on the line.

1. There is __an__ elephant who draws pictures.
2. It uses __a__ desk.
3. The desk has __a__ lamp.
4. The elephant wants to draw __an__ arrow.
5. The arrow is on __a__ table.

Extension: Have the children make a new list of words and say sentences that include them.

Name________ Date______ MECHANICS Grammar 170

Using Capital Letters

- A **proper noun** begins with a capital letter.
- An **abbreviation** of a person's title begins with a capital letter and ends with a period.

  Mr. James gave Tom a new basketball.

Read each sentence. Correct it. Write the correct sentence on the line.

1. mr. and mrs kress live in a apartment next door to my sister jane

   Mr. and Mrs. Kress live in an apartment next door to my sister Jane.
2. mr. kress works with an friend of mine

   Mr. Kress works with a friend of mine.
3. dr. kress is an doctor

   Dr. Kress is a doctor.
4. it seems like the kress family is an part of my family!

   It seems like the Kress family is a part of my family!

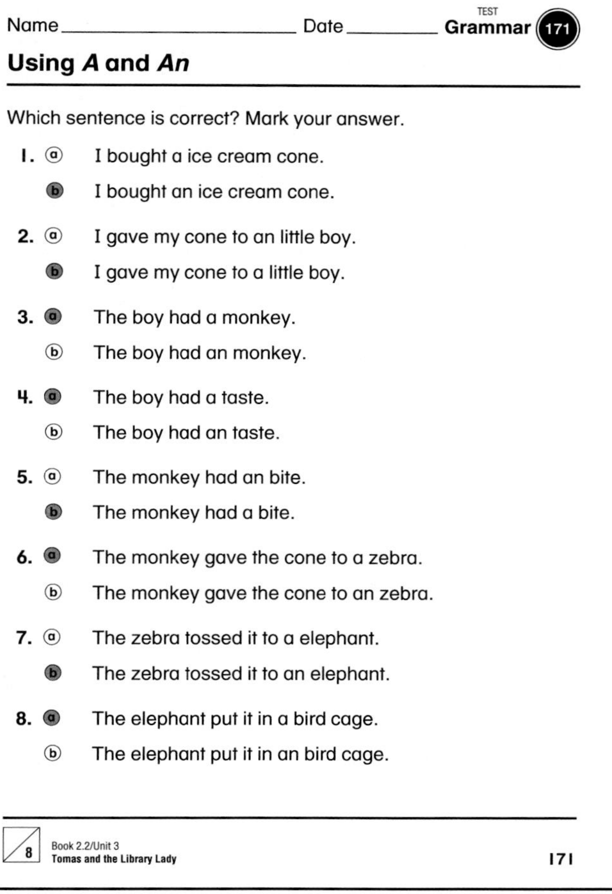

Name________________ Date________ TEST Grammar 171

Using *A* and *An*

Which sentence is correct? Mark your answer.

1. ⓐ I bought a ice cream cone.
   ⓑ I bought an ice cream cone.
2. ⓐ I gave my cone to an little boy.
   ⓑ I gave my cone to a little boy.
3. ⓐ The boy had a monkey.
   ⓑ The boy had an monkey.
4. ⓐ The boy had a taste.
   ⓑ The boy had an taste.
5. ⓐ The monkey had an bite.
   ⓑ The monkey had a bite.
6. ⓐ The monkey gave the cone to a zebra.
   ⓑ The monkey gave the cone to an zebra.
7. ⓐ The zebra tossed it to a elephant.
   ⓑ The zebra tossed it to an elephant.
8. ⓐ The elephant put it in a bird cage.
   ⓑ The elephant put it in an bird cage.

8 Book 2.2/Unit 3 Tomas and the Library Lady 171

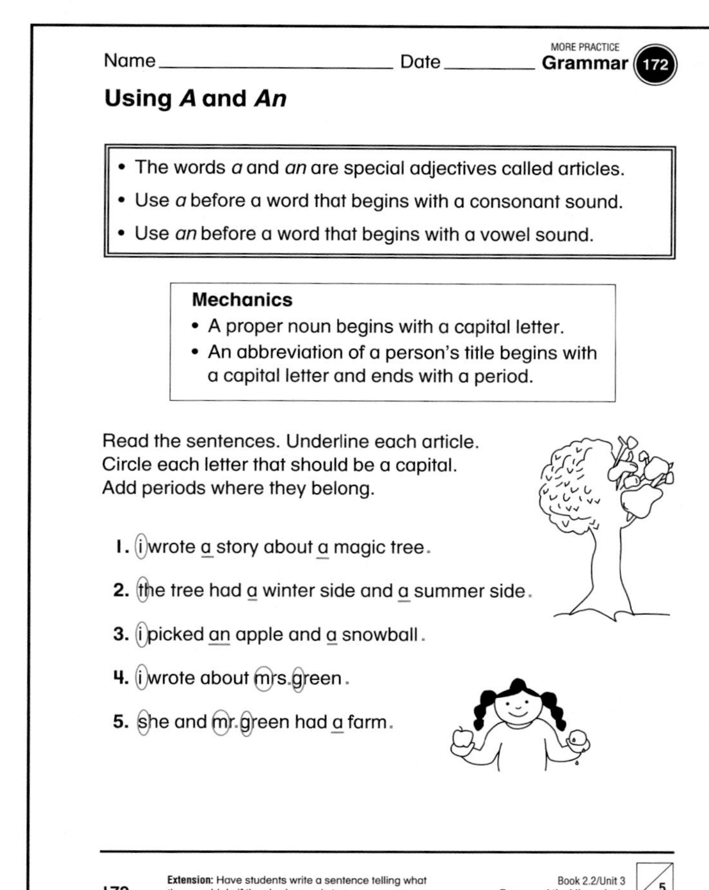

Name________________ Date________ MORE PRACTICE Grammar 172

Using *A* and *An*

- The words *a* and *an* are special adjectives called articles.
- Use *a* before a word that begins with a consonant sound.
- Use *an* before a word that begins with a vowel sound.

Mechanics
- A proper noun begins with a capital letter.
- An abbreviation of a person's title begins with a capital letter and ends with a period.

Read the sentences. Underline each article. Circle each letter that should be a capital. Add periods where they belong.

1. i wrote a story about a magic tree.
2. the tree had a winter side and a summer side.
3. i picked an apple and a snowball.
4. i wrote about mrs. green.
5. she and mr. green had a farm.

McGraw-Hill School Division

172 **Extension:** Have students write a sentence telling what they would do if they had a magic tree. Book 2.2/Unit 3 Tomas and the Library Lady 5

Name ______________________ Date __________ PRETEST SPELLING **167**

Words with Digraphs *sh, ch*

Pretest Directions

Fold back your paper along the dotted line. Use the blanks to write each word as it is said to you. When you finish the test, unfold the paper and correct any spelling mistakes. Practice those words for the Posttest.

1. ______	1. shift
2. ______	2. chair
3. ______	3. check
4. ______	4. shoe
5. ______	5. children
6. ______	6. shared
7. ______	7. shining
8. ______	8. shape
9. ______	9. chase
10. ______	10. cheek

Challenge Words

______	desert
______	evenings
______	midnight
______	package
______	shoulder

To Parents,
Here are the results of your child's weekly spelling Pretest. You can help your child study for the Posttest by following these simple steps for each word on the word list:

1. Read the word to your child.
2. Have your child write the word, saying each letter as it is written.
3. Say each letter of the word as your child checks the spelling.
4. If a mistake has been made, have your child read each letter of the correctly spelled word aloud and then repeat steps 1–3.

Name ______________________ Date __________ AT-HOME WORD STUDY SPELLING **168**

Words with Digraphs *sh, ch*

Using the Word Study Steps

1. LOOK at the word.
2. SAY the word aloud.
3. STUDY the letters in the word.
4. WRITE the word.
5. CHECK the word.
   Did you spell the word right?
   If not, go back to step 1.

Spelling Tip

Think of when you have seen the word before. Think of how it looked. Write the word in different ways to see which one looks correct.

~~shu~~, ~~shoo~~, **shoe**

Word Scramble

Unscramble each set of letters to make a spelling word.

1. raich	chair	2. khcec	check
3. fthis	shift	4. kehec	cheek
5. redsha	shared	6. hcsae	chase
7. eohs	shoe	8. rhienlcd	children
9. pesha	shape	10. ginnshi	shining

To Parents or Helpers:
Using the Word Study Steps above as your child comes across any new words will help him or her spell well. Review the steps as you both go over this week's spelling words.
Go over the Spelling Tip with your child. Help your child write new words in different ways to see which one looks right.
Help your child unscramble the letters to make words.

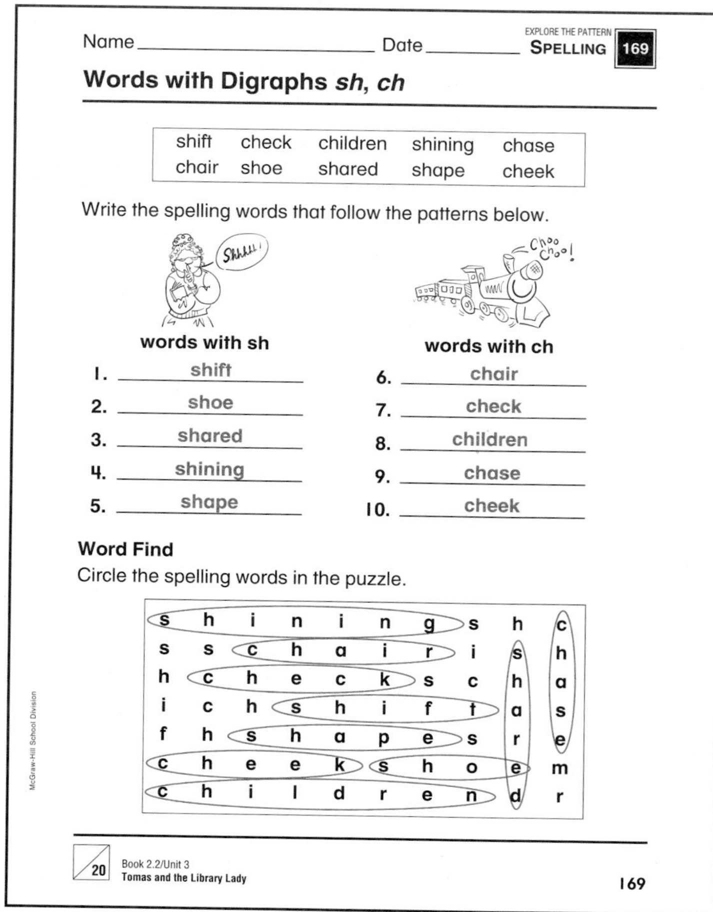

Name ______________________ Date __________ EXPLORE THE PATTERN SPELLING **169**

Words with Digraphs *sh, ch*

shift	check	children	shining	chase
chair	shoe	shared	shape	cheek

Write the spelling words that follow the patterns below.

words with sh	words with ch
1. shift	6. chair
2. shoe	7. check
3. shared	8. children
4. shining	9. chase
5. shape	10. cheek

Word Find

Circle the spelling words in the puzzle.

s	h	i	n	i	n	g	s	h	c
s	s	c	h	a	i	r	i	s	h
h	c	h	e	c	k	s	c	h	a
i	c	h	s	h	i	f	t	a	s
f	h	s	h	a	p	e	s	r	e
c	h	e	e	k	s	h	o	e	m
c	h	i	l	d	r	e	n	d	r

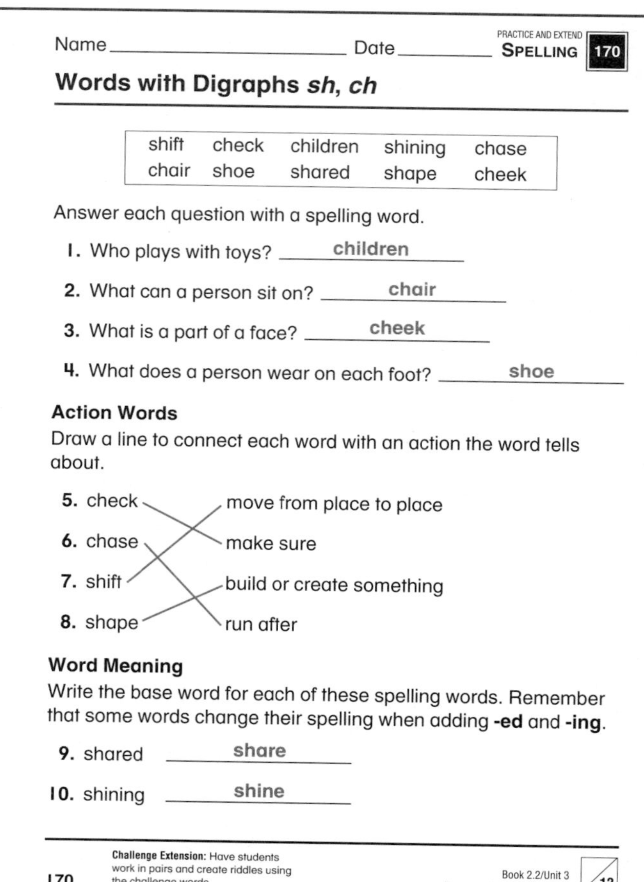

Name ______________________ Date __________ PRACTICE AND EXTEND SPELLING **170**

Words with Digraphs *sh, ch*

shift	check	children	shining	chase
chair	shoe	shared	shape	cheek

Answer each question with a spelling word.

1. Who plays with toys? children
2. What can a person sit on? chair
3. What is a part of a face? cheek
4. What does a person wear on each foot? shoe

Action Words

Draw a line to connect each word with an action the word tells about.

5. check	move from place to place
6. chase	make sure
7. shift	build or create something
8. shape	run after

Word Meaning

Write the base word for each of these spelling words. Remember that some words change their spelling when adding **-ed** and **-ing**.

9. shared share
10. shining shine

Challenge Extension: Have students work in pairs and create riddles using the challenge words.

Name______________________ Date__________ PROOFREAD AND WRITE SPELLING 171

Words with Digraphs *sh, ch*

Proofreading Activity

There are six spelling mistakes in the report below. Circle each misspelled word. Write the words correctly on the lines below.

Our class took a trip to Noisy Brook. Erin tried to chaise a frog, but she fell and cut her cheak. At lunch, all the shildren shareed their snacks. Bobby lost a shoo in the river. He took it off to see how cold the water was. We were lucky that the sun was shyning.

1. chase 2. cheek 3. children
4. shared 5. shoe 6. shining

Writing Activity

Write sentences about a field trip you would like to take. Use four spelling words in your sentences. Circle the spelling words you use.

____

____

____

____

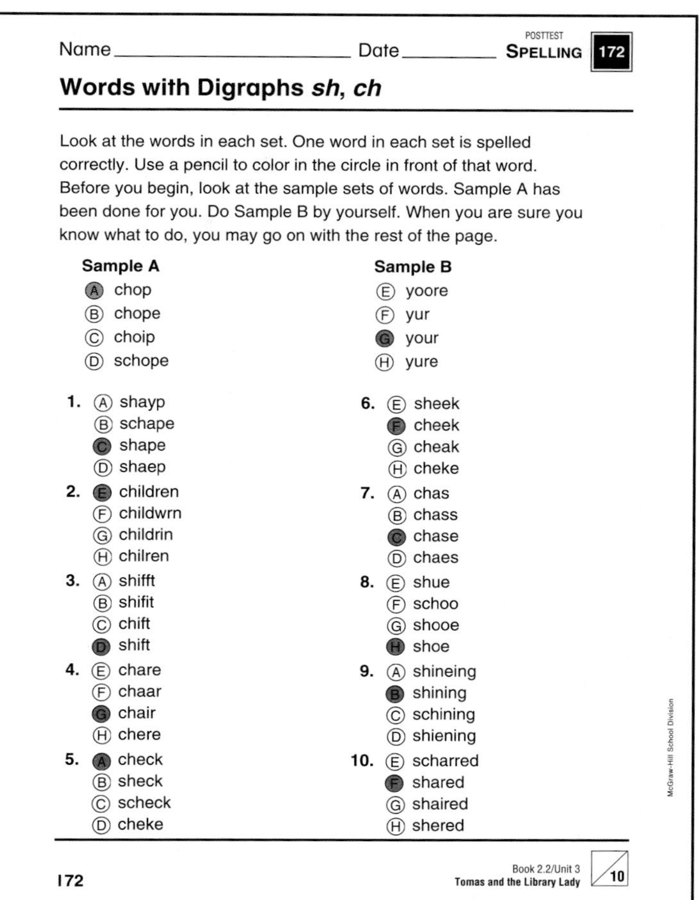

Name______________________ Date__________ POSTTEST SPELLING 172

Words with Digraphs *sh, ch*

Look at the words in each set. One word in each set is spelled correctly. Use a pencil to color in the circle in front of that word. Before you begin, look at the sample sets of words. Sample A has been done for you. Do Sample B by yourself. When you are sure you know what to do, you may go on with the rest of the page.

Sample A
- (A) chop
- (B) chope
- (C) choip
- (D) schope

Sample B
- (E) yoore
- (F) yur
- (G) your
- (H) yure

1. (A) shayp (B) schape (C) shape (D) shaep
2. (E) children (F) childwrn (G) childrin (H) chilren
3. (A) shifft (B) shifit (C) chift (D) shift
4. (E) chare (F) chaar (G) chair (H) chere
5. (A) check (B) sheck (C) scheck (D) cheke
6. (E) sheek (F) cheek (G) cheak (H) cheke
7. (A) chas (B) chass (C) chase (D) chaes
8. (E) shue (F) schoo (G) shooe (H) shoe
9. (A) shineing (B) shining (C) schining (D) shiening
10. (E) scharred (F) shared (G) shaired (H) shered

Princess Pooh • PRACTICE

Name__________ Date______ **Practice 227**

Long *a, o*

Complete each sentence with a word from the box below.

show	yellow	plain	raincoat	way	day	maid	toes

1. Could you ___show___ me the picture?
2. Polly knows the ___way___ across the lake .
3. Henry colors the sun ___yellow___.
4. The ___maid___ cleaned the room.
5. I wear my ___raincoat___ when it rains.
6. May said that her fingers and ___toes___ were cold.
7. Sue wore a ___plain___ dress to the party.
8. Today is a sunny ___day___.

8 Book 2.2/Unit 3 **Princess Pooh**

At Home: Ask children to think of more words that contain the sounds of long **a** spelled **ai**, **ay** and long **o**, spelled **oa**, **oe**, and **ow**.

227

Name__________ Date______ **Practice 228**

Vocabulary

Read the words in the box. Read the clues. Write the correct word on the line below each clue.

cousins	crowded	golden	princess	restaurant	world

1. This person might sit on a throne.
   princess
2. We like to go here when we're hungry.
   restaurant
3. These are people in your family you might visit.
   cousins
4. During a big sale, a store might be like this.
   crowded
5. A king might wear a crown this color.
   golden
6. You might fly around this in a plane someday.
   world

228

At Home: Have children make up new riddles for the vocabulary words.

Book 2.2/Unit 3 **Princess Pooh** 6

The Princess With a Heart

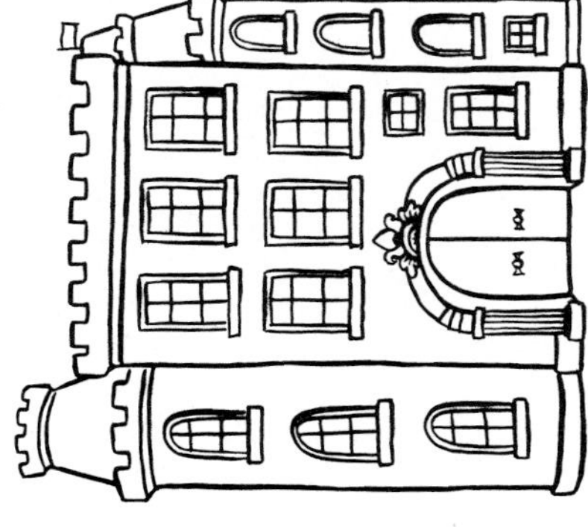

Once there was a princess named Rita. She and her sisters, Maria and Nina, lived in a golden palace.

Rita's sisters, Maria and Nina, worked hard every day. Rita braided her long, black hair.

Sometimes Maria and Nina would ask their sister to help. Rita always said no. She was too busy looking in the mirror.

2

One day a prince showed up from another part of the world. He asked Nina to marry him.

All of the girls' cousins and friends came to the wedding at a fancy restaurant. It was very crowded. Another prince also came. He asked Maria to marry him.

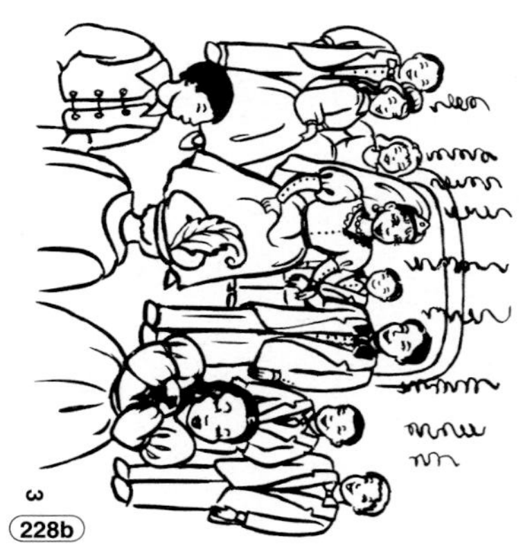

3

Everyone asked the prince, "Why not Rita? She has long, beautiful hair." He said, "I want someone who can see outside her window."

"What could he mean?" asked Rita. One day she left the mirror and looked out her window. Since that day Rita stopped looking in the mirror.

One day she saw a prince below her window. Soon they were married!

At Home: Have children write the next page for this book. Suggest they begin by telling what happened next to Princess Rita.

4

228a

228b

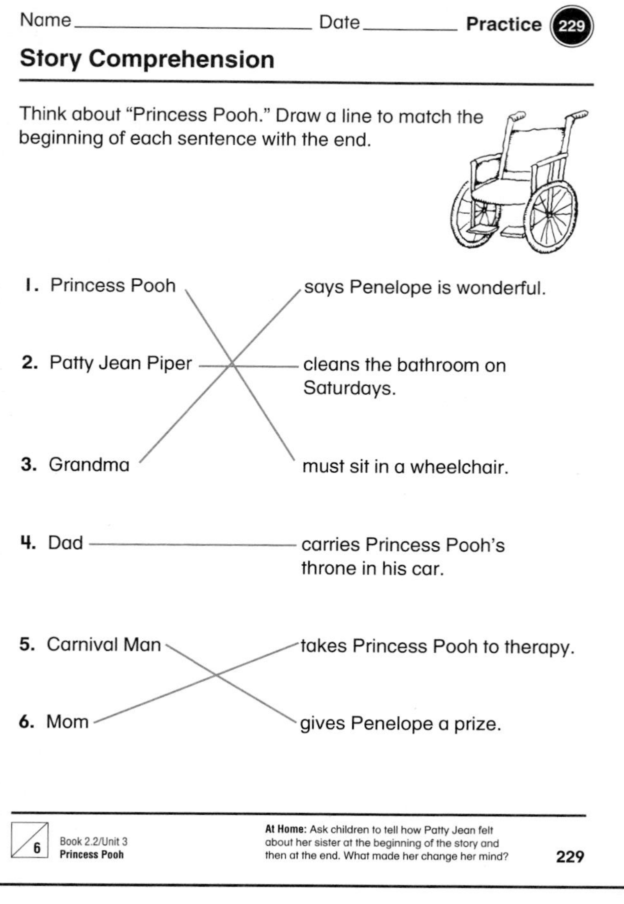

Name_______________ Date_________ **Practice 229**

Story Comprehension

Think about "Princess Pooh." Draw a line to match the beginning of each sentence with the end.

1. Princess Pooh — says Penelope is wonderful.
2. Patty Jean Piper — cleans the bathroom on Saturdays.
3. Grandma — must sit in a wheelchair.
4. Dad — carries Princess Pooh's throne in his car.
5. Carnival Man — takes Princess Pooh to therapy.
6. Mom — gives Penelope a prize.

At Home: Ask children to tell how Patty Jean felt about her sister at the beginning of the story and then at the end. What made her change her mind?

Name_______________ Date_________ **Practice 230**

Use an Encyclopedia

One of the best ways to learn more about a subject is to look at more than one entry in an encyclopedia. Sometimes an entry will direct you to another entry that contains related information.

BUMBLEBEE is a large, hairy, black and yellow bee that is often seen in summer. Bumblebees live in almost every country. Some islands in the Pacific never had bumblebees until man brought them. They range in size from one half to one inch. Unlike honeybees, they do not die after they sting. Bumblebees can sting again and again. They make a loud buzzing noise as they fly, scaring many people. The enemies of the bumblebee are beetles, flies, ants, mites, and wasps. *See also: Bee, Clover*

BEE is an insect that lives everywhere in the world except near the North and South Poles. There are 10,000 kinds of bees but only the honeybee makes honey. Most people are afraid of bees, but they only sting when scared or hurt. Honeybees are social insects. They live and work in a huge group called a colony. They fly about 12 miles an hour. Bees have been found in amber that was fifty million years old. *See also: Clover, Honey, Pollen, Pupa*

Use the encyclopedia entries to answer the questions.

1. Which entry discusses one kind of bee only? bumblebee
2. What entry does both of these entries tell you to see? clover
3. What fact about bees do both entries mention? that bees live almost everywhere
4. What are the other entries that are suggested for you to read? honey, pollen, pupa

At Home: Have children illustrate one of the facts they have learned about bees from the entries above.

Name_______________ Date_________ **Practice 231**

Long *a, o*

Circle the word that best completes each sentence. Then write the word on the line.

1. She knows what happened.
   (knows) row mow
2. Sarah watches the storm from the window.
   no (window) yellow
3. The rain pours down.
   bay plain (rain)
4. A big truck goes by.
   shows (goes) tows
5. Sarah stays inside the house until the rain stops.
   main ways (stays)
6. At the end of the storm, she sees a rainbow.
   (rainbow) show maid

At Home: Have children write words that rhyme with **bow, rain, goes, coat,** and **goes**.

Name_______________ Date_________ **Practice 232**

Long *a, o, e, i; tch, ch*

A. Write the word from the box that completes each sentence.

field	high	sky	find	catch

1. I find my lost shoe under the bed.
2. If I throw the ball, will you catch it?
3. We run in the field behind my house.
4. The rocket shot up into the sky.
5. How high can you jump?

B. Now draw a line from each sentence to the word that completes it.

6. His teeth __________ when he gets cold. — chatter
7. He will put on his __________ to get warm. — coat
8. Do you __________ a lot of books? — read
9. I like to __________ baseball. — play
10. The dirty water went down the __________. — drain

At Home: Have children illustrate one of the sentences above.

Name______________ Date________ **Practice 233**

Form Generalizations

Think about the story "Princess Pooh." Then write the answer to each question on the line.

1. Why does Patty Jean call Penny Princess Pooh?
   She thinks Penny acts like and is treated as a princess; everyone does things for her and she tells everyone what to do.
2. How does Patty Jean feel about Penny at the beginning of the story?
   She doesn't like her because she thinks Penny always gets her way.
3. How does Patty Jean think that other people feel about Penny?
   She thinks that other people like her and think she is sweet and wonderful.
4. Does Patty Jean think she is treated as well as Penny?
   No. She thinks she is treated like a servant.
5. Is everyone nice to Patty Jean when she rides in the wheelchair? Give examples.
   No. Some people look away as if frightened; some boys are mean and won't get out of her way.

At Home: Ask children to make another generalization about either Patty Jean or Penny.

Name______________ Date________ **Practice 234**

Figurative Language

What picture does each group of words make you think of?

like little stars
like a great, round orange
like people marching down the road
like a million dollars
as clear as glass

Complete each sentence by writing a phrase from above in the space. Use each phrase only once.

1. The trees looked
   like people marching down the road.
2. The sun looked
   like a great, round orange.
3. The dew on the grass was shining
   like little stars.
4. The lake was
   as clear as glass.
5. When I woke up this morning, I felt
   like a million dollars.

At Home: Choose two household items and ask children to invent a comparison to describe them. You may want to begin with your own example.

Name ______________ Date ________ **Reteach 227**

Long *a, o*

Read the following sentences

It is r**ai**ny every d**ay**.
I caught my t**oe** in the wind**ow** on the b**oa**t.

Circle the words that have the same long **a** or long **o** sound in each sentence. Then write the words.

1. The man wears a (coat) in his (boat).
   coat boat
2. Molly sees the (rainbow) through the (window).
   rainbow window
3. I hit my (toe) with the (hoe).
   toe hoe
4. There are (rains) on the (plains).
   rains plains
5. Do you (know) the people in the (show)?
   know show
6. Every (day) in (May) was sunny.
   day May

At Home: Have children write a sentence that uses two of the words they circled.

Name ______________ Date ________ **Reteach 228**

Vocabulary

Read the sentences. The underlined words are definitions of the words in the box. Write the word under its definition.

cousins crowded golden princess restaurant world

1. The room was full of people.
   crowded
2. We saw a movie about the daughter of a king and queen.
   princess
3. All the tables were taken at the place to eat.
   restaurant
4. The sun was a yellow-colored ball.
   golden
5. Two of my aunt and uncle's children came to see me.
   cousins
6. Millions of people live around the Earth.
   world

At Home: Have children draw a picture that illustrates two of the vocabulary words.

Name ______________ Date ________ **Reteach 229**

Story Comprehension

Think about "Princess Pooh." Circle the word that best completes each sentence.

1. Everyone says that Patty Jean grows like a ___.
   flower (weed)
2. When they shop, Patty Jean carries so many packages, she looks like a ___ with legs.
   throne (box)
3. The carnival man gave a stuffed ___ to Penny.
   (poodle) chair
4. When it rains, Patty Jean must wait for the ___ .
   throne (bus)
5. When she takes the wheelchair, Patty Jean learns how ___ it is for Penny.
   easy (hard)
6. In the end, Patty Jean just wants Penny to be ___ .
   (happy) sad

At Home: Ask children to talk about how Patty Jean felt about Penny at the end of the story.

Name ______________ Date ________ **Reteach 230**

Use an Encyclopedia

An **encyclopedia** provides general information on numerous topics.

Study the encyclopedia entry shown below.

Mercury–Mesa

MERRY-GO-ROUND is a machine that people ride for fun. It is often found at a fair or an amusement park. A merry-go-round is actually a platform that is in the shape of a circle. It turns slowly while music is played. Usually wooden horses are attached to poles for people to ride. Sometimes the poles go up and down. The horses are often brightly painted. The first merry-go-round was built in France in the late 1700s. It was called a *carrousel.* See also *rollercoaster.*

Use the encyclopedia entry to answer these questions.

1. What is the topic of this entry? a merry-go-round
2. Which guide words are found on this page? Mercury—Mesa
3. What was the name of the first merry-go-round? carousel
4. How do people use the wooden horses on the platform?
   they sit on them as the merry-go-round turns
5. What other topic does the encyclopedia suggest you see?
   roller coaster

At Home: Have children look up subjects that interest them in an encyclopedia and write reports about their findings.

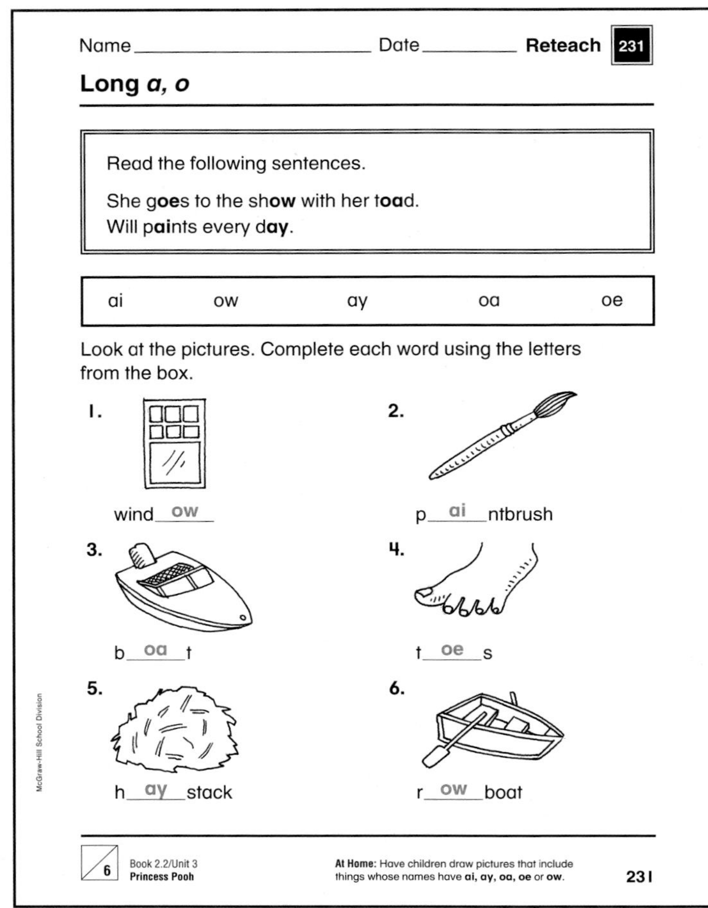

Name ______________ Date ________ **Reteach 231**

Long *a, o*

Read the following sentences.

She g**oe**s to the sh**ow** with her t**oa**d.
Will p**ai**nts every d**ay**.

ai	ow	ay	oa	oe

Look at the pictures. Complete each word using the letters from the box.

1. wind__ow__
2. p__ai__ntbrush
3. b__oa__t
4. t__oe__s
5. h__ay__stack
6. r__ow__boat

6 Book 2.2/Unit 3 **Princess Pooh**

At Home: Have children draw pictures that include things whose names have **ai, ay, oa, oe** or **ow**.

231

Name ______________ Date ________ **Reteach 232**

Long *a, o, e, i; tch, ch*

cry (fly)
fly

Circle the word that names each picture. Write the word.

1. (rainbow) sailboat — rainbow
2. stitch (crutch) — crutch
3. (sway) tray — sway
4. sleep (sweep) — sweep
5. (chair) cheese — chair
6. (island) siren — island

232

At Home: Challenge children to use three of the words they circled in a sentence.

Book 2.2/Unit 3 **Princess Pooh** 6

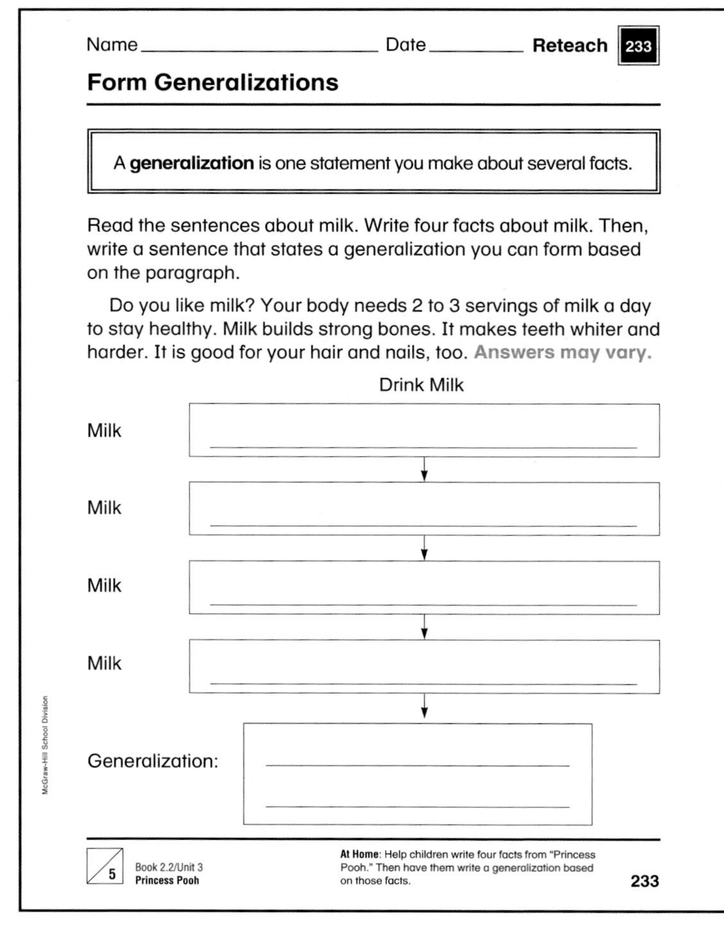

Name ______________ Date ________ **Reteach 233**

Form Generalizations

A **generalization** is one statement you make about several facts.

Read the sentences about milk. Write four facts about milk. Then, write a sentence that states a generalization you can form based on the paragraph.

Do you like milk? Your body needs 2 to 3 servings of milk a day to stay healthy. Milk builds strong bones. It makes teeth whiter and harder. It is good for your hair and nails, too. Answers may vary.

Drink Milk

Milk ______________

Milk ______________

Milk ______________

Milk ______________

Generalization: ______________

5 Book 2.2/Unit 3 **Princess Pooh**

At Home: Help children write four facts from "Princess Pooh." Then have them write a generalization based on those facts.

233

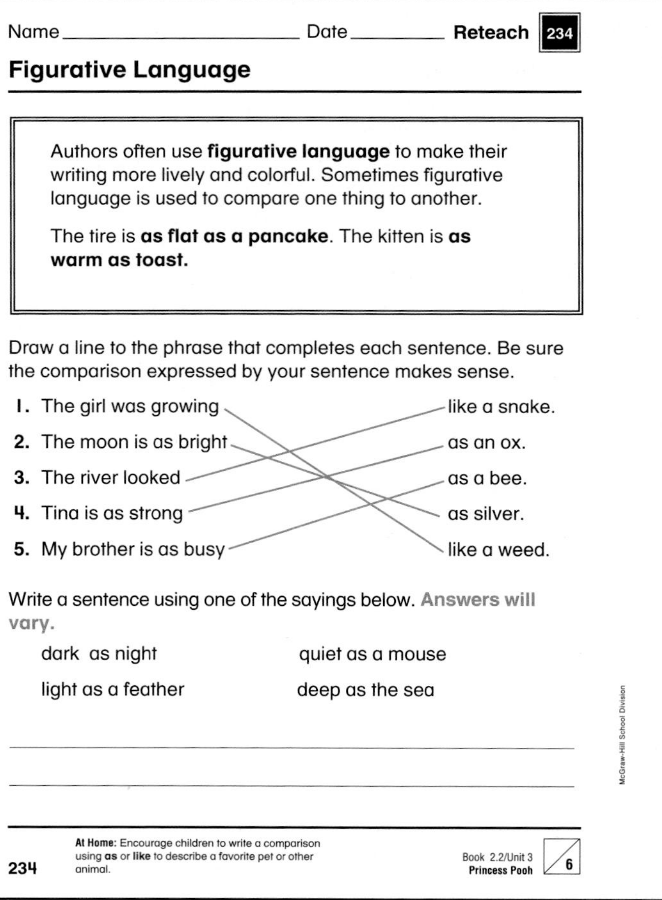

Name ______________ Date ________ **Reteach 234**

Figurative Language

Authors often use **figurative language** to make their writing more lively and colorful. Sometimes figurative language is used to compare one thing to another.

The tire is **as flat as a pancake**. The kitten is **as warm as toast.**

Draw a line to the phrase that completes each sentence. Be sure the comparison expressed by your sentence makes sense.

1. The girl was growing — like a snake.
2. The moon is as bright — as an ox.
3. The river looked — as a bee.
4. Tina is as strong — as silver.
5. My brother is as busy — like a weed.

Write a sentence using one of the sayings below. Answers will vary.

dark as night — quiet as a mouse
light as a feather — deep as the sea

____

____

234

At Home: Encourage children to write a comparison using **as** or **like** to describe a favorite pet or other animal.

Book 2.2/Unit 3 **Princess Pooh** 6

Name ______________ Date ________ Extend 227

Long *a, o*

Read the story. Circle all the words with the **long a** sound. Underline all the words with the **long o** sound.

Play Today

There is no school today. I am ready to play. I look out the window and see the rain. I put on my plain yellow raincoat and run next door. My friend knows that I am on my way. We play a game.

Which word has both **long a** and **long o** sounds?

raincoat

Use the word in a sentence.

Possible answer: The raincoat kept me dry.

At Home: Have children draw a picture of a rainy day scene. Label the picture with two sentences using **long a** and **long o** words.

Name ______________ Date ________ Extend 228

Vocabulary

cousins	crowded	golden
princess	restaurant	world

Choose words to match each clue. Fill in the puzzle.

Across

1. The children of your uncle or aunt.
2. Yellow and bright.
5. A place where people pay to eat meals.

Down

1. Filled with a lot of people packed together.
3. The daughter of a king or queen.
4. The earth.

Across: 1. COUSINS 2. GOLDEN 5. RESTAURANT
Down: 1. CROWDED 3. PRINCESS 4. WORLD

Write a sentence using three of the words from the box.

Answers could include: The restaurant was crowded with my cousins.

At Home: Challenge children to draw and label a picture that illustrates all the words from the puzzle.

Name ______________ Date ________ Extend 229

Story Comprehension

Finish the letter from Patty Jean to her sister.

Dear Penny,

I am sorry that I took your chair. I learned that it is not always fun to sit in the chair. Answers will vary.

Your sister,
Patty Jean

Draw a picture illustrating how Penny might feel after reading the letter.

At Home: Ask children to tell what happened in the story to change how Patty Jean felt about her sister.

Name ______________ Date ________ Extend 230

Use an Encyclopedia

Read about Helen Keller in this encyclopedia entry. Write a report about Helen Keller using facts from the entry.

Keller, Helen Adams (1880–1968)
Helen Keller was an American writer. She became blind and deaf at eight months old. When she was almost seven, Anne Sullivan came to take care of her. Miss Sullivan became Helen Keller's friend and teacher. Helen Keller learned quickly. She graduated from Radcliffe College. She wrote many books. She also raised money so other blind people could learn new jobs and skills. **See also *Macy, Anne Sullivan***

HELEN KELLER

At Home: Help children to look up Helen Keller in an actual encyclopedia. Allow them to pick out the volume that has the entry about Keller. Have them point out the guide words on the page about Keller.

Name____________________ Date__________ **Extend 231**

Long *a, o*

Circle the correct spelling of each word.

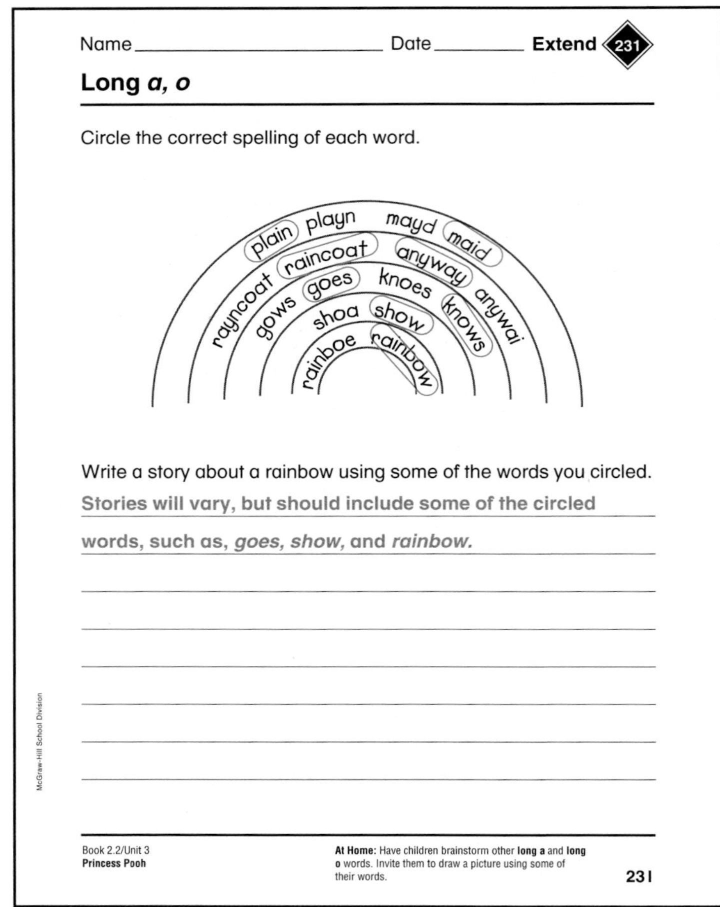

Write a story about a rainbow using some of the words you circled.

Stories will vary, but should include some of the circled words, such as, *goes, show,* and *rainbow.*

At Home: Have children brainstorm other **long a** and **long o** words. Invite them to draw a picture using some of their words.

Name____________________ Date__________ **Extend 232**

Long *a, o, e, i; tch, ch*

plain	yellow	chore
street	maid	sleep
window	wheel	drives
light	chair	myself
crutch	rain	knows
chin	hitch	match

Write each word in the correct list.

long a as in **main**	**long o** as in **snow**	**long e** as in **meet**
plain	yellow	street
maid	window	wheel
rain	knows	sleep

long i as in **sky**	**ch** as in **child**	**tch** as in **fetch**
myself	chin	crutch
light	chair	hitch
drives	chore	match

At Home: Have children make up silly rhymes using words from the lists.

Name____________________ Date__________ **Extend 233**

Form Generalizations

Read these facts.

A lot of people were in the park on Saturday.
The family did not have room to play ball.
The family did not find an empty table when it was time for lunch.
The playground was full.
The family wanted to go home.

Write a generalization about the park on Saturday.

Possible answer: The park was crowded on Saturday.

Do you think the family had fun at the park? Why?

No, there were too many people at the park.

Draw a picture showing what the park might have looked like on Saturday.

At Home: Have children write a generalization about playing in a crowded park.

Name____________________ Date__________ **Extend 234**

Figurative Language

throne with wheels	**like a box with legs**	**like a cloud**
a royal mess	**growing like a weed**	

Make the sentences more colorful. Write words from the box to take the place of the underlined words.

1. Penny sits on her wheelchair and gets a lot of attention.
   throne with wheels
2. At the store I look funny when I am hidden under all of our packages. like a box with legs
3. People tell Penny how wonderful she is and they tell me that I am getting taller. growing like a weed
4. When I sit down in Penny's chair it feels soft.
   like a cloud
5. I was very dirty the day I fell off the chair into the mud puddle.
   a royal mess

What do you think of when people say, "It's raining like cats and dogs"? Draw a picture. Then draw a picture showing what people really mean.

At Home: Have children write a sentence using a favorite expression.

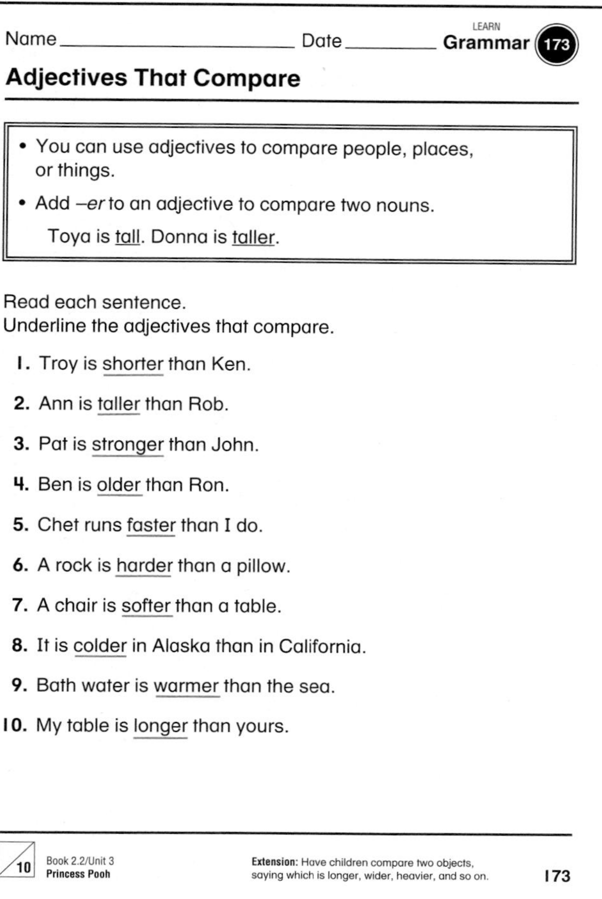

Name________________ Date________ LEARN Grammar 173

Adjectives That Compare

- You can use adjectives to compare people, places, or things.
- Add *–er* to an adjective to compare two nouns.

  Toya is tall. Donna is taller.

Read each sentence.
Underline the adjectives that compare.

1. Troy is shorter than Ken.
2. Ann is taller than Rob.
3. Pat is stronger than John.
4. Ben is older than Ron.
5. Chet runs faster than I do.
6. A rock is harder than a pillow.
7. A chair is softer than a table.
8. It is colder in Alaska than in California.
9. Bath water is warmer than the sea.
10. My table is longer than yours.

10 Book 2.2/Unit 3 Princess Pooh

Extension: Have children compare two objects, saying which is longer, wider, heavier, and so on.

173

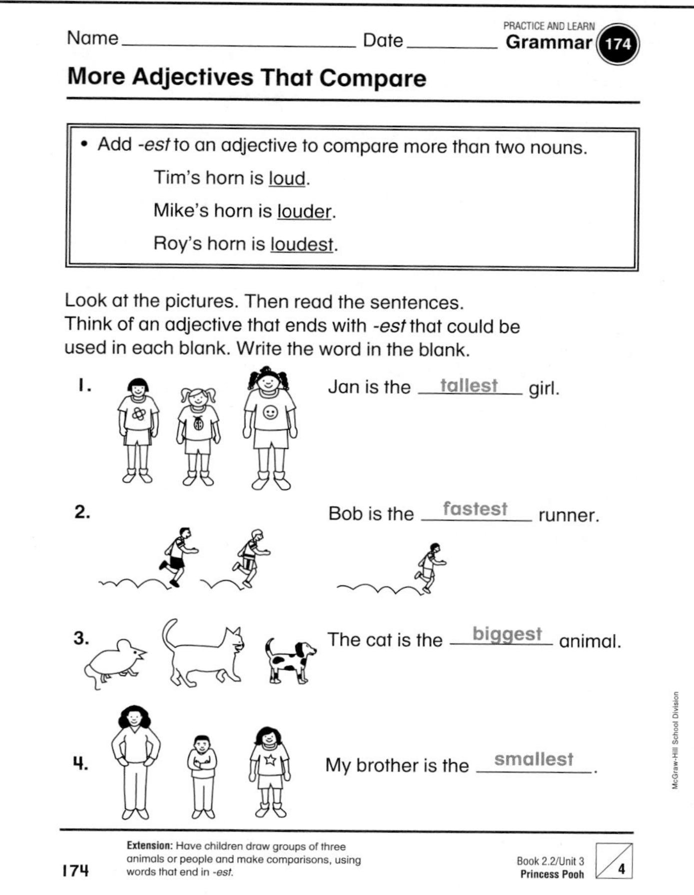

Name________________ Date________ PRACTICE AND LEARN Grammar 174

More Adjectives That Compare

- Add *-est* to an adjective to compare more than two nouns.

  Tim's horn is loud.

  Mike's horn is louder.

  Roy's horn is loudest.

Look at the pictures. Then read the sentences.
Think of an adjective that ends with *-est* that could be used in each blank. Write the word in the blank.

1. Jan is the __tallest__ girl.
2. Bob is the __fastest__ runner.
3. The cat is the __biggest__ animal.
4. My brother is the __smallest__.

174

Extension: Have children draw groups of three animals or people and make comparisons, using words that end in *-est*.

Book 2.2/Unit 3 Princess Pooh 4

McGraw-Hill School Division

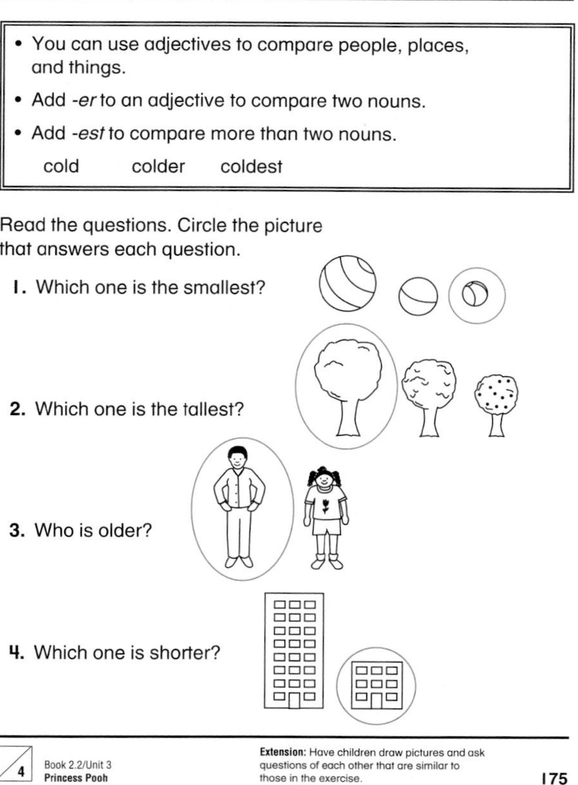

Name________________ Date________ REVIEW AND PRACTICE Grammar 175

Using Adjectives That Compare

- You can use adjectives to compare people, places, and things.
- Add *-er* to an adjective to compare two nouns.
- Add *-est* to compare more than two nouns.

  cold colder coldest

Read the questions. Circle the picture that answers each question.

1. Which one is the smallest?
2. Which one is the tallest?
3. Who is older?
4. Which one is shorter?

4 Book 2.2/Unit 3 Princess Pooh

Extension: Have children draw pictures and ask questions of each other that are similar to those in the exercise.

175

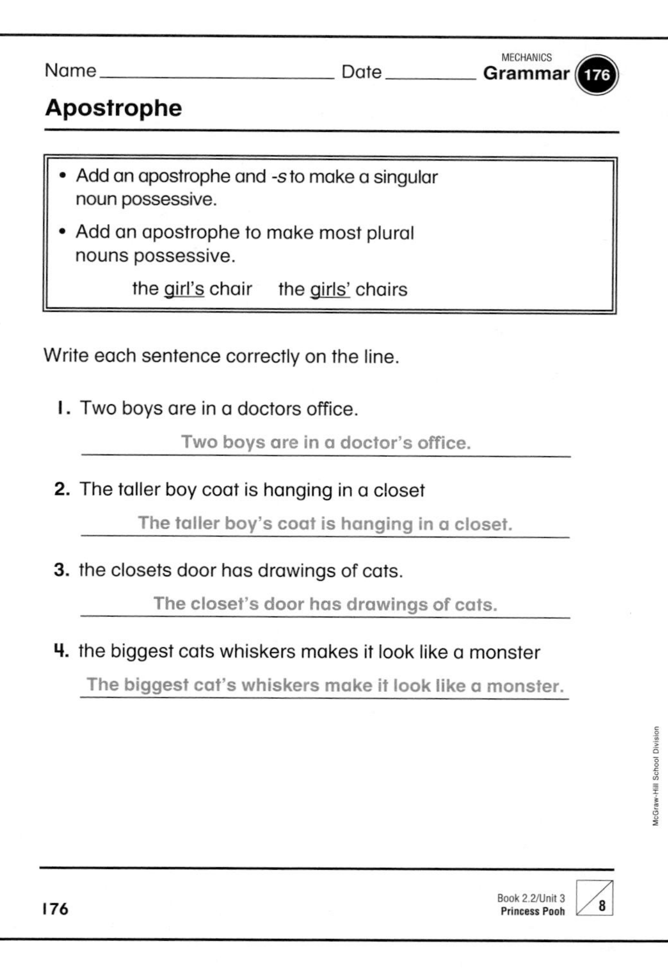

Name________________ Date________ MECHANICS Grammar 176

Apostrophe

- Add an apostrophe and *-s* to make a singular noun possessive.
- Add an apostrophe to make most plural nouns possessive.

  the girl's chair the girls' chairs

Write each sentence correctly on the line.

1. Two boys are in a doctors office.

   Two boys are in a doctor's office.
2. The taller boy coat is hanging in a closet

   The taller boy's coat is hanging in a closet.
3. the closets door has drawings of cats.

   The closet's door has drawings of cats.
4. the biggest cats whiskers makes it look like a monster

   The biggest cat's whiskers make it look like a monster.

McGraw-Hill School Division

176

Book 2.2/Unit 3 Princess Pooh 8

Name ____________ Date ________ TEST **Grammar 177**

Adjectives That Compare

A. Read each sentence. Add *-er* or *-est* to each adjective. Write the new adjective on the line.

1. That is the (tall) tree on the street. ___tallest___

2. It has the (hard) wood of all. ___hardest___

3. Wood is (strong) than paper. ___stronger___

B. Read each pair of sentences. Mark the one that is correct.

4. ⓐ My fingers are coldest than yours.

● My fingers are colder than yours.

5. ⓐ Jane is shortest than Emily.

● Jane is shorter than Emily.

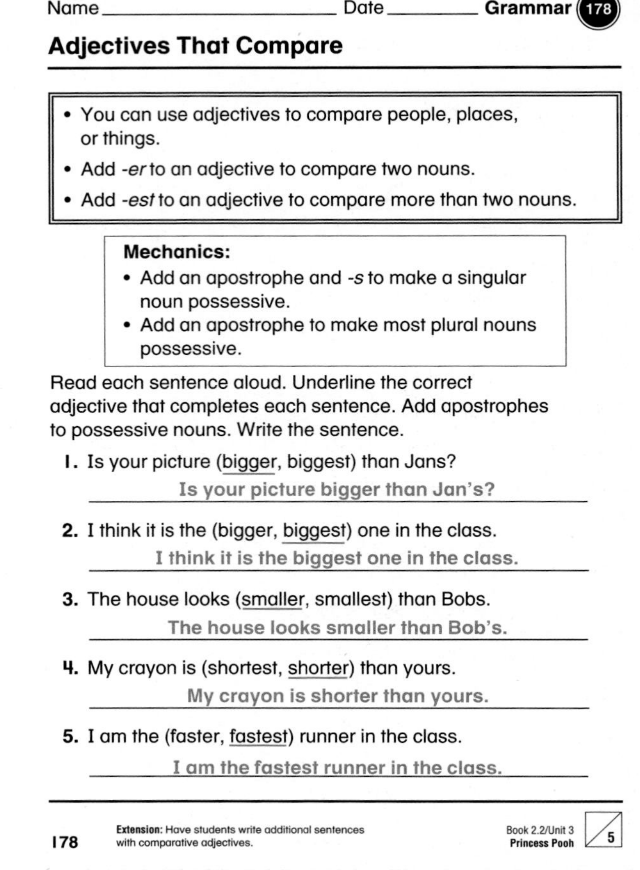

Name ____________ Date ________ MORE PRACTICE **Grammar 178**

Adjectives That Compare

- You can use adjectives to compare people, places, or things.
- Add *-er* to an adjective to compare two nouns.
- Add *-est* to an adjective to compare more than two nouns.

Mechanics:
- Add an apostrophe and *-s* to make a singular noun possessive.
- Add an apostrophe to make most plural nouns possessive.

Read each sentence aloud. Underline the correct adjective that completes each sentence. Add apostrophes to possessive nouns. Write the sentence.

1. Is your picture (bigger, biggest) than Jans?
Is your picture bigger than Jan's?

2. I think it is the (bigger, biggest) one in the class.
I think it is the biggest one in the class.

3. The house looks (smaller, smallest) than Bobs.
The house looks smaller than Bob's.

4. My crayon is (shortest, shorter) than yours.
My crayon is shorter than yours.

5. I am the (faster, fastest) runner in the class.
I am the fastest runner in the class.

 Extension: Have students write additional sentences with comparative adjectives.

Name________________________ Date__________ PRETEST SPELLING 173

Words with Digraphs *th, sh*

Pretest Directions
Fold back your paper along the dotted line. Use the blanks to write each word as it is said to you. When you finish the test, unfold the paper and correct any spelling mistakes. Practice those words for the Posttest.

1. ______ 1. with
2. ______ 2. push
3. ______ 3. both
4. ______ 4. rush
5. ______ 5. bath
6. ______ 6. mouth
7. ______ 7. brush
8. ______ 8. teeth
9. ______ 9. dash
10. ______ 10. fish

Challenge Words

______ cousins
______ golden
______ princess
______ restaurant
______ world

To Parents,
Here are the results of your child's weekly spelling Pretest. You can help your child study for the Posttest by following these simple steps for each word on the word list:

1. Read the word to your child.
2. Have your child write the word, saying each letter as it is written.
3. Say each letter of the word as your child checks the spelling.
4. If a mistake has been made, have your child read each letter of the correctly spelled word aloud and then repeat steps 1–3.

Name________________________ Date__________ AT-HOME WORD STUDY SPELLING 174

Words with Digraphs *th, sh*

Using the Word Study Steps

1. LOOK at the word.
2. SAY the word aloud.
3. STUDY the letters in the word.
4. WRITE the word.
5. CHECK the word.
   Did you spell the word right?
   If not, go back to step 1.

Spelling Tip
Think of a word that rhymes with a new word. Rhyming words often have the same spelling pattern.
Example:
w + ish = wish
f + ish = fish

Find and Circle
Where are the spelling words?

b	r	u	s	h	c	b	a	t	h	f	a
o	u	d	a	s	h	t	e	e	t	h	x
t	s	f	i	s	h	q	p	u	s	h	d
h	h	m	o	u	t	h	v	w	i	t	h

To Parents or Helpers:
Using the Word Study Steps above as your child comes across any new words will help him or her spell well. Review the steps as you both go over this week's spelling words.
Go over the Spelling Tip with your child. Help your child write new words that use beginnings and endings of words he or she can spell. Also, help your child form words related in meaning from other new words.
Help your child find and circle the spelling words in the puzzle.

Name________________________ Date__________ EXPLORE THE PATTERN SPELLING 175

Words with Digraphs *th, sh*

with	both	bath	brush	dash
push	rush	mouth	teeth	fish

Write the spelling words that follow the patterns in the crowns below.

Words ending with th
1. with
2. both
3. bath
4. mouth
5. teeth

Words ending with sh
6. push
7. rush
8. brush
9. dash
10. fish

Scramble
Unscramble each set of letters to make a spelling word. Write the words. Then circle the two letters that are the same in each word.

11. eehtt teeth
12. tohb both
13. thba bath
14. oumht mouth
15. ithw with

Name________________________ Date__________ PRACTICE AND EXTEND SPELLING 176

Words with Digraphs *th, sh*

with	both	bath	brush	dash
push	rush	mouth	teeth	fish

Gone Fishing
Use spelling words to complete each sentence below.

1. A fish swims in water.
2. Be careful not to push me.
3. The fish has a wide mouth.
4. Come with me in the boat.
5. We will have to rush if we want to be on time.
6. I'm late; now I'll have to dash.
7. I'll take a quick bath.
8. I'll brush my teeth.
9. Then I will brush my hair.
10. When we are ready, we'll both go and dance.

Word Meaning
Synonyms are words that have the same or similar meaning. Write a spelling word that has the same meaning as the word below.

11. hurry rush
12. run dash

Challenge Extension: Have students describe a new restaurant that opened and write a menu for it.

Name____________________ Date__________ PROOFREAD AND WRITE **SPELLING** 177

Words with Digraphs *th, sh*

Proofreading Activity

There are six spelling mistakes in the paragraph below. Circle each misspelled word. Write the words correctly on the lines below.

The big (fishe) began to (rusch) toward him. It wanted to bite him with its sharp (feith). What could he do? He waited for the fish to close its big (mout). Then he said, "Listen, I don't see why you want to (pussh) me. There's enough room for (botth) of us to swim here."

1. fish
2. rush
3. teeth
4. mouth
5. push
6. both

Writing Activity

What are the girls doing? Write sentences about the picture. Use four of your spelling words. Circle the spelling words you use.

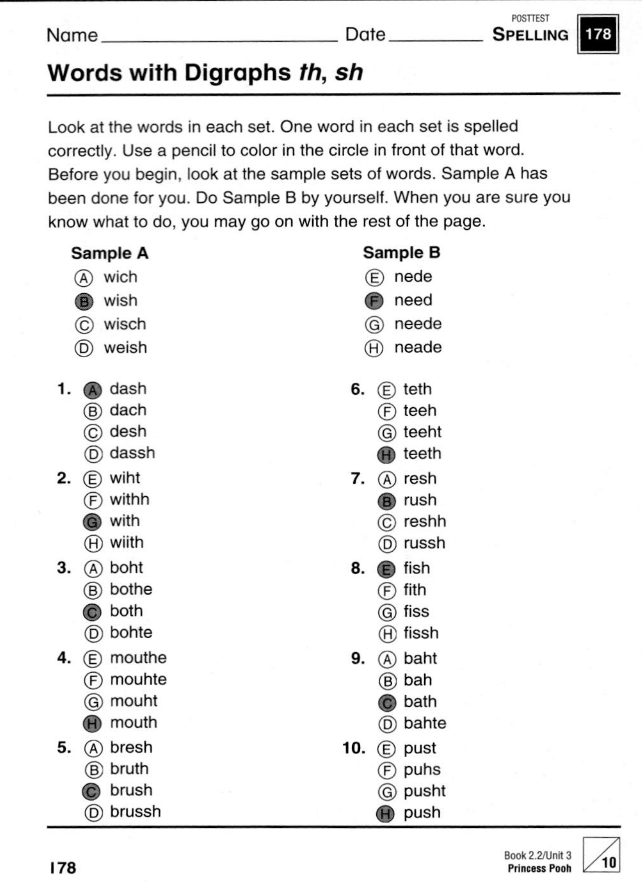

Name____________________ Date__________ POSTTEST **SPELLING** 178

Words with Digraphs *th, sh*

Look at the words in each set. One word in each set is spelled correctly. Use a pencil to color in the circle in front of that word. Before you begin, look at the sample sets of words. Sample A has been done for you. Do Sample B by yourself. When you are sure you know what to do, you may go on with the rest of the page.

Sample A
- Ⓐ wich
- ● wish
- Ⓒ wisch
- Ⓓ weish

Sample B
- Ⓔ nede
- ● need
- Ⓖ neede
- Ⓗ neade

1. Ⓐ● dash Ⓑ dach Ⓒ desh Ⓓ dassh

2. Ⓔ wiht Ⓕ withh Ⓖ● with Ⓗ wiith

3. Ⓐ boht Ⓑ bothe Ⓒ● both Ⓓ bohte

4. Ⓔ mouthe Ⓕ mouhte Ⓖ mouht Ⓗ● mouth

5. Ⓐ bresh Ⓑ bruth Ⓒ● brush Ⓓ brussh

6. Ⓔ teth Ⓕ teeh Ⓖ teeht Ⓗ● teeth

7. Ⓐ resh Ⓑ● rush Ⓒ reshh Ⓓ russh

8. Ⓔ● fish Ⓕ fith Ⓖ fiss Ⓗ fissh

9. Ⓐ baht Ⓑ bah Ⓒ● bath Ⓓ bahte

10. Ⓔ pust Ⓕ puhs Ⓖ pusht Ⓗ● push

Name____________________ Date_________ **Practice 235**

Soft *c* and Soft *g*

Complete the words that answer the riddles.

1. This is something that is cold and hard. You can also see through it.

   i_c_e

2. This is something that helps you cross over the water.

   brid_g_e

3. This is something you must run fast in to win.

   ra_c_e

4. These are small furry animals. Most of them like to eat cheese.

   mi_c_e

5. This is where small animals are kept.

   ca_g_e

6. Lions, tigers, and bears are this word.

   fier_c_e

7. This is what you turn in a book.

   pa_g_e

8. This is something you can cook on.

   ran_g_e

At Home: Have children write a silly sentence using some of the answers on this page.

Name____________________ Date_________ **Practice 236**

Vocabulary

Read each sentence. Write **T** if the sentence is true.
Write **F** if the sentence if false.

escaped	fierce	hidden	machine	swaying	swift

_T_ **1.** If you are hidden, you can't be seen.

_F_ **2.** A swift deer moves slowly.

_T_ **3.** The fish that escaped is free.

_F_ **4.** If you are swaying, you are very still.

_T_ **5.** You should be careful around a fierce dog.

_T_ **6.** If you are a swift runner, you might win the race.

_F_ **7.** Most machines are very slow.

_F_ **8.** A fierce animal is friendly to people.

_F_ **9.** A monkey that has escaped is still in a cage.

_F_ **10.** If you are hidden, everyone can see you.

_T_ **11.** A machine can do a lot of work.

_T_ **12.** The swaying branches on a tree are moving.

At Home: Have children make up other true and false statements about the vocabulary words.

Going to School

I have escaped many scary things! Sometimes when I'm afraid I hide in strange places. I dig into the sand. I even hide behind a rock.

My friends and I will stay hidden for hours. Life in the sea is dangerous and exciting!

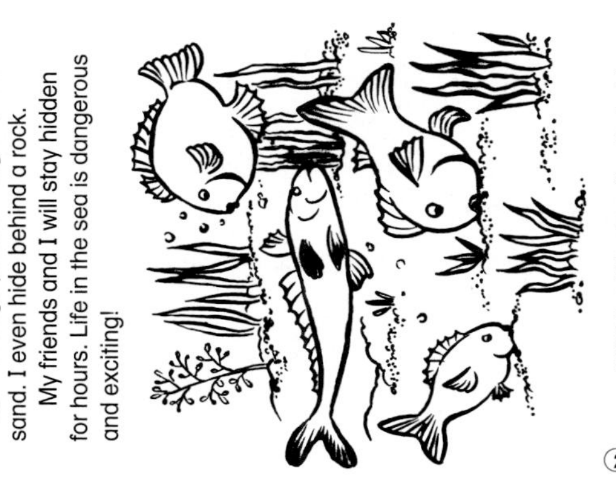

At Home: Have children draw a picture of a school of fish. Then have them draw some fish hiding behind the rocks.

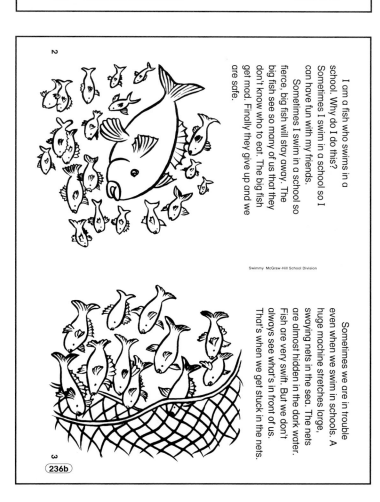

I am a fish who swims in a school. Why do I do this? Sometimes I swim in a school so I can have fun with my friends.

Sometimes I swim in a school so fierce, big fish will stay away. The big fish see so many of us that they don't know who to eat. The big fish get mad. Finally they give up and we are safe.

Sometimes we are in trouble even when we swim in schools. A huge machine stretches large, swaying nets in the sea. The nets are almost hidden in the dark water. Fish are very swift. But we don't always see what's in front of us. That's when we get stuck in the nets.

Name ______ Date ______ **Practice 237**

Story Comprehension

Think about "Swimmy." Read this passage about "Swimmy."

> Swimmy wanted to look all around. But the little red fish were afraid a large fish would eat them. Swimmy wanted to think of some way to have fun.

Write a complete sentence to answer each question.

1. What did Swimmy do right before this part of the story?
   He explored the deep wet world all by himself. Then he met a school of fish just like himself.
2. What did Swimmy do right after this part of the story?
   He organized the school of fish to look like one large fish moving through the water.
3. What is important about this part of the story?
   It shows that the little fish can solve a big problem if they all work together.
4. How do you think the little fish would describe Swimmy?
   Possible response: They would describe him as their leader.

At Home: Ask children to name things that Swimmy and the fish will see as they travel the deep, wet world.

Name ______ Date ______ **Practice 238**

Do an Author Search at the Library

When you do an **author search,** it is important to look closely at the description of the books listed. If you click on the icon that says "Full Record," you will find more information about a specific book.

Look at this result list of an author search. Let's say you read *Take Joy: The Tasha Tudor Christmas Book.* Now you want another book about the holidays. What would be a good choice?

1. Title: Take Joy: The Magical World of Tasha Tudor (video recording)
   Pub. Date: 1996 ■ **See Full Record**
2. Title: A Time to Keep: The Tasha Tudor Book of Holidays
   Pub. Date: 1992 ■ **See Full Record**
3. Title: Take Joy: The Tasha Tudor Christmas Book
   Pub. Date: 1966 ■ **See Full Record**

1. A Time to Keep: The Tasha Tudor Book of Holidays

To further help you decide, click on the Full Record icon. This is what you'd see. Use this information to answer the questions that follow.

Title: A Time to Keep: The Tasha Tudor Book of Holidays
Author: Tudor, Tasha
Publisher: Chicago: Rand McNally, © 1977; 58 pages, illustrations
Subjects: holidays in old New England

Library Location	Call Number
Wilson	J 394 TUD
East Treamer	J/394.26974/T

2. What is the subject of this book? holidays in old New England
3. Which library locations have a copy? Wilson and East Treamer
4. What is the call number of this book at Wilson library? J 394 TUD

At Home: Ask children what, besides books, is available by Tasha Tudor. (a videotape)

Name ______ Date ______ **Practice 239**

Soft *c* and Soft *g*

Below are pairs of words. The second word is scrambled. Unscramble the second word to make it rhyme with the first word and write your word on the line.

1. range	asgtrne	strange
2. race	epalc	place
3. rice	inec	nice
4. face	lcea	lace
5. cage	tsgae	stage
6. mice	cei	ice
7. page	gera	rage
8. twice	cmei	mice
9. brace	ctrae	trace
10. wage	gea	age
11. nice	lisce	slice
12. juice	ecrtu	truce

At Home: Have children write a sentence for two of the words they formed.

Name ______ Date ______ **Practice 240**

Soft *c, g;* Long *a, o, e, i*

Circle, then write, the word that completes each sentence.

1. Can you blow out all the candles?
   (blow) snow flow
2. I put ice in my drink.
   (ice) mice dice
3. He made a pot with some clay.
   hay (clay) say
4. The leaves fell from the tree.
   (tree) bee sneeze
5. Pam had a dream that she could fly.
   leap cream (dream)
6. I use my brain to think.
   stain chain (brain)
7. I change into pajamas before I go to bed.
   (change) strange page
8. Let's take the train to the beach.
   hail (train) rain

At Home: Have children write a one-paragraph story based on one of the sentences above.

Name_______________ Date________ **Practice 241**

Main Idea

Details are bits of information that support the main idea.

Read these sentences about "Swimmy." Then write the main idea for each section and one detail that supports it. Answers will vary.

A group of little fish lived in a small part of the great ocean. All were red except one of them. The little black fish swam faster than all the rest. Swimmy was his name.

1. **Main Idea:** The little fish lived in the ocean.
2. **Detail:** All were red except Swimmy; he was the fastest swimmer.

A tuna fish swallowed all the little red fish one day. But Swimmy escaped. He was very sad as he swam away.

3. **Main Idea:** A tuna fish ate all the fish except Swimmy.
4. **Detail:** Swimmy escaped; he was very sad.

Swimmy saw a school of little fish, just like him. They were afraid of the big fish. Swimmy taught them to swim close together like one giant fish.

5. **Main Idea:** Swimmy found another school of little fish.
6. **Detail:** They were afraid of the big fish; Swimmy taught them to swim close together.

At Home: Ask children to name one more detail for each main idea on this page.

Name_______________ Date________ **Practice 242**

Figurative Language

A writer will sometimes describe something by comparing it to something else.

Read the first sentence in each pair. Think about the picture the words bring to mind. Then complete the second statement to tell what the first sentence means.

1. My little dog can eat like a horse.
   My little dog can eat ___a lot___.
2. The hailstones were the size of baseballs.
   The hailstones were ___big___.
3. My sister is as light as a feather.
   My sister is not ___heavy___.
4. His shirt looked like an old rag.
   His shirt was not ___new or clean___.
5. Those deer can run like the wind.
   Those deer can run ___fast___.
6. The forest fire spread like lightning.
   The forest fire spread ___quickly___.

At Home: Point out that the last two sentences contain sayings that mean "quickly." Ask children to invent two more comparisons that mean the same thing.

Name ____________ Date ________ **Reteach 235**

Soft *c* and Soft *g*

Read the words.
br**ce** dan**ce** pa**ge** hu**ge**

Complete each sentence with a word from the box.

fierce	bridge	face	lace	place	change

1. The fierce tiger is hungry.
2. Sammy needs to change his wet socks.
3. Leslie drew a smiling face.
4. This dress has lace on it.
5. Loren walked over the bridge.
6. Tom's favorite place is the ocean.

At Home: Have children make a drawing of one of the sentences.

Name ____________ Date ________ **Reteach 236**

Vocabulary

Read each riddle. Circle the word that answers the riddle.

1. I am a monkey. I just got away from the zoo. I am very happy to be free. What did I do? — (escaped) sang jumped
2. I am not a person. But I do a lot of work. I make many things. I can lift heavy boxes. What am I? — ship (machine) artist
3. I am a wild lion. Don't come too close. If you try to catch me, watch out! What would you say I am? — friendly kind (fierce)
4. You can't see me. I'm not out in the open. I won't come out until you find me. What would you say I am? — (hidden) asleep hungry
5. I am a large tree. I am moving in the wind. I lean one way. Then I lean the other way. What am I doing? — walking running (swaying)
6. I am a bug. I can fly fast in the air. I fly so fast that you might not even see me. What might you say about me? — pretty (swift) slow

At Home: Have children write a sentence for each of the words they circled.

Name ____________ Date ________ **Reteach 237**

Story Comprehension

Complete the chart. Answers may vary.

Main Character: Swimmy
Setting: The ocean
Beginning of the Story: All of Swimmy's brothers and sisters are eaten by a big tuna fish.
Middle of the Story: Swimmy sees all of the different creatures that live in the sea. He meets another school of fish that are hiding.
End of the Story: Swimmy teaches the other fish how to swim so that they will be safe from bigger fish.
Draw a picture of Swimmy and his friends swimming safely.

At Home: Ask children to talk about why the school of little fish could scare away a big fish.

Name ____________ Date ________ **Reteach 238**

Do an Author Search at the Library

If you want to find a list of books by a particular author, you can do an **author search** at the computer in your library.

Below is an author search of books by Michelle Miller.

Results of Search

Top 8 matches (*author, Michelle Miller*)

1. Title: **Car Cat Rides Again** Published 1996
2. Title: **Car Cat** Published 1993
3. Title: **I Want to Be a Queen** Published 1993
4. Title: **A Garden for Mr. Rat** Published 1992
5. Title: **Nursery Rhymes A-B-C** Published 1992
6. Title: **I Want to Be a Doctor** Published 1992
7. Title: **I Want to Be a Dancer** Published 1991
8. Title: **I Want to Be a Teacher** Published 1990

Use the above list to answer these questions.

1. Which of the above books was published first? I Want to Be a Teacher
2. In which year was the first book in the "Car Cat" series published? 1993
3. If you liked "Car Cat", which book here would be good to read next? Car Cat Rides Again
4. Which book has something about the alphabet in its title? Nursery Rhymes A-B-C

At Home: Have children go to the library and do a computer author search of a favorite writer.

Name_______________ Date________ **Reteach 239**

Soft *c* and Soft *g*

Say these words. Listen for each sound made by the letters in dark type.
fen**ce** twi**ce** ed**ge** ra**ge**

Use a word from the box to answer each riddle.
Write the word on the line.

face	nice	cage	ice	stage	rice

1. This is a place where a mouse might live.
   cage
2. This is someone who is kind.
   nice
3. This is something everyone has.
   face
4. This is very cold.
   ice
5. This is where a play happens.
   stage
6. This is something we eat.
   rice

6 Book 2.2/Unit 3 **Swimmy**

At Home: Have children write two more words that contain the sounds /s/ spelled **ce** and /j/ spelled **ge**.

Name_______________ Date________ **Reteach 240**

Soft *c, g;* Long *a, o, e, i*

I _____ an apple.
read mean (eat)

Read the sentence. Circle the word that completes the sentence. Then write the word on the line.

1. The children hide in the garden.
   (hide) side high
2. I mow the lawn.
   know low (mow)
3. The dog wags her tail .
   nail (tail) jail
4. What day of the week is it?
   bay spray (day)
5. I bake a huge cake.
   age (huge) page
6. The mice share some bread.
   rice dice (mice)

At Home: Have children write three questions using some of the words they did not circle.

Book 2.2/Unit 3 **Swimmy** 6

Name_______________ Date________ **Reteach 241**

Main Idea

Remember: **Details** are bits of information that support the **main idea.**

Read the stories. Underline two details for each main idea.

Lighthouses beam light across the water to show ships the way to shore. Long ago, their light came from burning wood, coal, or oil. Today, most lighthouses use electric lights.

1. **Main Idea:**
   Lighthouses beam light across the water.
   Which details support the main idea?
   a. Lighthouses once used burning wood to make light.
   b. The light helps ships find their way.
   c. Seagulls make nests in lighthouses.

The Sankaty Head Lighthouse is sometimes called "Bright Eyes." Its electric beam is as bright as 3 million candles. It can be seen 29 miles away.

2. **Main Idea:**
   Sankaty Head is a bright lighthouse.
   Which details support the main idea?
   a. A fire burned the lighthouse down.
   b. Its nickname is "Bright Eyes."
   c. It is as bright as 3 million candles.

4 Book 2.2/Unit 3 **Swimmy**

At Home: Have children write another supporting detail for each of the main ideas.

Name_______________ Date________ **Reteach 242**

Figurative Language

To describe what something is like, a writer sometimes will compare it to something else.

That horse can race **like the wind.** My pet rabbit is **as soft as silk.**

Think about "Swimmy." Think about the things under the sea. Draw a line to the phrase that is a good comparison.

1. The sea is — as blue as the sky.
   as red as a rose.
2. Sea anemones look like a school of fish.
   — like pink palm trees.
3. The sea rocks look — like sugar candy.
   as light as a feather.
4. An eel is — as long as a rope.
   like a tooth
5. A clam is as big as a house.
   — as hard as a rock.

At Home: Have children draw a picture for one of the comparisons above. Ask them to write the comparison as a caption.

Book 2.2/Unit 3 **Swimmy** 5

Name ______________________ Date ________ **Extend 235**

Soft *c* and Soft *g*

The fish can only follow words with the same ending sound as **place** or **strange.** Color the fish's path blue.

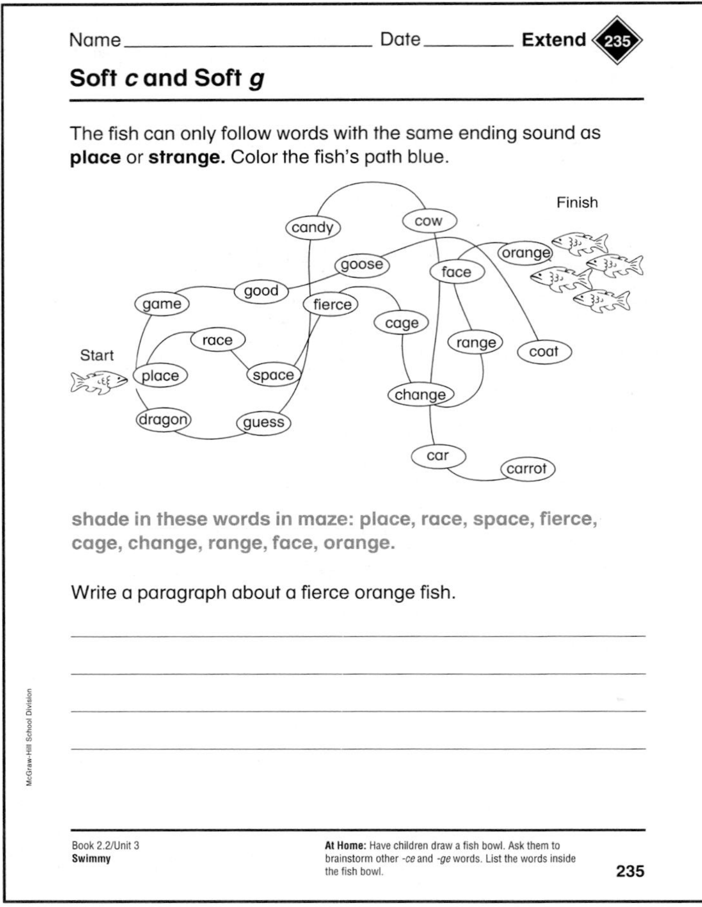

shade in these words in maze: place, race, space, fierce, cage, change, range, face, orange.

Write a paragraph about a fierce orange fish.

Book 2.2/Unit 3
Swimmy

At Home: Have children draw a fish bowl. Ask them to brainstorm other *-ce* and *-ge* words. List the words inside the fish bowl.

235

Name ______________________ Date ________ **Extend 236**

Vocabulary

machine	hidden	swaying
escaped	fierce	swift

The sentences tell what is happening in the picture. Write the words from the box that have nearly the same meaning as the underlined words.

1. The dog broke free and ran out the door. escaped
2. This dog looks mean and angry. fierce
3. The cat stays out of sight so the dog can't find it. hidden
4. A lawn mower is something with moving parts used to do a job. machine
5. The branches of the tree are moving back and forth in the wind. swaying
6. The cat will have to be fast when it comes down. swift

Will the dog find the cat? Will the cat escape? Write two sentences to tell what will happen next. Use words from the box.

Sample answers are shown.

The cat escaped by jumping over the dog.

The dog was not as swift as the cat.

236

At Home: Have children draw a picture illustrating the vocabulary words. Ask children to use the words to label their picture.

Book 2.2/Unit 3
Swimmy

Name ______________________ Date ________ **Extend 237**

Story Comprehension

Swimmy got his friends to work together to solve a problem. How could you get your friends to work together to change something?

Draw a picture of yourself. Write the words you would say to your friends. A sample answer is shown.

We could all bring in cans of food. Then we could give the food to people who need it.

Book 2.2/Unit 3
Swimmy

At Home: Ask children to think about other deep-sea problems that Swimmy and the other fish might work together to solve.

237

Name ______________________ Date ________ **Extend 238**

Do an Author Search at the Library

Choose your favorite author. Go to the library. Use the computer to do an author search. List the books the author has written below.

1. ____________
2. ____________
3. ____________
4. ____________
5. ____________
6. ____________

What kinds of books do you think your author likes to write?

Answers will vary.

How can you tell? Answers will vary, but should be based on the list generated by the computer.

238

At Home: Have children make a list of all their favorite authors. Encourage children to look in the library for books by these authors.

Book 2.2/Unit 3
Swimmy

Name_______________ Date________ **Extend 239**

Soft *c* and Soft *g*

Put an **X** on words that are not spelled correctly. Use the words left in the box to answer the riddles.

fiexse	strange	chanj	ras	place
fierce	stranj	change	race	plas

1. I am somewhere you can go. place
2. Some dangerous animals are like this. fierce
3. Something odd can also be this. strange
4. The runner at the finish line has just won this. race
5. This is what happens to the color of some trees in the fall. change

Write two or three sentences telling about your favorite place.

At Home: Have children write riddles for other **-ce** and **-ge** words.

Name_______________ Date________ **Extend 240**

Soft *c, g;* Long *a, o, e, i*

eel	**deep**	**fierce**	**giant**	**place**	**sky**
strange	**sea**	**swaying**	**swallowed**	**weeds**	

Unscramble the letters. Then write the words correctly. The first one is done for you.

caple	**place**
gsrtnae	strange
eeicrf	fierce
ele	eel
gwysnai	swaying
wdewlalso	swallowed
edep	deep
dwsee	weeds
esa	sea
ating	giant
ysk	sky

Use some of the words to write a sentence about what you might find in the sea.

Answers will vary.

At Home: Play a game of "Twenty Questions" in which you pick an object in the sea. Have children ask questions that can be answered with "yes" or "no."

Name_______________ Date________ **Extend 241**

Main Idea

Read the story.

At the library we read a book about dolphins. We found out that a dolphin is not a fish. A dolphin is a mammal that swims. Dolphins have fins just like fish do. Dolphins do not have gills. Dolphins breathe with their lungs just like other mammals do. Dolphins also have teeth. Dolphins live in family groups. They can be very smart. They "talk" to each other underwater using clicks and squeals.

Write a title for the story that shows the main idea.

Possible titles: All About Dolphins; A Fishy Mammal; Down Deep with Dolphins

Circle the picture that shows the main idea of the story.

Circle the dolphin swimming.

What do you think the most interesting part of the story is?

At Home: Children can create an illustrated poster about dolphins.

Name_______________ Date________ **Extend 242**

Figurative Language

Draw a line under the words in each sentence that help you form a picture in your mind. Draw a picture to go with each sentence.

1. A creature as flat as a pancake creeps along the bottom of the sea.
2. It looks like a forest of seaweed is growing from sugar-candy rocks.
3. An eel almost too long to remember swam by.
4. The sea anemones looked like pink palm trees swaying in the wind.

Write two new sentences. Use words that form pictures in the reader's mind. Sample answers shown.

The man crushed the box as flat as a pancake.

Sam felt like he had a mountain of homework to do.

At Home: Work with children to make a list of favorite descriptive expressions. Invite children to choose one to illustrate.

Name ______________ Date ________ LEARN Grammar 179

Adverbs

- An **adverb** tells more about a verb.
- An adverb can tell how.

  The man stood **still**.

  The people left **quickly**.

Circle the verb in each sentence.
Then write the adverb.

1. The dancers (moved) smoothly.
   smoothly
2. The people (spoke) loudly.
   loudly
3. Music (played) softly.
   softly
4. The woman happily (answered) questions.
   happily
5. The plane gently (landed).
   gently

Extension: Have one group of children write a list of verbs. Have another write adverbs that go with the verbs. Then have them switch tasks.

Name ______________ Date ________ LEARN AND PRACTICE Grammar 180

Adverbs

- An adverb can tell when or where.

  The bus leaves soon. (when)

  It will roll away. (where)

Circle the adverb in each sentence.
Write **when** if it tells when.
Write **where** if it tells where.

1. (Now) we see the bus. when
2. We climb (inside). where
3. (Finally,) the bus starts to move. when
4. We look (down). where
5. We stop (soon). when

Extension: Have the children underline the verb in each sentence.

Name ______________ Date ________ REVIEW AND PRACTICE Grammar 181

Adverbs

- An **adverb** tells more about a verb.
- An adverb can tell how, when, or where.

  Soon the bus is ready.

  The children sit inside.

  They talk loudly.

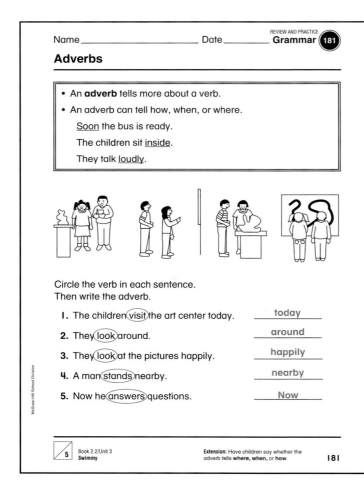

Circle the verb in each sentence.
Then write the adverb.

1. The children (visit) the art center today. today
2. They (look) around. around
3. They (look) at the pictures happily. happily
4. A man (stands) nearby. nearby
5. Now he (answers) questions. Now

Extension: Have children say whether the adverb tells **where, when,** or **how**.

Name ______________ Date ________ MECHANICS Grammar 182

Using Capital Letters

- The pronoun "I" is always a capital letter.
- A proper noun begins with a capital letter.

  I am going to Paris soon to visit Larry.

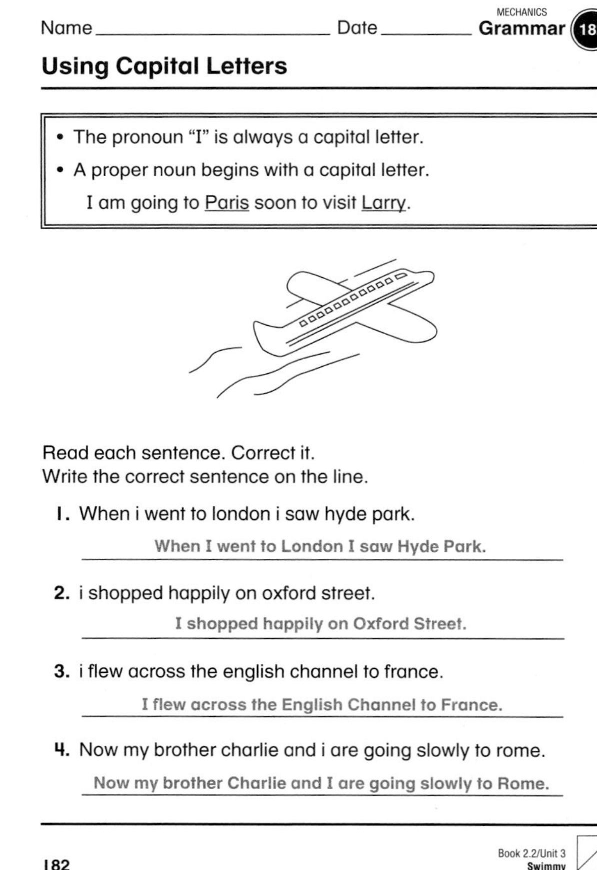

Read each sentence. Correct it.
Write the correct sentence on the line.

1. When i went to london i saw hyde park.
   When I went to London I saw Hyde Park.
2. i shopped happily on oxford street.
   I shopped happily on Oxford Street.
3. i flew across the english channel to france.
   I flew across the English Channel to France.
4. Now my brother charlie and i are going slowly to rome.
   Now my brother Charlie and I are going slowly to Rome.

Name______________________ Date_________ TEST Grammar 183

Adverbs

Read each question. Mark your answer.

1. Which sentence has an adverb that tells when?
   - ⓐ I like this large picture.
   - ⓑ It has great colors.
   - ● We are visiting the museum today.
2. Which sentence has an adverb that tells where?
   - ● A guard stands nearby.
   - ⓑ He has a small cell phone.
   - ⓒ He smiles at us.
3. Which sentence has an adverb that tells how?
   - ⓐ We like the museum.
   - ⓑ We look at the wall of pictures.
   - ● We talk quietly about them.
4. Which sentence has an adverb that tells when?
   - ⓐ We ask many questions.
   - ⓑ We want to know about the artists.
   - ● Now the teacher tells us about the pictures.
5. Which sentences has an adverb that tells how?
   - ⓐ The artists made the pictures.
   - ● The artists carefully drew the pictures.
   - ⓒ The artists are drawing the pictures.

Name______________________ Date_________ MORE PRACTICE Grammar 184

Adverbs

- An adverb tells more about a verb.
- An adverb can tell how, when, or where.

Mechanics:
- The pronoun "I" is always a capital letter.
- A proper noun begins with a capital letter.

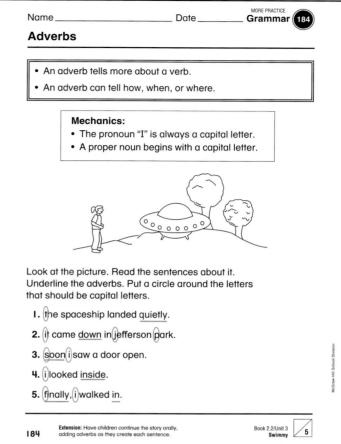

Look at the picture. Read the sentences about it. Underline the adverbs. Put a circle around the letters that should be capital letters.

1. the spaceship landed quietly.
2. it came down in jefferson park.
3. soon i saw a door open.
4. i looked inside.
5. finally, i walked in.

 Extension: Have children continue the story orally, adding adverbs as they create each sentence.

Name____________________ Date__________ PRETEST SPELLING 179

Words with Digraphs *th, wh*

Pretest Directions

Fold back your paper along the dotted line. Use the blanks to write each word as it is said to you. When you finish the test, unfold the paper and correct any spelling mistakes. Practice those words for the Posttest.

1. __________	1. there
2. __________	2. wheel
3. __________	3. than
4. __________	4. whale
5. __________	5. whimper
6. __________	6. thought
7. __________	7. whirl
8. __________	8. whisper
9. __________	9. through
10. __________	10. them
Challenge Words	
__________	escaped
__________	fierce
__________	hidden
__________	machine
__________	swift

To Parents,

Here are the results of your child's weekly spelling Pretest. You can help your child study for the Posttest by following these simple steps for each word on the word list:

1. Read the word to your child.
2. Have your child write the word, saying each letter as it is written.
3. Say each letter of the word as your child checks the spelling.
4. If a mistake has been made, have your child read each letter of the correctly spelled word aloud and then repeat steps 1–3.

Name____________________ Date__________ AT-HOME WORD STUDY SPELLING 180

Words with Digraphs *th, wh*

Using the Word Study Steps

1. LOOK at the word.
2. SAY the word aloud.
3. STUDY the letters in the word.
4. WRITE the word.
5. CHECK the word.
   Did you spell the word right?
   If not, go back to step 1.

Spelling Tip

Use words you know how to spell to help you spell new words. Word beginnings and endings can help.
Example:
when + f**eel** = wheel

Crossword Puzzle

Write the spelling word that best matches the clue. Put the spelling words in the boxes that start with the same number.

CROSSWORD CLUES

ACROSS
4. talk in a very quiet voice
5. from one end to the other
6. the people over there
7. spin

DOWN
1. in that place
2. idea
3. biggest sea mammal
4. one of two on a bike or one of four on a car

														1 T	
						2 T								H	
				3 W		H			4 W	H	I	S	P	E	R
			5 T	H	R	O	U	G	H					R	
				A		U			E			6 T	H	E	M
7 W	H	I	R	L		G			E						
				E		H			L						
						T									

To Parents or Helpers:

Using the Word Study Steps above as your child comes across any new words will help him or her spell well. Review the steps as you both go over this week's spelling words.

Go over the Spelling Tip with your child. Help your child use a computer spell-check feature to learn that it will not catch mistakes in sound-alike words.

Help your child solve the crossword puzzle.

Name____________________ Date__________ EXPLORE THE PATTERN SPELLING 181

Words with Digraphs *th, wh*

there	than	whimper	whirl	through
wheel	whale	thought	whisper	them

Write the spelling words that follow the patterns in the sea creatures below.

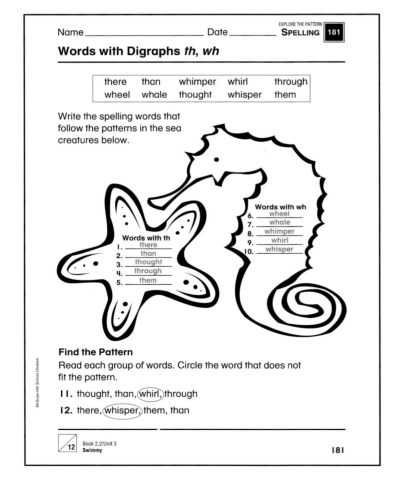

Words with th
1. there
2. than
3. thought
4. through
5. them

Words with wh
6. wheel
7. whale
8. whimper
9. whirl
10. whisper

Find the Pattern

Read each group of words. Circle the word that does not fit the pattern.

11. thought, than, (whirl), through
12. there, (whisper), them, than

Name____________________ Date__________ PRACTICE AND EXTEND SPELLING 182

Words with Digraphs *th, wh*

there	than	whimper	whirl	through
wheel	whale	thought	whisper	them

A Whale of a Time

Complete each sentence with a spelling word.

1. A __whale__ is a large animal that swims in the sea.
2. Do you see the whale over __there__ by the boat?
3. Whales are bigger __than__ any other animals.
4. People love whales and want to protect __them__.
5. Whales swim __through__ the sea.
6. She __thought__ she saw a whale, but it was only a big wave.
7. The captain turned the __wheel__ and headed home.

What's That Sound?

Choose the word below that tells about the sound in each sentence. Write the word.

whimper whisper

8. The dog was hurt and started to __whimper__.
9. Susan began to __whisper__ to Martin so no one else could hear her.
10. Which spelling word rhymes with **twirl**? __whirl__

Challenge Extension: Have students draw cartoon characters speaking to each other. They should use the Challenge Words in the dialogue.

Name_______________ Date_________ PROOFREAD AND WRITE SPELLING 183

Words with Digraphs *th, wh*

Proofreading Activity

There are five spelling mistakes in these lines from a play. Circle each misspelled word. Write the words correctly on the lines below.

Ike: Turn the (weel)! We want to go over (thre) by the store.
Ann: I (thoght) the store was down this street.
Ike: Be careful not to go (throogh) the yellow light.
Ann: Of course I will. It is better to be safe (thaen) sorry.

1. wheel 2. there 3. thought
4. through 5. than

Writing Activity

Use some of the spelling words to add lines to the play. Tell what Ann and Ike see or say when they go into a store.

6. Ann: ____________________
7. Ike: ____________________
8. Ann: ____________________
9. Ike: ____________________
10. Ann: ____________________

10 Book 2.2/Unit 3 Swimmy 183

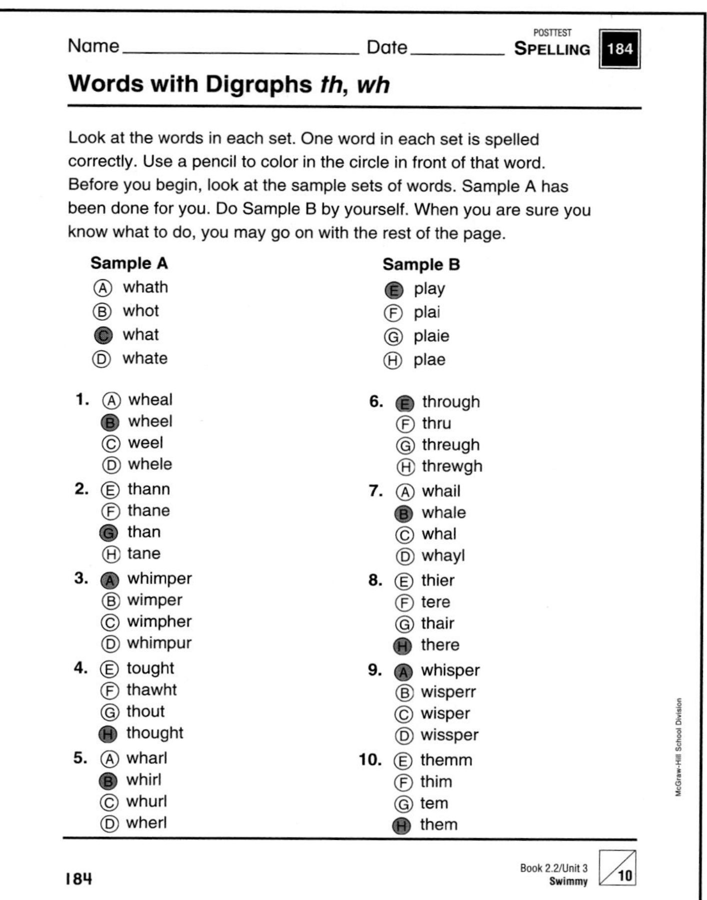

Name_______________ Date_________ POSTTEST SPELLING 184

Words with Digraphs *th, wh*

Look at the words in each set. One word in each set is spelled correctly. Use a pencil to color in the circle in front of that word. Before you begin, look at the sample sets of words. Sample A has been done for you. Do Sample B by yourself. When you are sure you know what to do, you may go on with the rest of the page.

Sample A
Ⓐ whath
Ⓑ whot
● what
Ⓓ whate

Sample B
● play
Ⓕ plai
Ⓖ plaie
Ⓗ plae

1. Ⓐ wheal ● wheel Ⓒ weel Ⓓ whele
2. Ⓔ thann Ⓕ thane ● than Ⓗ tane
3. ● whimper Ⓑ wimper Ⓒ wimpher Ⓓ whimpur
4. Ⓔ tought Ⓕ thawht Ⓖ thout ● thought
5. Ⓐ wharl ● whirl Ⓒ whurl Ⓓ wherl
6. ● through Ⓕ thru Ⓖ threugh Ⓗ threwgh
7. Ⓐ whail ● whale Ⓒ whal Ⓓ whayl
8. Ⓔ thier Ⓕ tere Ⓖ thair ● there
9. ● whisper Ⓑ wisperr Ⓒ wisper Ⓓ wissper
10. Ⓔ themm Ⓕ thim Ⓖ tem ● them

184 Book 2.2/Unit 3 Swimmy 10

The World's Plants Are in Danger • PRACTICE

Name____________________ Date________ **Practice 243**

Soft *c, g; ph, tch;* Long *a, o, e, i*

Circle the word that names each picture. Then write the word on the line.

1. ice (iron) — iron
2. (phone) tone — phone
3. sea (tree) — tree
4. catch (watch) — watch
5. (strange) large — strange

At Home: Ask children to choose two circled words and write two rhyming words for each one.

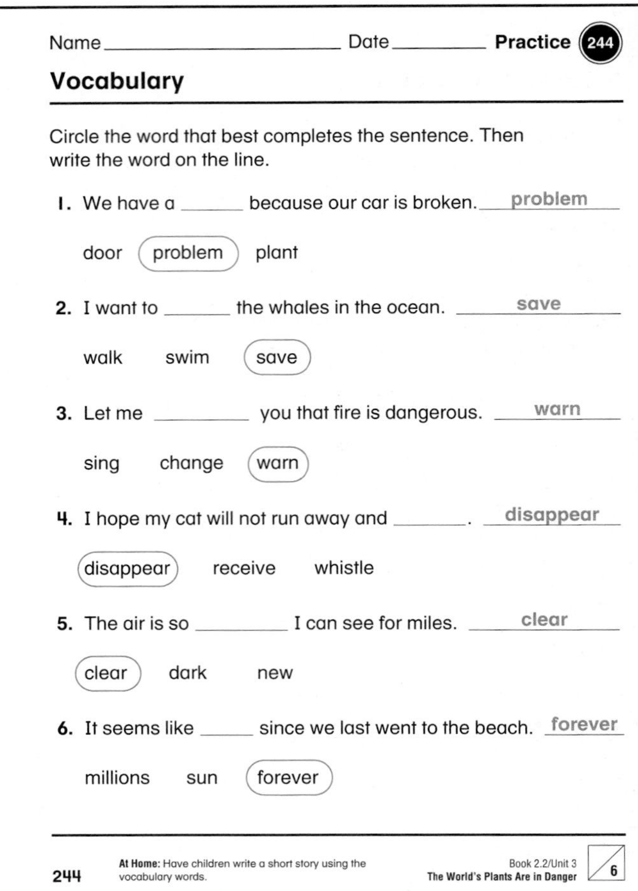

Name____________________ Date________ **Practice 244**

Vocabulary

Circle the word that best completes the sentence. Then write the word on the line.

1. We have a _____ because our car is broken. problem
   door (problem) plant
2. I want to _____ the whales in the ocean. save
   walk swim (save)
3. Let me _____ you that fire is dangerous. warn
   sing change (warn)
4. I hope my cat will not run away and _____. disappear
   (disappear) receive whistle
5. The air is so _____ I can see for miles. clear
   (clear) dark new
6. It seems like _____ since we last went to the beach. forever
   millions sun (forever)

At Home: Have children write a short story using the vocabulary words.

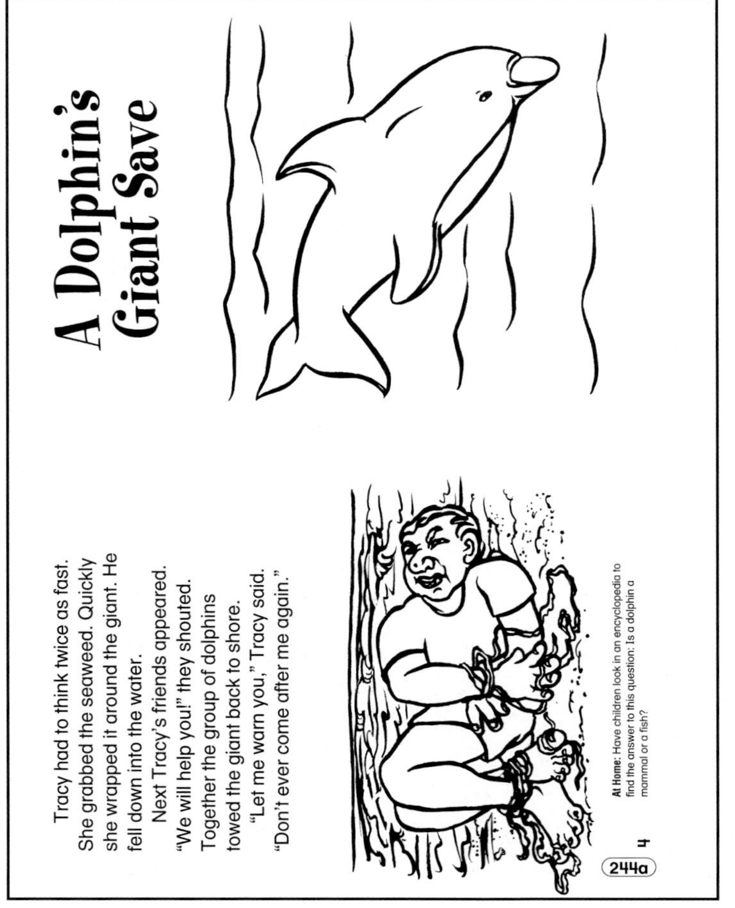

A Dolphin's Giant Save

Tracy had to think twice as fast. She grabbed the seaweed. Quickly she wrapped it around the giant. He fell down into the water.

Next Tracy's friends appeared. "We will help you!" they shouted. Together the group of dolphins towed the giant back to shore.

"Let me warn you," Tracy said. "Don't ever come after me again."

At Home: Have children look in an encyclopedia to find the answer to this question: Is a dolphin a mammal or a fish?

Long ago, there was a dolphin named Tracy. She lived in a deep sea of clear green water.

One day a giant named Pete came to the shore. "I am going to catch the biggest fish there is," he said.

Uh-oh, thought Tracy. This could be a problem.

The giant came marching into the sea. Poor Tracy tried to disappear behind some seaweed. The giant saw her and grabbed at the plants.

"I know you are in there!" he said. "You can't hide from me forever!"

Tracy didn't know what to do. She had to save herself!

Name________________ Date________ **Practice 245**

Story Comprehension

Think about "The World's Plants Are in Danger." Circle the correct answer to each question.

1. Why should you not pick wildflowers?
   - (They may be in danger of disappearing forever.)
   - They may belong to someone else.
2. About how many types of plants are in trouble?
   - about 1,000
   - (about 34,000)
3. What is true about nearly all of the plants in danger?
   - Each kind grows all around the world.
   - (Each kind grows in only one part of the world.)
4. How do humans destroy plants?
   - (Humans destroy the places where plants live.)
   - Humans make animal parks.
5. Why is it so important to save plants?
   - Plants live longer than humans.
   - (Plants clothe us, feed us, and provide us with medicines.)

At Home: Have children name three favorite plants found where they live.

Name________________ Date________ **Practice 246**

Choose a Reference Source

To find the information you need, you must sometimes look at more than one kind of **reference source**.
Look at the following four reference sources. Notice how each tells you something different.

Dictionary Entry

mall 1. a large enclosed shopping center 2. a large open space like a park (môl) noun, *plural* **malls**

Encyclopedia Entry

MALL. See SHOPPING CENTER
SHOPPING CENTER is a group of stores organized as a unit. The open area between them is usually called a mall. It may be covered and air conditioned. Some malls have restaurants, banks, hotels, medical care and theaters. Before World War II there were only ten malls in the U.S.

Nonfiction Book Title Page

THE MALL AS THE NEW TOWN: Are Malls Taking Over America?

by Dominick Sandstrom

Telephone Directory Yellow Pages

Malls/Shopping Centers— Malls
Heritage Mall 555-9876
Highway 98 Mall 555-2389

Use the reference sources above to answer these questions. Write **True** or **False**.

1. The encyclopedia entry would give you an idea what's in a mall. True
2. The nonfiction book includes a question as part of its title. True
3. The dictionary entry gives the names and addresses of the local malls. False
4. Under the entry "Malls/Shopping Centers," the telephone directory lists the phone numbers of all the separate stores in each mall. False

At Home: Have children use several sources to investigate a subject that interests them. Then compare the different reference sources.

Name________________ Date________ **Practice 247**

Main Idea

Read each story. Then read each main idea. Write two details from each story that support the main idea.

> A traffic light tells you to stop and go.
> A flashing light warns of danger ahead.
> Holiday lights are red and green.

Main idea: A light can be a safety signal.

Detail: A traffic light tells you to stop and go.

Detail: A flashing light warns of danger ahead.

> An ant has a pair of antennas on its head.
> Ants work hard to build their nests.
> Ants carry heavy loads of food to their nests.

Main idea: Ants are busy insects.

Detail: Ants work hard to build their nests.

Detail: Ants carry heavy loads of food to their nests.

At Home: Ask children to draw a picture about one detail from each story.

Name________________ Date________ **Practice 248**

Form Generalizations

Read the story. Then read the sentences below the story. Write **Yes** next to each fact from the story. Write **No** if it is not a fact from the story.

I love summer weather in Texas. It is hot in June, and we go swimming. In July, the temperature may reach 100 degrees. We like to go barefoot in this kind of heat. In August, we start school. We wear shorts and cotton shirts to keep cool.

1. June is a hot month in Texas. Yes
2. We can go swimming in June. Yes
3. The weather is hot when we start school. Yes
4. It is too cool to go barefoot in July. No
5. It may be 100 degrees in October. No

Read the sentences in the box. Write the generalization and then write two details that support the generalization.

> Going barefoot is fun.
> Summers are hot in Texas.
> Shorts are good clothes for school.

Generalization: Summers are hot in Texas.

Details: Going barefoot is fun.

Shorts are good clothes for school.

At Home: Have children write a generalization about the weather during the past week in your city.

The World's Plants Are in Danger • PRACTICE

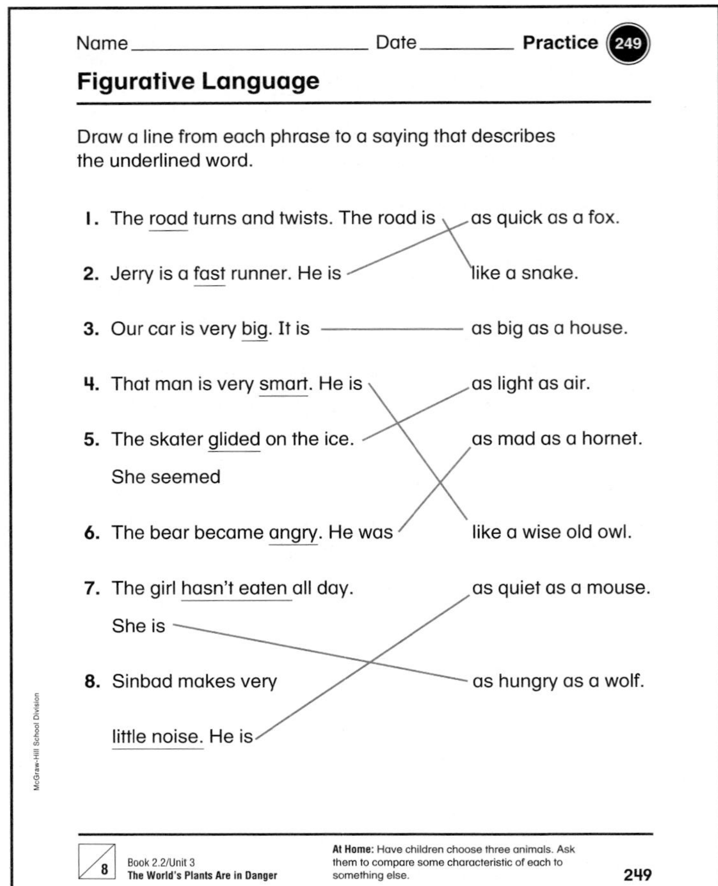

Name ______________________ Date __________ **Practice 249**

Figurative Language

Draw a line from each phrase to a saying that describes the underlined word.

1. The road turns and twists. The road is	as quick as a fox.
2. Jerry is a fast runner. He is	like a snake.
3. Our car is very big. It is	as big as a house.
4. That man is very smart. He is	as light as air.
5. The skater glided on the ice. She seemed	as mad as a hornet.
6. The bear became angry. He was	like a wise old owl.
7. The girl hasn't eaten all day. She is	as quiet as a mouse.
8. Sinbad makes very little noise. He is	as hungry as a wolf.

At Home: Have children choose three animals. Ask them to compare some characteristic of each to something else.

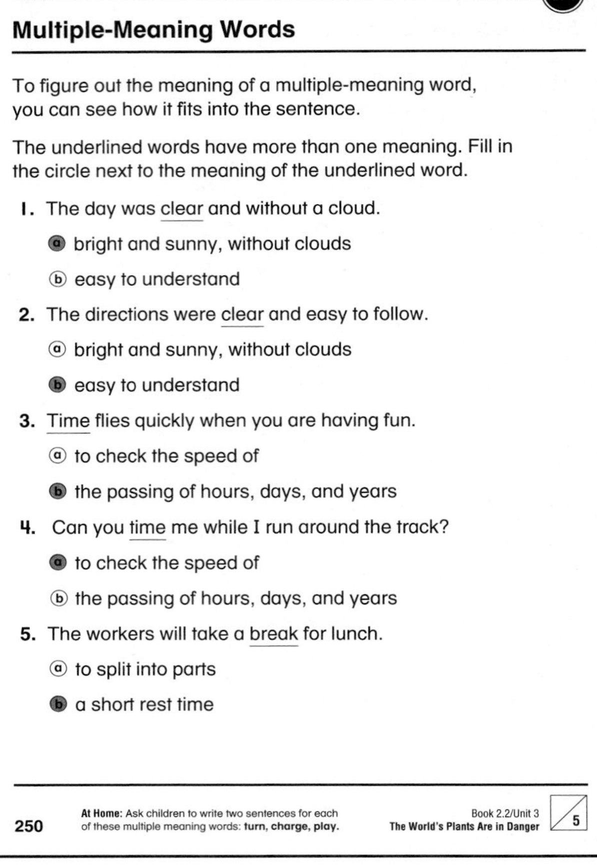

Name ______________________ Date __________ **Practice 250**

Multiple-Meaning Words

To figure out the meaning of a multiple-meaning word, you can see how it fits into the sentence.

The underlined words have more than one meaning. Fill in the circle next to the meaning of the underlined word.

1. The day was clear and without a cloud.
- ⓐ bright and sunny, without clouds
- ⓑ easy to understand

2. The directions were clear and easy to follow.
- ⓐ bright and sunny, without clouds
- ⓑ easy to understand

3. Time flies quickly when you are having fun.
- ⓐ to check the speed of
- ⓑ the passing of hours, days, and years

4. Can you time me while I run around the track?
- ⓐ to check the speed of
- ⓑ the passing of hours, days, and years

5. The workers will take a break for lunch.
- ⓐ to split into parts
- ⓑ a short rest time

At Home: Ask children to write two sentences for each of these multiple meaning words: **turn, charge, play.**

The World's Plants Are in Danger • RETEACH

Name_______________ Date_________ **Reteach 243**

Soft *c, g; ph, tch;* Long *a, o, e, i*

(mows) low

Circle the word that names each picture.

1. (feet) hands
2. green (rice)
3. (rainbow) valley
4. (lion) tiger
5. catcher (pitcher)
6. (raincoat) tie

6 Book 2.2/Unit 3 The World's Plants Are in Danger — **At Home:** Have children say the names of the circled words on this page. 243

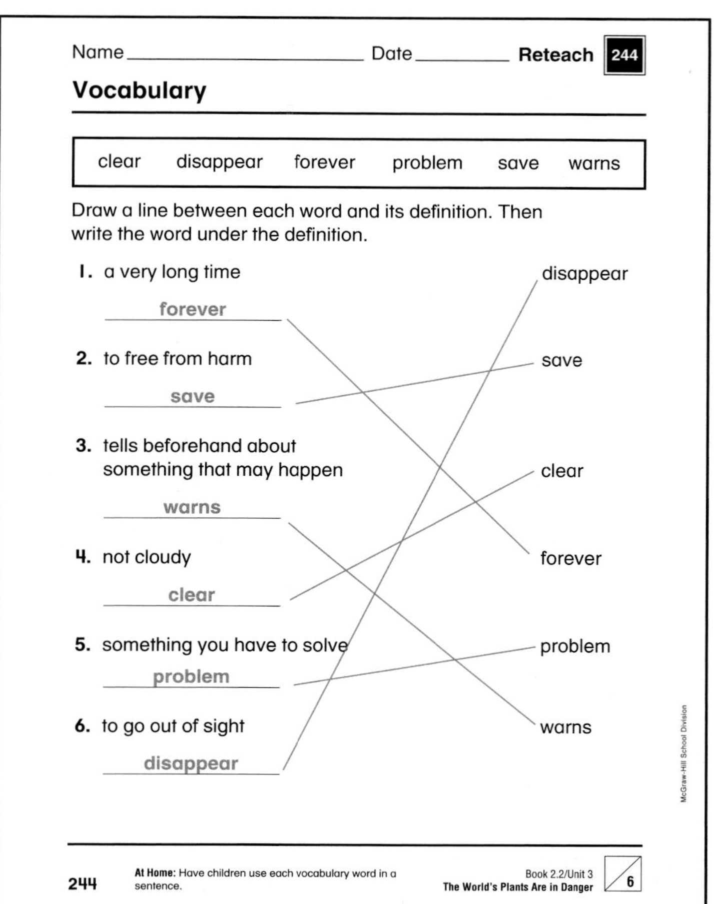

Name_______________ Date_________ **Reteach 244**

Vocabulary

clear	disappear	forever	problem	save	warns

Draw a line between each word and its definition. Then write the word under the definition.

1. a very long time — forever
2. to free from harm — save
3. tells beforehand about something that may happen — warns
4. not cloudy — clear
5. something you have to solve — problem
6. to go out of sight — disappear

disappear
save
clear
forever
problem
warns

244 **At Home:** Have children use each vocabulary word in a sentence. Book 2.2/Unit 3 The World's Plants Are in Danger 6

McGraw-Hill School Division

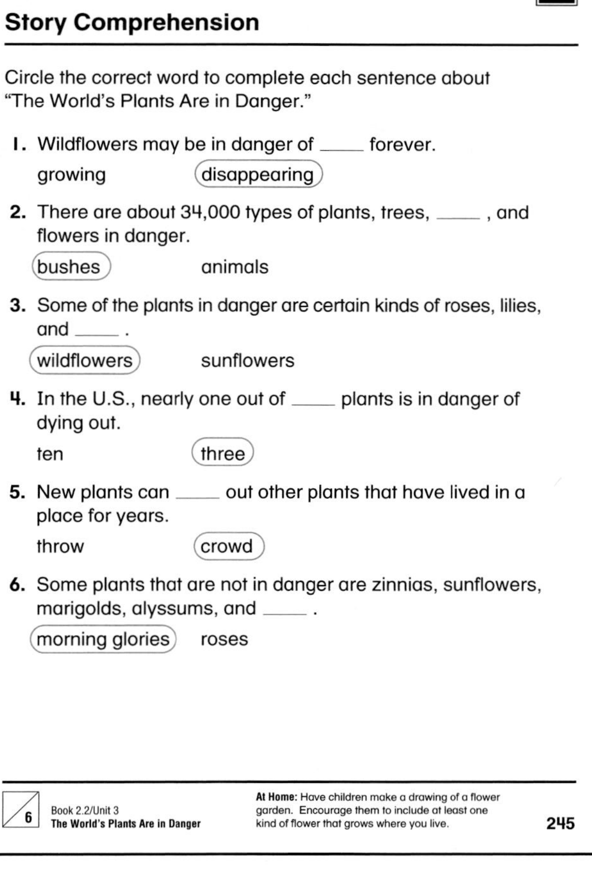

Name_______________ Date_________ **Reteach 245**

Story Comprehension

Circle the correct word to complete each sentence about "The World's Plants Are in Danger."

1. Wildflowers may be in danger of _____ forever.
   growing (disappearing)
2. There are about 34,000 types of plants, trees, _____, and flowers in danger.
   (bushes) animals
3. Some of the plants in danger are certain kinds of roses, lilies, and _____.
   (wildflowers) sunflowers
4. In the U.S., nearly one out of _____ plants is in danger of dying out.
   ten (three)
5. New plants can _____ out other plants that have lived in a place for years.
   throw (crowd)
6. Some plants that are not in danger are zinnias, sunflowers, marigolds, alyssums, and _____.
   (morning glories) roses

6 Book 2.2/Unit 3 The World's Plants Are in Danger — **At Home:** Have children make a drawing of a flower garden. Encourage them to include at least one kind of flower that grows where you live. 245

Name_______________ Date_________ **Reteach 246**

Choose a Reference Source

Reference books provide different kinds of information. A dictionary tells you about words. An encyclopedia tells you about topics. A nonfiction book tells you about facts. A telephone directory tells you the phone number of people or businesses.

The **dictionary** offers the following: definitions of words, part of speech, plural forms, pronunciation.

The **telephone directory** offers the following: phone numbers, addresses, spelling guides, business information.

The **encyclopedia** offers the following: facts about a wide variety of topics, charts, pictures, diagrams, graphs, outlines, suggestions of other topics.

Nonfiction books offer the following: facts and pictures about a topic.

Read the descriptions of the reference sources above. Tell which source would be best for doing the tasks listed.

1. You want to call your town mayor and ask some questions. telephone directory
2. You want to find out how to properly spell a word? dictionary
3. You to find out some general facts about a topic? encyclopedia
4. You want more detailed facts about a topic. nonfiction book

246 **At Home:** Ask children to write definitions for each of the types of reference books highlighted above. Book 2.2/Unit 3 The World's Plants Are in Danger 4

McGraw-Hill School Division

Name__________ Date______ **Reteach 247**

Main Idea

Remember: **Details** are bits of information that support the **main idea.**

Read the paragraphs. Underline two details for each main idea.

Many flowers are in danger of disappearing forever. There are about 34,000 types of plants in danger. Some of these are types of palm trees, roses, lilies, and wildflowers.

1. Main Idea:
   Many flowers are in danger.
   Which details support the main idea?
   a. There are about 34,000 plants in danger.
   b. Be careful when you plant flowers.
   c. Roses and lilies are in danger.

Humans have a lot to do with plants dying out. Humans destroy places where plants live. This happens when humans build roads, factories, and homes. Humans bring new plants to places. New plants can crowd out other plants that have been in that spot for hundreds of years.

2. Main Idea:
   Humans have a lot to do with plants dying out.
   Which details support the main idea?
   a. Humans protect plants.
   b. Humans build roads, factories, and homes.
   c. Humans bring new plants to places.

At Home: Have children write a poem or story about why it is important to keep plants from disappearing.

Name__________ Date______ **Reteach 248**

Form Generalizations

A **generalization** is a big idea based on facts. When you read, use facts from the story to form generalizations.

Read the story and the sentences. Write **Yes** beside each fact from the story. Write **No** if the sentence is not a fact from the story.

Do you like popcorn? Most people in America like it a lot! Some like plain popcorn. But many people prefer buttered popcorn or popcorn sprinkled with salt, cheese, or caramel. Americans eat more popcorn than any other people in the world. An average person eats about 42 quarts of popcorn a year. Altogether, that's about 2 billion large containers!

Is it a fact from the story?

Yes **1.** Some people like plain popcorn.

Yes **2.** Some people prefer buttered popcorn.

No **3.** Most people eat about 2 bags of popcorn a year.

No **4.** The Pilgrims didn't like popcorn.

Yes **5.** Americans eat about 2 billion large containers of popcorn a year.

Read the two sentences below. Decide which is a generalization about the story. Draw a line under the generalization.

Americans eat a lot of popcorn.
I don't like popcorn.

At Home: Help children write a generalization about "The World's Plants Are in Danger."

Name__________ Date______ **Reteach 249**

Figurative Language

Sometimes an author will describe something by comparing it to something else.

The sea looks **like a big blue blanket**.

The waves sound **like the beat of a drum**.

Read each sentence. Fill in the circle next to the saying that matches the underlined word or words.

1. The garden looks beautiful. It looks ________.
   ● as pretty as a picture.
   ○ as happy as a lark.
2. The air smells nice. It smells ________.
   ○ as dark as the night.
   ● as sweet as a rose.
3. Under the ground there is no light. It is ________.
   ○ as sweet as a rose.
   ● as dark as the night.
4. The popped balloon was very flat. It was ________.
   ● as flat as a pancake.
   ○ as big as a house.
5. My uncle Irv is big and wide. He is ________.
   ○ as quiet as a mouse.
   ● as big as a bear.
6. We will have to keep still. We will be ________.
   ○ as big as a barn.
   ● as quiet as mice.

At Home: Ask children to make up two comparisons that describe how they get ready for school.

Name__________ Date______ **Reteach 250**

Multiple-Meaning Words

Many words have more than one meaning. Look at the surrounding words to discover which meaning is being used.

After each sentence below, fill in the circle next to the phrase that defines the underlined word.

1. Martin plants carrots, beans, and flowers in his garden.
   ● to help something grow
   ○ a living thing that is not an animal
2. His favorite plants are the white roses.
   ○ to help something grow
   ● a living thing that is not an animal
3. In many states it is against the law to pick wildflowers.
   ● an area of the country
   ○ tells
4. Please stand up and state your name and age.
   ○ an area of the country
   ● tell
5. Wildflowers have lived in this spot for many years.
   ○ a mark
   ● a place
6. There is a spot on my new shirt.
   ● a mark
   ○ a place

At Home: Ask children to write two sentences using two meanings for **bat.**

The World's Plants Are in Danger • EXTEND

Name ____________ Date ________ **Extend 243**

Soft *c, g; ph, tch;* Long *a, o, e, i*

Color the words in the puzzle.

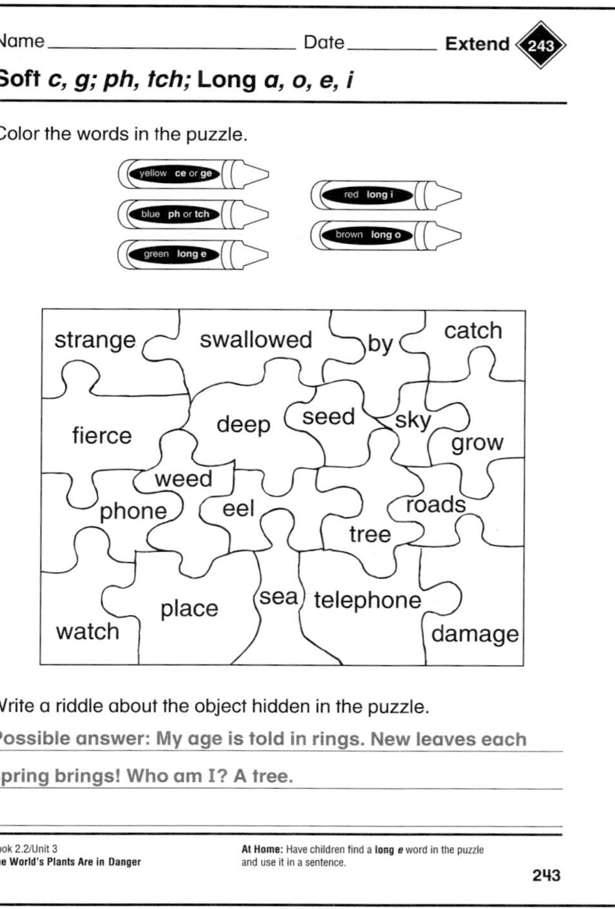

Write a riddle about the object hidden in the puzzle.

Possible answer: My age is told in rings. New leaves each spring brings! Who am I? A tree.

At Home: Have children find a **long *e*** word in the puzzle and use it in a sentence.

Name ____________ Date ________ **Extend 244**

Vocabulary

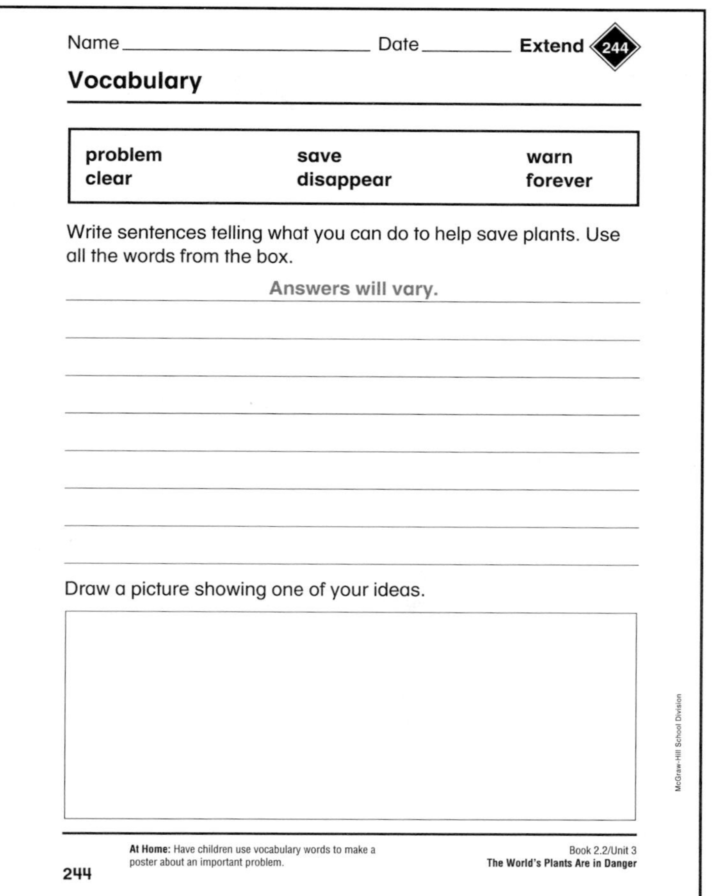

problem	save	warn
clear	disappear	forever

Write sentences telling what you can do to help save plants. Use all the words from the box.

Answers will vary.

Draw a picture showing one of your ideas.

At Home: Have children use vocabulary words to make a poster about an important problem.

Name ____________ Date ________ **Extend 245**

Story Comprehension

What would a world without plants be like? Write a sentence answering each question. Sample answers are shown.

1. What would your favorite park look like if there were no plants?
   It might look like a desert with nothing green growing.
2. What are some foods that we would no longer be able to eat?
   We wouldn't have any vegetables or meat since animals eat plants, too.
3. What might happen if the plants that medicines are made of were no longer around?
   People might find a way to make the medicines from chemicals or they might not have those medicines anymore.

Draw a picture to show one of the reasons plants disappear.

At Home: Have children talk and write sentences about the importance of plants in their lives.

Name ____________ Date ________ **Extend 246**

Choose a Reference Source

You want to grow some plants, but you need some facts first. Read the information in the reference sources below. Then answer the questions.

Dictionary Entries
plant 1. A living thing with a green pigment that allows it to make food from the sun, such as a flower. *Noun* 2. To put a plant or seed in the ground so that it can grow. *Verb* 3. The buildings and equipment used to make a product, such as cars; a factory. *Noun*

Title Page of Nonfiction Book
How to Grow Your Own Garden
by Bernard Beanpole
illustrations by I.C. Roses

Part of an Encyclopedia Entry
plant A living thing belonging to the plant kingdom. All plants have many cells and are usually anchored in one place. They make their own food and give off oxygen. Plants are the main source of food for animals.

Telephone Directory
Plant Stores
Pamela's Plants 555-4456
Perfect Planting 555-2244
Pick Your Plants 555-7799
Plants For You 555-5577

What reference source tells you:

Where to buy a plant?
telephone directory

How to grow a plant?
a book called *How to Grow Your Own Garden*

What to plant means?
dictionary

Who eats plants?
encyclopedia

Use these facts to write a report about plants on another piece of paper.

At Home: Children can use different reference books to make small booklets called "Kids Can Care for Plants."

Name________________ Date________ Extend 247

Main Idea

Make a list of five ideas you have for helping the earth.
Sample answers are shown.

1. We can plant more trees.
2. (We can reuse and recycle paper.)
3. ____
4. ____
5. ____

Circle the one idea that you think is most important.
Write four details that help support that idea.

1. When we reuse paper, we can save trees.
2. There will be less garbage in dumps if we use less paper.
3. ____
4. ____

Write a speech on a piece of recycled paper. Let people know what you think about helping the earth.

Use your main idea and supporting details in your speech. Read your speech to the class.

At Home: Ask children to think of supporting details for another one of their ideas.

Name________________ Date________ Extend 248

Form Generalizations

Read the story. Answer the questions.

Some plants are disappearing. The places where they grow are being destroyed. People are using the land to build new roads, factories, and homes. Even the flowers and trees that grow wild in parks and forests can disappear. People pick them or dig up the place where they are planted. Answers will vary.

Why are plants disappearing?

Plants are disappearing because the places where they live are being destroyed. They also are harmed when people pick them.

Think about the story.
What could you say that is nearly always true about people and plants?

People should think about saving plants when they plan new buildings.

Change these sentences to make them nearly always true.

People should leave all plants alone.

People should take care of plants.

Using land to build new buildings is bad.

People need places to live and work, but they should be careful to leave some trees and flowers alone.

At Home: Have children think of a statement that is nearly always true about wildflowers and illustrate it.

Name________________ Date________ Extend 249

Figurative Language

The words in the box can help make your writing more interesting. Use the words to write four sentences. Sample sentences shown.

like two peas in a pod	**fork in the road**
turn over a new leaf	**has a green thumb**

1. My sister and I are like two peas in a pod.
2. She has a green thumb.
3. I am going to turn over a new leaf.
4. The truck came to a fork in the road.

Draw a picture to show what you think of when you hear **fork in the road.**

What does **fork in the road** really mean? Draw a picture.

At Home: Have children list other favorite expressions. Let children tell what pictures they think of when they hear these words.

Name________________ Date________ Extend 250

Multiple-Meaning Words

Use words from the box to complete the sentences.

crowd	types	part	spot	safe

1. About one out of every ten ___types___ of wildflower is in danger of disappearing.
2. Planting too many new plants may ___crowd___ out other plants.
3. Planting a tree in a special ___spot___ will make that place more beautiful.
4. It is important for people to help keep the world's plants ___safe___ and out of danger.
5. Many of the plants in danger grow in one ___part___ of the world.

Use the same words to name these pictures.

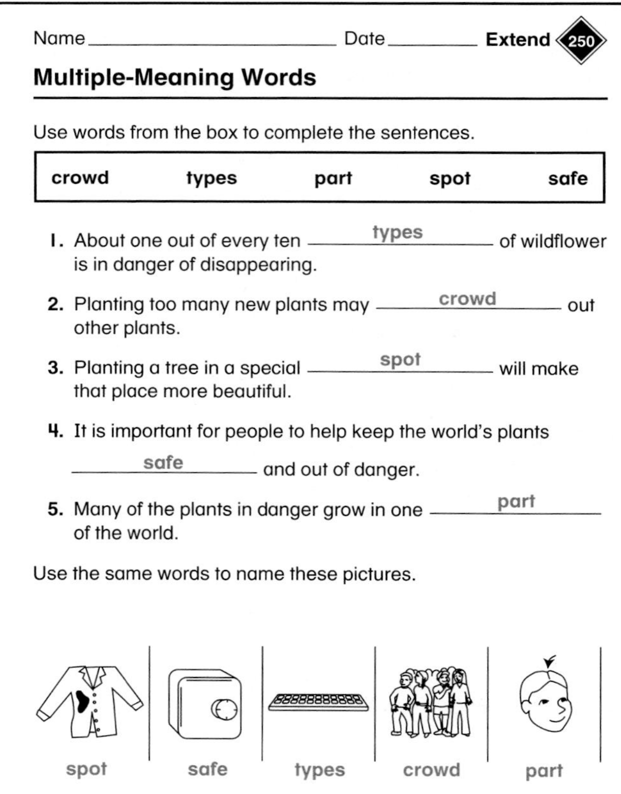

At Home: Challenge children to think of other words that have more than one meaning and use them in sentences.

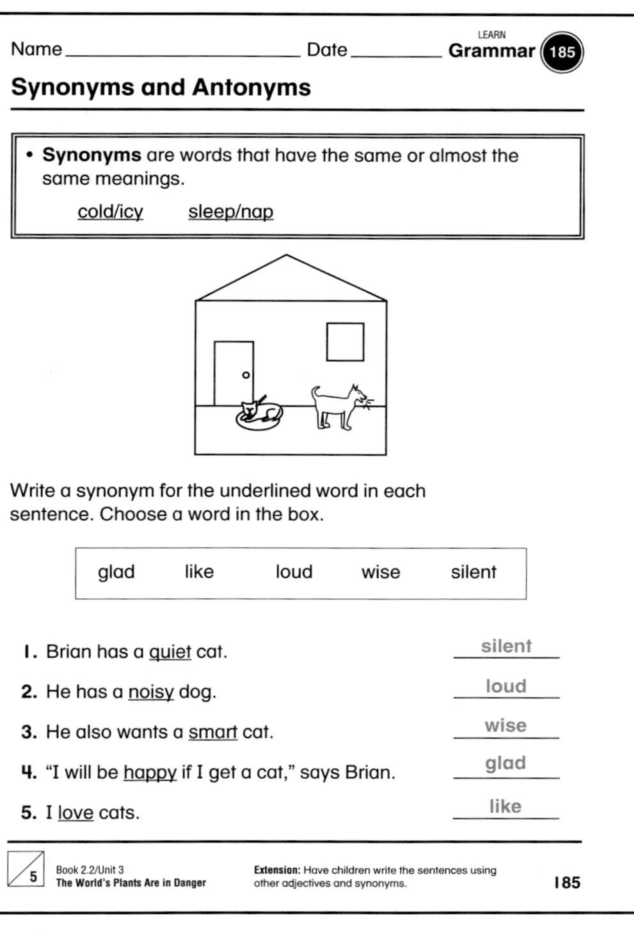

Name ______________ Date ________ LEARN Grammar 185

Synonyms and Antonyms

- **Synonyms** are words that have the same or almost the same meanings.
  cold/icy sleep/nap

Write a synonym for the underlined word in each sentence. Choose a word in the box.

glad	like	loud	wise	silent

1. Brian has a quiet cat. silent
2. He has a noisy dog. loud
3. He also wants a smart cat. wise
4. "I will be happy if I get a cat," says Brian. glad
5. I love cats. like

Extension: Have children write the sentences using other adjectives and synonyms.

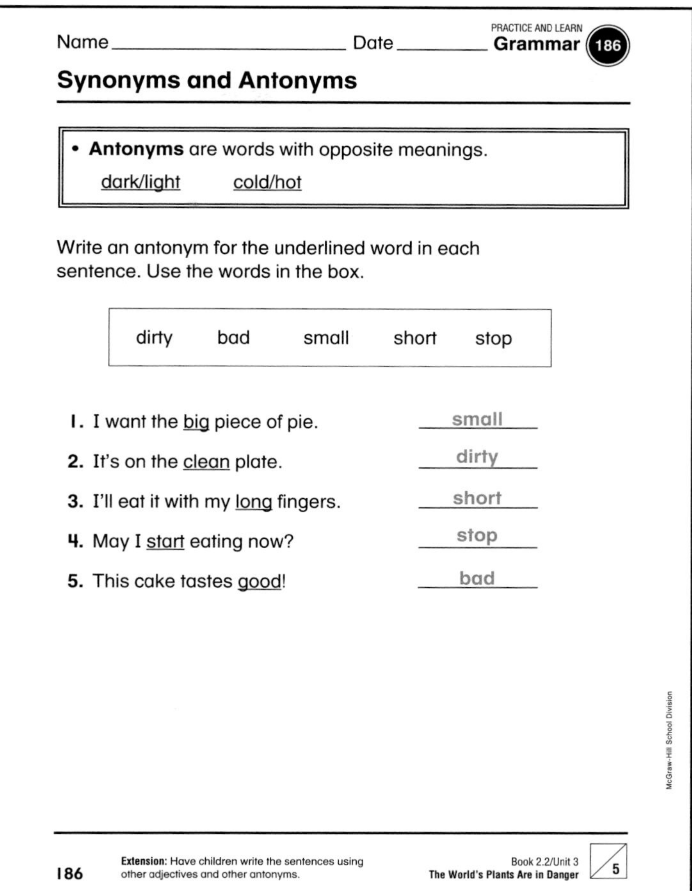

Name ______________ Date ________ PRACTICE AND LEARN Grammar 186

Synonyms and Antonyms

- **Antonyms** are words with opposite meanings.
  dark/light cold/hot

Write an antonym for the underlined word in each sentence. Use the words in the box.

dirty	bad	small	short	stop

1. I want the big piece of pie. small
2. It's on the clean plate. dirty
3. I'll eat it with my long fingers. short
4. May I start eating now? stop
5. This cake tastes good! bad

Extension: Have children write the sentences using other adjectives and other antonyms.

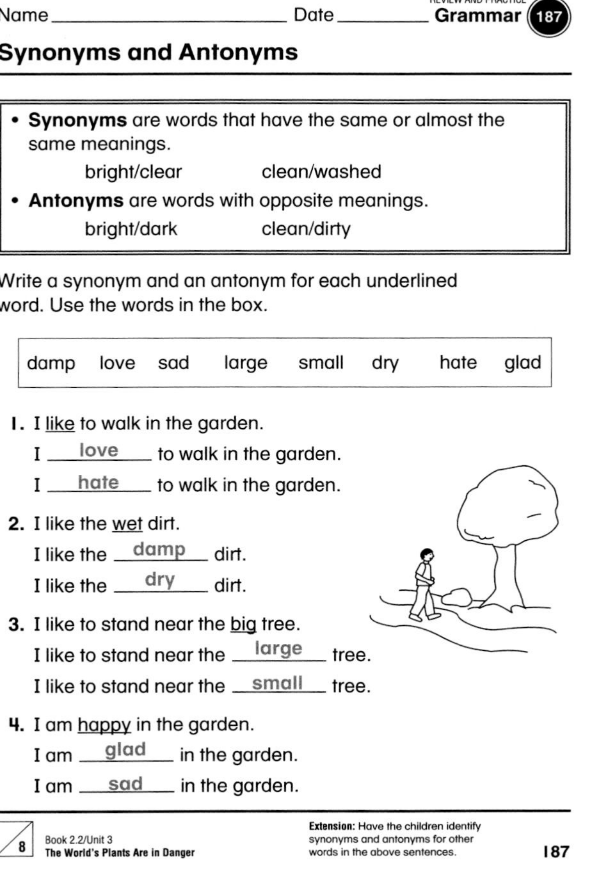

Name ______________ Date ________ REVIEW AND PRACTICE Grammar 187

Synonyms and Antonyms

- **Synonyms** are words that have the same or almost the same meanings.
  bright/clear clean/washed
- **Antonyms** are words with opposite meanings.
  bright/dark clean/dirty

Write a synonym and an antonym for each underlined word. Use the words in the box.

damp	love	sad	large	small	dry	hate	glad

1. I like to walk in the garden.
   I love to walk in the garden.
   I hate to walk in the garden.
2. I like the wet dirt.
   I like the damp dirt.
   I like the dry dirt.
3. I like to stand near the big tree.
   I like to stand near the large tree.
   I like to stand near the small tree.
4. I am happy in the garden.
   I am glad in the garden.
   I am sad in the garden.

Extension: Have the children identify synonyms and antonyms for other words in the above sentences.

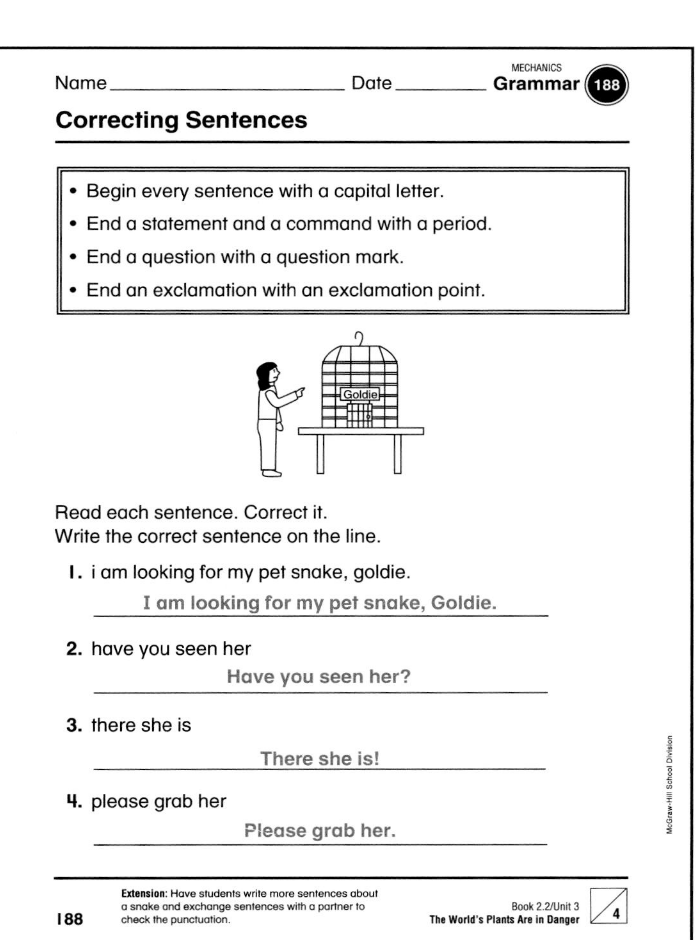

Name ______________ Date ________ MECHANICS Grammar 188

Correcting Sentences

- Begin every sentence with a capital letter.
- End a statement and a command with a period.
- End a question with a question mark.
- End an exclamation with an exclamation point.

Read each sentence. Correct it.
Write the correct sentence on the line.

1. i am looking for my pet snake, goldie.
   I am looking for my pet snake, Goldie.
2. have you seen her
   Have you seen her?
3. there she is
   There she is!
4. please grab her
   Please grab her.

Extension: Have students write more sentences about a snake and exchange sentences with a partner to check the punctuation.

Name__________ Date______ TEST Grammar 189

Synonyms and Antonyms

Write synonyms for the underlined words.

1. I have a large dog. big
2. She is very noisy. loud
3. She runs quickly. fast
4. Her bark sounds joyful. happy

Write the antonyms for the underlined words.

5. My cat is very large. small
6. He is always very good. bad
7. He plays quietly. loudly
8. He walks carefully. carelessly

Name__________ Date______ MORE PRACTICE Grammar 190

Synonyms and Antonyms

- **Synonyms** are words that have the same or almost the same meanings.
- **Antonyms** are words with opposite meanings.

Mechanics:
- Begin every sentence with a capital letter.
- End a statement with a period.
- End a question with a question mark.
- End a command with a period.
- End an exclamation with an exclamation point.

Look at the picture. Read the sentences. Circle the words that are the same as what the picture shows. Draw a line under the words that mean the opposite of what the picture shows. Write the sentences correctly.

1. it is a rainy day.
   It is a rainy day.
2. she is happy
   She is happy.
3. is it a sunny day
   Is it a sunny day?
4. oh, she is so sad
   Oh, she is so sad!

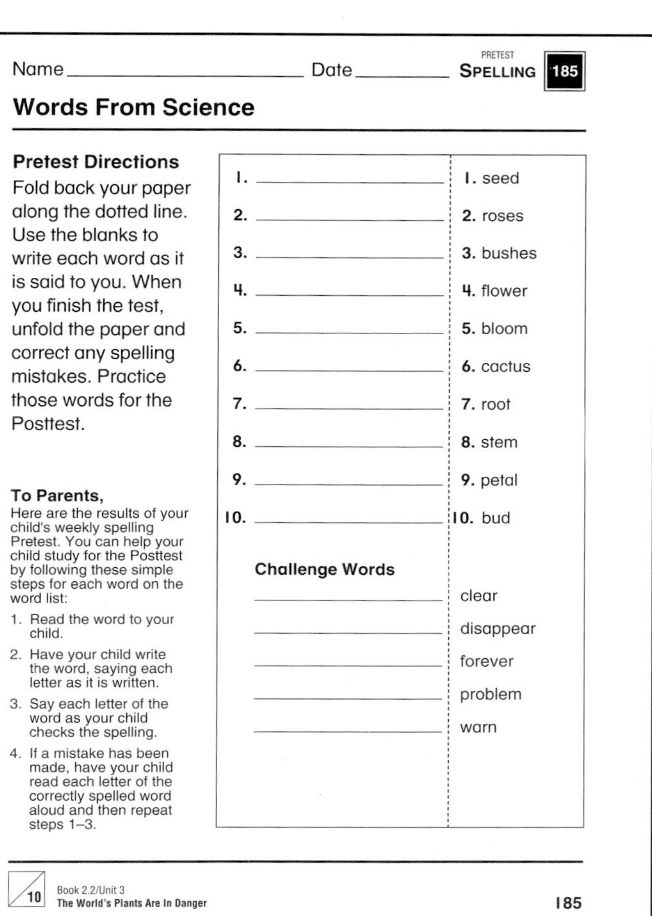

Name __________ Date __________ PRETEST SPELLING 185

Words From Science

Pretest Directions

Fold back your paper along the dotted line. Use the blanks to write each word as it is said to you. When you finish the test, unfold the paper and correct any spelling mistakes. Practice those words for the Posttest.

1. ______	1. seed
2. ______	2. roses
3. ______	3. bushes
4. ______	4. flower
5. ______	5. bloom
6. ______	6. cactus
7. ______	7. root
8. ______	8. stem
9. ______	9. petal
10. ______	10. bud

Challenge Words

______	clear
______	disappear
______	forever
______	problem
______	warn

To Parents,

Here are the results of your child's weekly spelling Pretest. You can help your child study for the Posttest by following these simple steps for each word on the word list:

1. Read the word to your child.
2. Have your child write the word, saying each letter as it is written.
3. Say each letter of the word as your child checks the spelling.
4. If a mistake has been made, have your child read each letter of the correctly spelled word aloud and then repeat steps 1–3.

10 Book 2.2/Unit 3 The World's Plants Are In Danger 185

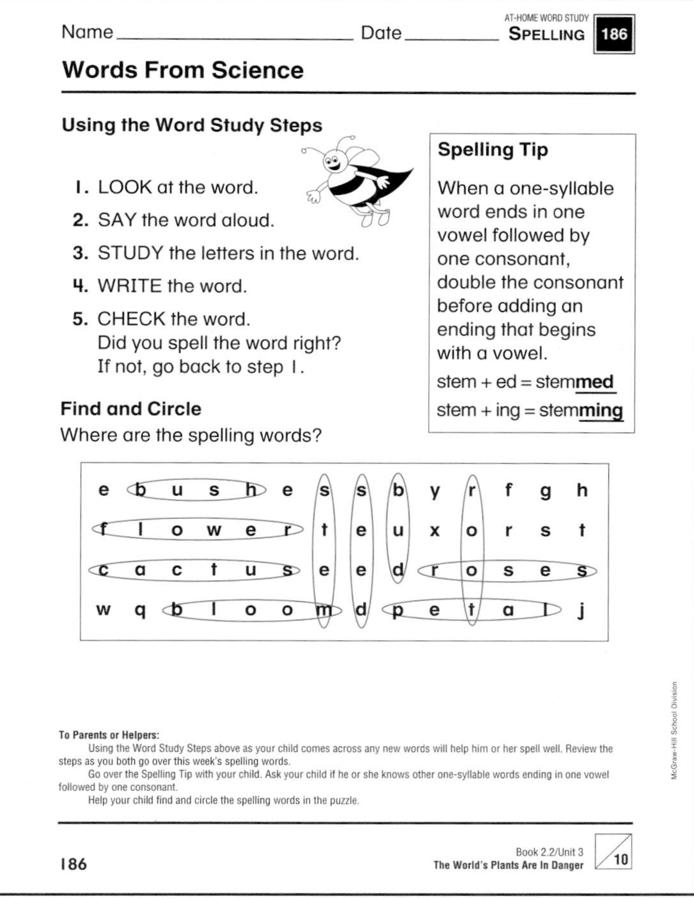

Name __________ Date __________ AT-HOME WORD STUDY SPELLING 186

Words From Science

Using the Word Study Steps

1. LOOK at the word.
2. SAY the word aloud.
3. STUDY the letters in the word.
4. WRITE the word.
5. CHECK the word. Did you spell the word right? If not, go back to step 1.

Spelling Tip

When a one-syllable word ends in one vowel followed by one consonant, double the consonant before adding an ending that begins with a vowel.

stem + ed = stem**med**

stem + ing = stem**ming**

Find and Circle

Where are the spelling words?

e	b	u	s	h	e	s	s	b	y	r	f	g	h
f	l	o	w	e	r	t	e	u	x	o	r	s	t
c	a	c	t	u	s	e	e	d	r	o	s	e	s
w	q	b	l	o	o	m	d	p	e	t	a	l	j

To Parents or Helpers:

Using the Word Study Steps above as your child comes across any new words will help him or her spell well. Review the steps as you both go over this week's spelling words.

Go over the Spelling Tip with your child. Ask your child if he or she knows other one-syllable words ending in one vowel followed by one consonant.

Help your child find and circle the spelling words in the puzzle.

186 Book 2.2/Unit 3 The World's Plants Are In Danger 10

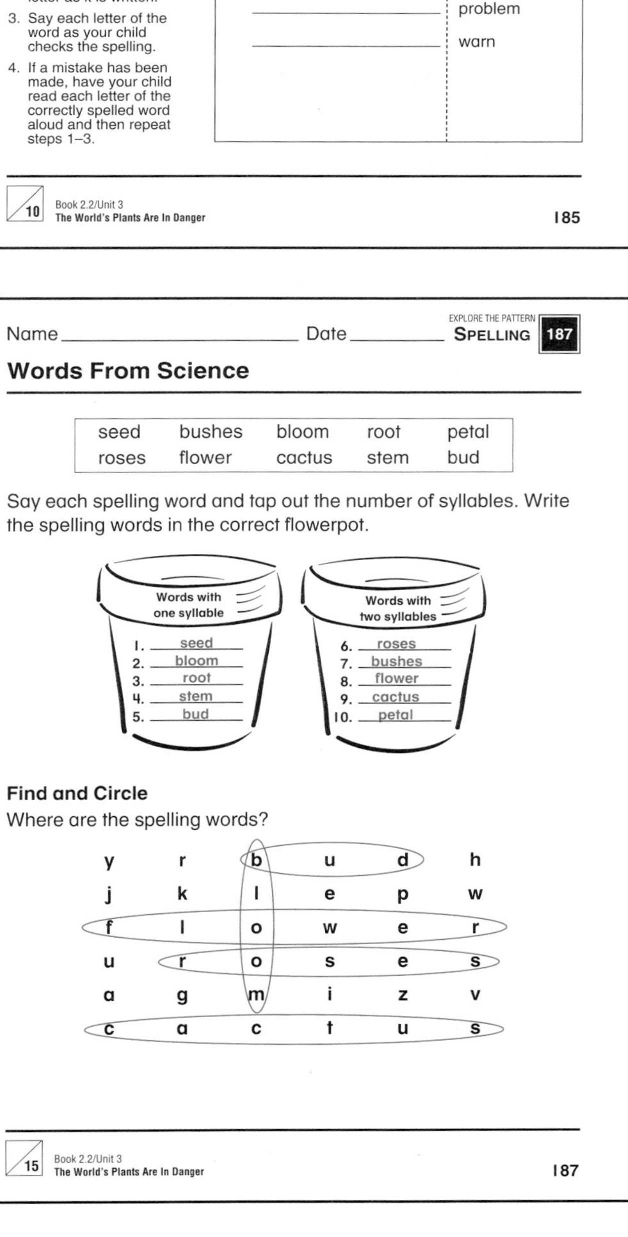

Name __________ Date __________ EXPLORE THE PATTERN SPELLING 187

Words From Science

seed	bushes	bloom	root	petal
roses	flower	cactus	stem	bud

Say each spelling word and tap out the number of syllables. Write the spelling words in the correct flowerpot.

Words with one syllable	Words with two syllables
1. seed	6. roses
2. bloom	7. bushes
3. root	8. flower
4. stem	9. cactus
5. bud	10. petal

Find and Circle

Where are the spelling words?

y	r	b	u	d	h
j	k	l	e	p	w
f	l	o	w	e	r
u	r	o	s	e	s
a	g	m	i	z	v
c	a	c	t	u	s

15 Book 2.2/Unit 3 The World's Plants Are In Danger 187

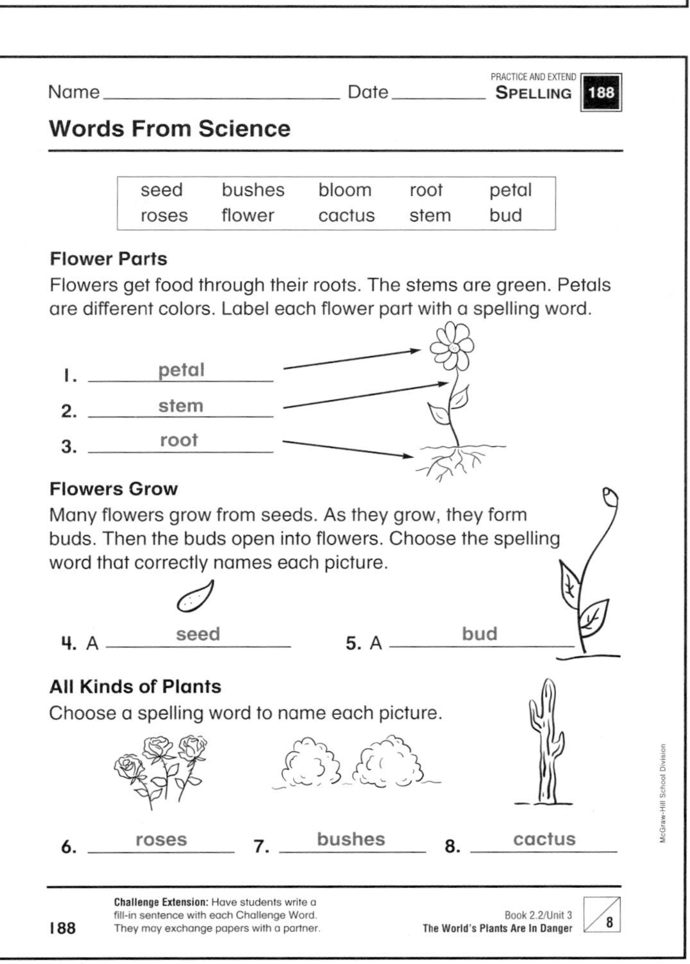

Name __________ Date __________ PRACTICE AND EXTEND SPELLING 188

Words From Science

seed	bushes	bloom	root	petal
roses	flower	cactus	stem	bud

Flower Parts

Flowers get food through their roots. The stems are green. Petals are different colors. Label each flower part with a spelling word.

1. petal
2. stem
3. root

Flowers Grow

Many flowers grow from seeds. As they grow, they form buds. Then the buds open into flowers. Choose the spelling word that correctly names each picture.

4. A seed 5. A bud

All Kinds of Plants

Choose a spelling word to name each picture.

6. roses 7. bushes 8. cactus

Challenge Extension: Have students write a fill-in sentence with each Challenge Word. They may exchange papers with a partner.

188 Book 2.2/Unit 3 The World's Plants Are In Danger 8

Name________________ Date________ PROOFREAD AND WRITE SPELLING 189

Words From Science

Proofreading Activity

There are six spelling mistakes in the journal below. Circle each misspelled word. Write the words correctly on the lines below.

July 7 Today, there are many (budes) on the rose (bushis). The (rowzis) will be in (blum) by next week, I think. I will be able to cut some pretty (flowrs) for the house.

July 15 Two weeks ago I planted two new plants. The wind last night broke the (steme) on one of the plants.

1. buds 2. bushes 3. roses
4. bloom 5. flowers 6. stem

Writing Activity

Pretend that you have a garden. Write a paragraph about how your garden grows. Use four spelling words to describe what happens.

____

____

____

____

____

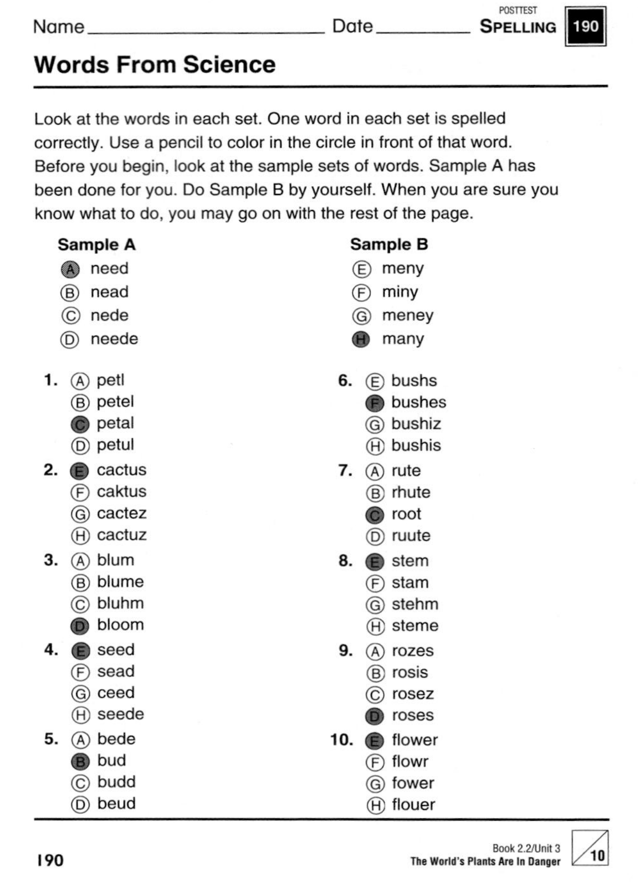

Name________________ Date________ POSTTEST SPELLING 190

Words From Science

Look at the words in each set. One word in each set is spelled correctly. Use a pencil to color in the circle in front of that word. Before you begin, look at the sample sets of words. Sample A has been done for you. Do Sample B by yourself. When you are sure you know what to do, you may go on with the rest of the page.

Sample A
- ● (A) need
- (B) nead
- (C) nede
- (D) neede

Sample B
- (E) meny
- (F) miny
- (G) meney
- ● (H) many

1. (A) petl (B) petel ● (C) petal (D) petul
2. ● (E) cactus (F) caktus (G) cactez (H) cactuz
3. (A) blum (B) blume (C) bluhm ● (D) bloom
4. ● (E) seed (F) sead (G) ceed (H) seede
5. (A) bede ● (B) bud (C) budd (D) beud
6. (E) bushs ● (F) bushes (G) bushiz (H) bushis
7. (A) rute (B) rhute ● (C) root (D) ruute
8. ● (E) stem (F) stam (G) stehm (H) steme
9. (A) rozes (B) rosis (C) rosez ● (D) roses
10. ● (E) flower (F) flowr (G) fower (H) flouer

Unit Review • PRACTICE and RETEACH

Name____________________ Date________ **Practice 251**

Unit 3 Vocabulary Review

A. Find a word that means almost the same thing. Write the matching word on the line.

fast	**1.** swift	always
rescue	**2.** save	fast
ran off	**3.** escaped	rescue
twelve A.M.	**4.** midnight	wild
always	**5.** forever	twelve A.M.
wild	**6.** fierce	ran off

B. Use the words in the box to complete the questions. Write the words on the lines.

hidden	restaurant	wipe	audience

1. When the play ended, what did the audience do?

2. Did you wipe up the milk you spilled?

3. Would you rather go to a restaurant or eat at home?

4. Where is the gift hidden?

10

At Home: Have children make up questions and answers for some of the words in Exercise A.

Name____________________ Date________ **Practice 252**

Unit 3 Vocabulary Review

A. Write a word from the box next to the word that means the opposite.

cheered	evenings	crowded	disappear

1. booed cheered **2.** empty crowded

3. show up disappear **4.** mornings evenings

B. Using the code below, write a word from the box next to the code.

accidents	desert	shoulder	cousins	golden	princess

<table>
<tr><td>a</td><td>b</td><td>c</td><td>d</td><td>e</td><td>f</td><td>g</td><td>h</td><td>i</td><td>j</td><td>k</td><td>l</td><td>m</td><td>n</td><td>o</td><td>p</td><td>q</td><td>r</td><td>s</td><td>t</td><td>u</td><td>v</td><td>w</td><td>x</td><td>y</td><td>z</td></tr>
<tr><td>!</td><td>@</td><td>#</td><td>$</td><td>%</td><td>^</td><td>&</td><td>*</td><td>(</td><td>)</td><td>_</td><td>~</td><td>=</td><td>+</td><td>{</td><td>[</td><td>}</td><td>]</td><td>|</td><td>\</td><td>></td><td>.</td><td>,</td><td>‘</td><td>?</td><td><</td></tr>
</table>

1. !##($%+\| accidents

2. $%|%]\ desert

3. &{~$%+ golden

4. [](+#%|| princess

5. |*{>~$%] shoulder

6. #{>|(+| cousins

At Home: Have children write two of the words from Exercise A in code.

10

Name____________________ Date________ **Reteach 251**

Unit 3 Vocabulary Review

A. Cross out the word that does not correctly complete the sentence.

1. He wore a ____ crown on his head.

- **a.** golden
- **b.** ~~crowded~~

2. Some flowers were ____ in the breeze.

- **a.** ~~cheered~~
- **b.** swaying

3. How can we solve this ____ ?

- **a.** ~~machine~~
- **b.** problem

4. She came to ____ us about the ice on the roads.

- **a.** warn
- **b.** ~~borrow~~

B. Match each definition below with the correct word. Write the letter of the word on the line.

b.	**1.** People who are watching a show	**a.** world
d.	**2.** A hot, dry, sandy place	**b.** audience
c.	**3.** The daughter of a king and queen	**c.** princess
a.	**4.** The earth	**d.** desert

8

At Home: Have children write a sentence using as many of the words from Exercise B as they can.

Name____________________ Date________ **Reteach 252**

Unit 3 Vocabulary Review

A. Circle the correct answer to each question below.

1. What should you do after you spill something?

(**a.** wipe it up) **b.** open a restaurant

2. Which is bigger—the world or a room?

(**a.** world) **b.** room

3. If you wanted to read one of the books in the library, what would you do?

(**a.** borrow it) **b.** save it

4. What is between your arm and your neck?

a. desert (**b.** shoulder)

B. Underline the correct word to complete each question below.

1. When did you get to the police ____ ?

a. audience **b.** desert <u>**c.** station</u> **d.** shoulder

2. When did your washing ____ break down?

a. midnight **b.** evenings <u>**c.** machine</u> **d.** problem

3. How long will it take to ____ the land?

a. disappear <u>**b.** clear</u> **c.** princess **d.** golden

4. Is she a slow runner or a ____ runner?

a. golden <u>**b.** swift</u> **c.** swaying **d.** midnight

At Home: Have children write answers for the questions in Exercise B.

8

Name________________ Date________ **Extend 251**

Vocabulary Review

Play with a friend. Flip a penny.
Move one space for heads.
Move two spaces for tails.
Make a sentence with the word you land on.
Take turns.

start — finish

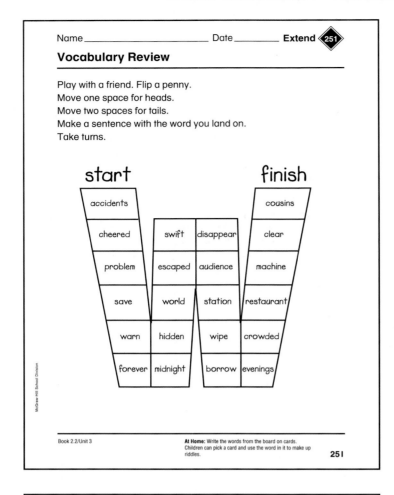

accidents			cousins
cheered	swift	disappear	clear
problem	escaped	audience	machine
save	world	station	restaurant
warn	hidden	wipe	crowded
forever	midnight	borrow	evenings

At Home: Write the words from the board on cards. Children can pick a card and use the word in it to make up riddles.

Name________________ Date________ **Extend 252**

Vocabulary Review

Follow the directions to draw a silly picture.

Draw a **princess** opening a **package** in the **desert.**
Draw a frog wearing a **golden** crown on its head.
Draw a **fierce** lion wearing a purse on its **shoulder.**
Draw a bear **swaying** on a swing.
Draw a giraffe **slipping** on a banana peel.

Write a silly story about your picture.

Stories will vary, but should include some of the boldfaced words.

At Home: Write a fairy tale together using the vocabulary words above.

Name________________ Date________ UNIT TEST **Grammar 191**

Adjectives and Adverbs

Read the passage and look at the underlined parts.
Is there a better way to say each part? If there is, which is the better way? Mark your answer.

> Jill took an long walk. (1) She passed an old house. She went inside mall. (2) She went home with a new pair of shoes.

1. ● Jill took a long walk.
   ⓑ Jill took long walk.
   ⓒ Jill walk.
   ⓓ No mistake.

2. ⓕ She went to big mall.
   ⓖ She went inside an mall.
   ● She went inside the big mall.
   ⓙ No mistake.

> We come in different sizes. My brother is tallest than my sister. (3) My sister is smaller than my mother. I am the taller of them all. (4)

3. ⓐ My brother is tallest.
   ● My brother is taller than my sister.
   ⓒ My brother is very tall.
   ⓓ No mistake

4. ● I am the tallest of them all.
   ⓖ I am the tall of them all.
   ⓗ I am tall.
   ⓙ No mistake.

Go On

Name________________ Date________ REVIEW **Grammar 192**

> The children are visiting the art center a day. (5) They look at the pictures. A man stands nearby. He answers questions glad. (6)

5. ⓐ The children are visiting the art center yesterday.
   ● The children are visiting the art center today.
   ⓒ The children are visiting the art center tomorrow.
   ⓓ No mistake

6. ⓕ He answers questions very glad.
   ⓖ He answers questions.
   ● He answers questions gladly.
   ⓙ No mistake.

> I want the big piece of pie. I don't want the large one. (7) Don't put it on a dirty plate. Put it on a clean plate. (8)

7. ● I don't want the small one.
   ⓑ I don't want the pie.
   ⓒ I don't want big.
   ⓓ No mistake

8. ⓕ Put it on plate.
   ⓖ Put it on dirty.
   ⓗ Put it on.
   ● No mistake.

Unit Review • SPELLING

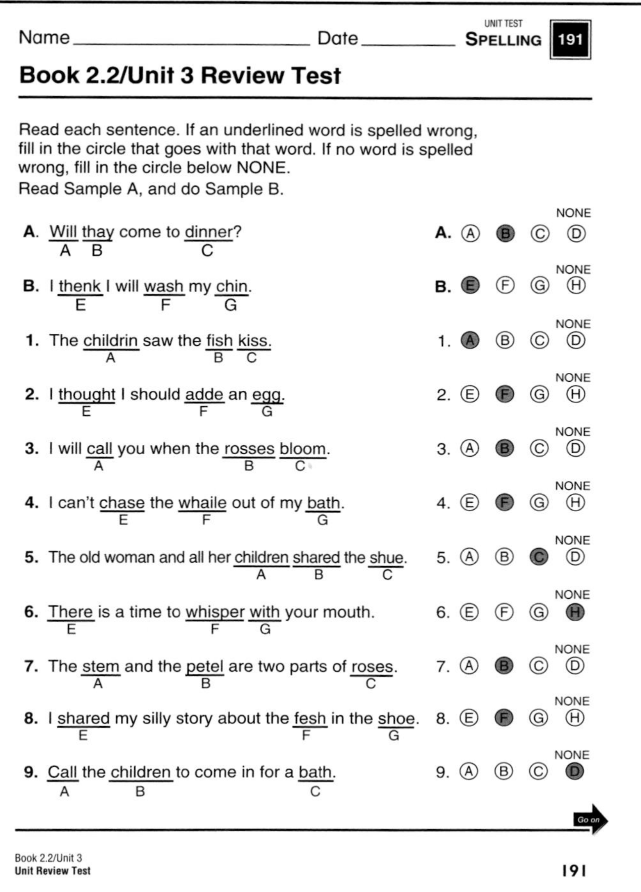

Name________________________ Date__________ UNIT TEST SPELLING 191

Book 2.2/Unit 3 Review Test

Read each sentence. If an underlined word is spelled wrong, fill in the circle that goes with that word. If no word is spelled wrong, fill in the circle below NONE.
Read Sample A, and do Sample B.

A. Will (A) thay (B) come to dinner (C)? — A. (A) (B) (C) (D) NONE

B. I thenk (E) I will wash (F) my chin (G). — B. (E) (F) (G) (H) NONE

1. The childrin (A) saw the fish (B) kiss (C). — 1. (A) (B) (C) (D) NONE
2. I thought (E) I should adde (F) an egg (G). — 2. (E) (F) (G) (H) NONE
3. I will call (A) you when the rosses (B) bloom (C). — 3. (A) (B) (C) (D) NONE
4. I can't chase (E) the whaile (F) out of my bath (G). — 4. (E) (F) (G) (H) NONE
5. The old woman and all her children (A) shared (B) the shue (C). — 5. (A) (B) (C) (D) NONE
6. There (E) is a time to whisper (F) with (G) your mouth. — 6. (E) (F) (G) (H) NONE
7. The stem (A) and the petel (B) are two parts of roses (C). — 7. (A) (B) (C) (D) NONE
8. I shared (E) my silly story about the fesh (F) in the shoe (G). — 8. (E) (F) (G) (H) NONE
9. Call (A) the children (B) to come in for a bath (C). — 9. (A) (B) (C) (D) NONE

Go on

Book 2.2/Unit 3
Unit Review Test 191

McGraw-Hill School Division

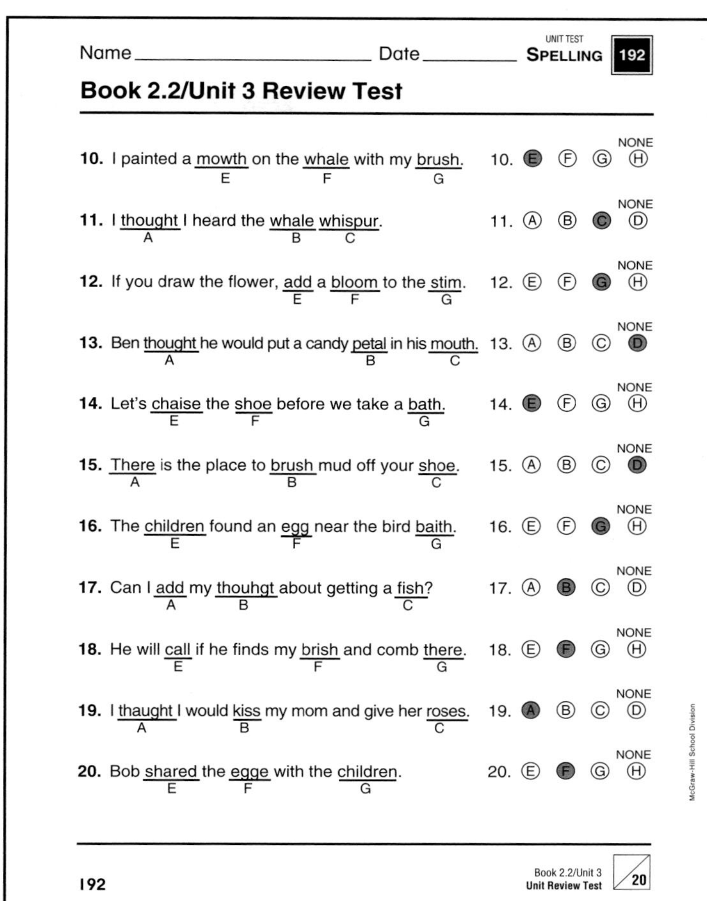

Name________________________ Date__________ UNIT TEST SPELLING 192

Book 2.2/Unit 3 Review Test

10. I painted a mowth (E) on the whale (F) with my brush (G). — 10. (E) (F) (G) (H) NONE
11. I thought (A) I heard the whale (B) whispur (C). — 11. (A) (B) (C) (D) NONE
12. If you draw the flower, add (E) a bloom (F) to the stim (G). — 12. (E) (F) (G) (H) NONE
13. Ben thought (A) he would put a candy petal (B) in his mouth (C). — 13. (A) (B) (C) (D) NONE
14. Let's chaise (E) the shoe (F) before we take a bath (G). — 14. (E) (F) (G) (H) NONE
15. There (A) is the place to brush (B) mud off your shoe (C). — 15. (A) (B) (C) (D) NONE
16. The children (E) found an egg (F) near the bird baith (G). — 16. (E) (F) (G) (H) NONE
17. Can I add (A) my thouhgt (B) about getting a fish (C)? — 17. (A) (B) (C) (D) NONE
18. He will call (E) if he finds my brish (F) and comb there (G). — 18. (E) (F) (G) (H) NONE
19. I thaught (A) I would kiss (B) my mom and give her roses (C). — 19. (A) (B) (C) (D) NONE
20. Bob shared (E) the egge (F) with the children (G). — 20. (E) (F) (G) (H) NONE

192 Book 2.2/Unit 3
Unit Review Test 20

McGraw-Hill School Division

Phonological Awareness

OBJECTIVES **Children will practice blending and segmenting sounds and deleting the second sound in blends.**

Alternate

Blend Sounds

TELEPHONE TALK

PARTNERS **Materials:** magazine pictures

Tell children that they will blend sounds to form words.

- Pair children to play "Telephone Talk." Ask partners to sit back to back. Give each pair three or four magazine pictures.
- Tell one partner to look at a picture and segment the sounds while pretending to talk on the phone.
- Have the other partner blend the sounds to form the word. Then have him or her say, "Did you say ______?"
- Ask the first partner to show the picture to the other partner to verify that he or she blended the sounds correctly.
- Continue by having partners switch roles.

Segment Sounds

MARK THAT SOUND

Materials: Word Building Boxes from *Word Building Kit,* dried beans

Tell children that as they say action words, they must mark each sound they hear in a word by moving a bean into a square of their Word Building Boxes.

- Give each child a set of Word Building Boxes and a handful of dried beans. Have children brainstorm some action words with you, such as *run, jump, swim, draw, itch, laugh, reach, stretch,* and so on.
- Children say the words aloud and then say the sounds that form the words, for example, *chatter* /ch/-/a/-/t/-/ər/. As children say each sound, they move a bean into a square of their Word Building Box. Note that children may need to draw extra squares on their sheet to accommodate all the sounds in the words.

Delete Sounds

WHICH ARE WORDS?

GROUP **Materials:** construction paper smiley faces

Tell children that they will play a game in which they delete the second sound in words with blends and decide whether the remaining sounds make a word.

- Have children make construction paper smiley faces.
- When they have finished, tell them that you will say a word and then you will say the sounds that form it. Children should repeat the word and the sounds.
- Then say the word without the second sound in the blend. Instruct children that if the remaining sounds make a word, they should hold up their smiley faces.
- Use the following words to get started: *black, track, twig, slight, snack, place, sketch, crouch, brat, glitch, branch, drive.*

Digraphs *ph, tch, ch*

OBJECTIVES **Students will recognize and decode words with digraphs *ph*, *tch*, and *ch*.**

Alternate Activities

Auditory

SINGING ALONG

Begin by humming a well-known tune, such as *Twinkle, Twinkle, Little Star.*

- Have students take turns changing the lyrics to create new silly verses with words that contain the digraphs *ph, tch, ch.* For example: *Twinkle, twinkle, little phone; You can't make a call alone.*
  ▶**Musical**

Visual

DIGRAPH LOTTO

Materials: lotto cards as described below, chips to cover pictures on the cards

Prepare lotto cards by drawing or cutting and pasting several pictures of objects whose names include the digraph *tch, ch* or *ph.* Include six pictures on each card. Prepare several sets of cards and make photocopies of each.

- Have students identify each picture by name and tell which digraph the name contains.
- Say a word with the sound of one of the digraphs. Keep a tally of how many of each digraph you use.
- Have students use a chip to cover an object whose name contains the same digraph as the word you say.
- Ask the first student who completely covers a card to say the name of each picture. Check the tally of digraphs to see that it matches.
  ▶**Linguistic**

Kinesthetic

TIC TAC TOE

Materials: tic tac toe grid, prepared as described below.

Prepare photocopies of a tic tac toe grid. At the top of each of the three columns, write the digraph *ph, ch,* or *tch.*

Have partners play *tic tac toe,* using the prepared grid. Instead of entering *Xs* and *Os,* tell students to write a word that includes the digraph written at the top of the column.

- The first player to complete three words in a row, column, or diagonal line, wins the round.
  ▶**Spatial**

CD-ROM

See Reteach 211, 215, 216, 224, 232, 243

Library/Media Center

OBJECTIVES **Students will identify and use resources in the library/media center.**

Alternate Activities

Kinesthetic

LIBRARY FINDS

Materials: a floor plan of the school or local public library

- Distribute copies of the floor plan, and display the plan with an overhead projector.
- Guide students through a discussion of the areas of the library.
- Take students to the library or media center. As you lead them to different sections, have them consult their floor plans to identify which resources are nearby. ▶**Spatial**

Visual

AUTHOR SEARCH

Materials: enlarged copy of a library author card from a card catalog

Display a large copy of an author card from a traditional or electronic card catalog. Explain the entries on the card.

- Give students a list of favorite authors, and have them search the catalog for titles by one of the authors.
- Tell students to check the shelves for books by the author they have chosen and, if copies are available, check one out for recreational reading. ▶**Logical/Mathematical**

Auditory

SUBJECT SEARCH

Materials: prepared list of subjects for research, such as: dogs, countries, oceans

At the library or media center, show students where the card catalog or automated catalog terminal is located.

- Give students step-by-step oral instructions for finding books on a particular subject.
- Tell each student to search for materials related to one of the subjects listed.

Have them write the call number for two or three references.

See Reteach 214, 222, 230, 238, 246

Form Generalizations

OBJECTIVES Students will form generalizations about conversations, the weather, and physical activities.

Alternate Activities

Auditory

CLUE WORDS

Materials: written list of generalization clue words

Explain that clue words used to state generalizations may include: *most, some, usually, often, always.*

- Post these words, and ask students to notice instances in which people use them throughout the day.
- Have students make notes about the generalizations they observe, and share their observations at the end of the day. ▶**Interpersonal**

Visual

WEATHER OR NOT

Over the course of a few days, have students note the weather and create symbols such as a sun, clouds, raindrops, or snow to indicate the weather each day. Tell them to draw one symbol for each day and keep a list.

- Ask volunteers to tell what the weather was mostly like over the past few days, asking them to note which symbol appears most often. ▶**Spatial**

Kinesthetic

FOLLOW THE LEADER

Play a quick game of *Follow the Leader*. Then ask a student to make a generalization about where you went or how you moved.

- Repeat, having different students take turns as the leader. Tell the leader to vary movements from the leader before.
- After each new leader, guide students in making a generalization about how the group moved. For example: *Most of the motions were like animals when Kelly was the leader. We all moved like ballet dancers when Sarah was the leader.*
- After several leaders have taken a turn, guide students to form a generalization about the entire activity, *e.g., We all had fun playing Follow the Leader.* ▶**Bodily/Kinesthetic**

See Reteach 217, 233, 248

Multiple-Meaning Words

OBJECTIVES Students will identify the appropriate meanings in context of multiple-meaning words.

Auditory

WELL, WELL, LISTEN WELL

GROUP Remind students that multiple-meaning words have more than one meaning. Other words in the sentences where they are used show which meaning is intended by the writer or speaker.

- Say a multiple-meaning word. Ask a volunteer to tell one of the meanings.
- Give students two sentences, each using a different meaning for the word.
- Have students listen to both sentences and hold up one finger or two to indicate whether the first or second sentence used the meaning that was given.
- Use sentences such as these:

That man did not look well.

The well had a bucket for water.

I stepped on a slug in the garden.

Did you see her slug that ball?

We keep tools in the shed.

A snake will shed its skin as it grows.

▶**Linguistic**

Kinesthetic

READY, ACTION!

GROUP **Materials:** prepared sentences as described below

Write several sentences with multiple-meaning words, and underline the multiple-meaning word in each.

- Have each student pick a sentence, read it aloud, and act out the correct meaning of the multiple-meaning word.
- Other students can raise their hand if they think the student demonstrated the correct meaning.
- Discuss any differences of opinion.
  ▶**Bodily/Kinesthetic**

Visual

SEEING DOUBLE

ONE **Materials:** drawing paper, markers or crayons

Provide a list of multiple-meaning words that can be depicted graphically, such as: *batter, bark, club, count, fly, hide, kind, loaf, palm, pound, school.*

- Have students choose one of the words. Instruct them to draw one picture that shows two meanings of the word. For example, they might show a loaf of bread loafing in a hammock.
- Have students display their completed drawings. Invite others to guess which multiple-meaning word is depicted and discuss both meanings shown. ▶**Spatial**

See Reteach 218, 226, 250

Phonological Awareness

OBJECTIVES Children will practice blending and segmenting sounds and deleting the second sound in blends.

Blend Sounds

GARDEN SIGNS

Materials: construction paper, craft sticks, and crayons or markers

Tell children that they will blend sounds to form words naming fruits and vegetables.

- Give each child a square-shaped sheet of white paper and a craft stick. Explain that they are going to make garden signs.
- Say the sounds of a fruit or vegetable.(Examples: *carrot, pea, corn, beet, bean, apple, pear, peach.*) Have children blend the sounds together to form the name of the fruit or vegetable. Then have them draw the garden sign showing a picture of the blended word.
- Attach the craft stick to make the completed garden sign.

Segment Sounds

CLAPPING GAME

Have pairs of children play a clapping game to segment sounds.

- Organize the class into pairs. Have partners face one another.
- One partner says the other partner's name. Then both children segment the name by saying the sounds aloud together. As they say the first sound in the name, children clap. For the second, they slap right hands together. For the third they clap, and for the fourth they slap left hands. They follow this pattern until they have segmented all the sounds in the name.
- Partners continue playing the game using words such as the following: *creek, bright, trees, nest, field, mice, graph, catch, treat,* and *laugh.*

Delete Sounds

LEAVE IT OUT

Materials: Word Building Boxes from *Word Building Kit,* game markers

Tell children that they will work in pairs to mark the sounds in a word with a blend, and then delete the second sound in each blend.

- Divide the class into pairs and give each pair a set of Word Building Boxes and a handful of game markers.
- Say the following words and the sounds that make up each word: *pleat* /p/-/l/-/ē/-/t/, *spit* /s/-/p/-/i/-/t/, *tree* /t/-/r/-/ē/, *steam* /s/-/t/-/ē/-/m/, *slip,* /s/-/l/-/i/-/p/, *bleat* /b/-/l/-/ē/-/t/, *grab* /g/-/r/-/a/-/b/. Have pairs work together to move a marker into a Word Building Box for each sound they hear.
- After they finish, have partners remove the second marker from the box and pronounce the sounds that remain after the second sound in the blend is removed. Then they say the new words. *(Pete, sit, tee, seam, sip, beat,* and *gab)*

Long *e* and Long *i*: /ē/ *ee, ie, ea*; /ī/ *i, y, igh*

TESTED OBJECTIVES **Students will recognize and decode words with long *e* and long *i*.**

Auditory

OLD SONGS, NEW VERSES

Sing a verse of *Old McDonald* to be sure all students are familiar with the song.

- Brainstorm long *e* and long *i* words that might fit new verses of *Old McDonald* and write them on a chalkboard.
- Have students work with partners to make up their own verses, using words that contain long *i* and long *e* sounds. For example: *Old McDonald had some mice, ee-i-ee-i-o/With a squeak squeak here,* etc.
- Encourage each pair to teach a verse to the group. ▶**Musical**

Visual

LONG VOWEL POSTERS

Materials: poster-sized cutouts of block letters *e* and *i*, magazines and newspapers for cutting, scissors, glue

Invite students to make posters. Have them write *ee, ie,* and *ea* at the top of one poster and *i, y,* and *igh* at the top of another.

- Provide magazines and newspapers. Have students cut out words with the long *i* and long *e* spellings.
- Tell students to paste words on the appropriate poster.
- When the posters are complete, have students read as many words as they can. ▶**Linguistic**

Kinesthetic

CLAP HANDS

Students can begin by sharing any common hand-clapping patterns they know.

- Have students practice this traditional hand-clapping rhyme:

A sailor went to sea, sea, sea,
To see what he could see, see, see,
But all that he could see, see, see,
Was the bottom of the deep blue sea, sea, sea.

- Have students innovate on text to create an original long /ī/ verse, such as the following:

A pilot went to fly, fly, sky
In the middle of the deep blue sky, sky, sky,
But all that she could spy, spy, spy
Was sky since she was up too high, high, high.

- Write the verses on chart paper for other students to recite. ▶**Bodily/Kinesthetic**

CD-ROM

See Reteach 219, 223, 224, 232, 240, 243

Main Idea

TESTED OBJECTIVES **Students will identify main ideas and supporting details.**

Auditory

WHAT'S IT ALL ABOUT?

GROUP **Materials:** storybook

Read students a short story, such as a fable.

- Ask students to think up a sentence that tells what the entire story was about. Remind them that a main idea should not include details; it should be a general statement that details relate to.
- Write students' ideas for a main idea statement on the board. Encourage discussion and revision of the statements to form a complete main idea statement. ▶**Interpersonal**

Kinesthetic

SUPPORTING DETAILS

PARTNERS **Materials:** writing paper, paper strips, tape

Copy sentences from a paragraph, omitting a main idea statement. Cut to make a separate strip of each sentence.

- Tell students to tape each sentence to a piece of paper.
- Have students read each detail (sentence) and talk it over with a partner.

WRITING Ask the pair to decide on a main idea statement that covers all of the details, and write it on another slip of paper.

- Have them tape the main idea statement to another piece of paper. Then they can arrange the sentences so that all of the supporting detail pages support the main idea page. ▶**Bodily/Kinesthetic**

Visual

MIX AND MATCH

ONE **Materials:** captioned photos from newspapers or magazines

Cut out photographs from a newspaper or news magazine. Then cut the captions apart from the pictures. Write corresponding numbers on the backs of matching pieces to allow for self-checking.

- Tell students a caption is a statement that tells the main idea of a photograph.
- Provide a pile of photos and a pile of captions for students to match. Explain that the caption should tell the main idea of the matching photograph. ▶**Spatial**

See Reteach 225, 241, 247

Phonological Awareness

OBJECTIVES **Children will practice blending and segmenting sounds and substituting beginning, middle, and ending sounds.**

Alternate

Blend Sounds

BLENDING CLUES

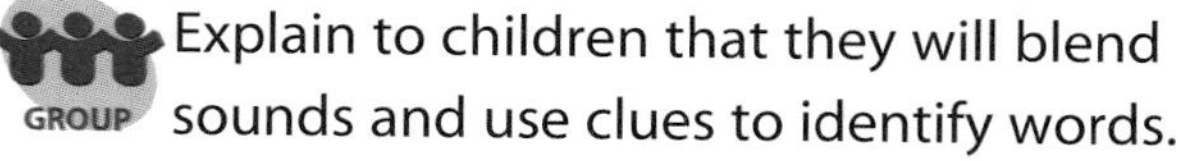

Explain to children that they will blend sounds and use clues to identify words.

- Tell children that you will say the sounds of some words. They will blend the sounds and say the words. To help them, you'll give them a clue for each word.
- Say the following sounds along with the clue for each word.

/p/-/l/-/ā/-/n/. It's the opposite of *fancy. (plain)*

/g/-/ō/-/t/. It's a farm animal. *(goat)*

/b/-/l/-/ō/-/z/. The wind does this. *(blows)*

/t/-/ō/-/z/. You've got five at the end of each foot. *(toes)*

/b/-/ē/-/ch/. This is where you can play in the sand. *(beach)*

/p/-/i/-/ch/-/ər/. This is the baseball player who throws the ball. *(pitcher)*

/s/-/t/-/ů/-/d/. It's the opposite of sat. *(stood)*

Segment Sounds

CHECK IT

Materials: chalkboard and chalk, or marker and erasable board

Have children make check marks on a board for sounds they hear in words.

- Tell children that you will say words and they will say the sounds that form the words.
- Ask two volunteers to go to the board for every word you pronounce. The first child repeats the word and then says it again, this time sound by sound. The second child makes a check mark on the board for each sound in the word. The rest of the class confirms that the volunteers have heard and marked the sounds correctly.
- Use words such as the following when pairs come to the board: *trace, niece, huge, sponge, catch, flight, winner,* and *great.*

Substitute Sounds

SOUND SWITCH

Materials: Phonics Pictures from *Word Building Kit*

Tell children that they will work in pairs to change sounds in words to match the sounds in Phonics Pictures.

- Organize the class into pairs. Give each pair eight or ten Phonics Pictures from the *Word Building Kit.*
- Explain that one partner should say a word for a color or a number and then say *beginning, middle,* or *end.* The other partner chooses a Phonics Picture and replaces the beginning, middle, or ending sound in their partner's word with the beginning sound of the Phonics Picture.
- Tell children that most of the new words they make will be nonsense words. For example, the first child might say *blue/beginning.* If the second child chooses the Phonics Picture for dinosaur, he or she would say /d/-/l/-/ü/, *dlue.*

Long *a* and Long *o*: /ā/ *ai, ay*; /ō/ *oa, oe, ow*

TESTED OBJECTIVES Students will recognize and decode words with long *a* and long *o*.

Visual

GO FISH

PARTNERS **Materials:** two sets of playing cards; each card has words and pictures of one of these long *o* and long *a* spellings: *ai, ay; oa, oe, ow* (e.g., *sail, pail, ray, hay, boat, goat, bow, slow, toe, hoe)*

- Players take turns asking each other for a card. They ask for a card by sound name, spelling, and by example, as in: *Do you have a long* o *card with* oa *as in* boat?
- If the partner has a card, the partner must give it to the player who asked. If a player gets a pair of matching vowels with the same spelling, the partner lays the pair down.
- Play continues until one player is out of cards. ▶**Logical/Mathematical**

Auditory

PLAY WITH SONG SOUNDS

GROUP Review the spellings of long *a* and long *o*.

- Sing *Row, Row, Row Your Boat* with students.
- Have group members collaborate to make up new lines for the song with long *o* and long *a* words. For example: *Grow, grow, grow your oats.* ▶**Musical**

Kinesthetic

SOUND SORTING

ONE **Materials:** cards, five book rings

Make several cards, each with one word that contains the long *a* or long *o* vowel spelling. Punch a hole in the corner of each card.

- Demonstrate how to open and close the book rings.
- Tell students they will sort the words on the cards by the long vowel spelling.
- Have them use a book ring to connect all the cards with the same vowel spelling. ▶**Spatial**

 **CD-ROM**

See Reteach 227, 231, 232, 240, 243

Figurative Language

OBJECTIVES Students will identify and interpret figurative language.

Auditory

SIMILE CIRCLE

GROUP Have students sit in a circle. Offer the phrases below, one at a time:

as quick as ______

as funny as ______

as soft as ______

as sad as ______

as sweet as ______

as graceful as ______

as cold as ______

as quiet as ______

- Go around the circle as quickly as possible, pausing for each student to complete the phrase with a few words. Encourage students to use original comparisons.
- Repeat with the next phrase, starting with a different student each time. ▶**Linguistic**

Kinesthetic

WHAT MAKES IT SPECIAL

GROUP **Materials:** stuffed animals or other toys

Have students bring in a favorite toy or stuffed animal, or hand out favorite classroom toys for children to describe. Invite students to sit in a circle.

- Ask each student to hold a toy or animal and describe it, using similes or other figurative language. Examples: *My car is as red as a fire engine, as fast as a rocket, and as noisy as a jet plane. My teddy is as soft as a kitten, as furry as a bear, and as special as a good friend.*
- Encourage students to pass their items around the circle and invite others to offer comparisons. ▶**Kinesthetic**

Visual

FIGURATIVE CLOUDS

PARTNERS Take students outside on a partly cloudy day. Have them sit comfortably and watch the sky and clouds.

- Ask students to describe what they see in the sky. Then have them add figurative language to modify their descriptions. ▶**Spatial**

See Reteach 234, 242, 249

Phonological Awareness

OBJECTIVES **Children will practice blending and segmenting sounds and substituting beginning, middle, and ending sounds.**

Blend Sounds

WHAT DO I SEE?

Materials: picture of a landscape or cityscape

Tell children that they will give each other clues to help blend sounds into words.

- Choose a detailed illustration of a country or city scene. Display the picture for the class. Divide the class into pairs and tell children that they will use the picture in a blending activity.
- One partner will look at the picture and choose something he or she sees in the picture. Then the child gives a hint and pronounces the sounds in the word. The partner repeats the sounds and blends them into the word. For example, if the child sees a tree in the picture, he or she might say, *It has branches.* /t/-/r/-/ē/ The second child repeats the sounds and says *tree.*
- Partners switch roles and continue the activity.

Segment Sounds

I SPY

GROUP **Materials:** construction paper, markers

Use this activity to help children practice segmenting words into individual sounds.

- Tell children that they are going to build a word pyramid.
- Have them draw three rows of boxes. Four on the bottom, three in the middle, and two on the top.
- Say the following groups of words in varied order: *it, lit, flit; an, can, scan; am, lamb, slam.* Ask the children how many sounds there are in each word.
- Have children work in small groups to figure out in which row a word belongs, putting check marks in the appropriate boxes with different colored markers.

Substitute Sounds

SUBSTITUTE ME

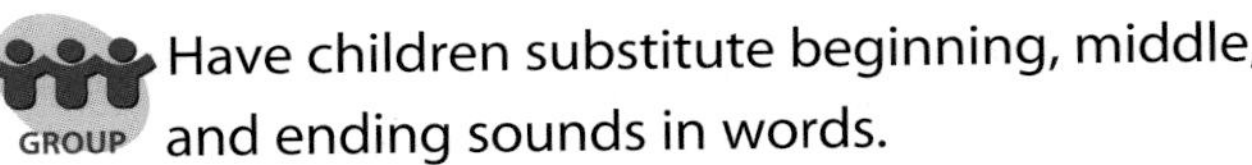

GROUP Have children substitute beginning, middle, and ending sounds in words.

- Say the word *cent*. Have one child stand for each sound. Tell children to say the sound they represent. Then blend the sounds together and say the word together.
- Ask another child to stand to represent the /r/ sound. Have that child tap the (/s/) child on the shoulder and stand in his or her place to indicate that the beginning sound is being switched.
- Tell children to say the sound they represent again with the new sound at the beginning. Then encourage the class to blend the sounds and say the word naturally. *(rent)*
- Continue using words such as the following: *crib, large, face, chain, better,* and *drip*. Be sure that beginning, middle, and ending sounds are substituted.

Soft *c* and Soft *g*: /s/ *ce*; /j/ *ge*

OBJECTIVES **Students will recognize and decode words with soft *c* and soft *g*.**

Auditory

TONGUE TWISTERS

GROUP **Materials:** paper and pencil

Have students brainstorm a list of words with soft *c* and soft *g* sounds.

- Display the list, and invite students to use it as they make up tongue twisters or silly sentences.
  ▶Linguistic

Kinesthetic

PUPPET FUN

PARTNERS **Materials:** odd socks, buttons, yarn, fabric glue

Invite students to make hand puppets and plan a short skit.

- Make a label for a puppet stage, and point out that the word *stage* has a soft *g* sound. Have students make up names that contain soft *c* or soft *g* for their puppets. Give examples, such as *George* and *Stacey.*
- Have students make up a brief skit that includes as many soft *c* and soft *g* sounds as possible.
  ▶Interpersonal

Visual

PLAY STORE

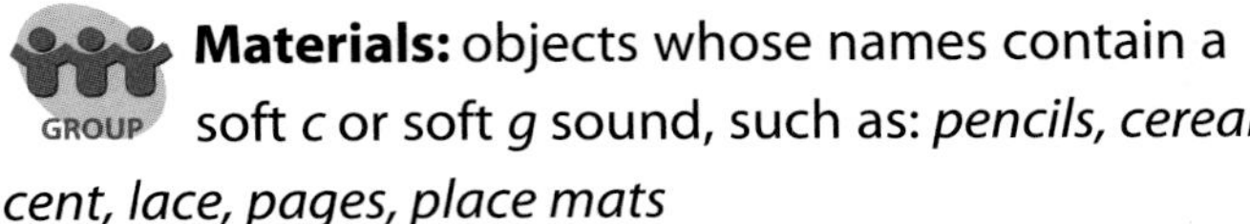

GROUP **Materials:** objects whose names contain a soft *c* or soft *g* sound, such as: *pencils, cereal, cent, lace, pages, place mats*

Prepare labels for objects whose names contain soft *c* or soft *g* sounds, and set up a corner of the classroom as a class store.

WRITING Have each student prepare a shopping list of items with soft *g* or soft *c* in the name.

- Invite students to go shopping and see if their items are in the store. They can pretend to buy the items, crossing them off their lists.
  ▶Bodily/Kinesthetic

CD-ROM

See Reteach 235, 239, 240, 243

A Communication Tool

Although typewriters and computers are readily available, many situations continue to require handwriting. Tasks such as keeping journals, completing forms, taking notes, making shopping or organizational lists, and the ability to read hand-written manuscript or cursive writing are a few examples of practical application of this skill.

BEFORE YOU BEGIN

Before children begin to write, certain fine motor skills need to be developed. Examples of activities that can be used as warm-up activities are:

- **Simon Says** Play a game of Simon Says using just finger positions.
- **Finger Plays and Songs** Sing songs that use Signed English, American Sign Language or finger spelling.
- **Mazes** Mazes are available in a wide range of difficulty. You can also create mazes that allow children to move their writing instruments from left to right.

Determining Handedness

Keys to determining handedness in a child:

- Which hand does the child eat with? This is the hand that is likely to become the dominant hand.
- Does the child start coloring with one hand and then switch to the other? This may be due to fatigue rather than lack of hand preference.
- Does the child cross midline to pick things up or use the closest hand? Place items directly in front of the child to see if one hand is preferred.
- Does the child do better with one hand or the other?

The Mechanics of Writing

DESK AND CHAIR

- Chair height should allow for the feet to rest flat on the floor.
- Desk height should be two inches above the level of the elbows when the child is sitting.
- The chair should be pulled in allowing for an inch of space between the child's abdomen and the desk.
- Children sit erect with the elbows resting on the desk.
- Children should have models of letters on the desk or at eye level, not above their heads.

PAPER POSITION

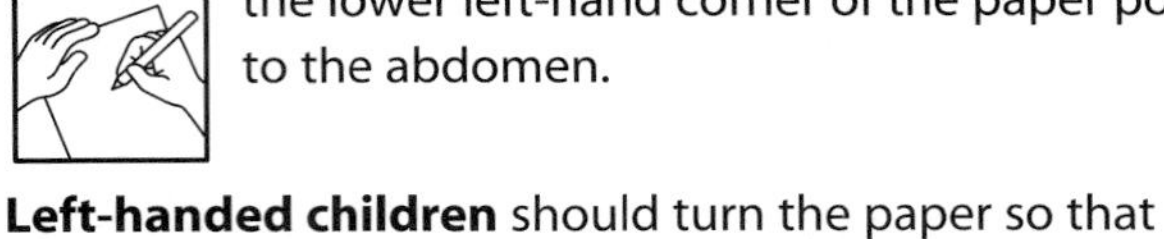

- **Right-handed children** should turn the paper so that the lower left-hand corner of the paper points to the abdomen.
- **Left-handed children** should turn the paper so that the lower right-hand corner of the paper points to the abdomen.
- The nondominant hand should anchor the paper near the top so that the paper doesn't slide.
- The paper should be moved up as the child nears the bottom of the paper. Many children won't think of this and may let their arms hang off the desk when they reach the bottom of a page.

The Writing Instrument Grasp

For handwriting to be functional, the writing instrument must be held in a way that allows for fluid dynamic movement.

FUNCTIONAL GRASP PATTERNS

- **Tripod Grasp** With open web space, the writing instrument is held with the tip of the thumb and the index finger and rests against the side of the third finger. The thumb and index finger form a circle.
- **Quadrupod Grasp** With open web space, the writing instrument is held with the tip of the thumb and index finger and rests against the fourth finger. The thumb and index finger form a circle.

INCORRECT GRASP PATTERNS

- **Fisted Grasp** The writing instrument is held in a fisted hand.

- **Pronated Grasp** The writing instrument is held diagonally within the hand with the tips of the thumb and index finger on the writing instrument but with no support from other fingers.
- **Five-Finger Grasp** The writing instrument is held with the tips of all five fingers.

TO CORRECT WRITING INSTRUMENT GRASPS

- Have children play counting games with an eye dropper and water.
- Have children pick up small objects with a tweezer.
- Do counting games with children picking up small coins using just the thumb and index finger.

FLEXED OR HOOKED WRIST

- The writing instrument can be held in a variety of grasps with the wrist flexed or bent. This is typically seen with left-handed writers but is also present in some right-handed writers. To correct wrist position, have children check their writing posture and paper placement.

Evaluation Checklist

Functional writing is made up of two elements, legibility and functional speed.

LEGIBILITY

MANUSCRIPT

Formation and Strokes

- ☑ Does the child begin letters at the top?
- ☑ Do circles close?
- ☑ Are the horizontal lines straight?
- ☑ Do circular shapes and extender and descender lines touch?
- ☑ Are the heights of all upper-case letters equal?
- ☑ Are the heights of all lower-case letters equal?
- ☑ Are the lengths of the extenders and descenders the same for all letters?

Directionality

- ☑ Are letters and words formed from left to right?
- ☑ Are letters and words formed from top to bottom?

Spacing

- ☑ Are the spaces between letters equidistant?
- ☑ Are the spaces between words equidistant?
- ☑ Do the letters rest on the line?
- ☑ Are the top, bottom and side margins even?

CURSIVE

Formation and Strokes

- ☑ Do circular shapes close?
- ☑ Are the downstrokes parallel?
- ☑ Do circular shapes and downstroke lines touch?
- ☑ Are the heights of all upper-case letters equal?
- ☑ Are the heights of all lower-case letters equal?
- ☑ Are the lengths of the extenders and descenders the same for all letters?
- ☑ Do the letters which finish at the top join the next letter? (*b, o, v, w*)
- ☑ Do the letters which finish at the bottom join the next letter? (*a, c, d, h, i, k, l, m, n, r, s, t, u, x*)
- ☑ Do letters with descenders join the next letter? (*f, g, j, p, q, y, z*)
- ☑ Do all letters touch the line?
- ☑ Is the vertical slant of all letters consistent?

Directionality

- ☑ Are letters and words formed from left to right?
- ☑ Are letters and words formed from top to bottom?

Spacing

- ☑ Are the spaces between letters equidistant?
- ☑ Are the spaces between words equidistant?
- ☑ Do the letters rest on the line?
- ☑ Are the top, bottom and side margins even?

SPEED

The prettiest handwriting is not functional for classroom work if it takes the child three times longer than the rest of the class to complete work assignments. After the children have been introduced to writing individual letters, begin to add time limitations to the completion of copying or writing assignments. Then check the child's work for legibility.

Handwriting Models—Manuscript

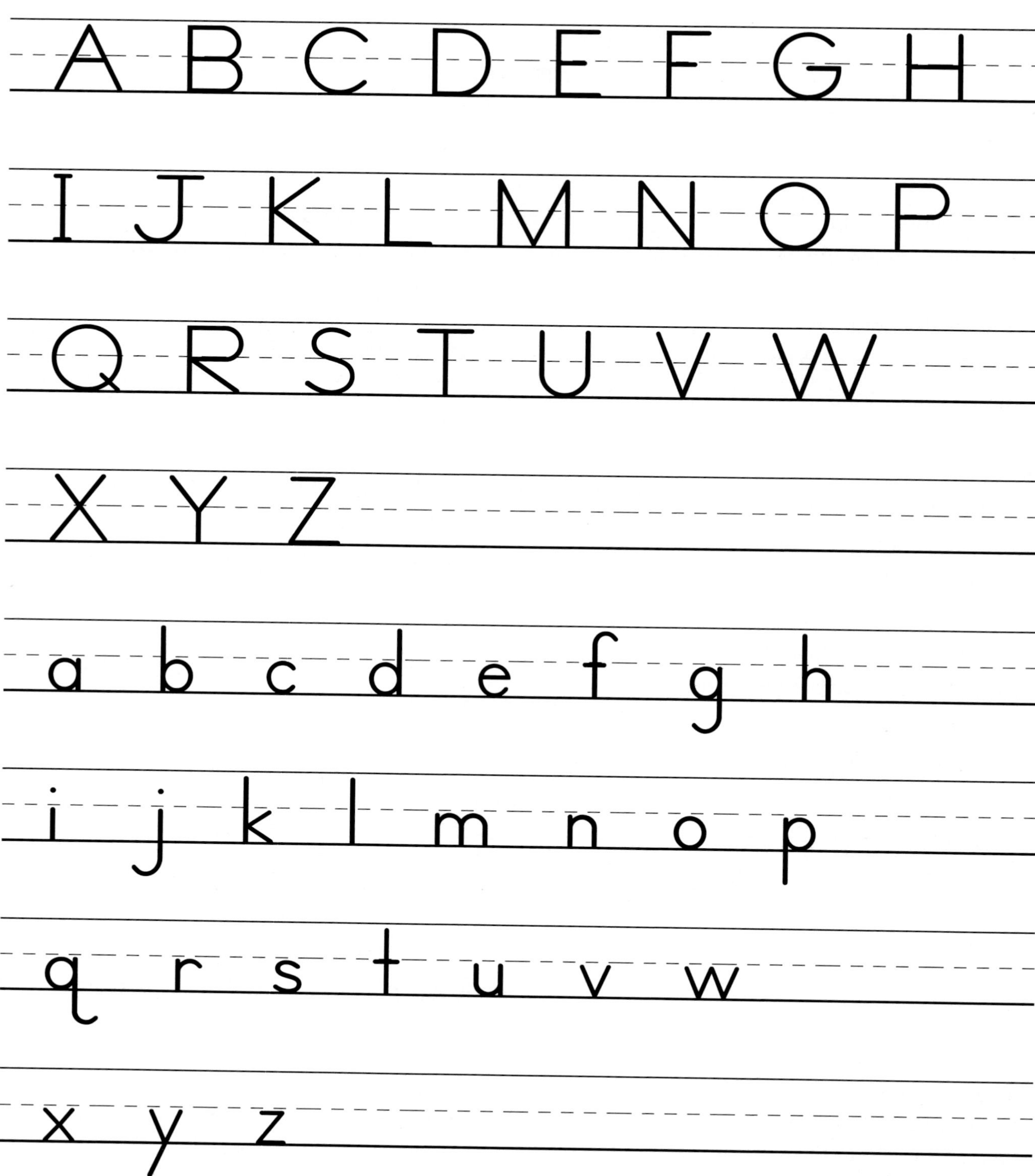

Handwriting Models—Cursive

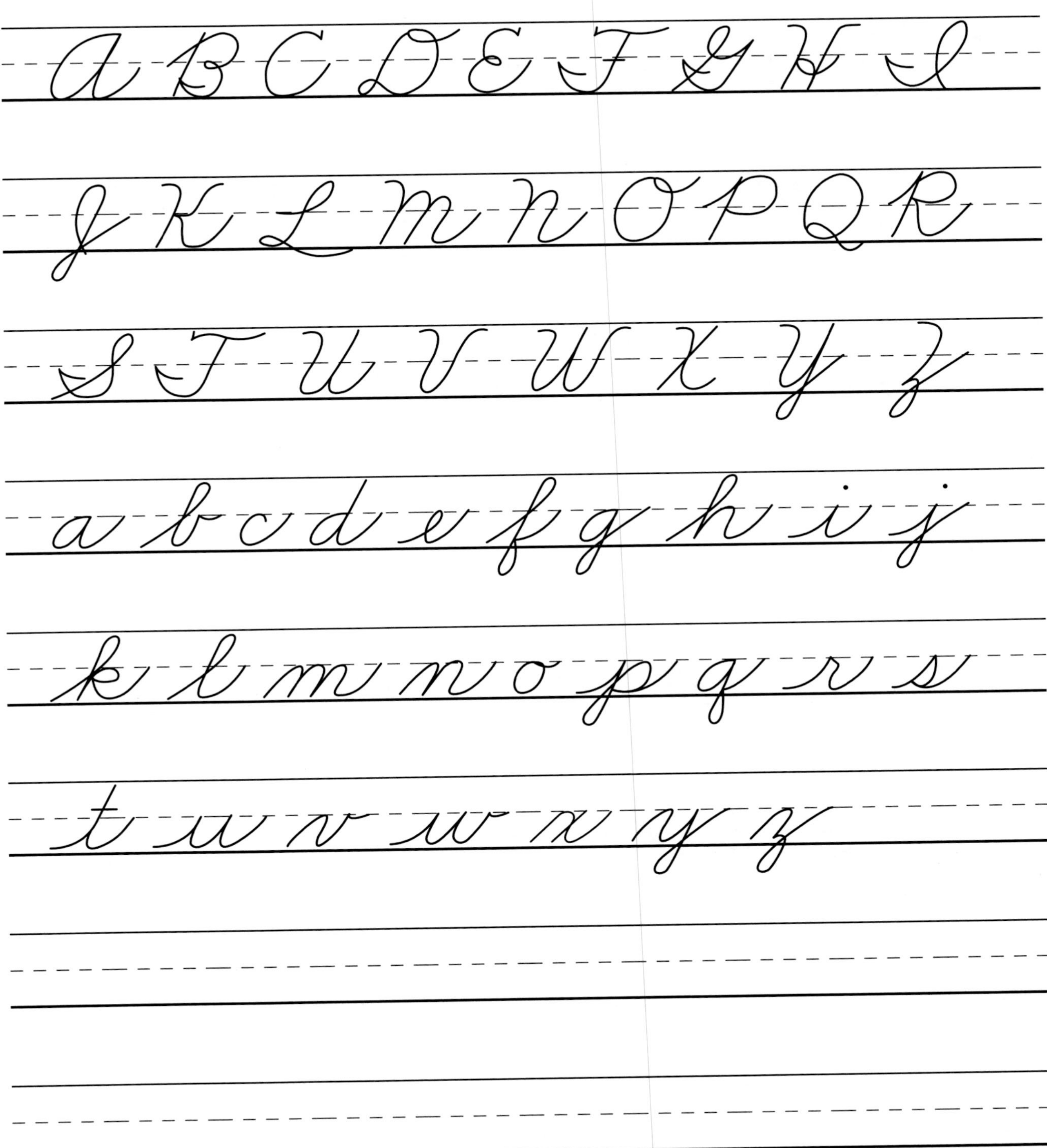

Handwriting Models—Slant

A B C D E F G H

I J K L M N O P

Q R S T U V W

X Y Z

a b c d e f g h

i j k l m n o p

q r s t u v w

x y z

Handwriting Practice

Selection Titles	Honors, Prizes, and Awards
 HENRY AND MUDGE Book 1, p.38 by ***Cynthia Rylant*** Illustrated by ***Suçie Stevenson***	**American Book Award Pick of the List (1987)** **Author: *Cynthia Rylant,*** winner of Caldecott Honor (1983) for *When I Was Young in the Mountains;* ALA Notable (1985) for *Waiting to Waltz: A Childhood: Poems;* ALA Notable, Caldecott Honor (1986), New York Times Best Illustrated (1985) for *The Relatives Came;* ALA Notable (1986) for *Blue-Eyed Daisy;* ALA Notable, Newbery Honor (1987) for *Fine White Dust;* ALA Notable (1988) for *Henry and Mudge Under the Yellow Moon;* ALA Notable (1991) for *Henry and Mudge and the Happy Cat;* ALA Notable (1992), Boston Globe-Horn Book Award (1991) for *Appalachia: The Voices of the Sleeping Birds;* ALA Notable (1993) for *Angel for Solomon Singer;* ALA Notable, Newbery Medal (1993), Boston Globe-Horn Book Award (1992) for *Missing May;* ALA Notable (1996) for *Mr. Putter and Tabby Pick the Pears;* ALA Notable (1996) for *Van Gogh Café* **Illustrator: *Suçie Stevenson,*** winner ALA Notable (1988) for *Henry and Mudge Under the Yellow Moon;* ALA Notable (1991) for *Henry and Mudge and the Happy Cat*
 ROUNDUP AT RIO RANCH Book 1, p.94 by ***Angela Shelf Medearis***	**Author: *Angela Shelf Medearis,*** winner of IRA-Teachers' Choice Award (1995) for *Our People*
 THE MERRY-GO-ROUND Book 1, p.124 by ***Myra Cohn Livingston***	**Poet: *Myra Cohn Livingston,*** winner of National Council of Teachers of English Award for Excellence in Poetry for Children (1980); ALA Notable (1984) for *Christmas Poems;* ALA Notable (1987) for *Cat Poems;* ALA Notable (1992) for *Poem-Making: Ways to Learn Writing Poetry*
 A LETTER TO AMY Book 1, p.158 by ***Ezra Jack Keats***	**Author/Illustrator: *Ezra Jack Keats,*** winner of Caldecott Medal (1963) for *The Snowy Day;* Caldecott Honor (1970) for *Goggles;* Boston Globe-Horn Book Award (1970) for *Hi, Cat!*
 THE BEST FRIENDS CLUB Book 1, p.194 by ***Elizabeth Winthrop*** Illustrated by ***Martha Weston***	**IRA-CBC Children's Choice (1990)** **Illustrator: *Martha Weston,*** winner of ALA Notable (1989) for *Big Beast Book: Dinosaurs and How They Got That Way*

Selection Titles	Honors, Prizes, and Awards
JAMAICA TAG-ALONG Book 1, p.218 by ***Juanita Havill***	**Author:** ***Juanita Havill,*** winner of Ezra Jack Keats Award (1987)
FOUR GENERATIONS Book 1, p.254 by ***Mary Ann Hoberman***	**Poet:** ***Mary Ann Hoberman,*** winner of American Book Award Paperback Picture Book (1983) for *A House Is a House for Me*
CLOUD DRAGONS Book 1, p.256 by ***Pat Mora***	**Author:** ***Pat Mora,*** winner of National Association for Chicano Studies Creative Writing Award (1983); New America: Woman Artists and Writers of the Southwest Award (1984); Smithsonian Magazine Notable Books for Children (1998) for *Tomás and the Library Lady*
ARTHUR WRITES A STORY Book 1, p.260 by ***Marc Brown***	**IRA-CBC Children's Choice (1997)** **Author/Illustrator:** ***Marc Brown,*** winner of Boston Globe-Horn Book Honor (1980) for *Why the Tides Ebb and Flow;* ALA Notable (1984) for *The Bionic Bunny Show*
BEST WISHES, ED Book 1, p.292 by ***James Stevenson***	**Author /Illustrator:** ***James Stevenson,*** winner of Boston Globe-Horn Book Honor (1998) for *Popcorn: Poems;* Christopher Award (1983) for *We Can't Sleep;* ALA Notable (1984) for *What's Under My Bed;* ALA Notable (1987) for *When I Was Nine;* ALA Notable, Boston Globe-Horn Book Honor (1987) for *Georgia Music;* ALA Notable (1988) for *Grandaddy's Place;* ALA Notable (1991) for *July;* ALA Notable (1993) for *Don't You Know There's a War On?;* ALA Notable (1994) for *Grandaddy and Janetta;* Texas Blue Bonnet Master List (1995), ALA Notable (1996) for *Sweet Corn: Poems;* ALA Notable (1996) for *Grandaddy's Stars*
TIME TO PLAY Book 1, p.380 by ***Nikki Grimes***	**Poet:** ***Nikki Grimes,*** winner of ALA Notable, Coretta Scott King Award (1979) for *Something on My Mind;* ALA Notable (1995) for *Meet Danitra Brown;* ALA Notable (1996) for *Come Sunday*

Selection Titles	Honors, Prizes, and Awards
RIVER WINDING Book 2, p.10 by ***Charlotte Zolotow***	**Poet: *Charlotte Zolotow,*** winner of Caldecott Honor (1953) for *Storm Book;* Caldecott Honor (1962) for *Mr. Rabbit and the Lovely Present;* Christopher Award (1975) for *My Grandson Leo;* ALA Notable (1996) for *When the Wind Stops*
CHARLIE ANDERSON Book 2, p.14 by ***Barbara Abercrombie*** Illustrated by ***Mark Graham***	**Redbook Children's Picture Book Award (1990)**
ZIPPING, ZAPPING, ZOOMING BATS Book 2, p.94 by ***Anne Earle*** Illustrated by ***Henry Cole***	**American Book Award Pick of the List (1995)**
WHAT IS IT? Book 2, p.128 by ***Eve Merriam***	**Poet: *Eve Merriam,*** winner of National Council of Teachers of English Award for Excellence in Poetry for Children (1981)
THE WEDNESDAY SURPRISE Book 2, p.182 by ***Eve Bunting*** Illustrated by ***Donald Carrick***	**ALA Notable Book (1990), IRA-CBC Children's Choice, IRA-Teachers' Choice, School Library Journal Best Book (1989)** **Author: *Eve Bunting,*** winner of ALA Notable (1990) for *Wall;* ALA Notable (1992) for *Fly Away Home;* Edgar Allen Poe Juvenile Award (1993) for *Coffin on a Case;* ALA Notable, Caldecott Medal (1995) for *Smoky Night;* ALA Notable (1997) for *Train to Somewhere;* National Council for Social Studies Notable Children's Book Award (1998) for *Moonstick,* and *I Am the Mummy Heb-Nefert,* and *On Call Back Mountain* **Illustrator: *Donald Carrick,*** winner of ALA Notable (1987) for *What Happened to Patrick's Dinosaurs?*
FOSSILS TELL OF LONG AGO Book 2, p.214 by ***Aliki***	**National Science Teachers' Association Outstanding Science Tradebook for Children (1990), Library of Congress Children's Book of 1972**

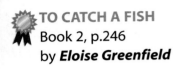

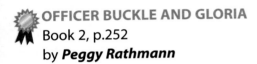

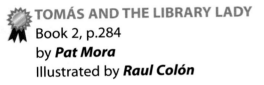

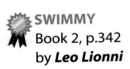

Selection Titles	Honors, Prizes, and Awards
TO CATCH A FISH Book 2, p.246 by ***Eloise Greenfield***	**Poet: *Eloise Greenfield,*** winner of Boston Globe-Horn Book Honor (1975) for *She Come Bringing Me That Little Baby Girl;* Jane Addams Book Award (1976) for *Paul Robeson;* Coretta Scott King Award (1978) for *Africa Dream;* Boston Globe-Horn Book Honor (1980) for *Childtimes: A Three Generation Memoir;* ALA Notable (1989) for *Grandpa's Face;* ALA Notable (1989) for *Under the Sunday Tree;* ALA Notable, Coretta Scott King Award (1990) for *Nathaniel Talking;* ALA Notable (1992) for *Night on Neighborhood Street;* National Council of Teachers of English Award for Excellence in Poetry for Children (1997)
OFFICER BUCKLE AND GLORIA Book 2, p.252 by ***Peggy Rathmann***	**Caldecott Medal, ALA Notable (1996)** **Author/Illustrator: *Peggy Rathmann,*** winner of ALA Notable (1995) for *Good Night, Gorilla*
TOMÁS AND THE LIBRARY LADY Book 2, p.284 by ***Pat Mora*** Illustrated by ***Raul Colón***	**Smithsonian Magazine Notable Books for Children (1998)** **Author: *Pat Mora,*** winner of National Association for Chicano Studies Creative Writing Award (1983); New America: Woman Artists and Writers of the Southwest Award (1984) **Illustrator: *Raul Colón,*** winner of ALA Notable (1996) for *My Mama Had a Dancing Heart*
SWIMMY Book 2, p.342 by ***Leo Lionni***	**Caldecott Honor (1961), *New York Times* Best Illustrated (1960)** **Author/Illustrator: *Leo Lionni,*** winner of Caldecott Honor (1961), *New York Times* Best Illustrated (1960) for *Inch by Inch;* Caldecott Honor (1968), *New York Times* Best Illustrated (1967) for *Frederick;* Caldecott Honor (1970) for *Alexander and the Wind-up Mouse*

Theme Bibliography

	Officer Buckle and Gloria	Tomás and the Library Lady
Trade Books **Additional fiction and nonfiction trade books related to each selection can be shared with children throughout the unit.**	**Rugby and Rosie** *Nan Parson Rossiter (Dutton Children's Books, 1997)* The story of how a family and their dog help prepare a puppy for training as a guide dog. *Realistic Fiction* **Chester, the Out-of-Work Dog** *Marilyn Singer, illustrated by Cat B. Smith (Henry Holt and Company, 1992)* Chester, a collie, is no longer responsible for certain chores when his family moves from the farm to the city. *Fiction* **Lyle at the Office** *Bernard Waber (Houghton Mifflin, 1994)* Lyle, a lovable crocodile, visits Mr. Primm's advertising office and receives a job offer. *Fiction*	**Potato: A Tale from the Great Depression** *Kate Lied, illustrated by Lisa Campbell Ernst (National Geographic Society, 1997)* A young girl recalls the story that her grandmother told her about how her grandparents had to keep moving in order to find work during the Great Depression. *Historical Fiction* **Radio Man** *Arthur Dorros (HarperCollins, 1993)* While traveling with his family of migrant workers, Diego uses his radio to keep in touch with people and places across the country. *Realistic Fiction* **Calling the Doves/El Canto de las Palomas** *Juan Felipe Herrera, illustrated by Elly Simmons (Children's Book Press, 1995)* A memoir in which the author shares the happy memories of his childhood in a family of migrant workers. *Autobiographical Story*
Technology **Multimedia resources can be used to enhance children's understanding of the selections.**	 ***Clown*** (Coronet/MTI) Video, 15 min. A child gives up his dog to a blind man.  ***Cops Are Tops: Our Police at Work*** (AIMS Multimedia) Video, 15 min. A look at how police are involved in community life, from school visits to protecting the people. 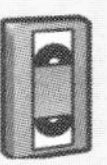 ***Firehouse Dog*** (BFA Educational Media) Video, 11 min. Firemen adopt a stray puppy and train it to become a fire dog.	 ***Ira Says Goodbye*** (SVE/Churchill) Video, 26 min. Two best friends say good-bye when one of them moves away. (Gold Apple Award, Best of Classroom)  ***Kazoo*** (BFA Educational Media) Video, 14 min. When a best friend moves away, his parting gift brings comfort to the friend he left behind. (CINE Eagle Award)  ***The New Kid*** (BFA Educational Media) Video, 11 min. This film focuses on the hardships of moving and the difficulties children have in approaching people in their new communities.

Princess Pooh

/ly Brother, Ant
'etsy Byars, illustrated by Marc Simont
Viking, 1997)

ı four separate stories, Ant's older
rother proves how helpful and under-
tanding an older brother can be.
'ealistic Fiction

'win Pickle
nn Doro, illustrated by Clare Mackie
Henry Holt and Company, 1996)

ead about the fun that Jenny
nd Ivory have as identical twins.
story in rhyme.
lumorous Fiction

/ly Rotten Redheaded Older
rother
atricia Polacco (Simon & Schuster,
994)

atricia learns that her obnoxious
rother Ralph is really a loving and
rotective person.
iction

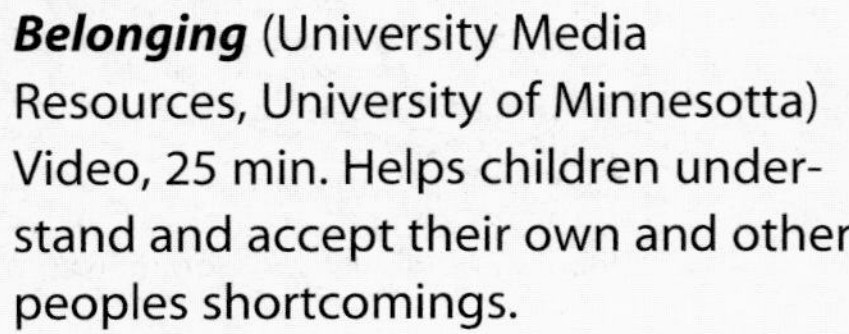

Belonging (University Media Resources, University of Minnesotta) Video, 25 min. Helps children understand and accept their own and other peoples shortcomings.

Regina: A Gift of Vision (Encyclopaedia Britannica Educational Corporation) Video, 11 min. A blind girl helps others understand the everyday life of a disabled person.

All I See (SRA McGraw-Hill) Video, 8 min. A movie about friendship and seeing.

Swimmy

Rainbow Fish
Marcus Pfister, J. Alison James (Translator) (North South Books, 1992)

When Rainbow Fish is shunned by the other fish for not giving them any of his beautiful scales, he learns a lesson about sharing and friendship.
Fiction

Baby Whale's Journey
Jonathan London, illustrated by Jon Van Zyle (Chronicle Books, 1999)

Baby Whale learns all he needs to know about surviving in the ocean from his mother and the other whales. This book has a simple poetic text and beautiful and dramatic illustrations.
Poetry

Whale
Judy Allen, illustrated by Tudor Humphries (Candlewick Press, 1994)

A young girl and her parents witness the seemingly magical rescue of a mother whale and her baby.
Fiction

Jr. Zoologist: Fish, Amphibians, Reptiles (SVE/Churchill Media) Video, 12 min. Explains and illustrates the unique anatomy and life cycles of these creatures.

See (Phoenix/BFA) Video, 13 min. A visual journey into the world of undersea creatures.

UnderSea Adventure (Educational Resources) CD-ROM, IBM. An interactive program about the oceans.

TIME FOR KIDS — The World's Plants Are In Danger

Pumpkin Circle
George Levenson, photographs by Shmuel Thaler (Tricycle Press, 1999)

A cycle of growth in a backyard pumpkin patch is told in upbeat rhymes and vibrant photographs.
Poetry

Someday a Tree
Eve Bunting, illustrated by Ronald Himler (Clarion Books, 1993)

A young girl, her parents, and their neighbors all try to save an old oak tree that has been poisoned by pollution.
Realistic Fiction

Earth Kids
Jill Wheeler (Abdo & Daughters, 1993)

Articles featuring students who are each working to save the environment, with suggestions for how others can participate.
Nonfiction

The Importance of Plants to Our World (United Learning) Video, 13 min. A look at how plants are used and needed in the world.

What Do Plants Do? (BFA Educational Media) Video, 12 min. An introduction to plants.

A World of Plants (National Geographic) CD-ROM, Macintosh and Windows. An interactive learning program that examines plants as well as the delicate balance of ecosystems.

Publishers Directory

Abdo & Daughters
4940 Viking Drive, Suite 622
Edina, MN 55435
(800) 458-8399 • www.abdopub.com

Aladdin Paperbacks
(Imprint of Simon & Schuster Children's Publishing)

Atheneum
(Imprint of Simon & Schuster Children's Publishing)

Bantam Doubleday Dell Books for Young Readers
(Imprint of Random House)

Blackbirch Press
260 Amity Rd.
Woodbridge, CT 06525
(203) 387-7525 • (800) 831-9183
www.blackbirch.com

Blue Sky Press
(Imprint of Scholastic)

Boyds Mills Press
815 Church Street
Honesdale, PA 18431
(570) 253-1164 • Fax (570) 253-0179 •
(877) 512-8366
www.boydsmillspress.com

Bradbury Press
(Imprint of Simon & Schuster Children's Publishing)

BridgeWater Books
(Distributed by Penguin Putnam)

Candlewick Press
2067 Masssachusetts Avenue
Cambridge, MA 02140
(617) 661-3330 • Fax (617) 661-0565
www.candlewick.com

Carolrhoda Books
(Division of Lerner Publications Co.)

Children's Press (Division of Grolier, Inc.)
P.O. Box 1795
Danbury, CT 06816-1333
(800) 621-1115 • www.grolier.com

Child's World
P.O. Box 326
Chanhassen, MN 55317-0326
(612) 906-3939 • (800) 599-READ •
www.childsworld.com

Chronicle Books
85 Second Street, Sixth Floor
San Francisco, CA 94105
(415) 537-3730 • Fax (415) 537-4460 •
(800) 722-6657 •
www.chroniclebooks.com

Clarion Books
(Imprint of Houghton Mifflin, Inc.)
215 Park Avenue South
New York, NY 10003
(212) 420-5800 • (800) 726-0600 •
www.houghtonmifflinbooks.com/clarion

Crowell (Imprint of HarperCollins)

Crown Publishing Group
(Imprint of Random House)

Dial Books
(Imprint of Penguin Putnam Inc.)

Dorling Kindersley (DK Publishing)
95 Madison Avenue
New York, NY 10016
(212) 213-4800 • Fax (212) 213-5240 •
(888) 342-5357 • www.dk.com

Doubleday (Imprint of Random House)

E. P. Dutton Children's Books
(Imprint of Penguin Putnam Inc.)

Farrar Straus & Giroux
19 Union Square West
New York, NY 10003
(212) 741-6900 • Fax (212) 741-6973 •
(888) 330-8477

Four Winds Press
(Imprint of Macmillan, see Simon & Schuster Children's Publishing)

Greenwillow Books
(Imprint of William Morrow & Co, Inc.)

Grosset & Dunlap
(Imprint of Penguin Putnam, Inc.)

Harcourt Brace & Co.
6277 Sea Harbor Drive
Orlando, Fl 32887
(407) 345-2000 •
(800) 225-5425 •
www.harcourtbooks.com

Harper & Row (Imprint of HarperCollins)

HarperCollins Children's Books
1350 Avenue of the Americas
New York, NY 10019
(212) 261-6500 • Fax (212) 261-6689 •
(800) 242-7737 •
www.harperchildrens.com

Holiday House
425 Madison Avenue
New York, NY 10017
(212) 688-0085 • Fax (212) 421-6134

Henry Holt and Company
115 West 18th Street
New York, NY 10011
(212) 886-9200 • (212) 633-0748 • (888) 330-8477 • www.henryholt.com/byr/

Houghton Mifflin
222 Berkeley Street
Boston, MA 02116
(617) 351-5000 • Fax (617) 351-1125 •
(800) 225-3362 •
www.houghtonmifflinbooks.com

Hyperion Books
(Division of ABC, Inc.)
77 W. 66th St. 11th floor
New York, NY 10023
(212) 456-0100 • (800) 343-9204 •
www.disney.com

Ideals Children's Books
(Imprint of Hambleton-Hill Publishing, Inc.)
1501 County Hospital Road
Nashville, TN 37218
(615) 254-2451 • (800) 327-5113

Joy Street Books
(Imprint of Little, Brown & Co.)

Just Us Books
356 Glenwood Avenue
E. Orange, NJ 07017
(973) 672-7701 • Fax (973) 677-7570
www.justusbooks.com

Alfred A. Knopf
(Imprint of Random House)

Lee & Low Books
95 Madison Avenue, Room 606
New York, NY 10016
(212) 779-4400 • Fax (212) 683-1894

Lerner Publications Co.
241 First Avenue North
Minneapolis, MN 55401
(612) 332-3344 • Fax (612) 332-7615 •
(800) 328-4929 • www.lernerbooks.com

Little, Brown & Co.
3 Center Plaza
Boston, MA 02108
(617) 227-0730 • Fax (617) 263-2864 •
(800) 759-0190 • www.littlebrown.com

Lothrop Lee & Shepard
(Imprint of William Morrow & Co.)

Macmillan
(Imprint of Simon & Schuster Children's Publishing)

Marshall Cavendish
99 White Plains Road
Tarrytown, NY 10591
(914) 332-8888 • Fax (914) 332-1888 •
(800) 821-9881 •
www.marshallcavendish.com

William Morrow & Co.
(Imprint of HarperCollins)

Morrow Junior Books
(Imprint of HarperCollins)

Mulberry Books
(Imprint of HarperCollins)

National Geographic Society
1145 17th Street, NW
Washington, DC 20036
(202) 857-7345 • (800) 638-4077 •
www.nationalgeographic.com

Northland Publishing
(Division of Justin Industries)
Box 1389
Flagstaff, AZ 86002
(520) 774-5251 • Fax (800) 744-0592 •
(800) 346-3257 • www.northlandpub.com

North-South Books
1123 Broadway, Suite 800
New York, NY 10010
(212) 463-9736 • Fax (212) 633-1004 •
(800) 722-6657 • www.northsouth.com

Orchard Books (A Grolier Company)
95 Madison Avenue
New York, NY 10016
(212) 951-2600 • Fax (212) 213-6435 •
(800) 433-3411 • www.grolier.com

Owlet (Imprint of Henry Holt & Co.)

Penguin Putnam, Inc.
375 Hudson Street
New York, NY 10014
(212) 366-2000 • Fax (212) 366-2636 •
(800) 631-8571 •
www.penguinputnam.com

Willa Perlman Books
(Imprint of Simon & Schuster Children's Publishing)

Philomel Books
(Imprint of Putnam Penguin, Inc.)

Puffin Books
(Imprint of Penguin Putnam, Inc.)

G.P. Putnam's Sons Publishing
(Imprint of Penguin Putnam, Inc.)

Random House
1540 Broadway
New York, NY 10036
(212) 782-9000 • (800) 200-3552 •
Fax (212) 782-9452
www.randomhouse.com/kids

Rourke Corporation
P.O. Box 3328
Vero Beach, FL 32964
(561) 234-6001 • (800) 394-7055 •
www.rourkepublishing.com

Scholastic
555 Broadway
New York, NY 10012
(212) 343-7500 • Fax (212) 965-7442 •
(800) SCHOLASTIC • www.scholastic.com

Charles Scribners's Sons
(Imprint of Simon & Schuster Children's Publishing)

Sierra Club Books for Children
85 Second Street, Second Floor
San Francisco, CA 94105-3441
(415) 977-5500 • Fax (415) 977-5793 •
(800) 935-1056 • www.sierraclub.org

Simon & Schuster Children's Books
1230 Avenue of the Americas
New York, NY 10020
(212) 698-7200 • (800) 223-2336 •
www.simonsays.com/kidzone

Smith & Kraus
177 Lyme Road
Hanover, NH 03755
(603) 643-6431 • Fax (603) 643-1831 •
(800) 895-4331 • www.smithkraus.com

Teacher Ideas Press
(Division of Libraries Unlimited)
P.O. Box 6633
Englewood, CO 80155-6633
(303) 770-1220 • Fax (303) 220-8843 •
(800) 237-6124 • www.lu.com

Ticknor & Fields
(Imprint of Houghton Mifflin, Inc.)

Usborne (Imprint of EDC Publishing)
10302 E. 55th Place, Suite B
Tulsa, OK 74146-6515
(918) 622-4522 • (800) 475-4522 •
www.edcpub.com

Viking Children's Books
(Imprint of Penguin Putnam Inc.)

Watts Publishing
(Imprint of Grolier Publishing; see Children's Press)

Walker & Co.
435 Hudson Street
New York, NY 10014
(212) 727-8300 • (212) 727-0984 •
(800) AT-WALKER

Whispering Coyote Press
300 Crescent Court, Suite 860
Dallas, TX 75201
(800) 929-6104 • Fax (214) 319-7298

Albert Whitman
6340 Oakton Street
Morton Grove, IL 60053-2723
(847) 581-0033 • Fax (847) 581-0039 •
(800) 255-7675 • www.awhitmanco.com

Workman Publishing Co., Inc.
708 Broadway
New York, NY 10003
(212) 254-5900 • Fax (800) 521-1832 •
(800) 722-7202 • www.workman.com

Multimedia Resources

AGC/United Learning
1560 Sherman Avenue, Suite 100
Evanston, IL 60201
(800) 323-9084 •
Fax (847) 328-6706 •
www.unitedlearning.com

AIMS Multimedia
9710 DeSoto Avenue
Chatsworth, CA 91311-4409
(800) 367-2467 •
www.AIMS-multimedia.com

BFA Educational Media
(see Phoenix Learning Group)

Broderbund
(Parsons Technology;
also see The Learning Company)
500 Redwood Blvd
Novato, CA 94997
(800) 395-0277
www.broderbund.com

Carousel Film and Video
260 Fifth Avenue, Suite 705
New York, NY 10001
(212) 683-1660 • e-mail:
carousel@pipeline.com

Cloud 9 Interactive
(888) 662-5683 • www.cloud9int.com

Computer Plus (see ESI)

Coronet/MTI
(see Phoenix Learning Group)

Davidson (see Knowledge Adventure)

Direct Cinema, Ltd.
P.O. Box 10003
Santa Monica, CA 90410-1003
(310) 636-8200 • Fax (310) 396-3233

Disney Interactive
(800) 900-9234 •
www.disneyinteractive.com

DK Multimedia (Dorling Kindersley)
95 Madison Avenue
New York, NY 10016
(212) 213-4800 • Fax: (800) 774-6733 •
(888) 342-5357 • www.dk.com

Edmark Corp.
P.O. Box 97021
Redmond, WA 98073-9721
(800) 362-2890 • www.edmark.com

Encyclopaedia Britannica Educational Corp.
310 South Michigan Avenue
Chicago, IL 60604
(800) 554-9862 • www.eb.com

ESI/Educational Software Institute
4213 S. 94th Street
Omaha, NE 68127
(800) 955-5570 • Fax (402) 592-2017 •
www.edsoft.com

GPN/Reading Rainbow
University of Nebraska-Lincoln
P.O. Box 80669
Lincoln, NE 68501-0669
(800) 228-4630 • Fax (800) 306-2330 •
www.gpn.unl.edu

Hasbro Interactive
(800) 683-5847 • www.hasbro.com

Humongous
13110 NE 177th Pl., Suite B101, Box 180
Woodenville, WA 98072
(800) 499-8386 • www.humongous.com

IBM Corp.
1133 Westchester Ave.
White Plains, NY 10604
(770) 863-1234 • Fax (770) 863-3030 •
(888) 411-1932 •
www.pc.ibm.com/multimedia/crayola

ICE, Inc.
(Distributed by Arch Publishing)
12B W. Main St.
Elmsford, NY 10523
(914) 347-2464 • (800) 843-9497 •
www.educorp.com

Knowledge Adventure
19840 Pioneer Avenue
Torrence, CA 90503
(800) 542-4240 • (800) 545-7677 •
www.knowledgeadventure.com

The Learning Company
6160 Summit Drive North
Minneapolis, MN 55430
(800) 395-0277 • www.learningco.com

Listening Library
A Subsidiary of Random House
One Park Avenue
Greenwich, CT 06870-1727
(800) 243-4504 • www.listeninglib.com

Macmillan/McGraw-Hill
(see SRA/McGraw-Hill)

Maxis
2121 N. California Blvd
Walnut Creek, CA 94596-3572
(925) 933-5630 • Fax (925) 927-3736 •
(800) 245-4525 • www.maxis.com

MECC
(see the Learning Company)

Microsoft
One Microsoft Way
Redmond, WA 98052-6399
(800) 426-9400 • www.microsoft.com/kids

National Geographic Society Educational Services
P.O. Box 10597
Des Moines, IA 50340-0597
(800) 368-2728 • Fax (515) 362-3366
www.nationalgeographic.com/education

National School Products
101 East Broadway
Maryville, TN 37804
(800) 251-9124 • www.ierc.com

PBS Video
1320 Braddock Place
Alexandria, VA 22314
(800) 344-3337 • www.pbs.org

Phoenix Films
(see Phoenix Learning Group)

The Phoenix Learning Group
2348 Chaffee Drive
St. Louis, MO 63146
(800) 221-1274 • e-mail:
phoenixfilms@worldnet.att.net

Pied Piper (see AIMS Multimedia)

Scholastic New Media
555 Broadway
New York, NY 10003
(800) 724-6527 • www.scholastic.com

Simon & Schuster Interactive
(see Knowledge Adventure)

SRA/McGraw-Hill
220 Danieldale Road
De Soto, TX 75115
(800) 843-8855 • Fax (972) 228-1982 •
www.sra4kids.com

SVE/Churchill Media
6677 North Northwest Highway
Chicago, IL 60631
(800) 829-1900 • Fax (800) 624-1678 •
www.svemedia.com

Tom Snyder Productions (also see ESI)
80 Coolidge Hill Rd.
Watertown, MA 02472
(800) 342-0236 • Fax (800) 304-1254 •
www.teachtsp.com

Troll Associates
100 Corporate Drive
Mahwah, NJ 07430
(800) 929-8765 • Fax (800) 979-8765 •
www.troll.com

Voyager (see ESI)

Weston Woods
12 Oakwood Avenue
Norwalk, CT 06850
(800) 243-5020 • Fax (203) 845-0498

Zenger Media
10200 Jefferson Blvd., Room 94,
P.O. Box 802
Culver City, CA 90232-0802
(800) 421-4246 • (800) 944-5432 •
www.Zengermedia.com

Word List

BOOK 1, UNIT 1

	Vocabulary	Spelling			
Ann's First Day		Words with short vowels			
	carrots **crawls** **homework** **hurry** **lucky** **shy**	bat **best** clock	**desk** fit hut	**just** **mom**	plant **still**
Henry and Mudge		Long vowels *a, i, o, u* with silent *e*			
	different **hundred** **parents** **searched** **weighed** **worry**	**alone** bike broke	fine joke late	mine same	take **used**
Luka's Quilt		Long *a* spelled *ai, ay* Long *e* spelled *ea, ee, ie*			
	answered **garden** **grandmother** **idea** **remember** **serious**	chief clay **dream**	**green** **keep** mail	mean **plain**	seat stay
Roundup at Rio Ranch		Long *o* spelled *oa, oe, ow,* and *o* Long *i* spelled *i, y,* and *igh*			
	broken **carefully** **cattle** **fence** **gently** **safety**	**by** dry **follow**	load mind old	row sigh	**slow** toe
Time for Kids: Welcome to a New Museum		Words from Social Studies			
	artist **body** **famous** **hour** **life** **visit**	**flags** law peace	**place** **slave** speech	tax time	trade vote

Boldfaced words appear in the selection.

BOOK 1, UNIT 2

	Vocabulary	Spelling			
Lemonade for Sale		/ü/ spelled *oo, ue, ew*			
	announced **empty** **melted** **poured** **squeezed** **wrong**	blew boot clue	few **new** **room**	school **too**	tool true
A Letter to Amy		/ou/ spelled *ou, ow;* /oi/ spelled *oi, oy*			
	candles **corner** **glanced** **repeated** **special** **wild**	brown coin cowboy	**down** **house** joy	loud **now**	**out** point
Best Friends Club		/âr/ spelled *are;* /ôr/ spelled *or, ore;* /îr/ spelled *ear*			
	allowed **leaned** **president** **promise** **rule** **whispered**	bare **care** corn	dear **more** **porch**	shore short	**tore** year
Jamaica Tag-Along		/är/ spelled *ar;* /ûr/spelled *ir, er, ur*			
	building **busy** **edge** **form** **giant** **repair**	arm birthday curl	dirt farm fur	hard **her**	herd **turned**
Time for Kids: Under Attack		Words from Science			
	afraid **chew** **danger** **lesson** **trouble** **understand**	**animals** fin **head**	**nets** river **seals**	senses **shark**	tide wave

Boldfaced words appear in the selection.

BOOK 1, UNIT 3

	Vocabulary	Spelling			
ARTHUR WRITES A STORY		**Silent letters *l, b, k, w, gh***			
	decided **float** **important** **library** **planet** **proud**	half **high** knee	knot **know** lamb	right thumb	write **wrote**
BEST WISHES, ED		**/ər/ spelled *er***			
	climbed **couple** **drifted** **half** **message** **notice**	corner driver farmer	father **letter** never	**other** **over**	**water** winter
THE PONY EXPRESS		**Short *e* spelled *ea***			
	arrive **early** **finish** **record** **rush** **success**	bread breakfast feather	instead **leather** meadow	meant ready	spread **weather**
NINE-IN-ONE, GRR! GRR!		**Long *e* spelled *y, ey***			
	earth **forget** **lonely** **memory** **mountain** **wonderful**	baby **every** **happy**	key lady **many**	money party	penny **tiny**
TIME FOR KIDS: CHANGE FOR THE QUARTER		**Words from Math**			
	collect **honors** **join** **order** **pocket** **worth**	buy **cent** cost	dime dollar exact	nickel price	**quarter** sum

Boldfaced words appear in the selection.

BOOK 2, UNIT 1

	Vocabulary	Spelling			
		/ů/ spelled *oo*			
CHARLIE ANDERSON	**chocolate** **clothes** **middle** **offered** **roof** **upstairs**	book brook cook	**foot** hood hook	shook stood	wood wool
		Soft *c* and soft *g*			
FERNANDO'S GIFT	**diving** **explains** **harm** **noisy** **soil** **village**	**age** cage charge	dance large mice	page race	**rice** space
		/ô/ spelled *a, aw, au, augh*			
THE BEST VACATION EVER	**brave** **guess** **museum** **practice** **vacation** **wonder**	**because** caught fault	**hawk** lawn paw	salt straw	talk taught
		Words with *ph, tch, ch*			
ZIPPING, ZAPPING, ZOOMING BATS	**disturb** **explore** **fact** **nature** **object** **several**	beach **catch** **each**	graph match patch	phone **pitch**	**sandwich** **touch**
		Words from Science			
TIME FOR KIDS: GOING BATTY FOR BATS	**breath** **cover** **crops** **darkness** **scary** **study**	blood **caves** den	**fly** **insects** **leaves**	nest sight	**sleep** wing

Boldfaced words appear in the selection.

BOOK 2, UNIT 2

	Vocabulary	Spelling			
Bremen Town Musicians	**daughter** **music** **scare** **third** **voice** **whistle**	Words with *c, k, ck*			
		act bake **come**	cover kind **like**	**luck** sick	**wake** **work**
Our Soccer League	**coaches** **field** **score** **stretches** **throws** **touch**	Initial *bl, br, dr, pl,* and *tr*			
		blow **blue** brag	brass drag draw	plan **play**	trap **try**
The Wednesday Surprise	**chance** **favorite** **heavy** **nervous** **office** **wrapped**	Initial *sl, sm, sp, st, sw*			
		slide slip **smart**	smooth speak spot	**start** **story**	sweet swim
Fossils Tell of Long Ago	**buried** **creatures** **fossil** **fresh** **layers** **millions**	Final *nk, nd, ft, st*			
		bank chest end	**ground** **hand** left	**past** **sank**	soft test
Time for Kids: Are You a Fossil Fan?	**change** **glue** **hunt** **magazine** **piece** **tooth**	Words from Social Studies			
		bone deep **digging**	drill hill land	ocean oil	**remains** **stone**

Boldfaced words appear in the selection.

BOOK 2, UNIT 3

	Vocabulary	Spelling
Officer Buckle and Gloria	**accidents** **audience** **cheered** **slips** **station** **wipe**	**Words with *ll, dd, ss, gg*** add call egg fill **kiss** odd press sell tell **well**
Tomás and the Library Lady	**borrow** **desert** **evenings** **midnight** **package** **shoulder**	**Words with initial *sh, ch*** **chair** chase **check** cheek **children** shape **shared** shift **shining** shoe
Princess Pooh	**cousins** **crowded** **golden** **princess** **restaurant** **world**	**Words with final *th* and *sh*** bath **both** brush dash fish mouth **push** **rush** teeth **with**
Swimmy	**escaped** **fierce** **hidden** **machine** **swaying** **swift**	**Words with initial *th* and *wh*** **than** **them** **there** **thought** **through** whale wheel whimper whirl whisper
Time for Kids: The World's Plants are in Danger	**clear** **disappear** **forever** **problem** **save** **warn**	**Words from Science** bloom bud **bushes** **cactus** **flower** petal root **roses** seed stem

Boldfaced words appear in the selection.

Listening, Speaking, Viewing, Representing

☑ Tested Skill

Tinted panels show skills, strategies, and other teaching opportunities

LISTENING	K	1	2	3	4	5	6
Learn the vocabulary of school (numbers, shapes, colors, directions, and categories)							
Identify the musical elements of literary language, such as rhymes, repetition, onomatopoeia, alliteration, assonance							
Determine purposes for listening (get information, solve problems, enjoy and appreciate)							
Understand and follow directions							
Listen critically and responsively; recognize barriers to effective listening							
Ask and answer relevant questions (for clarification; to follow up on ideas)							
Listen critically to interpret and evaluate							
Listen responsively to stories and other texts read aloud, including selections from classic and contemporary works							
Connect and compare own experiences, feelings, ideas, and traditions with those of others							
Apply comprehension strategies in listening activities							
Understand the major ideas and supporting evidence in spoken messages							
Participate in listening activities related to reading and writing (such as discussions, group activities, conferences)							
Listen to learn by taking notes, organizing, and summarizing spoken ideas							
Know personal listening preferences							
SPEAKING							
Use repetition, rhyme, and rhythm in oral texts (such as in reciting songs, poems, and stories with repeating patterns)							
Learn the vocabulary of school (numbers, shapes, colors, directions, and categories)							
Use appropriate language, grammar, and vocabulary learned to describe ideas, feelings, and experiences							
Ask and answer relevant questions (for clarification; to follow up on ideas)							
Communicate effectively in everyday situations (such as discussions, group activities, conferences, conversations)							
Demonstrate speaking skills (audience, purpose, occasion, clarity, volume, pitch, intonation, phrasing, rate, fluency)							
Clarify and support spoken messages and ideas with objects, charts, evidence, elaboration, examples							
Use verbal communication in effective ways, when, for example, making announcements, giving directions, or making introductions							
Use nonverbal communication in effective ways, such as eye contact, facial expressions, gestures							
Retell a story or a spoken message by summarizing or clarifying							
Connect and compare own experiences, ideas, and traditions with those of others							
Determine purposes for speaking (inform, entertain, compare, describe, give directions, persuade, express personal feelings and opinions)							
Recognize differences between formal and informal language							
Demonstrate skills of reporting and providing information							
Demonstrate skills of interviewing, requesting, and providing information							
Apply composition strategies in speaking activities							
Monitor own understanding of spoken message and seek clarification as needed							
VIEWING							
Demonstrate viewing skills (focus attention, organize information)							
Understand and use nonverbal cues							
Respond to audiovisual media in a variety of ways							
Participate in viewing activities related to reading and writing							
Apply comprehension strategies in viewing activities, including main idea and details							
Recognize artists' craft and techniques for conveying meaning							
Interpret information from various formats, such as maps, charts, graphics, video segments, technology							
Know various types of mass media (such as film, video, television, billboards, and newspapers)							
Evaluate purposes of various media, including mass media (information, appreciation, entertainment, directions, persuasion)							
Use media, including mass media, to compare ideas, information, and points of view							
REPRESENTING							
Select, organize, or produce visuals to complement or extend meanings							
Produce communication using appropriate media to develop a class paper, multimedia or video reports							
Show how language, medium, and presentation contribute to the message							

Reading: Alphabetic Principle, Sounds/Symbols

✓ Tested Skill

Tinted panels show skills, strategies, and other teaching opportunities

PRINT AWARENESS	K	1	2	3	4	5	6
Know the order of the alphabet							
Recognize that print represents spoken language and conveys meaning							
Understand directionality (tracking print from left to right; return sweep)							
Understand that written words and sentences are separated by spaces							
Know the difference between individual letters and printed words							
Understand that spoken words are represented in written language by specific sequences of letters							
Recognize that there are correct spellings for words							
Know the difference between capital and lowercase letters							
Recognize how readers use capitalization and punctuation to comprehend							
Recognize the distinguishing features of a letter, word, sentence, paragraph							
Understand appropriate book handling							
Recognize that parts of a book (such as cover/title page and table of contents) offer information							
PHONOLOGICAL AWARENESS							
Listen for environmental sounds							
Identify spoken words and sentences							
Divide spoken sentence into individual words							
Produce rhyming words and distinguish rhyming words from nonrhyming words							
Identify, segment, and combine syllables within spoken words							
Blend and segment onsets and rimes							
Identify and isolate the initial, medial, and final sound of a spoken word							
Add, delete, or substitute sounds to change words (such as *cow* to *how*, *pan* to *fan*)							
Blend sounds to make spoken words							
Segment one-syllable spoken words into individual sounds							
PHONICS AND DECODING							
Alphabetic principle: Letter/sound correspondence	✓	✓	✓				
Blending CVC words	✓	✓					
Segmenting CVC words	✓						
Blending CVC, CVCe, CCVC, CVCC, CVVC words	✓	✓	✓				
Segmenting CVC, CVCe, CCVC, CVCC, CVVC words and sounds	✓	✓	✓				
Initial and final consonants: /n/n, /d/d, /s/s, /m/m, /t/t, /k/c, /f/f, /r/r, /p/p, /l/l, /k/k, /g/g, /b/b, /h/h, /w/w, /v/v, /ks/x, /kw/qu, /j/j, /y/y, /z/z	✓	✓					
Initial and medial short vowels: *a, i, u, o, e*	✓	✓	✓				
Long vowels: *a-e, i-e, o-e, u-e* (vowel-consonant-e)		✓	✓				
Long vowels, including *ay, ai; e, ee, ie, ea; o, oa, oe, ow; i, y, igh*		✓	✓				
Consonant Digraphs: *sh, th, ch, wh*		✓					
Consonant Blends: continuant/continuant, including *sl, sm, sn, fl, fr, ll, ss, ff*		✓					
Consonant Blends: continuant/stop, including *st, sk, sp, ng, nt, nd, mp, ft*		✓					
Consonant Blends: stop/continuant, including *tr, pr, pl, cr, tw*		✓					
Variant vowels: including /ů/*oo*; /ô/*a, aw, au*; /ü/*ue, ew*		✓	✓				
Diphthongs, including /ou/*ou, ow*; /oi/*oi, oy*		✓	✓				
r-controlled vowels, including /âr/*are*; /ôr/*or, ore*; /îr/*ear*			✓				
Soft *c* and soft *g*			✓				
nk		✓	✓				
Consonant Digraphs: *ck*	✓	✓					
Consonant Digraphs: *ph, tch, ch*			✓				
Short *e: ea*			✓				
Long *e: y, ey*			✓				
/ü/*oo*		✓	✓				
/är/*ar*; /ûr/*ir, ur, er*		✓	✓				
Silent letters: including *l, b, k, w, g, h, gh*			✓				
Schwa: /ər/*er*; /ən/*en*; /əl/*le*;			✓				
Reading/identifying multisyllabic words		✓	✓				
Using graphophonic cues							

✓ Tested Skill

Tinted panels show skills, strategies, and other teaching opportunities

Reading: Vocabulary/Word Identification

WORD STRUCTURE	K	1	2	3	4	5	6
Common spelling patterns							
Syllable patterns							
Plurals		✓					
Possessives		✓					
Contractions		✓					
Root, or base, words and inflectional endings (*-s, -es, -ed, -ing*)		✓	✓	✓		✓	
Compound Words		✓	✓	✓	✓	✓	✓
Prefixes and suffixes (such as *un-, re-, dis-, non-; -ly, -y, -ful, -able, -tion*)			✓	✓	✓	✓	✓
Root words and derivational endings				✓	✓	✓	✓
WORD MEANING							
Develop vocabulary through concrete experiences, word walls, other people							
Develop vocabulary through selections read aloud							
Develop vocabulary through reading							
Cueing systems: syntactic, semantic, graphophonic							
Context clues, including semantic clues (word meaning), syntactical clues (word order), and graphophonic clues	✓	✓	✓	✓	✓	✓	✓
High-frequency words (such as *the, a, and, said, was, where, is*)	✓	✓					
Identify words that name persons, places, things, and actions							
Automatic reading of regular and irregular words							
Use resources and references (dictionary, glossary, thesaurus, synonym finder, technology and software, and context)							
Classify and categorize words							
Synonyms and antonyms			✓	✓	✓	✓	✓
Multiple-meaning words			✓		✓	✓	✓
Figurative language			✓	✓	✓	✓	✓
Decode derivatives (root words, such as *like, pay, happy* with affixes, such as *dis-, pre-, un-*)							
Systematic study of words across content areas and in current events							
Locate meanings, pronunciations, and derivations (including dictionaries, glossaries, and other sources)							
Denotation and connotation							✓
Word origins as aid to understanding historical influences on English word meanings							
Homophones, homographs							
Analogies							✓
Idioms							

Reading: Comprehension

PREREADING STRATEGIES	K	1	2	3	4	5	6
Preview and predict							
Use prior knowledge							
Set and adjust purposes for reading							
Build background							
MONITORING STRATEGIES							
Adjust reading rate							
Reread, search for clues, ask questions, ask for help							
Visualize							
Read a portion aloud, use reference aids							
Use decoding and vocabulary strategies							
Paraphrase							
Create story maps, diagrams, charts, story props to help comprehend, analyze, synthesize and evaluate texts							

(continued on next page)

✓ Tested Skill

Tinted panels show skills, strategies, and other teaching opportunities

(Reading: Comprehension continued)

SKILLS AND STRATEGIES	K	1	2	3	4	5	6
Recall story details, including character and setting	✓	✓					
Use illustrations	✓	✓					
Distinguish reality and fantasy	✓	✓	✓				
Classify and categorize	✓						
Make predictions	✓	✓	✓	✓	✓	✓	✓
Recognize sequence of events (tell or act out)	✓	✓	✓	✓	✓	✓	✓
Recognize cause and effect	✓	✓	✓	✓	✓	✓	✓
Compare and contrast	✓	✓	✓	✓	✓	✓	✓
Summarize	✓	✓	✓	✓	✓	✓	✓
Make and explain inferences		✓	✓	✓	✓	✓	✓
Draw conclusions		✓	✓	✓	✓	✓	✓
Distinguish important and unimportant information				✓	✓	✓	✓
Recognize main idea and supporting details	✓	✓	✓	✓	✓	✓	✓
Form conclusions or generalizations and support with evidence from text			✓	✓	✓	✓	✓
Distinguish fact and opinion (including news stories and advertisements)				✓	✓	✓	✓
Recognize problem and solution			✓	✓	✓	✓	✓
Recognize steps in a process		✓	✓	✓	✓	✓	✓
Make judgments and decisions				✓	✓	✓	✓
Distinguish fact and nonfact				✓	✓	✓	✓
Recognize techniques of persuasion and propaganda							✓
Evaluate evidence and sources of information, including checking other sources and asking experts							✓
Identify similarities and differences across texts (including topics, characters, problems, themes, cultural influences, treatment, scope, or organization)							
Practice various questions and tasks (test-like comprehension questions)							
Paraphrase and summarize to recall, inform, and organize							
Answer various types of questions (open-ended, literal, interpretative, test-like such as true-false, multiple choice, short-answer)							
Use study strategies to learn and recall (preview, question, reread, and record)							
LITERARY RESPONSE							
Listen to stories being read aloud							
React, speculate, join in, read along when predictable and patterned selections are read aloud							
Respond to a variety of stories and poems through talk, movement, music, art, drama, and writing							
Show understanding through writing, illustrating, developing demonstrations, and using technology							
Connect ideas and themes across texts							
Support responses by referring to relevant aspects of text and own experiences							
Offer observations, make connections, speculate, interpret, and raise questions in response to texts							
Interpret text ideas through journal writing, discussion, enactment, and media							
TEXT STRUCTURE/LITERARY CONCEPTS							
Distinguish forms and functions of texts (lists, newsletters, signs)							
Use text features to aid comprehension							
Understand story structure							
Identify narrative (for entertainment) and expository (for information) text							
Distinguish fiction from nonfiction, including fact and fantasy							
Understand literary forms (stories, poems, plays, and informational books)							
Understand literary terms by distinguishing between roles of author and illustrator							
Understand title, author, and illustrator across a variety of texts							
Analyze character, character's motive, character's point of view, plot, setting, style, tone, mood		✓	✓	✓	✓	✓	✓
Compare communication in different forms							
Understand terms such as *title, author, illustrator, playwright, theater, stage, act, dialogue,* and *scene*							
Recognize stories, poems, songs, myths, legends, folktales, fables, tall tales, limericks, plays, biographies, autobiographies							
Judge internal logic of story text							
Recognize that authors organize information in specific ways							
Recognize author's purpose: to inform, influence, express, or entertain							
Describe how author's point of view affects text				✓	✓	✓	✓
Recognize biography, historical fiction, realistic fiction, modern fantasy, informational texts, and poetry							
Analyze ways authors present ideas (cause/effect, compare/contrast, inductively, deductively, chronologically)							
Recognize literary techniques such as imagery, repetition, flashback, foreshadowing, symbolism							

(continued on next page)

☑ Tested Skill

Tinted panels show skills, strategies, and other teaching opportunities

(Reading: Comprehension continued)

VARIETY OF TEXT	K	1	2	3	4	5	6
Read a variety of genres and understand their distinguishing features							
Use expository and other informational texts to acquire information							
Read for a variety of purposes							
Select varied sources when reading for information or pleasure							
Know preferences for reading literary and nonfiction texts							
FLUENCY							
Read regularly in independent-level and instructional-level materials							
Read orally with fluency from familiar texts							
Self-select independent-level reading							
Read silently for increasingly longer periods of time							
Demonstrate characteristics of fluent and effective reading							
Adjust reading rate to purpose							
Read aloud in selected texts, showing understanding of text and engaging the listener							
CULTURES							
Connect own experience with culture of others							
Compare experiences of characters across cultures							
Articulate and discuss themes and connections that cross cultures							
CRITICAL THINKING							
Experiences (comprehend, apply, analyze, synthesize, evaluate)							
Making connections (comprehend, apply, analyze, synthesize, evaluate)							
Expression (comprehend, apply, analyze, synthesize, evaluate)							
Inquiry (comprehend, apply, analyze, synthesize, evaluate)							
Problem solving (comprehend, apply, analyze, synthesize, evaluate)							
Making decisions (comprehend, apply, analyze, synthesize, evaluate)							

Study Skills

INQUIRY/RESEARCH AND STUDY STRATEGIES	K	1	2	3	4	5	6
Follow and give directions							
Use alphabetical order							
Use text features and formats to help understand text (such as boldface, italic, or highlighted text; captions; headings and subheadings; numbers or symbols)							
Use study strategies to help read text and to learn and recall information from text (such as preview text, set purposes, and ask questions; use SQRRR; adjust reading rate; skim and scan; use KWL)							
Identify/frame and revise questions for research							
Obtain, organize, and summarize information: classify, take notes, outline, web, diagram							
Evaluate research and raise new questions							
Use technology for research and/or to present information in various formats							
Follow accepted formats for writing research, including documenting sources							
Use test-taking strategies							
Use text organizers (book cover; title page—title, author, illustrator; contents; headings; glossary; index)		☑	☑	☑	☑	☑	☑
Use graphic aids, such as maps, diagrams, charts, graphs, schedules, calendars		☑	☑	☑	☑	☑	☑
Read and interpret varied texts, such as environmental print, signs, lists, encyclopedia, dictionary, glossary, newspaper, advertisement, magazine, calendar, directions, floor plans, online resources		☑	☑	☑	☑	☑	☑
Use print and online reference sources, such as glossary, dictionary, encyclopedia, telephone directory, technology resources, nonfiction books		☑	☑	☑	☑	☑	☑
Recognize Library/Media Center resources, such as computerized references; catalog search—subject, author, title; encyclopedia index		☑	☑	☑	☑	☑	☑

Writing

☑ Tested Skill

Tinted panels show skills, strategies, and other teaching opportunities

MODES AND FORMS	K	1	2	3	4	5	6
Interactive writing							
Descriptive writing			☑				
Personal narrative			☑	☑	☑	☑	☑
Writing that compares		☑	☑	☑	☑	☑	☑
Explanatory writing			☑	☑	☑	☑	☑
Persuasive writing				☑	☑	☑	☑
Writing a story		☑	☑	☑	☑	☑	☑
Expository writing; research report		☑	☑	☑	☑	☑	☑
Write using a variety of formats, such as advertisement, autobiography, biography, book report/report, comparison-contrast, critique/review/editorial, description, essay, how-to, interview, invitation, journal/log/notes, message/list, paragraph/multi-paragraph composition, picture book, play (scene), poem/rhyme, story, summary, note, letter							
PURPOSES/AUDIENCES							
Dictate sentences and messages, such as news and stories, for others to write							
Write labels, notes, and captions for illustrations, possessions, charts, and centers							
Write to record, to discover and develop ideas, to inform, to influence, to entertain							
Exhibit an identifiable voice							
Use literary devices (suspense, dialogue, and figurative language)							
Produce written texts by organizing ideas, using effective transitions, and choosing precise wording							
PROCESSES							
Generate ideas for self-selected and assigned topics using prewriting strategies							
Develop drafts							
Revise drafts for varied purposes, elaborate ideas							
Edit for appropriate grammar, spelling, punctuation, and features of published writings							
Proofread own writing and that of others							
Bring pieces to final form and "publish" them for audiences							
Use technology to compose, revise, and present text							
Select and use reference materials and resources for writing, revising, and editing final drafts							
SPELLING							
Spell own name and write high-frequency words							
Words with short vowels (including CVC and one-syllable words with blends CCVC, CVCC, CCVCC)							
Words with long vowels (including CVCe)							
Words with digraphs, blends, consonant clusters, double consonants							
Words with diphthongs							
Words with variant vowels							
Words with r-controlled vowels							
Words with /ər/, /əl/, and /ən/							
Words with silent letters							
Words with soft *c* and soft *g*							
Inflectional endings (including plurals and past tense and words that drop the final *e* and double a consonant when adding *-ing, -ed*)							
Compound words							
Contractions							
Homonyms							
Suffixes such as *-able, -ly, -ful,* or *-less,* and prefixes such as *dis-, re-, pre-,* or *un-*							
Spell words ending in *-tion* and *-sion*, such as *station* and *procession*							
Accurate spelling of root or base words							
Orthographic patterns and rules such as *keep/can; sack/book; out/now; oil/toy; match/speech; ledge/cage;* consonant doubling, dropping *e,* changing *y* to *i*							
Multisyllabic words using regularly spelled phonogram patterns							
Syllable patterns (including closed, open, syllable boundary patterns)							
Synonyms and antonyms							
Words from Social Studies, Science, Math, and Physical Education							
Words derived from other languages and cultures							
Use resources to find correct spellings, synonyms, and replacement words							
Use conventional spelling of familiar words in writing assignments							
Spell accurately in final drafts							

(continued on next page)

Tested Skill

Tinted panels show skills, strategies, and other teaching opportunities

(Writing continued)

GRAMMAR AND USAGE	K	1	2	3	4	5	6
Understand sentence concepts (word order, statements, questions, exclamations, commands)							
Recognize complete and incomplete sentences							
Nouns (common, proper, singular, plural, irregular plural, possessive)							
Verbs (action, helping, linking, irregular)							
Verb tense (present, past, future, perfect, and progressive)							
Pronouns (possessive, subject and object, pronoun-verb agreement)							
Use objective case pronouns accurately							
Adjectives							
Adverbs that tell how, when, where							
Subjects, predicates							
Subject-verb agreement							
Sentence combining							
Recognize sentence structure (simple, compound, complex)							
Synonyms and antonyms							
Contractions							
Conjunctions							
Prepositions and prepositional phrases							
PENMANSHIP							
Write each letter of alphabet (capital and lowercase) using correct formation, appropriate size and spacing							
Write own name and other important words							
Use phonological knowledge to map sounds to letters in order to write messages							
Write messages that move left to right, top to bottom							
Gain increasing control of penmanship, pencil grip, paper position, beginning stroke							
Use word and letter spacing and margins to make messages readable							
Write legibly by selecting cursive or manuscript, as appropriate							
MECHANICS							
Use capitalization in sentences, proper nouns, titles, abbreviations and the pronoun *I*							
Use end marks correctly (period, question mark, exclamation point)							
Use commas (in dates, in addresses, in a series, in letters, in direct address)							
Use apostrophes in contractions and possessives							
Use quotation marks							
Use hyphens, semicolons, colons							
EVALUATION							
Identify the most effective features of a piece of writing using class/teacher-generated criteria							
Respond constructively to others' writing							
Determine how his/her own writing achieves its purpose							
Use published pieces as models for writing							
Review own written work to monitor growth as a writer							

Scoring Chart

The Scoring Chart is provided for your convenience in grading your students' work.

- Find the column that shows the total number of items.
- Find the row that matches the number of items answered correctly.
- The intersection of the two rows provides the percentage score.

NUMBER CORRECT / TOTAL NUMBER OF ITEMS	1	2	3	4	5	6	7	8	9	10	11	12	13	14	15	16	17	18	19	20	21	22	23	24	25	26	27	28	29	30
1	100	50	33	25	20	17	14	13	11	10	9	8	8	7	7	6	6	6	5	5	5	5	4	4	4	4	4	4	3	3
2		100	66	50	40	33	29	25	22	20	18	17	15	14	13	13	12	11	11	10	10	9	9	8	8	8	7	7	7	7
3			100	75	60	50	43	38	33	30	27	25	23	21	20	19	18	17	16	15	14	14	13	13	12	12	11	11	10	10
4				100	80	67	57	50	44	40	36	33	31	29	27	25	24	22	21	20	19	18	17	17	16	15	15	14	14	13
5					100	83	71	63	56	50	45	42	38	36	33	31	29	28	26	25	24	23	22	21	20	19	19	18	17	17
6						100	86	75	67	60	55	50	46	43	40	38	35	33	32	30	29	27	26	25	24	23	22	21	21	20
7							100	88	78	70	64	58	54	50	47	44	41	39	37	35	33	32	30	29	28	27	26	25	24	23
8								100	89	80	73	67	62	57	53	50	47	44	42	40	38	36	35	33	32	31	30	29	28	27
9									100	90	82	75	69	64	60	56	53	50	47	45	43	41	39	38	36	35	33	32	31	30
10										100	91	83	77	71	67	63	59	56	53	50	48	45	43	42	40	38	37	36	34	33
11											100	92	85	79	73	69	65	61	58	55	52	50	48	46	44	42	41	39	38	37
12												100	92	86	80	75	71	67	63	60	57	55	52	50	48	46	44	43	41	40
13													100	93	87	81	76	72	68	65	62	59	57	54	52	50	48	46	45	43
14														100	93	88	82	78	74	70	67	64	61	58	56	54	52	50	48	47
15															100	94	88	83	79	75	71	68	65	63	60	58	56	54	52	50
16																100	94	89	84	80	76	73	70	67	64	62	59	57	55	53
17																	100	94	89	85	81	77	74	71	68	65	63	61	59	57
18																		100	95	90	86	82	78	75	72	69	67	64	62	60
19																			100	95	90	86	83	79	76	73	70	68	66	63
20																				100	95	91	87	83	80	77	74	71	69	67
21																					100	95	91	88	84	81	78	75	72	70
22																						100	96	92	88	85	81	79	76	73
23																							100	96	92	88	85	82	79	77
24																								100	96	92	89	86	83	80
25																									100	96	93	89	86	83
26																										100	96	93	90	87
27																											100	96	93	90
28																												100	97	93
29																													100	97
30																														100

Writing a Story: Characters Solving a Problem

Scoring Rubric: 6-Trait Writing					
6. Exceptional	**5. Excellent**	**4. Good**	**3. Fair**	**2. Poor**	**1. Unsatisfactory**
• **Ideas & Content** crafts a highly entertaining, detailed original story; each character is distinct and plays a special role. • **Organization** carefully-planned story sequence moves the reader smoothly through the events; has an inviting beginning and a satisfying ending. • **Voice** shows originality and wit; strong personal message speaks directly to the reader. • **Word Choice** inventive use of advanced language creates striking pictures in the reader's mind. • **Sentence Fluency** varied, effective sentences flow in a natural rhythm that strengthens the story line. • **Conventions** is skilled in most conventions; proper use of the rules of English enhances clarity, meaning, and narrative style; editing is largely unnecessary.	• **Ideas & Content** creates a cohesive original story, with details that bring events to life. • **Organization** unfolds a well-organized story line that moves the reader easily through the events from beginning to end. • **Voice** shows originality and a personal feeling that connects with the reader. • **Word Choice** thoughtful use of both challenging and everyday language creates clear pictures for the reader. • **Sentence Fluency** varied, effective sentences flow smoothly and add interest to the story. • **Conventions** is skilled in most conventions; proper use of the rules of English enhances clarity and narrative style.	• **Ideas & Content** presents a solidly-crafted story, with details that express the main idea. • **Organization** has a well-planned narrative strategy; events and characters are connected; has a clear beginning and ending. • **Voice** makes a strong effort to convey a genuine personal style to the reader. • **Word Choice** uses a variety of words that fit the story intention; experiments with some new words; overall message is clear. • **Sentence Fluency** careful, varied sentences cohere and are easy to read aloud. • **Conventions** may make some errors in spelling, capitalization, punctuation or usage which do not interfere with understanding the text; some editing may be needed.	• **Ideas & Content** attempts to write a story; may not elaborate adequately, or may lose control of the narrative line. • **Organization** may not have a clear story structure, or may have trouble connecting ideas; reader may be confused by order of events, or placement of new characters. • **Voice** may get a basic idea across, without a sense of involvement in telling a story. • **Word Choice** may not use words that express a strong feeling, or create clear images for the reader. • **Sentence Fluency** most sentences are understandable; some may be incomplete or awkward; text is somewhat hard to read aloud. • **Conventions** makes noticeable mistakes which interfere with a smooth reading of the story.	• **Ideas & Content** may not show a narrative purpose; may retell events from a familiar story or film; may create indistinct characters. • **Organization** shows extreme lack of organization; beginning and ending are undeveloped or missing; events and ideas are disconnected. • **Voice** is not involved in entertaining a reader; does not share a message of personal importance or interest. • **Word Choice** does not choose words that express clear feelings or pictures; some word choices may detract from understanding the story. • **Sentence Fluency** makes incomplete, awkward, or confusing sentences; may have trouble fitting words and sentences together. • **Conventions** makes repeated errors in spelling, word choice, punctuation and usage; frequent mistakes interfere with following the text.	• **Ideas & Content** does not tell a story; writer may go off in several directions, without a sense of purpose; characters, if any, do not connect to events. • **Organization** extreme lack of organization interferes with following the text; there may be no evident structure at all. • **Voice** does not address a reader, or has no grasp of sharing understandable feelings and ideas. • **Word Choice** uses words that do not relate to storytelling, or are vague and confusing to the reader. • **Sentence Fluency** constructs incomplete, rambling, or confusing sentences; text is hard to follow, and to read aloud. • **Conventions** makes severe errors in most or all conventions, so as to interfere with readability; some parts of the text may be impossible to follow or understand.

Incomplete 0: This piece is either blank, or fails to respond to the writing task. The topic is not addressed, or the student simply paraphrases the prompt. The response may be illegible or incoherent.

8-Point Writing Rubric

Writing a Story: Characters Solving a Problem

8-Point Writing Rubric							
8	**7**	**6**	**5**	**4**	**3**	**2**	**1**
The writer • has crafted an entertaining and highly original story with interesting characters, a well-described setting, and an intriguing plot. • has developed unique characters who each play a distinctive role in the story line. • has shown unusual wit, depth, and imagination in unfolding the events of the story. • has created a story arc that contains a strong beginning, an engaging middle, and a satisfying ending. • has displayed an especially keen sense of knowing how to appeal to an audience.	The writer • has crafted an entertaining story with characters, setting, and a plot. • has developed characters who each play an appropriate part in the story line. • exhibits wit and imagination in her/his unfolding of events. • has set down a clear-cut progression of events with a beginning, middle, and end. • exhibits a keen sense of entertaining an audience.	The writer • has made a strong effort to create an original story. • has made a strong effort to create distinctive characters who play a part in the story line. • may exhibit wit or imagination in her/his unfolding of events. • has made a largely successful attempt to unfold events in an organized structure. • attempts to entertain an audience.	The writer • has attempted to create an original story. • has created characters whose actions move the story along. • has attempted to unfold events in an organized structure but may show some gaps in story line or sequence. • exhibits an awareness of audience.	The writer • may have attempted to write an original story. • has created characters but may show little distinction between them. • may exhibit difficulty in developing a story structure. • may have retold events from a storybook or film. • may show little awareness of audience. • may exhibit a limited grasp of descriptive language and writing conventions.	The writer • has made a largely unsuccessful attempt at telling a story. • may present minimal or no ideas or descriptions of characters, events, or setting. • may present few connections between any ideas or details. • may show a limited vocabulary range. • may lack an awareness of audience. • may have difficulty grasping writing conventions.	The writer • has made an unsuccessful attempt at telling a story. • presents minimal ideas or descriptions of characters, events, or setting. • may make no connections between any ideas or details. • may use words inappropriately in ways that confuse the reader. • may display serious problems with writing conventions. • shows no awareness of audience.	The writer • has made no attempt at telling a story. • presents no ideas or descriptions of characters, events, or setting. • makes no connections between any ideas or details. • exhibits a vocabulary too limited for the demands of the task. • exhibits extreme problems with writing conventions.

0: This piece is either blank, or fails to respond to the writing task. The topic is not addressed, or the student simply paraphrases the prompt. The response may be illegible or incoherent.